2017 Valuation Handbook

U.S. Guide to Cost of Capital

Market Results Through 2016

Duff & Phelps

WILEY

About the Data

The information and data presented in the *2017 Valuation Handbook – U.S. Guide to Cost of Capital* and the online *Risk Premium Toolkit* and the online *Cost of Capital Analyzer* has been obtained with the greatest of care from sources believed to be reliable, but is not guaranteed to be complete, accurate or timely. Duff & Phelps, LLC (www.duffandphelps.com) and/or its data providers expressly disclaim any liability, including incidental or consequential damages, arising from the use of the *2017 Valuation Handbook – U.S. Guide to Cost of Capital* and/or the online *Risk Premium Toolkit* and/or the *Cost of Capital Analyzer* or any errors or omissions that may be contained in the *2017 Valuation Handbook – U.S. Guide to Cost of Capital* and/or the online *Risk Premium Toolkit* and/or the online *Cost of Capital Analyzer*, or any other product (existing or to be developed) based upon the methodology and/or data published herein. One of the sources of raw data used to produce the derived data and information herein is Morningstar, Inc. Use of raw data from Morningstar to produce the derived data and information herein does not necessarily constitute agreement by Morningstar, Inc. of any investment philosophy or strategy presented in this publication.

About Duff & Phelps

Duff & Phelps is the premier global valuation and corporate finance advisor with expertise in complex valuation, disputes and investigations, M&A, real estate, restructuring, and compliance and regulatory consulting. The firm's more than 2,000 employees serve a diverse range of clients from offices around the world. For more information, visit www.duffandphelps.com.

M&A advisory, capital raising, and secondary market advisory services in the United States are provided by Duff & Phelps Securities, LLC. Member FINRA/SIPC. Pagemill Partners is a Division of Duff & Phelps Securities, LLC. M&A advisory and capital raising advisory services are provided in a number of European countries through Duff & Phelps Securities Ltd, UK, which includes branches in Ireland and Germany. Duff & Phelps Securities Ltd, UK, is regulated by the Financial Conduct Authority.

Additional Resources

Duff & Phelps authors *five* books that focus on U.S. and international valuation theory, data, and risk premia (e.g., equity risk premia, risk-free rates, size premia, industry risk premia, betas, industry multiples and other statistics, etc.) for use in valuation models. The *Valuation Handbook − U.S. Guide to Cost of Capital* (this book) is one of these five books.

Duff & Phelps produces *one* book that focuses on U.S. capital markets performance data (i.e., the history of returns of the capital markets in the U.S. from 1926 to the present). This resource, the *Stocks, Bonds, Bills, and Inflation® (SBBI®) Yearbook*, has been published for over 30 years.[i.1] The *SBBI Yearbook* does not provide extensive valuation data or methodology.[i.2]

The six books are:[i.3]

U.S. and International Valuation Theory and Data

- *Cost of Capital: Applications and Examples (5th edition)*
- *Valuation Handbook − U.S. Guide to Cost of Capital*
- *Valuation Handbook − U.S. Industry Cost of Capital*
- *Valuation Handbook − International Guide to Cost of Capital*
- *Valuation Handbook − International Industry Cost of Capital*

U.S. Capital Markets Performance Data

- *Stocks, Bonds, Bills, and Inflation (SBBI) Yearbook*

All six Duff & Phelps books are published by John Wiley & Sons (Hoboken, NJ). Each of the six books is summarized in the following sections.

To learn more about cost of capital issues, and to ensure that you are using the most recent Duff & Phelps Recommended ERP, visit www.duffandphelps.com/CostofCapital.

[i.1] "Stocks, Bonds, Bills, and Inflation" and "SBBI" are registered trademarks of Morningstar, Inc. All rights reserved. Used with permission.

[i.2] Morningstar previously published two "Ibbotson SBBI" yearbooks: (i) The *SBBI "Classic" Yearbook*, which is now produced by Duff & Phelps and published by John Wiley & Sons as the "SBBI Yearbook" starting in 2016 (the word "Classic" was dropped from the title), and (ii) the *SBBI "Valuation" Yearbook*, which was discontinued by Morningstar in 2013. The former *SBBI Valuation Yearbook* was replaced by the *Valuation Handbook − U.S. Guide to Cost of Capital* (this book), also produced by Duff & Phelps and published by John Wiley & Sons, starting in 2014.

[i.3] In 2014, 2015, and 2016 the four books comprising the Valuation Handbook series were named as follows: *Valuation Handbook − Guide to Cost of Capital, Valuation Handbook − Industry Cost of Capital, International Valuation Handbook − Guide to Cost of Capital*, and *International Valuation Handbook − Industry Cost of Capital*. Starting with the 2017 Valuation Handbook editions, the names of the four books were changed to: *Valuation Handbook − U.S. Guide to Cost of Capital, Valuation Handbook − U.S. Industry Cost of Capital, Valuation Handbook − International Guide to Cost of Capital*, and *Valuation Handbook − International Industry Cost of Capital*, respectively. For simplicity, in all 2017 books, intra-year updates, marketing materials, online tools, etc., the new names are used (even when referring to pre-2017 editions).

Cost of Capital: Applications and Examples **5th edition**

The authoritative, comprehensive overview of valuation theory, best practices, and proper use of data. This book puts an emphasis on practical application.

To learn more about the latest theory and practice in cost of capital estimation, see *Cost of Capital: Applications and Examples* 5th edition, by Shannon P. Pratt and Roger J. Grabowski (John Wiley & Sons, Inc., 2014).

The *Cost of Capital: Applications and Examples* 5th edition is a one-stop shop for background and current thinking on the development and uses of rates of return on capital. This book contains expanded materials on estimating the basic building blocks of the cost of equity capital, the risk-free rate, and equity risk premium, plus in-depth discussion of the volatility created by the 2008 financial crisis, the subsequent recession and uncertain recovery, and how those events have fundamentally changed how we need to interpret the inputs to the models we use to develop these estimates.

The *Cost of Capital: Applications and Examples* 5th edition includes case studies providing comprehensive discussion of cost of capital estimates for valuing a business and damages calculations for small and medium-sized businesses, cross-referenced to the chapters covering the theory and data. This book puts an emphasis on practical application. To that end, this updated edition provides readers with exclusive access to a companion website filled with supplementary materials, allowing you to continue to learn in a hands-on fashion long after closing the book.

The *Cost of Capital: Applications and Examples* has been published since 1998, and is updated every three to four years. The 6th edition of this book is scheduled to be available in early 2018.

"Shannon Pratt and Roger Grabowski have produced a remarkably comprehensive review of the subject...it is a work that valuation practitioners, CFOs, and others will find an invaluable reference".

– Professor Richard Brealey, Emeritus Professor of Finance, London Business School (from the Foreword)

"Estimating the cost of capital is critical in determining the valuation of assets, in evaluating the capital structure of corporations, and in estimating the long-run expected return of investments. Shannon Pratt and Roger Grabowski have the most thorough text on the subject, not only providing various estimation methods, but also numerous ways to use the cost of capital".

– Professor Roger G. Ibbotson, Professor Emeritus of Finance at the Yale School of Management, Chairman and Chief Investment Officer of Zebra Capital LLC, and former Chairman and founder of Ibbotson Associates, now part of Morningstar, Inc.

Valuation Handbook – U.S. Guide to Cost of Capital (this book)

This annual book includes the U.S. cost of capital data inputs (equity risk premia, size premia, industry risk premia, risk premia over the risk-free rate, risk-free rates) that were previously published in the Morningstar/Ibbotson *Stocks, Bonds, Bills, and Inflation (SBBI) Valuation Yearbook* and the Duff & Phelps *Risk Premium Report*.

The *Valuation Handbook – U.S. Guide to Cost of Capital* can be used to develop cost of equity capital estimates (using both the build-up method and CAPM) for an individual business, business ownership interest, security, or intangible asset. This includes many examples for using the data properly.

The *Valuation Handbook – U.S. Guide to Cost of Capital* has been published since 2014, and is updated annually with data through December 31 of the previous year (e.g., the *2014 Valuation Handbook – U.S. Guide to Cost of Capital* is "data through" December 31, 2013; the *2015 Valuation Handbook – U.S. Guide to Cost of Capital* is "data through" December 31, 2014, etc.). This book includes three optional intra-year quarterly updates (March, June, and September).

Valuation Handbook – U.S. Industry Cost of Capital

This annual book provides industry-level cost of capital estimates (cost of equity capital, cost of debt capital, and weighted average cost of capital, or WACC), plus detailed industry-level statistics for sales, market capitalization, capital structure, various levered and unlevered beta estimates (e.g., ordinary-least squares (OLS) beta, sum beta, peer group beta, downside beta, etc.), valuation (trading) multiples, financial and profitability ratios, equity returns, aggregate forward-looking earnings-per share (EPS) growth rates, and more. Over 300 critical industry-level data points are calculated for approximately 180 U.S. industries (depending on data availability). Industries are organized by standard industrial classification (SIC) code.

The *Valuation Handbook – U.S. Industry Cost of Capital* can be used to benchmark, augment, and support the analyst's own custom analysis of the industry in which a subject business, business ownership interest, security, or intangible asset resides.

The *Valuation Handbook – U.S. Industry Cost of Capital* has been published since 2014, and is updated annually with data through March 31 of the current year (e.g., the *2014 Valuation Handbook – U.S. Industry Cost of Capital* is "data through" March 31, 2014; the *2015 Valuation Handbook – U.S. Industry Cost of Capital* is "data through" March 31, 2015, etc.). This book includes three optional intra-year quarterly updates (June, September, and December).

Valuation Handbook – International Guide to Cost of Capital

This annual book provides country-level equity risk premia (ERPs), relative volatility (RV) factors, and country risk premia (CRPs).

This book can be used to estimate country-level cost of equity capital globally, for up to 188 countries, from the perspective of investors based in any one of up to 56 countries (depending on data availability).

The *Valuation Handbook – International Guide to Cost of Capital* has been published since 2014, and is updated annually with data through December of the previous year and March of the current year (e.g., the *2014 Valuation Handbook – International Guide to Cost of Capital* is "data through" December 31, 2013 and March 31, 2014; the *2015 Valuation Handbook – International Guide to Cost of Capital* is "data through" December 31, 2014 and March 31, 2015, etc.). This book includes one optional semi-annual update with data through June and September.

"Measuring the impact of country risk in determining the international cost of capital is one of the most vexing issues in finance. Any company doing international cost of capital estimation must, at minimum, consult the International Valuation Handbook – U.S. Guide to Cost of Capital".

– **Campbell R. Harvey**, Professor of International Business at the Fuqua School of Business, Duke University

Valuation Handbook – International Industry Cost of Capital

This annual book provides the same type of rigorous industry-level analysis published in the U.S.-centric *Valuation Handbook – U.S. Industry Cost of Capital*, on a global scale.

This book includes industry-level analyses for four global economic areas: (i) the "World", (ii) the European Union, (iii) the Eurozone, and (iv) the United Kingdom.[i.4] Industries in the book are identified by their Global Industry Classification Standard (GICS) code. Each of the four global economic area's industry analyses are presented in three currencies: (i) the euro (€ or EUR), (ii) the British pound (£ or GBP), and (iii) the U.S. dollar ($ or USD).

This annual book provides industry level cost of capital estimates (cost of equity capital, cost of debt capital, and weighted average cost of capital, or WACC), plus detailed industry-level statistics for sales, market capitalization, capital structure, various levered and unlevered beta estimates (e.g., ordinary-least squares (OLS) beta, sum beta, peer group beta, downside beta, etc.), valuation (trading) multiples, financial and profitability ratios, equity returns, aggregate forward-looking earnings-per share (EPS) growth rates, and more. Over 300 critical industry-level data points are calculated for each industry (depending on data availability). Industries are organized by global industry classification standard (GICS) code.

[i.4] In the *Valuation Handbook – International Industry Cost of Capital*, "World" companies are defined as companies that (i) are components of the MSCI ACWI IMI, and (ii) satisfy the rigorous screening requirements that are employed to define the company sets used therein.

The *Valuation Handbook − International Industry Cost of Capital* can be used to benchmark, augment, and support the analyst's own custom analysis of the industry in which a subject business, business ownership interest, security, or intangible asset resides.

The *Valuation Handbook − International Industry Cost of Capital* has been published since 2015, and is updated annually with data through March 31 of the current year (e.g., the *2015 Valuation Handbook − International Industry Cost of Capital* is "data through" March 31, 2015; the *2016 Valuation Handbook − International Industry Cost of Capital* is "data through" March 31, 2016, etc.). This book includes one optional semi-annual update with data through September.

Stocks, Bonds, Bills, and Inflation (SBBI) Yearbook

This annual book has been the definitive annual resource for historical U.S. capital markets performance data for over 30 years.

Starting with the 2016 edition, the *Stocks, Bonds, Bills, and Inflation (SBBI) Yearbook* is now produced by Duff & Phelps and published by John Wiley & Sons. The *SBBI Yearbook* was previously published by Morningstar, Inc. under the name "Ibbotson *Stocks, Bonds, Bills, and Inflation (SBBI) Classic Yearbook*".[i.5]

This book includes returns, index values, and statistical analyses of U.S. large company stocks, small company stocks, long-term corporate bonds, long-term government bonds, intermediate-term government bonds, U.S. Treasury bills, and inflation from January 1926 to present (monthly).

Anyone serious about investments or investing needs an appreciation of capital market history. Such an appreciation, which can be gained from this book, is equally valuable to the individual and institutional investor, practitioners and scholars in finance, economics, and business; portfolio strategists; and security analysts seeking to benchmark their own investment performance. The *SBBI Yearbook* is a thinking person's guide to using historical data to understand the financial markets and make decisions.

[i.5]   The *SBBI Yearbook* was published by Morningstar, Inc. from 2007 through 2015, and by Ibbotson Associates in years prior to 2007.

Purchasing Information

U.S. and International Valuation Theory and Data

- *Cost of Capital: Applications and Examples (5th edition)*
- *Valuation Handbook – U.S. Guide to Cost of Capital*
- *Valuation Handbook – U.S. Industry Cost of Capital*
- *Valuation Handbook – International Guide to Cost of Capital*
- *Valuation Handbook – International Industry Cost of Capital*

To order additional copies of the *2017 Valuation Handbook – U.S. Guide to Cost of Capital* (this book), or other Duff & Phelps valuation data resources published by John Wiley & Sons, please visit www.wiley.com/go/ValuationHandbooks, or call: U.S. (800) 762-2974 International (317) 572-3993 or fax (317) 572-4002.

U.S. Capital Markets Performance Data

- *Stocks, Bonds, Bills, and Inflation (SBBI) Yearbook*

To order copies of the *SBBI Yearbook*, please visit www.wiley.com/go/sbbiyearbook, or call: U.S. (800) 762-2974 International (317) 572-3993 or fax (317) 572-4002.

Table of Contents

Acknowledgements

Authors

Roger J. Grabowski, FASA
Managing Director, Duff & Phelps

James P. Harrington
Director, Duff & Phelps

Carla Nunes, CFA
Managing Director, Duff & Phelps

Thank you

The authors give special thanks to Senior Associate Kevin Madden and Analysts Aaron Russo and Andrew Vey of Duff & Phelps for their assistance in assembling the exhibits presented herein, analysis, editing, and quality control. We thank Executive Assistant Michelle Phillips for production assistance, Director Kelly Hunter for securing data permissions, and Trevor Boake and Daniel Eliades for technology support.

Introduction

The *Valuation Handbook – U.S. Guide to Cost of Capital* is not designed to duplicate the contents of comprehensive, learned treatises on estimating the cost of equity capital such as, Shannon P. Pratt and Roger J. Grabowski, *Cost of Capital: Applications and Examples* 5th edition (John Wiley & Sons, Inc., 2014). That book, for example, covers the latest theory and practice in cost of capital estimation, including cost of capital for uses in business valuation, project assessment and capital budgeting, divisional cost of capital, reporting unit valuation and goodwill impairment testing, valuing intangible assets for financial reporting, and transfer pricing.

Rather, the *Valuation Handbook – U.S. Guide to Cost of Capital* is designed to complement such works, providing a brief refresher for valuation analysts on the approaches to valuation and estimating the cost of equity capital, but primarily focusing on the data sources commonly available for estimating the cost of equity capital.

Who Should Use the *Valuation Handbook – U.S. Guide to Cost of Capital*

The *Valuation Handbook – U.S. Guide to Cost of Capital* is designed to assist financial professionals in estimating the cost of equity capital (k_e) for a subject company. Cost of equity capital is the return necessary to attract funds to an equity investment. The valuation data and methodology in the *Valuation Handbook – U.S. Guide to Cost of Capital* can be used to develop cost of equity capital estimates using both the build-up method and the capital asset pricing model (CAPM). In addition to the traditional professional valuation analyst, the *Valuation Handbook – U.S. Guide to Cost of Capital*, and the online *Risk Premium Toolkit,* and online *Cost of Capital Analyzer*, are designed to serve the needs of:[i.6]

- Corporate finance officers for pricing or evaluating mergers and acquisitions, raising private or public equity, property taxation, and stakeholder disputes.

- Corporate officers for the evaluation of investments for capital budgeting decisions.

- Investment bankers for pricing public offerings, mergers and acquisitions, and private equity financing.

- CPAs who deal with either valuation for financial reporting or client valuations issues.

- Judges and attorneys who deal with valuation issues in mergers and acquisitions (M&A), shareholder and partner disputes, damage cases, solvency cases, bankruptcy reorganizations, property taxes, rate setting, transfer pricing, and financial reporting.

[i.6] The *Risk Premium Toolkit* (previously called the "*Risk Premium Calculator*") and *Cost of Capital Analyzer* are web-based companion applications that are based on the same data and methodology that is published in the *Valuation Handbook – U.S. Guide to Cost of Capital*. Both the *Risk Premium Toolkit* and the *Cost of Capital Analyzer* can be used by the valuation analyst to estimate cost of equity capital for a   subject company dependent on its size and risk characteristics using multiple models (including the build-up method and CAPM). The *Risk Premium Toolkit* is available from Business Valuation Resources, LLC (BVR) (website: www.bvresources.com/costofcapital; phone: 1 (503) 291-7963 ext. 2).
The *Cost of Capital Analyzer* is available from ValuSource, (website: www.valuationhandbook.com; phone: 1 (800) 825-8763).

About the *Valuation Handbook – U.S. Guide to Cost of Capital*

The *2017 Valuation Handbook – U.S. Guide to Cost of Capital* includes two sets of valuation data:

- Data previously available in the Duff & Phelps *Risk Premium Report* (no longer published as a stand-alone publication), and

- Data previously available in the Morningstar/Ibbotson *Stocks, Bonds, Bills, and Inflation SBBI Valuation Yearbook*.[i.7]

The *Risk Premium Report* has been published annually since 1996 and, like the former *SBBI Valuation Yearbook*, provides data and methodology to assist financial professionals in estimating the cost of equity capital for a subject company using various build-up models and the CAPM.

The size premia data previously published in the *SBBI Valuation Yearbook* is referred to as the "CRSP Deciles Size Premia" exhibits in the *Valuation Handbook – U.S. Guide to Cost of Capital*, while the size and risk premia data published in the Duff & Phelps *Risk Premium Report* continues to be titled "Risk Premium Report" exhibits.

"Data Through" Date

The *2017 Valuation Handbook – U.S. Guide to Cost of Capital* includes data through December 31, 2016, and is intended to be used for 2017 valuation dates.

[i.7] Morningstar, Inc. announced in September 2013 that it would no longer publish the Morningstar/Ibbotson *SBBI Valuation Yearbook* and other valuation publications and products.

Same Data Sources

The same data sources used to produce the size premia and other risk premia in the Duff & Phelps *Risk Premium Report* and the former Morningstar/Ibbotson *SBBI Valuation Yearbook* are used to produce the data in the *2017 Valuation Handbook − U.S. Guide to Cost of Capital*:

- The universe of companies used to perform the analyses presented in the Risk Premium Report Study presented herein is comprised of those companies that are found in both (i) the Center for Research in Securities Prices (CRSP) equities database at the University of Chicago Booth School of Business, and (ii) Standard & Poor's *Compustat* database.

- The equity portfolios, asset class data, and individual company data used to perform the analyses presented in the CRSP Deciles Size Study presented herein are (i) the CRSP standard market-capitalization-based NYSE/NYSE MKT/NASDAQ indices, (ii) the *SBBI* Series from Morningstar's *Direct* database, and (iii) Standard & Poor's *Research Insight* database.

To learn more about CRSP, visit www.crsp.com. To learn more about Morningstar's *Direct* database, visit www.corporate.morningstar.com. To learn more about Standard & Poor's, visit www.standardandpoors.com.

New in the *2017 Valuation Handbook − U.S. Guide to Cost of Capital*

The *Valuation Handbook − U.S. Guide to Cost of Capital* is in its fourth year of publication with the release of the 2017 edition (this book). The inaugural 2014 edition was self-published by Duff & Phelps; starting in 2015, the *Valuation Handbook − U.S. Guide to Cost of Capital* is published by John Wiley & Sons, marking a significant milestone for the *Valuation Handbook − U.S. Guide to Cost of Capital*.

We have updated and added to our discussion in Chapter 3 of the risk-free rate and the equity risk premium with analyses of the effects of flight to quality and massive central bank monetary interventions on these two important cost of capital inputs.

We have added to Chapter 12, "Answers to Commonly Asked Questions" some of the many thoughtful questions we received from valuation analysts throughout the year about the *Valuation Handbook − U.S. Guide to Cost of Capital*.

For more information about Duff & Phelps valuation data resources published by John Wiley & Sons, please go to: www.wiley.com/go/ValuationHandbooks.

Chapter 1
Cost of Capital Defined

Introduction

"The cost of capital is the expected rate of return that the market requires in order to attract funds to a particular investment."

– Shannon P. Pratt and Roger J. Grabowski, co-authors of *Cost of Capital*, 5th edition[1.1]

"The opportunity cost of capital is one of the most important concepts in finance. For example, if you are a chief finance officer contemplating a possible capital expenditure, you need to know what return you should look to earn from the investment. If you are an investor who needs to plan for future expenditures, you need to ask what return you can expect to earn on your portfolio."

– Richard Brealey, London Business School

"The opportunity cost of capital is equal to the return that could have been earned on alternative investments at a similar level of risk and liquidity."

– Roger Ibbotson, Yale University

"The cost of capital is the price charged by investors for bearing the risk that the company's future cash flows may differ from what they anticipated when they made the investment."

– McKinsey[1.2]

The cost of capital may be described in simple terms as the expected return appropriate for the expected level of risk.[1.3] The cost of capital is also commonly called the *discount rate*, the *expected return*, or the *required return*.[1.4]

Before elaborating on the specifics of estimating cost of capital inputs, we begin the *Valuation Handbook – U.S. Guide to Cost of Capital* with a basic framework. In many instances, valuations are performed by applying a combination of three broad valuation approaches: (i) the income approach, (ii) the market approach, or (iii) the asset approach. The market and asset approaches, however, do not generally rely on a cost of capital input. Income-based methods, on the other hand, are highly dependent on the use of an appropriate cost of capital estimate. There are a wide variety of

---

[1.1] Shannon P. Pratt and Roger J. Grabowski, *Cost of Capital: Applications and Examples* 5th ed. (Hoboken, NJ: John Wiley & Sons, 2014): 2.

[1.2] Tim Koller, Marc Goedhart, and David Wessels, *Valuation: Measuring and Managing the Value of Companies*, 5th ed. (Hoboken, NJ: John Wiley & Sons, 2010): 33.

[1.3] Investors tend to try to maximize return for a given amount of risk, or minimize risk for a given amount of return.

[1.4] When a business uses a given cost of capital to evaluate a commitment of capital to an investment or project, it often refers to that cost of capital as the "hurdle rate". The hurdle rate is the minimum expected rate of return that the business would be willing to accept to justify making the investment.

methods within the income approach, but they are not the subject of this text. Instead, we limit our discussion to the broad categories of single period versus multi-period approaches to distinguish between the notions of capitalizing and discounting.

We then proceed to provide an overview of basic cost of capital concepts, outline general sources of capital, and finally conclude by summarizing some general ways to estimate the cost of typical capital structure components.

Income Approach Overview

Broadly speaking, the income approach can be defined as a way of determining a value indication of an investment (e.g., business, business ownership interest, security, or intangible asset) using one or more methods that convert the expected future economic benefits associated with an investment into a single "present value" amount. The basic steps of valuing a business are summarized in Exhibit 1.1.

Exhibit 1.1: Basic Steps in Valuing a Business

Step 1
Estimate expected future cash flows.
This is the *numerator* in a discounting and capitalization formula.

Step 2
Estimate the cost of capital (i.e., the "discount rate").
This is a key input in the *denominator* in a discounting and capitalization formula.

Step 3
Use the *cost of capital* to "discount" the expected future cash flows back to present value.

Throughout this book, the terms "business" or "entity" are used to generically represent the subject investment being valued. In reality, the subject investment could include a wholly owned business, a business ownership interest, a security, or an intangible asset, among many others.

Discounting versus Capitalizing Concepts

Income approaches, in general, derive the present value of expected future economic benefits by either capitalizing a single period benefit amount or discounting to present value a multi-period projection. Depending on the nature of the projections and the subject investment being valued, both methods can be acceptable. The single period and multi-period approaches are summarized as follows:

- **Single Period:** When expected benefits are capitalized, a *single* (representative or normalized) benefit level is divided by an appropriate capitalization factor to convert the benefit to present value. This method would be appropriate when the economic benefits are expected to increase (or decline) at a *constant* rate into the future (i.e., akin to a constant-growth annuity). As such, capitalization is a simplified version of a multi-period analysis.

- **Multi-period**: When expected benefits are discounted, annual benefits are estimated for *each* of the future periods in which they are expected to occur. This stream of economic benefits is converted to present value by applying an appropriate discount rate (or cost of capital) and using present value techniques. Discounting tends to be more appropriate in situations where the economic benefits are expected to increase (or decrease) at *varying* rates into the future.

In its most basic form, the present value concept embedded in the income approach may be represented in equation format as:

Formula 1.1

$$PV = \frac{NCF_0\left(1+g\right)^1}{\left(1+k\right)^1} + \frac{NCF_0\left(1+g\right)^2}{\left(1+k\right)^2} + \ldots + \frac{NCF_0\left(1+g\right)^n}{\left(1+k\right)^n}$$

Where:

PV	=	Present value
NCF_0	=	Net cash flow at "time zero" (i.e., "now" or the most recently completed period as of the valuation date)
k	=	Discount rate
g	=	Expected rate of change (growth) in net cash flows
n	=	Total number of periods

Expected future economic benefits are typically measured by net cash flows (sometimes called free cash flows, or simply, cash flows). Net cash flow represents discretionary cash available to be paid out to stakeholders (providers of capital) of an entity or project (e.g., interest, debt payments, dividends, withdrawals) without jeopardizing the projected ongoing operations of the entity or project. Net cash flow is typically defined as an after-tax concept (specifically, *after* corporate income taxes and *before* investor income taxes) because the sources of the discount rate measures are typically drawn from rates of return after corporate income taxes and before investor income taxes.

Capitalization Rates versus Discount Rates

These terms are sometimes confused with each other, but the process of capitalizing is really just a shorthand form of discounting. The data in this book can be used to develop both capitalization rates and discount rates.

As discussed in the previous section, with capitalization rates, we focus on the expected benefit of just a *single* period, usually the expected net cash flow projected for the first year immediately following the valuation date. This amount represents the long-term normalized base level of net cash flows or a base from which the level of cash flows is expected to increase or decline at a more or less *constant* rate. This single-year net cash flow is then divided by the capitalization rate.

A challenge with capitalizing is that for most investments, expected net cash flows are rarely projected to increase at a constant rate into perpetuity from either the year preceding or the year following the valuation date. We do note that such a simplifying assumption is commonly used to estimate the residual year value (sometimes called terminal year value or continuing value) in a multi-period analysis; however, that residual year net cash flow is intended to represent the sustainable or normalized level of cash flows into perpetuity.

Alternatively, discount rates are applied in the context of a *multi*-period analysis. There, annual expected net cash flows from the subject investment are projected over the life of that investment. Again, this is appropriate when the expected cash flows are *not* constant, or are *not* changing at a constant growth rate. In these cases, the expected cash flows are divided by a present value factor (the terms "$(1 + k)^1$" through "$(1 + k)^n$" in Formula 1.1), which includes a discount rate (k) estimate. Common practice in business valuation is to assume that the net cash flows are received on average continuously throughout the year (approximately equivalent to receiving the net cash flows in the middle of the year), in which case the present value factor is generally based on a mid-year convention (e.g., $(1+k)^{0.5}$).

A challenge associated with discounting (for most investments) is the accuracy of the projection of expected net cash flows for each specific projection period several years into the future. Nevertheless, since the future cash flows of businesses (and capital projects) are typically not constant, and in some cases vary significantly from period to period, these types of investments lend themselves to discounting, more so than to capitalizing.

Relationship Between Capitalization Rates and Discount Rates

If the expected increase or decrease (i.e., growth) in net cash flows for the investment is stable and sustainable over a long period of time, then a discount rate (cost of capital) can reasonably be converted into a capitalization rate. We could even say that the capitalization rate is a function of the discount rate and growth rate under these conditions. The relationship between the discount rate and the capitalization rate can be put into equation form as shown in Formula 1.2:[1.5]

Formula 1.2

Capitalization Rate = Discount Rate − Expected Growth Rate

Can the discount rate and capitalization rate ever be the same value? Yes − the discount rate and capitalization rate are equivalent when the expected growth rate is equal to zero.[1.6]

Lastly, notable to Formula 1.1 is its use of g, a constant expected rate of growth in net cash flows.

[1.5] A critical assumption in Formula 1.2 is that the expected rate of increase (growth) in the net cash flow from the investment is reasonably constant over the long term (technically into perpetuity).

[1.6] A simple example of when the growth rate could be equal to zero is a preferred stock that is issued in perpetuity, is not callable, for which there is not prospect of liquidation, and which pays a set dividend at the end of each year.

This formula can be extended to include different variations of growth stages (e.g., multi-stage growth model), but this level of detail is beyond the scope of this book. For greater detail, see Chapter 4, "Discounting versus Capitalizing" in the *Cost of Capital*, 5th Edition.

As presented in Formula 1.1, a series of annual net cash flows (expected to increase at a constant annual rate *g*) are individually discounted to present value. A constant growth rate enables this formula to be simplified to a single period capitalization. This constant growth capitalization formula is commonly known as the Gordon Growth Model:

$$PV = \frac{NCF_0(1+g)}{(k-g)}$$

Note that for this model to make economic sense, NCF_0 must represent a normalized amount of net cash flow from the investment for the previous year, from which a steady rate of growth is expected to proceed. Therefore, NCF_0 may not need to be the actual net cash flow for period 0 but may reflect certain normalization adjustments, such as elimination of the effect of one or more non-recurring factors.

This capitalization formula serves as the basis for estimation of the residual value in many multi-stage growth models. Often the residual value represents a significant portion of the estimated value of the investment. But because the inputs to the discount rates are imprecise, the goal is to obtain an unbiased estimate of the discount rate. But research has shown that this commonly used formula does not provide an unbiased estimate of the residual value and an adjustment is needed. We discuss this adjustment in section entitled "Estimates of Cost of Capital are Imprecise" at the end of Chapter 1.

Valuation Date

The valuation date is the specific point in time as of which the valuation analyst's opinion of value applies. The valuation date is sometimes referred to as the "effective date" or "appraisal date".

A guiding principle in conducting valuations is that you should incorporate facts that are known or reasonably knowable at the time of the valuation date.

The *2017 Valuation Handbook – U.S. Guide to Cost of Capital* includes data through December 31, 2016, and is intended to be used for 2017 valuation dates.

Basic Cost of Capital Concepts

Cost of Capital Is Forward-Looking

The cost of capital (like valuation itself) is based on investors' expectations of what will happen in the *future*, and it is therefore "forward-looking". Cost of capital is used to discount the expected future economic benefits (or income) associated with the ownership of an investment to their present value. The term "expected" represents the average of probability-weighted possible economic benefits (or income) that are usually measured in terms of expected future cash flows.

Exhibit 1.2: Valuation Is Equating Expected Future Economic Benefits (Cash Flows) to Present Value

Expected Future Economic Benefits (Cash Flows)

$$ \boxed{\$} \quad \boxed{\$} \quad \boxed{\$} \quad \boxed{\$} $$

| 1 | 2 | 3 | ...n |

Present Value ⟵————————————————

Does History Repeat Itself?

Uncertainty about what is going to happen in the future is the very nature of risk. In the absence of being able to tell the future with anything approaching certainty, we naturally oftentimes look to the past (e.g., analyzing historical market data) in an attempt to gauge what may happen in the future.

For example, the equity risk premium (ERP) – a key variable in estimating the cost of equity capital – is defined as the incremental return that investors demand for investing in equities (stocks) rather than investing in a risk-free asset. As discussed in Chapter 3, one common method for estimating the ERP is to examine the historical differences between equity returns and risk-free returns, and make an assumption that this historical relationship will hold in the future. This method of estimating the ERP "works" only to the extent that history does repeat itself, which is by no means guaranteed.

Past returns may provide, at best, some guidance as to what returns in the future will be (given an expected level of risk). This is not to say that analyzing what happened in the past for hints of what may happen in the future is unhelpful – it generally *is* helpful – especially when compared to the alternative of trying to guess the future without the benefit of learning from the past.

The use of historical data in the formulation of cost of capital inputs is discussed in greater detail in Chapter 3, "Basic Building Blocks of the Cost of Equity Capital – Risk-free Rate and ERP".

Cost of Capital Is a Function of the Investment, Not the Investor

The cost of capital is a function of the investment, not the investor.[1.7] In other words, the characteristics of a particular investor does not directly change the characteristics of the investment being analyzed.

The cost of capital comes from the marketplace, and the marketplace is comprised of a pool of investors "pricing" the risk of a particular asset. It therefore represents the consensus assessment of the pool of investors that are participants in a particular market. The term "market" refers to the universe of investors who are reasonable candidates to fund a particular investment.

[1.7]   Ibbotson Associates, "What Is the Cost of Capital?" *1999 Cost of Capital Workshop* (Chicago: Ibbotson Associates, 1999).

Cost of Capital Is Based on Market Value

When estimating the value of an investment – as defined under a particular standard of value (i.e., fair market value, fair value, etc.) – the measurement is performed using market-based concepts, rather than by relying on the book value, par value, or carrying value of that investment. Although not directly observable, the cost of capital is also estimated by using market data. As stated earlier, the cost of capital is the expected rate of return on alternative investments with similar levels of risk. Investors will compare these alternative investments based on their market value, not their book or carrying amounts.

For example, the yield to maturity shown in the bond quotations in the financial press is based on the closing market price of a bond, not on its face value. Similarly, the implied cost of equity capital for a company's stock is based on the share price at which it trades, and not on the company's book value per share.

Cost of Capital Is Usually Stated in Nominal Terms

The data for developing discount and capitalization rates described in this book are expressed in nominal terms. Estimating cost of capital in "nominal" terms means that it includes investors' expectations of future inflation. Conversely, estimating cost of capital in "real" terms means that it does not include investors' inflation expectations.

Cost of capital is usually stated in nominal terms because the return that investors demand is typically going to be at least enough to keep up with what they expect future inflation to be. In other words, investors will require compensation for the expected future erosion of an asset's value due to inflation.

Cost of Capital Is Usually Stated in Terms of After-tax Returns

Just as net cash flow is an after-tax concept (i.e., measured after entity-level income taxes), the discount and capitalization rates as developed in this book are also after-tax (specifically, after entity level or corporate income taxes, but before individual investor taxes). The equity "total returns" published in the financial press include both dividends (income) and price (i.e., capital appreciation) returns (reflecting *after*-tax performance at the corporate level), but are *before* taxation at individual investor level.[1.8]

As-if Publicly traded

The discount and capitalization rates as developed in this book are "as-if publicly traded". The data used in the *Valuation Handbook – U.S. Guide to Cost of Capital* are drawn from information on public companies and, therefore, the resulting cost of capital estimates using the data are "as if public".

Discounting expected future expected cash flows for a non-publicly traded investment (e.g., a closely held business) using an "as if publicly-traded" cost of capital may not provide an accurate

---

[1.8] Total return consists of three components: (i) price (i.e., capital appreciation) returns, (ii) income returns (e.g., dividends), and (iii) reinvestment (e.g., of dividends) returns.

estimate of value to the extent that market participants would consider other risks associated with non-publicly traded investments. For example, when estimating the cost of equity capital for a closely held company, the risks will more than likely differ from the risks of the sample of guideline public companies to which it is being compared (i.e., the "peer group"), and valuation analysts may therefore deem additional adjustments to the cost of capital estimate necessary.

Minority Interest

Some valuation analysts argue that the income approach always produces a publicly traded minority basis of value because the build-up method and the capital asset pricing model (CAPM) develop discount and capitalization rates from minority transaction data in the public markets. This is not correct. The discount and capitalization rates as developed in this book do not include an implied "minority interest" discount in them. There is little or no difference in the rate of return that most investors require for investing in a public, freely tradable minority interest versus a controlling interest.[1.9]

The Delaware Court of Chancery recognizes that discount rates derived from public company data should not be adjusted for an implied minority discount.[1.10] The Court of Chancery first rejected this adjustment in 1991[1.11] and, except for one anomalous exception, it has continued to reject adding a control premium to valuations where the valuation experts used the discounted cash flow method, a form of the income approach.

Controlling Interest

Investors typically do not reduce their required rate of return because they are buying a controlling interest in an investment, rather than a minority interest.

Generally, the cost of capital is the same for minority interest investments as for controlling interest investments. While a premium above current market trading prices is often paid to acquire a controlling equity interest, this premium is typically paid because buyers expect to implement some measures to increase future cash flows of the target investment, not because of a lower cost of capital associated with control.

Varying Cost of Capital

When we value an investment, we are estimating the present value of the expected future economic benefits or income associated with that investment. Like all valuation inputs, the cost of capital should also reflect future expectations. In theory, when dealing with multiple periods in the forecast period, the risk profile of the annual future cash flows will likely differ from period to period. As a

---

[1.9] Pratt, *Business Valuation Discounts and Premiums* (Hoboken, NJ: John Wiley & Sons, 2001): 30, cited in Lane, 2004 Del. Ch. LEXIS 108.

[1.10] Valuation analysts should be aware of the influence that the Delaware Court of Chancery has on other courts, such as the U.S. Tax Court. The Delaware Court of Chancery hears more valuation-related cases than any other court, and many courts look, even informally, at the decisions of that court for guidance. To learn more, visit: www.courts.delaware.gov/chancery.

[1.11] *In re Radiology Associates*, 611 A.2d 485, 494 ("The discounted cash flow method purports to represent the present value of Radiology's cash flow. . .The discounted cash flow analysis, as employed in this case, fully reflects this value without need for an adjustment").

result, the cost of capital associated with any investment would arguably also change from period to period. This can quickly become a very complex exercise.

As a simplification, valuation analysts generally estimate a single cost of capital and apply it to each of the periods in the forecast.

Sources of Capital

Thus far the term cost of capital has been used in generic terms. As stated earlier, the cost of capital is the expected rate of return required to attract funds to a particular investment. The word "capital" in "cost of capital" refers to the components of an entity's capital structure. The capital structure is a function of how the entity raises capital to fund its business operations (i.e., the funding sources). Businesses typically raise capital by issuing (i) common equity, (ii) preferred equity, and/or (iii) debt.[1.12, 1.13]

The capital structure can include a combination of these three components, each of which has its own cost of capital.[1.14] When valuing the overall business enterprise, these three types of cost of capital are "blended" together to form a "weighted average cost of capital", or WACC.

The basic forms of cost of capital when referring to an entity's capital structure are defined as follows:

- **Common equity capital:** The cost of equity capital is the expected return to common equity (i.e., stock) investors. Often referred to as simply the cost of equity. Common stocks are the most widely held form of equity, and thus the most familiar type of equity investment for most people. Common stock owners hope to gain from rising share prices, and from dividend distributions. Dividends to common equity investors are typically paid after dividends to preferred equity investors have already been paid. Also, common equity investors are typically "last in line" in the case of liquidation or bankruptcy. Common equity is generally *riskier* than either preferred equity or debt instruments, but over the long term may provide a higher return. (Note that the higher the risk of an investment, the higher the expected return.)

- **Preferred equity capital:** The cost of preferred equity capital is the expected return to preferred equity (i.e., stock) investors. Usually referred to as simply the cost of preferred equity. Preferred shares often pay a fixed dividend, and this dividend is typically paid prior to any dividend payments to common equity shareholders. Because the preferred equity's dividend is often fixed, it often trades like a bond with a coupon and its price will

---

1.12 There may be more than one subcategory in any or all of the listed categories of capital. Also, there may be related forms of capital, such as warrants or options.

1.13 Equity securities are generically referred to as "stocks", and debt securities are generically referred to as "bonds".

1.14 The cost of raising capital should include the costs of raising capital from external capital sources. These costs, commonly termed flotation or transaction costs, reduce the actual proceeds received by the firm. Some of these are direct out-of-pocket outlays, such as fees paid to underwriters, legal expenses, and prospectus preparation costs. Because of this *reduction* in proceeds, the business's required returns must be *greater* to compensate for the additional costs.

fluctuate (inversely) with market interest rates.[1.15] However, certain forms of preferred stock (e.g., convertible preferred) have features that resemble common equity. Preferred equity is generally *less* risky than common equity, but *riskier* than debt instruments.

- **Debt capital:** The cost of debt capital is the expected return to debt (e.g., bond) investors. Usually referred to as simply cost of debt. Note that the cost of debt is estimated prior to the tax effect (without regard to the tax shield). Debt capital is generally *less* risky than preferred equity and common equity.

- **Weighted average cost of capital (WACC):** The cost of capital to the overall business is commonly called the WACC. WACC represents the market-capitalization-weighted cost of capital for both equity holders (both common and preferred) and debt holders. WACC is sometimes referred to as "blended cost of capital", or simply "overall cost of capital". WACC is typically estimated on an after-tax basis, as explained later in this chapter.

Cost of Capital Input Assumptions

Data and methodology in the Valuation Handbook – U.S. Guide to Cost of Capital can be used to estimate the cost of common equity capital. Estimating the costs of the other components of the capital structure – preferred equity capital and debt capital – is typically more straightforward than estimating the cost of common equity capital. This is because the cost of capital (risk) of fixed-income securities (bonds) and fixed-income-like securities (preferred stocks) are usually directly observable in the market, while the cost of equity capital is not. We discuss these components only briefly here.[1.16]

Estimating the Cost of Preferred Equity Capital

If the capital structure includes preferred equity capital and it is publicly traded, the market yield (dividend ÷ market price) can be used as the cost of that component. If the preferred security does not trade publicly or trades infrequently, the current market yield for preferred stocks with comparable features and risk can be used as a proxy. Standard & Poor's integrates debt and preferred stock in the same rating scale, according to its published criteria.[1.17] According to this publication, preferred stock is rated generally below subordinated debt. When the corporate credit rating on a company is investment grade, its preferred stock is generally rated two notches below the corporate credit rating. When the corporate credit rating is below investment grade, the preferred stock is rated at least three notches (i.e., one full rating category) below the corporate credit rating. Other adjustments may be appropriate. Moody's also uses similar criteria when assigning a preferred stock rating. It is noted that separate rating criteria would apply, if dealing with

---

[1.15] The price of preferred equity will fluctuate as similar-risk investments' yields vary. Because of the similarities of certain preferred equities and bonds, these preferred equities' prices will tend to fluctuate with the generic concept of "interest rates".

[1.16] To learn more about the cost of preferred capital and debt capital, see Pratt and Roger J. Grabowski, op.cit.: Chapter 20, "Other Components of a Business's Capital Structure".

[1.17] Source: Standard & Poor's "Criteria – Corporates – General: 2008 Corporate Criteria: Rating Each Issue", published originally on April 15, 2008, and republished on January 1, 2016. According to this document, prior to 1999, Standard & Poor's used a separate preferred stock scale. In February 1999, the debt and preferred stock scales were integrated.

hybrid securities.[1.18]

Valuation analysts can use this information to assess where the subject company's preferred stock would fit within the corporate rating scale, given the actual (or synthetic) credit rating of the subject entity, and then select the yields for preferred stocks with similar features and ratings.

Estimating the Cost of Debt Capital

If the capital structure includes debt capital, valuation analysts should estimate a current market rate for that component of the entity's capital structure. The interest rate should be consistent with the financial condition of the subject business, based on a comparative analysis of the subject business's operating ratios.

If the entity has been assigned a credit rating, one can estimate the cost of debt using a yield curve analysis. If the entity is not formally rated, one can estimate a credit rating (often called a "synthetic" rating). This typically entails calculating certain financial ratios for the subject company and benchmarking them against key median ratios by rating category, as published by rating agencies.

Major rating agencies such as Standard & Poor's and Moody's publish their credit rating criteria, making it generally available to investors. They also publish periodically certain key ratios observed historically by rating category. For example, S&P Capital IQ's *CreditStats Direct*™ provides median credit ratios by rating category for several industries. *CreditStats Direct*™ is a module within *RatingsDirect*® that offers financial statement data and ratios as adjusted by Standard & Poor's rating analysts. *RatingsDirect*® is a web-based product within the S&P Capital IQ's *Global Credit Portal*®, which provides access to Standard & Poor's global credit ratings and research. Standard & Poor's also offers an application called *CreditModel*, which is a proprietary suite of statistical models that create credit scores for public and private mid-cap and large firms. These calculations are based on, yet differ from Standard & Poor's Ratings Services' criteria.

All of these are examples of tools that can help valuation analysts assess where the subject investment would fit within the credit rating scale and then find the market yields corresponding to the estimated rating.

Debt capital can also include forms of off-balance sheet liabilities such as operating leases and unfunded pension liabilities. Estimating the cost of debt associated with these off-balance items is outside the scope of this book, which focuses primarily on estimating the cost of equity capital.

[1.18] Source: Moody's "Rating Methodology – Updated Summary Guidance for Notching Bonds, Preferred Stocks and Hybrid Securities of Corporate Issuers", published on February 2007. To access this document, visit: https://www.moodys.com/sites/products/AboutMoodysRatingsAttachments/2006400000430106.pdf.

An excellent source of statistics that enable the valuation analyst to gauge the impact of debt-like off-balance sheet items in the capital structure of the subject industry is the *Valuation Handbook – U.S. Industry Cost of Capital*.[1.19] These debt-equivalent liabilities (specifically, operating leases and unfunded pension obligations) are not only taken into account by credit rating agencies when assigning a debt rating for a company, but should likely be considered as well when ascertaining the true financial (and equity) risk of the subject company.

For example, in Exhibit 1.3 an abbreviated section of Appendix A from the *2016 Valuation Handbook – U.S. Industry Cost of Capital* is shown. Appendix A in the industry book lists the "Latest" debt-to-total-capital ratios of all U.S. industries analyzed therein (approximately 180) *before* and *after* adjusting for capitalized operating leases and unfunded liabilities. For example, when debt-to-total-capital is calculated using "Book Debt" (i.e., *unadjusted* debt), the "Latest" debt-to-total-capital ratio for SIC 45 (Transportation by Air) is 27.5%, but when debt-to-total-capital is calculated using "Book Debt + Off-Balance-Sheet Debt" (i.e., debt *adjusted* to include capitalized operating leases and unfunded pensions), the "Latest" debt-to-total capital ratio for SIC 45 is 44.9%, a difference of 17.4% (44.9% – 27.5%).

[1.19] The *Valuation Handbook – U.S. Industry Cost of Capital* provides cost of capital estimates (i.e., equity capital, debt capital, and WACC) for approximately 180 U.S. industries and size groupings (i.e., Large-, Mid-, Low-, and Micro-capitalization companies), plus a host of detailed statistics that can be used for benchmarking purposes (over 300 critical industry-level data points calculated for each industry, depending on data availability). This annual book provides industry-level cost of capital estimates (cost of equity capital, cost of debt capital, and weighted average cost of capital, or WACC), plus detailed industry-level statistics for sales, market capitalization, capital structure, various levered and unlevered beta estimates, valuation (trading) multiples, financial and profitability ratios, equity returns, aggregate forward-looking earnings-per share (EPS) growth rates, and more. Industries are organized by standard industrial classification (SIC) code. The *Valuation Handbook – U.S. Industry Cost of Capital* has been published since 2014, and is updated annually with data through March 31 of the current year (e.g., the *2014 Valuation Handbook – U.S. Industry Cost of Capital* is "data through" March 31, 2014; the *2015 Valuation Handbook – U.S. Industry Cost of Capital* is "data through" March 31, 2015, etc.). This book includes three optional intra-year quarterly updates (June, September, and December). To order copies of the *Valuation Handbook – Industry Cost of Capital* and its quarterly updates, please go to www.wiley.com/go/ValuationHandbooks.

Exhibit 1.3: Abbreviated Section of Appendix A from the *2016 Valuation Handbook − U.S. Industry Cost of Capital* (as of March 31, 2016)

SIC	Industry Description	Calculated Using Book Debt Debt-to-total Capital (%)	Calculated Using Book Debt + Off-Balance-Sheet Debt Debt-to-total Capital (%)
45	Transportation By Air	27.5	44.9
591	Drug Stores and Proprietory Stores	19.7	31.2
3711	Motor Vehicles and Passenger Car Bodies	62.7	65.4

SIC	Industry Description	Relative Impact: Operating Leases versus Unfunded Pension Liabilies Primary Driver of Change in Capital Structure	Operating Leases (%)	Unfunded Pension Liabilities (%)
45	Transportation By Air	Operating Leases	72.6	27.4
591	Drug Stores and Proprietory Stores	Operating Leases	99.6	0.4
3711	Motor Vehicles and Passenger Car Bodies	Unfunded Pension Liabilities	8.8	91.2

Note that for each industry in Exhibit 1.3, the off-balance-sheet debt item (capitalized operating leases or unfunded pensions) that is the "primary driver" of the change in capital structure is *identified*, and its relative impact *quantified*. For example, the primary driver of the change in capital structure of SIC 591 (Drug Stores and Proprietary Stores) is "Operating Leases", which accounted for 99.6% of the change. Alternatively, the primary driver of the change in capital structure of SIC 3711 (Motor Vehicles and Passenger Car Bodies) was "Unfunded Pension Liabilities", which accounted for 91.2% of the change.

Appendix B of the *Valuation Handbook − U.S. Industry Cost of Capital* builds on the statistics provided in Appendix A. In Appendix B, the "unlevered" (i) Raw (OLS) betas, (ii) Blume-Adjusted betas, (iii) Peer Group betas, (iv) Vasicek-Adjusted betas, (v) Sum betas, and (vi) Downside betas of each industry are calculated two ways: (i) *with* and (ii) *without* capitalized operating leases and unfunded pension liabilities being considered in the unlevering formula. In the analyses presented in *Valuation Handbook − U.S. Industry Cost of Capital*, the "Miles-Ezzell" formulas are used to unlever all beta estimates.[1.20]

In addition to the aforementioned statistics, the *Valuation Handbook − U.S. Industry Cost of Capital* provides eight (8) cost of equity capital estimates for each of the industries covered in the book, cost of debt capital and weighted average cost of capital (WACC) estimates, plus capital structure, valuation multiples, industry betas, and more (depending on data availability). Exhibit 1.4 is a sample industry analysis page from the *2016 Valuation Handbook − U.S. Industry Cost of Capital*.

[1.20] See James A. Miles and John R. Ezzell, "The Weighted Average Cost of Capital, Perfect Capital Markets and Project Life: A Clarification", *Journal of Financial and Quantitative Analysis* (1980): 719–730.

Data Updated Through March 31, 2016

4

Number of Companies: 184
Transportation, Communications, Electric, Gas, and Sanitary Services

Industry Description
This division includes establishments providing, to the general public or to other business enterprises, passenger and freight transportation, communications services, or electricity, gas, steam, water or sanitary services.

Sales (in millions)

Three Largest Companies

AT&T Inc.	$146,801.0
Verizon Communications Inc.	131,620.0
Comcast Corp.	74,510.0

Three Smallest Companies

York Water Co.	$47.1
Providence And Worcester Railroad	34.3
U.S. Geothermal Inc.	31.0

Total Assets (in millions)

Three Largest Companies

AT&T Inc.	$402,672.0
Verizon Communications Inc.	244,640.0
Comcast Corp.	166,574.0

Three Smallest Companies

RGC Resources, Inc.	$148.1
Providence And Worcester Railroad	111.9
Hudson Technologies Inc.	85.0

Annualized Monthly Performance Statistics (%)

Industry	Geometric Mean	Arithmetic Mean	Standard Deviation	S&P 500 Index	Geometric Mean	Arithmetic Mean	Standard Deviation
1-year	2.9	3.7	13.3	1-year	1.8	2.8	15.1
3-year	9.9	10.4	11.1	3-year	11.8	12.5	12.7
5-year	12.4	13.0	11.2	5-year	11.6	12.4	13.6

Return Ratios (%)

	Return on Assets Latest	5-Yr Avg	Return on Equity Latest	5-Yr Avg	Dividend Yield Latest	5-Yr Avg	Current Ratio Latest	5-Yr Avg	Operating Margin Latest	5-Yr Avg	Long-term EPS Analyst Estimates
Median (184)	3.3	3.4	7.4	7.8	2.7	2.8	1.1	1.1	17.6	16.4	6.6
SIC Composite (184)	4.1	3.4	5.9	5.5	3.4	3.3	0.9	1.0	18.7	16.3	7.0
Large Composite (18)	5.1	3.7	7.0	5.7	3.5	3.7	0.8	0.9	18.7	15.4	7.0
Small Composite (18)	4.7	5.1	5.0	6.4	2.5	3.6	2.5	2.1	14.9	18.2	10.6
High-Financial Risk (27)	-4.4	-2.4	-15.3	-6.2	2.4	2.6	1.0	1.2	3.1	5.4	17.1

Liquidity Ratio: Current Ratio. Profitability Ratio (%): Operating Margin. Growth Rates (%): Long-term EPS.

Betas (Levered)

	Raw (OLS)	Blume Adjusted	Peer Group	Vasicek Adjusted	Sum	Downside
Median	0.8	0.9	0.7	0.8	0.8	1.0
SIC Composite	0.6	0.8	0.7	0.6	0.6	0.6
Large Composite	0.6	0.7	0.8	0.6	0.5	0.6
Small Composite	0.7	0.8	0.6	0.7	0.6	0.7
High Financial Risk	1.1	1.1	0.6	1.1	1.6	1.4

Betas (Unlevered)

	Raw (OLS)	Blume Adjusted	Peer Group	Vasicek Adjusted	Sum	Downside
Median	0.6	0.6	0.5	0.6	0.6	0.8
SIC Composite	0.5	0.6	0.5	0.5	0.4	0.5
Large Composite	0.4	0.5	0.6	0.4	0.4	0.4
Small Composite	0.6	0.7	0.5	0.6	0.5	0.6
High Financial Risk	0.7	0.6	0.5	0.7	0.8	0.7

Equity Valuation Multiples

	Price/Sales Latest	5-Yr Avg	Price/Earnings Latest	5-Yr Avg	Market/Book Latest	5-Yr Avg
Median	1.8	1.5	20.9	18.6	1.7	1.5
SIC Composite	1.7	1.4	16.9	18.3	1.7	1.6
Large Composite	1.5	1.3	14.3	17.5	1.9	1.7
Small Composite	2.5	2.0	20.1	15.7	1.7	1.7
High Financial Risk	0.6	0.7	–	–	1.8	2.0

Enterprise Valuation (EV) Multiples

	EV/Sales Latest	5-Yr Avg	EV/EBITDA Latest	5-Yr Avg
Median	2.6	2.4	9.7	9.0
SIC Composite	2.5	2.2	8.5	8.1
Large Composite	2.2	1.9	7.5	7.1
Small Composite	2.9	2.6	12.5	9.3
High Financial Risk	1.8	1.7	12.4	10.2

Enterprise Valuation — SIC Composite

EV/Sales: Latest 2.5, 5-Yr Avg 2.2. EV/EBITDA: Latest 8.5, 5-Yr Avg 8.1.

Fama-French (F-F) 5-Factor Model

	Fama-French (F-F) Components F-F Beta	SMB Premium	HML Premium	RMW Premium	CMA Premium
Median	1.2	2.2	0.3	1.0	-2.4
SIC Composite	0.7	-0.4	-0.9	0.0	3.3
Large Composite	0.7	-0.9	-1.7	0.0	0.0
Small Composite	0.6	2.7	1.7	0.3	1.4
High Financial Risk	–	–	–	–	–

Leverage Ratios (%)

	Debt/MV Equity Latest	5-Yr Avg	Debt/Total Capital Latest	5-Yr Avg	Cost of Debt (%) Latest
Median	52.1	57.6	34.2	36.6	5.5
SIC Composite	54.4	55.7	35.2	35.8	5.5
Large Composite	47.3	49.5	32.1	33.1	5.2
Small Composite	28.8	40.9	22.4	29.0	6.5
High Financial Risk	–	145.5	67.5	59.3	8.3

Capital Structure — SIC Composite (%) Latest

D/TC 35.2, E/TC 64.8

Cost of Equity Capital (%)

	CRSP Deciles CAPM	CAPM +Size Prem	Build-Up	Risk Premium Report CAPM +Size Prem	Build-Up	Discounted Cash Flow 1-Stage	3-Stage	Fama-French 5-Factor Model
Median	8.2	9.5	8.5	11.5	12.9	9.6	7.9	11.6
SIC Composite	7.5	7.6	7.6	8.6	10.6	10.3	8.4	9.7
Large Composite	7.2	6.9	7.7	7.5	9.7	10.4	9.0	5.2
Small Composite	7.6	10.1	9.7	11.7	15.5	12.6	11.0	13.2
High Financial Risk	–	–	–	30.1	30.3	–	–	–

Cost of Equity Capital (%) — SIC Composite

Avg CRSP 7.6, Avg RPR 9.6, 1-Stage 10.3, 3-Stage 8.4, 5-Factor Model 9.7

Weighted Average Cost of Capital (WACC) (%)

	CRSP Deciles CAPM	CAPM +Size Prem	Build-Up	Risk Premium Report CAPM +Size Prem	Build-Up	Discounted Cash Flow 1-Stage	3-Stage	Fama-French 5-Factor Model
Median	7.2	7.9	7.4	9.2	9.9	7.8	7.0	9.6
SIC Composite	6.4	6.4	6.4	7.1	8.3	8.2	7.0	7.8
Large Composite	6.2	6.0	6.5	6.4	7.9	8.3	7.4	4.8
Small Composite	7.1	9.0	8.7	10.3	13.3	10.9	9.7	11.4
High Financial Risk	–	–	–	15.0	15.1	–	–	–

WACC (%) — SIC Composite

Low 6.4, High 8.3, Average 7.3, Median 7.1

Calculating the Weight of Capital Structure Components

By definition, the WACC formulation requires us to calculate the weight (i.e., percentage of the total) for each component within the capital structure. In theory, the relative weightings of debt and equity or other capital structure components are based on the market values of each of those components, not on their book values. In practice, most valuation analysts tend to assume that the carrying value of debt capital on the balance sheet is a reasonable proxy for its market value. While this is a common practice, doing so when book values differ significantly from market values can distort cost of capital calculations.

The weight of each component of the capital structure is calculated as follows:

Formula 1.3

$$W_e = \frac{M_e}{M_e + M_p + M_d}, \qquad W_p = \frac{M_p}{M_e + M_p + M_d}, \qquad W_d = \frac{M_d}{M_e + M_p + M_d}$$

Where:

W_e	=	Weight of common equity capital in the capital structure
W_p	=	Weight of preferred equity capital in the capital structure
W_d	=	Weight of debt capital in the capital structure
M_e	=	Market value of common equity capital
M_p	=	Market value of preferred equity capital
M_d	=	Market value of debt capital

For example, if M_e = $90, M_p = $15, and M_d = $60, the weight of each of the capital structure components is calculated as follows:

$$W_e = \frac{M_e}{M_e + M_p + M_d} = \frac{\$90}{\$90 + \$15 + \$60} = 0.55 \ \text{or } 55\%$$

$$W_p = \frac{M_p}{M_e + M_p + M_d} = \frac{\$15}{\$90 + \$15 + \$60} = 0.09 \ \text{or } 9\%$$

$$W_d = \frac{M_d}{M_e + M_p + M_d} = \frac{\$60}{\$90 + \$15 + \$60} = 0.036 \ \text{or } 36\%$$

Capital Structure Considerations

The traditional view of the optimal capital structure is that a firm should increase the proportion of debt until its WACC is minimized, and therefore its enterprise value is maximized. However, there is a trade-off between the incremental tax benefits of additional debt and increasing bankruptcy risks.

The ability to carry and service debt (also known as "debt capacity") can vary significantly among firms. For example, as operational profitability increases, debt capacity will tend to increase (and vice versa). In addition, entities with high corporate-level taxes tend to carry more debt, presumably because the "tax effect" (the interest tax shield) associated with their debt is worth more to them relative to entities paying lower tax rates.[1.21]

The mechanical application of the WACC formula ignores the cost of financial distress, thereby systematically underestimating WACC for highly levered companies. As the proportion of debt is increased in the capital structure, the formulas commonly used for levering equity betas (and increasing the cost of equity capital as debt increases) are linear, and therefore likely to *understate* the cost of equity capital at high amounts of leverage. Similarly, the traditional depiction of the cost of debt capital fails to consider the gradually increasing cost of debt as debt is added to the capital structure due to a potential decrease in ability to service.

Many valuation analysts' WACC templates are especially prone to error when leverage is high. WACC templates often give results that do not increase with increases in leverage, which cannot be true when debt exceeds certain thresholds. One possible solution is to migrate the capital structure over time from the current leverage level to the optimal or target level. The inputs (e.g., cost of debt) would have to be internally consistent with the leverage assumption in each forecast period.

Varying Capital Structure Assumptions

Again, when we value something, we are valuing the present value of the expected future economic benefits or income associated with the investment. It follows that the capital structure used in the valuation analysis (like all valuation inputs) should also reflect future expectations. In other words, "the relevant weights should be based on the proportions of debt and equity that the firm targets for its capital structure over the long-term planning period".[1.22] The target capital structure is the mix of debt, preferred equity, and common equity the firm plans to use over the long-run to finance its operations.

Two questions often arise when selecting the capital structure assumption: (i) whether an actual or a hypothetical capital structure should be used, and (ii) whether to assume a constant or a variable capital structure.

[1.21] Interest payments to service debt capital are typically tax deductible. This "tax shield" effect results in a *lower* net cost of debt. The *greater* the tax rate, the *greater* the value of the "shield".

[1.22] Alfred Rappaport, *Creating Shareholder Value: A Guide for Managers and Investors*, revised ed. (New York: Free Press, 1997): 37.

In answer to the first question, if an entity (or an interest in that entity) is required to be valued as is, assuming the capital structure will remain intact, then the amount of debt in the entity's actual capital structure should be used. One simple example might be the case of a non-controlling (or minority) equity interest versus a controlling equity interest. If a non-controlling interest is to be valued, the entity's existing level of debt as of the valuation date may be appropriate because it might be beyond the power of a minority stockholder to change the capital structure. Alternatively, if a controlling interest is being valued, an argument could be made that a hypothetical capital structure may be used because a controlling owner would presumably have the power to alter the capital structure. Facts and circumstances specific to the valuation will dictate which of these arguments is appropriate.

In answer to the second question, as a simplification most valuation analysts develop a single discount rate (e.g., WACC) when applying the income approach. This means that a single capital structure assumption is generally used (either the current capital structure or a target capital structure) when computing a WACC. When relying on a single point estimate, valuation analysts frequently adopt the average or median capital structure of guideline companies in the subject company's industry with the assumption that the subject company would finance its operations over the long term in a similar fashion as the guideline companies.

Notwithstanding this general practice, there may be circumstances when a migrating or varying capital structure is considered appropriate, as suggested above. To the extent that an entity's capital structure (at market value weights) varies over time, using a constant capital structure and constant WACC to discount the projected cash flows in each period will misstate the value of the entity. When dealing with overlevered entities, to the extent that the proportion of debt is expected to migrate downward over time, using a constant WACC with the initial capital structure would likely undervalue the business (assuming that appropriate adjustments had been made to increase the cost of debt and equity to reflect current excess debt levels, which would result in the current WACC being greater than the optimal target WACC). WACC in this case would likely *decline* over time because the cost of debt would arguably decrease as the proportion of debt drops and the influence of financial distress is mitigated in the cost of equity.

Calculating WACC

WACC is based on the cost of each capital structure component net of any corporate-level tax effect of that component. Because we are interested in cash flows after entity-level taxes, literature and valuation analysts typically refer to this formulation of the WACC as an after-tax WACC.

The basic formula for computing the after-tax WACC for an entity with three capital structure components is:

Formula 1.4

$$WACC = \left(k_e \times W_e\right) + \left(k_p \times W_p\right) + \left(k_{d(pt)}[1-t] \times W_d\right)$$

Where:

$WACC$	=	Weighted average cost of capital (after-tax)
k_e	=	Cost of common equity capital
W_e	=	Weight of common equity capital in the capital structure
k_p	=	Cost of preferred equity capital
W_p	=	Weight of preferred equity capital in the capital structure
$k_{d(pt)}$	=	Cost of debt capital (pre-tax)
t	=	Income tax rate
W_d	=	Weight of debt capital in the capital structure

For example, using the weight of capital structure components calculated in the previous example (W_e = 55%, W_p = 9%, W_d = 36%), and assuming a hypothetical cost of equity capital of 16%, a cost of preferred equity capital of 10%, a (pre-tax) cost of debt capital of 6%, and a tax rate of 39%, WACC is calculated as follows:

$$WACC = \left(k_e \times W_e\right) + \left(k_p \times W_p\right) + \left(k_{d(pt)}[1-t] \times W_d\right)$$

$$WACC = \left(16\% \times 55\%\right) + \left(10\% \times 9\%\right) + \left(6\%[1-39\%] \times 36\%\right)$$

$$WACC = \left(8.8\%\right) + \left(0.9\%\right) + \left(1.3\%\right) = 11.0\%$$

If the capital structure varies significantly over time, using a constant WACC will probably result in the incorrect value of the company or project. While Formula 1.4 is by far the most widely used discount rate for valuing the business enterprise, it is based on certain simplifying assumptions that may or may not be true in specific circumstances. For example, the formula assumes that the income tax deductions from interest expense (i.e., the interest tax shield) results in reduced cash income taxes in the period in which the interest is paid. The formula should not be used when the interest tax shields do not result in reduced cash taxes. Nor should the constant WACC formula be used when the ratio of equity to invested capital is not expected to be constant over time in market value terms (though the varying WACC method can adjust for this error).

For entities with publicly traded common stock, preferred stock and debt, the weights can be derived from observed market values. For entities for which some or all of their preferred stock and debt are not publicly traded, the market values must be estimated (after estimating the cost of preferred equity or the cost of debt, as outlined earlier in the chapter). But when dealing with closely held common stock, the weights for the common equity can only be determined at the end of the valuation process. That methodology requires using an iterative calculation process.[1.23]

Estimates of Cost of Capital Are Imprecise

The cost of capital is used to discount expected net cash flows of a business, business ownership interest, security, or intangible asset to present value, and as such represents the expected (i.e., *future*) rate of return of an investment. Cost of capital is therefore (by definition) a forward-looking concept, and is an *imprecise* measure with regard to its exact value. After all, the future cannot be predicted with anything approaching certainty. Because the true (future) returns are not observable, they are typically estimated by looking to historical data, with the expectation that the past will repeat itself (which is *not* always true).

Even if the estimate of the cost of capital is unbiased, the resulting estimated investment or firm value (which is, at least in part, a function of the cost of capital) will be biased (i.e., under- or over-stated) in the presence of estimation errors associated with the cost of capital. These have to be adjusted to enable an unbiased estimation of the investment or firm value. These considerations are particularly important when estimating terminal values consisting of the net cash flows generated after a period of detailed forecast that typically ends after 5–10 years. This terminal value is in most cases a significant portion of the investment or firm value, thus an unbiased estimation is essential.

Various authors have tackled the problem of imprecise estimation and methods to adjust the discount rates to obtain an unbiased estimate of the terminal value. In one recent paper the authors derive adjustments to the cost of capital that account for estimation uncertainty as to the cost of capital inputs.[1.24] Using their estimation risk-adjusted cost of capital, the authors obtain unbiased investment or firm values when applying the terminal value formula. Their adjustment is a function of the uncertainty as to the cost of capital.

For example, assume the analyst estimates the cost of capital for Business A to be equal to 10%. In this case, assume that the analyst is highly certain of the cost of capital inputs (e.g., the beta estimate has a small standard error and has been relatively constant over the recent past). The authors calculate that the bias-corrected discount rate would be as close as 10.113%. But assume that the analyst estimates the cost of capital for Business B to be 10% but due to the relative uncertainty as to the accuracy of the inputs (e.g., the beta estimate has a large standard error and has fluctuated in recent periods) as of the valuation date there is greater uncertainty as to the correct

---

[1.23] Pratt and Grabowski, op.cit., Chapter 21, "Weighted Average Cost of Capital".

[1.24] Simon Elsner and Hans-Christian Krumholz, "Corporate valuation using imprecise cost of capital", *Journal of Business Economics*, Vol. 83 (9): 985–1014.

cost of capital. The authors calculate that the bias-corrected discount rate under those circumstances could be as different as 12.136%. We refer the reader to that paper for a discussion of the theory and their Table 3 of adjusted costs of capital. The authors point out that their work deals with the uncertainty of the discount rate estimation and not the uncertainty of the expected net cash flow estimates.

Key Things to Remember about Cost of Capital

- The cost of capital is the expected rate of return that market participants require in order to attract funds to a particular investment. The cost of capital is an opportunity cost.

- The cost of capital is also commonly called the discount rate, the expected return, or the required return.

- There are three broad valuation approaches: the (i) income approach, (ii) the market approach, and (iii) the asset-based approach. We focus on income-based methods in this book, since these are the methodologies that require cost of capital estimates.

- Capitalizing and discounting are two ways to bring expected cash flows back to present value under the income approach. In capitalizing, we focus on the cash flow of just a single normalized period. In discounting, we project the annual expected cash flows from the subject investment over the life of that investment.

- The cost of capital (like all valuation inputs) is forward-looking. Cost of capital is used to discount expected *future* cash flows to present value. Because the future cannot be predicted with anything approaching certainty, estimates of cost of capital are inherently imprecise.

- Past returns may provide some guidance as to what returns in the future will be, but there is no guarantee that the past will "repeat itself".

- Cost of capital is a function of the investment, not the investor.

- Cost of capital is based on market value, and is usually stated in nominal, after-tax terms (after corporate taxes, but before individual investor taxes).

- The data used in the *Valuation Handbook – U.S. Guide to Cost of Capital* are drawn from information on public companies and, therefore, the resulting cost of capital estimates developed using this book are "as if public". Valuation analysts may deem additional adjustments to be necessary.

- The cost of capital to the overall business is commonly called the WACC. WACC represents the market-capitalization-weighted cost of capital for both equity holders (both common and preferred) and debt holders.

- The data and methodology in the *Valuation Handbook – U.S. Guide to Cost of Capital* can be used to estimate cost of common equity capital.

Chapter 2
Methods for Estimating the Cost of Equity Capital

Basic Framework[2.1]

All of the methods commonly used to estimate the cost of equity capital have the same basic framework: they start with a "risk-free" rate, and then add a premium for "risk", as summarized in Exhibit 2.1.

Exhibit 2.1: The Basic Framework of the Models Used to Estimate the Cost of Equity Capital

Two of the most widely used methods of estimating the cost of equity capital are the Build-up method and the capital asset pricing model (CAPM). Both methods are predicated on this basic framework. In this book we focus on how to use the two valuation data sets (CRSP Deciles Size Premia Study exhibits and Risk Premium Report Study exhibits) contained herein to estimate the cost of equity capital using these two methods.

The nominal risk-free rate (R_f) is in theory a function of the real (risk-free) rate of interest plus expected inflation. The risk-free rate is the return available on a security that the market generally regards as free of the risk of default.[2.2] The nominal risk-free rate serves as an inflation adjustment mechanism, increasing or decreasing the cost of equity capital as inflation estimates change. During periods of increased inflation expectations, nominal risk-free rates increase, thereby increasing the expected returns estimated through cost of equity capital models. Similarly, during periods of decreased inflation expectations, nominal risk-free rates decrease, thereby decreasing the expected returns estimated through cost of equity capital models.

As the market's perception of an investment's riskiness increases, the risk premium, *RP*, also increases; accordingly, the rate of return that the market requires (the discount rate) will likewise increase for a given set of expected cash flows. The *greater* the market's required rate of return, the *lower* the present value of the investment, and the *lower* the market's required rate of return, the *greater* the present value of the investment.

[2.1]   This chapter is excerpted in part from Shannon P. Pratt and Roger J. Grabowski, *Cost of Capital: Applications and Examples* 5th ed. (Hoboken, NJ: John Wiley & Sons, 2014).

[2.2]   The yield on a 20-year constant maturity U.S. government bond is used as a proxy for the risk-free rate in the *2017 Valuation Handbook — U.S. Guide to Cost of Capital*, unless otherwise noted.

Defining Risk

Probably the most widely accepted definition of risk in the context of investment valuations is the degree of uncertainty of achieving future expectations at the times and in the amounts expected.[2.3] The definition implies uncertainty as to both the *amounts* and the *timing* of expected economic income. By expected economic income, in a technical sense, we mean the expected value (i.e., weighted mean/average) of the probability distribution of possible economic income for each forecast period.

In Chapter 1, we discussed the valuation process of present value as applied to expected cash flows. Any one year's distribution of possible net cash flows can be thought of as a bundle of possible outcomes. The present value of this series of expected cash flows can be depicted in the following formula (assuming a constant growth rate g):

Formula 2.1

$$PV = \frac{NCF_0(1+g)^1}{(1+k)^1} + \frac{NCF_0(1+g)^2}{(1+k)^2} + \ldots + \frac{NCF_0(1+g)^n}{(1+k)^n}$$

Where:

PV	=	Present value
NCF_0	=	Net cash flow at "time zero" (i.e., "now" or the most recently completed period as of the valuation date)
k	=	Discount rate
g	=	Expected rate of change (growth) of net cash flows
n	=	Total number of periods

This can also be written as:

$$PV = \frac{NCF_1}{(1+k)^1} + \frac{NCF_2}{(1+k)^2} + \ldots + \frac{NCF_n}{(1+k)^n}$$

Where:

NCF_n	=	Expected net cash flow at the end of period n (implicitly, the NCF in each period may be growing at a constant or at a varying growth rate from the prior period)

Market Returns Increase as Risk Increases by Asset Class

In finance theory, investors are generally assumed to be risk averse. Risk aversion can be measured by the amount of additional expected payoff an investor requires to accept additional risk.

[2.3] David Laro and Shannon P. Pratt, *Business Valuation and Federal Taxes: Procedure, Law, and Perspective*, 2nd ed. (Hoboken, NJ: John Wiley & Sons, 2010), Chapter 12.

If we plot the observed relationship of risk and return over time, we observe a strong linear relationship between risk and return, which is referred to as the capital market line (CML). The CML is defined as a line used in the capital asset pricing model that plots the rates of return for efficient portfolios,[2.4] depending on the rate of return and the level of risk (as measured by standard deviation) for a particular portfolio. Because investors are risk averse, the market requires an increasing rate of return as the risk of a bad outcome increases.

Exhibit 2.2: Capital Market Line; Empirical Estimate based on Realized Total Returns by U.S. Asset Class 1926–2016

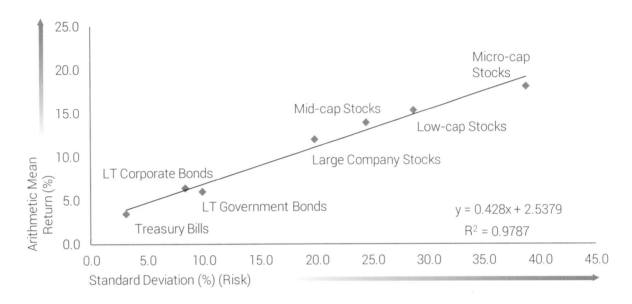

How do we know the market demands and receives greater returns for taking on greater risk? In Exhibit 2.2, the empirical estimate of the CML shows the market's pricing of portfolios of different U.S. asset classes over the period 1926 through 2016. As the risk (as measured by the standard deviation of returns) increases, the realized return increases.

Exhibit 2.3 provides summary statistics of total returns, income returns, and capital appreciation returns of basic U.S. asset classes over the time period 1926–2016. The 1926–2016 time period matches the time horizon over which the size premia, equity risk premia, and other statistics in the CRSP Deciles Size Study exhibits are calculated.

Exhibit 2.4 provides summary statistics of total returns, income returns, and capital appreciation returns of basic U.S. asset classes, as measured over the time period 1963–2016. The 1963–2016 time horizon matches the time horizon over which the size premia, "risk premia over the risk-free rate", and other statistics in the Risk Premium Report Study exhibits are calculated.

[2.4]   CML is the tangent line drawn from the risk-free point to the feasible region for risky assets. This line shows the relationship between the return and total risk for efficient portfolios. Efficient portfolios are a combination of risky assets plus the risk-free asset, which minimizes risk for a given level of return (i.e., the lowest-risk highest-reward set of portfolios), or maximizes return for a given level of risk.

Exhibit 2.3: Summary Statistics of Annual Total Returns, Income Returns, and Capital Appreciation Returns of Basic U.S. Asset Classes
1926–2016

1926–2016	Geometric Mean Returns (%)	Arithmetic Mean Returns (%)	Standard Deviation of Returns (%)
Large Company Stocks			
Total Return	10.0	12.0	19.9
Income Return	4.0	4.0	1.6
Capital Appreciation Return	5.8	7.7	19.2
Small Company Stocks			
Total Return	12.1	16.6	31.9
Mid-cap Stocks (Decile 3-5)			
Total Return	11.1	13.8	24.4
Income Return	3.8	3.8	1.8
Capital Appreciation Return	7.1	9.8	23.7
Low-cap Stocks (Decile 6-8)			
Total Return	11.5	15.3	28.7
Income Return	3.4	3.5	2.0
Capital Appreciation Return	7.9	11.6	28.1
Micro-cap Stocks (Decile 9-10)			
Total Return	12.1	18.0	38.8
Income Return	2.5	2.5	1.7
Capital Appreciation Return	9.7	15.4	38.0
Long-term Corporate Bonds			
Total Return	6.0	6.3	8.4
Long-term Government Bonds			
Total Return	5.5	6.0	9.9
Income Return	5.0	5.0	2.6
Capital Appreciation Return	0.3	0.7	8.9
Intermediate-term Government Bonds			
Total Return	5.1	5.3	5.6
Income Return	4.4	4.4	2.9
Capital Appreciation Return	0.6	0.7	4.5
US Treasury Bills			
Total Return	3.4	3.4	3.1
Inflation	2.9	3.0	4.1

Source of underlying data in both Exhibit 2.3 and 2.4: (i) Stocks, Bonds, Bills, and Inflation® (SBBI®) return series from the Morningstar *Direct* database. Series used: Large Company Stocks (IA SBBI US Large Stock TR USD Ext). The "SBBI US Large Stock" return series is essentially the S&P 500 index; Small Company Stocks (IA SBBI US Small Stock TR USD); Long-term Corp. Bonds (IA SBBI US LT Corp TR USD); Long-term Gov't Bonds (IA SBBI US LT Govt TR USD); Intermediate-term Gov't Bonds (IA SBBI US IT Govt TR USD); T-bills (IA SBBI US 30 Day TBill TR USD); Inflation (IA SBBI US Inflation). All rights reserved. Used with permission. (ii) CRSP U.S. Stock Database and CRSP U.S. Indices Database © 2017 Center for Research in Security Prices (CRSP®), University of Chicago Booth School of Business. *(continued on next page)*

Exhibit 2.4: Summary Statistics of Annual Total Returns, Income Returns, and Capital Appreciation Returns of Basic U.S. Asset Classes
1963–2016

1963–2016	Geometric Mean Returns (%)	Arithmetic Mean Returns (%)	Standard Deviation of Returns (%)
Large Company Stocks			
Total Return	10.1	11.5	16.6
Income Return	3.2	3.2	1.2
Capital Appreciation Return	6.8	8.1	16.1
Small Company Stocks			
Total Return	13.6	16.3	24.5
Mid-cap Stocks (Decile 3-5)			
Total Return	11.9	13.7	19.5
Income Return	2.8	2.8	1.4
Capital Appreciation Return	9.0	10.7	18.9
Low-cap Stocks (Decile 6-8)			
Total Return	12.6	15.1	23.4
Income Return	2.4	2.4	1.3
Capital Appreciation Return	10.2	12.6	22.7
Micro-cap Stocks (Decile 9-10)			
Total Return	12.3	16.1	29.8
Income Return	1.9	1.9	1.0
Capital Appreciation Return	10.4	14.2	29.2
Long-term Corporate Bonds			
Total Return	7.4	7.8	10.0
Long-term Government Bonds			
Total Return	7.1	7.7	11.9
Income Return	6.4	6.5	2.5
Capital Appreciation Return	0.4	0.9	10.8
Intermediate-term Government Bonds			
Total Return	6.6	6.8	6.4
Income Return	5.8	5.9	2.9
Capital Appreciation Return	0.5	0.7	5.3
US Treasury Bills			
Total Return	4.8	4.8	3.2
Inflation	3.9	4.0	2.9

(continued from previous page) CRSP standard market-cap-weighted NYSE/NYSE MKT/NASDAQ deciles 1–10. Mid-cap stocks represented by a market-capitalization weighted portfolio comprised of CRSP deciles 3-5; Low-cap stocks represented by a market-capitalization weighted portfolio comprised of CRSP deciles 6-8; Micro-cap stocks represented by a market-capitalization weighted portfolio comprised of CRSP deciles 9-10. Total return is equal to sum of three components returns: income return, capital appreciation, and reinvestment return. Used with permission. All rights reserved. Calculations performed by Duff & Phelps, LLC.

Types of Risk

Although risk arises from many sources, this chapter addresses risk in the economic sense, as generally used in the conventional methods of estimating cost of capital. In this context, capital market theory divides risk into four components:

1. Maturity risk

2. Market risk

3. Company-specific risk

4. Liquidity and marketability risk

Maturity Risk

Maturity risk (also called horizon risk, interest rate risk, or term risk) is the risk that the value of the investment may increase or decrease because of changes in the level of interest rates. The longer the term of an investment, the greater the maturity risk. For example, market prices of long-term bonds fluctuate much more in response to changes in levels of interest rates than do market prices of short-term bonds or notes. When we refer to the yields on long-term U.S. government bonds as risk-free rates, we mean that we regard them as free from the prospect of default. We recognize that they do incorporate maturity risk: the only part of the yield that is arguably risk-free is the income return component. That is, the interest payments promised are risk-free, or so we assume. But the market price or value of the bonds move up or down as interest rates move, creating a capital gain or loss. Thus, there is a risk (i.e., an opportunity cost) to capital embedded in these bonds.

The longer the maturity, the greater the susceptibility to changes in market price in response to changes in market rates of interest. With regard to interest rates, much of the uncertainty derives from the uncertainty of future inflation levels.

Market Risk

Market risk (also called systematic or undiversifiable risk in the context of the pure textbook CAPM) is the uncertainty of future returns due to the sensitivity of the return on a subject investment to variability in returns for the investment market as a whole. Although this is a broad conceptual definition, for many U.S. companies, the investment market as a whole is generally limited to the U.S. equity markets, and typically returns are measured on either the New York Stock Exchange (NYSE) Composite Index or the Standard & Poor's (S&P) 500 Index. For multi-national companies, the investment market may be more appropriately considered the world equity markets with returns measured on the S&P Global 1200 Index or one of the MSCI Global Standard indices.

The term that is commonly used for sensitivity to market risk is beta. In the context of the CAPM, beta measures the expected sensitivity of changes in returns of a security (either an individual company or a portfolio of companies) to changes in returns of the "market". In the U.S., the market proxy, or benchmark, is often the S&P 500 Index or the NYSE Composite Index.

While beta has come to have a specific meaning in the context of the CAPM, beta is used in finance literature as a more general term meaning the sensitivity of an investment to any of a variety of risk factors. Bonds have beta risks (e.g., risks to changes in interest rates and to general economic conditions as reflected in the broad stock market). Individual stocks have beta risks (e.g., to general economic conditions as reflected in the broad stock market and to the relative risks of large company stocks to small company stocks).

Some theorists hold that the only risk that capital markets reward with an expected premium rate of return (over the risk-free asset) is market risk, because other company-specific risks can be eliminated by holding a well-diversified portfolio of investments. Recent research increasingly shows that the market prices other risks as well (i.e., other risks are systematic).

For example, the size premium is a risk factor that is systematic (priced by the market) and is an adjustment to pure CAPM. Empirical evidence indicates that beta alone does not measure the risk of smaller companies. We discuss the size premium in Chapter 4.

Company-specific Risk

Company-specific risk (sometimes called unique or idiosyncratic risk) is the uncertainty of expected returns arising from factors other than those factors correlated with the investment market as a whole. These factors may include characteristics of the industry and/or the individual company. In international investing, they also can include characteristics of a particular country.

Some of the unique risk of an investment may be captured in systematic risk factors priced by the market such as the size premium. Fully capturing company-specific risk in the discount rate requires analysis of the company in comparison with other companies. However, while the size premium captures many risk factors, valuation analysts must be careful to capture all the risk factors and at the same time avoid double-counting of risk.

Capital market theory assumes efficient markets. That is, it assumes prices change concurrent with changes in the economic fundamentals (economy, industry, or company factors) such that the market prices of public stocks represent the consensus of investors as to the present value of cash flows and that changes in such fundamentals are "instantly" recognized in market prices. One study supports the rationality of stock prices where data on expected cash flows are available to investors.[2.5]

But market inefficiency can (and does) occur for public stocks, particularly for smaller company stocks that do not have sufficient investor following such that their prices react to changes in fundamentals in a timely fashion. We do recognize that market prices may not correctly or fully account for the fundamentals of a smaller, thinly traded public company at particular points in time. Studies on returns of small public companies that quantify the size premium, capture the average effect. A company-specific adjustment may still be appropriate (either positive or negative) even if size is already considered.

[2.5]   Aharon R. Ofer, Oded Sarig, and Keren Bar-Hava, "New Tests of Market Efficiency Using Fully Identifiable Equity Cash Flows" Working paper, February 2007. Available at http://www.ssrn .com/abstract=965242.

While the pure CAPM holds that any risk beyond market or beta risk can be diversified away (hence the term diversifiable risk often being equated with company-specific risk) researchers have found other risk factors are priced by the market (i.e., other risk factors are also systematic risk factors). We discuss the company-specific risk premium in Chapter 6.

Liquidity and Marketability Risk

Discussions of capital market theory generally assume that investments are "liquid", and many of the observations about risk and return are drawn from information about liquid investments. Liquidity generally refers to the ability to readily convert an investment into cash without significant loss of principal – the *less* liquid an investment is, the *riskier* it is, and vice versa. In other words, investors *like* liquidity, and *dislike* illiquidity, and will therefore demand more compensation for investing in illiquid investments. These risks, while listed here separately, are systematic risks in that the pricing of these risks for a particular investment moves with the overall market pricing of liquidity and marketability risks. The risk premia for lack of liquidity and marketability can be embedded in the discount rate or as a separate adjustment from an "as if liquid" ("as if freely traded") estimate of value.

Marketability and liquidity are major risks facing closely held companies (both minority and controlling interests), and can have a significant impact on the ultimate value. However, valuation analysts (except for venture capitalists) typically do not factor these risks into the discount rate. Instead, the common approach is to value the closely held company or interest in the company "as if freely traded" and then subtract a discount that incorporates a discount for lack of marketability and a discount for lack of liquidity because most of the valuation metrics that we use are drawn from the public markets.

Cost of Equity Capital Estimation Methods

In practice, the build-up method and CAPM are the most frequently used methods to estimate the cost of equity capital. The risk premia and size premia presented in the *Valuation Handbook – U.S. Guide to Cost of Capital's* data exhibits can be used to develop cost of equity capital estimates using build-up and CAPM, and so we focus on these two methods here.

The *Valuation Handbook – U.S. Guide to Cost of Capital* provides two sets of valuation data that analysts can use to estimate the cost of equity capital:

- **CRSP Deciles Size Premia Exhibits:** These exhibits provide the size premia and other valuation data previously published in the Morningstar/Ibbotson *SBBI Valuation Yearbook*.

- **Risk Premium Report Exhibits:** These exhibits provide the size premia and other valuation data previously published in the Duff & Phelps *Risk Premium Report*.

The build-up method and the CAPM method are the most frequently used methods for estimating cost of equity capital. These methods are summarized in Exhibit 2.5. All of the methods start with a risk-free rate (R_f), and then add various premia for risk.[2.6]

Exhibit 2.5: The Build-up Methods and CAPM Models

CRSP Decile Size Premia Exhibits

Build-Up	*CAPM*
$k_e = R_f + RP_m + RP_i + RP_s$	$k_e = R_f + \beta \times (RP_m) + RP_s$

Risk Premium Report Exhibits

Build-Up	*CAPM*
$k_e = R_f + RP_{m+s} + ERP\ Adjustment$	$k_e = R_f + \beta \times (RP_m) + RP_s$

NOTE: *All cost of equity estimates developed using the Valuation Handbook – U.S. Guide to Cost of Capital are prior to the addition of any company-specific risks (RP_c) that the individual analyst deems appropriate.*

Where:

k_e	=	Cost of equity capital
R_f	=	Risk-free rate
RP_m	=	Equity risk premium (also referred as ERP)
RP_s	=	Size premium
RP_i	=	Industry risk premium
RP_c	=	Company-specific risk premium
β	=	Beta
RP_{m+s}	=	Equity (market) risk premium plus size premium combined
ERP Adjustment	=	An adjustment to account for the difference between the forward-looking ERP that the analyst has selected and the historical (1963–present) ERP that was used as a *convention* in the calculations performed to create the Risk Premium Report Exhibits. Used only when using the Risk Premium Report exhibits. See Chapter 9, "Risk Premium Report Exhibits – General Information".

[2.6]   The Risk Premium Report exhibits provides eight methods of estimating the cost of equity capital, including unlevered cost of equity capital and high-financial-risk cost of equity capital. For detailed examples of these cost of equity capital methods, see Chapter 10.

Build-up

The build-up method is an additive model commonly used for calculating the cost of equity capital. As the name implies, successive "building blocks" are summed, each representing the additional risk inherent to investing in alternative assets. Both of the sets of valuation data presented in the *2017 Valuation Handbook – U.S. Guide to Cost of Capital* (CRSP Deciles Size Premia exhibits and Risk Premium Report exhibits) can be used to develop cost of equity capital estimates using the build-up method.

CRSP Deciles Size Premia – Build-up Method

The first set of valuation data in the *Valuation Handbook – U.S. Guide to Cost of Capital* that valuation analysts can use to estimate the cost of equity capital is the CRSP Deciles Size Premia exhibits. These exhibits provide the size premia and other valuation data previously published in the *SBBI Valuation Yearbook*. Formula 2.2 presents the CRSP Deciles Size Premia build-up method.

Formula 2.2

$$k_e = R_f + RP_m + RP_i + RP_s$$

The CRSP Deciles Size Premia build-up method follows the basic framework of all cost of equity capital estimation models: a premium for risk is added to the risk-free rate. In this case, the "premium for risk" is deconstructed into three components:

- **Equity risk premium (RP_m):** The equity risk premium is the extra return that investors demand to compensate them for investing in a diversified portfolio of large common stocks rather than investing in risk-free securities. The equity risk premium is sometimes referred to as the "market" risk premium.

- **Size premium (RP_s):** The size premium represents the difference between actual historical excess return and the excess return predicted by beta. The "size effect" is based on the empirical observation that companies of smaller size are associated with greater risk and, therefore, have greater cost of capital. All size premia in the *Valuation Handbook – U.S. Guide to Cost of Capital* are "beta-adjusted", meaning that they have been adjusted to remove the portion of excess return that is attributable to beta, leaving only the size effect's contribution to excess return.

- **Industry risk premium (RP_i):** A measure of beta risk scaled around 0. An $RP_i < 0$ implies that the industry is *less* risky than the market, an $RP_i = 0$ implies that the industry has the *same* risk as the market, and an $RP_i > 0$ implies that the industry is *riskier* than the market. RP_i are not appropriate for use with CAPM, but are only appropriately used in "build-up" methods of estimating cost of equity capital that do not already have a measure of beta. An RP_i is used solely within the context of a build-up method. RP_i are a necessary cost of capital ingredient for those valuation analysts who like to use a build-up method in their valuation analysis (alone, or in addition to the CAPM).

Risk Premium Report – Build-up Method

The second set of valuation data in the *Valuation Handbook – U.S. Guide to Cost of Capital* that valuation analysts can use to estimate the cost of equity capital is the Risk Premium Report exhibits. These exhibits provide the size premia and other valuation data previously published in the Duff & Phelps *Risk Premium Report*. Formula 2.3 presents the Risk Premium Report build-up 1 method.

Formula 2.3

$$k_e = R_f + RP_{m+s} + ERP\, Adjustment$$

The Risk Premium Report build-up 1 method, just like the CRSP Deciles Size Premia build-up method, follows the basic framework of all cost of equity capital estimation models: a premium for risk is added to the risk-free rate. In this case, the "premium for risk" is deconstructed into two components:

- **Risk Premia over the Risk-free Rate (RP_{m+s}):** Risk premia over the risk-free rate represents the difference between the historical (observed) return of equities over the risk-free rate, and are a measure of risk in terms of the combined effect of *market* risk and *size* risk.

- **ERP Adjustment:** The ERP Adjustment is needed to account for the difference between the forward-looking ERP as of the valuation date that the analyst has selected to use in his or her cost of equity capital calculations, and the historical (in this case, 1963–present) ERP that was used as a *convention* in the calculations performed to create the Risk Premium Report exhibits. See Chapter 9 for detailed discussion of the ERP adjustment.

The Risk Premium Report exhibits provide valuation analysts with eight methods of estimating the cost of equity capital. The Build-up 1 and the CAPM are the most commonly used in practice. For detailed examples on the various methods of estimating the cost of equity capital using the Risk Premium Report exhibits, see Chapter 9.

CAPM

The CAPM has served as the foundation for pricing risk for nearly fifty years. Financial theorists generally have favored using the CAPM as the preferred method to estimate the cost of equity capital and the CAPM has become the most widely used method for estimating the cost of equity capital.

As with any model, certain assumptions are made in developing CAPM, and those assumptions also represent limitations. Outlining the CAPM's several assumptions and criticisms is beyond the scope of this book. Despite its many criticisms, the CAPM is still one of the most widely used models for estimating the cost of equity capital, especially for larger companies in its pure textbook form, and even for smaller companies and closely held companies in its expanded or adjusted form (a.k.a. modified CAPM). The pure textbook CAPM formula is shown in Formula 2.4:

Formula 2.4

$$k_e = R_f + \beta \times (RP_m)$$

Where:

k_e	=	Cost of equity capital
R_f	=	Risk-free rate
β	=	Beta
RP_m	=	Equity risk premium (also referred as ERP)

The primary difference between the CAPM and the (basic) build-up method is the introduction of a market or systematic risk factor for a specific stock, which acts as a modifier to the general equity risk premium. In the context of the CAPM, market risk is measured by a risk factor called beta. Beta measures the sensitivity of excess total returns (total returns over the risk-free rate of return) on any individual security (or portfolio of securities) to the excess total returns on some measure of the market, such as the Standard & Poor's (S&P) 500 Index or the New York Stock Exchange (NYSE) Composite Index.

In theory, beta can be defined as:

Formula 2.5

$$\beta = \frac{cov(R_i, R_m)}{var(R_m)}$$

Where:

β	=	Beta
R_i	=	Return on security
R_m	=	Return on market portfolio
$Cov(R_i, R_m)$	=	Expected covariance between the return on security i and the market return R_m. Can also be measured in terms of excess returns of security i $(R_i - R_f)$ and the excess market return $(R_m - R_f)$
$Var(R_m)$	=	Expected variance of excess return on the overall stock market

Covariance measures the degree to which the return on a particular security and the overall market's return move together. Covariance is not volatility. Covariance is a measure of the two variables' tendency to vary in the same direction and in the same relative amounts.

Estimation of Equity Beta

Beta is a forward-looking concept. However, the most widely used techniques for estimating beta generally use historical data over a sample or look-back period and assume that the future will be sufficiently similar.

Research shows that betas are time-varying (i.e., sensitive to market changes as the economy changes; betas differ during improving economic conditions compared with periods when economic conditions are declining). Using a historical method based on a sample period may not provide a reliable indication of expected beta when economic conditions are changing. The current and expected future economic conditions may differ from the economic conditions during the look-back period. Therefore, the beta estimated using the data for the look-back period may not reflect the future.

Academics prefer to estimate beta by comparing the excess returns on an individual security relative to the excess returns on the relevant market index. By *excess return*, we mean the total return (which includes both dividends and capital gains and losses) over and above the return available on a risk-free investment (e.g., U.S. government securities). Use of excess returns allows for normalizing changes in returns for changes in inflation during the look-back period.

For publicly traded securities, valuation analysts can estimate beta via regression (ordinary least squares (OLS) regression), by regressing the excess returns on the individual stock $(R_i - R_f)$ against the excess returns on the market $(R_m - R_f)$ during the look-back period. The resulting slope of the best-fit line is the beta estimate.

On a final note, because closely held companies, divisions, and reporting units have generally no market price, their betas cannot be measured directly. Thus, to use the CAPM to estimate the cost of capital for a closely held company, division, or reporting unit, it is necessary to estimate a proxy beta for that business. This is often accomplished by using an average or median beta for the industry group or by selecting specific guideline public companies and using some composite of their betas. The goal is to match the risk of that subject business to the risks of the guideline public companies.[2.7]

[2.7] An excellent source of industry and peer group beta statistics for use in CAPM estimates of cost of equity capital is the *Valuation Handbook – U.S. Industry Cost of Capital* (Wiley & Sons). The *Valuation Handbook – U.S. Industry Cost of Capital* provides cost of capital estimates (i.e., equity capital, debt capital, and WACC) for approximately 180 U.S. industries and size groupings (i.e., Large-, Mid-, Low-, and Micro-capitalization companies), plus a host of detailed statistics that can be used for benchmarking purposes (over 300 critical industry-level data points calculated for each industry, depending on data availability). The *Valuation Handbook – U.S. Industry Cost of Capital* has been published since 2014 with data through March 31 of the edition year (e.g., the *2014 Valuation Handbook – U.S. Industry Cost of Capital* was data through March 31, 2014; the *2015 Valuation Handbook – U.S. Industry Cost of Capital* was data through March 31, 2015, etc.). This book includes three optional quarterly updates (June, September, and December). See Exhibit 1.4 for a sample industry analysis page from the *2016 Valuation Handbook – U.S. Industry Cost of Capital*. To order copies of the *Valuation Handbook – U.S. Industry Cost of Capital* and its optional quarterly updates, please go to: www.wiley.com/go/ValuationHandbooks.

Modified CAPM

If we modify the CAPM to also reflect the size effect (RP_s), we can expand the cost of equity capital formula as follows:[2.8]

Formula 2.6

$$k_e = R_f + \beta \times \left(RP_m \right) + RP_s$$

Where:

k_e	=	Cost of equity capital
R_f	=	Risk-free rate
β	=	Beta
RP_m	=	Equity risk premium (also referred as ERP)
RP_s	=	Size premium

CRSP Deciles Size Premia and Risk Premium Report – CAPM

Both sets of valuation data (CRSP Deciles Size Premia exhibits and Risk Premium Report exhibits) presented herein can be used to develop cost of equity capital estimates using the CAPM and share the same variables (see Formula 2.6). A premium for risk is added to the risk-free rate. In this case, the "premium for risk" is deconstructed into three components:

- **Equity risk premium (RP_m):** The equity risk premium is the extra return that investors demand to compensate them for investing in a diversified portfolio of large common stocks rather than investing in risk-free securities. The equity risk premium is sometimes referred to as the "market" risk premium.

- **Size premium (RP_s):** The size premium represents the difference between actual historical excess returns and the excess return predicted by beta. The "size effect" is based on the empirical observation that companies of smaller size are associated with greater risk and, therefore, have greater cost of capital. All size premia in the *Valuation Handbook – U.S. Guide to Cost of Capital* are "beta-adjusted", meaning that they have been adjusted to remove the portion of excess return that is attributable to beta, leaving only the size effect's contribution to excess return.

- **Beta (β):** Measure of the systematic risk of a stock; the tendency of a stock's price to correlate with changes in the market. It is used as a modifier to the equity risk premium (ERP) in the context of the CAPM. Beta is the sole risk measure of equity capital of the pure CAPM, the form of the CAPM most often shown in textbooks. The combination of equity beta for the subject business multiplied by the ERP for the market equals the estimated risk premium for the subject business.

[2.8] Formula 2.6 represents textbook CAPM *after* the addition of a size premium (RP_s), but prior to any additional "company-specific" risk premia (RP_c) that may be deemed applicable by the individual valuation analyst.

Other Cost of Equity Capital Estimation Methods

The pure "textbook" CAPM (see Formula 2.4) provides fundamental insights about risk and return. Textbook CAPM (i) provides a framework to fundamental concepts of asset pricing and portfolio theory and (ii) is simple to understand and easy to apply. However, textbook CAPM is fraught with empirical problems, and its empirical record is poor.[2.9]

Because of that poor record, a number of alternative models have been developed that better explain differences in rates of return among stocks of companies. Many of these models are multi-factor models; they include risk factors that have been shown to be priced by the market, other than simple market beta. Generally, the multi-factor models begin with a risk-free rate of return and add one or more factors based on the risks of the investment.[2.10] For example, the "modified" CAPM introduces a size premium and a company-specific risk premium to the pure CAPM (see Formula 2.6).[2.11]

Alternatively, the valuation analyst can estimate the expected rate of return *implied* by the existing price for publicly traded securities. In this approach, the analyst typically uses the income approach to reverse-engineer the cost of capital given (i) estimates of expected future net cash flows of the subject company, and (ii) the observable market price of the company.

In any case, these methods are designed to help us understand how the market prices *risk*. But defining the relationship among risk measures and returns is not an easy task, and researchers often observe what they term anomalies (i.e., a result that differs from what is expected). For example, Ibbotson and Idzorek discuss the concepts of risk in a 2014 article:[2.12]

"We believe that most of the best-known market premiums and anomalies can be explained by an intuitive and naturally occurring (social or behavioral) phenomenon observed in countless settings: popularity. Popularity is often defined as a social phenomenon associated with being admired, sought after, well known, and/or accepted... How can we apply popularity to the relative performance of different asset classes and different securities? Asset pricing theories have long recognized that expected returns should not be the same for the various instruments in the marketplace. The primary explanation for these differences has been differences in risk. Of course, risk is unpopular — investors do not like risk and want to be compensated for it".

[2.9] Pratt and Grabowski, op.cit., Chapter 13, "Criticism of CAPM and Beta versus Other Risk Measures". See also: Mike Dempsey, "The Capital Asset Pricing Model (CAPM): The History of a Failed Revolutionary Idea in Finance", *Abacus* Vol. 49 (Supplement) and Pablo Fernandez, "CAPM: An Absurd Model", working paper (November 19, 2015). Available at SSRN: http://ssrn.com/abstract=2505597.

[2.10] Pratt and Grabowski, op.cit., Chapter 18, "Other Methods of Estimating the Cost of Equity Capital".

[2.11] In the *Valuation Handbook – U.S. Industry Cost of Capital*, we present the following cost of equity capital estimates: (i) Capital Asset Pricing Model (CAPM), (ii) CAPM + Size Premium (using the CRSP Deciles Size Study), (iii) Build-up + Industry Risk Premium (using the CRSP Deciles Size Study), (iv) CAPM + Size Premium (using the Risk Premium Report Study), (v) Build-up + Risk Premium Over the Risk-free Rate (using Risk Premium Report Study), (vi) 1-Stage Discounted Cash Flow (DCF) model, (vii) 3-Stage DCF model, (viii) Fama-French (F-F) 5-Factor Model. Cost of debt capital and weighted average cost of capital (WACC) are also presented for each industry (depending on data availability). WACC is calculated using the cost of equity capital estimated by each of the eight models, plus the cost of preferred capital input and the cost of debt capital input. For more information about Duff & Phelps valuation data resources published by John Wiley & Sons, please go to: www.wiley.com/go/ValuationHandbooks.

[2.12] Roger G. Ibbotson and Thomas M. Idzorek, "Dimensions of Popularity", *The Journal of Portfolio Management* Vol 40 (5):68–74.

Ibbotson and Idzorek continue: "Although risk is clearly unpopular, it is only one dimension of popularity. Popularity can include all sorts of other characteristics that do not fit well into the risk and return paradigm". One example of this is "liquidity", or the risk of not being able to turn your investment into cash extremely quickly without a price concession. Liquidity cannot easily be squeezed into a traditional risk and return paradigm since *less* liquid assets are not necessarily *more* volatile, nor do they necessarily have *higher* betas.

Studies have shown that although risk may be the main driver of return differences *across* asset classes, there is increasing evidence that risk is not the primary driver *within* asset classes in that within the stock market, the lower-risk characteristics are often associated with higher returns – the *opposite* of underlying capital market theory. The term "risk" has become synonymous for the sum total of all attributes investors do not like. In Chapter 4 we further discuss the relationship between liquidity, size, and returns, as illiquidity is one of those attributes that is "unpopular".

The authors conclude: "Academics have sought to explain and understand asset prices, with a strong emphasis on market premiums and market anomalies. Generally, these academics end up falling into one of two camps: the equilibrium efficient market camp or the behavioral economics camp. Popularity offers an explanation that is consistent with both approaches".

In a 2016 extension of the 2014 article, Ibbotson and Chen conclude that "value and low liquidity have the largest impact on returns, while low beta, low volatility, and low liquidity have the best performance when measured on a risk adjusted basis. Contrary to the conventional wisdom on risk and reward, most portfolio sorting metrics exhibit an inverse risk-return relationship, with lower risk portfolios outperforming higher risk portfolios. A broad theme that emerges from the empirical evidence is that popularity *underperforms*." (emphasis added).[2.13]

This research demonstrates that we are indeed in the relative infancy of understanding how the market prices risk. We provide in this book multiple sources of data so the user can develop cost of equity capital estimates using several models and then check the results of applying these models with observed returns.

[2.13] Roger G. Ibbotson and Daniel Y.-J. Kim, "Risk and Return Within the Stock Market: What Works Best?", January 8, 2016. To learn more, visit http://www.zebracapm.com/, and click on "Our Research".

Key Things to Remember about the Methods for Estimating the Cost of Equity Capital

- The build-up method for estimating the cost of equity capital has the following five components:

  1. A risk-free rate

  2. A general equity risk premium (ERP)

  3. A size premium

  4. An industry adjustment factor

  5. A company-specific risk adjustment (which can be either positive or negative, depending on the differences in risks comparing the subject company to the guideline companies from which the size premium was derived)

- The CAPM differs from the build-up method by introducing the beta coefficient, β, the sensitivity of excess returns for the subject company stock to excess returns for the market.

- The CAPM, like most economic models, offers a theoretical framework for how certain relationships would exist subject to certain assumptions.

- The pure textbook CAPM has several underlying assumptions, which may be met to a greater or lesser extent for the market as a whole or for any particular company or investment. While some question whether empirical evidence is consistent with the predictions resulting from the theory, CAPM is widely used today.

- All cost of equity estimates developed using the *Valuation Handbook – U.S. Guide to Cost of Capital* are prior to the addition of any company-specific risks (RP_c) that the individual analyst deems appropriate.

- There are all sorts of other characteristics that do not fit well into the risk and return paradigm. We are in the relative *infancy* of understanding how the market prices risk. Generally, academics end up falling into one of two camps: the equilibrium efficient market camp or the behavioral economics camp. "Popularity" may offer an explanation that is consistent with both approaches.

Chapter 3

Basic Building Blocks of the Cost of Equity Capital – Risk-free Rate and Equity Risk Premium

The basic building blocks for the build-up methods and the modified capital asset pricing model (CAPM) are:

- Risk-free rate

- Equity risk premium

- Size premium

- Beta (in CAPM) or industry risk premium (in build-up method)

- Company-specific risk premium

We will discuss the risk-free rate (R_f) and the equity risk premium (ERP) in this chapter. We will discuss the remaining building blocks in later chapters.

The Risk-free Rate and Equity Risk Premium: Interrelated Concepts

A risk-free rate is the return available, as of the valuation date, on a security that the market generally regards as free of the risk of default.

For valuations denominated in U.S. dollars, valuation analysts have typically used the spot yield to maturity (as of the valuation date) on U.S. government securities as a proxy for the risk-free rate. The two most commonly used risk-free bond maturities have been the 10- and 20-year U.S. government bond yields.

The use of (i) long-term U.S. government bonds, and (ii) an ERP estimated relative to yields on long-term bonds most closely match the investment horizon and risks that confront business managers who are making capital allocation decisions and valuation analysts who are applying valuation methods to value a "going concern" business.

The risk-free rate and the ERP are interrelated concepts. All ERP estimates are, by definition, developed *in relation* to the risk-free rate. Specifically, the ERP is the extra return investors expect as compensation for assuming the additional risk associated with an investment in a diversified portfolio of common stocks, compared to the return they would expect from an investment in risk-free securities.

This brings us to an important concept. When developing cost of capital estimates, the valuation analyst should match the term of the risk-free rate used in the CAPM or build-up formulas with the duration of the expected net cash flows of the business, asset, or project being evaluated.[3.1] Further, the term of the risk-free rate should *also* match the term of the risk-free rate used to develop the ERP, as illustrated in Exhibit 3.1.

Exhibit 3.1: The Risk-free Rate and ERP Should Be Consistent with the Duration of the Net Cash Flows of the Business, Asset, or Project Being Evaluated

Term of risk-free rate used in CAPM or Build-up equation	=	Expected duration of the net cash flows of the business, asset, or project being evaluated	=	Term of risk-free rate used to develop the ERP

In many of the cases in which one is valuing a business, a "going concern" assumption is made (the life of the business is assumed to be indefinite), and therefore selecting longer-term U.S. government bond yields (e.g., 20 years) as the proxy for the risk-free rate is appropriate.

The risk-free rate and the ERP, like all components of the cost of equity capital (and the cost of equity capital itself), are *forward-looking* concepts. The reason that the cost of capital is a forward-looking concept is straightforward: when we value a company (for instance), we are trying to value how much we would pay (now) for the *future* economic benefits associated with owning the company. Since we will ultimately use the cost of capital to discount these future economic benefits (usually measured as *expected* cash flows) back to their present value, the cost of capital itself must *also* be forward-looking.

Spot Risk-free Rates versus Normalized Risk-free Rates

Beginning with the global financial crisis of 2008 (the "Financial Crisis"), analysts have had to reexamine whether the "spot" rate is still a reliable building block upon which to base their cost of equity capital estimates. The Financial Crisis challenged long-accepted practices and highlighted potential problems of simply continuing to use the spot yield-to-maturity on a safe government security as the risk-free rate, without any further adjustments.

During periods in which risk-free rates appear to be abnormally low due to flight to quality or massive central bank monetary interventions, valuation analysts may want to consider normalizing the risk-free rate. By "normalization" we mean estimating a risk-free rate that more likely reflects the *sustainable* average return of long-term U.S. Treasuries.

[3.1]   Certain sections of this chapter are excerpted in part from Shannon P. Pratt and Roger J. Grabowski, *Cost of Capital: Applications and Examples* 5th ed. (Hoboken, NJ: John Wiley & Sons, 2014)

Why Normalize the Risk-free Rate?

The yields of U.S. government bonds in certain periods during and after the Financial Crisis may have been *artificially* repressed, and therefore likely unsustainable. Many market participants will agree that nominal U.S. government bond yields have been artificially low over the last several years. Even members of the Federal Open Market Committee (FOMC) have openly discussed the need to "normalize" interest rates, as documented in the minutes of meetings held over the last few years, as well as in a statement released in September 2014, entitled "Policy Normalization Principles and Plans".[3.2, 3.3]

The Federal Reserve ("Fed"), the central bank of the United States, kept a zero-interest-rate policy (dubbed "ZIRP" in the financial press) for seven years, from December 2008 until December 2015.

At its December 15–16, 2015 meeting, the Fed decided to raise the target range for the federal funds rate for the first time in nine years, from a range of 0.00%–0.25% to 0.25%–0.50% (effectively, a 25-basis-point-increase). At the time, FOMC participants believed that the target level for the federal funds rate should increase another three or four times during 2016, with the median projections suggesting it could rise by 100 basis points in total.[3.4]

However, the path to normalization slowed down considerably relative to original expectations. It took another 12 months – until the December 2016 meeting – for the FOMC to finally increase rates again, the second time in 10 years. The target range for the Federal funds rate was raised from a range of 0.25%–0.50% to 0.50%–0.75% (again, effectively a 25 basis points increase). Even then, officials were very cautious about how to characterize the timing of normalization policies, signaling that further increase in interest rates would likely be gradual in the future:[3.5]

> *"The Committee expected that economic conditions would evolve in a manner that would warrant only gradual increases in the federal funds rate and that the federal funds rate was likely to remain, for some time, below levels that are expected to prevail in the longer run."*

[3.2] The "Policy Normalization Principles and Plans", released on September 17, 2014, is available at: https://www.federalreserve.gov/newsevents/press/monetary/20140917c.htm. To access minutes of FOMC meetings visit: http://www.federalreserve.gov/monetarypolicy/fomccalendars.htm.

[3.3] The Federal Reserve Bank ("Fed") has the responsibility for setting monetary policy in the United States. To do so, the Fed controls the three tools of monetary policy: open market operations, the discount rate, and reserve requirements. The Board of Governors of the Federal Reserve System is responsible for setting the discount rate and reserve requirements, while the FOMC is the committee charged under U.S. law with overseeing the nation's open market operations (i.e., the Fed's buying and selling of U.S. Treasury securities). To learn more about the FOMC, visit: https://www.federalreserve.gov/monetarypolicy/fomc.htm.

[3.4] "Minutes of the Federal Open Market Committee December 15–16, 2015", Board of Governors of the Federal Reserve System. For details visit: http://www.federalreserve.gov/monetarypolicy/fomccalendars.htm.

[3.5] "Minutes of the Federal Open Market Committee December 13–14, 2016", Board of Governors of the Federal Reserve System. For details visit: http://www.federalreserve.gov/monetarypolicy/fomccalendars.htm.

In conjunction with the December 13–14, 2016 meeting, FOMC participants also submitted their projections of the most likely outcomes for real GDP growth, unemployment rate, inflation, and the federal funds rate for each year from 2016 to 2019 and over the longer run.[3.6] All 17 FOMC participants believed that the target level for the federal funds rate should rise further during 2017, with the median projections suggesting three 25-basis-point-increases, for a combined total of 75 basis points. The median estimate for the longer-term federal funds rate was projected to be 3.0% (down from the 3.5% estimate made one year earlier), to be reached sometime *after* 2019. Note that in the near-term (i.e., 2017), investors are also generally projecting a much slower pace for rate hikes and of lower magnitude. [3.7]

John C. Williams, President of the Federal Reserve Bank of San Francisco (an FOMC participant, but not currently a voting FOMC member), has been very vocal about the need to start normalizing interest rates. During 2015 and 2016, he gave several presentations and speeches, where he mentioned the need to raise interest rates to more "normal" levels. For example, in a presentation delivered in October 2016, he said:[3.8]

> *"Given the progress we have made and signs of continued solid momentum in the economy, and consistent with our agreed-upon monetary policy approach, it makes sense for the Fed to gradually move interest rates toward more normal levels."*

However, he acknowledged in the same speech that even after normalization takes place, interest rates may simply be lower than in pre-Financial Crisis years. Discussing the Fed's short-term benchmark interest rate (the target federal funds rate), he elaborated on that topic:[3.9]

> *"The key takeaway from these global trends is that interest rates are going to stay lower than we've come to expect in the past. This does not mean they will be zero, but when juxtaposed with pre-recession normal short-term interest rates of, say, 4 to 4½ percent, it may be jarring to see the underlying r-star guiding us towards a new normal of 3 to 3½ percent – or even lower. Importantly, this future of low interest rates is not due to easy monetary policy; instead, it is the rate expected to prevail when the economy is at full strength and the stance of monetary policy is neutral."* [3.10]

[3.6] FOMC participants, who all submit economic projections, include not only the current FOMC voting members, but also other non-voting, regional Federal Reserve Bank presidents. For a current list of FOMC participants, visit: https://www.stlouisfed.org/fomcspeak. For a current list of FOMC committee members, visit: https://www.federalreserve.gov/monetarypolicy/fomc.htm.

[3.7] See, for example, the CME Group FedWatch Tool. The FedWatch Tool is based on CME Group 30-Day Fed Fund futures prices, which are used to express the market's views on the likelihood of changes in U.S. monetary policy. This tool allows market participants to view the probability of an upcoming Fed Rate hike up to one year out. For details visit: http://www.cmegroup.com/trading/interest-rates/countdown-to-fomc.html.

[3.8] Presentation to the Federal Home Loan Bank of San Francisco's 2016 Member Conference San Francisco, CA entitled "Assessing the New Normal(s)", delivered on delivery on October 21, 2016. A copy of the remarks can be found here: http://www.frbsf.org/our-district/press/presidents-speeches/williams-speeches/2016/october/assessing-the-new-normals/. For a list of speeches and presentations by President Williams, visit: http://www.frbsf.org/our-district/press/presidents-speeches/williams-speeches/.

[3.9] The federal funds rate is the interest rate at which depository institutions lend balances to each other overnight. The target federal funds rate is a short-term rate and is used as the benchmark interest rate to implement U.S. monetary policies, such as raising or reducing interest rates.

[3.10] The so-called r* (r-star) stands for the longer-run value of the neutral rate. President Williams defined r-star as essentially what inflation-adjusted interest rates (i.e., real rates) will be once the economy is back to full strength. However, note that when citing estimates of 3.0% to 3.5% (or even lower) as the new normal, President Williams is referring to the target Fed funds rate, which is expressed in nominal terms.

James Bullard, President of the Federal Reserve Bank of St. Louis and an FOMC member, concurs. In a recent presentation entitled "Safe Real Interest Rates and Fed Policy" he concluded that interest rates are expected to remain low for quite a while:[3.11]

> "Safe real rates of return are exceptionally low and are not expected to rise soon, a "low-safe-real-rate regime." This means, in turn, that the policy rate should be expected to remain exceptionally low over the forecast horizon."

In subsequent speeches, Bullard indicated that this is still the case even after the newly-inaugurated U.S. President and his Administration start implementing new polices, unless these are directed towards improving medium-term U.S. productivity growth. Either way, the new policies would not be expected to materially affect this "low-safe-real-rate regime" in 2017.[3.12]

While the views of regional Fed Presidents or individual FOMC members do not reflect the official positions of the committee, the bottom line is that interest rates are expected to go up to a more "normal" level in the medium-term. Yet, what is considered "normal" today may be lower than ever imagined prior to the 2008 Financial Crisis. We will elaborate on the consequences of this statement later in this chapter.

So what does it mean when someone says the current U.S. Treasury yields are not "normal"? And even if interest rates are not considered "normal", why is that any different from other periods in history? Remember, the risk-free rate is intended to adjust the cost of equity capital for expected future inflation. Typically, valuation analysts use a 20-year U.S. government bond yield when developing a U.S. dollar-denominated cost of equity capital. Therefore, the risk-free rate should reflect an average expected return over those years.

To be clear, in most circumstances we would prefer using the "spot" yield (i.e., the yield available in the market) on safe government bonds as a proxy for the risk-free rate.[3.13] However, during times of flight to quality and/or high levels of central bank intervention (such as the period beginning with the Financial Crisis) those *lower* observed yields imply a *lower* cost of capital (all other factors held the same), just the opposite of what one would expect in times of relative economic distress and/or uncertainty. During these periods, using a non-normalized risk-free rate (with no corresponding adjustments to the ERP) would likely lead to an *underestimated* cost of equity capital, and so a "normalization" adjustment may be a reasonable approach to address the apparent inconsistency.

[3.11] "Safe Real Rates and Fed Policy", presentation at the Commerce Bank 2016 Annual Economic Breakfast in St. Louis, M.O., November 10, 2016. A copy of the presentation can be found here:
https://www.stlouisfed.org/from-the-president/speeches-and-presentations/2016/safe-real-interest-rates-and-fed-policy.
For a list of speeches and presentations by President Bullard, visit:
https://www.stlouisfed.org/from-the-president/speeches-and-presentations.

[3.12] See for example "The 2017 Outlook for U.S. Monetary Policy", presented at the St. Louis Financial Forum, Olin Business School, Washinton University in St. Louis on February 9, 2017. A copy of the presentation can be found here:
https://www.stlouisfed.org/from-the-president/speeches-and-presentations/2017/outlook-for-us-monetary-policy.

[3.13] Government bond yields can be found at the Board of Governors of the Federal Reserve System website at:
http://www.federalreserve.gov/releases/h15/data.htm.

Why isn't the Current Spot Risk-Free Rate Considered "Normal"?

Part of the reason that U.S. Treasury yields are likely "artificially repressed" is that the "Fed" has been *telling* us that its actions were intended to push rates down, and thus boost asset prices (e.g., stocks, housing). For example, at the September 13, 2012 FOMC press conference, the Fed Chairman at the time, Ben Bernanke, stated:[3.14]

> *"...the tools we have involve affecting financial asset prices...To the extent that home prices begin to rise, consumers will feel wealthier, they'll feel more disposed to spend ... So house prices is one vehicle. Stock prices – many people own stocks directly or indirectly...and if people feel that their financial situation is better because their 401(k) looks better or for whatever reason, their house is worth more, they are more willing to go out and spend, and that's going to provide the demand that firms need in order to be willing to hire and to invest."*

Even now, after the Fed has initiated the process of normalizing interest rates, its statements and actions still talk about the need for an accommodative stance (i.e., maintaining interest rates low). At its January 2017 meeting, when deciding not to raise interest rates further, the FOMC indicated that:[3.15]

> *"After assessing current conditions and the outlook for economic activity, the labor market, and inflation, members agreed to maintain the target range for the federal funds rate at 1/2 to 3/4 percent. They judged that the stance of monetary policy remained accommodative, thereby supporting some further strengthening in labor market conditions and a return to 2 percent inflation."*

In Exhibit 3.2, the balance sheet of the U.S. Federal Reserve is shown over time. Since the Financial Crisis, the Fed has been purchasing massive quantities of U.S. Treasuries and mortgage backed securities (MBS) through a series of so-called quantitative easing (QE) measures. At the end of December 2016, the Fed's balance sheet summed to $4,461,980 million ($4.5 *trillion*), essentially unchanged from December 2015.

[3.14] FOMC: Press Conference on September 13, 2012. To obtain the press conference transcript, visit:
https://www.federalreserve.gov/monetarypolicy/fomcpresconf20120913.htm.

[3.15] "Minutes of the Federal Open Market Committee January 31–February 1, 2017", Board of Governors of the Federal Reserve System.
For details visit: http://www.federalreserve.gov/monetarypolicy/fomccalendars.htm.

Exhibit 3.2: Balance Sheet of the Federal Reserve (vis-à-vis Credit Easing Policy Tools) January 2007–December 2016

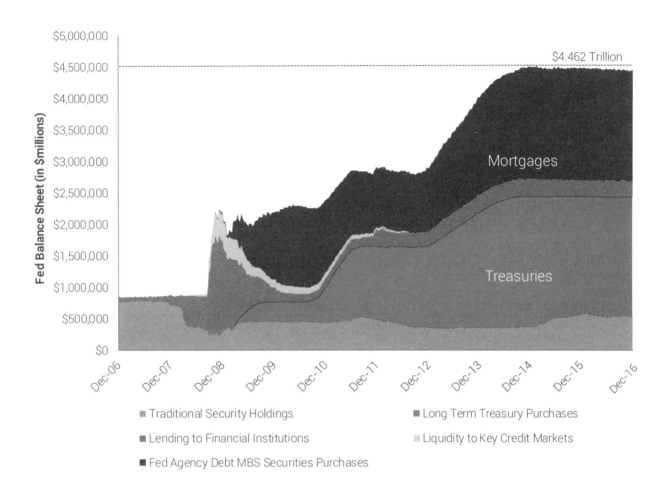

Source of underlying data: Federal Reserve Bank of Cleveland. To learn more, visit: https://www.clevelandfed.org.

In the post-crisis period, some analysts estimated that the Fed's purchases accounted for a growing majority of new Treasury issuance. In early 2013 in the online version of the *Financial Times*, one analyst wrote, *"The Fed, the biggest buyer in the market, has been the driver of artificially low Treasury yields"*.[3.16] In Exhibit 3.3 we show the aggregate dollar amount of marketable securities issued by the U.S. Department of Treasury (e.g., bills, notes, bonds, inflation-indexed securities, etc.) from 2003 through December 2016. We also display how much of the U.S. public debt is being held by the Fed, foreign investors (including official foreign institutions), and other investors.

[3.16] Michael Mackenzie, "Fed injects new sell-off risk into Treasuries", FT.com, January 8, 2013.

Exhibit 3.3: Marketable U.S. Treasury Securities Held by the Public
December 2003–December 2016

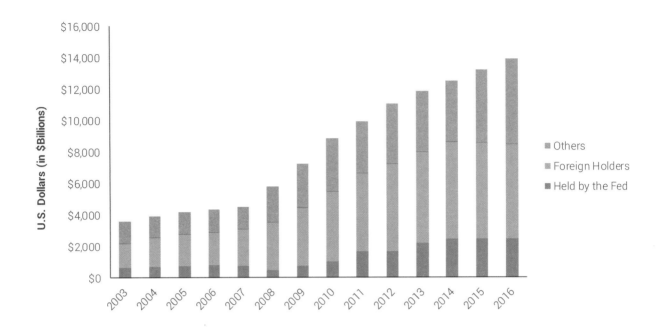

Source of underlying data: Federal Reserve Bank of St. Louis Economic Research; U.S. Department of the Treasury. Compiled by Duff & Phelps, LLC.[3.17]

Notably, the issuance of marketable interest-bearing debt by the U.S. government to the public increased threefold between the end of 2007 and 2016. Keeping everything else constant (*ceteris paribus*), the law of supply and demand would tell us that the dramatic increase in supply would lead to a significant decline in government bond prices, which would translate into a surge in yields. But that is not what happened. During the same period, the Fed more than tripled its holdings of U.S. Treasury securities, representing a 14% compound annual growth rate through the end of 2016.[3.18] Between 2003 and 2008, the Fed's holdings of U.S. Treasuries had held fairly constant in the vicinity of $700 to $800 billion, with December 2008 being the significant exception, when holdings dropped to approximately $476 billion. The first QE program was announced by the FOMC in November 2008, and formally launched in mid-December 2008. After that period, the various QE programs implemented by the Fed have contributed to absorb a sizable portion of the increase in U.S. Treasuries issuance. It is noted that for the first time since 2008, the Fed's holding of marketable U.S. Treasury securities stayed constant at the end of 2016 (in dollar amount) relative to the prior year. Nevertheless, the share held by the Fed at the end of 2016 continues to be at similar levels as those observed between 2013 and 2015.

[3.17] Sources included: (i) Board of Governors of the Federal Reserve System (US), U.S. Treasury securities held by the Federal Reserve: All Maturities [TREAST], retrieved from FRED, Federal Reserve Bank of St. Louis https://research.stlouisfed.org/fred2/series/TREAST/, February 23, 2017; (ii) Monthly Statements of the Public Debt (MSPD) retrieved from https://www.treasurydirect.gov/govt/reports/pd/mspd/mspd.htm, February 23, 2017 ; and (iii) U.S. Department of the Treasury International Capital (TIC) System's Portfolio Holdings of U.S. and Foreign Securities – A. Major Foreign Holders of U.S. Treasury Securities retrieved from http://www.treasury.gov/resource-center/data-chart-center/tic/Pages/ticsec2.aspx, February 23, 2017.

[3.18] If the comparison had been made between 2008 and 2016, the increase would be even more staggering: holdings by the Fed increased 418%, or a 23% compound annual growth rate.

Likewise, broad demand for safe government debt by foreign investors, amid the global turmoil that followed the Financial Crisis, has absorbed another considerable fraction of new U.S. Treasuries issuance. How significant are these purchases by the Fed and foreign investors? Exhibit 3.4 shows the same information as in Exhibit 3.3, but displays the relative share of each major holder of marketable U.S. Treasuries since 2003 until 2016.

Exhibit 3.4: Relative Holdings of Marketable U.S. Treasury Securities Held by the Public (in percentage terms) December 2003–December 2016

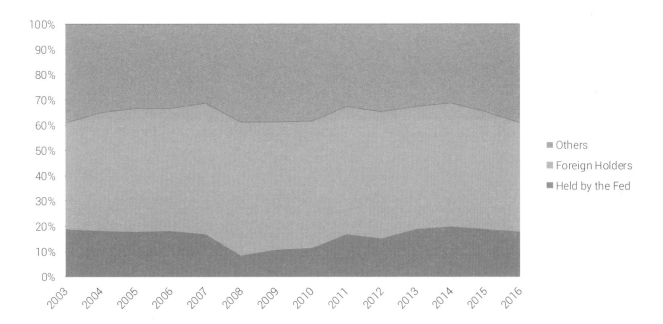

Source of underlying data: Federal Reserve Bank of St. Louis Economic Research; U.S. Department of the Treasury. Compiled by Duff & Phelps, LLC.

At the end of 2016, the relative share of U.S. Treasuries held by the Fed and foreign investors was approximately 18% and 43% respectively, for a combined 61%, compared to 65% in 2015. From 2011 to 2015, this combined level was actually close to the 69% observed at the end of 2007, prior to the onset of the Financial Crisis. As indicated above, the dollar amount of U.S. Treasuries has tripled after 2007, which means that the Fed and foreign investors have absorbed around two-thirds of the available stock in the post-crisis period until 2015.

Curiously, 2016 marked the first year when the aggregate amount of U.S. Treasuries held by foreign investors dropped noticeably (in the prior year, it had declined by a negligible amount). The relative share of U.S. Treasuries held by foreign investors declined from 47% to 43%, the lowest proportion since 2003 (even though the drop in dollar amount was only 2%). In particular, China lost to Japan its top spot as the country with the largest holdings of U.S. Treasuries, reducing its investments to their lowest level since 2010. Should this trend continue, there could be some upward pressure in U.S. interest rates.

Interestingly, a look at the composition of foreign investors reveals that from 2006 through 2015 over two-thirds are actually foreign official institutions (i.e., central banks and central governments of foreign countries); this declined to approximately 64% in 2016.[3.19, 3.20] Thus, despite the recent decline, a large majority of U.S. Treasuries are still currently held by either foreign governments or central banks around the world (including the Fed).

A team of researchers has recently studied the impact that this massive amount of U.S. Treasury purchases by foreign investors and the Fed have had on long-term real rates. Specifically, using data through November 2012, the authors estimated that by 2008 foreign purchases of U.S. Treasuries had cumulatively reduced 10-year real yields by around 80 basis points. The subsequent Fed purchases through the various QE programs implemented in the 2008–2012 period was estimated to incrementally depress 10-year real yields by around 140 basis points. Combining the impact of Fed and foreign investor purchases of U.S. Treasuries, real 10-year yields were depressed by 2.2% at the end of 2012, according to these authors' estimates.[3.21]

When the Fed concluded its third round of QE measures (in October 2014) and signaled that an increase in the target federal funds rate might be on the horizon, the salient question was what would happen to rates as one of the largest purchasers in the market (the Fed) discontinued its QE operations. All other things held the same, rates would be expected to rise. But again, that is not what happened. In fact, the yield on 10-year U.S. Treasury bonds dropped from 2.4% at the end of October to 2.2% at the end of December 2014. Likewise, the 20-year yield dropped from 2.8% to 2.5% over the same period.

Somewhat puzzling was the behavior of interest rates following the Fed's decision on December 16, 2015 to raise its target range for the federal funds rate for the first time in nine years. At first, the yield on 10- and 20-year U.S. Treasury bonds increased, reaching 2.3% and 2.7% respectively at December 31, 2015. Indeed, yields had already been rising since October 2015, in anticipation of such a rate hike decision. However, with the early 2016 global financial market turmoil, yields declined once more. In fact, global interest rates went through a rollercoaster ride in 2016, with record low yields being reached by mid-year in some countries, while a year-end reversal pushed rates back to similar levels as of year-end 2015.

Why is that?

It may be useful to first distinguish short-term drivers versus long-term trends in interest rates.

It is almost undisputed that aggressive monetary policies implemented as a response to the Financial Crisis drove long-term interest rates in the U.S. and several advanced economies to historically low levels. But many economists claim that the current low rate environment is not just a cyclical story and that we can expect to see a lower level of interest rates in the long term (although not as low as today's). A number of explanatory factors and theories have emerged, some more pessimistic than others.

[3.19] Source: Treasury International Capital (TIC) System's Portfolio Holdings of U.S. and Foreign Securities – A. Major Foreign Holders of U.S. Treasury Securities retrieved from
http://www.treasury.gov/resource-center/data-chart-center/tic/Pages/ticsec2.aspx, February 23, 2017.

[3.20] For a description of foreign official institutions, visit "TIC Country Codes and Partial List of Foreign Official Institutions" at:
http://www.treasury.gov/resource-center/data-chart-center/tic/Pages/foihome.aspx.

[3.21] Kaminska, Iryna and Zinna, Gabriele, "Official Demand for U.S. Debt: Implications for U.S. Real Interest Rates". IMF Working Paper No. 14/66 (April 2014).

We do not select which, amongst the various theories, is more (or less) correct. Instead, we suggest that valuation specialists read different sources to get acquainted with such theories. A recent survey conducted by the Council of Economic Advisers lists various factors that could help explain why long-term interest rates are currently so low. According to the study, the following is a list of possible factors, bifurcated between those that are likely transitory in nature and those that are likely longer-lived: [3.22, 3.23]

Factors that Are Likely Transitory

- Fiscal, Monetary, and Foreign-Exchange Policies

- Inflation Risk and the Term Premium

- Private-sector Deleveraging

Factors that Are Likely Longer-Lived

- Lower Global Long-run Output and Productivity Growth

- Shifting Demographics

- The Global "Saving Glut"

- Safe Asset Shortage

- Tail Risks and Fundamental Uncertainty

The report concludes that it remains an open question whether the underlying factors linked to the currently low rates are transitory, or do they imply that the long-run equilibrium for long-term interest rates is lower than before the Financial Crisis.

The bottom line is that the future path of interest rates is currently uncertain.[3.24] So, for now, we will focus on some the factors that may be keeping interest rates still very low in the near term and discuss whether one can expect an increase from these levels in the medium term.

First of all, the size of the Fed's balance sheet is still considered enormous by historical standards and the Fed has expressed the intent to keep its holdings for a long time. For example, at its December 2016 meeting, when announcing the increase by 25 basis points of the target range for

---

[3.22] The Council of Economic Advisers, an agency within the Executive Office of the President of the United States, is charged with providing economic advice to the U.S. President on the formulation of both domestic and international economic policy.

[3.23] "Long-Term Interest Rates: A Survey", July 2015. The full report can be accessed here: https://obamawhitehouse.archives.gov/sites/default/files/docs/interest_rate_report_final.pdf. See also "The Decline in Long-Term Interest Rates", July 14, 2015, a short blog article by Maurice Obstfeld and Linda Tesar discussing the various possible drivers of low long-term interest rates listed in the report. The article can be accessed here: https://www.whitehouse.gov/blog/2015/07/14/decline-long-term-interest-rates.

[3.24] For another analysis of current long-term interest rates, see Jonathan Wilmot, "When bonds aren't bonds anymore", *Credit Suisse Global Investment Returns Yearbook 2016*, February 2016.

the federal funds rate from 0.25%–0.50% to 0.50%–0.75%, the FOMC stated that:[3.25]

> *"The Committee is maintaining its existing policy of reinvesting principal payments from its holdings of agency debt and agency mortgage-backed securities in agency mortgage-backed securities and of rolling over maturing Treasury securities at auction, and it anticipates doing so until normalization of the level of the federal funds rate is well under way. This policy, by keeping the Committee's holdings of longer-term securities at sizable levels, should help maintain accommodative financial conditions."*

Translation: the Fed is likely keeping the size of its balance sheet constant for the foreseeable future, because it still wants to keep long-term interest rates low.

A report released in November 2014 (following the conclusion of QE3) by Standard & Poor's (S&P) appears to concur with our interpretation:[3.26]

> *"Since QE works via a stock effect, as long as a central bank is maintaining a certain stock of QE, it is still 'doing' QE. If a central bank has reached the maximum point of expanding its balance sheet, it is a little perverse to describe it as having 'ended QE.' Rather, what it will have ended are the asset purchases required to get it to the point of having done the maximum amount of QE it has decided to put in place."*

The impact that such a large balance sheet is having on interest rates was also implicitly acknowledged by the FOMC at its January 2017 meeting:[3.27]

> *"... it was noted that the downward pressure on longer-term interest rates exerted by the Federal Reserve's asset holdings was expected to diminish in the years ahead in light of an anticipated gradual reduction in the size and duration of the Federal Reserve's balance sheet."*

Secondly, another phenomenon has helped push U.S. interest rates lower over time: purchases of U.S. Treasury securities by foreign investors have grown at a fast pace over the last several years.[3.28] While 2016 was the first time that net purchases decreased by a noticeable amount (with a negligible decline in 2015), the reality is that the total share of U.S. Treasuries owned by foreign investors is still very high (refer back to Exhibit 3.4). Should 2016 become a trend and foreign demand for U.S. Treasury securities continue to decline, it would still likely take years for these holdings to be unwound (especially given the level of globalization of the world economy). Notably, there are academic studies that document a significant impact of foreign investors on U.S. interest rates even prior to the onset of 2008 Financial Crisis. One such study (not to be confused with the research cited previously) estimated that absent the substantial foreign

---

[3.25] Press Release of FOMC's Monetary Policy Statement, December 16, 2015. For details visit: http://www.federalreserve.gov/monetarypolicy/fomccalendars.htm.

[3.26] S&P *Ratings Direct* report entitled "Economic Research: The Fed Is Continuing, Not 'Ending,' Quantitative Easing", November 4, 2014.

[3.27] "Minutes of the Federal Open Market Committee January 31–February 1, 2017", Board of Governors of the Federal Reserve System. For details visit: http://www.federalreserve.gov/monetarypolicy/fomccalendars.htm.

[3.28] Source: Treasury International Capital (TIC) System's Portfolio Holdings of U.S. and Foreign Securities – A. "Major Foreign Holders of U.S. Treasury Securities" retrieved from http://www.treasury.gov/resource-center/data-chart-center/tic/Pages/ticsec2.aspx, February 23, 2017.

inflows into U.S. government bonds, the (nominal) 10-year Treasury yield would be 80 basis points higher using data through 2005.[3.29, 3.30]

Thirdly, an environment of geopolitical and economic uncertainty led to flight-to-quality movements during certain periods of 2015 and 2016, which helped drive interest rates even lower for major safe-havens countries. In 2016, there were three events of significant equity volatility:

- Early 2016 concerns about a slowing global economy and deflationary pressures ("Period 1" in Exhibit 3.5 on the next page).

- The June decision by U.K. voters in favor of leaving the European Union (EU), popularly known in the financial press as "Brexit" ("Period 2" in Exhibit 3.5).

- The election of Mr. Donald Trump as the new U.S. president in November ("Period 3" in Exhibit 3.5).

Periods 1 and 2 were accompanied by *decreases* in global yields in a flight to quality dynamic; Period 3 was succeeded by *increases* in global yields in seeming anticipation of higher growth and inflation with the new U.S. administration's promise of tax and regulatory reform.

[3.29] Warnock, Francis E., and Veronica Cacdac Warnock, "International Capital Flows and U.S. Interest Rates," *Journal of International Money and Finance* 28 (2009): 903–919.

[3.30] The impact of foreign financial flows on long-term interest rates is not confined to the U.S. A recent research paper estimates that the increase in foreign holdings of Eurozone bonds between early 2000 and mid-2006 is associated with a reduction of Eurozone long-term interest rates by 1.55%. See: Carvalho, Daniel and Michael Fidora, "Capital inflows and euro area long-term interest rates", ECB Working Paper 1798, June 2015. Note that the 'euro' was introduced to financial markets on January 1, 1999 as the new 'single currency' of what is now known as the Eurozone.

Exhibit 3.5: 10-year Yields on Government Bonds for United States, United Kingdom, Germany, and Japan
December 2015–December 2016

Source of Underlying Data: S&P *Capital IQ* Database. Compiled by Duff & Phelps, LLC.

Global Turbulence and Impact on Interest Rates

Global investors had enough reasons to seek safe haven investments during 2016. In general, political conflicts continued in 2016 in various regions of the world. In Europe and the U.S., there was a rise in populist candidates and political parties, with anti-immigration and anti-globalization undertones. In Europe, the Islamic State of Iraq and Syria (ISIS) continued to launch acts of terrorism, with significant attacks carried out in Belgium, France, and Germany, for example. These terrorist acts exacerbated the growing aversion to open borders. In fact, this sentiment was likely a leading cause of the surprising Brexit vote and also contributed to the unexpected U.S. election results.

In addition, concerns about a slowing global economy and deflationary pressures have also led global investors to seek safe haven investments, such as government bonds issued by the U.S., Germany, and Switzerland, to name a few. Oil prices continued to tumble from their mid-2014 highs, reinforcing investor anxiety over stagnant growth in the Eurozone and Japan, as well as a deceleration in China and several other emerging-market countries.

The sharp decline in oil prices placed additional pressure on an already very low inflation environment, considered by many as bordering on deflation territory. For perspective, the price of Brent crude oil was at $115/barrel in mid-June 2014; since then prices declined to $38/barrel at the end of 2015, a cumulative 67% decline in the space of a year and a half. The collapse of oil prices continued in early 2016.[3.31] Oil prices have since made a recovery, with Brent crude oil doubling from the January low of $29 to $57 at year-end 2016, but still far below the peak level reached in mid-2014. These higher oil prices have helped raise inflation expectations in the U.S. and the Eurozone. However, core inflation (i.e., excluding food and energy prices) continues to be below the central bankers' target of 2.0% in the Eurozone, Japan, and to a lesser extent, the United States.

Deflation risks and economic stagnation are precisely what led central banks in Japan and Eurozone to boost their respective monetary easing policies over the last two years. In October 2014, Japan's central bank surprised the world by announcing a second easing program self-dubbed as "quantitative and qualitative easing" (QQE).[3.32] In November, after the announcement of a second consecutive quarter of economic contraction, Japan's prime minister Shinzo Abe also proclaimed snap parliamentary elections, explicitly seeking endorsement to continue with the government's expansionary economic policies (also known as "Abenomics").

In another surprise move, the BOJ announced on January 29, 2016 a landmark decision to implement a negative interest rate policy (dubbed "NIRP" in the financial press), in conjunction with its QQE. The BOJ joined the European Central Bank (ECB), as well as the Danish, the Swedish and the Swiss central banks in adopting this new form of unconventional monetary policies. NIRP entails financial institutions paying interest on the liabilities that the central bank issues to them. The main idea of NIRP is to discourage savings, while creating incentives for consumers to increase their spending and companies to expand their investment. However, the consequence of such measures is to also pressure interest rates further downwards. According to an S&P research report:[3.33]

> "Negative interest rate policy appears to be able to exert downward pressure on the whole yield curve via the portfolio rebalance effect, as security prices, perturbed by the central bank's fixing of one price, adjust to restore equilibrium."

In September 2016, the BOJ again surprised markets by introducing a new "Quantitative and Qualitative Monetary Easing (QQE) with Yield Curve Control". The BOJ is now targeting the nominal yield of 10-year Japanese government bonds to around 0.0%. No other central bank targets both the level and the slope of the yield curve.

[3.31]   Source: S&P *Capital IQ* database.

[3.32]   For a list of BOJ's monetary policy decisions, visit: http://www.boj.or.jp/en/mopo/mpmdeci/index.htm/.

[3.33]   Standard & Poor's *Ratings Direct* report entitled "Negative Interest Rates: Why Central Banks Can Defy 'Time Preference'", February 3, 2016.

According to Fitch Ratings, global negative-yielding sovereign debt stood at $9.1 trillion as of December 29, 2016, although this actually represents a decline from prior months.[3.34]

In the Eurozone, lackluster growth trends, coupled with deflation fears, induced the ECB to announce an unprecedented measure to charge negative interest rates on deposits held at the central bank.[3.35] Responding to a weak third quarter, the ECB revealed in September 2014 details for two different securities purchase programs. The continued threat of deflation led the ECB to announce a larger scale sovereign debt buying program in January 2015, consisting of €60 billion in monthly asset purchases. This program was launched in March with an original target end-date of September 2016. Real GDP growth did improve in the first quarter of 2015, but decelerated once again in the second and third quarters. The November terrorist attacks in Paris, the Syrian refugee crisis, and the mounting political uncertainty in Spain and Portugal were all risk factors affecting the Eurozone at the end of 2015. Inflation was also virtually stagnant in October and November. As a result, the ECB announced in December 2015 a further cut of the already-negative deposit facility rate and an extension of monthly asset purchases to March 2017. In March 2016, the ECB unveiled further rate cuts and an expansion of its QE program, including increased monthly asset purchases from €60 to €80 billion. Investment-grade corporate bonds were added to the program, which drove their yields to record lows.

Finally, in December 2016, after signs that economic recovery in the Eurozone became stronger, and threats of deflation virtually disappeared, the ECB announced an extension of its QE program from March to December 2017, but reduced monthly purchases to be made after March back to a pace of €60 billion. Despite this projected slowdown in purchases, some analysts are predicting that by year-end 2017, the ECB will have a larger balance sheet than the Fed.[3.36]

Exhibit 3.6 illustrates how the combination of these QE programs has been driving down government bond yields globally. In this exhibit, we show how total assets of the Fed, BOJ, ECB, and the Bank of England have evolved from 2006 until the end of 2016. Note that his this an imperfect measure of sovereign debt instruments held by these central banks, since balance sheets will include other types of assets. Nonetheless, it is striking that at the end of 2016, the combined assets amounted to approximately $13.0 trillion, which is more than triple the level registered in August 2008 of $4.2 trillion, just before the onset of the Financial Crisis.

Notwithstanding these recent trends, central banks in the Eurozone, U.K., and Japan have not shown signs of scaling back their QE programs in a material way during 2017. This is in contrast to the U.S., where the Fed is likely to continue to raise rates in 2017, as previously discussed. The divergence in monetary policies in the U.S. versus other major economic regions could actually create some downward pressure in U.S. Treasury yields, making the path towards normalization somewhat slower. Ultimately, U.S. government bonds will likely offer more-attractive yields than bonds issued by other safe-haven countries, and a stronger U.S. dollar may enable foreign investors to pick up extra returns on U.S. investments.

[3.34] "Fitch: Less Global Negative-Yielding Debt No Easier on Investors, January 25, 2017. This article can be accessed here: https://www.fitchratings.com/site/pr/1018089.

[3.35] For a list of ECB's monetary policy decisions, visit: https://www.ecb.europa.eu/press/govcdec/html/index.en.html.

[3.36] "The Size of ECB Balance Sheet Will Surpass the Feds in Just 8 Months", Gavekal Capital, December 12, 2016. This article can be accessed here: http://blog.gavekalcapital.com/?p=12376.

Exhibit 3.6: Total Assets Held by Central Banks in the United States, Eurozone, Bank of Japan, and Bank of England (in U.S. Dollars)
December 2006–December 2016

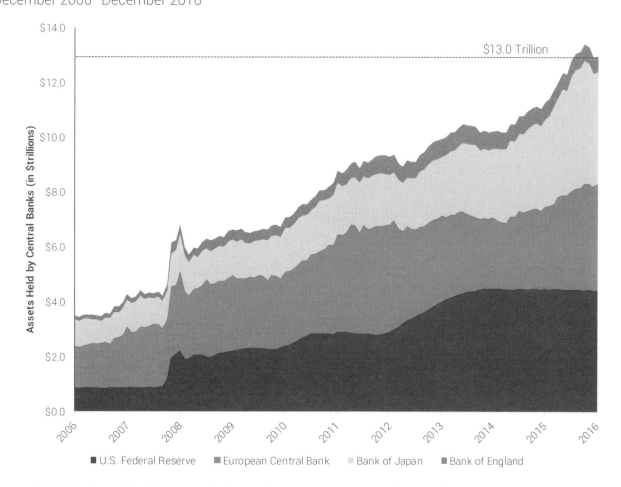

Source of Underlying Data: Federal Reserve Bank of St. Louis Economic Research. Compiled by Duff & Phelps, LLC.

Looking forward to 2017, many of the forces behind disappointing U.S. stock market performance during 2016, such as low commodity prices, sluggish global growth, and shrinking corporate profits (partly due to a strong U.S. dollar), may be fading in the coming year. This could contribute to an upward pressure on global interest rates, including those in the U.S., but perhaps not as drastic as some initially thought.

So, are artificially repressed U.S. Treasury yields sustainable? The accommodative monetary policy (including the massive QE programs) implemented by the Fed since the Financial Crisis "cannot go on forever", meaning that the Fed may really not have much of a choice in whether to "stop" or not. Put simply, things that are destined to stop will stop by their own accord, one way or another. Whether it will be a "graceful dismount" is yet to be seen.

In the short-term, there are probably still enough significant factors that will keep interest rates at artificial low levels. However, in the medium-term, borrowing any major setback in the global economy, investors seem to be expecting U.S. interest rates to start rising after 2017, although to lower levels than in the pre-Financial Crisis period. We compiled consensus forecasts from reputable sources published close to year-end 2016. Exhibit 3.7 displays the average of consensus forecasts for 10-year U.S. Treasury bond yields through 2022 from a variety of surveys.[3.37, 3.38] We then added a maturity premium to the 10-year yield, to arrive at an implied forecast for the 20-year government bond yield.[3.39]

Exhibit 3.7: Average forecasted 10-year U.S. Treasury Bond Yield and Implied 20-year U.S. Risk-free Rate (in percentage terms) at year-end 2016

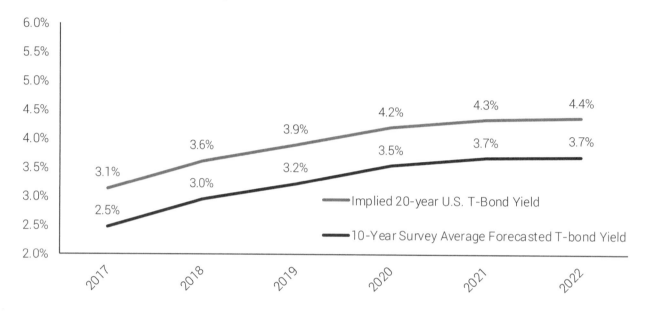

Sources of underlying data: Survey of Professional Forecasters; Livingston Survey; U.S. Consensus Forecasts; Blue Chip Economic Indicators; and Blue Chip Financial Forecasts; S&P Capital IQ database. Compiled by Duff & Phelps, LLC.

The Congressional Budget Office (CBO), a non-partisan agency supporting the U.S. Congressional budgeting process, was less optimistic on how fast rates will rise.

In its August 2016 update to "The Budget and Economic Outlook: 2016 to 2026" report, the CBO estimated the 10-year yield to average 3.1% in 2019, which would imply a 20-year yield around 3.8% using a maturity premium of 66 basis points. Its long-term forecast for the 10-year yield has been downgraded to 3.6% starting in 2022, again implying a long-term 20-year yield around 4.2%.[3.40]

[3.37]   Sources: "Survey of Professional Forecasters: Fourth Quarter 2016", Federal Reserve Bank of Philadelphia (November 14, 2016); "The Livingston Survey: December 2016", Federal Reserve Bank of Philadelphia (December 9, 2016); "Consensus Forecasts Global Outlook 2016–2026", Consensus Economics Inc. (October 2016); "Consensus Forecasts – A Digest of International Economic Forecasts", Consensus Economics Inc. (December 2016); Blue Chip Economic Indicators (October 10, 2016 and December 10, 2016); Blue Chip Financial Forecasts (December 1, 2016 and January 1, 2017); S&P Capital IQ™ database.

[3.38]   Not all surveys provided consensus forecasts through 2022. At a minimum, all five sources included forecasts for 2017 and 2018.

[3.39]   A maturity premium of approximately 66 basis points was added to the 10-year yield. This was based on the average yield spread between the 20- and the 10-year U.S. Treasury constant maturity bonds from December 2008 through December 2016. Had more recent data been used, when the yield spread has declined to a range of 30 to 40 basis points, would not materially change our main conclusion. While the magnitude of the maturity premium can be debated, using even the most recent 30 to 40 bps average yield spread would imply that at year-end 2016, market participants expected the 20-year yield to reach close to 3.6% by 2019 (3.2% + approximately 0.4%).

[3.40]   "The Budget and Economic Outlook: 2016 to 2026", released August 23, 2016. Again, using a maturity premium of 40 basis points would imply a 20-year yield of 3.5% in 2019 and a long-term 20-year yield of 4.0% starting in 2022. For more details on this report, visit: https://www.cbo.gov/publication/51908.

Methods of Risk-free Rate Normalization

Estimating a normalized risk-free rate can be accomplished in a number of ways, including (i) simple averaging, or (ii) various "build-up" methods.

The first method of estimating a normalized risk-free rate entails calculating averages of yields to maturity on long-term government securities over various periods. This method's implied assumption is that government bond yields revert to the mean. In Exhibit 3.8, the solid red line is the spot yield on a 20-year U.S. government bond (December 2007–December 2016), whereas the dashed gray line shows a 3.4% average monthly yield of the 20-year U.S. government bond over the previous 10 years ending on December 31, 2016. Government bond spot yields at the end of December 2016 were lower than the monthly average over the last 10 years. Taking the average over the last 10 years is a simple way of "normalizing" the risk-free rate. An issue with using historical averages, though, is selecting an appropriate comparison period that can be used as a reasonable proxy for the future.

Exhibit 3.8: Spot and Average Yields on 20-year U.S. Government
December 2007–December 2016

Source of underlying data: 20-year U.S. government bond series. Board of Governors of the Federal Reserve System website at: http:// www.federalreserve.gov/releases/h15/data.htm.

The second method of estimating a normalized risk-free rate entails using a simple build-up method, where the components of the risk-free rate are estimated and then added together. Conceptually, the risk-free rate can be (loosely) illustrated as the return on the following two components:[3.41]

Risk-free Rate = Real Rate + Expected Inflation

The first component, the *real rate*, has recently spiked the interest of academics, analysts, and financial media alike. The research agenda in this area has been particularly active in the last 12 to 18 months. Until the 2016 edition of the *Valuation Handbook – U.S. Guide to Cost of Capital*, we had relied on certain academic studies that suggested the long-term *"real"* risk-free rate to be somewhere in the range of 1.2% to 2.0%, based on the study of inflation swap rates and/or yields on long-term U.S. Treasury Inflation Protected Securities (TIPS). [3.42, 3.43, 3.44, 3.45]

Fast forward to the end of 2016, and we now have several other studies from which to draw an estimate for real rates. As highlighted earlier in this chapter, academic researchers and economic analysts have proposed a number of explanations for the secular (i.e., not cyclical or temporary) decline in global real interest rates, which they argue precedes the onset of the 2008 Financial Crisis. Some of those studies have proposed new measures to estimate the real rate for the United States and other countries. Based on those studies, we are now relying on a long-term real rate estimate of 0.0% to 2.0% for the United States, which represents a lower range relative to prior Duff & Phelps analyses.[3.46, 3.47]

[3.41] This is a simplified version of the "Fisher equation", named after Irving Fisher. Fisher's *"The Theory of Interest"* was first published by Macmillan (New York), in 1930.

[3.42] TIPS are marketable securities whose principal is adjusted relative to changes in the Consumer Price Index (CPI).

[3.43] Haubrich, Joseph, George Pennacchi, and Peter Ritchken, "Inflation Expectations, Real Rates, and Risk Premia: Evidence from Inflation Swaps," *Review of Financial Studies* Vol. 25 (5) (2012): 1588–1629. The results of the authors' work are updated on a monthly basis and published in the Federal Reserve Bank of Cleveland's website. The 'Inflation Expectations' monthly series published in the 'Inflation Central' section of the website, contains an expected 10-year Real Risk Premia (as predicted by the model), which would be a proxy for the maturity premium of the 10-year *real yield* over the short-term real risk-free rate. For example, in December 2016, this expected 10-year Real Risk Premia was 1.3%. The 'Inflation Central' is located here: https://www.clevelandfed.org/en/our-research/inflation-central.aspx.

[3.44] Andrew Ang and Geert Bekaert "The Term Structure of Real Rates and Expected Inflation," *The Journal of Finance*, Vol. LXIII (2) (April 2008).

[3.45] Olesya V Grishchenko and Jing-zhi Huang "Inflation Risk Premium: Evidence From the TIPS Market," *The Journal of Fixed Income*, Vol. 22 (4) (2013): 5–30.

[3.46] Pescatori, Andrea and Jarkko Turunen, "Lower for Longer: Neutral Rates in the United States", IMF Working Paper No. 15/135 (June 2015); Kiley, Michael T., "What Can the Data Tell Us About the Equilibrium Real Interest Rate?", Finance and Economics Discussion Series 2015–077. Washington: Board of Governors of the Federal Reserve System (August 2015); Lubik, Thomas A. and Christian Matthes "Calculating the Natural Rate of Interest: A Comparison of Two Alternative Approaches", Richmond Fed Economic Brief (October 2015); Reza, Abeer and Subrata Sarker, "Is Slower Growth The New Normal In Advanced Economies?", Bank Of Canada Review (Autumn 2015); Lansing, Kevin J., "Projecting the Long-Run Natural Rate of Interest", FRBSF Economic Letter 2016–25 (August 2016); Hamilton, James, Ethan Harris, Jan Hatzius, and Kenneth West, "The Equilibrium Real Funds Rate: Past, Present and Future", *IMF Economic Review*, November 2016, Vol. 64, Issue 4, p. 660–707; Holston, Kathryn, Thomas Laubach, and John C. Williams, "Measuring the Natural Rate of Interest: International Trends and Determinants", Federal Reserve Bank of San Francisco Working Paper 2016–11 (December 2016).

[3.47] We continue to also rely on the results of Haubrich et al (2012) work, which are updated on a monthly basis and published in the Federal Reserve Bank of Cleveland's website.

Note that these lower estimates can coexist with the post-U.S. election optimism for policies that will boost real growth for the U.S. economy. While the ultimate net effect is still unknown, economists still do not appear to be convinced that this will translate into a higher long-term potential for real GDP (gross domestic product). Consensus long-term real GDP estimates continue to be below the levels seen in post-World War II recoveries.

The second component, *expected inflation*, can also be estimated in a number of ways. Monetary policymakers and academics have been monitoring several measures of market expectations of future inflation. One method of estimating long-term inflation is to take the difference between the yield on a 20-year U.S. government bond yield and the yield of a 20-year U.S. TIPS. This is also known as the "breakeven inflation".[3.48] This calculation is shown in Exhibit 3.9 over the time period July 2004–December 2016. Over this period, the average monthly breakeven long-term inflation estimate using this method was 2.3% (3.72% government bond yield − 1.46% TIPS).

Exhibit 3.9: Breakeven Long-term Inflation Estimate (20 year Government Bond Yield − 20 year TIPS Yield)
July 2004–December 2016

Source of underlying data: 20-year U.S. government bond series and 20-year TIPS series, Board of Governors of the Federal Reserve System website at: http://www.federalreserve.gov/releases/h15/data.htm. Calculated by Duff & Phelps, LLC.

[3.48] Breakeven inflation is based on the differential between nominal and TIPS yields with equivalent maturity. However, several studies have documented that the breakeven inflation has not been a good predictor for inflation expectations. The differential between nominal and real rates is not only complicated by a liquidity premium, but also by the potential presence of the inflation risk premium, with both of these premiums varying through time. For a more detailed list of academic studies documenting the magnitude of the liquidity premium and the inflation risk premium, refer back to Chapter 7 of Shannon P. Pratt and Roger J. Grabowski, *Cost of Capital: Applications and Examples*, 5th ed. (Hoboken, NJ: John Wiley & Sons, 2014).

Additionally, in the U.S., there are a number of well-established surveys providing consensus estimates for expected inflation. One academic study has examined various methods for forecasting inflation over the period 1952–2004 and found that surveys significantly outperform other forecasting methods.[3.49] Exhibit 3.10a outlines some of the most prominent surveys in this area. Altogether, the year-end 2016 estimates of longer-term inflation range from 1.9% to 2.3%.

Exhibit 3.10a: Long-term Expected Inflation Estimates
Year-end 2016 (approx.)

Source	Estimate (%)
Livingston Survey (Federal Reserve Bank of Philadelphia)	2.3
Survey of Professional Forecasters (Federal Reserve Bank of Philadelphia)	2.2
Blue Chip Financial Forecasts	2.3
Blue Chip Economic Indicators	2.3
Consensus Economics	2.3
Cleveland Federal Reserve	1.9
Aruoba Term Structure of Inflation Expectations	2.3
University of Michigan Survey 5-10 Year Ahead Inflation Expectations	2.3
Range of Expected Inflation Forecasts	1.9% to 2.3%

Sources of underlying data: "The Livingston Survey: December 2016," Federal Reserve Bank of Philadelphia (December 9, 2016); "Survey of Professional Forecasters: Fourth Quarter 2016," Federal Reserve Bank of Philadelphia (November 14, 2016); *Blue Chip Financial Forecasts* (December 1, 2016 and January 1, 2017); *Blue Chip Economic Indicators* (October 10, 2016 and December 10, 2016); "Consensus Forecasts Global Outlook 2016–2026", Consensus Economics Inc. (October 2016); "Consensus Forecasts – A Digest of International Economic Forecasts", Consensus Economics Inc. (December 2016); Federal Reserve Bank of Cleveland (estimates as of December 2016); Philadelphia Federal Reserve, Aruoba Term Structure of Inflation Expectations (estimates as of December 2016); the University of Michigan Inflation Expectations, December 2016.

Adding the estimated ranges for the "real" risk-free rate and longer-term inflation together produces an estimated normalized risk-free rate range of 1.9% to 4.3%, with a midpoint of 3.1% (see Exhibit 3.10b).

[3.49] Ang, A., G. Bekaert, and M. Wei. "Do macro variables, asset markets, or surveys forecast inflation better?" *Journal of Monetary Economics*. 54, 1163-1212.

Exhibit 3.10b: Estimated Range of Normalized Risk-free Rate Using Simple Build-up Method

Range of Estimated Long-term Real Rate	0.0% to 2.0%
Range of Estimated Expected Inflation Forecasts	1.9% to 2.3%
Range of Estimated Long-term Normalized Risk-free Rate	1.9% to 4.3%
Midpoint	3.1%

While the results of the U.S. presidential election seem to have spurred higher inflation expectations for global investors as manifested by higher yields, consensus long-term inflation expectations (see Exhibit 3.10a) have seemingly not moved higher at this point. Partly, this is due to the fact that inflation was virtually non-existent for two years and now we are simply returning to pre-2014 "normal" conditions, as the impact of the collapse in oil prices subsides. We will continue to closely monitor the aftermath of the U.S. presidential election and its potential impact on inflation expectations and consequent effects on the normalized long-term risk-free rate.

Spot Yield or Normalized Yield?

Should the valuation analyst use the current market yield on risk-free U.S. government bonds or use a "normalized" risk-free yield when estimating the cost of equity capital?

As stated earlier, in most circumstances we would prefer to use the "spot" yield on U.S. government bonds available in the market as a proxy for the U.S. risk-free rate. However, during times of flight to quality and/or high levels of central bank intervention, those lower observed yields imply a lower cost of capital (all other factors held the same) – just the opposite of what one would expect in times of relative economic distress – so a "normalization" adjustment may be considered appropriate. By "normalization" we mean estimating a rate that more likely reflects the sustainable average return of long-term risk-free rates. *If spot yield-to-maturity were used at these times, without any other adjustments, one would arrive at an overall discount rate that is likely inappropriately low vis-à-vis the risks currently facing investors.* Exhibit 3.11 shows the potential problems of simply using the spot yield-to-maturity on 20-year U.S. government bonds in conjunction with unadjusted U.S. historical equity risk premia. Data is displayed for year-end 2007 through year-end 2016. For example, in December 2008, at the height of the Financial Crisis (when risks were arguably at all-time highs), using the 1926–2008 historical ERP of 6.5% together with the spot 20-year yield of 3.0% would result in a base cost of equity capital of 9.5%. In contrast, the base cost of equity would be 11.6% (4.5% plus 7.1%) at year-end 2007, implying that risks were actually higher at the end of 2007 than at the end of 2008. From both a theoretical and practical standpoint, the reality is that investors likely perceived risks to be much higher in December 2008, relative to the December 2007. This demonstrates that a mechanical application of the data may result in nonsensical results.[3.50]

[3.50] More detailed information on historical ERPs can be found later in this chapter.

Exhibit 3.11: Spot 20-year U.S. Treasury Yield in Conjunction with Unadjusted "Historical" Equity Risk Premium

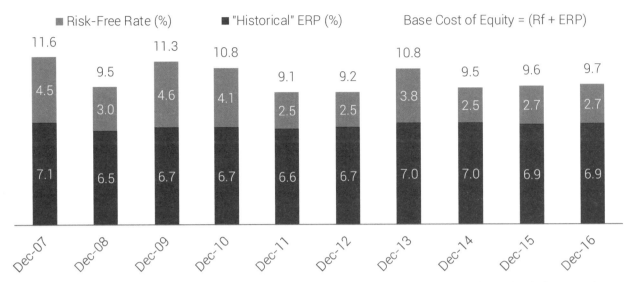

Source of underlying data: Morningstar *Direct* database. Exhibit 3.11 is constructed using the long-horizon "historical" ERP, and SBBI long-term U.S. government bond series, as published in the former 2008–2013 *SBBI Valuation Yearbook* and the 2014–2017 *Valuation Handbook – U.S. Guide to Cost of Capital*. Full-precision decimals were used in the calculations; some values may not add up due to rounding issues. Used with permission. All rights reserved. Calculations performed by Duff & Phelps, LLC.

Adjustments to the ERP or to the risk-free rate are, in principle, a response to the same underlying concerns and should result in broadly similar costs of capital. Adjusting the risk-free rate in conjunction with the ERP is only one of the alternatives available when estimating the cost of equity capital.

For example, one could use a spot yield for the risk-free rate, but *increase* the ERP or other adjustment to account for higher (systematic) risk. If the valuation analyst chooses to use the spot yield to estimate the cost of capital during periods when those yields are less than "normal," the valuation analyst must use an estimated ERP that is *matched* to (or implied by) those *below-normal* yields. However we note that the most commonly used data sources for ERP estimates are long-term series measured when interest rates were largely not subject to such market intervention. Using those data series with an abnormally low spot yield creates a mismatch.

Alternatively, if the valuation analyst chooses to use a normalized risk-free rate in estimating the cost of capital, the valuation analyst must again use an estimated ERP that is *matched* to those *normalized* yields. Normalizing the risk-free rate is likely a more direct (and more easily implemented) analysis than adjusting the ERP due to a *temporary* reduction in the yields on risk-free securities, while *longer-term* trends may be more appropriately reflected in the ERP.

We examined interest rates for the months since the Financial Crisis began. We also estimated a "normalized" yield each month using trailing averages and a build-up model.

Concluded Normalized Risk-free Rate

In the examples in this book, we are using data as of December 2016.

We examined interest rates for the months since the Financial Crisis began. We also estimated a "normalized" yield using trailing averages (3.4%; see Exhibit 3.8) and a build-up model (3.1%; see Exhibit 3.10b). Based on the combination of these quantitative and qualitative factors, we have concluded 3.5% as a reasonable normalized risk-free rate of return. As of December 31, 2016, the Duff & Phelps recommended ERP is 5.5% (discussed in the next section), implying a base U.S. cost of equity capital of 9.0% (3.5% + 5.5%) at that time.

Exhibit 3.19 (at the end of this chapter) provides a summary of both the Duff & Phelps recommended equity risk premium and the accompanying risk-free rate (either "spot" or "normalized") over the time period December 2007 through December 2016. Please note that the Duff & Phelps recommended ERP is developed in *relation to* (and should be used in *conjunction with*) the risk-free rate it was developed in relation to (either "spot" or "normalized", as indicated in Exhibit 3.19).

Equity Risk Premium[3.51]

The ERP (often interchangeably referred to as the *market risk premium*) is defined as the extra return (over the expected yield on risk-free securities) that investors expect to receive from an investment in the market portfolio of common stocks, represented by a broad-based market index (e.g., S&P 500 Index or the NYSE Index).

In a relatively recent paper, the authors conclude that "The ERP is almost certainly the most important variable in finance."[3.52]

The ERP (or notational RP_m) is defined as:

Formula 3.1

$$RP_m = R_m - R_f$$

Where:

RP_m =   Equity risk premium

R_m =   Expected return on a diversified portfolio of equity securities, most often measured as the S&P 500 Index or the NYSE Index (for the U.S. market)

R_f =   Expected risk-free rate

ERP is a forward-looking concept. It is an expectation as of the valuation date for which no market quotes are directly observable. ERP is a function of expected returns on a diversified portfolio of equities minus an expected yield on a risk-free security to which it is compared over a specified time period.

The ERP can be thought of in terms of an *unconditional* ERP (i.e., the long-term average through the business cycle) and a *conditional* ERP based on current levels of the stock market and economy relative to the long-term average.[3.53]

In this chapter, we are addressing returns of publicly traded stocks relative to an expected yield on a risk-free security. The ERP in conjunction with the risk-free rate, either normalized or actual, also establishes a beginning benchmark for estimating the appropriate discount rates for securities of closely held businesses.

[3.51]   Excerpted in part from Pratt and Grabowski, op.cit.: Chapters 8 and 8A and updated through December 31, 2013.

[3.52]   Richard C. Grinold, Kenneth K. Kroner, and Laurence B. Siegel, "A Supply Model of the Equity Premium," in *Rethinking the Equity Risk Premium*, ed. P. Brett Hammond, Jr., Martin L. Leibowitz, and Lawrence B. Siegel (The Research Foundation of CFA Institute, 2011): 53.

[3.53]   Robert D. Arnott, "Historical Results," *Equity Risk Premium Forum, AIMR* (November 8, 2001): 27.

Estimating the Equity Risk Premium

There is no single universally accepted methodology for estimating the ERP. A wide variety of premiums are used in practice and recommended by academics and financial advisors. These differences are often due to differences in how ERP is estimated.

Generally, we can categorize approaches for estimating the ERP as either an *ex post* approach or an *ex ante* approach.

For example, some valuation analysts define expected returns on common stocks in terms of averages of realized (historical) single-period returns while others define expected returns on common stocks in terms of realized multi-year compound returns. These are *ex post* approaches.

Some valuation analysts estimate the ERP using the returns on the diversified portfolio implied by expected (future) stock prices or expected dividends. These are *ex ante* approaches.

From an investment return perspective, the ERP is typically defined as the expected average annual compound return on a diversified portfolio of equity securities, most often measured as the S&P 500 Index or the NYSE Index for the U.S. market, minus the expected return on a risk-free security.[3.54]

If one is using *historical* risk premiums (sometimes called a "long-term historical ERP") as an estimator of *future* risk premiums (an *ex post* approach), the geometric average of realized returns is the estimator one should use in compounding future returns to estimate future wealth. But if one is using historical risk premiums as the estimator of the ERP for use in cost of capital models intended for discounting expected cash flows, the most widely used statistic is the arithmetic average of realized risk premiums.

Even if one is simply looking forward at prospective returns for the S&P 500 and the implied ERP (an *ex ante* approach), the arithmetic average equivalent of the implied ERP is a better statistic to use in cost of capital models intended for discounting expected cash flows.

Historical return and risk premium data is most often expressed in terms of one-year returns. In the *Valuation Handbook – U.S. Guide to Cost of Capital*, we have attempted to convert varying indications of the ERP such that they are measured in a consistent framework (e.g., a statistical estimator of the ERP in excess of 20-year U.S. government bonds).

Ex Post Approaches

While a valuation analyst can observe premiums realized over time by referring to historical data (i.e., realized risk premium approach or *ex post* approach), such realized premium data do not represent the ERP expected in those prior periods, nor do they represent the current ERP estimate. Rather, to the extent that realized premiums on the average equate to expected premiums in prior periods, such samples *may be* representative of current expectations. But to the extent that prior

---

[3.54] For example, see Peng Chen, "Will Bonds Outperform Stocks over the Long Run? Not Likely," in *Rethinking the Equity Risk Premium*, ed. P. Brett Hammond, Jr., Martin L. Leibowitz, and Lawrence B. Siegel (The Research Foundation of CFA Institute, 2011): 128.

events that were not expected to occur caused realized returns to differ from prior expectations, such samples need to be adjusted to remove the effects of these nonrecurring events. One needs to understand which events might be considered nonrecurring and then adjust the data for them in order to improve the predictive power of the sample.

Further, *ex post* realized returns on stocks and realized risk premiums will be affected by differences between expected inflation at the time of an ERP estimate was made and the realized inflation subsequent to the date of the estimate. This difference will cause *ex post* stock returns and *ex post* risk premiums to differ from ERP estimates made in prior periods.

Ex Ante Approaches

Valuation analysts can derive forward-looking estimates for the ERP from forward-looking data at the time of the analysis (*ex ante* approach).[3.55] We can generally categorize four types of forward-looking data used in estimating the expected returns on a diversified portfolio of equities and, in turn, the ERP:

    i.   Data on the underlying expectations of growth in overall corporate earnings and dividends.

    ii.   Data aggregated from projections of analysts following the companies comprising the broad portfolio as to their expectations of dividends and future stock prices.

    iii.   Data on observations of risk premiums evidenced in the level of the S&P 500, corporate bond spreads (e.g., differences in yields on corporate bonds rated Baa and Aaa), or prices for credit default swaps.

    iv.   Surveys of expectations of respondents.

The goal of both the *ex post* and *ex ante* approaches is to estimate the *expected* ERP as of the valuation date.

Any estimate of the ERP must be made in relation to a risk-free security. That is, the ERP is measured as the difference between the expected return on a well-diversified portfolio of large company common stocks and the rate of return expected on a risk-free security.

In valuing going-concern businesses and long-term investments made by businesses, valuation analysts generally use long-term U.S. government bonds as the risk-free security and use an estimate of ERP developed relative to long-term U.S. government bonds. This convention both represents a realistic, simplifying assumption and is consistent with the theory of the CAPM.[3.56]

[3.55] See, for example, the discussion in Eugene F. Fama and Kenneth R. French, "The Equity Premium," *Journal of Finance* (April 2002): 637–659.

[3.56] Eugene F. Fama, "Risk-Adjusted Discount Rates and Capital Budgeting Under Uncertainty," *Journal of Financial Economics* 5(1) (1977): 3–24. This is true for both the original CAPM of Sharpe-Lintner-Mossin and the extension of the textbook CAPM, the intertemporal CAPM of Merton.

Most business investments have long durations and suffer from a reinvestment risk just as long-term government bonds do. As such, the use of long-term U.S. government bonds and an ERP estimated relative to such bonds more closely matches the investment horizon and risks confronting business managers in capital budgeting decisions, as well as in valuation issues.

Therefore, in the remainder of this chapter, we have translated all estimates of ERP to estimates relative to 20-year U.S. government bonds rates.

Unconditional ERP

We will first examine the *unconditional ERP* (i.e., long-term average) using realized risk premium data (the *ex post* approach). While academics and valuation analysts agree that ERP is a forward-looking concept, some valuation analysts, including taxing authorities and regulatory bodies, use historical data to estimate the ERP under the assumption that historical data are a valid proxy for current investor expectations. They like the appearance of accuracy, and we do emphasize the word *appearance.*

In the realized risk premium approach, the estimate of the ERP is the risk premium (realized return on stocks in excess of the risk-free rate) that investors have, on average, realized over some historical holding period. The underlying theory is that the past provides a reasonable indicator of how the market will behave in the future, and also that investors' expectations are influenced by the historical performance of the market.

A more direct justification for use of the realized risk premium approach is the contention that, for whatever reason, securities in the past have been priced in such a way as to earn the returns observed. By using an estimated cost of equity capital incorporating the average of realized risk premiums, you may to some extent replicate this level of pricing.

The long-term average of realized risk premiums is calculated from varying rates of returns on common stocks over fluctuating risk-free rates. They are generally reported annually. A common practice adds the same long-term average realized risk premium (an *ex post* estimate of the ERP) to the market interest rate of the risk-free security throughout the following year regardless of the level of the rate on that security as of the valuation date.

This common practice implicitly either assumes that during upcoming periods the difference between the expected return on common stocks and U.S. government bonds is constant. Alternatively, this common practice implicitly assumes that any decrease or increase in the ERP as of the valuation date is short-term in nature and that the ERP is mean-reverting to the long-term average of realized risk premiums rather quickly.

Let us look at an example of the consequences of this common practice. If a valuation analyst were using the long-term average of realized risk premiums from 1926–2007 of 7.1% as the appropriate ERP estimate during 2008, that 7.1% ERP would have been added to the spot risk-free rate at any valuation date during 2008 regardless of the level of the risk-free rate during that year and regardless of any changes in risks in the economy.

For example, the yield on 20-year U.S. government bonds was 4.8% on October 31, 2008, resulting in a base cost of equity of 11.9% (4.8% + 7.1%). But due to the increase in economic risks as the Financial Crisis unfolded, the yield had fallen due to flights to quality to 3.7% as of November 30, 2008. Following this common practice, the 7.1% would have been added to this lower yield, resulting in a base cost of equity capital of 10.8% (3.7% + 7.1%), even though risk had clearly increased.[3.57]

In applying the historical (i.e., "realized") risk premium approach, an important consideration is the number of years of historical return data to include when calculating the average. One school of thought holds that the future is best estimated using a very long horizon of past returns, commonly going back to 1926. While the selection of 1926 as a starting point corresponds to the initial publishing of the forerunner to the current S&P 500 (the S&P Composite Index of 90 stocks), the choice of that date was otherwise arbitrary.

Another school of thought holds that the future is best measured by the (relatively) recent past. The average realized risk premium is sensitive to the period chosen for the average.

A summary of some of the issues that should likely be considered when selecting a time period over which to calculate a "historical" ERP estimate are as follows (this list is not exhaustive):

Reasons to focus on recent history:

- The recent past may be most relevant to an investor.

- Return patterns may change over time.

- The longer period includes "unusual events" which may not be representation of today's economy.

- The relationship between stocks and bonds may have changed in more recent years compared to less recent years.

Reasons to focus on long-term history:

- Long-term historical returns have shown surprising stability.

- Short-term observations may lead to illogical forecasts.

- Every period has dramatic historical events, and we do not know what major events lie ahead.

- Law of large numbers: More observations lead to a more accurate estimate.

Differences in one's approach to estimating the ERP hinge even more on the measure of expected return on equity securities.

[3.57] *2013 Ibbotson SBBI Valuation Yearbook* (Chicago: Morningstar, 2013): 57–61. The *SBBI Valuation Yearbook* was discontinued in 2013.

Realized Historical Stock and Bond Returns

The highest-quality data are available for periods beginning in 1926 from the Center of Research in Security Prices (CRSP) at the University of Chicago. The *Valuation Handbook – U.S. Guide to Cost of Capital* contains summaries of returns on U.S. stocks and bonds derived from those data series. The reported returns include the effects from the reinvestment of dividends.

Returns on common stocks have been assembled by various sources (and with various degrees of quality) for earlier periods. Reasonably good stock market return data are available back to 1872, and less reliable data are available back to the end of the eighteenth century. In the earliest period, the market consisted almost entirely of bank stocks, and by the mid-nineteenth century, the market was dominated by railroad stocks.[3.58] Data for government bond yield data have also been assembled for these periods. Exhibit 3.12 presents the realized average annual risk premiums for stocks assembled from various sources for alternative periods through 2016.

We measure the realized risk premium by comparing the stock market returns during the period to the income return on long-term U.S. government bonds (or total returns for the years before 1926).

Exhibit 3.12 displays the arithmetic average of realized risk premiums, the standard errors of estimate and the geometric average of the realized risk premiums.

Exhibit 3.12: Realized Equity Risk Premiums: Stock Market Returns Minus U.S. Government Bonds Through 2016

Length (Yrs.)	Period Dates	Arithmetic Average (%)	Standard Deviation (%)	Standard Error (%)	Geometric Average (%)
20	1997–2016	4.92	18.71	4.18	3.09
30	1987–2016	6.07	17.08	3.12	4.40
40	1977–2016	5.68	16.10	2.55	4.15
50	1967–2016	4.92	16.75	2.37	3.33
91	1926–2016	6.94	19.97	2.09	4.81
117	1900–2016	6.65	19.63	1.81	4.60
145	1872–2016	5.90	18.68	1.55	4.07
219	1798–2016	5.12	17.91	1.21	3.46

Sources of underlying data: Data compiled from R. Ibbotson and G. Brinson, *Global Investing* (New York: McGraw-Hill, 1993); W. Schwert, "Indexes of U.S. Stock Prices from 1802 to 1987", *Journal of Business* Vol. 63 (July 1990): 399–426; S. Homer and R. Sylla, *A History of Interest Rates*, 3rd ed. (Piscataway, NJ: Rutgers University Press, 1991); and CRSP and Morningstar *Direct* database. Calculations by Duff & Phelps, LLC. Used with permission. All rights reserved.

While some may question the relevance of averages including early periods for estimating today's ERP, what is striking is that the largest arithmetic average of one-year returns (of all the periods displayed in Exhibit 3.12) is the 91 years from 1926 to 2016.

[3.58]   See Pratt and Grabowski, op.cit.: 143.

Why use the income return on long-term government bonds? The income return in each period represented the expected yield on the bonds at the time of the investment. Investors make a decision to invest in the stock market today by comparing the expected return from that particular investment to the rate of return today on a benchmark risk-free security (in this case, the long-term U.S. government bond). While investors did not know the stock market return when they invested at the beginning of each year, they did know the rate of interest promised on long-term U.S. government bonds when they were first issued. To try to match the expectations at the beginning of each year, we measure historical stock market returns on an expectation that history will repeat itself over the expected return on bonds in each year.

The realized risk premiums vary year to year, and the estimate of the *true* ERP resulting from this sampling is subject to some degree of error. We display the standard errors of estimate in Exhibit 3.12. The standard error of estimate allows you to measure the likely accuracy of using the realized risk premium as the estimate of the *true* ERP assuming that the observations are drawn from a distribution of returns that is still relevant. This statistic indicates the estimated range within which the *true* ERP falls (i.e., assuming normality, the true ERP can be expected to fall within two standard errors with a 95% level of confidence).

In choosing the years one includes in the estimate, the valuation analyst is looking for a period in which the realized returns best represent what might be expected in future periods. One might consider eliminating from the sample periods influenced by abnormal circumstances. Or one might consider a sample period with risk characteristics more comparable to the risk characteristics confronting investors today.

World War II Interest Rate Bias

Some observers have suggested that the period including the 1940s and the immediate post-World War II boom years may have exhibited unusually high average realized return premiums due to the Fed's intervention in the bond markets to control interest rates.[3.59]

We consider the years 1942 through 1951 particularly problematic as they reflected a period of government-imposed stability in U.S. government bond yields. During World War II, the U.S. Treasury (Treasury) decreed that interest rates had to be kept at artificially low levels in order to reduce government financing costs. This led to the Fed's April 1942 public commitment to maintain interest rates at prescribed levels on U.S. government debt, both long-term and short-term.[3.60]

With regard to short-term interest rates, the Fed agreed to make a market in 3-month T-bills at a yield of 3/8 percent. With regard to longer-term securities, the Fed agreed to support interest rate ceilings; for example, it agreed to support 25-year U.S. government bond prices at a level consistent with a 2.5% interest rate ceiling. For perspective, the current policy being implemented by the central bank of Japan, by targeting 0.0% (zero) on 10-year Japanese government bonds, is a variant of what the Fed did back in the 1940s.

[3.59] Jeremy Siegel, *Stocks for the Long Run* (New York: McGraw-Hill, 1994): 20.

[3.60] Mark Toma, "Interest Rate Controls: The United States in the 1940's," *The Journal of Economic History* 52(3) (September 1992): 633–634.

After World War II, the Fed continued to maintain an interest rate ceiling due to the Treasury's pressure and, to a lesser extent, a fear of returning to the high unemployment levels of the Great Depression. The Treasury and the Fed ended the pegging of interest rates on T-bills in July 1947. But interest rate controls on long-term rates continued until postwar inflationary pressures caused the Treasury and the Fed to reach an accord announced March 4, 1951, freeing the Fed of its obligation of pegging interest rates.[3.61] Including this period in calculating realized returns is analogous to valuing airline stocks today by looking at prices of airline stocks when domestic airline fares were regulated.

To better understand the impact of the interest rate controls on the ERP, we examined the annual arithmetic average of realized risk premiums for the period 1926–2016 and the annual arithmetic average of realized risk premiums for the period 1926–2016 *excluding 1942 through 1951*. Exhibit 3.13 displays these results.

Exhibit 3.13: Realized Risk Premiums Including and Excluding the Years 1942–1951

Period Dates	Realized Risk Premiums (arithmetic average) (%)	Standard Deviations (%)
1926–2016	6.94	19.97
1926–2016 (excluding 1942–1951)	5.85	20.44

Source of underlying data: Morningstar *Direct* database. Copyright © 2017 Morningstar, Inc. All rights reserved. Calculations by Duff & Phelps, LLC.

Eliminating the years 1942 through 1951 from the sample reduced the realized risk premium from the 6.94% to 5.85% for 1926–2016. One can interpret the realized risk premium data reported herein as being biased high by as much as 1.08% (6.94% − 5.85%) (difference due to rounding). We will call this the "WWII Interest Rate Bias." We use 1.08% as the adjustment below to indicate the extent of the possible bias created by this period in the indicated ERP estimates we display.

We are not questioning the accuracy of the realized risk premiums reported using the *SBBI®* data. Rather, we believe that if one were using the realized return data as a basis for forecasting ERP, demonstrated biases should be removed where possible. Removing the data from 1942–1951 from the sample allows the valuation analyst to make the data more representative of what might be expected in future years. We believe that valuation analysts should consider the WWII Interest Rate Bias when estimating ERP using realized risk premium data.[3.62]

"Market" rates subject to control are really not market rates reflective of real interest rates plus the market's expectations of inflation. This was true during the 1942–1951 period and is true as we are writing this book due to the actions of the Fed through quantitative easing.

The summarized data in Exhibit 3.12 represent the arithmetic and geometric averages of realized risk premiums for one-year returns. That is, the dollars invested (including reinvested dividends) are

---

[3.61] Jerry W. Markham, *A Financial History of the United States*, vol. 1 (Armonk, NY: M.E. Sharpe, 2002): 299–300.

[3.62] Some disagree with our conclusion. See for example, Kevin Piccolo, "The Dangers of Normalization: An Interest-Rate Perspective," *The Value Examiner* (March/April 2012): 23–32.

reallocated to available investments annually, and the return is calculated for each year. The arithmetic average is the mean of the annual returns. The geometric average is the single compound return that equates the initial investment with the ending investment, assuming annual reallocation of investment dollars and reinvestment of dividends.

For example, assume the following series of stock prices (assuming no dividends):

Period	Stock Price ($)	Period Return (%)
1	10	n/a
2	20	100
3	10	-50

The arithmetic average of periodic returns equals $(100\% + -50\%)/2 = 25\%$, and the geometric average equals $[(1+r_1)(1+r_2)]^{1/2} - 1 = [(1+1.0 \times 1 - 0.5)]^{1/2} - 1 = 0\%$.

Realized risk premiums measured using the geometric (compound) averages are always less than those using the arithmetic average. The geometric mean is the lower boundary of the arithmetic mean, and the two are equal in the unique situation that every observation is identical. The more variable the period returns however, the greater the difference between the arithmetic and geometric averages of those returns. This is simply the result of the mathematics of a series that has experienced deviations.

The choice between using the geometric and arithmetic average is a matter of disagreement among academics and valuation analysts. Using the arithmetic average for discounting net cash flow receives the most support in the literature.[3.63] Some authors recommend a geometric average.[3.64]

Comparing Investor Expectations to Realized Risk Premiums

Much has been written comparing the realized risk premiums as reported in sources – such as past editions of the *Ibbotson SBBI Valuation Yearbooks* – and the ERP that must have been expected by investors, given the underlying economics of publicly traded companies (e.g., expected growth in earnings or expected growth in dividends) and the underlying indicators for the economy (e.g., expected growth in gross domestic product (GDP)). Such studies conclude that investors could not have expected as large an ERP as the risk premiums actually realized historically.[3.65]

[3.63] See, for example, Paul Kaplan, "Why the Expected Rate of Return Is an Arithmetic Mean," *Business Valuation Review* (September 1995); *2012 Ibbotson® SBBI® Valuation Yearbook*: 56–57; Mark Kritzman, "What Practitioners Need to Know about Future Value, " *Financial Analysts Journal* (May/June 1994): 12–15; Zvi Bodie, Alex Kane, and Alan J. Marcus, *Investments* (Chicago: Irwin Professional Publishing, 1989): 720–723; Elroy Dimson, Paul Marsh and Mike Staunton, *Credit Suisse Global Investment Returns Sourcebook 2016* (London: Credit Suisse/London Business School, 2016).

[3.64] See, for example, Aswath Damodaran, *Investment Valuation: Tools and Techniques for Determining the Value of Any Asset*, 3rd ed. (Hoboken, NJ: John Wiley & Sons, 2012): 162–163; Aswath Damodaran, "Equity Risk Premiums: Determinants, Estimation and Implications – the 2016 Edition," (March 2016): 33–34, available at: https://papers.ssrn.com/sol3/papers2.cfm?abstract_id=2742186.

[3.65] Several of those studies are summarized in Pratt and Grabowski, op.cit., Chapter 8A, "Deriving ERP Estimates": 147–153.

Ibbotson and Chen report on a study in which they estimated forward-looking long-term sustainable equity returns and expected ERPs since 1926. They first analyzed realized equity returns by decomposing returns into factors including inflation, earnings, dividends, price-to-earnings ratios, dividend payout ratios, book values, returns on equity, and GDP per capita (the fundamental building blocks of equity returns being "supplied" by companies).

They forecasted the ERP through supply-side models built from historical data by removing the price-to-earnings ratio inflation (a top-down approach for estimating the market's re-pricing due to the underlying economic changes in aggregate). Those authors determined that the long-term ERP that could have been expected, given the underlying economics, was less than the realized premium.[3.66]

We updated the "supply side" ERP over the 1926–2016 for the *2017 Valuation Handbook – U.S. Guide to Cost of Capital*. The supply-side ERP estimate is 3.99% (on a geometric basis), and 5.97% (on an arithmetic basis). In comparison, the realized (historical) 1926–2016 ERP was 4.81% (on a geometric basis), and 6.94% (on an arithmetic basis).[3.67]

We are using the methodology consistent with that used in the discontinued *SBBI® Valuation Yearbook*. We examined the compound annual growth in price-to-earnings ratios from 1926 to the current year where the current year's price-to-earnings ratio is calculated using a three-year average of earnings. Using the three-year average allows the adjustment to smooth out the volatility of extraordinary events and allows earnings to better reflect a normalized trend.

In order to keep the measurement of the three-year average earnings consistent with the price of the S&P 500 index at the time that the supply side adjustment is calculated (e.g., the price of the S&P 500 at December 31, 2016, for the supply-side long-term ERP estimate as of the end of 2016), we used the three-year average based on the prior-year's earnings, the current year's earnings estimated at year-end, and the forecast earnings in the following year.

For example, the adjustment is based on the S&P 500 price at December 31, 2016, divided by the average of the earnings for the S&P 500 companies in 2015, which are known, 2016, which are estimated, and 2017, which are forecasted.[3.68] Obviously since the actual 2016 will not be known until 2017 and the forecast 2017 earnings will not be known until 2018, the adjustment as of the end of 2016 will change in the *Valuation Handbook – U.S. Guide to Cost of Capital* editions to be

---

[3.66] Roger G. Ibbotson and Peng Chen, "Long-Run Stock Market Returns: Participating in the Real Economy, " *Financial Analysts Journal* (January–February 2003): 88–98; see also Charles P. Jones and Jack W. Wilson, "Using the Supply Side Approach to Understand and Estimate Stock Returns," Working paper, June 6, 2006.

[3.67] The long-term 1926–present "historical" and "supply-side" ERPs were published on the "back page" (i.e., "Key Variables in Estimating the Cost of Capital") of the Morningstar/Ibbotson *SBBI Valuation Yearbook* from 1999–2013 and 2004–2013, respectively. The long-term 1926–present historical and supply-side ERPs, calculated using the same data and methodology as were used in the former *SBBI Valuation Yearbook*, are found in Appendix 3, "CRSP Deciles Size Premia Study: Key Variables" in the *2017 Valuation Handbook – U.S. Guide to Cost of Capital* (this book).

[3.68] The estimated top-down earnings estimate for the S&P 500 for the calendar year (in the analysis herein, 2017) *following* the most recently completed calendar year (in the analyses herein, 2016) used in the supply side ERP estimate is provided by Standard & Poor's at http://us.spindices.com/indices/equity/sp-500.

published as of the end of 2017 and 2018.[3.69] The choice in constructing the three-year average is an exercise in judgment.[3.70] We then adjusted the realized risk premiums from 1926 to the current year by removing this observed growth in price-to-earnings ratios, which has occurred primarily in the past 30 years.

William Goetzmann and Roger Ibbotson, commenting on the supply side approach of estimating expected risk premiums, note:

> "These forecasts tend to give somewhat lower forecasts than historical risk premiums, primarily because part of the total returns of the stock market have come from price-earnings ratio expansion. This expansion is not predicted to continue indefinitely, and should logically be removed from the expected risk premium."[3.71]

Chen estimated the ERP as of early 2011 relying on the supply side model exclusively.[3.72] To the authors of this book, this certainly indicates his preference of the supply side estimate to the straight historical average estimate.

Since this adjustment for the growth in price-to-earnings ratios reflects primarily changes observed during the past 30 years and the supply-side analysis (as we have implemented it) makes no other adjustments to the realized returns, one might interpret that a forward estimate of the long-term ERP derived from data in this *2017 Valuation Handbook – U.S. Guide to Cost of Capital* should be 5.97% (supply-side model on an arithmetic average basis) minus the 1.08% WWII Interest Rate Bias discussed earlier, or 4.89% for one-year holding period returns.

Unconditional ERP Estimates

The following summarizes the long-term unconditional ERP estimates as of 2016:

Exhibit 3.14: Long-term Realized Risk Premiums Measured Relative to Long-term U.S. Government Bonds

Adjusted Realized Risk Premium	Period	Arithmetic Average (%)	Geometric Average (%)
Long-term "Historical" ERP	1926–2016	6.94	4.81
Long-term "Supply-side" ERP	1926–2016	5.97	3.99
"Supply-side" minus WWII Interest Rate Bias ERP	1926–2016	4.89	n/a

Source of underlying data: Morningstar *Direct* database. Copyright © 2017 Morningstar, Inc. All rights reserved. Calculations by Duff & Phelps, LLC.

[3.69] The geometric average supply-side ERP of 3.99% (see Exhibit 3.14) was converted into an (estimated) arithmetic average using the standard deviation of the annual returns of the S&P 500 total returns index, as measured over the period 1926–2016 (19.97%, see Exhibit 3.13), which resulted in a supply-side arithmetic average ERP of 5.97%. The extra return attributable to the price-to-earnings multiple expansion was 0.79% per annum, when calculating the supply side ERP based on the three-year averaging convention. The extra return due to the price-to-earnings multiple expansion through 2016 was 0.87% per annum using 1-year periods.

[3.70] Magdalena Mroczek, "Unraveling the Supply-Side Equity Risk Premium," *The Value Examiner* (January/February 2012): 19–24.

[3.71] William N.Goetzmann and Roger G.Ibbotson, "History and the Equity Risk Premium," Chapter 12 in *Handbook of the Equity Risk Premium,* ed. Rajnish Mehra (Amsterdam: Elsevier, 2008): 522–523.

[3.72] Peng Chen, "Will Bonds Outperform Stocks over the Long Run? Not Likely," in *Rethinking the Equity Risk Premium,* ed. P. Brett Hammond, Jr., Martin L. Leibowitz, and Lawrence B. Siegel (The Research Foundation of CFA Institute, 2011): 117–129.

The analyses summarized in Exhibit 3.14 are estimates of ERP measured relative to U.S. government bonds and that, with the exception of periods of governmental intervention in U.S. government long-term bonds (i.e., the period resulting in the WWII Interest Rate Bias (1942–1951) as discussed above), the returns on bonds generally reflected a market based pricing of yields, not impacted by actions by the Fed to suppress yields on long-term U.S. government bonds.

One could argue, for example, that if a "historical" ERP were adjusted for periods in which nonmarket forces artificially depressed Treasury yields, then matching the Duff & Phelps normalized risk-free rate with this "adjusted" historical ERP might be appropriate. We agree, but with *significant* qualifications. For example, in Exhibit 3.13 and Exhibit 3.14 we report what the long-term "historical" ERP and the long-term "supply-side" ERP would be if the WWII interest rate bias were subtracted from each. The differences are significant: these analyses suggest (for example) that the long-term historical ERP as measured over the 1926–2016 period is overstated by up to 1.08%. While this analysis is compelling, and adjusting the "historical" ERP in this fashion likely does make the concept of matching the Duff & Phelps normalized risk-free rate with an "adjusted" historical ERP more correct, the reality is that this approach is not as internally consistent as compared to that of matching the Duff & Phelps normalized risk-free rate with the Duff & Phelps recommended ERP.

We express the unconditional ERP in terms over an arithmetic average equivalent, which is appropriate for estimating single-period discount rates for discounting net cash flows to present value (e.g., the build-up method, the CAPM, etc.)

Conditional ERP

Prior to September 2008 and the Financial Crisis, it was quite common for analysts to be content to make an ERP estimate once each year. Even if the ERP changed month to month, the magnitude of the change was not very great. But beginning in September 2008, the stock market and the economy started to tumble into crisis and valuation analysts began to question the stability of their ERP estimates: (i) should one be adjusting their ERP more often than annually and (ii) if the answer to this question was "yes," then how should one estimate the ERP? Clearly, simply using a long-term average of realized risk premiums was not going to work during the Financial Crisis. This became very obvious at the end of December 2008.

If one simply added an estimate of the ERP taken from sources commonly used before the Financial Crisis to the spot yield on 20-year U.S. government bonds at month-end December 2008, one would have arrived at an estimate of the cost of equity capital that was too low.

For example, as illustrated in Exhibit 3.11, at December 2007 the yield on 20-year U.S. government bonds equaled 4.5%, and the realized risk premium reported based on the average realized risk premiums for 1926–2007 was 7.1%. But at December 2008, the yield on 20-year U.S. government bonds was 3.0%, and the realized risk premium reported based on the average realized risk premiums for 1926–2008 was 6.5%.

So just at the time that the risk in the economy *increased* to arguably the highest point, the base cost of equity capital using realized risk premiums *decreased* from 11.6% (4.5% plus 7.1%) to 9.5% (3.0% plus 6.5%).[3.73]

Research has shown that ERP varies through business cycles.[3.74] We use the term *conditional ERP* to mean the ERP that reflects current market conditions. Those market conditions reflect both the risk of investments as viewed through the collective eyes of the marginal investors (those investors moving money into and out of investments at a particular date; i.e., those investors setting prices) and the collective risk aversion as viewed through those same marginal investors. For example, the ERP should be greater when uncertainty is greater and smaller when uncertainty is smaller.[3.75]

When the economy is near or in recession (as reflected in relatively low returns on stocks and greater economic uncertainty), the *conditional* ERP is likely at the higher end of the range (e.g., at December 31, 2008). When the economy improves (with expectations of improvements reflected in recent increasing stock returns), the *conditional* ERP likely moves toward the midpoint of the range. When the economy is near its peak (and reflected in relatively high stock returns and increased economic certainty), the *conditional* ERP is likely at the lower end of the range.

Duff & Phelps Recommended U.S. ERP

In estimating the conditional ERP, valuation analysts cannot simply use the long-term historical ERP, whether as reported or adjusted as we discussed above. A better alternative would be to examine approaches that are sensitive to the current economic conditions.

Duff & Phelps employs a multi-faceted analysis to estimate the conditional ERP that takes into account a broad range of economic information and multiple ERP estimation methodologies to arrive at its recommendation.[3.76]

First, a reasonable range of normal or unconditional ERP is established.

Second, based on current economic conditions, Duff & Phelps estimates where in the range the true ERP likely lies (top, bottom, or middle) by examining the current state of the economy (both by examining the level of stock indices as a forward indicator and examining economic forecasts), as well as the implied equity volatility and corporate spreads as indicators of perceived risk.

[3.73] While some commentators proposed that analysts adjust their cost of capital estimates as of December 2008 by using a company-specific risk premium, the authors of this book believe that mischaracterizes the observed risks in the markets. Rather, risk-free interest rates declined dramatically due to primarily a flight-to-quality and the expected ERP increased. Neither of these events were company-specific risk issues. However, if the inclusion of increased market risk were done properly, the result should be the same.

[3.74] See for example, Robert D. Arnott, "Equity Risk Premium Myths," and Antti Ilmanen, "Time Variation in the Equity Risk Premium," in *Rethinking the Equity Risk Premium*, ed. P. Brett Hammond, Jr., Martin L. Leibowitz, and Lawrence B. Siegel (The Research Foundation of CFA Institute, 2011).

[3.75] See Martin Lettau, S. C. Ludvigson, and J. A. Wachter, "The Declining Equity Risk Premium: What Role Does Macroeconomic Risk Play?," *Review of Financial Studies* 21 (2008): 1675–1687. The authors linked changes in the ERP to changes in the volatility of economic variables such as employment, consumption, and growth in Gross Domestic Product.

[3.76] For details on the Duff & Phelps recommended ERP over time, go to www.DuffandPhelps.com/CostofCapital.

Economic and Financial Market Indicators

Relative to January 31, 2016 – the last time that Duff & Phelps changed its *conditional* U.S. ERP recommendation – we saw some indications that equity risk in financial markets has declined, in particularly towards the end of 2016. Exhibit 3.15 summarizes the primary economic and financial market indicators we analyzed at December 31, 2016 and how they have moved since January 31, 2016, with the corresponding relative impact on ERP indications:

Exhibit 3.15: Economic and Financial Market Indicators Considered in Duff & Phelps' ERP Recommendation as of December 31, 2016

Factor	Change	Effect on ERP
U.S. Equity Markets	↑	↓
Implied Equity Volatility	↓	↓
Corporate Spreads	↓	↓
EPU and Equity Uncertainty	↓	↓
GDP Growth and GDP Growth Forecasts	↑	↓
Unemployment Environment	↓	↓
Consumer and Business Sentiment	↑	↓
Sovereign Credit Ratings	↔	↔

To better understand where these indicators stand at year-end 2016, it may be helpful to first review how they evolved throughout the year. Looking back, 2016 turned out to be a year full of surprises and extreme events. In broad strokes, 2016 saw three distinct periods with significant spikes in equity volatility, both in the U.S. and in other major developed economies:

- January–February: concerns about slowing global economy and deflationary pressures ("Period 1")

- June–July: "Brexit" vote aftermath ("Period 2")

- November: U.S. presidential elections ("Period 3")

Period 1: The beginning of 2016 was characterized by a big equity market sell-off (e.g., from January 2016 through the end of February 2016, the S&P 500 fell 5.1%), stemming from concerns about a slowing global economy and deflationary pressures. Tumbling oil and other commodity prices (e.g., Brent Crude oil price hit a 12-year low in January) reinforced investor anxiety over stagnant growth in the Eurozone and Japan, as well as a deceleration in several emerging-market countries, with a particularly focus on China (considered by many analysts as the engine of growth for the global economy). As a result, broad equity indices (e.g., the S&P 500) across the globe suffered significant losses, market volatility spiked, and credit spreads of U.S. high-yield over U.S.

investment-grade corporate bonds widened substantially (also affecting companies outside the oil and mining sectors). This led global investors to seek safe haven investments, such as securities issued by the U.S., Germany, and United Kingdom governments, to name a few, causing sharp declines in government bond yields for these countries.

Turbulence continued in February, with credit spreads of U.S. high-yield over U.S. investment-grade corporate bonds widening to levels not seen since 2009, at the height of the Financial Crisis. While equity markets started to progressively recover from their February lows, bond yields continued to fall, pressured by fears of global deflation and declining real growth rates.

Period 2: An event in late June set off a second period of high volatility, abruptly halting the recovery in equity markets. On June 23rd, 2016, the United Kingdom held a referendum to decide whether to leave or remain as member of the European Union (EU). Against prior poll predictions, 51.9% of U.K. voters were in favor of leaving the EU, while 48.1% voted to remain a member. This decision is popularly known in the financial press as "Brexit".

The Brexit vote sent shockwaves to global financial markets. The immediate aftermath of the Brexit vote was a predictable "flight-to-safety", a similar reaction to that observed after other well-reported geopolitical events that occurred since the 2008 global financial crisis. "Flights-to-safety" are typically characterized by an increased demand for gold, as well as safe-haven government bonds and investment-grade corporate bonds (with a corresponding decline in yields), while equity markets decline, volatility spikes, and default spreads for speculative-grade (a.k.a. high-yield or "junk") bonds widen.

The initial state of panic was then ensued by a recovery in various market indicators. Several analysts have called Brexit the biggest non-event of the year. Supporting this argument, analysts will cite the recovery of broad equity indices, such as the FTSE 100 and FTSE 250, of all the losses suffered in the weeks that followed the Brexit vote. In addition, several U.K. economic indicators turned out to be more robust than most analysts had expected, suggesting the negative impact may have been temporary (or illusory). The natural conclusion may be that the impact of the Brexit vote is less severe than many had previously believed, and that the immediate reaction by financial markets was overblown. However, on the other side of the spectrum, some economists and market analysts will point out that this recent data does not completely rule out negative medium and long-term effects. The reality is that it is still too early to ascertain what the ultimate impact will be to the United Kingdom and other European economies, once the U.K. formally notifies the EU that it is leaving under Article 50 of the Lisbon Treaty. Concerns have also deepened about the possibility of a so-called "hard" Brexit.

Period 3: Fast forward to the end of 2016, and the U.S. presidential election results marked the second major political surprise of the year. On November 8, 2016, candidate Donald Trump won the election, despite polls predicting the opposite. Populist politics shook the world in 2016, with voters in the United States and the United Kingdom displaying highly polarized views towards globalization and establishment politics. Donald Trump capitalized on such sentiment and his promises of pro-growth policies ultimately won the electorate.

As measured by the CBOE "VIX" Index, equity volatility hiked in the days preceding the election (see Exhibit 3.16). However, contradicting prior expectations, the win by Mr. Trump was accompanied by a major shift in sentiment. Equity markets have set record highs, credit spreads have tightened materially, the VIX has collapsed, and U.S. Treasury yields have risen in the weeks since Mr. Trump's election victory.

Exhibit 3.16: CBOE Volatility S&P 500 Index (VIX)
January 2016–December 2016

It is almost eight years since the global economy began its recovery from the Financial Crisis. This makes it one of the longest expansions on record, but real growth rates have fallen short of the rebound observed in other post-World War II recessions. The U.S. economy has been expanding at a modest rate – although better than other major developed economies – with the risks of a recession seemingly tempered.

The employment situation has improved, with the unemployment rate declining since the beginning of 2016 and the U.S. economy moving close to full employment. However, the labor force participation rate is at its lowest level since the late 1970s.

Thus far, the global economic recovery has been supported by unprecedented monetary policies. At the beginning of 2017, however, investors may expect a shift away from QE policies towards fiscal measures, as a boost to economic expansion. Consumer confidence and business sentiment have improved markedly, with the former at its highest level since June 2004 and well above its long-term average.

In general, investors seem to be expecting that President Trump's policies will accelerate economic growth and increase corporate profits significantly, via some key areas:

- Fiscal stimulus through corporate and individual tax cuts and cash repatriation holidays for multinationals;

- Infrastructure spending; and

- Deregulation.

However, some of his other policies, including trade protectionism and immigration controls, could erase some or all of that growth, according to some analysts. Ultimately, there is still very little detail about the new policy proposals, and the net impact on growth still uncertain.

Some are beginning to question the record highs in stock markets and that the extremely low levels of volatility (as measured by the VIX Index) could be a sign of complacency. For example, a recent Wall Street Journal article noted that:[3.77]

> "The last time U.S. stock market volatility started the year this low was in 2007, shortly before the subprime crisis hit. Before that, it was 1994, a year when the U.S. Federal Reserve shocked markets and hedge funds blew up.
>
> The historical parallels are scary because when investors anticipate that volatility will be low, it can be sign of excessive complacency. But there are good reasons not to worry too much about the low level of the VIX, the Chicago Board Options Exchange's Volatility Index—and one very good reason to keep a close eye on it nonetheless.
>
> Here's why the VIX scares people: Complacency."

Unexpected outcomes, such as the Brexit vote and the U.S. presidential election, can raise market volatility in the near term. In 2017, a number of events on the political calendar may crystallize these risks. As can be observed in Exhibit 3.17, these include, for example, the general (parliamentary) elections in the Netherlands, the presidential election in France, and the general elections in Germany. Against the rising tide of anti-establishment sentiment, mainstream parties may feel compelled to adopt some of the policies advocated by populist parties, such as a shift towards looser fiscal policies and a step back from globalization.

[3.77] James Mackintosh, "What the Vix Is Really Telling the Markets Now", www.wsj.com, updated February 14, 2016.

Exhibit 3.17: 2017 Global Political Calendar – Selected Events

Month	Country	Political Event
January	United States	Donald Trump inaugurated as President
March	United Kingdom	Likely to Trigger Article 50 of Lisbon Treaty (Brexit)
April	France	Presidential Elections - Round 1
	Turkey	Constitutional Referendum
May	France	Presidential Elections - Round 2
	Iran	Presidential Elections
June	France	Parliamentary Elections
September	Germany	Parliamentary (Federal) Elections

Source of underlying data: "Bundestag election 2017", retrieved on February 21, 2017 from:
https://www.bundeswahlleiter.de/en/bundestagswahlen/2017.html.
OSCE (Organization for Security and Co-Operation in Europe) Elections Calendar, retrieved from on February 21, 2017 from:
http://www.osce.org/odihr/elections/calendar.
Open Europe's political calendar for 2017, retrieved from on February 21, 2017 from:
http://openeurope.org.uk/today/blog/open-europes-political-calendar-2017/.
NDI's Global Elections Calendar, retrieved from on February 21, 2017 from: https://www.ndi.org/elections-calendar.

Considering the level of unknowns going into 2017, some analysts suggest that the current level of optimism in financial markets may need some tempering. A recent Vanguard research report summarized the current situation succinctly:[3.78]

> *"By late 2016, market sentiment had quickly shifted from an overly pessimistic outlook of cyclically weak stagnation toward an overly optimistic expectation of a growth acceleration. Both views are incorrect."*

The prospect of higher policy uncertainty in the U.S. and the rising political risks in Europe and other regions of the globe present opportunities, but also risks for financial markets in 2017.

[3.78] "2017 economic and market outlook: Stabilization, not stagnation", Vanguard Research, December 2016. This white paper can be accessed here:
https://advisors.vanguard.com/VGApp/iip/site/advisor/researchcommentary/article/IWE_InvRes2017EconomicOutlook .

Quantitative Models

We examine other indicators that may provide a more quantitative view of where we are within the range of reasonable long-term estimates for the U.S. ERP.

Duff & Phelps currently uses several models as corroborating evidence. We reviewed these indicators at year-end 2016.

- **Damodaran Implied ERP Model** – Professor Aswath Damodaran calculates implied ERP estimates for the S&P 500 and publishes his estimates on his website. Damodaran estimates an implied ERP by first solving for the discount rate that equates the current S&P 500 index level with his estimates of cash distributions (dividends and stock buybacks) in future years. He then subtracts the current yield on 10-year U.S. government bonds. Duff & Phelps then converts his estimate to an arithmetic average equivalent measured against the 20-year U.S. government bond rate.

  In 2014, Prof. Damodaran introduced new capabilities to his implied equity risk premium calculator. The new features allow the user to select a variety of base projected cash flow yields, as a well as several expected growth rate choices for the following five years in the forecast. Each option for cash flow yields is independent of the growth rate assumptions, which means that the user can select up to 35 different combinations to estimate an implied ERP. More recently, Prof. Damodaran added a new feature that allows the terminal year's projected cash flows to be adjusted to what he considers a more sustainable payout ratio. This sustainable payout is computed using the long-term growth rate (g) and the trailing 12-month return on equity (ROE), as follows: Sustainable Payout = 1 − g/ROE. If the user selects this option, the payout ratio over the next (projected) five years is based on a linear interpolation between today's payout ratio and the Sustainable Payout. Otherwise, the terminal year payout ratio will be the same as today's value throughout the entire forecast.

  Exhibit 3.18 shows the current options that a user can select to arrive at an implied ERP indication. Each of these combinations can then be adjusted for a sustainable payout, if the user so decides.

Exhibit 3.18: Professor Damodaran's Implied Equity Risk Premium Calculator Cash Flow Yield (Dividends + Buybacks) and Growth Rate Options

S&P 500 Cash Flow Yield (Dividends + Buybacks)	S&P Earnings Growth Rates for Years 1 through 5 in the Projections	Adjustment for Sustainable Payout
Trailing 12-months Dividend + Buyback Yield	Historical Growth Rate for the last 10 years	Adjust Cash Flow Yield for Sustainable Payout
Average Dividend + Buyback Yield for the last 10 years	Bottom-up Forecasted Growth Rate for next 5 years (with growth in the 5th year assumed to be equal to the current 10-year U.S. Treasury yield)	Do Not Adjust Cash Flow Yield for Sustainable Payout
Average Dividend + Buyback Yield for the last 5 years	Top-Down Forecasted Growth Rate for next 5 years (with growth in the 5th year assumed to be equal to the current 10-year U.S. Treasury yield)	
Average Payout for the last 10 years, multiplied by Trailing 12-month Earnings	Fundamental Growth Rate (i.e., Earnings Retention Rate * Current ROE)	
Average Payout for the last 5 years, multiplied by Trailing 12-month Earnings	Fundamental Growth Rate (i.e., Earnings Retention Rate * 10-year Average ROE)	
Average Payout for the last 10 years, using S&P 500 Normalized Earnings		
Trailing 12-month Dividend + Buyback Yield, Net of Stock Issuance		

Note: ROE = Return on Equity

Source of underlying data: Downloadable dataset entitled "Spreadsheet to compute ERP". To obtain a copy, visit: http://people.stern.nyu.edu/adamodar/.

Based on Prof. Damodaran's estimates of the trailing 12-month cash flow yield (dividends plus buybacks) of S&P 500 constituents – as published on the home page of his website – his implied ERP (converted into an arithmetic average equivalent) was approximately 6.75% measured against an abnormally low 20-year U.S. government bond yield (2.79%).[3.79] The equivalent normalized implied ERP estimate was 6.04% measured against a normalized 20-year U.S. government bond yield (3.5%), which represents an increase of 21 basis points relative to December 2015 (5.83%), and 19

[3.79] Damodaran's implied rate of return (based on the actual 10-year yield) on the S&P 500 = 8.14% as of January 1, 2017, minus 2.79% actual rate on 20-year U.S. government bonds plus an adjustment to equate the geometric average ERP to its arithmetic equivalent. The result reflects conversion of the implied ERP to an arithmetic average equivalent.

basis points relative to January 31, 2016 (5.85%) [(the latter being the last time D&P Changed its recommended U.S. ERP from 5.0% to 5.5%)].[3.80] Testing the first two options outlined in Exhibit 3.18 (S&P 500 cash flow yield [dividends plus buybacks] and S&P 500 earnings growth rates for years one through 5 in the projections), we obtained a range of indications for a normalized arithmetic-average implied ERP estimate between 4.11% and 7.20% (once again, measured against a normalized 20-year U.S. government bond yield of 3.5%), representing an increase in the range observed last year. Alternatively, if projected cash flows were adjusted for the third option in Exhibit 3.18 (Adjustment for Sustainable Payout), the implied ERP indications would narrow to a range between 3.52% and 5.42%.

- **Default Spread Model (DSM)** – The Default Spread Model is based on the premise that the long term average ERP (the unconditional ERP) is constant and deviations from that average over an economic cycle can be measured by reference to deviations from the long term average of the default spread between corporate bonds rated in the Baa category by Moody's versus those in the Aaa rating category.[3.81]

  At the end of December 2016, the conditional ERP calculated using the DSM model was 4.95%, a decline from the ERP indications of 5.51% and 5.65% at the end of December 2015 and January 2016, respectively. This model notably removes the risk-free rate itself as an input in the estimation of ERP. However, the ERP indication resulting from the DSM is still interpreted as an estimate of the relative return of stocks in excess of risk-free securities. Nevertheless, in periods where corporate default spreads for investment-grade bonds (i.e., those in the Aaa through Baa rating categories) are significantly compressed due to a significant investor demand for yield (i.e., a search for a current yield-producing investment) in a high-quality, lower risk asset class, the DSM model may result in ERP indications less consistent with the risk perceived in equity markets.[3.82] This appears to be the case in the recent months leading up to December 2016. This

---

[3.80] Damodaran's implied rate of return (based on the actual 10-year yield) on the S&P 500 – 8.14% as of January 1, 2017 minus 3.50% normalized rate on 20-year U.S. government bonds plus an adjustment to equate the geometric average ERP to its arithmetic equivalent. The resulting 6.04% reflects the conversion of the implied ERP into an arithmetic average equivalent, which is then compared to similarly-calculated ERP indications of 5.83% and 5.85% as of December 31, 2015 and January 31, 2016, respectively.

[3.81] The Default Spread Model presented herein is based on Jagannathan, Ravi, and Wang, Zhenyu," The Conditional CAPM and the Cross -Section of Expected Returns," *The Journal of Finance*, Volume 51, Issue 1, March 1996: 3–53. See also Elton, Edwin J. and Gruber, Martin J., Agrawal, Deepak, and Mann, Christopher "Is There a Risk Premium in Corporate bonds?", Working Paper, http://pages.stern.nyu.edu/~eelton/working_papers/corp%20bonds/Is%20there%20a%20risk%20premium%20in%20corporate%20bonds.pdf. Duff & Phelps uses (as did Jagannathan, Ravi, and Wang) the spread of high-grade corporates (proxied by yields on Aaa rated bonds) against lesser grade corporates (proxied by yields on Baa rated bonds). Corporate bond series used in analysis herein: Barclays US Corp Baa Long Yld USD (Yield) and Barclays US Corp Aaa Long Yld USD (Yield); Source: Morningstar *Direct*.

[3.82] Also, note that returns on below-investment grade corporate bonds (a.k.a., "high-yield" or "junk" bonds) tend to move more closely with equity returns than do investment-grade corporate bonds. See for example S&P Global Market Intelligence Fridson's newsletter from November 2, 2016 entitled "Stocks versus HY bonds, plus monthly recap". In this Newsletter, analyst Marty Fridson stated that "...stocks and high-yield bonds do tend to move together. For the 29 years (1987–2015) for which full-year returns are available on the BofA Merrill Lynch US High Yield Index, its annual total return correlation with the S&P 500 is 65%." In addition, Fridson discussed the impact of a strong search for yield, which led to significantly higher returns for junk bonds (and correspondingly lower yields) in the January–October 2016 period than expected for this asset class (bond prices move in opposite direction to yields). So, just prior to the U.S. presidential election on November 8, 2016, when stock markets had shown lackluster performance for the year, Fridson wrote that "(w)e hypothesize that high-yield bonds have responded more dramatically than stocks – and excessively – to this year's improvement in economic and financial conditions because of investors' desperate search for yield. Stocks, other than this year's strongly performing high-dividend variety, do not satisfy that appetite."

was also the case back in 2011, for example, in the midst of the Euro sovereign debt crisis, where other ERP indicators pointed to high risk in equity markets, but the DSM model indicated an ERP close to the long-term unconditional ERP (5.0% as applied by Duff & Phelps).

- **Hassett Implied ERP (Hassett)** – Stephen Hassett has developed a model for estimating the implied ERP, as well as the estimated S&P 500 index level, based on the current yield on long-term U.S. government bonds and a risk premium factor (RPF).[3.83] The RPF is the empirically derived relationship between the risk-free rate, S&P 500 earnings, real interest rates, and real GDP growth to the S&P 500 index over time. The RPF appears to change only infrequently. The model can be used monthly to estimate the S&P 500 and the conditional ERP based on the current level of interest rates.[3.84]

  Hassett's analysis uses the spot 10-year risk-free rate for the period from January 2008 through July 2011; thereafter, his analysis uses a normalized yield on U.S. Treasuries of 4.0% (2.0% real risk-free rate plus 2.0% inflation) and 4.5% (2.0% real risk-free rate plus 2.5% inflation).[3.85, 3.86] Using a normalized 4.0% risk-free rate at year-end 2016, the S&P 500 index appeared to be somewhat overvalued based on the Hassett model's predictions, whereas using a 4.5% normalized risk-free rate would imply the index is substantially overvalued. Alternatively, based on the S&P 500 index level at the end of December 2016, the implied risk-free rate commensurate with the index closing price was 3.69%. This indication for the risk-free rate is very close to the Duff & Phelps concluded normalized risk-free rate of 3.5%, effective November 15, 2016 and thereafter (until further notice).

While these additional models may be useful in suggesting the direction of changes in the conditional ERP, they are, like *all* methods of estimating the ERP, imperfect. Both the Damodaran Implied ERP Model, the Default Spread Model, and the Hassett model utilize assumptions that are subjective in nature. For example, the Damodaran Implied ERP Model assumes a long-term growth rate for dividends and buybacks that is largely a matter of judgment. Likewise, in the default spread model, the changes in spread are applied to a "benchmark" ERP estimate; the choice of that benchmark ERP is largely a matter of judgment.

Again, the inherent "imperfection" of any single ERP estimation model is precisely why Duff & Phelps takes into account a *broad* range of economic information and *multiple* ERP estimation methodologies to arrive at our conditional ERP recommendation.

[3.83] Stephen D. Hassett, "The RPF Model for Calculating the Equity Risk Premium and Explaining the Value of the S&P with Two Variables," *Journal of Applied Corporate Finance* 22, 2 (Spring 2010): 118–130.

[3.84] For a more detailed description of Hassett's Risk Premium Factor model see Pratt and Grabowski, op.cit., Chapter 8A, "Deriving ERP Estimates": 167–168".

[3.85] "Dissecting S&P 500's 2016 Performance Using The RPF Model", January 3, 2017, by Steve Hassett, Retrieved from: http://seekingalpha.com/article/4034011-dissecting-s-and-p-500s-2016-performance-using-rpf-model.

[3.86] To confirm, Stephen Hassett uses a 2.0% real rate in his analysis for a normalized yield on U.S. Treasures. As discussed previously and illustrated in Exhibit 3.10b, Duff & Phelps uses a range of 0.0% to 2.0% for the long-term real rate.

While the current evidence seems to be pointing to a decline in equity risk in financial markets relative to January 31, 2016, from a qualitative perspective we deem it prudent to let some time elapse, in order to better assess the impact of the U.S. presidential election results in the forward-looking ERP. We took a similar "wait-and-see" approach when evaluating the impact of Brexit on cost of capital assumptions. After considering all of the evidence, Duff & Phelps recommends a conditional U.S. ERP at year-end 2016 equal to 5.5% used in conjunction with a normalized risk-free rate of 3.5%.

Concluding on an ERP

What is a reasonable estimate of the *unconditional* or long-term average ERP for the United States?

As of December 31, 2016

Based on the data summarized above, we have the following evidence:

Historical Long-term ERP (1926–2016)	6.94%
Supply-side Long-term ERP (1926–2016)	5.97%
Supply-side Long-term ERP adjusted for WWII Interest Rate Bias	4.89%

Some valuation analysts expressed dismay over the necessity of considering a forward ERP since that would require changing their current cookbook practice of relying exclusively on the post-1925 historical arithmetic average of one-year realized risk premiums as their estimate of the ERP.

But valuation is a forward-looking concept, not an exercise in mechanical application of formulas. Correct valuation methodology requires applying value drivers reflected in today's market pricing. We need to mimic the market. In our experience, you often cannot match current market pricing for equities using the post-1925 historical arithmetic average of one-year realized premiums as the basis for developing discount rates. The entire valuation process is based on applying reasoned judgment to the evidence derived from economic, financial, and other information and arriving at a well-reasoned opinion of value. Estimating the ERP is no different.

For example, court case decisions have supported and adopted the Ibbotson and Chen supply-side ERP estimate; as a result, it would be an error to blindly assume that the post-1925 average of realized risk premiums is to be used as an ERP estimate by default.

Valuation analysts are advised to be familiar with the various choices regarding the ERP including the supply-side long-term ERP. This includes an understanding of the methodology and data in forward-looking models based on analysts' estimates, estimates based solely on historical data, "supply-side" ERP models and surveys. All of these methods can be informative. But *each* model has weaknesses that may disqualify it from being utilized as "the" single model.

For valuation dates as of December 31, 2016 (and thereafter, until further notice), we conclude on a *conditional* U.S. ERP of 5.5%, matched with a normalized yield on 20-year U.S. government bonds equal to 3.5%, implying a 9.0% base cost of equity capital in the United States (see Exhibit 3.19).

The ERPs in Exhibit 3.19 are expressed in terms of an arithmetic average equivalent, which is appropriate for estimating single period discount rates for discounting net cash flows to present value (e.g., the build-up method and the CAPM).

Were we to use the spot yield-to-maturity on 20-year U.S. Treasuries of 2.79% as of December 31, 2016, one would have to increase the ERP assumption accordingly.[3.87] One can determine the ERP against the spot 20-year yield as of December 31, 2016, inferred by our recommended U.S. ERP (used in conjunction with the normalized risk-free rate), by using the following formula :

U.S. ERP Against Spot 20-Year Yield (Inferred)

D&P Recommended U.S. ERP + Normalized Risk-Free Rate − Spot 20-Year U.S. Treasury Yield = 5.50% + 3.50% − 2.79% = 6.21%

[3.87] Source of underlying data: 20-year U.S. government bond series. Board of Governors of the Federal Reserve System website at: http:// www.federalreserve.gov/releases/h15/data.htm.

Exhibit 3.19: Duff & Phelps Recommended U.S. ERP and Corresponding Risk-Free Rates January 2008–Present

Date	Risk-free Rate (R $_f$)	R $_f$ (%)	Duff & Phelps Recommended ERP (%)	What Changed
Current Guidance:				
November 15, 2016 – UNTIL FURTHER NOTICE	**Normalized 20-year U.S. Treasury yield**	3.50	5.50	R $_f$
January 31, 2016 – November 14, 2016	Normalized 20-year U.S. Treasury yield	4.00	5.50	ERP
December 31, 2015	Normalized 20-year U.S. Treasury yield	4.00	5.00	
December 31, 2014	Normalized 20-year U.S. Treasury yield	4.00	5.00	
December 31, 2013	Normalized 20-year U.S. Treasury yield	4.00	5.00	
February 28, 2013 – January 30, 2016	Normalized 20-year U.S. Treasury yield	4.00	5.00	ERP
December 31, 2012	Normalized 20-year U.S. Treasury yield	4.00	5.50	
January 15, 2012 – February 27, 2013	Normalized 20-year U.S. Treasury yield	4.00	5.50	ERP
December 31, 2011	Normalized 20-year U.S. Treasury yield	4.00	6.00	
September 30, 2011 – January 14, 2012	Normalized 20-year U.S. Treasury yield	4.00	6.00	ERP
July 1 2011 – September 29, 2011	Normalized 20-year U.S. Treasury yield	4.00	5.50	R $_f$
June 1, 2011 – June 30, 2011	Spot 20-year U.S. Treasury yield	Spot	5.50	R $_f$
May 1, 2011 – May 31, 2011	Normalized 20-year U.S. Treasury yield	4.00	5.50	R $_f$
December 31, 2010	Spot 20-year U.S. Treasury yield	Spot	5.50	
December 1, 2010 – April 30, 2011	Spot 20-year U.S. Treasury yield	Spot	5.50	R $_f$
June 1, 2010 – November 30, 2010	Normalized 20-year U.S. Treasury yield	4.00	5.50	R $_f$
December 31, 2009	Spot 20-year U.S. Treasury yield	Spot	5.50	
December 1, 2009 – May 31, 2010	Spot 20-year U.S. Treasury yield	Spot	5.50	ERP
June 1, 2009 – November 30, 2009	Spot 20-year U.S. Treasury yield	Spot	6.00	R $_f$
December 31, 2008	Normalized 20-year U.S. Treasury yield	4.50	6.00	
November 1, 2008 – May 31, 2009	Normalized 20-year U.S. Treasury yield	4.50	6.00	R $_f$
October 27, 2008 – October 31, 2008	Spot 20-year U.S. Treasury yield	Spot	6.00	ERP
January 1, 2008 – October 26, 2008	Spot 20-year U.S. Treasury yield	Spot	5.00	
December 31, 2007	Spot 20-year U.S. Treasury yield	Spot	5.00	Initialized

Normalized in this context means that in months where the risk-free rate is deemed to be abnormally low, a proxy for a longer-term sustainable risk-free rate is used.

To ensure you are always using the most recent ERP recommendation, visit: www.DuffandPhelps.com/CostofCapital.

Chapter 4

Basic Building Blocks of the Cost of Equity Capital – Size Premium

Size as a Predictor of Equity Returns

The size effect is based on the empirical observation that companies of smaller size are associated with greater risk and, therefore, have greater cost of capital. The "size" of a company is one of the most important risk elements to consider when developing cost of equity capital estimates for use in valuing a business simply because size has been shown to be a *predictor* of equity returns. In other words, there is a significant (negative) relationship between size and historical equity returns – as size *decreases*, returns tend to *increase*, and vice versa.[4.1]

Traditionally, researchers have used market value of equity (market capitalization, or simply "market cap") as a measure of size in conducting historical rate of return studies. However, as we discuss later in this chapter, market cap is not the only measure of size that can be used to predict return, nor is it necessarily the best measure of size to use.

The creation of the Center for Research in Security Prices (CRSP) databases at the University of Chicago in the early 1960s was a big advancement in the research of security prices. The CRSP database includes U.S. equity total returns (capital appreciation plus dividends) going back to 1926.

Possibly the most notable reason that the establishment of the CRSP databases was so important was that it enabled researchers to look at stocks with different characteristics and analyze how their returns differed. One of the first characteristics that researchers analyzed was large-market-capitalization (large-cap) companies versus small-market-capitalization (small-cap) companies.

For example, a 1981 study by Rolf Banz examined the returns of New York Stock Exchange (NYSE) small-cap companies compared to the returns of NYSE large-cap companies over the period 1926–1975.[4.2] What Banz found was that the returns of small-cap companies were *greater* than the returns for large-cap companies. Banz's 1981 study is often cited as the first comprehensive study of the size effect.

[4.1] This chapter is excerpted in part from Shannon P. Pratt and Roger J. Grabowski, *Cost of Capital: Applications and Examples* 5th ed. (Hoboken, NJ: John Wiley & Sons, 2014).

[4.2] Rolf W. Banz, "The Relationship between Return and Market Value of Common Stocks", *Journal of Financial Economics* (March 1981): 3–18. This paper is often cited as the first comprehensive study of the size effect.

Possible Explanations for the Greater Returns of Smaller Companies

Some valuation analysts erroneously treat small firms as equivalent to scaled-down large firms. Valuation analysts know that small firms have risk characteristics that differ from those of large firms. For example, large firms may have greater ability to enter the market of the small firm and take market share. Large companies likely have more resources to "weather the storm" in economic downturns. Large firms can generally spend more on R&D, advertising, and typically even have greater ability to hire the "best and brightest". Larger firms may have greater access to capital, broader management depth, and less dependency on just a few customers. A larger number of analysts typically follow large firms relative to small firms, so there is probably more information available about large firms. Small firms have fewer resources to fend off competition and redirect themselves after changes in the market occur.[4.3]

Any one of these differences (not an all-encompassing list) would tend to *increase* investors' required rate of return to induce them to invest in small companies rather than investing in large companies.

The size effect is not without controversy, nor is this controversy something new. Traditionally, small companies are believed to have greater required rates of return than large companies because small companies are inherently riskier. It is not clear, however, whether this is due to size itself, or to other factors closely related to or correlated with size (e.g., liquidity).[4.4] The qualification that Banz noted in his 1981 article remains pertinent today:

> *"It is not known whether size [as measured by market capitalization] per se is responsible for the effect or whether size is just a proxy for one or more true unknown factors correlated with size."*

In this chapter, we first present empirical evidence for the size effect, followed by a discussion of common criticisms of the size effect.

The Size Effect: Empirical Evidence

Summary statistics over the 1926–2016 period for CRSP NYSE/NYSE MKT/NASDAQ[4.5] deciles 1–10 are shown in Exhibit 4.1. As size (in this case, as measured by market cap) *decreases*, return tends to *increase*. For example, the annual arithmetic mean return of decile 1 (the largest-cap companies) was 11.05% over the 1926–2016 period, while the annual arithmetic mean return of decile 10 (the smallest-cap companies) was 20.27%. Note that this increased return comes at a price: risk (as measured by standard deviation) increases from 18.92% for decile 1 to 42.45% for

---

[4.3] M. S. Long and J. Zhang, "Growth Options, Unwritten Call Discounts and Valuing Small Firms", EFA 2004 Maastricht Meetings Paper no. 4057, March 2004. Available at http://www.ssrn.com/abstract=556203.

[4.4] Even after controlling for size, research suggests that liquidity is still a systematic factor and a predictor of returns. See Roger G. Ibbotson, Zhiwu Chen, Daniel Y.-J. Kim, and Wendy Y. Hu, "Liquidity as an Investment Style", *Financial Analysts Journal* Vol 69(3): 30–44, May/June 2013, and Roger G. Ibbotson, Ph.D. and Daniel Y.-J. Kim, Ph.D., "Liquidity as an Investment Style: 2016 Update". Copies available at www.zebracapm.com.

[4.5] On October 1, 2008, NYSE Euronext acquired the American Stock Exchange (AMEX). The "NYSE MKT" is the former American Stock Exchange, or AMEX. The CRSP standard market-cap-based NYSE/AMEX/NASDAQ indices are now called the NYSE/NYSE MKT/NASDAQ indices.

decile 10. The relationship between risk and return is a fundamental principle of finance and for estimating the cost of capital.

Exhibit 4.1: Summary Statistics of Annual Returns (CRSP NYSE/NYSE MKT/NASDAQ Deciles) 1926–2016

Decile	Geometric Mean (%)	Arithmetic Mean (%)	Standard Deviation (%)
1-Largest	9.31%	11.05%	18.92%
2	10.56%	12.82%	21.49%
3	11.04%	13.57%	23.35%
4	10.85%	13.80%	25.56%
5	11.49%	14.62%	26.18%
6	11.37%	14.81%	27.11%
7	11.58%	15.41%	29.02%
8	11.56%	16.14%	33.01%
9	11.56%	16.97%	37.18%
10-Smallest	13.31%	20.27%	42.45%

Source of underlying data: CRSP U.S. Stock Database and CRSP U.S. Indices Database © 2017 Center for Research in Security Prices (CRSP®), University of Chicago Booth School of Business. CRSP NYSE/NYSE MKT/NASDAQ deciles 1–10. Used with permission. All rights reserved. Calculations performed by Duff & Phelps, LLC.

The Size Effect Over Longer Periods

Exhibit 4.2 illustrates the size effect. As size (measured by market cap in this case) *decreases*, return tends to *increase*. For example, an investment of $1 in CRSP decile 1 (comprised of the largest companies) at the end of 1925 would have grown to $3,293 by the end of 2016, and an investment in CRSP decile 6 (comprised of medium-sized companies) would have grown to $18,039. However, an investment of $1 in CRSP decile 10 (comprised of the smallest companies) would have grown to $86,590 over the same period.

Exhibit 4.2: Terminal Index Values of CRSP NYSE/NYSE MKT/NASDAQ Deciles 1–10
Index (Year-end 1925 = $1.00)
January 1926–December 2016

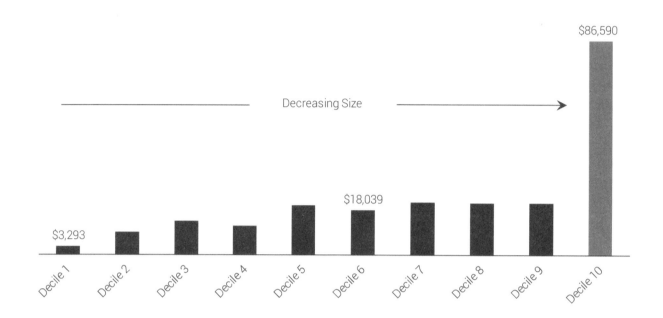

Exhibit 4.2 illustrates two other important concepts. The first is that the size effect is not "linear" – the size effect is clearly concentrated in the smallest-cap companies.[4.6]

The second is that over longer periods of time the size effect is *not* just evident for the smallest companies, but is evident for all but the largest groups of companies, including companies with a market capitalization in excess of several billions of dollars.

To illustrate this, decile 1 (large-cap companies) is compared to a portfolio comprised of equal parts of deciles 6–9 in Exhibit 4.3. An investment of $1 in decile 1 at the end of 1925 would have grown to $3,293 by the end of 2016, while an investment of $1 in a portfolio comprised of equal parts of deciles 6–9 at the end of 1925 would have grown to $22,042 by the end of 2016 (remember decile 10, which is comprised of the smallest-cap companies, is *excluded* from this analysis). Even with decile 10 *excluded*, the portfolio made up of deciles 6–9 outperformed large-cap companies over the 1926–2016 period.

[4.6] Some researchers have suggested that the size effect is concentrated in even smaller firms than discussed here. Horowitz, Loughran, and Savin found that if "...firms less than $5 million in value are excluded from the sample universe...", the size effect becomes insignificant, at least as measured over the 1963–1997 time period. Joel L. Horowitz, Tim Loughran, and N.E. Savin, "The disappearing size effect", *Research in Economics* (2000), 83–100.

Exhibit 4.3: Terminal Index Values of CRSP NYSE/NYSE MKT/NASDAQ Decile 1 and a Portfolio Comprised of equal parts of Deciles 6–9
Index (Year-end 1925 = $1.00)
January 1926–December 2016

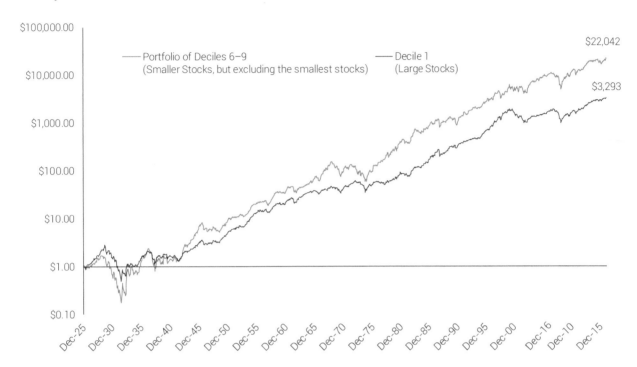

Small-cap companies do not always outperform large-cap companies. As a matter of fact, small-cap companies' shorter-term behavior relative to large-cap companies can be quite erratic, so analyzing small-cap companies' performance relative to large-cap companies' performance over varying holding periods may be instructive in revealing longer-term trends.

In Exhibit 4.4, the percentage of periods in which small-cap companies outperformed large-cap companies is analyzed over 1-, 5-, 10-, 20- and 30-year holding periods. As the holding period is increased, small-cap companies tend to outperform large-cap companies in a greater number of periods. In other words, the *longer* small-cap companies are given to "race" against large-cap companies, the greater the chance that small-cap companies outpace their larger counterparts. For example, small-cap companies outperformed large-cap companies 81.4% of the time over all 20-year holding periods from January 1926 through December 2016. In contrast, large-cap companies outperformed small-cap companies only 18.6% over the same holding and time period.

Exhibit 4.4: Percentage of Periods that Small-cap Companies Outperform Large-cap Companies over 1-, 5-, 10-, 20-, and 30-year Holding Periods (1926–2016)

Holding Period	1-year	5-years	10-years	20-years	30-years
Small-cap Companies Outperform (%)	52.9%	57.2%	70.0%	81.4%	90.3%
Large-cap Companies Outperform (%)	47.1%	42.8%	30.0%	18.6%	9.7%

Source of underlying data: CRSP U.S. Stock Database and CRSP U.S. Indices Database © 2017 Center for Research in Security Prices (CRSP®), University of Chicago Booth School of Business. Small-cap companies are represented by CRSP NYSE/NYSE MKT/NASDAQ decile 10; Large-cap companies are represented by CRSP NYSE/NYSE MKT/NASDAQ decile 1. The number of 1-, 5-, 10-, 20-, and 30-year holding periods over the January 1926–December 2016 time horizon is 1,081, 1,033, 973, 853, and 733, respectively. Used with permission. All rights reserved. Calculations performed by Duff & Phelps, LLC.

The Size Effect Tends to Stabilize Over Time

It may be instructive to examine the tendencies of small-cap stocks' performance versus large-cap stocks' performance over time periods with *fixed* starting dates and *variable* ending dates. This will help to see what happens as more time periods are added (and thus the importance of "unusual" time periods is diminished).

In Exhibit 4.5, the average difference in annual returns for small-cap companies minus large-cap companies was calculated for periods with fixed starting dates of 1926 (the first year data is available from CRSP), 1963 (the Risk Premium Report exhibits are calculated over the time period 1963–2016), and 1982 (the year following publication of Banz's 1981 article).[4.7]

On the far left side of Exhibit 4.5 for the series "Fixed Beginning Date Starting 1926", the first data point is the average difference in annual return for small-cap companies minus large-cap companies in 1926, the second data point (moving to the right) is the average difference in annual return for small-cap companies minus large-cap companies over the period 1926–1927, and then 1926–1928, etc., until the final data point on the far right is the average difference in annual return for small-cap companies minus large-cap companies over the period 1926–2016.

The same analysis is displayed for "Fixed Beginning Date Starting 1963", with the leftmost data point being the average difference in annual return for small-cap companies minus large-cap companies in 1963, and then (again, moving to the right) the average difference in annual return for small-cap companies minus large-cap companies over the periods 1963–1964, 1963–1965, etc., until the final data point on the far right is the average difference in annual return for small-cap companies minus large-cap companies over the period 1963–2016.

And finally, the same analysis for "Fixed Beginning Date 1982" is shown, with the leftmost data point being the average difference in annual return for small-cap companies minus large-cap companies in 1982, and the rightmost data point being the average difference in annual return for small-cap companies minus large-cap companies over the period 1982–2016.

[4.7] Banz, Rolf W. "The Relationship between Return and Market Value of Common Stocks". *Journal of Financial Economics* (March 1981): 3–18. Banz's 1981 article demonstrated that smaller-cap stocks exhibited significantly greater performance over larger-cap stocks over the period from 1926 to 1975.

Exhibit 4.5 suggests that while the size effect measured over shorter time periods may be quite erratic (and even negative at times), there seems to be an overall tendency toward stability as time periods are added and the longer the period over which it is measured (regardless of the start date). Further, this stability seems to be reached in "positive territory" (the rightmost points in Exhibit 4.5), suggesting a positive size effect over time.

Exhibit 4.5: CRSP Decile 10 minus Decile 1, Average Difference in Annual Returns
Fixed beginning date, variable ending dates
1926–2016, 1963–2016, 1982–2016

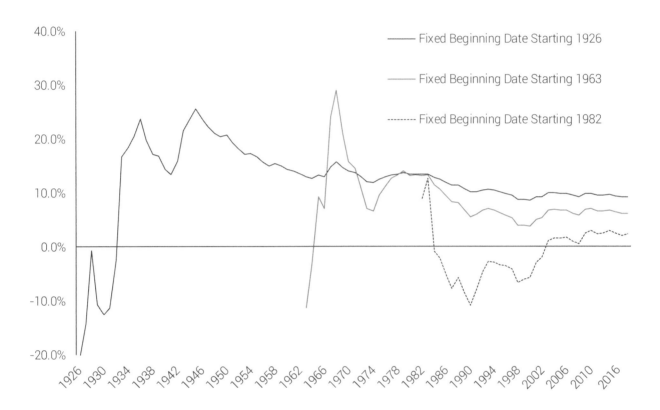

The Size Effect Changes Over Time

The variability of the size effect is illustrated in Exhibit 4.6. In Exhibit 4.6, the size premium for CRSP decile 10 (comprised of the smallest companies) is calculated as of each year-end from1962–2016 using the same methodology and data set as is currently used in the *Valuation Handbook – U.S. Guide to Cost of Capital* in the CRSP Deciles Size Premia study (and the same methodology and data set used previously in the former *SBBI Valuation Yearbook*).

For example, a hypothetical *Valuation Handbook* published in 1969 would have used data available from 1926–1968 to calculate CRSP decile 10's size premium, and this would have resulted in a size premium of approximately 9.2%. In a hypothetical *2000 Valuation Handbook – U.S. Guide to Cost of*

Capital, using data from 1926–1999, the size premium for CRSP decile 10 would have been approximately 4.5%. And, in the *2017 Valuation Handbook – U.S. Guide to Cost of Capital* (this book), the size premium for CRSP decile 10 reported in Appendix 3, "CRSP Deciles Size Premia Study: Key Variables", is 5.6%.

Exhibit 4.6: CRSP Decile 10 Size Premium
Year-end 1962 to Year-end 2016

Sources of underlying data: (i) CRSP U.S. Stock Database and CRSP U.S. Indices Database © 2017 Center for Research in Security Prices (CRSP®), University of Chicago Booth School of Business; Small-cap companies are represented by CRSP NYSE/NYSE MKT/ NASDAQ decile 10. (ii) Morningstar *Direct* database. The betas used as an input in calculating size premia were calculated using excess total returns over 30-day U.S. Treasury Bills. The market benchmark used in beta calculations is the S&P 500 total return index. Used with permission. All rights reserved. All calculations performed by Duff & Phelps, LLC.

These examples provide evidence that the size effect is *cyclical*. That cyclicality is part of the risk of small companies; if small size companies *always* performed better than large companies, small size companies would be *less* risky than large-cap companies, not riskier. This is true even though the expected returns are higher for small-cap companies in the long-term. By analogy, bond returns occasionally outperform stock returns. For example, over the 10-year period ending December 2011, long-term U.S. government bonds returned 133.2% and the S&P 500 Index return 33.4%, yet few would contend that over time the expected return on bonds is greater than the expected return on stocks.[4.8]

Criticisms of the Size Effect

The size effect is *not* without controversy, though, and various commentators question its validity. In fact, some commentators contend that the historical data are so flawed that valuation analysts can dismiss all research results that support the size effect. For example, is the size effect merely the result of not measuring beta correctly? Are there market anomalies that simply cause the size effect to appear? Is size just a proxy for one or more factors correlated with size, suggesting that

---

[4.8]   Source of underlying data: Morningstar *Direct* database. Calculations performed by Duff & Phelps, LLC.

valuation analysts should use those factors directly rather than size to measure risk? Is the size effect hidden because of unexpected events?

Is the Size Effect the Result of Incorrectly Measuring Betas?

Some commentators have held that the size effect is in part a function of underestimating betas for troubled firms (which tend to populate the smaller deciles where size is measured by market cap). Including troubled companies could cause the size premium to be overestimated in the CRSP 10th decile and the subdeciles 10a (and its upper and lower halves 10w and 10x) and 10b (and its upper and lower halves 10y and 10z), which are populated with the smallest companies as measured by market cap.

The most commonly used size premia is derived based on an ordinary least squares regression (OLS) beta. We examine two alternative methods of calculating the beta in order to compute a size premia, sum betas and annual betas.

Effects of the Size Premia when Using OLS Betas, Annual Betas, and Sum Betas

First, we calculated sum betas. Smaller companies generally trade more infrequently and exhibit more of a lagged price reaction (relative to the market) than do larger companies. One of the ways of capturing this lag movement is called "sum" beta. Sum betas are designed to compensate for the more infrequent trading of smaller company stocks.

Second, we calculated betas based on *annual* return data (rather than *monthly* data).

Both of these methods appear to correct for the low beta estimates of smaller companies. The sum beta estimates are greater for smaller companies than OLS betas, which are derived using non-lagged market benchmark data. The annual betas are also greater for smaller companies than the betas derived using monthly return data. The net result of the *greater* sum betas (or greater annual betas) is *smaller* size premia.

In Exhibit 4.7, OLS betas, sum betas, and annual betas are calculated for the CRSP standard deciles, decile 10 subdeciles, and size groupings. In Exhibit 4.7, annual betas tend to be greater than OLS betas, and sum betas tend to be larger than both OLS and annual betas. The OLS betas and sum betas for the portfolios comprised of larger companies are approximately the same.

For example, the OLS beta for decile 1 (comprised of the largest companies) is 0.92, and the sum beta for decile 1 is 0.92. Alternatively, the OLS beta for decile 10 (comprised of the smallest companies) is 1.39, while the sum beta for decile 10 is 1.69. All things held the same, the *larger* sum beta of decile 10 implies a *smaller* size premia (3.55%) than implied for its OLS beta counterpart (5.59%)

Sum betas and annual betas tend to be larger for smaller companies than when using OLS betas. As a result, they tend to be less plagued by the overestimation problem due to incorrectly measuring beta.

Exhibit 4.7: OLS Betas, Sum Betas, and Annual Betas, and their Respective Implied Size Premia
As of December 31, 2016

Decile	OLS Beta	Size Premium (%)	Annual Beta	Size Premium (%)	Sum Beta	Size Premium (%)
1-Largest	0.92	-0.35	0.94	-0.51	0.92	-0.33
2	1.04	0.61	1.04	0.57	1.06	0.46
3	1.11	0.89	1.10	0.94	1.14	0.66
4	1.13	0.98	1.17	0.64	1.20	0.49
5	1.17	1.51	1.19	1.32	1.25	0.94
6	1.17	1.66	1.21	1.42	1.28	0.90
7	1.25	1.72	1.29	1.43	1.39	0.73
8	1.30	2.08	1.37	1.64	1.48	0.83
9	1.34	2.68	1.47	1.73	1.55	1.23
10-Smallest	1.39	5.59	1.60	4.19	1.69	3.55
Breakdown of 10th Decile						
10a	1.41	4.09	1.52	3.31	1.67	2.26
10w	1.38	3.10	1.41	2.92	1.58	1.74
10x	1.45	5.33	1.67	3.77	1.80	2.86
10b	1.37	8.64	1.74	6.04	1.71	6.27
10y	1.42	7.21	1.80	4.55	1.75	4.93
10z	1.28	11.63	1.60	9.43	1.64	9.17
Size Grouping						
Mid-Cap (3–5)	1.12	1.02	1.14	0.91	1.18	0.65
Low-Cap (6–8)	1.22	1.75	1.27	1.45	1.36	0.82
Micro-Cap (9–10)	1.35	3.67	1.52	2.51	1.59	2.01

Sources of underlying data: (i) CRSP U.S. Stock Database and CRSP U.S. Indices Database © 2017 Center for Research in Security Prices (CRSP®), University of Chicago Booth School of Business. (ii) Morningstar *Direct* database. Used with permission. All rights reserved. Calculations performed by Duff & Phelps, LLC.

OLS and Sum betas are estimated from monthly return data in excess of the 30-day U.S. Treasury bill total return, January 1926–December 2016. Annual betas are estimated from annualized return data in excess of the 30-day U.S. Treasury bill total return, 1926–2016.

Historical risk-free rate represented by the 91-year arithmetic mean income return component of 20-year U.S. government bonds (5.02%).

Calculated in the context of the CAPM by multiplying the historical equity risk premium by beta. The historical equity risk premia in this example is estimated as the arithmetic annual mean return of the S&P 500 Index (11.95%) minus the arithmetic annual mean income return component of 20-year U.S. government bonds (5.02%) from 1926–2016.

A problem with annual betas is that oftentimes there are simply not enough annual periods to calculate a statistically significant beta (e.g., 5 periods of *annual* return data is likely not enough periods to estimate a meaningful beta). So in many cases, the choice distills down to a choice between OLS and sum beta.

In applying the capital asset pricing model (CAPM) (particularly for smaller businesses), we are looking for the most *accurate* estimate, and not the most *expedient* one. If you use an OLS beta for a small company by multiplying the OLS beta times the equity risk premium (ERP) estimate and adding an OLS-based size premium, you may not arrive at as accurate an estimate of the cost of equity capital as by multiplying a sum beta times the ERP estimate and adding a sum-beta-based size premium. You should be using the most accurate estimate of beta and the most accurate measure of the appropriate size premium. Having said that, whatever type of beta you ultimately choose to employ, you should match the source of the size premium (OLS or sum beta) with the type of beta estimate you have chosen for your subject company.

For example, for internal consistency, one should use a size premium derived using an OLS beta when the subject company beta is an OLS beta, and one should use a size premium derived using sum betas when the subject company beta is a sum beta (Exhibit 4.8).

Exhibit 4.8: Potential Impact on Cost of Equity Capital; Matching (or Mismatching) the Type of Beta Used in the CAPM Equation to the Type of Beta Used to Develop the Size Premium

		Beta Used in CAPM Equation	
		OLS Beta	Sum Beta
Beta Used to Develop Size Premia	OLS Beta	A – even –	B Higher COE
	Sum Beta	C Lower COE	D – even –

The resulting cost of equity capital resulting in the "matched" cases (Case A and Case D) do not necessarily have to equal (and likely will not), but they will tend to be within a reasonable range of each other. Using Cases B and C may lead to an incorrect estimate of cost equity capital. To be clear, we recommend using sum betas for the development of size premia, and to also use sum beta within the CAPM, (particularly if dealing with smaller companies), because sum betas tend to better explain the returns of smaller companies. However, in cases in which you do use OLS betas in CAPM, you should use an OLS beta derived size premium.

Data Issues

Critics of the size effect point out various issues with the data used, resulting in anomalies that people mistakenly have observed as the size effect. These data issues may include seasonality, bid/ask bounce bias, and delisting bias, among others.[4.9] In the following sections, we discuss the different compositions of portfolios in the CRSP Deciles Size Premia study data set and the Risk Premium Report study data set.

Composition of the Smallest CRSP Deciles

We divided the CRSP 10th decile into subdeciles 10a and 10b (10a is the top half of the 10th decile, and 10b is the bottom half of the 10th decile) and further divided subdecile 10a into 10w and 10x, and subdecile 10b into 10y and 10z. This is the same breakdown of CRSP decile 10 that was previously presented in the former Morningstar/Ibbotson *SBBI Valuation Yearbook*.

As of December 31, 2016, the reported size premium for the smallest 5% of companies by market capitalization as represented by CRSP subdecile 10b is 8.64%, and the size premium for the next smallest 5% of companies (as represented by CRSP subdecile 10a) is 4.09%, a difference of 4.55%.

What kind of companies populate subdeciles 10b and its top and bottom halves, 10y and 10z? The CRSP Deciles Size Premia include all companies with no exclusion of speculative (e.g., start-up) or distressed companies whose market capitalization may be small because they are speculative or distressed. The inclusion of speculative or distressed companies in the database is one basis for criticism of the size effect. Exhibit 4.9 and Exhibit 4.10 display information about the types of companies that are included in decile 10y and decile 10z, respectively.[4.10]

[4.9] For a complete discussion of these issues, please refer to Pratt and Grabowski, op.cit.: Chapter 15A, "Other Data Issues Regarding the Size Effect".

[4.10] Exhibits 4.9 and 4.10 are as of September 2016 rather than December 2016 in order to mimic how the CRSP standard market-cap based portfolios are formed. The CRSP deciles portfolio compositions are reset quarterly (March, June, September, December), and then portfolio returns are calculated for these portfolio compositions over the *subsequent* quarter. As of December 2016, the most recent "reset" is September 2016.

Exhibit 4.9: Breakdown of Decile 10y Companies: Market Value of Equity between $73.561 and $127.279 million
September 30, 2016

Decile 10y	Market Value of Equity (in $millions)	Book Value of Equity (in $millions)	5-Year Average Net Income (in $millions)	Market Value of Invested Capital (in $millions)
95th Percentile	$123.589	$181.402	$11.539	$694.333
75th Percentile	109.944	103.051	4.860	198.683
50th Percentile	96.018	69.078	(1.500)	121.770
25th Percentile	82.854	27.766	(16.279)	99.799
5th Percentile	74.678	(4.808)	(37.147)	77.794

Decile 10y	Total Assets (in $millions)	5-Year Average EBITDA (in $millions)	Sales (in $millions)	Return on Book Equity (%)
95th Percentile	$1,332.366	$69.393	$516.086	17.9
75th Percentile	681.630	17.890	151.971	8.0
50th Percentile	155.707	3.986	51.495	(1.6)
25th Percentile	62.955	(10.610)	29.228	(42.7)
5th Percentile	22.811	(22.001)	8.279	(103.6)

Decile 10y	OLS Beta	Sum Beta
95th Percentile	2.24	3.16
75th Percentile	1.24	1.77
50th Percentile	0.65	0.98
25th Percentile	0.29	0.36
5th Percentile	0.11	0.18

Sources of underlying data: (i) CRSP U.S. Stock Database and CRSP U.S. Indices Database © 2017 Center for Research in Security Prices (CRSP®), University of Chicago Booth School of Business. (ii) S&P *Capital IQ*. Used with permission. All rights reserved. Calculations performed by Duff & Phelps, LLC.

Exhibit 4.10: Breakdown of Decile 10z Companies: Market Value of Equity between $2.516 and $73.504 million
September 30, 2016

Decile 10z	Market Value of Equity (in $millions)	Book Value of Equity (in $millions)	5-Year Average Net Income (in $millions)	Market Value of Invested Capital (in $millions)
95th Percentile	$70.114	$85.864	$4.600	$176.784
75th Percentile	53.104	42.925	0.709	72.135
50th Percentile	34.343	18.007	(3.958)	46.750
25th Percentile	18.846	5.866	(13.929)	25.493
5th Percentile	6.657	(5.338)	(25.146)	9.759

Decile 10z	Total Assets (in $millions)	5-Year Average EBITDA (in $millions)	Sales (in $millions)	Return on Book Equity (%)
95th Percentile	$660.828	$22.767	$248.603	15.5
75th Percentile	106.517	3.179	67.029	2.5
50th Percentile	40.658	(1.547)	25.303	(23.0)
25th Percentile	17.456	(9.474)	8.086	(94.5)
5th Percentile	6.319	(18.669)	1.329	(222.4)

Decile 10z	OLS Beta	Sum Beta
95th Percentile	2.71	3.45
75th Percentile	1.35	1.79
50th Percentile	0.70	1.01
25th Percentile	0.28	0.43
5th Percentile	0.09	0.13

Sources of underlying data: (i) CRSP U.S. Stock Database and CRSP U.S. Indices Database © 2017 Center for Research in Security Prices (CRSP®), University of Chicago Booth School of Business. (ii) S&P *Capital IQ*. Used with permission. All rights reserved. Calculations performed by Duff & Phelps, LLC.

From these data we can conclude:

- Betas used for calculating the size premium for subdecile 10y and subdecile 10z (using the OLS method of calculating betas) generally *understate* the beta, and therefore *overstate* the size premium. Note the small betas for companies in the 25th and 5th percentiles.

- Subdecile 10y and subdecile 10z are populated by many large (but highly leveraged) companies with small market capitalizations that probably do not match the characteristics of financially healthy but small companies (see "Total Assets", 95th percentile measures).

Stocks of the *troubled* companies included in the data probably are trading like call options (unlimited upside, limited downside). Even if you were to use the sum beta method, the beta estimates would likely be underestimated and the size premium overstated (see "Return on Book Equity", 25th percentile and 5th percentile).

Before using the size premium data for 10b or its top and bottom halves, 10y and 10z, the valuation analyst likely should determine if the mix of companies that comprise the subdeciles are indeed comparable to the subject company.

Composition of the Smallest Risk Premium Report Studies Portfolio

The Risk Premium Report studies use a different methodology from the CRSP Deciles Size Premia studies. The Risk Premium Report studies screen out speculative start-ups, distressed (i.e., bankrupt) companies, and other high-financial-risk companies. These studies measure beta using the sum beta method. This methodology was chosen to counter the criticism of the size effect by some that the size premium is a function of the high rates of return for speculative companies and distressed companies in the data set.

The Risk Premium Report studies use the sum beta method to measure the size premium because it finds that betas of small companies in the data set (even after removing speculative, distressed, and other high-financial-risk companies) are underestimated if one uses the OLS method of estimating betas. Even after eliminating speculative, distressed, and other high-financial-risk companies and using the sum beta in measuring size, we still observe the size effect for a more recent period (since 1963).

The Risk Premium Report exhibits include a total of eight size measures, including six that are not based on market capitalization. Exhibit 4.11 shows the breakdown of companies in the Risk Premium Report exhibits in portfolio 25 (portfolio 25 is comprised of the smallest companies) for each of the eight size measures.

If the subject company is not highly levered, the companies in portfolio 25 may be more comparable to a small subject company, and therefore the size premium data for portfolio 25 may be more appropriate to use when dealing with very small companies.

Exhibit 4.11: Size Measure of Companies That Comprise Portfolio 25 of the *Risk Premium Report* December 31, 2016

Portfolio 25	Market Value of Equity (in $millions)	Book Value of Equity (in $millions)	5-Year Average Net Income (in $millions)	Market Value of Invested Capital (in $millions)
Largest Company	$291.526	$159.204	$11.274	$387.281
95th Percentile	260.490	151.276	10.302	355.585
75th Percentile	189.941	116.879	7.292	257.179
50th Percentile	99.386	74.349	4.148	141.789
25th Percentile	48.289	33.630	1.976	67.336
5th Percentile	16.848	13.868	0.669	20.342
Smallest Company	4.784	4.756	0.054	8.190

Portfolio 25	Total Assets (in $millions)	5-Year Average EBITDA (in $millions)	Sales (in $millions)	Number of Employees
Largest Company	$346.465	$39.386	$307.857	686
95th Percentile	318.170	36.761	276.458	641
75th Percentile	249.862	26.608	200.273	485
50th Percentile	163.579	15.120	118.960	272
25th Percentile	62.163	6.991	55.810	131
5th Percentile	24.577	2.109	18.314	10
Smallest Company	9.283	1.130	2.619	1

Sources of underlying data: (i) CRSP U.S. Stock Database and CRSP U.S. Indices Database © 2017 Center for Research in Security Prices (CRSP®), University of Chicago Booth School of Business. (ii) S&P *Research Insight*. Used with permission. All rights reserved. Calculations performed by Duff & Phelps, LLC.

Financial services companies (i.e., SIC code 6; those companies in finance, insurance, or real estate) are *excluded* from Risk Premium Report portfolios, primarily because some of the financial data used in the Risk Premium Report is difficult to apply to companies in the financial sector (e.g., "sales" at commercial banks). In addition, financial services companies tend to support a much higher ratio of debt-to-equity than do other industries, and so including them with non-financial firms may be an apples-to-oranges comparison that could lead to improperly skewed results. Moreover, companies in the financial services sector were poorly represented during the early years of the Standard & Poor's *Compustat* database.

Because companies in SIC code 6 are excluded from the set of companies used to perform the analyses presented in the Risk Premium Report, the data should not be used by an analyst estimating the cost of equity capital for a financial services company or other company in SIC code 6.

We also publish accounting-based fundamental risk information about the companies that comprise the 25 size-ranked portfolios for *each* of the eight size measures analyzed in the Risk Premium Report exhibits. This information includes:

- Five-year average operating income margin

- Coefficient of variation in operating income margin

- Coefficient of variation in return on book equity

The first statistic measures profitability, and the latter two statistics measure volatility of earnings.

This information provides the analyst with two important capabilities:

1. Additional tools to determine if the mix of companies that comprise the Risk Premium Report's portfolios are indeed comparable to the subject company.

2. The opportunity to gauge whether an increase (or decrease) adjustment to a risk premium or size premium (and thus cost of equity capital) is indicated, based on the company-specific differences of the subject company's fundamental risk and the average fundamental risk of companies that make up the portfolios from which the risk premia are derived. (for more information, see the section entitled "Comparative Risk Study" in Chapter 10).

Has the Size Effect Disappeared in More Recent Periods?

Some research has suggested that in more recent years the size effect is greatly diminished, or has disappeared altogether. The point in time usually identified as the year after which the size effect is diminished is 1981. The primary reason for this is that in 1981 Banz examined the returns of NYSE small-cap companies compared to the returns of NYSE large-cap companies over the period 1926–1975, and found that there was a negative relationship between size as measured by market capitalization and return (i.e., as market capitalization *decreases*, returns *increase*). In effect, Banz is said to have "let the cat out of the bag" that small-cap companies offered greater returns, and that attracted more investment in small-cap companies. Prices were bid up, thus ultimately reducing the overall returns.

Hou and van Dijk posited that the apparent disappearance of the size effect after the early 1980s was due to cash flow shocks. Realized returns for small companies were generally less than expected because of negative cash flow shocks, and realized returns for large companies were generally greater than expected because of positive cash flow shocks.[4.11]

4.11 Kewei Hou and Mathijs A. van Dijk, "Resurrecting the size effect: Firm size, profitability shocks, and expected stock returns", Ohio State University Fisher College of Business working paper, March 31, 2014. Copy available at:
http://papers.ssrn.com/sol3/papers.cfm?abstract_id=1536804.

What caused the cash flow shocks? The number of newly public firms in the United States increased dramatically in the 1980s and 1990s compared with prior periods, and the profitability and survival rate of the newly public firms was generally less than the profitability and survival rates for firms that went public in previous years. After adjusting realized returns for the cash flow shocks, the result was that returns of small firms on a pro forma basis exceeded the returns of large firms by approximately 10% per annum, consistent with the size premium in prior periods.

A more direct reason often cited for a diminished size effect in more recent years was possibly most succinctly stated by Horowitz, Loughran, and Savin, who suggested that "it is quite possible that as investors became aware of the size effect, small firm prices increased (thus lowering subsequent returns)".[4.12] This conjecture may be supported by the sheer number of small-cap companies that have come into existence since Banz's 1981 article that demonstrated that smaller-cap companies exhibited significantly greater performance over the period from 1926 to 1975.[4.13]

We performed analyses to investigate which of two hypothetical investors would have ended up with more money in their pocket over various holding periods within the full range of monthly CRSP decile data (January 1926–December 2016): the first investor invests only in small-cap companies, and the second investor only invests in large-cap companies.

To do this, we first calculated the terminal index value of $1.00 invested for every possible combination of monthly beginning dates and end dates for CRSP decile 1 (the largest-cap companies) and CRSP decile 10 (the smallest-cap companies) over the January 1926–December 2016 period.[4.14] The total number of monthly begin dates and end dates combinations between January 1926 and December 2016 is 596,778.

We then subtracted the terminal index value of large-cap companies from the terminal index value of small-cap companies for *each* of the 596,778 beginning date/end date combinations. If the terminal index value of small-cap companies was greater than the terminal index value of large-cap companies, this would indicate small-cap companies returned a higher return over that period for the investor.

Example: $1.00 invested in large-cap companies from January 1926 would have grown to $3,293.43 by the end of December 2016. Alternatively, $1.00 invested in small-cap companies from January 1926 would have grown to $86,589.99 by the end of December 2016. Investing in small-cap companies would have resulted in $83,296.56 ($86,589.99 − $3,293.43) *more* money in one's pocket than investing in large-cap companies over this period.

These calculations were performed for *every* possible monthly beginning date and end date combination between January 1926 and December 2016.

[4.12]   Joel L. Horowitz, Tim Loughran, and N.E. Savin, "The disappearing size effect", *Research in Economics* (2000), page 98.

[4.13]   Banz, Rolf W. "The Relationship between Return and Market Value of Common Stocks". *Journal of Financial Economics* (March 1981): 3–18. Professor Banz's 1981 article is often cited as the first comprehensive study of the size effect.

[4.14]   The terminal index value in all cases presented here is the amount that $1 invested on the begin date would have grown to (or decreased to) as of the end date.

The result of this analysis was that small-cap companies outperformed large-cap companies in 503,127 of the cases (84%), and large-cap companies outperformed small-cap companies in 93,651 cases of the (16%).

If hypothetical Investor A, who invests *only* in CRSP Decile 1 (comprised of the largest companies), had invested $1 in each of the 596,778 possible start-month/end-month investment horizons between January 1926 and December 2016, her $596,778 total investment would have become $98,468,279.

Alternatively, if hypothetical Investor B, who invests *only* in CRSP Decile 10 (composed of the smallest companies), had invested $1 in each of those 596,778 possible start-month/end-month investment horizons between January 1926 and December 2016, his $596,778 total investment would have become $1,867,196,551.

In Exhibit 4.12, an abbreviated summary of these results is shown, where the holding periods are limited to *exactly* 1 month, 5-years, 10-years, 20-years, and 30-years, instead of all 596,778 possible start- and end-date combinations. Start dates covering the entire January 1926–December 2016 period are examined, as well as three more recent start date windows: January 1982–December 2016, January 1990–December 2016, and January 2000–December 2016. All three of the more recent start date windows are *after* Banz wrote his 1981 article that identified the size effect, and so they are labeled as "Post Banz". Also, in Exhibit 4.12 the number of periods examined is shown first, followed by the outperformance percentage of the total periods in parentheses.

In the top row of Exhibit 4.12 (in which the holding period is restricted to a single month), large-cap companies outperformed small-cap companies in the majority of cases (52%) over the entire 1926–2016 start date window, and in the 1982–2016 start date window (53%); in the 1990–2016 start date window large-cap and small-cap stocks tied at 50% each. In the 2000–2016 start date window, however, small-cap companies outperform, although barely (54%).

As the holding period is increased from 1 month to 60 months (and longer), and as the time that small-cap companies and large-cap companies are given to "race" against each other is lengthened, small-cap companies again tend to outperform. For example, over the entire range of start dates (1926–2016), there are a total of 733 (662 + 71) holding periods that are exactly 360 months (30 years) long, with small-cap companies outperforming large-cap companies in 662 (90%) of them (bottom row, left column).

Exhibit 4.12: Small-cap Companies' Performance minus Large-cap Companies' Performance Over Periods of *Exactly* 1, 60, 120, 240, and 360 Months

Holding Period	All Dates 1926–2016	Post Banz 1982–2016	Post Banz 1990–2016	Post Banz 2000–2016
Exactly 1 month				
Small Stocks Outperform	519 (48%)	196 (47%)	162 (50%)	111 (54%)
Large Stocks Outperform	573 (52%)	224 (53%)	162 (50%)	93 (46%)
Exactly 60 months (5 years)				
Small Stocks Outperform	591 (57%)	177 (49%)	172 (65%)	108 (74%)
Large Stocks Outperform	442 (43%)	184 (51%)	93 (35%)	37 (26%)
Exactly 120 months (10 years)				
Small Stocks Outperform	681 (70%)	168 (56%)	168 (82%)	69 (81%)
Large Stocks Outperform	292 (30%)	133 (44%)	37 (18%)	16 (19%)
Exactly 240 months (20 years)				
Small Stocks Outperform	694 (81%)	143 (79%)	85 (100%)	–
Large Stocks Outperform	159 (19%)	38 (21%)	0 (0%)	–
Exactly 360 months (30 years)				
Small Stocks Outperform	662 (90%)	46 (75%)	–	–
Large Stocks Outperform	71 (10%)	15 (25%)	–	–

Source of underlying data: CRSP U.S. Stock Database and CRSP U.S. Indices Database © 2017 Center for Research in Security Prices (CRSP®), University of Chicago Booth School of Business. Large-cap companies and small-cap companies are represented by CRSP NYSE/NYSE MKT/NASDAQ decile 1 and 10, respectively. Used with permission. All rights reserved. Calculations performed by Duff & Phelps, LLC.

These analyses suggest:

- The size effect is *cyclical.* Sometimes small-cap companies outperform large-cap companies, and sometimes large-cap companies outperform small-cap companies.

- The *longer* the holding period over which small-cap companies and large-cap companies are given to "race" against each other, the *more likely* it is that small-cap companies will outperform large-cap companies. This implies that over the longer-term (which is the default period over which most business valuations are done), the size effect is indeed a significant factor that should likely be accounted for in the development of cost of capital estimates.

- The 1980s were *not kind* to small capitalization stocks. During this period, the size effect likely was on a cyclical low, or even significantly negative.

Relationship of Size and Liquidity

Liquidity affects the cost of capital. For this purpose, *liquidity* refers to the speed at which a large quantity of a security can be traded with a minimal impact on the price and at the lowest cost. Banz's 1981 musing as to whether "...size per se is responsible for the effect or whether size is just a proxy for one or more true unknown factors correlated with size" may have been cannily prescient. Research on returns as related to "size" is abundant, but over time a growing body of work investigating the impact of "liquidity" on returns has emerged.

Capital market theory also assumes liquidity of investments. Many of the observations about risk and return are drawn from information for liquid investments. Investors desire liquidity and require greater returns for illiquidity. But the degree of liquidity is one of the risk factors for all investments. Any discussion of a liquidity premium, therefore, would be incomplete without accounting for underlying stock risks before considering relative liquidity.

Stocks of small companies generally do not have the same level of liquidity as large-company stocks. This is likely a function of the mix of shareholders and underlying risk characteristics. Many institutional investors do not own stocks in small companies because they have too much money to invest. Were they to invest as little as 1% of their available funds in a small company, they would be likely to control the company. Institutional investors generally want liquidity to move into and out of positions in a single firm. Therefore, one does not see the breadth of investors investing in small-company stocks.

Further, small companies are followed by only a small window of analysts, if at all. This makes it more difficult for investors to evaluate small firms.

Is the size premium simply the result of differences in liquidity? If one is valuing a small business, that business, if it were publicly traded, would likely never have the same breadth of shareholders as a large publicly traded company, and whatever impact the relative illiquidity of small companies has on the cost of capital will carry over to any small business.

Some analysts have suggested that the size effect should be set aside because various studies have ignored transaction costs in measuring rates of return. The analysts point out that small stocks often have higher transaction costs than large stocks. In addition, the historical size premium can be greatly reduced if one makes certain assumptions about transaction costs and holding periods. However, in applying the income approach to valuation, analysts typically use projected net cash flows that do not make any adjustment for an investor's hypothetical transaction costs. It may be that small stocks are priced in a way that increases the rates of return so as to reward investors for the costs of executing a transaction. If so, it would be a distortion to express the discount rate on a net-of-transaction-cost basis while the net cash flow projections are on a before-transaction-cost basis.

Academic studies support the hypotheses that illiquidity is a factor in pricing and returns of stocks and that returns of small firms are more sensitive to market liquidity. Moreover, any reasonable adjustment for transaction costs should recognize that investors can mitigate these costs on an annual basis by holding their stocks for a longer period. In fact, investors in small companies tend to have longer holding periods than investors in large companies.

First, let's examine some of the research.

As early as 1986, Amihud and Mendelson, demonstrated that "...market-observed average returns are an increasing function of the spread..." (i.e., less liquid stocks, as measured by a larger bid-ask spread, outperform more liquid stocks), and further concluded that the "...higher yields required on higher-spread stocks give firms an incentive to increase the liquidity of their securities, thus reducing their opportunity cost of capital".[4.15]

In a 2013 article, Ibbotson, Chen, Kim, and Hu suggested that while the typical measures of liquidity employed in the literature are each "...highly correlated with company size", they demonstrate that liquidity, as measured by annual stock turnover, "...is an economically significant investment style that is just as strong, but distinct from traditional investment styles such as size, value/growth, and momentum".[4.16] Analyzing the performance of a broad universe of U.S. stocks from 1972–2011, the authors go on to say that "...there is an incremental return from investing in less liquid stocks even after adjusting for the market, size, value/growth, and momentum factors", and conclude that "...equity liquidity is the missing equity style".

The authors identify two main sources of the greater returns of less liquid stocks. The first is that "investors like liquidity and dislike illiquidity", and "...a premium has to be paid for any characteristic that investors demand, and a discount must be given for any characteristic investors seek to avoid". Thus, "...the investor in less liquid stocks gets lower valuations, effectively buying stocks at a discount".

As we discussed in Chapter 2, one can think of risk in terms of popularity. For example, illiquidity is typically considered a risk, and less liquid stocks are considered less popular. One can classify less liquid stocks as less popular than brand name stocks that are in the news, having more analyst coverage and greater trading volume. Similarly, the size premium can be thought of as a risk measure that encompasses both illiquidity risk and underlying business risk; small capitalization stocks are typically less popular.

[4.15] Amihud, Yakov and Haim Mendelson, 1986, "Asset Pricing and the Bid-Ask Spread", *Journal of Financial Economics* 17, 223–249.

[4.16] See Roger G. Ibbotson, Zhiwu Chen, Daniel Y.-J. Kim, and Wendy Y. Hu, "Liquidity as an Investment Style", *Financial Analysts Journal* Vol 69(3): 30–44, May/June 2013. Copy available at www.zebracapm.com.

In a 2017 update to the 2013 article, Ibbotson and Kim examine market data from 1972–2016 and conclude that liquidity, as measured by stock turnover, meets the four criteria that characterize a benchmark investment style that William F. Sharpe defined in a 1992 article: (i) "identifiable before the fact", (ii) "not easily beaten", (iii) "a viable alternative", and (iv) "low in cost":[4.17, 4.18]

Identifiable Before the Fact: Given that Ibbotson and Kim's measure of liquidity was the previous year's turnover of the stock, the liquidity measure used is (by definition) *"identifiable before the fact"*.[4.19]

Not Easily Beaten: Ibbotson and Kim then compared the 1st quartile returns of the various styles, and these all outperformed the equally weighted market portfolio. The returns from the low liquidity quartile were comparable to the other styles, beating size and momentum, but trailing value. They consider all four styles to be *"not easily beaten"*.

A Viable Alternative: Ibbotson and Kim examined double sort portfolios comparing liquidity with size, value, and momentum in four-by-four matrices. The impact of liquidity on returns was somewhat stronger than size and momentum, and roughly comparable to value. It was also additive to each style. Thus they determined that liquidity was *"a viable alternative"* to size, value, and momentum.

Low in Cost: Ibbotson and Kim demonstrated that less liquid portfolios could be formed *"at low cost"*. The portfolios they examined were formed only once per year, and 64.21% of the stocks stayed in the same quartile. The high-performing low quartile had 78.50% of the stocks stay in that quartile. Thus the liquidity portfolios themselves exhibit low turnover, which can keep their costs low.

Ibbotson and Kim demonstrate that liquidity is "a viable alternative" to each of the three other well established styles (size, value/growth, and momentum) by focusing on distinguishing turnover from size, value, and momentum by constructing "double-sort" quartile portfolios that combine liquidity with each of the other styles (in turn). In each of these analyses, the "liquidity effect" held regardless of size, value/growth, and momentum groupings.

For example, it is often presumed that investing in less liquid stocks is equivalent to investing in small-cap stocks. To determine if liquidity is effectively a proxy for size, they constructed equally weighted double-sort portfolios in capitalization and turnover quartiles. Exhibit 4.13 reports the annualized geometric mean (compound) return, arithmetic mean return, and standard deviation of returns along with the average number of stocks in each intersection portfolio.

[4.17] The "2017 update to the 2013 article" is Roger G. Ibbotson and Daniel Y.-J.Kim, "Liquidity as an Investment Style, 2017 Update", January 27, 2017. The section on the 2017 update herein is largely excerpted from Roger G. Ibbotson and Daniel Y.-J.Kim's writing in same. Copies of the 2017 update are available at www.zebracapm.com. Roger Ibbotson is Professor Emeritus of Finance, Yale School of Management, and Chairman & CIO, Zebra Capital Management, LLC. Daniel Y.-J.Kim is Director of Research, Zebra Capital Management, LLC.

[4.18] Sharpe, William F., 1992, "Asset Allocation: Management Style and Performance Measurement". *Journal of Portfolio Management*, Vol. 18, No. 2 (Winter):7–19.

[4.19] Other liquidity measures could have met that criteria as well, but Ibbotson and Kim chose turnover because it was simple, easy to measure, and has a significant impact on returns.

Exhibit 4.13: Summary Statistics of Size and Liquidity "Double Sort" Quartile Portfolios 1972–2016

	Low Liquidity	Mid-Low Liquidity	Mid-High Liquidity	High Liquidity	Liquidity Effect (%)
Micro-Cap					
Geometric Mean (%)	16.03	15.66	9.65	-0.29	**16.32**
Arithmetic Mean (%)	18.41	19.28	14.97	4.91	
Standard Deviation (%)	22.93	28.84	34.91	33.37	
Avg. Number of Stocks	342	182	125	98	
Small-Cap					
Geometric Mean (%)	15.68	14.35	12.20	5.77	**9.91**
Arithmetic Mean (%)	17.35	16.93	15.52	9.96	
Standard Deviation (%)	19.56	23.99	27.16	30.41	
Avg. Number of Stocks	198	201	174	175	
Mid-Cap					
Geometric Mean (%)	14.19	13.90	12.67	8.15	**6.04**
Arithmetic Mean (%)	15.57	15.60	14.81	11.69	
Standard Deviation (%)	17.75	19.68	21.75	27.63	
Avg. Number of Stocks	131	177	202	237	
Large-Cap					
Geometric Mean (%)	11.20	12.05	11.75	8.89	**2.31**
Arithmetic Mean (%)	12.44	13.18	13.27	11.87	
Standard Deviation (%)	16.33	15.50	17.76	24.79	
Avg. Number of Stocks	75	188	247	237	
Size Effect (%)	**4.83**	**3.61**	**-2.10**	**-9.18**	

Source: Roger G. Ibbotson and Daniel Y.-J.Kim, "Liquidity as an Investment Style, 2017 Update", January 27, 2017. To learn more, visit www.zebracapm.com.

Across the micro-cap quartile in Exhibit 4.13, the low-liquidity portfolio earned a geometric mean return of 16.03% per year in contrast to the high-liquidity portfolio returning -0.29% per year, suggesting that the liquidity effect is the *strongest* among micro-cap stocks, and then declines from small- to mid- to large-cap stocks. Note that the micro-caps row contains both the *highest* return and the *lowest* returns.

Across the large-cap quartile, the low- and high-liquidity portfolios returned 11.20% and 8.89% respectively, producing a liquidity effect of 2.31%.

Within the two mid-size portfolios, the liquidity return spread is also significant. Therefore, size does not capture liquidity (i.e., the liquidity premium *holds* regardless of size group). Conversely, the size effect does *not* hold across all liquidity quartiles, especially in the highest turnover quartile (-9.18%).

A "heat map" of the size and liquidity "double sort" quartile portfolios is presented in Exhibit 4.14. In Exhibit 4.14, the deeper the red, the *higher* the return, and the darker the gray, the *lower* the return. For example, the highest return over the 1972–2016 period was produced by low-liquidity/micro-cap stocks. Alternatively, the lowest return was produced by high-liquidity/micro-cap stocks.

Exhibit 4.13: Heat Map of Size and Liquidity "Double Sort" Quartile Portfolios (%), Compound Annual Returns
1972–2016

Source of underlying data: Roger G. Ibbotson and Daniel Y.-J.Kim, "Liquidity as an Investment Style, 2017 Update", January 27, 2017. To learn more, visit www.zebracapm.com.

In the 2017 update on liquidity, Ibbotson and Kim reach four broad conclusions: (i) liquidity should be given equal standing to size, value/growth, and momentum as an investment style, (ii) liquidity, as measured by stock turnover, is an economically significant indicator of long run returns, (iii) returns from liquidity are sufficiently different from the other styles, so that it is not merely a substitute, and finally, (iv) a stock's liquidity is relatively stable over time, with changes in liquidity associated with changes in valuation.

Ashok Abbott also investigated the relative importance of the size and liquidity risk factors.[4.20] The author used a multi-factor model including a trading cost measure and a liquidity premium factor to assess the absolute contribution for each factor individually, as well as in combination with other factors, to form an estimate of the combined contribution of the factors considered in the estimate of the cost of equity capital.[4.21]

[4.20] Ashok Bhardwaj Abbott (2015). Available from the author.
[4.21] A measure of an individual stock's liquidity, with higher levels signifying that the current order flow in the market can absorb larger volumes of trading without significantly affecting prices.

Abbott found significant negative relationships between the size of the companies as measured by market value of equity and his trading cost measure; stocks of larger firms can be traded at a lower cost. He found a similar relationship between liquidity and cost of trading. As stocks become more liquid, trading costs and price impact both decline, as suggested by theory.

The Risk Premium Report Study exhibits in this book demonstrate that size and fundamental risk of small companies are correlated (displayed in the "C" exhibits presented in Appendix 4 and discussed in Chapter 10). This leads one to consider that size may, in part at best, be a coincident indicator of fundamental company risk.

That same relationship may be creating the liquidity effect. That is, the underlying risks of small companies being greater than those of larger companies may cause investors to shy away from small companies, valuing their liquidity. Thus, reduced liquidity may also be a coincident indicator of fundamental risk.

In measuring the appropriate size premium when estimating the cost of equity capital for a division or reporting unit of a large public company or a closely held business, one need not separate the portion of the size premium that may be attributable to an illiquidity factor. One is estimating the cost of capital as if the market were pricing the risks of the subject business based on the average risk of other companies of comparable size including any portion of the risks due to illiquidity.

Key Things to Remember about the Size Premium

- The size effect is based on the empirical observation that companies of smaller size are associated with greater risk and, therefore, have greater costs of capital. In other words, there is a significant (negative) relationship between the size and historical equity returns – as size *decreases*, returns tend to *increase*, and vice versa.

- Traditionally, small companies are believed to have greater required rates of return than large companies because small companies are inherently riskier. It is not clear, however, whether this is due to size itself, or to another factor closely related to size.

- The size effect is not evident just for the smallest companies; it is evident for all but the largest groups of companies, including companies with a market capitalization in excess of several billions of dollars. However, the size effect is greatest with the smallest companies.

- Small-cap companies tend to outperform large-cap companies over longer periods. The longer the period over which small-cap companies and large-cap companies are given to "race" against each other, the more likely it is that small-cap companies will outperform large-cap companies. The size effect tends to stabilize over time.

- Use sum betas for the development of size premia, and use sum beta within the CAPM (particularly if dealing with very small companies), because sum betas tend to better explain the returns of smaller companies. However, in cases in which you do use OLS betas in CAPM, you should use an OLS-beta derived size premium.

- Risk Premium Report portfolios do not include start-up and high-financial-risk companies. The returns on these companies could be expected to be high because of their risk, not because of their size.

- Despite many criticisms of the size effect, it continues to be observed in data sources. Further, observation of the size effect is consistent with a modification of the pure CAPM. Studies have shown the limitations of beta as a sole measure of risk. The size premium is an empirically derived correction to the pure CAPM.

- While the 1980s were *not* kind to small-cap companies (the size effect likely was on a cyclical low, or even negative), the evidence suggests that after the 1980s, the size effect may again be entering a cyclical period of strength.

- If the valuation analyst is estimating the cost of equity capital of a closely held subject company on an "as if publicly" basis, the valuation assumption is that the subject company would have liquidity (if it was public) to approximately the average of comparable size public companies. The size premium published in the *Valuation Handbook – U.S. Guide to Cost of Capital* are appropriate to use in developing the cost of equity capital without separating the size effect from the liquidity effect.

- The size effect is not without controversy, nor is this controversy something new. Traditionally, small companies are believed to have greater required rates of return than large companies because small companies are inherently riskier. It is not clear, however, whether this is due to size itself, or to other factors closely related to or correlated with size (e.g., liquidity).

- One can think of risk in terms of popularity. Characteristics of investments that investors *desire* are "popular", while characteristics of investments that investors do *not* desire are not popular. All other things being equal, assets with popular characteristics will be priced higher and have lower returns than assets with unpopular characteristics, which will be priced lower and have higher returns. Popularity can include all sorts of other characteristics that do not fit well into the risk and return paradigm.

Chapter 5

Basic Building Blocks of the Cost of Equity Capital – Betas and Industry Risk Premia

In this chapter we first discuss beta, which is an important input needed when estimating cost of equity capital under the capital asset pricing model (CAPM), and then discuss industry risk premia (RP_i), which are a special type of beta modified for use within the build-up model.

Beta

Beta is a measure of the systematic risk of a stock; the tendency of a stock's price to correlate with changes in the market. The "market" is typically represented by a broad-based equity index that includes a wide range of industries, and arguably behaves like the market as a whole.

The market's beta is 1.0 by definition. A company with a beta equal to 1.0 has the same risk as the market (it theoretically moves up and down with the market *in tandem*), a company with a beta greater than 1.0 is riskier than the market (it theoretically moves up and down to a *greater* degree than the market), and a company with a beta less than 1.0 is less risky than the market (it theoretically moves up and down to a *lesser* degree than the market).

Betas for equity capital are used as a modifier to the equity risk premium (ERP) in the context of CAPM. Beta is the sole risk factor of the pure CAPM, the form of the CAPM most often shown in textbooks. The combination of equity beta for the subject business multiplied by the ERP equals the estimated risk premium for the subject business.[5.1]

Equity betas increase with the risk of the business. For example, the beta of an entity with greater business (operating) risk will tend to be greater than the beta of an entity with lesser business risk. Similarly, the beta of a entity with more debt in the capital structure will tend to be greater than the beta of an entity with lesser financial risk.

Beta estimates are generally derived from returns data of publicly traded securities. If one is valuing a closely held business or a non-public division or reporting unit, for example, one likely will be using the beta estimate of publicly traded securities as a proxy for the non-public business.

Published and calculated beta estimates for public stocks typically reflect the capital structure in place during the look-back period. In other words, individual leverage decisions by each publicly traded company will impact its published (equity) beta. The beta estimates are typically made using realized returns for the subject business's stock and an index that represents the stock market as a whole. For example, many analysts use the S&P 500 Index as a proxy for the U.S. market. In the *2017 Valuation Handbook – U.S. Guide to Cost of Capital* the proxy for the market is the S&P 500 Index, unless otherwise stated.

[5.1]   This portion of the chapter is excerpted in part from Pratt and Grabowski, op.cit.: Chapter 11, "Beta: Differing Definitions and Estimates".

Other broad-based indices can be used as well, such as the Wilshire 5000, or the Morningstar U.S. Market Index (among others). As a matter of fact, as long as the index is broad-based and is representative of the market as a whole, it is arguably suitable for use as a market benchmark, and generally similar betas will be produced.

In Exhibit 5.1 the ordinary least squares (OLS) betas for the 60-month period ending December 2016 are calculated for 10 publicly traded U.S. companies, using three different broad-based U.S. equities indices. The OLS beta estimates are similar, regardless of the broad-based equities index chosen.

Exhibit 5.1: Company Betas Using Different Market Benchmarks
December 31, 2016

Company	S&P 500 Index	Wilshire 5000 Index	Morningstar U.S. Market Index
Apple Inc.	1.30	1.23	1.25
Caterpillar Inc.	1.36	1.40	1.39
The Coca-Cola Company	0.65	0.58	0.59
Expedia, Inc.	0.72	0.67	0.69
Exxon Mobil Corporation	0.89	0.86	0.85
Johnson & Johnson	0.72	0.68	0.68
Monsanto Company	1.01	1.00	1.00
Nvidia Corporation	1.30	1.32	1.30
The Procter & Gamble Company	0.59	0.53	0.54
Wells Fargo & Company	0.99	0.99	0.98

Source of underlying data: (i) Standard & Poor's *Capital IQ* database (ii) Morningstar's *Direct* database. Used with permission. All rights reserved. Betas calculated over the time period January 2012–December 2016 using excess total returns over 30-day U.S. Treasury Bills. Calculations performed by Duff & Phelps, LLC.

The reason that the results are similar is because the correlation of the three market benchmark indices is very high. In Exhibit 5.2 a simple cross-correlation matrix is shown. The three broad-based market indices selected for this example are highly correlated over the January 2012–December 2016 time period that these betas were calculated (and highly correlated over longer time periods as well).

Exhibit 5.2: Correlation Matrix of the S&P 500 Index, the Wilshire 5000 Index, and the Morningstar U.S. Market Index

January 2012–December 2016

	S&P 500 Index	Wilshire 5000 Index	Morningstar U.S. Market Index
S&P 500 Index	1.000		
Wilshire 5000 Index	0.996	1.000	
Morningstar U.S. Market Index	0.996	1.000	1.000

Source of underlying data: Morningstar's *Direct* database. Used with permission. All rights reserved. Calculations performed by Duff & Phelps, LLC.

These betas sometimes are referred to as levered betas, since these beta estimates reflect the actual leverage in a company's capital structure. The adjustment for leverage differences is called unlevering and levering beta estimates.[5.2]

Estimation of Equity Beta

Beta, like cost of capital itself, is a forward-looking concept. It is intended to be a measure of the *expected* future relationship between the return on an individual security (or portfolio of securities) and the return on the market. In the CAPM, beta should be the expected beta.

The market, as measured by a broad-based equities index, is ultimately a proxy for the broader economy. In this context, beta is theoretically the expected sensitivity of the individual security to changes in the overall economy. The sensitivity of individual security returns is the sensitivity of the company to cash flow risks and discount rate risk. It represents the sensitivity of changing expectation about expected cash flows of the business relative to changing expectations about expected cash flows of the economy as a whole (i.e., the market) changing expectations for the ERP.[5.3]

Valuation analysts typically use beta estimates derived from regressions over look-back periods or other techniques to develop the expected beta for use in the CAPM. Newer estimation techniques use implied volatility derived from options to estimate expected betas.

There are two general ways for estimating betas:

1. A direct beta estimate (sometimes called a top-down estimate) for a public company comes from regressing excess returns of the public company's stock on the excess returns of a market portfolio over a look-back period.

[5.2] For a comprehensive discussion of unlevering and levering beta estimates, see Pratt and Grabowski, op.cit.: Chapter 12, "Unlevering and Levering Equity Betas".

[5.3] John Y. Campbell and Jianping Mei, "Where Do Betas Come From? Asset Price Dynamics and the Sources of Systematic Risk" *Review of Financial Studies* 6(3) (1993): 567–592.

2. A *proxy* beta can be estimated by:

    i.   Identifying the businesses in which the subject entity operates.

    ii.   Identifying guideline public companies and estimating their levered betas.

    iii. Unlevering the guideline public company beta estimates to get estimates of unlevered (asset) betas.

    iv. Taking an average, often a weighted average, of these unlevered betas, where the weights are based on the relative values (or operating income) of the businesses in which the subject entity operates.

    v.   Levering the beta estimate using an appropriate debt-to-equity ratio for the subject entity.

You need to use a proxy beta when the subject business is a division, reporting unit, or closely held business.

The most widely used techniques for estimating beta generally use historical data over a sample or look-back period and assume that the future will be sufficiently similar to this past period to justify extrapolation of betas calculated using historical data.

For a publicly traded stock, you can estimate beta via regression (ordinary least squares (OLS) regression), regressing the excess returns on the individual security $(R_i - R_f)$ against the excess returns on the market $(R_m - R_f)$ during the look-back period. Formula 5.1 shows the regression formula.

Formula 5.1

$$\left(R_i - R_f\right) = \alpha + \beta \times \left(R_m - R_f\right) + \varepsilon$$

Where:

R_i	=	Historical return for publicly traded stock, i
R_f	=	Risk-free rate
α	=	Regression constant
β	=	Estimated beta based on historical data over the look-back period
R_m	=	Historical return on market portfolio, m
ε	=	Regression error term

The resulting slope of the best-fit line is the beta estimate. In Exhibit 5.3 a "scatterplot" graph of Starbucks Corporation's excess returns and the S&P 500 excess returns are shown over the 60-month period January 2012–December 2016. The dashed trend line is defined by the equation y=mx+b, where "b" is the y-intercept, and "m" is the slope. The slope of the dashed trend line (0.7964) is the beta of Starbucks Corporation for the 60-month period ending December 31, 2016.

Exhibit 5.3: Starbucks Corp. Excess Returns versus S&P 500 Index Excess Returns Scatterplot
January 2012–December 2016

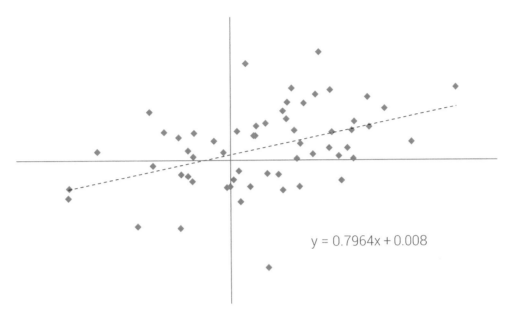

$$y = 0.7964x + 0.008$$

Source of underlying data: (i) Standard & Poor's *Capital IQ* database (ii) Morningstar *Direct* database. Used with permission. All rights reserved. Betas calculated over the time period January 2012–December 2016 using excess total returns over 30-day U.S. Treasury Bills. Calculations performed by Duff & Phelps, LLC.

We use excess returns in all of our beta computations.[5.4] Some valuation analysts and other financial data services calculate betas using total returns for the subject security and for the market returns instead of excess returns. Other valuation analysts calculate returns for the subject security and for the market simply using changes in price and ignoring dividend returns.

Comparisons of beta estimates using excess returns or total returns show that, as a practical matter, it generally makes little difference in the aggregate. However, if one uses only changes in price and ignores dividend return, it may make a difference, at least for a stock whose returns are predominantly comprised of dividends.

Because beta is an expected sensitivity, any estimation using historical methods is subject to error. The analyst can gauge the quality of the beta by examining various statistics resulting from the regression used to estimate the beta. Two important statistics are:

- ***t-statistic:*** Indicates if the beta estimate is statistically different from zero, and is an indication of how useful the regression results are in estimating the relationship between the returns of the stock and the returns of the market. For example, a regression to calculate a beta using 60 months of data has 59 degrees of freedom, and needs to have a t-statistic of ± 1.67 (two-tailed test) for the beta to be "statistically different from 0" at a 90% confidence level.[5.5]

[5.4]   *SBBI* beta calculations also used excess returns. For example, see *2013 SBBI Valuation Yearbook*: 72.

[5.5]   t-stat critical values *change* depending on the degrees of freedom and the confidence level. In the case of beta estimates using simple regression techniques, the degrees of freedom will be the number of periods minus 1. t-stat tables are available in almost any statistics book, and can also be looked up using Microsoft *Excel*'s TINV function (TINV assumes a two-tailed test, which is the proper test in this case).

- **Standard error of estimate:** Standard deviation of the estimate of the beta made by the sample used in the regression. This gives an indication of how close the estimated beta is to the "true" beta. For example, if Company ABC has a beta of 1.5 with standard error of 0.2, there is an approximate 68% probability that Company ABC's "true" beta falls between 1.3 (1.5 − 0.2) and 1.7 (1.5 + 0.2), and an approximate 95.5% chance that the company's "true" beta falls between 1.1 (1.5 − 0.4) and 1.9 (1.5 + 0.4).

In Exhibit 5.4, high standard error beta estimates are compared to low standard error beta estimates. Microsoft Corporation and Mannkind Corporation's beta estimates have an average standard error of 0.05 and 0.22, respectively, over the 60-month period January 2012–December 2016. The stability of Microsoft's beta (lower standard error) compared to the instability of Mannkind's beta (higher standard error) is apparent. Betas can (and do) change over time, but lack of stability may indicate that the beta is not of high statistical quality.

The concept that examining the beta estimate's standard error "gives an indication of how close the estimated beta is to the 'true' beta" can be illustrated by simple inspection of Exhibit 5.4 and asking the following questions: First, how confident would you be of claiming that Microsoft's "true" beta is around 1.0? Second, would you be *more* confident or *less* confident about making a similar claim about where Mannkind's "true" beta probably falls? The likely answer for many valuation analysts would be that Microsoft's estimated beta's *stability* over the 60-month period gives them more confidence in it than they might have in Mannkind's estimated betas, which are relatively unstable over the 60-month period.

Exhibit 5.4: 60-month Rolling Betas
High Standard Error Beta Estimate versus Low Standard Error Beta Estimates
January 2012–December 2016

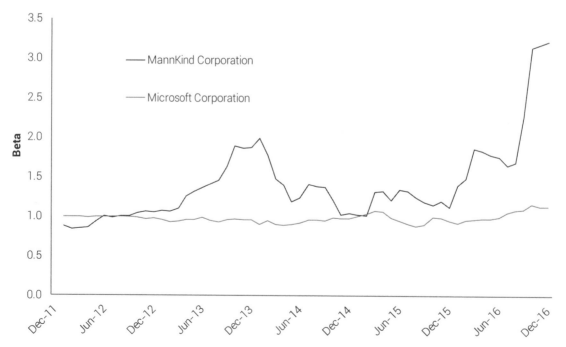

Also, the analyst must be cautious of beta estimates using smaller public companies where there is no active market, as their betas tend to be underestimated using OLS beta estimates and by reference sources. The sum beta method of estimating betas helps correct for the tendency for OLS methods to underestimate betas. We discuss the use of the sum beta method of estimating beta later in this chapter. Further, the *greater* the sample of beta estimates drawn from guideline public companies of similar size as the subject business you use as the basis for the beta estimate of the subject business, generally the *better* the accuracy because the standard error of estimate is reduced.

Differences in Estimation of Equity Betas

Note that significant differences can exist among beta estimates for the same stock published by different financial reporting services. One of the implications of this is that a valuation analyst should try to use betas for guideline companies used in a valuation from the *same source*. While we recommend that valuation analysts calculate their own beta estimates, if you are *not* calculating beta yourself, and if the betas for all of the selected guideline companies are not available from a single source, the best solution probably may be to use the source providing betas for the *greatest* number of guideline companies, and not use betas from other sources for the others. This helps to avoid "an apples-and-oranges" mixture of betas calculated using different methodologies.

Differences in the beta measurement derive primarily from choices within four variables:

1. The length of the time period over which the historical returns are measured (i.e., the length of the look-back period)

2. The periodicity (frequency) of return measurement within that time period (e.g., weekly versus monthly, etc.)

3. The risk-free rate above which the excess returns are measured

4. The choice of which index to use as a market proxy

The length of time period over which the historical returns are measured can have significant impact on the beta estimate. If a fundamental change in the business environment in which an individual company (or even an industry) operates occurs, the valuation analyst should consider whether using historical data from *before* the change should be included in the overall analysis.

A simple example of this concept is provided in Exhibit 5.5. In Exhibit 5.5, a rolling 60-month beta is shown for the Financials sector over the time period January 2005–December 2016, a period which includes the 2008 Financial Crisis. Clearly something fundamentally changed in the Financials sector post-crisis (see area of heightened beta values in the middle of the graph in Exhibit 5.5). In mid- 2014 the heightened beta values of the Financial sector returned to the lower values similar to those seen in pre-crisis, likely primarily due to the months most deeply affected by the 2008 Financial Crises dropping out of the 60-month rolling beta calculation.

An analyst assessing Financial sector betas as of, say, December 31, 2016 has to decide if the information embedded in the post-crisis returns through mid-2014 is still pertinent. If not, then the valuation analyst should consider shortening the lookback period over which the beta is calculated to exclude the post-crisis returns information.

Exhibit 5.5: 60-month Rolling Beta of Financial Sector
January 2006–December 2016

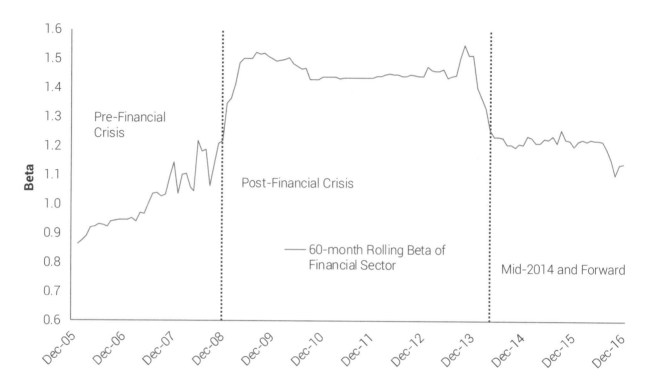

Source of underlying data: (i) Standard & Poor's *Capital IQ* database (ii) Morningstar's *Direct* database. The financials sector is represented by the S&P Composite 1500 Financials Index. The S&P Composite 1500 Financial Index® are comprised of members of the GICS® financial sector. Used with permission. All rights reserved. Calculations by Duff & Phelps, LLC.

The overall goal is to look for the best beta estimate, reflecting the expected risk of the guideline companies, and ideally derived using the *same* data sets, methodologies, and time periods.

Tendency Toward Market or Industry Average

One technique used by Bloomberg and *Value Line* for adjusting historical betas weights the historical beta estimate by approximately two-thirds, and the market beta of 1.0 by approximately one-third. This adjustment is sometimes referred to as the "Blume" adjustment, or the "one third/two thirds" adjustment.[5.6] This is a *mechanical* "one size fits all" adjustment that has the net effect of adjusting historical betas that are *less* than 1.0 *upward*, and adjusting historical betas that are *greater* than 1.0 *downward*. The adjustment is said to create a "forward" (or prospective) estimated beta because this adjustment is based on the assumption that betas tend to move toward the

---

[5.6]   Blume, M.E., "On the Assessment of Risk", *Journal of Finance*, Vol. 26, 1971, pp.1–10. This adjustment is sometimes referred to as the "Blume" adjustment, or the "one third/two thirds" adjustment. The equation for this adjustment is $Beta_{adjusted} = 0.371 + 0.635 Beta_{historical}$.

market's beta (1.0) over time. It does not indicate that any adjustment to the data used in calculating the historical beta estimate was made.

Another technique for adjusting beta estimates is a more sophisticated technique called *Vasicek shrinkage*.[5.7] The general idea is that betas with the highest statistical standard errors are the least reliable estimates and are, therefore, adjusted toward the market, peer group, or industry average *more* than are betas with lower standard errors.[5.8] The Vasicek shrinkage technique is not a "one size fits all" technique like the Blume adjustment, and also offers the flexibility to adjusting to the market, peer group, or industry average.

Whether betas tend to move toward market averages or industry averages over time is an issue open to debate, although it seems more intuitive that companies in say, the pharmaceuticals industry, will become more like the average *pharmaceutical* company over time, rather than look more like the average company in *any* industry. In 2010's *Global GT LP and Global GT LTD v. Golden Telecom, Inc.*, the Delaware Court of Chancery wrote that "... the historic beta is considered to have a fair amount of predictive power, and to be a reliable proxy for unobservable forward-looking betas ...there is support for the notion that more extreme betas tend to revert to the *industry mean* (emphasis added) over time". Furthermore, the Court noted that "... no reliable literature or evidence was presented to show that the beta of a telecom company like Golden, which operates in a risky market, will revert to 1.0".[5.9]

Lag effect

For all but the largest companies, the prices of individual stocks tend to react in part to movements in the overall market with a lag. The smaller the company, generally the greater the lag in the price reaction. This does not necessarily imply that the market itself is wholly inefficient, although the market for some stocks *is* more efficient than for other stocks. Large-cap companies tend to be followed by more analysts and are owned by more institutional investors than are small-cap companies. Therefore, large-cap companies tend to react more quickly to changes in the economy or changes in the business (e.g., introduction of a new product, signing of a new major contract) nearly instantaneously, while smaller companies' stocks tend to react at a slower rate.

Because of the lag in all but the largest companies' sensitivity to movements in the overall market, traditional OLS betas tend to understate systematic risk. A *sum beta* consists of a multiple regression of a stock's current month's excess returns over the 30-day T-bill rate on the market's *current* month's excess returns and on the market's *previous* month's excess returns, and then a summing of the resulting coefficients. This helps to capture more fully the lagged effect of co-movement in a company's returns with returns on the market (market or systematic risk). Exhibit 5.6 includes a sampling of OLS and sum betas for companies across the size spectrum as of December 2016.

[5.7] The formula was first suggested by Oldrich A. Vasicek, "A Note on Using Cross-Sectional Information in Bayesian Estimation of Security Betas", *Journal of Finance* (1973).

[5.8] This was the adjustment used in the *Ibbotson Beta Book*, where this adjusted beta was labeled *Ibbotson Beta*. The *Ibbotson Beta Book* and the individual beta "tear" sheets previously available on the Morningstar website are no longer published.

[5.9] *Global GT LP v. Golden Telecom, Inc.*, 993 A.2d 497 (Del. Ch. 2010); aff'd, 11 A.3d 214 (Del 2010).

Exhibit 5.6: Comparison of OLS Betas and Sum Betas for Companies of Varying Size Market Capitalization as of December 2016

Company	Market Capitalization (in $millions)	OLS Beta	Sum Beta	Difference
Merck & Co., Inc.	162,312.686	0.77	0.77	0.00
CVS Health Corporation	84,152.715	0.84	0.86	0.02
Anthem, Inc.	37,874.107	0.63	0.72	0.09
Celanese Corporation	11,275.568	1.25	1.41	0.16
Steven Madden, Ltd.	2,167.334	0.54	0.79	0.25
MTS Systems Corporation	945.472	1.57	1.84	0.26
Handy & Harman Ltd.	312.751	1.63	2.09	0.46
Commercial Vehicle Group, Inc	167.831	1.05	1.39	0.34

Source of underlying data: (i) Standard & Poor's *Capital IQ* database (ii) Morningstar *Direct* database. Used with permission. All rights reserved. Betas are estimated from monthly return data in excess of the 30-day U.S. Treasury bill total return, January 2012–December 2016. The S&P 500 Index was used as the market benchmark. Calculations performed by Duff & Phelps, LLC.

In Exhibit 5.6, the *larger* the company, the *smaller* the difference between the OLS beta and the sum beta tend to be, and the *smaller* the company, the *greater* the difference between the OLS beta and the sum beta tend to be.[5.10] The research suggests that this understatement of systematic risk by the traditional beta measurements accounts in part, but certainly not totally, for the fact that small-cap companies achieve excess returns over their apparent CAPM-required returns (where the market equity risk premium is adjusted for beta).

The formula for the sum beta is:

Formula 5.2

$$\left(R_n - R_{f,n}\right) = \alpha + \beta_n \times \left(R_{m,n} - R_{f,n}\right) + \beta_{n-1} \times \left(R_{m,n-1} - R_{f,n-1}\right) + \varepsilon$$

$$Sum\,Beta\ = \beta_n + \beta_{n-1}$$

[5.10] Exceptions to this pattern can be found, of course, but this is the general trend in the overall population of companies.

Where:

R_n	=	Return on individual security in current month
$R_{f,n}$	=	Risk-free rate in current month
α	=	Regression constant
β_n	=	Estimated market coefficient based on sensitivity to excess returns on market portfolio in current month
R_m	=	Historical return on market portfolio
$(R_{m,n} - R_{f,n})$	=	Excess return on the market portfolio in the current month
β_{n-1}	=	Estimated lagged market coefficient based on sensitivity to excess returns on market-portfolio last month
$(R_{m,n-1} - R_{f,n-1})$	=	Excess return on market portfolio last month
ε	=	Regression error term

Sum betas for individual stocks can be calculated using a spreadsheet such as Microsoft *Excel* and historical return data, which is available from several sources (e.g., Standard & Poor's *Capital IQ*). Some analysts prefer to calculate their own sum betas for a peer group of public companies (which they use as a proxy for the beta of their subject private business in the context of CAPM) and thus make a smaller adjustment for the size effect. The theory is that the sum beta helps correct for the larger size effect that is principally due to a misspecification of beta when using traditional OLS betas for smaller companies. It should be noted that sum beta estimates may at times be statistically "noisy". When estimating a proxy beta using any look back method, valuation analysts should always be cautious when dealing with a small number of guideline companies.

Full-Information Beta

Ideally, one would like to have a sampling of betas from many "pure play" guideline public companies when estimating a proxy beta. "Pure play" companies are companies with say, at least 75% of revenue from a single Standard Industrial Classification (SIC) code. In some industries the *largest* participants may be conglomerates for which participation in the given industry is a *small* part of their overall revenues. In a strictly pure-play analysis, these companies would be *excluded*, even though they may be the dominant participant in the industry. The full-information beta approach enables the *inclusion* of these companies' participation in the industry in the beta calculation.[5.11]

The full-information beta methodology is based on the premise that a business can be thought of as a portfolio of assets. The full-information methodology is designed to capture the impact that the individual segments have upon the overall business beta. After identifying all companies having segment sales in an industry, the analyst calculates a beta estimate of those companies. The analyst then runs a multiple regression with betas as the dependent variables (applying a weight to each beta based on its relative market capitalization to the industry market capitalization) and sales

---

[5.11] Paul D. Kaplan, and James D. Peterson. "Full-Information Industry Betas", *Financial Management*, Summer 1998.

of the segments of each of the companies in the industry as the independent variable. That is, one is measuring the relative impact on the betas of companies in an industry based on the relative contributed (as measured typically by sales) each company has within the industry.

Applying market capitalization weights in the process tends to reduce the beta estimates because large capitalization companies on the average have lower betas than smaller companies. Measuring the impact on betas using segment sales data may present a problem in that the market weights profits, not sales. This procedure may over-weight the relative importance of business segments having high sales and low profits.

Industry Risk Premia

Industry risk premia (RP_i) in the *2017 Valuation Handbook – U.S. Guide to Cost of Capital* are full-information betas that have been adjusted so that they can be added as a simple "up or down" adjustment in the build-up method.[5.12] The need for an industry risk adjustment within the context of the build-up method can be demonstrated simply by comparing the modified CAPM formula to the build-up formula.

The modified CAPM formula is:

Formula 5.3

$$k_e = R_f + \beta \times (RP_m) + RP_s$$

And the build-up formula is:

Formula 5.4

$$k_e = R_f + RP_m + RP_s + RP_i$$

Where:

$k_{e,i}$	=	Expected rate of return on security i
R_f	=	Risk-free rate of return
β	=	Beta
RP_m	=	Equity risk premium (market risk)
RP_s	=	Size premium
RP_i	=	Industry risk premium

[5.12] Industry Risk Premia were previously published in Table 3-5, "Industry Premia Estimates" in the *Morningstar/Ibbotson SBBI Valuation Yearbook*. In the *Valuation Handbook – U.S. Guide to Cost of Capital* these premia are still called "industry risk premia", but the nomenclature used within equations for this term is changed from "*IRP*" to "*RP$_i$*".

There are several common elements in the two equations. Both equations include a risk-free rate (R_f), an equity risk premium or market premium (RP_m), a size premium (RP_s), and (if the analyst deems it necessary) an additional adjustment for company-specific risk (RP_c). But, while the CAPM equation *includes* a beta (β), the build-up equation does *not*. This is where the industry risk premium comes in – the industry risk premium (RP_i) introduces a measure of beta risk into the build-up equation so that it more closely approximates the CAPM.

The *2017 Valuation Handbook – U.S. Guide to Cost of Capital* provides industry risk premia (RP_i) in Appendix 3a "Industry Risk Premium (RP_i)". The industries for which industry risk premia are calculated are based on Standard Industrial Classification (SIC) codes. Each company's contribution to the adjustment shown is based on a full-information beta with each company's contribution to the full-information beta based on the segment sales reported in the company's 10-K for that SIC code.[5.13]

The analyst can download the list of companies included in the full-information beta calculation for each industry (and thus the industry risk premium), and can inspect the 10-Ks filed with the Securities and Exchange Commission for the companies included.[5.14] The descriptions of the companies included in the 10-K filings may provide the analyst with additional support for the similarities of the subject company to the companies (and business segments of companies) included in the full-information beta calculations. The segment information in the 10-K will also show the proportionate contribution to earnings, which may be very different from the proportionate contribution to revenue. While we use revenues because they are always positive numbers, in theory one should rely on segment profitability because stock returns are a function of profit, not revenue, and use of revenue segmenting may result in overweighting the low-profit segment.

The formula used to calculate industry risk premium (RP_i) is as follows:

Formula 5.5

$$RP_i = (FIB \times RP_m) - RP_m$$

Where:

RP_i	=	Industry risk premium
FIB	=	Full-information beta for the industry
RP_m	=	ERP estimate used to calculate RP_i

[5.13] Consistent with past *SBBI Valuation Yearbooks*.
[5.14] To view the full list of companies, download the Industry Risk Premia Company List Report at www.DuffandPhelps.com/CostofCapital.

Appendix 3a displays the following data:

- SIC code

- SIC code description

- The number of companies included in the full-information beta calculation for each industry

- Full-information beta for each SIC code as of December 2016

- Three industry risk premia calculated, using different ERP estimates:[5.15]

  Long-term, "historical" (i.e., realized) ERP: As of the end of 2016, the long-horizon historical equity risk premium was 6.94%.[5.16]

  Long-term "supply-side" ERP: As of the end of 2016, the long-horizon supply-side equity risk premium was 5.97%.[5.17]

  Duff & Phelps Recommended ERP: As of the end of 2016, the Duff & Phelps recommended ERP is 5.5% (developed in conjunction with a "normalized" long-term risk-free rate of 3.5%).[5.18]

The industry risk premia previously published in Table 3-5 of the *SBBI Valuation Yearbook* were full-information betas converted to industry risk premia using only the long-term "historical" ERP in Formula 5.5. Appendix 3a provides industry risk premia calculated using the long-term "historical" ERP in the first column of industry risk premia (these industry risk premia are equivalent to the ones previously published in Table 3-5 of the former *SBBI Valuation Yearbook*).

In recognition that valuation analysts may use different ERP estimates, we have pre-calculated industry risk premia using two additional ERP estimates: (i) the long-term "supply-side" ERP, and (ii) the Duff & Phelps Recommended ERP.

For example, if you select SIC 281(Industrial Inorganic Chemicals), the full-information beta equals 1.04. Using the three ERP estimates, the following displays the calculation of the pre-calculated industry risk premia:

[5.15] The industry risk premia *previously* published in Table 3-5 of the Morningstar/Ibbotson *SBBI Valuation Yearbook* were full-information betas converted to industry risk premia using only the "historical" long-term equity risk premium.

[5.16] Calculated as the average annual return of the S&P 500 total return index minus the average annual return of the SBBI long-term (20-year) government bond income return series over the 1926–2016 time period. The long-horizon historical equity risk premium was previously published on the "back page" of the Morningstar/Ibbotson *SBBI Valuation Yearbook* (discontinued).

[5.17] The supply-side equity risk premium was also previously published on the "back page" of the Morningstar/Ibbotson *SBBI Valuation Yearbook* (discontinued).

[5.18] To learn more about cost of capital issues, and to ensure that you are using the most recent Duff & Phelps Recommended ERP, visit www.duffandphelps.com/CostofCapital.

Using the long-term "historical" ERP:

$$RP_i = (FIB \times RP_m) - RP_m$$
$$0.29\% = (1.04 \times 6.94\%) - 6.94\% \text{ (difference due to rounding)}$$

Using the long-term "supply-side" ERP:

$$RP_i = (FIB \times RP_m) - RP_m$$
$$0.25\% = (1.04 \times 5.97\%) - 5.97\% \text{ (difference due to rounding)}$$

Using the Duff & Phelps Recommended ERP:

$$RP_i = (FIB \times RP_m) - RP_m$$
$$0.23\% = (1.04 \times 5.50\%) - 5.50\% \text{ (difference due to rounding)}$$

If you have concluded on a different ERP from what is shown, a custom industry risk premium can be calculated in conjunction with Formula 5.5 . For example, if you have concluded that the future long-term ERP is 5.0%, then the custom industry risk premium for a full-information beta of 1.04 is:

$$RP_i = (FIB \times RP_m) - RP_m$$
$$0.20\% = (1.04 \times 5.00\%) - 5.00\%$$

Alternatively, if you have calculated your own custom peer group beta, you can use Formula 5.5 to calculate a custom industry risk premium. For example, say you have calculated a peer group beta of 0.87, and that you are using the supply-side ERP, then the custom industry risk premium would be calculated as:

$$RP_i = (Peer\,Group\,Beta \times RP_m) - RP_m$$
$$-0.78\% = (0.87 \times 5.97\%) - 5.97\%$$

The industry risk premia (RP_i) can then be added to the build-up method as a simple up-or-down adjustment for "beta" risk:

$$k_e = R_f + RP_m + RP_s + RP_i$$

NOTE: *Industry risk premia are a measure of "beta" risk. Industry risk premium should not be used within the context of the CAPM or any other method of cost of capital estimation that already has a beta, because by doing so you will be double-counting beta risk.*

Full-Information Beta Methodology

The methodology used to calculate the full information betas (and thus the industry risk premia) in Appendix 3a is nearly identical with how they were calculated in the former SBBI.[5.19] For example, the same database and data was used (Standard & Poor's *Research Insight*). The 3,502 U.S. companies included in the analysis had to have revenues of at least $100,000 in the most recent fiscal year, and have a market cap of at least $10,000 in the most recent month. The companies had to have an OLS beta greater than 0.0 and less than 5.0, and any resulting full information betas that were less than 0.0 or greater than or equal to 3.0 were eliminated.

However, there are also differences with the *2017 Valuation Handbook – U.S. Guide to Cost of Capital's* methodology for calculating industry risk premia compared to the former *SBBI Valuation Yearbook's* methodology.

For example, instead of requiring that each company had to have "36 months of [return] data in the previous 60 months", we required "36 months of *contiguous* return data, ending December 31, 2016". The goal of our more stringent criteria was to *lessen* the threshold for excluding companies that had "spotty" data, and thus *increase* the data quality of the overall set.

A second difference was in the minimum number of companies participating in an industry (by SIC code) required in order to be included in the full-information beta regression analysis. We required a minimum of 10 participants in each industry; the former *SBBI* required 5 participants. The goal of this more stringent requirement was to eliminate SICs that have few participant companies, and are prone to high volatility from period to period.

[5.19] The full-information betas published in the *2017 Valuation Handbook – U.S. Guide to Cost of Capital* (and in the former *SBBI Valuation Yearbook*) are based on an article by Paul D. Kaplan and James D. Peterson: "Full-Information Industry Betas", *Financial Management*, Summer 1998.

Debt Betas

The risk of debt capital can be measured by the beta of the debt capital (β_d). In cases where the debt capital is publicly traded, the β_d can be measured in a manner identical to measuring the beta of equity. For publicly traded debt, a regression of returns provides an estimate of β_d.

The general formula for estimating the beta for debt (e.g., traded bonds) is:[5.20]

Formula 5.6

$$R_d = \alpha + \beta_d \times \left(R_m - R_f \left(1 - t \right) \right) + \varepsilon$$

Where:

R_d	=	Rate of return on subject debt (e.g., bond) capital
α	=	Regression constant
β_d	=	Estimated beta for debt capital based on historical data
R_m	=	Historical rate of return on the "market"
t	=	Income tax rate
ε	=	Regression error term

That estimate indicates how the market views the riskiness of the debt as the rate of return on the stock market changes (i.e., as riskiness of equity changes).

The risk implied by debt beta is a function of the amount of debt in the capital structure; the variability of earnings before interest, taxes, depreciation, and amortization (EBITDA); the level and variability of EBITDA/sales; and so on. These are fundamental risks that the interest (and principal) will or can be paid when due.

Betas of debt generally correlate with credit ratings. While there is no data source that we know of that publishes debt betas for individual debt issuances at this time, Appendix 3b, "Debt Betas", (top panel) displays debt betas by credit rating as of year-end 2016. An analyst needs to estimate an approximate credit rating (synthetic credit rating) for the business debt that is not rated by Moody's, Standard & Poor's, or Fitch (discussed in Chapter 1 in in the section entitled "Estimating the Cost of Debt Capital"). The observed betas by debt rating can be used in conjunction with the equity beta unlevering and levering formulas which require debt beta estimates.

In Appendix 3b (bottom panel), the 60-month rolling average debt beta of Barclays U.S. credit grade indices (investment grade and non-investment grade) are plotted over the time horizon December 2008–December 2016. Intuitively, the debt betas of non-investment grade credit ratings are consistently larger (implying greater systematic risk) than debt betas of investment grade credit ratings.

[5.20] Simon Benninga, *Financial Modeling* 2nd ed. (Cambridge, MA: MIT Press, 2000): 414.

Unlevering and Levering Equity Betas

Published and calculated betas for publicly traded stocks typically reflect the capital structure of each respective company at market values. These betas are sometimes referred to as *levered betas*, that is, betas reflecting the leverage in the company's capital structure.

Levered betas incorporate two risk factors that bear on systematic risk: business (or operating) risk and financial (or capital structure) risk. Removing the effect of financial leverage (i.e., unlevering the beta) leaves the effect of business risk only. The unlevered beta is often called an asset beta. Asset beta is the beta that would be expected were the company financed only with equity capital. When a firm's beta estimate is measured based on observed historical total returns (as most beta estimates are), its measurement necessarily includes volatility related to the company's financial risk. In particular, the equity of companies with higher levels of debt is riskier than the equity of companies with less leverage (all else being equal).

If the leverage of the division, reporting unit, or closely held company subject to valuation differs significantly from the leverage of the guideline public companies selected for analysis, or if the debt levels of the guideline public companies differ significantly from one another, it typically is desirable to remove the effect that leverage has on the betas before using them as a proxy to estimate the beta of the subject company.

Various authors have proposed alternative methodologies for unlevering and levering betas. These methodologies are generally functions of the risk of realizing the tax savings resulting from the tax deductions resulting from the interest expense of the debt component of the capital structure.

For example, if the guideline public company is losing money, has tax-loss carry-forwards from prior periods, or is marginally profitable, the tax savings from current interest payments will not be recognized in the current period; in essence, the cost of debt is greater by the loss or deferral of the income tax savings. This risk is captured both in the levered equity beta observed in the market and by the observed debt beta.

The debt beta captures the sensitivity recognized by the market to the risk of the debt as business conditions improve or deteriorate. The greater the debt beta, the more the market recognizes that the debt is sharing risk with the equity. If there were no assumed risk sharing, then the observed debt beta would be zero.

In Chapter 10 in the section entitled "Overview of the Methodology and Assumptions Used to Unlever Risk Premia" we discuss how we unlever the reported risk premia. That formula incorporates a debt beta.

Key Things to Remember about Betas and the Industry Risk Premia

- An equity beta is a measure of the sensitivity of the movement in returns on a particular stock to movements in returns on some measure of the market. As such, beta scales market or systematic risk. In cost of capital estimation, beta is used as a modifier to the general equity risk premium in using the CAPM.

- There are many variations on the way betas are estimated by different sources of published betas and by valuation analysts. Thus, a beta for a stock estimated by one source may be very different from a beta estimated for the same stock by another source.

- Betas are an important element in estimating the cost of equity capital. The process of estimating beta requires considerable diligence, effort, and judgment on the part of the analyst.

- Industry risk premia are used to have the build-up method more closely approximate the CAPM.

- Industry risk premia are valid only to the extent that the subject company's risk characteristics are similar to the weighted average of the companies that make up the industry for the SIC code.

- Industry risk premia in the *2017 Valuation Handbook – U.S. Guide to Cost of Capital* are full-information betas that have been adjusted so that they can be added as a simple "up or down" adjustment in the build-up method. Industry risk premium should not be used within the context of the CAPM or any other method of cost of capital estimation that already has a beta, because by doing so you will be double-counting beta risk.

Chapter 6

Basic Building Blocks of the Cost of Equity Capital – Company-specific Risk Premia

Introduction

In this chapter we turn our attention to the last of the basic building blocks of the cost of equity capital, the company-specific risk premium (C-SRP). Identifying and quantifying a C-SRP is one of the most controversial and elusive areas of business valuation.[6.1] It is an adjustment common to both the build-up methods and CAPM.

The term company-specific risk is used to describe a variety of adjustments to the cost of equity capital. In a purely theoretical sense, the models used to estimate cost of capital generally assume that risks that can be "diversified away" are not compensable; this risk is properly called "unsystematic risk". Having said that, part of the problem that has been created in practice is that the intended meaning of the term "company-specific risk" can vary from person to person. For example, is a "company-specific" risk adjustment necessary in a hypothetical case in which the guideline public companies and the subject company are identical in every way? Many analysts would contend that the answer to this question is "no" – although this answer probably has very little to do with the theoretical definition of company-specific risk. What is probably intended is that no further adjustment may be necessary because the peer group in this hypothetical case (being identical to the subject) acts as a perfect proxy.

Different adjustments to the cost of equity capital are made in practice under the heading C-SRP. Among the adjustments labeled C-SRP are:

- **Adjustments for differences in risk:** Adjustments to cost of equity capital estimates derived from a sample of guideline public companies to account for differences in risk between a subject company that is not public (e.g., a closely held business, a division, or a reporting unit) and the guideline public companies.

- **Adjustments for Risk in Net Cash Flows and Biased Projections:** Adjustments to cost of equity capital estimates to account for risk in the net cash flows and biased projections provided for use in the valuation process.

- **Adjustments for Other Risk Factors:** For example, adjustments to cost of equity capital estimates to account for risks accepted by investors that may not hold diversified portfolios of investments.

[6.1]   This chapter is excerpted in part from Shannon P. Pratt and Roger J. Grabowski, *Cost of Capital: Applications and Examples* 5th ed. (Hoboken, NJ: John Wiley & Sons, 2014)

This inconsistent use of the term C-SRP has led to considerable confusion in addition to its subjective nature. Former Chancellor Strine of the Delaware Court of Chancery stated the court's perspective on this issue:

> *Much more heretical to CAPM, however, the build-up method typically incorporates heavy dollops of what is called "company-specific risk", the very sort of unsystematic risk that the CAPM believes is not rewarded by the capital markets and should not be considered in calculating a cost of capital. The calculation of a company-specific risk is highly subjective and often is justified as a way of taking into account competitive and other factors that endanger the subject company's ability to achieve its projected cash flows. In other words, it is often a back-door method of reducing estimated cash flows rather than adjusting them directly....*[6.2]

Others add a note of caution to an indiscriminant use of a C-SRP. They point out that many of the characteristics that are often cited as reasons for the addition of a company-specific risk adjustment are "the very attributes that generally define small companies", and therefore adding a company-specific risk may be double counting risks already embodied in the size premium adjustment.[6.3]

Adjustments for Differences in Risk

Let us begin by addressing C-SRP in the context of an adjustment to cost of equity capital estimates derived from a sample of guideline public companies to account for differences in risk between a subject company that is not public and the guideline public companies. Many analysts are able to express qualitative reasons for C-SRPs, but rarely provide data relating those qualitative factors to actual measurements in expected return. This lack of empirical support adds to the skepticism about the use of company-specific risk factors.

To help focus the discussion, let us assume that we are estimating the cost of equity capital by using the modified version of the CAPM. Many of the same issues surface if one were using a build-up method including an industry risk premium, which is a special type of beta modified for use within the build-up model.

Beta Suffers from Measurement Error

When an analyst is estimating the cost of equity capital for a public company, the analyst can directly observe the market's pricing of risk specific for the subject company. Every change in the public company's stock price signals the market's assessment of the company's risk relative to its expected returns given the current economic environment.

The beta estimate for the public company derived from a look-back method is an estimate of that specific company's measure of market risk (i.e., a company-specific risk factor). The public

---

[6.2] *Delaware Open MRI Radiology Associates, P.A. v. Howard B. Kessler et al.* (Court of Chancery of State of Delaware, Cons C.A. No. 27–N).

[6.3] Ted Israel, "The Generous Helping of Company-Specific Risk that May Already be Included in Your Size Premia", *Business Valuation Update*, Vol. 17, No. 6, June 2011.

company is generally its own best guideline public company; the market is confronted with pricing that company's own characteristics.

Some analysts may jump to the conclusion that this beta estimate captures the entirety of the market's pricing of risk. But, beta estimates suffer from measurement error.

For example, while beta is a forward-looking risk concept, the most commonly employed method for estimating beta uses regression analysis of *prior* period excess returns. During that prior period (look-back period, typically 60 months), some of the observed excess returns of the subject company stock are explained by the market risk expected by and priced by the market.

But some of the excess returns of the subject company stock resulted from unexpected events that the market could never have anticipated at the beginning of the look-back period, so they could never have been included in the pricing of risk by the market at the beginning of the look-back period, nor likely ever can be expected to be repeated in the future.

Therefore, in estimating the beta using a regression of excess returns over a look-back period, one can only estimate expected *future* beta with error. Valuation analysts are accustomed to adjusting subject company historical financial statements for non-recurring events that are unrepresentative of the expected future financial results, but it is quite another thing to separate the relationship between expected returns that are likely to continue and be priced by the market from observations during the look-back period that one would consider non-recurring.

One may find that estimating betas using observed returns over a look-back period at times provides an illogical estimate of beta. For example, for new public companies, there may not be enough data over the look-back period to produce a meaningful estimate of beta. Or, the subject company may have experienced a significant change during the look-back period that fundamentally changes the company (for example, a merger during the look-back period, or a downward assessment by the market in the future prospects of the business leading to a downward repricing of the company's stock price during the look-back period), and thus changes the way the market views the risk of the company. In such circumstances, if one needs to estimate a beta for a publicly traded company or provide a double check to the result provided by a regression, a commonly used method is to compare the beta estimate for the subject company to the median of the beta estimates of a sampling of guideline public companies (bottom-up approach). But the risks of the subject public company often do not match those of the median of the guideline public companies and may not even really match the risks of any of the guideline public companies used to develop the median.

Proxy Beta Estimates

When an analyst is estimating the cost of capital for a division or reporting unit of a public company or a closely held company, no direct observations of returns are available. This means that there are two major tasks confronting the analyst:

1. Develop a proxy beta estimate by matching the subject company's business risk characteristics to guideline public companies to understand how the market might price the market risk of the subject business if it in fact were public (i.e., what would be its beta estimate were it public).

2. Estimating additional risk factors priced by the market.

Let us address the task of matching business risk characteristics to develop a beta or proxy beta estimate. In the ideal situation, the analyst could identify "pure play" public companies (companies whose revenues are predominantly derived from a single business line such that their business risks would mirror those of the subject company). The beta estimates would likely fall into a tight range, and a measure of central tendency would likely be a good proxy beta estimate.

But finding pure play companies with the mix of business risks that *exactly* match those of the subject business can be difficult, if not impossible. Often the matching is done in terms of the SIC codes of the guideline public companies, but their actual mix of businesses can be quite different. Accordingly, the valuation analyst then must assess whether factors affecting a company's competitive position in the industry or its unique characteristics would cause investors to view that company's risk *differently* from the average risk characteristics of the guideline public companies to which it is being compared.

Alternatively, if there were sufficient pure play guideline public companies that had nearly the same risk characteristics as the subject company such that the market pricing of those risk characteristics could be observed, there would be no need to adjust for market risks that differ from those of the pure play guideline public companies.

However, there are often insufficient or even no pure play guideline public companies with risk characteristics matching those of the subject company. In those cases the analyst must look to how the market prices various risk characteristics to develop an estimate of the market risk. That is, if a sample of guideline public companies provides a poor or even meaningless estimate of the market risk that the subject company would experience were it public, it is appropriate to add or subtract a C-SRP to mimic the hypothetical pricing of the subject company's market risk.

The proper estimation of beta should help the valuation analysts better match the risk and return as priced by the market as observed in the guideline public companies with the appropriate risk and return for the subject division, reporting unit, or closely held business.[6.4]

[6.4] See Pratt and Grabowsk, op.cit.: Chapter 11, "Beta: Differing Definitions and Estimates," and Chapter 12, "Unlevering and Levering Equity Betas".

Even for a company whose stock is publicly traded, one may need to develop a "proxy" beta by relying on inputs derived from a sampling of guideline public companies, because the beta estimate derived from the publicly traded stock itself may result in an unreliable estimate of the cost of equity capital.

Beta alone is not the only risk factor priced by the market (i.e., beta is not the only systematic risk factor).[6.5] So even having a direct estimate of beta stills leaves the analyst with the task of estimating other risk factors that are priced by the market.

Adjustments for Risk in Net Cash Flows and Biased Projections

Another commonly cited reason for a C-SRP is that the projections provided do not adequately capture the range of possible outcomes or there is bias, management or otherwise, reflected in the projections. According to the generally held theory surrounding using the CAPM, for example, as the basis for estimating the cost of capital, bad outcomes should be reflected in the various possible cash flows, with the expected cash flows reflecting both the more likely scenarios but also scenarios that will have a negative impact on net cash flows.

For example, assume that the subject business is an agribusiness operation, located in South Texas, which "dry farms" (relying only on rainfall) its tillable acres to grow cotton and milo crops. The pure play guideline public companies raise many more crop types; their holdings are geographically dispersed around the United States and Mexico, and, generally, they both dry farm and irrigate their crops, depending on the crops.

The underlying variability of the net cash flows of the South Texas agribusiness operation is much greater than that of the guideline public companies, year after year. Adding downside scenarios for negative events would serve to lower the mean of the distribution and better approximate the expected cash flows. Some would argue that there is greater inherent variability in the net cash flows that can be addressed through a variety of scenarios. While it may be appropriate to adjust for this greater risk by including a C-SRP in the cost of capital, a discussion of this issue is beyond the scope of this text.

The analyst must show how the distribution of possible net cash flows may differ in order to justify adding a C-SRP in estimating the cost of capital. The following discussion on bias in projections provides some guidance in this regard.

[6.5]   See Pratt and Grabowski, op.cit.: Chapter 13, "Criticism of CAPM and Beta versus Other Risk Measures".

Bias in Projections

Adding a company-specific risk premium to the discount rate is a commonly applied method to account for the overly optimistic forecasts.[6.6]

In the context of the modified CAPM we get the following:

$$k_e = R_f + \beta \times (RP_m) + RP_s \pm RP_c$$

Where:

k_e	=	Cost of equity capital
R_f	=	Risk-free rate
β	=	Beta
RP_m	=	Equity risk premium (also referred as ERP)
RP_s	=	Size premium
RP_c	=	Company-specific risk premium (C-SRP) due to biased cash flow estimates

This commonly applied method of adjusting the discount rate does have a conceptual basis in cases where the range of possible cash flows included in the estimate of the expected cash flows omits a scenario that results in a permanent downside impact on the range of cash flows.

One of the first tasks is to test the forecasts to determine if forecasts prepared in prior periods have consistently been biased. Even in circumstances where the forecasts have been prepared in the normal course of business, it is not unusual for the forecast to be aspirational, rather than expectational. That is, they represent management's belief as to what can be accomplished if they succeed in carrying out their business plan. Businesspeople by their nature are optimists. Rarely are the projections tempered for possible downside outcomes.[6.7] One common method to assess for aspirational bias is to compare a series of historical forecasts to the actual subsequent performance and derive a "batting average" of sorts to consider in adjusting the current projections.

Expected cash flows should account for downside scenarios, of course, but sometimes the forecasts prepared by management and used in a valuation can be somewhat rosy in that they may reflect successful outcomes only, rather than reflecting the range of possible outcomes (both good and bad) that should be included in estimated expected cash flows.

Forecasts may also be biased high because they do not take into account the possibility that cash flows will in fact stop because of a possible downside risk that simply causes the business to stop operating (e.g., loss of the contract with the sole customer of the business). If such risks exist, it is common to simply increase the discount rate to account for the risk (i.e., add a C-SRP).

[6.6] On the other hand, projections prepared in conjunction with some litigation disputes are often biased downward.

[6.7] Richard Ruback, "Downsides and DCF: Valuing Biased Cash Flow Forecasts", *Journal of Applied Corporate Finance* 23(2) (Spring 2011): 8–17.

The risks to a company's cash flow may also *change* (in addition to ceasing operations) over time. For example, a parts supplier to an automobile manufacturer may have a contract to supply parts for an existing model of automobile (the contract likely specifies pricing but does not guarantee quantity). The risks to the cash flows during the current life of that model are significantly less than the risks to the cash flows after the current model life ends. As planning for a replacement model moves ahead before the current model life ends, the parts supplier will need to bid against other parts suppliers for that new model. This may indicate that the discount rate should change (be increased) after the current model life ends. There is a risk that net cash flows will be reduced if the parts supplier is unsuccessful in gaining a contract on a subsequent model. Possible net cash flows will likely not end if the parts supplier is not awarded a subsequent contract, as there will be replacement parts to be supplied, but the risks to the net cash flows have increased significantly.

Some Possible Courses of Action

It is often difficult for the analyst to obtain from management a distribution of possible outcomes, though the analyst should investigate the impacts on possible net cash flow outcomes if various events may take place. For example, what would be the impact on net cash flow if the subject company's largest customer reduced its purchases by, say, 25%? Or what would be the impact on net cash flows if competition caused the subject company to reduce its pricing by 10%? In this way, even if the analyst chooses to adjust the discount rate for the biased cash flow estimates rather than adjust the distribution of net cash flows, the analyst can test the impact of the addition to the cost of capital by hypothesizing a reasonable distribution of net cash flows. The key is to gain an understanding of the business risks through the interviews with management and through careful analysis of the income statements. Assessing risks initiates the valuation process and continues throughout.

Furthermore, developing a probability analysis of possible net cash flows with one of the outcomes predicting net cash flows equal to zero can assist the analyst in understanding the relative magnitude of his or her subjective assessment of the risk represented by the addition of a C-SRP. We recommend that an analyst closely examine the probability of a zero net cash flow scenario in the distribution of possible net cash flows as a check on any C-SRP added to the discount rate to account for the chance that the subject company may be forced to shut down because of a company-specific risk factor.[6.8]

Adjustments for Other Risk Factors

The cost of equity capital under pure CAPM is based on a company's systematic (or market) risk as measured by beta and not on any other risk factors. Investors are much less diversified than expected, even after consideration of the efforts of investment advisors urging them to diversify. Further, many do not hold the market portfolio as predicted by the pure CAPM. Based on these findings, it is reasonable to assume that investor rates of return expectations are influenced by risk factors beyond beta. The market has been found to price other risk factors beyond beta.

[6.8] See also Atuna Saha and Burton G. Malkiel, "Valuation of Cash Flows with Time-Varying Cessation Risk", *Journal of Business Valuation and Economic Loss Analysis* 7(1) (2012): Article 3.

One such risk factor, firm size, is priced by the market as a risk factor (or as a proxy for other risk factors). While the pure CAPM would classify the size premium as unsystematic, we have found the size premium to be systematic. There is a predictable pattern of how the market prices this risk. Another company-specific risk issue is distress.[6.9]

Matching Fundamental Risk and Return

Valuation analysts typically have quantified the relationship between risk and expected return only by measuring risk in terms of beta and size. While company size is a risk factor in and of itself, Grabowski and King, original co-authors of what is now the Risk Premium Report's Risk Study, were interested in understanding whether the stock market recognized risk as measured by fundamental or accounting information.

The measures of company risk derived from accounting information may also be called fundamental or accounting measures of company risk to distinguish them from a stock–market–based measure of equity risk such as beta. The Risk Premium Report Risk Study uses three alternative measures of company risk, the first of which is a measure of profitability; the latter two are measures of earnings variability):

1. Operating margin (the lower the operating margin, the greater the risk)

2. Coefficient of variation in operating margin (the greater the coefficient of variation in operating margin, the greater the risk)

3. Coefficient of variation in return on equity (the greater the coefficient of variation in return on equity, the greater the risk)

Exhibit 6.1: Operating Margin (i.e., "profitability") and Variability of Earnings versus Risk

Operating Margin   Risk   Variability of Earnings   Risk

[6.9] See Pratt and Grabowski, op.cit.: Chapter 17, "Distressed Businesses".

The Risk Premium Report's Risk Study documents the relationship between equity returns and the three fundamental risk measures. Exhibit 6.2 displays the observed relationships for the three risk measures and the risk premia. By each measure of risk covered in the Risk Study, the result is a clear relationship between risk and historical equity returns. The portfolios of companies with higher risk have yielded higher rates of return. How to use the Risk Study is discussed in detail in Chapter 10.

In the first graph (upper left), one sees that as the average operating profit margin decreases (more risk), the returns increase. In the second graph (upper right), one sees that as the variability in the operating income increases (more risk), the returns increase. In the third graph (bottom), one sees that as the variability in the return on equity (ROE) increases (more risk), the returns increase.

Exhibit 6.2: Risk Premium Report-Risk Study

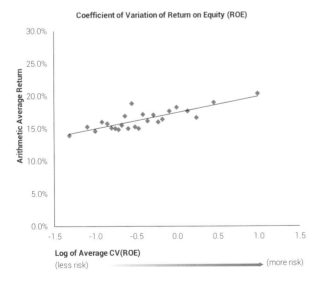

Source of underlying data: Derived from data from the Center for Research in Security Prices. © 2017 CRSP, Center for Research in Security Prices, University of Chicago Booth School of Business. Used with permission. All rights reserved. Calculations by Duff & Phelps, LLC.

A variety of academic studies have examined the relationship between financial statement data and various aspects of business risk.[6.10] Research has shown that measures of earnings volatility can be useful in explaining credit ratings, predicting bankruptcy, and explaining the CAPM beta.

Cost to Cure

One way to account for company-specific risk is to estimate the *cost to cure* that risk. For example, if a company-specific risk is reliant on a key salesperson for a large amount of sales, then the cost of buying life insurance sufficient to reimburse the company for the possible loss of that person due to death is one measure of the cost to cure that risk. Another company-specific risk that may be accounted for by estimating the cost to cure is potential environmental cleanup costs. One can estimate the probability-weighted costs of remediation, given the possibility that a cleanup will be required and the possible timing of a required cleanup.

Applying an adjustment for company-specific risk using the cost to cure is completely consistent with capital market theories, as these are adjustments to the expected cash flows.

Key Things to Remember about Company-specific Risk Premia

- Quantifying company-specific risk is one of the most controversial and elusive areas of business valuation.

- Valuation analysts who have written on company-specific risk reinforce the fact that the courts disapprove of unsubstantiated company-specific risk premia. Those authors advise valuation professionals that courts do not find the company-specific risk premium to be reliable, and therefore caution them to avoid utilizing *unsubstantiated* premia when offering expert testimony.

- Many of the characteristics that are often cited as reasons for the addition of a company-specific risk adjustment are the very attributes that generally define small companies, and therefore adding a company-specific risk may be double counting risks already embodied in the size premium adjustment. Thus the company-specific risk premium should be used judiciously.

- The company-specific risk premium is an adjustment that can be made by the valuation analyst to the data contained in the *Valuation Handbook – U.S. Guide to Cost of Capital*.

[6.10] A survey of the academic research can be found in Gerald White, Ashwinpaul Sondi, and Haim Fried, *The Analysis and Use of Financial Statements*, 3rd ed. (Hoboken, NJ: John Wiley & Sons, 2003): Chapter 18.

Chapter 7

The CRSP Deciles Size Premia Studies and the Risk Premium Report Studies – A Comparison

The CRSP Deciles Size Premia Study had been published in the Morningstar/Ibbotson *SBBI Valuation Yearbook* since 1999; the Risk Premium Report's Size Study was first published in 1996.

Both studies are now published in the *2017 Valuation Handbook – U.S. Guide to Cost of Capital*.

The CRSP Deciles Size Premia Study and the Risk Premium Report's Size Study examine the relationship between size and return, and both find that size and return are negatively correlated (as size *decreases*, return tend to *increase*, and vice versa).

However, there are significant differences between the two data sets used in the studies that the valuation analysts should be aware of. In this chapter, we first provide a brief history of both studies, and then discuss the two studies' similarities and differences.

History of the CRSP Deciles Size Premia Studies[7.1]

In 1976, Professor Roger Ibbotson co-published a seminal study analyzing the long-term returns of the principal asset classes in the United States economy. His findings documented the relationship between risk and return and quantified the ability to reduce risk through diversification. The study of long-term returns on asset classes also led to the development of such relevant cost of capital concepts as the equity risk premium and the size premium. The original 1976 study was extended into the *Ibbotson Stocks, Bonds, Bills, and Inflation (SBBI) Classic Yearbook* which has been published for more than 30 years.

In 2016, Morningstar announced that it would no longer publish the *Ibbotson Stocks, Bonds, Bills, and Inflation (SBBI) Classic Yearbook*. Starting with the 2016 edition, the *Ibbotson Stocks, Bonds, Bills, and Inflation (SBBI) Classic Yearbook* is now produced by Duff & Phelps, and published by John Wiley & Sons (Hoboken, NJ). The book has a slightly different name: the *Stocks, Bonds, Bills, and Inflation (SBBI) Yearbook* (or simply, "*SBBI Yearbook*").[7.2]

A separate version of the original *SBBI Classic* publication was developed based upon a series of workshops Ibbotson Associates held on the cost of capital. This publication was called the *Ibbotson SBBI Valuation Yearbook*, and was published from 1999–2013. In late 2013, Morningstar (which acquired Ibbotson Associates in 2006) announced that it will no longer publish the *Ibbotson SBBI*

[7.1] This section is excerpted from the former *2013 SBBI Valuation Yearbook*, Introduction, page 1 (Morningstar, Chicago, 2013). The *SBBI Valuation Yearbook* is discontinued.

[7.2] The *2016 SBBI Yearbook* (with data through December 31, 2015) was the first edition of the former *SBBI "Classic" Yearbook* produced by Duff & Phelps and published by John Wiley & Sons. The *2017 SBBI Yearbook* (with data through December 31, 2016) became available in March 2017. The *SBBI Yearbook* provides historical "performance" data of U.S. asset classes and does not provide extensive valuation data or methodology.

Valuation Yearbook and other valuation publications and products.

The size premia and industry risk premia data previously published in the *Ibbotson SBBI Valuation Yearbook* are now published in the *Valuation Handbook – U.S. Guide to Cost of Capital* (updated annually, since 2014).

History of the Risk Premium Report Studies

In 1990, Roger Grabowski began closely studying the relationship between company size and stock returns.[7.3] Grabowski's early research focused on size as measured by market capitalization, but quickly advanced to two additional areas of inquiry: whether stock returns were predicted by (i) measures of size other than market capitalization, and also whether stock returns were predicted by (ii) fundamental risk measures based on accounting data. To investigate these questions, in 1992 Grabowski, working with a colleague, contracted with CRSP to build a database that combined stock prices, number of shares, and dividend data from the CRSP database with accounting and other fundamental accounting data from the Standard & Poor's *Compustat* database.

What they found was that as size *decreases*, or risk *increases* (as measured by fundamental accounting data), returns tend to *increase* (and vice versa). Thereafter, Grabowski and his colleague published a series of articles reporting their findings, culminating with a seminal 1996 article and a subsequent article in 1999 which together serve as the foundation of the Risk Premium Report Size and Risk Studies.[7.4, 7.5]

Data Sources

The methodologies and data used to form the CRSP Decile portfolios are similar to the methodologies and data used to form the Risk Premium Report portfolios. However, there are significant differences, including:

- Financial service companies are *not* excluded from the CRSP Decile portfolios.

- The CRSP Deciles do *not* exclude "high-financial-risk" companies from the portfolios used to create its size premia.

- The CRSP Deciles portfolios are rebalanced quarterly, rather than annually.

- The CRSP Deciles portfolios' returns are market-cap-weighted, rather than equal-weighted.

[7.3] Roger Grabowski, FASA, is a managing director in the Duff & Phelps Chicago office and part of the firm's Valuation Advisory Service practice. He is also co-author with Dr. Shannon Pratt of *Cost of Capital: Applications and Examples*, 5th Edition (John Wiley & Sons, 2014).

[7.4] Roger J. Grabowski and David King, "New Evidence on Size Effects and Equity Returns", *Business Valuation Review* (September 1996, revised March 2000), & Roger J. Grabowski and David King, "New Evidence on Equity Returns and Company Risk", *Business Valuation Review* (September 1999, revised March 2000). The research began when King and Roger Grabowski were at Price Waterhouse, predecessor firm to PricewaterhouseCoopers.

[7.5] The *Risk Premium Report* studies were published as the *Standard & Poor's Corporate Value Consulting Risk Premium Report* for reports from 2002 to 2004 and as the *PricewaterhouseCoopers Risk Premium Reports* and *Price Waterhouse Risk Premium Reports* for years before 2002.

CRSP Deciles Size Premia[7.6]

The data sources and methodologies used in the former *Ibbotson SBBI Valuation Yearbook* are the *same* as those used for the CRSP Deciles Size Premia in the *2017 Valuation Handbook – U.S. Guide to Cost of Capital*. The portfolios used in the CRSP Deciles Size Premia are created by CRSP.

CRSP has refined the methodology of creating size-based portfolios and has applied this methodology to the entire universe of NYSE/NYSE MKT/NASDAQ-listed securities going back to 1926. The New York Stock Exchange universe excludes:

- Closed-end mutual funds

- Preferred stocks

- Real estate investment trusts

- Foreign stocks

- American Depositary Receipts

- Unit investment trusts

- Americus Trusts

All companies on the NYSE are ranked by the combined market capitalization of their eligible equity securities. The companies are then split into 10 equally populated groups, or deciles. Eligible companies traded on the NYSE MKT (the former AMEX) and the Nasdaq National Market (NASDAQ) are then assigned to the appropriate deciles according to their capitalization in relation to the NYSE breakpoints.

The portfolios are rebalanced quarterly, using closing prices for the last trading day of March, June, September, and December. Securities added during the quarter are assigned to the appropriate portfolio when two consecutive month-end prices are available. If the final NYSE price of a security that becomes delisted is a month-end price, then that month's return is included in the quarterly return of the security's portfolio. When a month-end NYSE price is missing, the month-end value of the security is derived from merger terms, quotations on regional exchanges, and other sources. If a month-end value still is not determined, the last available daily price is used. Base security returns are monthly holding period returns. All distributions are added to the month-end prices, and appropriate price adjustments are made to account for stock splits and dividends. The return on a portfolio for one month is calculated as the weighted average of the returns for its individual stocks.

[7.6] This section is excerpted from the former *2013 SBBI Valuation Yearbook*, page 85 (Morningstar, Chicago, 2013). The *SBBI Valuation Yearbook* is discontinued.

Annual portfolio returns are calculated by compounding the monthly portfolio returns.[7.7]

Risk Premium Report Portfolios

The universe of companies used to perform the analyses presented in the Risk Premium Report is comprised of those companies that are found in *both* the CRSP and Standard & Poor's *Compustat* database. The following types of firms are then excluded:

- American depositary receipts (ADRs)

- Non-operating holding companies

- Financial service companies (SIC code 6)

- Unseasoned companies

- High-financial-risk companies[7.8]

Financial service companies (those companies in finance, insurance, or real estate) are *excluded* because some of the financial data used is difficult to apply to companies in the financial sector (e.g., "sales" at a commercial bank). In addition, financial service companies tend to support a much higher ratio of debt to equity than do other industries, and so including them in with non-financial firms may be an "apples to oranges" comparison that could lead to improperly skewed results.

Valuation analysts should *not* use the Risk Premium's Size Study or Risk Study results to estimate cost of equity capital for a financial services company. Financial services companies include those companies in finance, insurance, or real estate (i.e., companies with an SIC Code that begins with "6").

The small-cap universe may consist of a disproportionate number of start-up companies and recent initial public offerings. These "unseasoned" companies may be inherently riskier than companies with a track record of viable performance. For this reason (for each year since 1963), the universe of companies is screened to exclude companies with any of the following characteristics:

- Companies lacking 5 years of publicly traded price history.

- Companies with sales below $1 million in any of the previous five fiscal years.

[7.7] According to CRSP, in 2016 CRSP "performed a comprehensive check and found changes to index levels back to 1977. Almost all of the changes are due to CRSP adding factor[s] to adjust price values for distribution codes 5663 & 5773. These edits were made in the 201612 iteration...". These edits are detailed in the CRSP document "STOCK & INDEX RELEASE NOTES, December 2016 Annual UPDATE" (available at: http://www.crsp.com/files/images/release_notes/mdaz_201612_annual.pdf). This review of the database caused small changes in the returns over the 1926–2015 period (calculated using the December 31, 2015 data cut) compared to the returns over the 1926–2015 period (calculated using the December 31, 2016 data cut). These changes were not material: the largest/smallest change to the geometric mean return of CRSP standard market-cap-weighted deciles 1–10 over this period was 0.0044%/-0.0146%; the average/median change was -0.0007%/0.0003%.

[7.8] This division of the universe of companies between seasoned and low financial risk companies and unseasoned and high financial risk companies is consistent with the valuation theory that matching risk characteristics provides more accurate valuation results. See for example Friedrich Sommer, Christian Rose and Arnt Wöhrmann, "Negative Value Indicators in Relative Valuation – An Empirical Perspective," *Journal of Business Valuation and Economic Loss Analysis* 2014 Vol. 9(1): 23–54.

- Companies with a negative 5-year-average EBITDA (earnings before interest, taxes, depreciation and amortization) for the previous five fiscal years.

- Companies not listed on one of the major U.S. stock exchanges (NYSE, NYSE MKT[7.9] or NASDAQ).

The Risk Premium Report portfolios exclude "high-financial-risk" companies from the portfolios used to create its premia, but provide further analysis of these companies *separately* in its High-Financial-Risk study. These companies have any of the following characteristics:

- Companies that Standard & Poor's has identified in the *Compustat* database as in bankruptcy or in liquidation.

- Companies with a "5-year average net income available to common equity" less than zero for the previous five years (either in absolute terms or as a percentage of the book value of common equity).

- Companies with "5-year-average operating income" (net sales minus cost of goods sold; selling, general, and administrative expenses; and depreciation) less than zero for the previous five years (either in absolute terms or as a percentage of net sales).

- Companies with negative book value of equity at any one of the company's previous five fiscal year-ends.

- Companies with a debt-to-total capital ratio exceeding 80%, (debt is measured in book value terms, and total capital is measured as book value of debt plus market value of equity).

After these exclusions, the next step is to determine portfolio breakpoints for each of the eight size measures' 25 portfolios. Similar to the CRSP Decile portfolios, the upper and lower "boundaries" of each portfolio (i.e., breakpoints) for the Risk Premium Report portfolios are represented by the largest and smallest New York Stock Exchange (NYSE) company, respectively, in each of the 25 portfolios.

For example, to determine the breakpoints for the 25 portfolios ranked by "Total Assets", all of the companies in the base set that are traded on the NYSE are ranked from largest (in total assets) to smallest (in total assets), and then divided into 25 equally populated portfolios. Portfolio 1 made up of the largest companies and Portfolio 25 made up of the smallest companies.

Once portfolio breakpoints are determined, companies from the NYSE MKT (formerly the AMEX) universe and the NASDAQ universe are added to the appropriate portfolio, depending on their size with respect to the breakpoints (this is also very similar to what is done to form the CRSP Decile portfolios). Since NYSE MKT and NASDAQ companies are generally small relative to NYSE companies, their addition to the data set produces portfolios that are more heavily populated at the "small cap" end of the spectrum. The portfolios are rebalanced annually.

[7.9]   The "NYSE MKT" is the former American Stock Exchange, or AMEX.

The equity returns for each of the 25 portfolios returns are calculated using an equal-weighted average of the companies in the portfolio, and these returns are then used to calculate the size premia and risk premia (and other useful information and statistics) for each.

Equal-weighted rather than market-cap-weighted returns are used in the formation of the Risk Premium Report portfolios because one could consider the former type of returns most relevant to the analyst applying the results of the Risk Premium Report in practice.

Specifically, the Risk Premium Report analysis of equal-weighted returns mimics the approach of the valuation analyst matching his or her subject company with a group of guideline firms based on a set of risk characteristics that includes size and financial risk. As the returns of each firm in the group of guideline firms are potentially equally informative about the effect of matching (risk) characteristics on the cost of equity, the equal-weighted realized returns of the peer group are likely more relevant to the analysis than are the market-cap-weighted returns. Using equal-weighted returns is also analogous to analysts using equal-weighted valuation multiples in the market approach to valuation.

Definitions of "Size"

Likely the most significant difference between the two studies is that the CRSP Deciles Size Premia measures "size" solely by market value of equity ("market capitalization", or simply "market cap"), while the Risk Premium Report measures size by market capitalization, plus seven additional measures of size:

    i.   Market capitalization

    ii.   Book value of equity

    iii.   5-year average net income

    iv.   Market value of invested capital (MVIC)

    v.   Total assets

    vi.   5-year average EBITDA

    vii.   Sales

    viii. Number of employees

Time Period Examined

The CRSP Deciles Size Premia are calculated over the time horizon 1926–present year. The Risk Premium Report size and risk premia are calculated over the time horizon 1963–present year.[7.10]

Generally, advocates of using the longest period for which returns are available argue that long-term returns are stable and that using shorter horizons would exclude events that could potentially re-occur. Advocates of using a shorter time horizon argue that some previous events are unlikely to re-occur, or that the relationship between stocks and bonds has changed in more recent years.

Number of Portfolios

The CRSP Deciles Size Premia have 10 portfolios (i.e., deciles) for which size premia are calculated. Decile 1 is comprised of the largest companies, and decile 10 is comprised of the smallest companies. Decile 10 is further split into 10a (and its upper and lower halves 10w and 10x) and 10b (and its upper and lower halves 10y and 10z).

The Risk Premium Report Size and Risk Studies have 25 portfolios. Portfolio 1 is comprised of the largest companies, and portfolio 25 is comprised of the smallest companies.

Portfolio Overlap

The CRSP Deciles Size Premia portfolios and size groupings *overlap*. The Risk Premium Report portfolios do *not* overlap. "Overlap" occurs when a subject company can properly be placed in *multiple* portfolios or size groupings, and can lead to significantly different cost of equity estimates.

For example, say Company ABC has an estimated market cap of no more than $10 million. A valuation analyst using the CRSP Deciles Size Premia exhibits can properly place Company ABC into *four* different size groupings: Micro-Cap, Decile 10, portfolio 10b, and portfolio 10z. In the *2017 Valuation Handbook – U.S. Guide to Cost of Capital*, these size grouping have size premia of 3.67%, 5.59%, 8.64%, and 11.63%, respectively. Choosing the appropriate size grouping is left to the valuation analyst.

A valuation analyst using the Risk Premium Report exhibits can properly place Company ABC into only a *single* market capitalization grouping. For example, Company ABC, with a market capitalization of $10 million, can be properly placed into portfolio 25 of Exhibit B-1 only, which has a smoothed size premium of 7.22%.

Some valuation analysts argue that size grouping "overlap" introduces a level of subjectivity that may lead to "goal-seeking" of cost equity capital estimates. For example, using the CRSP Deciles Size Premia cited in the previous example, the difference in Company ABC's cost of equity capital estimate could vary by as much as nearly 7.96%, depending on which size grouping the valuation

---

[7.10]   In the *2017 Valuation Handbook – U.S. Guide to Cost of Capital*, the *CRSP Decile* studies and *Risk Premium Report* studies examine the time periods 1926–2016 and 1963–2016, respectively.

professional decides to place the subject company into (Micro-Cap, Decile 10, portfolio 10b, or portfolio 10z).[7.11] Others argue that valuation analysts need this flexibility in order to "choose the size premium that is most statistically relevant for their application".[7.12]

Guideline Portfolio Method and Regression Equation Method

The CRSP Deciles Size Premia provide a *single* way to match their subject company's market capitalization with the appropriate size premium (which is, in essence, the "guideline portfolio" method).

The Risk Premium Report portfolios provide *two* ways to match the subject company's size (or risk) characteristics to the appropriate size (or risk) premium (the "guideline portfolio method" and the "regression equation method").

For more about matching the subject company's characteristics with the appropriate premium, please see Chapter 8, "CRSP Deciles Size Premia Examples" and Chapter 9 "Risk Premium Report Exhibit – General Information".

Risk Premia Over CAPM (Size Premia)

The CRSP Deciles Size Premia study and the Risk Premium Report's Size Study provide the traditional "risk premia over CAPM", commonly referred to as "size premia". Size premia represent the difference between historical (observed) excess return and the excess return predicted by the capital asset pricing model (CAPM). Size premia can be added to cost of capital estimation models as an adjustment for the additional risk of smaller companies relative to large companies.

Both the CRSP Deciles Size Premia and the Risk Premium Report are "beta-adjusted". A "beta-adjusted" size premium has been adjusted to remove the portion of excess return that is attributable to beta, leaving only the size effect's contribution to excess return. The size premia in both studies are calculated in essentially the same way – as the difference in historical portfolio excess returns (i.e., what *actually* happened), and the excess returns that CAPM would have *predicted*. Excess returns are defined here as portfolio returns over and above the risk-free asset's returns.

Exhibit 7.1 provides an overview of the CRSP deciles and size groupings in terms of relative size (by aggregate market capitalization) and number of companies as of December 31, 2016.

Decile 1 has 191 companies in it, and accounts for nearly two-thirds of aggregate market cap (66.12%). Decile 10 has 790 companies in it, and accounts for less than 1% of aggregate market cap (0.40%).

[7.11] The 7.96% that the cost of equity capital estimate could vary is the "high" size premium estimate (11.63%) minus the "low" size premium estimate (3.67%).

[7.12] Michael W. Barad, "Size Matters: How to Apply Size Premium Metrics When Size-Based Category Breakpoints Overlap", *The Value Examiner* (November/December 2009).

In Exhibit 7.2, the largest company in each of the CRSP (NYSE/NYSE MKT/NASDAQ) deciles and size groupings (by market capitalization) as of September 30, 2016.[7.13]

Exhibit 7.1: Aggregate Market Capitalization and Company Counts of the CRSP (NYSE/NYSE MKT/NASDAQ) Deciles and Size Groupings
December 31, 2016

Decile	Historic Average Percentage of Total Capitalization	Recent Number of Companies	Recent Decile Market Capitalization (in $thousands)	Recent Percentage of Total Capitalization
1-Largest	63.13%	191	15,290,475,300	66.12%
2	13.95%	200	3,010,671,018	13.02%
3	7.55%	202	1,609,575,618	6.96%
4	4.73%	221	1,010,851,810	4.37%
5	3.26%	227	677,120,067	2.93%
6	2.41%	259	541,037,999	2.34%
7	1.79%	283	384,129,198	1.66%
8	1.33%	361	297,164,943	1.28%
9	1.03%	487	212,609,644	0.92%
10-Smallest	0.82%	790	92,882,169	0.40%
Mid-Cap 3-5	15.54%	650	3,297,547,494	14.26%
Low-Cap 6-8	5.53%	903	1,222,332,139	5.29%
Micro-Cap 9-10	1.85%	1,277	305,491,813	1.32%

Source of underlying data: Calculated (or derived) based on data from CRSP © 2017 Center for Research in Security Prices (CRSP®), The University of Chicago Booth School of Business (2017). Calculations by Duff & Phelps, LLC.

[7.13] The CRSP deciles are re-constituted and rebalanced at the end of each calendar quarter (March, June, September, and December). These quarter-end portfolios are then followed for the subsequent three months. For example, the breakpoints in Exhibit 7.2 were a key input in defining the companies placed in each decile at the end of September 2016; these portfolio compositions were then used to calculate the October, November, and December 2016 returns associated with each decile.

Exhibit 7.2: Largest Company (by market capitalization) in CRSP (NYSE/NYSE MKT/NASDAQ) Deciles and Size Groupings
September 30, 2016

Decile	Company Name	Recent Market Capitalization (in $thousands)
1-Largest	Apple Inc.	609,163,498
2	Apache Corp.	24,233,747
3	Textron Inc.	10,711,194
4	C F Industries Holdings Inc.	5,676,716
5	Ellie Mae Inc.	3,512,913
6	Generac Holdings Inc.	2,390,899
7	Flagstar Bancorp Inc.	1,569,984
8	SEACOR Holdings Inc.	1,030,426
9	Kadant Inc.	567,843
10-Smallest	Pioneer Energy Services Corp.	262,891

Source of underlying data: CRSP databases © 2017 Center for Research in Security Prices (CRSP®), The University of Chicago Booth School of Business (2017).

In the following sections we provide an example of (i) calculating a CRSP Deciles Size Premium and (ii) a Risk Premium Report size premium, using example data from each of the two data sets.

Size Premium Calculation: CRSP Deciles Size Premia

In the *2017 Valuation Handbook – U.S. Guide to Cost of Capital*, the CRSP Deciles Size Premia are calculated over the years 1926–2016. The following statistics are calculated over this time period:

- The "historical" average annual long-term equity risk premium is 6.94%.

- The average annual risk-free rate is 5.02%.

- CRSP portfolio 10b average annual return equals 23.14%.

- CRSP portfolio 10b OLS beta equals 1.37.

The beta-adjusted size premium for CRSP portfolio 10b is calculated as follows:

10b Size Premium = actual excess return – excess return predicted by CAPM

Looking at Exhibit 7.3, the *actual* excess return of portfolio 10b is 18.12% (23.14% – 5.02%), and the excess return that CAPM *predicted* is 9.49% (1.37 x 6.94%) (difference due to rounding). The size premium for CRSP portfolio 10b is therefore 8.64%, which is "what actually happened" (18.12%) minus "what CAPM predicted" (9.49%) (difference due to rounding). This is what is meant when we say that the beta of smaller companies doesn't explain all of their returns. In this simple example, beta fell 8.64% short of explaining what actually happened.

Exhibit 7.3: CRSP (NYSE/NYSE MKT/NASDAQ) Deciles; Returns in Excess of CAPM (i.e., beta-adjusted Size Premium, as of December 31, 2016)

Size Grouping		OLS Beta	Arithmetic Mean	Return in Excess of Risk-free Rate (actual)	Return in Excess of Risk-free Rate (as predicted by CAPM)	Size Premium
Mid-Cap (3–5)		1.12	13.82%	8.80%	7.79%	1.02%
Low-Cap (6–8)		1.22	15.26%	10.24%	8.49%	1.75%
Micro-Cap (9–10)		1.35	18.04%	13.02%	9.35%	3.67%
Breakdown of Deciles 1–10						
1-Largest		0.92	11.05%	6.04%	6.38%	-0.35%
2		1.04	12.82%	7.81%	7.19%	0.61%
3		1.11	13.57%	8.55%	7.66%	0.89%
4		1.13	13.80%	8.78%	7.80%	0.98%
5		1.17	14.62%	9.60%	8.09%	1.51%
6		1.17	14.81%	9.79%	8.14%	1.66%
7		1.25	15.41%	10.39%	8.67%	1.72%
8		1.30	16.14%	11.12%	9.04%	2.08%
9		1.34	16.97%	11.96%	9.28%	2.68%
10-Smallest		1.39	20.27%	15.25%	9.66%	5.59%
Breakdown of 10th Decile						
10a		1.41	18.85%	13.84%	9.75%	4.09%
	10w	1.38	17.69%	12.67%	9.58%	3.10%
	10x	1.45	20.37%	15.36%	10.03%	5.33%
10b		1.37	23.14%	18.12%	9.49%	8.64%
	10y	1.42	22.07%	17.06%	9.85%	7.21%
	10z	1.28	25.54%	20.53%	8.90%	11.63%

Source of underlying data: Calculated (or derived) based on data from CRSP © 2017 Center for Research in Security Prices (CRSP®), The University of Chicago Booth School of Business (2017). Calculations by Duff & Phelps, LLC.

Size Premium Calculation: Risk Premium Report

In the *2017 Valuation Handbook – U.S. Guide to Cost of Capital*, the Risk Premium Report size studies are calculated over the years 1963–2016. The following statistics are calculated over this time period:

- The "historical" average annual long-term equity risk premium is 5.02%.

- The average annual risk-free rate is 6.46%.

- In Risk Premium Report Exhibit B-3 (25 portfolios sorted from largest companies to smallest companies by net income), portfolio 25 average annual return equals 21.44%.

- In Risk Premium Report Exhibit B-3, portfolio 25 has a sum beta of 1.31.

The beta-adjusted size premium for Risk Premium Report Exhibit B-3, portfolio 25, is calculated as follows:

Exhibit B-3, portfolio 25 Size Premium = actual excess return − excess return predicted by CAPM

The *actual* excess return of Exhibit B-3, portfolio 25 is 14.98% (21.44% − 6.46%), and the excess return that CAPM *predicted* is 6.60% (1.31 x 5.02%) (difference due to rounding). The (un-smoothed; see next section) size premium for Exhibit B-3 portfolio 25 is therefore 8.39%, which is "what actually happened" (14.98%) minus "what CAPM predicted" (6.60%) (difference due to rounding).

"Smoothed" Premia versus "Average" Premia

The CRSP Deciles Size Premia are not smoothed.

We recommend using the "smoothed" size premia (and risk premia) in the Risk Premium Report. Smoothing the premia essentially averages out the somewhat scattered nature of the raw average premia. The "smoothed" average risk premium is generally the more appropriate indicator for most of the portfolio groups. It should be noted, however, that at the largest-size and smallest-size ends of the range, the average historical risk premia may tend to jump off of the smoothed line, particularly for the portfolios ranked by size measures that incorporate market capitalization (Exhibits A-1 and A-4).

OLS Beta versus Sum Beta

The CRSP Deciles Size Premia use ordinary least square (OLS) betas to calculate the size premia shown in Appendix 3 (the size premia in Appendix 3 are the *same* size premia previously published on the *SBBI Valuation Yearbook*'s "back page" ("Key Variables in Estimating the Cost of Capital"). Sum beta equivalents to these OLS size premia estimates are available in Chapter 4, "Basic Building Blocks of the Cost of Equity Capital − Size Premium".

The Risk Premium Report uses "sum" betas in all calculations. Sum betas have been shown to be better predictors of smaller companies' expected returns. To learn more about sum betas, see Chapter 5, "Basic Building Blocks of the Cost of Equity Capital − Betas and Industry Risk Premia".

Risk Premia Over the Risk Free Rate

The Risk Premium Report exhibits also provides a second type of premia, "risk premia over the risk-free rate". Risk premia over the risk-free rate are provided in the Size Study's A exhibits, and in the Risk Study's D exhibits.

Risk premia over the risk-free rate in the Size Study's A exhibits and the Risk Study's D exhibits represent the overall difference between the historical (observed) return of equities over the risk-free rate, and are therefore a measure of risk in terms of the combined effect of *market* risk and *size* risk. These premia are simply added to the risk-free rate, within the context of the build-up method.

The CRSP Deciles Size Premia do not include "risk premia over the risk-free rate".

Unlevered Premia

The Risk Premium Report provides "levered" and "unlevered" size and risk premia. Unlevered premia are used to estimate cost of equity capital assuming a firm is financed 100% with equity and 0% debt.

The CRSP Deciles Size Premia do not include "unlevered" premia.

Risk Study

The Risk Premium Report includes the Risk Study in addition to the Size Study. The CRSP Deciles Size Premia include only a size study.

The Risk Study is an extension of the Size Study. The main difference between them is that while the Size Study analyzes the relationship between size and return, the Risk Study analyzes the relationship between fundamental risk measures (based on accounting data) and return. These are called "fundamental" measures of company risk to distinguish these risk measures from a stock market based measure of equity risk such as beta. As in the Size Study, 25 portfolios are created, but instead of being ranked by eight alternative measures of size as is done in the Size Study, the Risk Study portfolios are ranked by three fundamental risk measures:

- Five-year average operating income margin

- Coefficient of variation in operating income margin

- Coefficient of variation in return on book equity

The first statistic measures profitability and the other two statistics measure volatility of earnings. All have been shown to be predictors of equity returns. The Risk Study exhibits provide the valuation analyst with an additional method for estimating cost of equity capital.

Characteristics of Companies in Portfolios

The Risk Premium Report includes detailed information about the characteristics of the companies that comprise the portfolios used to create its premia, and provides the valuation analyst with a mechanism to further refine cost of equity estimates by gauging how "alike or different" the subject company is compared to the companies that make up the portfolios (see the section entitled "Comparative Risk Study" in Chapter 10).

The CRSP Deciles Size Premia Study provides some information about the characteristics of the companies that comprise the portfolios used to create the published size premia, but does not presently provide a mechanism for using this information to further refine cost of equity estimates.

Online Applications

The Risk Premium Report Study and CRSP Deciles Size Premia Study have online companion applications that automatically calculate levered and unlevered cost of equity estimates using both the build-up method and the CAPM, and then provides full summary output in both Microsoft *Word* and Microsoft *Excel* format.[7.14]

Exhibit 7.4 (next page) summarizes the similarities and differences between the Risk Premium Report Study and the CRSP Deciles Size Premia Study.

[7.14] Business Valuation Resources (BVR) and ValuSource have both developed online companion applications to the *2017 Valuation Handbook − U.S. Guide to Cost of Capital*. Both BVR's online version, the *"Risk Premium Toolkit"* (previously named the *"Risk Premium Calculator"*), and ValuSource's version, the *"Cost of Capital Analyzer"*, are designed to help the valuation analyst use the *2017 Valuation Handbook − U.S. Guide to Cost of Capital's* data as efficiently as possible (both the CRSP Deciles Size Premia Studies and the Risk Premium Report Studies data are included). Both versions automatically calculate and properly apply the ERP Adjustment to all methods of cost of equity capital methods available when using the Risk Premium Report exhibits. The online *"Risk Premium Toolkit"* is available from BVR at www.BVResources.com/DuffPhelps or by calling 1 (503) 291-7963 extension 2. The *"Cost of Capital Analyzer"* is available from ValuSource at www.valuationhandbook.com or by calling 1 (800) 825-8763.

Exhibit 7.4: Risk Premium Report Study and the CRSP Deciles Size Premia Study Comparison Table

	CRSP Deciles Size Premia Study	Risk Premium Report Study
Time horizon over which data is analyzed	1926–present year	1963–present year
Size study included	Yes	Yes
Size measures used	Market Cap	Market Cap + 7 alternative size measures
Premia over CAPM (i.e., size premia)	Yes	Yes
"Risk premia over the risk-free rate"	No	Yes
Unlevered premia (in addition to levered premia)	No	Yes
Risk Study (in addition to Size Study)	No	Yes
Risk measures used	NA	Operating Margin, CV Operating Margin, CV ROE
Can be used to estimate COE using build-up method	Yes	Yes
Can be used to estimate COE using CAPM model	Yes	Yes
Number of portfolios	10 Deciles + 10w, 10x, 10y, 10z	25
Regression formulas available for estimating "exact" interpolated premia "in between" portfolios, or for estimating premia for very small companies	No	Yes
Portfolio overlap*	Yes	No
Exclusion of financial companies	No	Yes
Exclusion of high-financial-risk companies	No	Yes
Analysis of high-financial-risk companies	NA	Yes
Specific information about the companies that comprise the portfolios	Yes	Yes
Mechanism to further refine cost of equity estimates by gauging how "alike or different" the subject company is when compared to the companies that make up the portfolios	No	Yes
Online *Risk Premium Toolkit* included	Yes	Yes

* Portfolio overlap refers to whether a subject company can be be properly placed in multiple size groupings.

Chapter 8
CRSP Deciles Size Premia Examples

The *2017 Valuation Handbook – U.S. Guide to Cost of Capital's* "CRSP Deciles Size Premia" are the same size premia that were previously published in the *SBBI Valuation Yearbook*. The CRSP Deciles Size Premia can be used to estimate the cost of equity capital using the build-up method and the capital asset pricing model (CAPM). In this chapter, examples for using the data properly are provided. For more information about the theoretical basis of the build-up and CAPM models, see Chapter 2, "Methods for Estimating the Cost of Equity Capital".

A size premium is necessary for both the build-up method and the CAPM when using the CRSP Deciles Size Premia data set to estimate the cost of equity capital. Examination of market evidence shows that within the context of CAPM, beta does not fully explain the difference between small company returns and large company returns. In other words, the *actual* (historical) excess return smaller companies earn tends to be greater than the excess return *predicted* by the CAPM for these companies. This "premium over CAPM" is commonly known as a "beta-adjusted size premium" or simply "size premium".

The size premia in both data sets (CRSP Deciles Size Premia exhibits and Risk Premium Report exhibits) in the *2017 Valuation Handbook – U.S. Guide to Cost of Capital* are "beta-adjusted". In other words, the portion of excess return that is not attributable to beta is controlled for, or *removed*, leaving only the size effect's contribution to excess return. These premia are appropriate for use in the CAPM, and in build-up methods that *do not otherwise already have a measure of size risk*.

Industry risk premia (RP_i) in the *2017 Valuation Handbook – U.S. Guide to Cost of Capital* are full-information betas that have been adjusted so that they can be added as a simple "up or down" adjustment when the build-up method is employed to estimate the cost of equity capital. Adding both a size premium and an industry risk premium to the build-up method is *not* double-counting. The size premium is "beta-adjusted", and the industry risk premium is the beta risk. These two premia are designed to account for two *different* types of risk. Industry risk premia are found in Appendix 3a.

Build-up Example

The build-up method is an additive model used for calculating the required rate of return on equity capital. As the name implies, successive "building blocks" are summed, each representing the additional risk inherent to investing in alternative assets. An example of this is the extra return (i.e., "premium"), that investors demand for investing in stocks versus investing in a riskless security. The build-up equation for use with the CRSP Deciles Size Premia exhibits is as follows:[8.1]

$$k_{e,i} = R_f + RP_m + RP_s + RP_i$$

[8.1] The *2017 Valuation Handbook – U.S. Guide to Cost of Capital* (this book) provides data and methodology that can be used to estimate cost of equity capital *prior* to any additional "company-specific" risk premia (RP_c) that may be deemed applicable by the individual valuation analyst.

Where:

$k_{e,i}$	=	Expected rate of return on security i (this is "cost of equity capital")
R_f	=	Risk-free rate as of the valuation date (typically a long-term U.S. government bond yield)
RP_m	=	General equity risk premium (i.e., "ERP") estimate for the "market"
RP_s	=	Risk premium for smaller size (i.e., "premium over CAPM", or "size premium")
RP_i	=	Industry risk premium

In the build-up method, we start with the risk-free rate (R_f), and then add the general equity risk premium or market premium (RP_m), a premium for small size (RP_s), and an industry risk premium (RP_i).[8.2]

All of the information to estimate cost of equity using the CRSP Deciles Size Premia data exhibits as of December 31, 2016 (the "data through" date of the *2017 Valuation Handbook – U.S. Guide to Cost of Capital*) can be found in the following two tables:

Appendix 3, "CRSP Deciles Size Premia: Key Variables"[8.3]

- R_f (risk-free rate)

- RP_m (equity risk premium)

- RP_s (size premium)

Appendix 3a, "Industry Risk Premia (RP_i)"[8.4]

- RP_i (industry risk premium)

Estimate the cost of equity capital for a company in SIC 36 (Electronic and Other Electrical Equipment and Components, Except Computer Equipment) with an estimated market cap of $300 million using the build-up equation:

$$k_{e,i} = R_f + RP_m + RP_s + RP_i$$

[8.2] The industry risk premium was referred to as "IRP" in equations in the former *SBBI Valuation Yearbook*. In the *2017 Valuation Handbook – U.S. Guide to Cost of Capital*, the industry risk premium is referred to as "RP_i" in equations. Other than that, the industry risk premia in the *2017 Valuation Handbook – U.S. Guide to Cost of Capital* are exactly the same concept as they were in the former *SBBI Valuation Yearbook* – an adjustment that inserts a measure of "beta" risk into the build-up equation to make it more comparable to the CAPM. For more information, see Chapter 5, "Basic Building Blocks of the Cost of Equity Capital – Betas and Industry Risk Premia".

[8.3] Appendix 3, "CRSP Deciles Size Premia Study: Key Variables" includes all of the data previously published on the *SBBI Valuation Yearbook's* "back page", which was entitled "Key Variables in Estimating the Cost of Capital".

[8.4] Appendix 3a, "Industry Risk Premia (RP_i)" is the equivalent of Table 3-5, "Industry Premia Estimates" in the former Morningstar/Ibbotson *SBBI Valuation Yearbook*.

Referring to Appendix 3, the risk-free rate (R_f) is the "Long-term (20-year) U.S. Treasury Coupon Bond Yield" (2.72%):

$$k_{e,i} = 2.72\% + RP_m + RP_s + RP_i$$

Referring again to Appendix 3, the equity risk premium (RP_m) is the "Long-horizon expected equity risk premium (historical)" (6.94%):

$$k_{e,i} = 2.72\% + 6.94\% + RP_s + RP_i$$

Referring again to Appendix 3, the size premium (RP_s) is the "Size Premium (Return in Excess of CAPM)". The estimated market cap of $300 million places the company in the Micro-Cap category, which has a size premium of 3.67%. The company's market cap of $300 million could also place it in Decile 9, which has a size premium of 2.68%. The choice of which size category the company more properly belongs in falls ultimately to the valuation analyst (and his or her intimate knowledge of the subject company). However, placing the company in the broader size category (Micro-Cap) is likely the more *conservative* estimate. The $300 million estimated market capitalization falls comfortably in the *middle* of the smallest and largest companies of the Micro-Cap size category ($2.516 million and $567.843 million, respectively), and $300 million falls closer to the *bottom* of the Decile 9 size category's range of smallest and largest companies ($263.715 million and $567.843 million, respectively).

In this example we will use the more conservative size premium of the broader Micro-Cap category, 3.67%:

$$k_{e,i} = 2.72\% + 6.94\% + 3.67\% + RP_i$$

Finally, referring to Appendix 3a, the industry risk premium (RP_i) is the "Industry Risk Premia (%) calculated using" either (i) the "Long-term *Historical* ERP", (ii) the Long-term Supply-Side ERP, or (iii) the Duff & Phelps Recommended ERP. We selected the "Long-horizon expected equity risk premium (historical)" as our market premium in this example (6.94%), and so the appropriate industry risk premium to select is the industry risk premium calculated using the long-term *historical* ERP.[8.5] For SIC 36, this is 1.94%. The cost of equity capital estimate for this company using the build-up method is 15.27%:

$$15.27\% = 2.72\% + 6.94\% + 3.67\% + 1.94\%$$

Alternatively, if you have calculated your own *custom* peer group beta you can calculate a custom industry risk premium. For example, if you have calculated a custom peer group beta of 1.15, and you are using the "historical" ERP, then the custom industry risk premium (RP_i) is:[8.6]

[8.5]   Alternatively, had we selected the "Long-horizon expected equity risk premium (*supply-side*)" as our market premium from Appendix 3, the appropriate industry risk premium from Appendix 3a would be the industry risk premium calculated using the long-term *supply-side* ERP.

[8.6]   See Formula 5.5 in Chapter 5, "Basic Building Blocks of the Cost of Equity Capital – Betas and Industry Risk Premia".

$$RP_i = (Peer\,Group\,Beta \times RP_m) - RP_m$$
$$1.04\% = (1.15 \times 6.94\%) - 6.94\%$$

NOTE: *Industry risk premia (RP_i) are a measure of "beta" risk. Industry risk premium should not be used within the context of the CAPM or any other method of cost of capital estimation that already has a beta, because by doing so you will be double-counting beta risk.*

CAPM Example

The capital asset pricing model (CAPM) is the most widely used method for estimating the cost of equity capital. For example, one survey found that while many firms use multiple methods of estimating the cost of equity capital, 75% of them use the CAPM.[8.7] Despite its criticisms, the CAPM has been one of the most widely used models for estimating the cost of equity capital for more than 30 years.

The CAPM equation for use with the CRSP Deciles Size Premia exhibits is as follows:[8.8]

$$k_{e,i} = R_f + (\beta \times RP_m) + RP_s$$

Where:

$k_{e,i}$	=	Expected rate of return on security i (this is "cost of equity capital")
R_f	=	Risk-free rate as of the valuation date (typically a long-term U.S. government bond yield)
β	=	A measure of market (i.e., systematic) risk of a stock; the sensitivity of changes in the returns (dividends plus price changes) of a stock relative to changes in the returns of a specific market benchmark or index.
RP_m	=	General equity risk premium (i.e., "ERP") estimate for the "market"
RP_s	=	Risk premium for smaller size (i.e., "premium over CAPM", or "size premium")

With CAPM, we start with the risk-free rate (R_f), and then add the equity risk premium (RP_m) multiplied by a beta (β), and then add a premium for size (RP_s).

All of the information to estimate cost of equity using the CRSP Deciles Size Premia exhibits as of December 31, 2016 (the "data through" date of this book) can be found in the following table (with the exception of beta):

[8.7] John R. Graham and Campbell R. Harvey, "The Theory and Practice of Corporate Finance," *Journal of Financial Economics* (May 2001): 187–243.

[8.8] The *2017 Valuation Handbook – U.S. Guide to Cost of Capital* provides data and methodology that can be used to estimate cost of equity capital *prior* to any additional "company-specific" risk premia (RP_c) that may be deemed applicable by the individual valuation analyst.

Appendix 3, "CRSP Deciles Size Premia Study: Key Variables"[8.9]

- R_f (risk-free rate)

- RP_m (equity risk premium)

- RP_s (size premium)

Estimate the cost of equity capital for a company in SIC 36 (Electronic and Other Electrical Equipment and Components, Except Computer Equipment) with a market cap of $300 million using the CAPM equation:

$$k_{e,i} = R_f + \left(\beta \times RP_m \right) + RP_s$$

Referring to Appendix 3, the risk-free rate (R_f) is the "Long-term (20-year) U.S. Treasury Coupon Bond Yield" (2.72%):

$$k_{e,i} = 2.72\% + \left(\beta \times RP_m \right) + RP_s$$

Referring again to Appendix 3, the equity risk premium (RP_m) is the "Long-horizon expected equity risk premium (historical)" (6.94%):

$$k_{e,i} = 2.72\% + \left(\beta \times 6.94\% \right) + RP_s$$

Referring again to Appendix 3, the size premium (RP_s) is the "Size Premium (Return in Excess of CAPM)". The estimated market cap of $300 million places the company in the Micro-Cap category, which has a size premium of 3.67%. The company's market cap of $300 million could also place it in Decile 9, which has a size premium of 2.68%. The choice of which size category the company more properly belongs in falls ultimately to the valuation analyst (and his or her intimate knowledge of the subject company). However, placing the company in the broader size category (Micro-Cap) is likely the more *conservative* estimate. The $300 million estimated market capitalization falls comfortably in the *middle* of the smallest and largest companies of the Micro-Cap size category ($2.516 million and $567.843 million, respectively), and $300 million falls closer to the *bottom* of the Decile 9 size category's range of smallest and largest companies ($263.715 million and $567.843 million, respectively).

In this example we will use the more conservative size premium of the broader Micro-Cap category, 3.67%:

$$k_{e,i} = 2.72\% + \left(\beta \times 6.94\% \right) + 3.67\%$$

[8.9] Appendix 3, "CRSP Deciles Size Premia Study: Key Variables" includes all of the data previously published on the Morningstar/Ibbotson *SBBI Valuation Yearbook's* "back page", which was entitled "Key Variables in Estimating the Cost of Capital".

The only input not available from Appendix 3 is the beta (β). The analyst could use the "full-information" beta for SIC code 36 (1.28) from Appendix 3a, which would result in a cost of equity capital estimate of 15.27%:

$$15.27\% = 2.72\% + (1.28 \times 6.94\%) + 3.67\%$$

An excellent source of industry and peer group betas for use in the analyst's custom CAPM estimate of cost of equity capital is the *Valuation Handbook − U.S. Industry Cost of Capital*.[8.10, 8.11] For example, in the *2016 Valuation Handbook − U.S. Industry Cost of Capital*, the median adjusted peer group beta for SIC 36 is 1.2.

In addition to industry and peer group betas (both levered and unlevered), the *Valuation Handbook − U.S. Industry Cost of Capital* provides eight (8) cost of equity capital estimates for each of the industries covered in the book (depending on data availability), cost of debt capital and weighted average cost of capital (WACC) estimates, plus capital structure, valuation multiples, industry betas, and more. The analyst can use this information to (i) benchmark, (ii) supplement, and (iii) strengthen his or her own custom cost of capital analysis.[8.12]

Alternatively, analysts can calculate their own *custom* peer group beta estimates using the guideline companies they have selected as the best proxies for their particular subject company, or select a group of published betas from another published source such as Bloomberg.

[8.10] The *Valuation Handbook − U.S. Industry Cost of Capital* provides industry-level cost of capital estimates (cost of equity capital, cost of debt capital, and weighted average cost of capital, or WACC), plus detailed industry-level statistics for sales, market capitalization, capital structure, various levered and unlevered beta estimates (e.g., ordinary-least squares (OLS) beta, sum beta, peer group beta, downside beta, etc.), valuation (trading) multiples, financial and profitability ratios, equity returns, aggregate forward-looking earnings-per share (EPS) growth rates, and more. Over 300 critical industry-level data points are calculated for approximately 180 U.S. industries (depending on data availability). Industries are organized by standard industrial classification (SIC) code. The *Valuation Handbook − U.S. Industry Cost of Capital* has been published since 2014, and is updated annually with data through March 31 of the current year (e.g., the *2014 Valuation Handbook − U.S. Industry Cost of Capital* is "data through" March 31, 2014; the *2015 Valuation Handbook − U.S. Industry Cost of Capital* is "data through" March 31, 2015, etc.). This book includes three optional intra-year quarterly updates (June, September, and December). To order the *2017 Valuation Handbook − U.S. Industry Cost of Capital or* other Duff & Phelps valuation data resources published by John Wiley & Sons, please visit: www.wiley.com/go/ValuationHandbooks.

[8.11] See Exhibit 1.4 herein for a sample industry analysis page from the *2016 Valuation Handbook − U.S. Industry Cost of Capital*.

[8.12] A normal and prudent step in any analysis is to perform some benchmarking as a "reasonableness" test. The information in the *Valuation Handbook − U.S. Industry Cost of Capital* helps the analyst answer the question, "How does my own analysis of the subject company compare to the subject company's peers (i.e., the industry)?"

Key Things to Remember about the CRSP Deciles Size Premia

- When using the CRSP Deciles Size Premia exhibits, a size premium is added to both the build-up and CAPM estimates of cost of equity capital.

- The size premia in both data sets (CRSP Deciles Size Premia exhibits and Risk Premium Report exhibits) in the *2017 Valuation Handbook – U.S. Guide to Cost of Capital* are "beta-adjusted". In other words, the portion of excess return that is not attributable to beta is controlled for, or removed, leaving only the size effect's contribution to excess return.

- Size premia are appropriate for use in the capital asset pricing model (CAPM), and in build-up methods that *do not otherwise already have a measure of size risk.*

- Industry risk premia (RP_i) are a measure of "beta" risk. Industry risk premium should not be used within the context of the CAPM or any other method of cost of capital estimation that already has a beta, because by doing so you will be double-counting beta risk.

- The size premia in Appendix 3 use ordinary least square (OLS) betas to derive the size premia. Equivalent size premia calculated using sum betas are available in Exhibit 4.7 in Chapter 4.

- When using the CRSP Deciles Size Premia data set, if the analyst has selected the long-term "historical ERP or long-term "supply-side" ERP, the corresponding risk-free rate should be the spot rate. Alternatively, the Duff & Phelps recommended ERP should be used with the risk-free rate that it was developed *in relation* to, per the schedule provided in Exhibit 3.19. The Duff & Phelps recommended ERP as of December 31, 2016 was developed *in relation* to a 3.5% "normalized" risk-free rate. When using the CRSP Deciles Size Premia data set, if the analyst has selected the Duff & Phelps recommended ERP as of December 31, 2016 (5.5%), the corresponding risk-free rate should be 3.5%, implying a 9.0% (5.5% + 3.5%) base cost of equity capital in the U.S. as of that time.

Chapter 9
Risk Premium Report Exhibits – General Information

In Chapter 9, general information about the Risk Premium Report exhibits is presented. In Chapter 10, detailed examples for estimating cost of equity capital using the Risk Premium Exhibits are provided.

Appropriate Use of the Risk Premium Report Exhibits

The risk premia and size premia reported in the Risk Premium Report exhibits can be used to develop cost of equity capital estimates using both the build-up method and the capital asset pricing model (CAPM). The Risk Premium Report exhibits are primarily designed to be used to develop cost of equity capital estimates for the large majority of companies that are fundamentally healthy, and for which a "going concern" assumption is appropriate. As such, high-financial-risk (i.e., "distressed") companies are excluded from the base dataset and analyzed separately in the Risk Premium Report exhibits' "High-Financial-Risk Study".

Because financial services companies are excluded from the base set of companies used to develop the analyses presented in the Risk Premium Report exhibits, these exhibits should *not* be used to estimate cost of equity capital for financial services companies. Financial services companies include those companies in finance, insurance, or real estate (i.e., companies with an SIC Code that begins with "6").

The data used in the Risk Premium Report exhibits are drawn from information on public companies. Therefore, the resulting cost of equity capital estimates using the data are "as if public".

The Risk Premium Report exhibits can be used to develop estimates of cost of equity capital for divisions, reporting units and closely held businesses without "guessing" at the value of the business before one begins the analysis. Rather, fundamental measures of firm size (e.g., sales, net income, EBITDA) and risk (e.g., operating margin) can be used to directly estimate cost of equity capital for non-public businesses.

How the Risk Premium Report Exhibits Are Organized

The Risk Premium Report exhibits include the Size Study, the Risk Study, the High-Financial-Risk Study, and the Comparative Risk Study.

- **Size Study:** Comprised of Exhibits A-1 through A-8 (used in the build-up method) and Exhibits B-1 through B-8 (used in CAPM). Analyzes the relationship between equity returns and company size, using eight measures of company size:

    i. Market capitalization

    ii. Book value of equity

    iii. 5-year average net income

    iv. Market value of invested capital (MVIC)

    v. Total assets

    vi. 5-year average EBITDA

    vii. Sales

    viii. Number of employees

- **Risk Study:** Comprised of Exhibits D-1, D-2, and D-3 (fundamental measures of risk based on accounting data). Analyzes the relationship between equity returns and three accounting-based fundamental risk measures:

    i. Five-year average operating income margin

    ii. Coefficient of variation in operating income margin

    iii. Coefficient of variation in return on book equity

- **High-Financial-Risk Study:** Comprised of Exhibits H-A, H-B, and H-C. Exhibit H-A is the high-financial-risk equivalent to the A exhibits, Exhibit H-B is the high-financial-risk equivalent to the B exhibits, and Exhibit H-C is the high-financial-risk equivalent to the C exhibits. Analyzes the relationship between equity returns and high-financial-risk, as measured by the Altman z-Score.

- **Comparative Risk Study:** Comprised of the C exhibits, when used in conjunction with the D exhibits. The C Exhibits can help valuation analysts further refine their cost of equity capital estimates by comparing their subject company's fundamental risk factors to the fundamental risk factors of the companies that comprise the 25 Size Study portfolios.

Exhibit 9.1: The Size Study, Risk Study, High-Financial-Risk Study, Comparative Risk Study, and Corresponding Exhibits

Size Study	Risk Study
Exhibits A-1 through A-8	Exhibits D-1 through D-3
Exhibits B-1 through B-8	

High-Financial-Risk Study	Comparative Risk Study
Exhibits H-A, H-B, and H-C	Exhibits C-1 through C-8

Cost of Equity Capital Estimation Methods Available

Exhibit 9.2 provides a complete list of the methods available when using the Risk Premium Report exhibits to estimate cost of equity capital, their respective equations, and which data exhibit the inputs for each of the methods is found in.

Exhibit 9.2: All Available Cost of Equity Capital Estimation Methods in the Risk Premium Report

Study	Method	Cost of Equity Capital Formula	Data Exhibit	ERP Adjustment?
Size Study	Build-up 1	$k_e = R_f + RP_{m+s}$ $+ ERP\ Adjustment$	A Exhibits	Yes
Size Study	Build-up 1-unlevered	$k_e = R_f + RP_{m+s,\ unlevered}$ $+ ERP\ Adjustment$	C Exhibits	Yes
Size Study	CAPM	$k_e = R_f + (\beta * ERP) + RP_s$	B Exhibits	No
Size Study	Build-up 2	$k_e = R_f + ERP + RP_s + RP_i$	B Exhibits	No
Risk Study	Build-up 3	$k_e = R_f + RP_{m+c}$ $+ ERP\ Adjustment$	D Exhibits	Yes
Risk Study	Build-up 3-unlevered	$k_e = R_f + RP_{m+c,\ unlevered}$ $+ ERP\ Adjustment$	D Exhibits	Yes
High-Financial-Risk Study	Build-up 1-High-Financial-Risk	$k_e = R_f + RP_{m+s,\ high\text{-}financial\text{-}risk}$ $+ ERP\ Adjustment$	H-A Exhibits	Yes
High-Financial-Risk Study	CAPM-High-Financial-Risk	$k_e = R_f + (\beta * ERP) + RP_{s,\ high\text{-}financial\text{-}risk}$	H-B Exhibits	No

Exhibit 9.2 also identifies which of the estimation methods require an "ERP Adjustment". The ERP Adjustment is an important additional step that must be taken when using certain kinds of Risk Premium Report risk premia. The ERP adjustment is discussed in detail in the next section.

Proper Application of the Equity Risk Premium (ERP) Adjustment[9.1]

In this section, the following topics are discussed:

- The ERP Adjustment Defined

- When the ERP Adjustment is Necessary

- Calculating the ERP Adjustment

The ERP Adjustment Defined

The equity risk premium (ERP) Adjustment is needed to account for the difference between the forward-looking ERP as of the valuation date that the analyst has selected to use in his or her cost of equity capital calculations, and the historical (1963–present) ERP that was used as a *convention* in the calculations performed to create the Risk Premium Report exhibits.[9.2] In other words, if a user's estimate of the ERP on a forward-looking basis is materially different from the historical ERP as measured over the time horizon 1963–present, it is reasonable to assume that the *other* historical portfolio returns reported here would differ on a forward-looking basis by a similar amount. The ERP Adjustment accounts for this difference.

The historical 1963–present ERP is used as the convention to use in the calculations for two straightforward reasons.

First, it would be quite impractical to recalculate and publish the Risk Premium Report exhibits using *every* conceivable ERP that a valuation analyst might select. We know that there is a wide diversity in practice among academics and valuation analysts regarding ERP estimates, and we also know that there is also a wide diversity of ERP estimates used by financial professionals in valuation engagements. So, a *single* ERP is selected as a convention to calculate all of the size and risk premia, and the individual analyst adjusts accordingly, relative to their selected ERP as of the valuation date.

Second, the 1963–present time horizon corresponds to when the accounting and returns data are available from the CRSP and Compustat databases, and so selecting the same time horizon seemed a natural choice.

[9.1] Business Valuation Resources (BVR) and ValuSource have both developed online companion applications to the *Valuation Handbook – U.S. Guide to Cost of Capital*. Both BVR's online version, the *"Risk Premium Toolkit"* (previously named the *"Risk Premium Calculator"*), and ValuSource's version, the *"Cost of Capital Analyzer"*, are designed to help the valuation analyst use the *Valuation Handbook – U.S. Guide to Cost of Capital's* data as efficiently as possible (both the CRSP Deciles Size Premia Studies and the Risk Premium Report Studies data are included). Both versions automatically calculate and properly apply the ERP Adjustment to all methods of cost of equity capital methods available when using the Risk Premium Report exhibits. The online *"Risk Premium Toolkit"* is available from BVR at BVResources.com/DuffPhelps or by calling 503-291-7963 extension 2. The *"Cost of Capital Analyzer"* is available from ValuSource at valuationhandbook.com or by calling 1 (800) 825-8763.

[9.2] All data in the *2017 Valuation Handbook – U.S. Guide to Cost of Capital's* Risk Premium Report exhibits is calculated over the time horizon 1963–2016 (54 years). All data in the *2017 Valuation Handbook – U.S. Guide to Cost of Capital's* CRSP Decile Size Premium exhibits are calculated over the time horizon 1926–2016 (91 years).

When the ERP Adjustment is Necessary

The general rules of whether the ERP Adjustment is necessary are:

- If you are using a "risk premium over the risk-free rate" (RP_{m+s}) from the A, C, D, H-A, or H-C Risk Premium Report exhibits, then the ERP Adjustment is *always* needed.

- If you using a Risk Premium Report "size premium" (RP_s), from Exhibits B-1 through B-8, or from the Exhibit H-B (Exhibit H-B is the "high-financial-risk" version of the "B" exhibits), then the ERP Adjustment is *never* needed, regardless of what ERP you select in your cost of equity capital estimates

This information is summarized in Exhibit 9.3.

Exhibit 9.3: When the ERP Adjustment is Necessary

ERP Adjustment *Always* Necessary (these premia are all "Risk Premia Over the Risk-free Rate")	ERP Adjustment *Never* Necessary (these premia are all "Size Premia")
Exhibits A-1 through A-8	Exhibits B-1 through B-8
Exhibits C-1 through C-8	Exhibit H-B
Exhibits D-1 through D-3	
Exhibits H-A or H-C	

Note that in Exhibit 9.2, the "Build-up 1" method and the "CAPM" method are highlighted. These two methods are probably the most commonly used methods of estimating cost of equity capital using the Risk Premium Report exhibits. The first one (Build-up 1) uses a risk premium over the risk-free rate (from the A Exhibits) as an input, and the second one (CAPM) uses a size premium (from the B Exhibits) as an input. Thus, in many cases the question of whether the ERP Adjustment is necessary reduces to the following:

- If you are using Build-up 1, *apply* the ERP Adjustment to your cost of capital estimate.

- If you are using CAPM, do *not* apply the ERP Adjustment to your cost of capital estimate.

Why Is the ERP Adjustment Necessary?

There are two types of premia in the Risk Premium Report exhibits. The first type of premia is "risk premia over the risk-free rate" (RP_{m+s}), which are a measure of risk in terms of the combined effect of *market* risk and *size* risk. Risk premia over the risk-free rate are simply added to a risk-free rate to estimate cost of equity capital when using the build-up method.

The second type of premia published in the Risk Premium Report exhibits is "risk premia over CAPM" (RP_s), which are commonly referred to as "beta adjusted size premia", or simply "size premia", and are a measure of *size* risk. Size premia can be added as an adjustment for the additional risk of smaller companies when using the CAPM.

The ERP adjustment is necessary when using risk premia over the risk-free rate because these premia measure risk in terms of the combined effect of *market* risk and *size*, the historical *market* risk premium used to calculate these premia is embedded in them. If the user selects an ERP for use in his or her cost of equity capital calculations that is *different* from the historical market risk premium that is *embedded* in these premia, it is reasonable to assume that the historical portfolio returns used in the exhibits would differ on a forward-looking basis by a similar differential, and an adjustment must therefore be made to account for this difference.

On the other hand, the Risk Premium Report's beta-adjusted size premia measure risk in terms of the effect of *size* risk only, and therefore do *not* have the historical 1963–present historical *market* risk premium embedded in them. Methods that utilize the Risk Premium Report's size premia (RP_s) therefore do not require an ERP adjustment in any case, regardless of the ERP that is selected for use in the cost of equity capital calculations.

What if the ERP Adjustment is not made to the models in Exhibit 9.2 that indicate that the adjustment is necessary? In cases where the ERP Adjustment is not applied as indicated in Exhibit 9.2, the net effect is that the historical 1963–2016 ERP used in the calculations to create the *2017 Valuation Handbook – U.S. Guide to Cost of Capital's* Risk Premium Report exhibits is *embedded* in the user's cost of equity capital estimate. This may (or may not) be the ERP that the user wishes to use as of his or her valuation date.

For example, the ERP used as a convention in the calculations to create the *2017 Valuation Handbook – U.S. Guide to Cost of Capital's* Risk Premium Report exhibits was the historical 1963–2016 market risk premium (5.02%). If the user estimates cost of equity capital using the "Build-up 1" method (which requires an ERP Adjustment) the ERP embedded in his or her estimate is 5.02% even though it is not "visible" in the equation. If in the same valuation engagement the user has estimated cost of equity capital using CAPM and selects say, the supply-side ERP (5.97%) to use in the CAPM equation, then *two different ERPs* have effectively been used in the *same* engagement (5.02% in the case of the Build-up 1 estimate, and 5.97% in the case of the CAPM estimate). The way to bring them back into harmony is simply to always apply the ERP Adjustment as indicated in Exhibit 9.2.

Calculating the ERP Adjustment for Use with the *2017 Valuation Handbook – U.S. Guide to Cost of Capital* Data

The ERP Adjustment is calculated as the simple difference between the ERP the user has selected for use in his or her cost of equity capital estimates *minus* the historical 1963–present ERP. In the *2017 Valuation Handbook – U.S. Guide to Cost of Capital*, the historical ERP used as a convention in the calculations of the Risk Premium Report exhibits was 5.02% (5.0% rounded).[9.3] The ERP adjustment for Risk Premium Report data published in the *2017 Valuation Handbook – U.S. Guide to Cost of Capital* is therefore calculated as follows:

[9.3] Calculated as the average annual return difference between the total return of the S&P 500 Index and the income return of long-term U.S. government bonds. Source of underlying data: Morningstar *Direct* database.

ERP Adjustment = ERP that User has selected − Historical ERP (1963−2016)

ERP Adjustment = ERP that User has selected − 5.0%

For example, if you selected the Duff & Phelps' recommended ERP of 5.5% to use in your year-end 2016 cost of capital estimates, then the ERP adjustment would be 0.5% (5.5% − 5.0%).[9.4] Alternatively, if you selected the *2017 Handbook − U.S. Guide to Cost of Capital's* supply-side ERP of 5.97% (6.0%, rounded), then the ERP Adjustment would be 1.0% (6.0% − 5.0%).[9.5]

Calculating the ERP Adjustment in Prior Years

In Exhibit 9.4, additional information about the historical ERP used as a convention to calculate the premia in previous versions of the *Risk Premium Report* is included for completeness and convenience.[9.6]

Exhibit 9.4: Historical Market Risk Premia Used in *Previous* Risk Premium Report Calculations 2013 Report − 2017 Report

Report Year	Period	Historical ERP (%)
2017 Risk Premium Report	1963–2016	5.0
2016 Risk Premium Report	1963–2015	4.9
2015 Risk Premium Report	1963–2014	5.1
2014 Risk Premium Report	1963–2013	4.9
2013 Risk Premium Report	1963–2012	4.5

"Smoothed" Premia versus "Average" Premia

The premia presented in the Risk Premium Report exhibits are "smoothed" across portfolios using regression analysis.[9.7] This regression analysis is also used as the basis for the "regression equation method" discussed in the next section. Smoothing the premia essentially averages out the somewhat scattered nature of the raw average premia. The "smoothed" average risk premium is generally the most appropriate indicator for most of the portfolio groups. It should be noted, however, that at the largest-size and smallest-size ends of the range, the average historical risk premia may tend to jump off of the smoothed line, particularly for the portfolios ranked by size measures that incorporate market capitalization (Exhibits A-1 and A-4).

[9.4] As of December 31, 2016 the Duff & Phelps recommended ERP is 5.5%, developed relative to a *normalized* risk-free rate of 3.5%. Within the context of cost of equity capital estimation models, the Duff & Phelps recommended ERP should be used in conjunction with the risk-free rate it was developed in relation to (in this case, 3.5%). For more information, see Exhibit 3.19 in Chapter 3, "Basic Building Blocks of the Cost of Equity Capital − Risk-free Rate and Equity Risk Premium".

[9.5] The supply-side ERP is developed relative to a "spot" risk-free rate (as opposed to "normalized" risk-free rate). Within the context of cost of equity capital estimation models, the supply-side should therefore be used in conjunction with the risk-free rate it was developed in relation to (in this case, the spot rate).

[9.6] The *Risk Premium Report* was published annually from 1996–2013. Starting in 2014, the *Report's* data is published in the hardcover *Valuation Handbook − U.S. Guide to Cost of Capital.* The *Risk Premium Report* itself is no longer published as a stand-alone publication.

[9.7] The "average" risk premia serve as the dependent variable in the regression (the thing being "predicted"); the base-10 log values of the average size (or risk) serve as the independent variable (the "predictor"). Because the size (or risk) measure is expressed in logarithms, this is equivalent to the change in size (or risk) premium given the percentage change in the size (or risk) of the companies from portfolio to portfolio.

The "Guideline Portfolio Method" versus the "Regression Equation Method"

The Risk Premium Report exhibits provide two ways for valuation analysts to match their subject company's size characteristics with the appropriate smoothed premium to be used to estimate the cost of equity capital: the "guideline portfolio" method and the "regression equation" method.

The major difference between the guideline portfolio method and the regression equation method is illustrated in Exhibits 9.5a and 9.5b, which are abbreviated portions of Portfolio 24 and Portfolio 25 from Risk Premium Report Exhibit A-3.[9.8]

Exhibit 9.5a represents the guideline portfolio method. In Exhibit 9.5a the average net income of Portfolio 24 is $15 million, and the average net income of Portfolio 25 is $5 million. If you are using the guideline portfolio method and Subject Company ABC's 5-year average net income is, say, $7 million, you would select Portfolio 25's published smoothed risk premium of 12.97%, because $7 million is closer to $5 million than it is to $15 million. Alternatively, if Subject Company XYZ's 5-year average net income is, say, $3 million, you would *again* select Portfolio 25's published risk premium of 12.97%, because $3 million is closest to Portfolio 25's average net income of $5 million.

The regression equation method, however, allows the valuation analyst to calculate a custom *interpolated* risk premium "in between" portfolios, and also to calculate custom *interpolated* smoothed risk premia for companies with size characteristics less than the average size in Portfolio 25.

Exhibit 9.5b represents the regression equation method. In Exhibit 9.5b, Subject Company ABC's net income of $7 million falls *in between* the average net income of Portfolio 24 ($15 million) and Portfolio 25 ($5 million), and the regression equation method enables the valuation analyst to calculate an exact interpolated smoothed risk premium of 12.55%, which is *in between* the published risk premia of Portfolio 24 (11.70%) and Portfolio 25 (12.97%).

In the second case, Subject Company XYZ's net income of $3 million is *smaller* than the average size of $5 million in Portfolio 25, and an exact interpolated smoothed risk premium of 13.50% is calculated, which is *higher* than the 12.97% risk premium of Portfolio 25.

These results are intuitive – as size decreases, risk premia (and thus cost of equity capital) tend to increase. In the next section, an example of how to calculate custom "interpolated" smoothed

---

[9.8] Exhibit A-3 consists of 25 portfolios sorted from largest (Portfolio 1) to smallest (Portfolio 25) according to 5-year average net income (Portfolios 3 through 23 are not shown in Exhibits 9.5a and 9.5b).

premium using the Risk Premium Report's regression equation method is provided.

Exhibit 9.5a: Guideline Portfolio Method   **Exhibit 9.5b**: Regression Equation Method

Portfolio Rank By Size	Average Net Inc. (in $millions)	Smoothed Average Risk Premium
1	10,101	4.45%
2	2,747	5.90%
///	///	///
24	15	11.70%
Subject Company ABC ------▶ (7)		
	(5) ------▶	12.97%
25		
Subject Company XYZ ------▶ (3)		

Portfolio Rank By Size	Average Net Inc. (in $millions)	Smoothed Average Risk Premium
1	10,101	4.45%
2	2,747	5.90%
///	///	///
24	15	11.70%
Subject Company ABC ------▶ (7) ------▶		12.55%
25	(5)	12.97%
Subject Company XYZ ------▶ (3) ------▶		13.50%

Example: Calculating an Interpolated Premium Using the Regression Equation Method

In almost all cases, the subject company's size will not exactly match the average size characteristics of the guideline portfolio (in the Risk Premium Report exhibits) or the decile (in the CRSP Deciles Size Premia exhibits). The Risk Premium Report exhibits provide both the "guideline portfolio method" and "regression equation method" for matching the subject company's size (and risk) characteristics to the appropriate size (or risk) premium. The regression equation method enables Risk Premium Report exhibits users to calculate an interpolated smoothed premium "in between" portfolios based upon the subject company' specific size characteristics.[9.9]

The regression equation method is outlined in this section first. Then, a discussion (and guidance) is provided on what to do when the size characteristics of subject company are *less* than the characteristics of the average size of the companies that comprise the Risk Premium Report exhibits' 25th portfolios.

In each of the Risk Premium Report exhibits, regression equations are provided. For example, the regression equation for Risk Premium Report Exhibit A-3 is:

*= 14.722% − 2.565% * LOG(Net Income)*

The 5-year average net income of the companies that comprise Exhibit A-3's Portfolio 24 is $15 million, and the 5-year average net income of the companies comprising Portfolio 25 is $5 million. If you were using the guideline portfolio method and the subject company had 5-year net income of say, $7 million, you would select Portfolio 25's risk premium of 12.97% when employing the

---

[9.9] The CRSP Size Premia exhibits presently provide the "guideline portfolio" method, but have no mechanism in place for calculating custom size premia "in between" deciles.

build-up method because $7 million is closer to $5 million than it is to $15 million.

But the subject company's 5-year net income of $7 million is *in between* the average net income of Portfolios 24 and 25, and you may prefer to calculate a custom interpolated smoothed premium in *between* portfolios 24 and 25 rather than using the published 12.97% premium. This is easy to do using the "regression equation" method – just substitute the 5-year net income (in $ millions) of your subject company (in this case, "7") for "net income" into the regression equation listed on Exhibit A-3:[9.10]

$$= 14.722\% - 2.565\% * LOG(7)$$

$$= 14.722\% - 2.565\% * 0.8451$$

$$= 12.55\%$$

Portfolio 24's published smoothed premium is 11.70%, Portfolio 25's published smoothed premium is 12.97%, and the calculated interpolated smoothed premium based on the subject company's 5-year net income of $7 million is in between these two premia, at 12.55%. Each exhibit in the Risk Premium Report will have a *different* regression equation. We recommend using as many of the size and risk measures as possible for best results.

Tips Regarding the Regression Equation Method

- The regression equations are *different* for each exhibit.

- Estimate cost of equity capital using as many of the eight A exhibits (A-1 through A-8) that are available for the subject company, and then calculate the average and median of all of these estimates. This principle is also true when using the B exhibits (B-1 through B-8) to estimate cost of equity capital using the CAPM.

Can the Regression Equation Method Be Used If the Subject Company Is Small?

The previous example was for a subject company whose size characteristics were *greater* than the average company in Portfolio 25 (comprised of the smallest companies). Can we apply the Risk Premium Report data for a subject company whose size characteristics are *less* than the average company included in Portfolio 25?

The short answer is "Yes". It may be appropriate to extrapolate the risk premium for companies whose size characteristics are less than the average characteristics of the companies comprising the bottom half of Portfolio 25 using the regression equation method. While extrapolating a statistical relationship far beyond the range of data used in analysis is generally not recommended, in cost of capital analyses (or any analysis for that matter), there is always the question of "compared to what?" Put simply, while it may not be ideal to extrapolate a statistical relationship

---

[9.10] In this equation, rather than using the traditional multiplication symbol "x", we put the equation into the Microsoft Excel format by using the character "*". Also, remember to enter the amount in "millions" (e.g., $7,000,000 should be entered as 7).

beyond a certain range, one may be confronted with a situation in which no better measure is available.

Specifically, in cases where the size characteristic of the subject company is significantly *less* than that of the average company included in Portfolio 25 for any given size measure, the valuation analyst may report the individual, average and the median premia (and corresponding cost of equity capital estimates) using both the guideline portfolio method and the regression equation method (using all of the subject company size characteristics that are available). However, we recommend that the valuation analyst consider disclosing that the subject company's selected size metric is less than, for instance, the smallest of companies included in Portfolio 25 of a particular size measure. Once again, reporting all of the information in a transparent way is preferable to not reporting it at all, especially in cases where no better alternative is available.

For more information, see the section in Chapter 10 entitled "Calculating Custom Interpolated Premia for Smaller Companies".

Size Study or Risk Study?

Use both. Analysts can use the Size Study if it has been determined that the risks of the subject company are comparable to the average of the portfolio companies of comparable size (e.g., comparable operating margin). One can determine the relative risk characteristics by looking at Exhibits C-1 through C-8. But, we do not know precisely how the market prices risk. The Risk Study provides returns based on risk measures regardless of size. One would likely expect that returns are greater for say, Portfolio 25, in the size measured portfolios rather than Portfolio 25 in the risk measured portfolio because sometimes a large company has risk measures more like a small company, and vice versa. How much higher/lower can these returns be? The D exhibits may help identify the magnitude of the return adjustment. Detailed examples on how to use the Risk Study can be found in Chapter 10.

Key Things to Remember About the Risk Premium Report Exhibits

- The Risk Premium Report exhibits include the Size Study, the Risk Study, the High-Financial-Risk Study, and the Comparative Risk Study.

- The risk premia and size premia reported in the Risk Premium Report exhibits can be used to develop cost of equity capital estimates using both the build-up method and the capital asset pricing model (CAPM).

- Because financial services companies are excluded from the base set of companies used to develop the analyses presented in the Risk Premium Report exhibits, these exhibits should *not* be used to estimate cost of equity for financial services companies.

- If you using a Risk Premium Report "size premium" (RP_s), then the ERP Adjustment is *never* needed, regardless of what ERP you select to use in your cost of equity capital estimates. If you are using a Risk Premium Report "risk premium over the risk-free rate" (RP_{m+s}), then the ERP Adjustment is *always* needed.

- The "smoothed" average risk premium is generally the most appropriate indicator for most of the portfolio groups. The valuation analyst can use either the smoothed average premium *published* for each guideline portfolio, or *calculate* a "custom" interpolated smoothed average premium using the regression equations associated with each exhibit.

- The Risk Premium Report exhibits provide two ways for valuation analysts to match their subject company's size characteristics with the appropriate smoothed premium to be used to estimate the cost of equity capital: the "guideline portfolio" method and the "regression equation" method. The regression equation method allows the valuation professional to calculate a custom *interpolated* risk premia "in between" portfolios, and also to calculate custom *interpolated* risk premia for companies with size characteristics less than the average size in Portfolio 25.

- It may be appropriate to extrapolate the risk premium for companies whose size characteristics are *less* than the average characteristics of the companies comprising the bottom half of Portfolio 25 using the regression equation method.

Chapter 10
Risk Premium Report Exhibits – Examples

In this chapter, we first discuss concepts that are specific to each of the four Risk Premium Report studies (Size Study, Risk Study, High-Financial-Risk Study, Comparative Risk Study), and then provide detailed examples for using the data in each to estimate the cost of equity capital.

Size Study

The size of a company is one of the most important risk elements to consider when developing cost of equity estimates for use in valuing a firm. Traditionally, researchers have used market value of equity (i.e., "market capitalization" or simply "market cap") as a measure of size in conducting historical rate of return research. For example, the Center for Research in Security Prices (CRSP) "deciles" are developed by sorting U.S. companies by market capitalization. Another example is the Fama-French "Small minus Big" (SMB) series, which is the difference in return of "small" stocks minus "big" (i.e., large) stocks, as defined by market capitalization.[10.1, 10.2]

Reasons for Using Additional Measures of Size

There are several reasons for using other measures of size in *addition* to the traditional measure of size, market value of equity.

First, financial literature indicates a bias may be introduced when ranking companies by market value of equity because a company's market value of equity may be affected by characteristics of the company other than size.[10.3] In other words, some companies might be small because they are risky (high discount rate), rather than risky because they are small (low market capitalization). One simple example could be a company with a large asset base, but a small market capitalization as a result of high leverage or depressed earnings. Another example could be a company with large sales or operating income, but a small market capitalization due to being highly leveraged.

Second, market capitalization may be an imperfect measure of the risk of a company's operations.

Third, using alternative measures of size may have the practical benefit of removing the need to first make a "guesstimate" of size in order to know which portfolio's premium to use (this issue is commonly referred to as the "circularity" issue). When you are valuing a closely held company, you are trying to determine market value of equity. If you need to make a guesstimate of the subject

---

[10.1] To learn more about the Center for Research in Security Prices (CRSP) at the University of Chicago Booth School of Business, visit www.CRSP.com.

[10.2] Eugene Fama, 2013 Nobel laureate in economic sciences, is the Robert R. McCormick Distinguished Service Professor of Finance at the University of Chicago, and Ken French is the Roth Family Distinguished Professor of Finance at the Tuck School of Business at Dartmouth College. Fama and French are prolific researchers and authors who have contributed greatly to the field of modern finance. Fama and French's paper "The Cross-Section of Expected Stock Returns" was the winner of the 1992 Smith Breeden Prize for the best paper in the *Journal of Finance*. Fama is also chairman of the Center for Research in Security Prices (CRSP) at the University of Chicago Booth School of Business.

[10.3] "A Critique of Size Related Anomalies", Jonathan Berk, *Review of Financial Studies*, vol. 8, no. 2 (1995).

company's market value of equity first in order to know which size premium to use, the "circularity" problem is introduced. While market capitalization, at least for a closely held firm, is *not* generally available, other size measures, such as total assets or net income, *are* generally available.[10.4]

Finally, when doing analysis of any kind it is generally prudent to approach things from multiple directions if at all possible. This is good practice for several reasons, with the most important being that it has the potential of strengthening the conclusions of the analysis.

The Difference Between the Size Study's A Exhibits and the B Exhibits

The results of the Size Study are presented in Exhibits A-1 through A-8 and Exhibits B-1 through B-8. The main difference between the A and B exhibits is how they are used. The A exhibits are used if you are using a "build-up" method to develop cost of equity capital estimates, and the B exhibits are used if you are using the capital asset pricing model (CAPM) to develop cost of equity capital estimates. This difference in usage is a function of the type of "risk premia" presented in each of the exhibits:

The A exhibits provide "risk premia over the risk-free rate" (RP_{m+s}) in terms of the combined effect of *market* risk and *size* risk for 25 portfolios ranked by eight alternative measures of size. These premia can be added to a risk-free rate (R_f) to estimate cost of equity capital in a build-up model.

The B exhibits provide "risk premia over CAPM" (i.e., size premia) (RP_s) in terms of size risk for 25 portfolios ranked by eight alternative measures of size. These premia are commonly known as beta-adjusted size premia, or simply size premia. These premia can be added as a size adjustment to a basic CAPM to estimate cost of equity capital.[10.5]

The Difference Between "Risk Premia Over the Risk-free Rate" and "Risk Premia Over CAPM"

Risk Premium Over Risk-Free Rate (RP_{m+s})

"Risk premia over the risk-free rate" represent the difference between the historical (observed) total return of equities over the risk-free rate.[10.6] A long-run average historical risk premium is often used as an indicator of the expected risk premium of a typical equity investor. Total returns are based on dividend income plus capital appreciation and represent returns after corporate taxes (but before owner-level taxes). To estimate the historical risk premia in the *2017 Valuation Handbook – U.S. Guide to Cost of Capital*, the average total return for each of the 25 size-ranked portfolios is calculated over the sample period, and then the average income return of long-term U.S. government bonds (using SBBI data) over the same period is subtracted.

[10.4] For further discussion of the history of the size premium and criticisms of the size premium, see Chapters 14 and 15 in *Cost of Capital: Applications and Examples* 5th ed. by Shannon Pratt and Roger Grabowski, Wiley (April, 2014).

[10.5] The basic CAPM formula is *Cost of Equity Capital = Risk-Free Rate + (Beta x ERP)*. A "modified CAPM" usually refers to the common modification to the CAPM formula that is used to incorporate an adjustment for size: *Cost of Equity Capital = Risk-Free Rate + (Beta x ERP) + Size Premium*. Please note that the modified CAPM as presented is after addition of a size premium and prior to the addition of any "company-specific" risk premia that the individual valuation analyst may deem appropriate.

[10.6] Risk premia over the risk-free rate and size premia are presented in the Risk Premium Report Exhibits. The CRSP Deciles Size Premia exhibits present size premia, but do not include risk premia over the risk-free rate.

For example, the average annual arithmetic return for portfolio 25 in Exhibit A-3 (size measure: 5-year average net income) over the time period 1963–2016 is 21.44%, and the average annual income return of long-term U.S. government bonds over the same period is 6.46%. This implies that the "risk premium over the risk-free rate" is 14.98% (21.44% − 6.46%) for this portfolio. This difference is a measure of risk in terms of the combined effect of *market* risk and *size* risk.

As of December 31, 2016, the average risk premium over the risk-free rate for portfolio 1 (comprised of the largest companies) for all *eight* of the size measures analyzed in the Size Study was 5.97%, and the average risk premium over the risk-free rate for portfolio 25 (comprised of the smallest companies) for all *eight* of the size measures was 14.97%, a difference of 9.0% (14.97% − 5.97%). There is a clear negative relationship between "size" and premium over long-term bonds (i.e., as size decreases, the return over the risk-free rate increases).

Because risk premia over the risk-free rate have an embedded measure of market (i.e., "beta") risk, these premia *are* appropriate for use in "build-up" methods that do *not* already include a measure of market risk, but are *not* appropriate for use in models (e.g., CAPM) that already have a measure of market risk.

Risk premia over the risk-free rate (RP_{m+s}) are presented in Exhibits A-1 through A-8. In the *2017 Valuation Handbook – U.S. Guide to Cost of Capital*, these risk premia are calculated over the period 1963 (the year that the *Compustat* database was inaugurated) through December 2016.

Both risk premia over the risk-free rate *and* size premia are presented in the Risk Premium Report Exhibits. The CRSP Deciles Size Premia exhibits present size premia, but do not include risk premia over the risk-free rate.

Size Premia (RP_s)

"Risk Premia over CAPM" represent the difference between historical (observed) excess return and the excess return predicted by CAPM. Years ago, the "small stock premium" was calculated as the simple difference in small company returns versus large company returns.[10.7] However, an examination of the betas of large stocks versus small stocks revealed that within the context of the capital asset pricing model (CAPM), beta (a measure of market risk) did not fully explain all of the difference between large company returns and small company returns. The observed (i.e., historical) excess return of portfolios comprised of smaller stocks tended to be greater than the excess return predicted by the CAPM. What followed from this observation is what is now commonly referred to as the "size premium". To learn more about the size effect, see Chapter 4.

Size premia are presented in both the Risk Premium Report Exhibits and the CRSP Deciles Size Premia exhibits. The methodology employed to calculate the size premia in both data sets is very similar, and distills down to measuring the difference in historical excess returns (i.e., "what actually

---

[10.7] For example, in early versions of what would evolve into the *SBBI Classic Yearbook* (Morningstar, Chicago 2015) the "small stock premium" was calculated as the simple difference between a "small company stock" series and the Standard & Poor's (S&P) Composite Index (i.e., the S&P 500 Index). Starting in 2016, the *SBBI "Classic" Yearbook"* is updated annually by Duff & Phelps, and published by John Wiley & sons, and is renamed "SBBI Yearbook" (the word "Classic" has been removed). To order copies of the *SBBI Yearbook*, please visit www.wiley.com/go/sbbiyearbook, or call: U.S. (800) 762-2974 International (317) 572-3993 or fax (317) 572-4002.

happened"), and the excess returns that CAPM would have predicted. Detailed examples of the derivation of size premia for both data sets are provided in Chapter 7, "The CRSP Deciles Size Premia Studies and the Risk Premium Report Studies – A Comparison".

The "A" and "B" Exhibits: Summary of Data Presented

While the A and B exhibits present different types of risk premia, both the A and B exhibits' 25 portfolios are ranked by the same eight alternative measures of size, which are described in Exhibit 10.1.[10.8] Each of the exhibits A-1 through A-8 and B-1 through B-8 displays one line of data for each of the 25 size-ranked portfolios.

Exhibit 10.1: Eight Alternative Measures of Size

Exhibits A-1 and B-1
Market value of common equity (common stock price times number of common shares outstanding).

Exhibit A-2 and B-2
Book value of common equity (does not add back the deferred tax balance)

Exhibit A-3 and B-3
5-year average net income for previous five fiscal years (net income before extraordinary items).

Exhibit A-4 and B-4
Market value of invested capital (MVIC) (market value of common equity plus carrying value of preferred stock plus long-term debt (including current portion) and notes payable).

Exhibit A-5 and B-5
Total Assets (as reported on the balance sheet).

Exhibit A-6 and B-6
5-year average earnings before interest, income taxes, depreciation and amortization (EBITDA) for the previous five fiscal years (operating income before depreciation plus non-operating income).

Exhibit A-7 and B-7
Sales (net).

Exhibit A-8 and B-8
Number of employees (number of employees, either at year-end or yearly average, including part-time and seasonal workers and employees of consolidated subsidiaries; excludes contract workers and unconsolidated subsidiaries).

The A and B exhibits include the statistics outlined in Exhibit 10.2 for each of the size measures outlined in Exhibit 10.1.

[10.8] For a detailed description of the Standard & Poor's *Compustat* data items used in the Risk Premium Report exhibits, please see Appendix 1.

For comparative purposes, the average returns from the SBBI series for Large Companies (essentially the S&P 500 Index), Small Companies, and Long-Term Government Bond Income Returns for the period 1963 through the latest year are also reported in each exhibit.[10.9]

Exhibit 10.2: Statistics Reported for 25 size-ranked portfolios in the Size Study's A and B Exhibits

Exhibits A-1 through A-8	Exhibits B-1 through B-8
• Average of the sorting criteria (e.g., average number of employees) for the latest year used in determining the size of the companies (i.e., the size criteria when the latest year's portfolios are formed). For example, the market value in exhibit B-1 is the market value of equity at the beginning of the latest year. The other size criteria are based on what was known at the beginning of the latest year when the portfolios are formed.	• Average of the sorting criteria (e.g., average number of employees) for the latest year used in determining the size of the companies (i.e., the size criteria when the latest year's portfolios are formed). For example, the market value in exhibit B-1 is the market value of equity at the beginning of the latest year. The other size criteria are based on what was known at the beginning of the latest year when the portfolios are formed.
• The number of companies in each portfolio at the beginning of the latest year.	• Beta estimate calculated using the "sum beta" method applied to monthly returns for 1963 through the latest year (see Chapter 5 for a description of the "sum beta" method).
• Beta calculated using the "sum beta" method applied to monthly returns for 1963 through the latest year (see Chapter 5 for a description of the "sum beta" method).	• Arithmetic average historical equity return since 1963.
• Standard deviation of annual historical equity returns.	• Arithmetic average historical risk premium over long-term Treasuries (average return on equity in excess of long-term Treasury bonds) since 1963 (RP_{m+s}).
• Geometric average historical equity return since 1963.	• Indicated CAPM premium, calculated as the beta of the portfolio multiplied by the average historical market risk premium since 1963 (measured as the difference between SBBI Large Stock total returns and SBBI income returns on long-term Treasury bonds).
• Arithmetic average historical equity return since 1963.	• Premium over CAPM, calculated by subtracting the "Indicated CAPM Premium" from the "Arithmetic Risk Premium" (RP_s).
• Arithmetic average historical risk premium over long-term Treasuries (average return on equity in excess of long-term Treasury bonds) since 1963 (RP_{m+s}).	• "Smoothed" Premium over CAPM: the fitted premium from a regression with the historical "Premium over CAPM" as dependent variable and the logarithm of the average sorting criteria as independent variable (RP_s).
• "Smoothed" average historical risk premium: the fitted premium from a regression with the average historical risk premium as dependent variable and the logarithm of the average sorting criteria as independent variable. (We present the coefficients and other statistics from this regression analysis in the top right hand corner of the exhibits) (RP_{m+s}).	
• Average carrying value of preferred stock plus long-term debt (including current portion) plus notes payable ("Debt") as a percent of MVIC since 1963.	

[10.9] Source: Morningstar *Direct* database.

Calculating Custom Interpolated Premia for Smaller Companies

The Risk Premium Report exhibits provide two ways for valuation analysts to match their subject company's size characteristics with the appropriate smoothed premium: the "guideline portfolio" method and the "regression equation" method. The regression equation method allows the valuation analyst to calculate a custom *interpolated* risk premia "in between" portfolios, and also to calculate custom *interpolated* risk premia for companies with size characteristics smaller than the average size in Portfolio 25.

In order to assess the appropriateness of using the regression equations for small companies, Exhibit 10.3 is provided. Exhibit 10.3 can help the valuation analyst gauge the size characteristics of the subject company relative to the size characteristics of companies that comprise Portfolio 25 for each of the eight size measures, and provide support for the additional adjustment provided by the regression equations.

Portfolio 25

The size characteristics for portfolio 25 for each of the eight size measures in both the Risk Premium Report exhibits A-1 through A-8 and B-1 through B-8 are shown in Exhibit 10.3. While the A and B exhibits present *different* types of risk premia, the A and B exhibits are:

- Comprised of the *same* set of companies, and

- Ranked by the *same* eight alternative measures of size.

This is done intentionally. It ensures that the "risk premia over the risk-free rate" that are published in the A exhibits and used in the build-up method are "apples to apples" when compared to the size premia that are published in the B exhibits and used in the CAPM.

Exhibit 10.3: Size Characteristics of the Companies that Comprise Portfolio 25, by Percentile

Portfolio 25	Market Value of Equity (in $millions)	Book Value of Equity (in $millions)	5-Year Average Net Income (in $millions)	Market Value of Invested Capital (in $millions)
Largest Company	$291.526	$159.204	$11.274	$387.281
95th Percentile	260.490	151.276	10.302	355.585
75th Percentile	189.941	116.879	7.292	257.179
50th Percentile	99.386	74.349	4.148	141.789
25th Percentile	48.289	33.630	1.976	67.336
5th Percentile	16.848	13.868	0.669	20.342
Smallest Company	4.784	4.756	0.054	8.190

Portfolio 25	Total Assets (in $millions)	5-Year Average EBITDA (in $millions)	Sales (in $millions)	Number of Employees
Largest Company	$346.465	$39.386	$307.857	686
95th Percentile	318.170	36.761	276.458	641
75th Percentile	249.862	26.608	200.273	485
50th Percentile	163.579	15.120	118.960	272
25th Percentile	62.163	6.991	55.810	131
5th Percentile	24.577	2.109	18.314	10
Smallest Company	9.283	1.130	2.619	1

The use of Exhibit 10.3 is straightforward. For example, the "95th Percentile" of size in Portfolio 25 for "5-year Average Net Income" is $10.302 million, which means that 95% of the companies in Portfolio 25 have average income that is *less* than $10.302 million (alternatively this means that 5% of the companies in Portfolio 25 have average income that is *greater* than $10.302 million). Or, looking to the 5th percentile, 5% of the companies in Portfolio 25 have average income that is *less* than $0.669 million (alternatively, this means that 95% of the companies in Portfolio 25 have average income that is *greater* than $0.669 million).

To provide even greater detail about the composition of the portfolios used to calculate the premia in the Risk Premium Report Study, Exhibit 10.3 also includes the *smallest* and *largest* companies in the 25th portfolio of each of the eight size measures. For example, the largest company in Portfolio 25 for "5-year Average Net Income" is $11.274 million. Alternatively, the smallest company in Portfolio 25 for "5-year Average Net Income" is $0.054 million.

When using the Risk Premium Report exhibits to estimate cost of equity capital for a subject company in Portfolio 25, three cases are possible:

Case 1: *All* of the subject company's size characteristics are *greater* than the smallest companies in Portfolio 25 of each of the eight size measures, reported in Exhibit 10.3.

In Case 1, the valuation professional can report the individual, average and median premia (and corresponding cost of equity capital estimates) using both the guideline portfolio method and calculated using the regression equation method (using all of the subject company size characteristics that are available).[10.10]

Case 2: *Some* of the subject company's size characteristics are *greater* than the smallest companies in Exhibit 10.3, and *some* of the subject company's size metrics are *less* than the smallest companies in Exhibit 10.3.

In Case 2, the valuation analyst may consider reporting the individual, average and median premia (and corresponding cost of equity capital estimates) using both the guideline portfolio method and calculated using the regression equation method (using all of the subject company size characteristics that are available) segregated in three different groupings:

- The premia calculated using subject company size characteristics that are *greater* than the smallest company;

- The premia calculated using subject company size characteristics that are *less* than the smallest company; and

- A combined grouping of all the premia calculated using subject company size characteristics (both those *greater* than, and *less* than, the smallest company).

In many cases, the difference between the three groupings' concluded cost of equity capital estimates will be small.

Case 3: *None* of the subject company's size characteristics are *greater* than the smallest companies as reported in Exhibit 10.3.

In Case 3, the valuation analyst may report the individual, average and median premia (and corresponding cost of equity capital estimates) using both the guideline portfolio method and calculated using the regression equation method (using all of the subject company size characteristics that are available). We recommend that the valuation analyst disclose that the subject company's size characteristics are less than the smallest companies included in Portfolio 25 for all size measures.

[10.10] The Risk Premium Report Study analyzes the relationship between return and eight different measures of size. It would *not* be unusual for fewer than the maximum number of eight size measures or fewer than the maximum number of three risk measures to be used when estimating cost of equity using the Risk Premium Report exhibits. When using the Risk Premium Report's "Size Study", the minimum number of size measures required is one. However, we recommend using as many size measures as possible for best results.

Overview of Methods Used to Estimate Cost of Equity Capital Using the Size Study

The Risk Premium Report's Size Study provides a total of four different ways to estimate the cost of equity capital.

There are two methods of estimating cost of equity capital for a subject company, Build-up 1 and CAPM, plus one method for estimating *unlevered* cost of equity capital (assuming a firm is financed 100% with equity and 0% debt).[10.11] A fourth method is provided, we call "Build-up 2".[10.12] The Size Study can be used in conjunction with the industry risk premia previously published in the *SBBI Valuation Edition Yearbook*, and now published in the *2017 Valuation Handbook – U.S. Guide to Cost of Capital* (see Appendix 3a). Build-up 2 incorporates a separate variable for the industry risk premium. To do this, a rudimentary adjustment is made to a full-information beta to calculate an industry risk premium that can be used within the context of Risk Premia Report data.

The cost of equity capital estimation methods provided by the Risk Premium Report's Size Study are summarized in Exhibit 10.4. An example of each (using the guideline portfolio method and the regression equation method) is provided in the following section.

Exhibit 10.4: Methods of Estimating Cost of Equity Capital Using the Risk Premium Report's Size Study

Study	Method	Cost of Equity Capital Formula
Size Study	Build-up 1	$k_e = R_f + RP_{m+s} + ERP \text{ Adjustment}$
Size Study	Build-up 1-Unlevered	$k_e = R_f + RP_{m+s, unlevered} + ERP \text{ Adjustment}$
Size Study	CAPM	$k_e = R_f + (\beta * ERP) + RP_s$
Size Study	Build-up 2	$k_e = R_f + ERP + RP_s + RP_i$

All of the examples herein are calculated using full precision decimals. Differences may arise if the user were to hand calculate the examples due to rounding differences.

[10.11] Unlevered risk premia over the risk-free rate are presented in Exhibits C-1 through C-8.

[10.12] There are various "Build-up" methods in the *2017 Valuation Handbook – U.S. Guide to Cost of Capital*. Giving them names like "Build-up 1", "Build-up 2", etc., was necessary so as to differentiate them from one another.

Size Study Examples: Assumptions Used

Valuation Date

The *2017 Valuation Handbook – U.S. Guide to Cost of Capital* is calculated with "data through" December 31, 2016, and so for all examples of estimating the cost of equity capital using the Risk Premium Report exhibits presented herein, the *valuation date* is December 31, 2016.

ERP and Risk-free Rate

As of December 31, 2016, the Duff & Phelps recommended equity risk premium (ERP) was 5.5%, developed relative to a "normalized" long-term treasury yield of 3.5%. For all examples of estimating the cost of equity capital using the Risk Premium Report exhibits, the assumed ERP is therefore 5.5%, and the risk-free rate used is 3.5%. For more information about the Duff & Phelps recommended ERP and normalized risk-free rates, see Chapter 3, "Basic Building Blocks of the Cost of Equity Capital – Risk-free Rate and Equity Risk Premium".

The use of the Duff & Phelps recommended ERP of 5.5% and a 3.5% normalized risk-free rate in no way precludes valuation analysts from using different ERP estimates or different risk-free-rates. However, it is important to *match* the ERP with the risk-free rate it was developed in relation to. For example, the long-term "historical" ERP and long-term supply-side ERP reported herein (see Appendix 3, "CRSP Deciles Size Premia Study: Key Variables") were both developed in relation to long-term spot risk-free rates (for the most part), and not normalized rates. So if the long-term "historical" ERP or the long-term supply-side ERP is selected, analysts should likely use "spot" rates rather than a "normalized" rates.[10.13]

Beta and Industry Risk Premium

For the CAPM examples (which require a beta), a beta of 1.2 is assumed. For the Build-up 2 examples, which requires an industry risk premium (RP_i), a "full-information" (FIB) beta of 1.2 is assumed, implying an RP_i (when using the assumed 5.5% ERP used in these examples) of 1.1% calculated as follows:

$$RP_i = (FIB \times RP_m) - RP_m$$

$$1.1\% = (1.20 \times 5.50\%) - 5.50\%$$

For a detailed discussion about betas and industry risk premia, see Chapter 5, "Basic Building Blocks of the Cost of Equity Capital – Betas and Industry Risk Premia".

[10.13] Exhibit 3.19 summarizes the Duff & Phelps recommended ERP and corresponding risk-free rate *over time* (January 2008–present).

Hypothetical Subject Company Size Characteristics

There are up to eight alternative size measures that can be used with any of the four methods of estimating cost of equity capital provided by the *Size Study*. It would *not* be unusual for fewer than eight of these measures to be available for any given subject company. For example, market value of equity will probably not be available for a closely held company, nor will market value of invested capital (in which market value of equity is embedded). In cases where fewer than eight size measures are available, it is generally acceptable to use the size measures that *are* available.

In each of the examples of using the Size Study to estimate cost of equity capital, the hypothetical subject company size measures summarized in Exhibit 10.5 will be used (total assets of $300 million, for instance, will be used in all examples).

Exhibit 10.5: Hypothetical Subject Company Size Characteristics
(Used in all Size Study examples)

Size Measure (in $millions, except for Number of Employees)		Appropriate Exhibit			
		Build-up 1	Build-up 1 -Unlevered	CAPM	Build-up 2
Market Value of Equity	$120	A-1	C-1	B-1	B-1
Book Value of Equity	$100	A-2	C-2	B-2	B-2
5-year Average Net Income	$10	A-3	C-3	B-3	B-3
Market Value of Invested Capital	$180	A-4	C-4	B-4	B-4
Total Assets	$300	A-5	C-5	B-5	B-5
5-year Average EBITDA	$30	A-6	C-6	B-6	B-6
Sales	$250	A-7	C-7	B-7	B-7
Number of Employees	200	A-8	C-8	B-8	B-8

Exhibit 10.5 also includes the data exhibits in which the appropriate risk premia for each of the size measures can be found. For example, for use in the Build-up 1 method, risk premia over the risk-free rate (RP_{m+s}) for "Total Assets" are found in Exhibit A-5. For use in the CAPM method, the appropriate premia over CAPM (RP_s, or "size premia") for "Total Assets" are found in Exhibit B-5.

Please note that for any given valuation engagement these inputs may be (and probably will be) different from the ones used in the examples.

Size Study Examples

Build-up 1

The Build-up 1 method is an additive model commonly used for calculating the required rate of return on equity capital. As the name implies, successive "building blocks" are summed, each representing the additional risk inherent to investing in alternative assets. The Size Study calculates average "risk premia over the risk-free rate" (RP_{m+s}) from 1963 through December 2016 for each of the 25 size-ranked portfolios. These RP_{m+s} premia are found in Exhibits A-1 through A-8, and can be added to a risk-free rate to estimate cost of equity capital (k_e) using the Build-up 1 method.

The Build-up 1 equation is:

$$k_{e\ build\text{-}up\ 1} = R_f + RP_{m+s} + ERP\ Adjustment$$

Note that the "ERP Adjustment" is a necessary adjustment when using Build-up 1. The equity risk premium adjustment is made to reconcile the historical data presented in the Risk Premium Report exhibits with the forward-looking ERP chosen by the individual analyst as of the valuation date. For a detailed discussion of the ERP Adjustment, see the section in Chapter 9 entitled, "Proper Application of the Equity Risk Premium (ERP) Adjustment".

The historical ERP from 1963–2016 (5.0%) was used as an input in performing the analysis in the 2017 Report, and is thus embedded in the RP_{m+s} premia. In these examples we have selected to use an ERP of 5.5%, and the ERP Adjustment is:

$$ERP\ Adjustment = User's\ ERP - Historical\ (1963-2016)\ ERP$$
$$ERP\ Adjustment = 0.5\% = 5.5\% - 5.0\%$$

This implies that on a forward-looking basis as of the valuation date, investors expected to earn 0.5% more than they realized on average over the period 1963–2016. It is reasonable to assume that the other historical portfolio returns reported here would differ on a forward-looking basis by a similar differential.

Examples of both the guideline portfolio method and the regression equation method follow, starting with the simpler guideline portfolio method. In general, the regression equation method is preferred because this method allows for interpolation between the individual guideline portfolios, although the guideline portfolio method is less complicated, and more direct.

Example 1a: Build-up 1 Method (using guideline portfolios)

To estimate the cost of equity capital (k_e) with the Build-up 1 method using "guideline portfolios", three pieces of information are needed:

- Risk-free rate (R_f)

- Risk premium over the risk-free rate (RP_{m+s})

- Equity risk premium Adjustment *(ERP Adjustment)*

We have assumed a risk-free rate of 3.5% for all examples, and the ERP Adjustment has been calculated as 0.5%, so the only missing input is the risk premium over the risk-free rate (RP_{m+s}).

$$k_{e\ build-up\ 1} = 3.5\% + RP_{m+s} + 0.5\%$$

Gathering the RP_{m+s} premia is straightforward. Match the various size measures of the subject company with the guideline portfolios composed of companies of similar size in Exhibits A-1 through A-8, and identify the corresponding *smoothed average risk premium*.

For example, according to Exhibit 10.5, our hypothetical subject company has a market value of equity of $120 million, and the appropriate data exhibit is Exhibit A-1 (25 portfolios sorted by market value of equity). An abbreviated version of Exhibit A-1 is shown in Exhibit 10.6. Of the 25 portfolios, the portfolio that has an average market value *closest* to the subject company's $120 million market value is Portfolio 25 ($121 million). The corresponding *smoothed average risk premium* is 14.02% (14.0%, rounded).

Exhibit 10.6: Companies Ranked by Market Value of Equity (Exhibit A-1)

Portfolio Rank by Size	Average Mkt. Value (in $millions)	Log of Average Mkt. Value	Number as of 2014	Beta (SumBeta) Since '63	Standard Deviation of Returns	Geometric Average Return	Arithmetic Average Return	Arithmetic Average Risk Premium	*Smoothed Average Risk Premium*	Average Debt/ MVIC
1	238,299	5.38	45	0.83	15.90%	9.64%	11.66%	5.20%	*2.41%*	14.59%
2	60,613	4.78	36	0.96	16.96%	8.52%	10.64%	4.18%	*4.50%*	19.02%
3	35,630	4.55	38	0.92	15.90%	9.62%	11.70%	5.24%	*5.32%*	20.92%
					///					
24	370	2.57	86	1.24	24.14%	15.71%	19.35%	12.89%	*12.31%*	24.92%
25	121	2.08	249	1.29	36.29%	18.48%	24.39%	17.94%	***14.02%***	27.08%

This process is continued for each of the eight size characteristics that are available for the subject company. Looking again to Exhibit 10.5, our hypothetical subject company has a book value of equity of $100 million, and the appropriate data exhibit is Exhibit A-2 (25 portfolios ranked by book value of equity). An abbreviated version of Exhibit A-2 is shown in Exhibit 10.7. Of the 25 portfolios, the portfolio that has an average book value of equity value *closest* to the subject company's $100 million market value is Portfolio 25 ($76 million). The corresponding *smoothed average risk premium* is 12.07% (12.1%, rounded).

Exhibit 10.7: Companies Ranked by Book Value of Equity (Exhibit A-2)

Portfolio Rank by Size	Average Book Val. (in $millions)	Log of Average Book Val.	Number as of 2014	Beta (SumBeta) Since '63	Standard Deviation of Returns	Geometric Average Return	Arithmetic Average Return	Arithmetic Average Risk Premium	*Smoothed Average Risk Premium*	Average Debt/ MVIC
1	67,532	4.83	40	0.78	15.49%	10.72%	12.78%	6.32%	*5.00%*	25.50%
2	21,719	4.34	33	0.84	15.91%	9.87%	11.91%	5.45%	*6.18%*	29.95%
3	14,074	4.15	33	0.92	16.78%	10.68%	12.93%	6.47%	*6.63%*	28.42%
←					///					→
24	207	2.32	135	1.27	24.71%	13.87%	17.89%	11.43%	*11.03%*	22.68%
25	76	1.88	249	1.25	25.42%	14.47%	18.68%	12.22%	**12.07%**	23.06%

After all of the available size measures for the subject company have been matched to the closest guideline portfolio in the appropriate exhibit and the corresponding *smoothed average risk premium* has been identified for each, the subject company's cost of equity capital can be estimated, as shown in Exhibit 10.8.

Exhibit 10.8: Build-up 1 Method Cost of Equity Capital Estimate (using guideline portfolios)

	Size Measure (in $millions, except for Number of Employees)	Appropriate Exhibit	Guideline Portfolio	Risk-Free Rate, R_f	Smoothed Premia Over Risk-Free Rate, RP_{m+s}	ERP Adjustment	Cost of Equity Capital k_e
Market Value of Equity	$120	A-1	25	3.5% +	14.0% +	0.5% =	**18.0%**
Book Value of Equity	$100	A-2	25	3.5% +	12.1% +	0.5% =	16.0%
5-year Average Net Income	$10	A-3	24	3.5% +	11.7% +	0.5% =	15.7%
Market Value of Invested Capital	$180	A-4	25	3.5% +	13.5% +	0.5% =	17.4%
Total Assets	$300	A-5	24	3.5% +	11.6% +	0.5% =	**15.6%**
5-year Average EBITDA	$30	A-6	25	3.5% +	12.5% +	0.5% =	16.5%
Sales	$250	A-7	25	3.5% +	12.6% +	0.5% =	16.6%
Number of Employees	200	A-8	25	3.5% +	12.7% +	0.5% =	16.6%
Mean (average) values				3.5% +	12.6% +	0.5% =	**16.6%**
Median (typical) values				3.5% +	12.6% +	0.5% =	**16.6%**

The cost of equity capital for the hypothetical subject company in this example has an estimated cost of capital ranging from 15.6% to 18.0%, with a mean (average) and median (typical) cost of equity capital of 16.6%.

Example 1b: Build-up 1 Method (using regression equations)

When the subject company size measures do not exactly match the respective average company size of the guideline portfolios, the data exhibits provide a straightforward way to interpolate an "exact" risk premium over the risk-free rate (RP_{m+s}) between guideline portfolios using the "regression equation" method.

The *only* difference between estimating cost of equity capital using the Build-up 1 method using "guideline portfolios method" (as in the previous example) and using the "regression equation method" (this example) is how the risk premia over the risk-free rate (RP_{m+s}) are identified.

In the previous example, the *smoothed average risk premia* published in the Risk Premium Report exhibits for the appropriate guideline portfolios were used to estimate cost of equity capital. In this example, the regression equations found on each of the data exhibits will be used to calculate a "custom" interpolated *smoothed average risk premia*, based upon the specific size measures of the subject company.

This example utilizes the same long-term risk-free rate (3.5%) and the ERP Adjustment (0.5%) established in the previous example, so the only missing input is the risk premium over the risk-free rate (RP_{m+s}). Again, according to Exhibit 10.5, our hypothetical subject company has a market value of equity of $120 million, and the appropriate data exhibit is Exhibit A-1 (25 portfolios sorted by market value of equity).

The regression equation provided in Exhibit A-1 (25 portfolios ranked by market value of equity), is:

Smoothed Risk Premium (RP_{m+s}) = 21.363% − 3.525% ∗ Log (Market Value)

To calculate an interpolated risk premium, substitute the subject company's $120 million market value into the regression equation as follows:[10.14]

Smoothed Risk Premium (RP_{m+s}) = 21.363% − 3.525% ∗ Log (120)

The interpolated smoothed risk premium for "market value of equity" is therefore 14.0%:

14.0% = 21.363% − 3.525% ∗ 2.079

This process is continued for each of the eight size characteristics that are available for the subject company. Our hypothetical subject company has a book value of equity of $100 million, and the appropriate data exhibit is Exhibit A-2 (25 portfolios ranked by book value of equity).

The regression equation provided in Exhibit A-2 (25 portfolios ranked by book value of equity), is:

Smoothed Risk Premium (RP_{m+s}) = 16.589% − 2.401% ∗ Log (Book Value)

To calculate an interpolated smoothed risk premium, substitute the subject company's $100 million book value of equity into the regression equation as follows:

Smoothed Risk Premium (RP_{m+s}) = 16.589% − 2.401% ∗ Log (100)

The interpolated smoothed risk premium for "book value of equity" is therefore 11.8%:

11.8% = 16.589% − 2.401% ∗ 2.000

[10.14] Please note that the logarithmic relationship is base-10, and that the financial size data is in millions of dollars, such that the log of $120 million is log (120), not log (120,000,000). The formula to calculate a value's base-10 logarithm in Microsoft Excel is "=log (value)". The "∗" used in the regression equation is the symbol used in Microsoft Excel to denote the multiplication symbol, "x". The "∗" format is also used to denote multiplication in the regression equations in the data exhibits.

Exhibit 10.9 shows the calculations for each of the eight size measure's "custom" interpolated smoothed average risk premia over the risk-free rate (RP_{m+s}).

Exhibit 10.9: Build-up 1 Method Calculation of RP_{m+s} Premia (using regression equations)

	Size Measure (in $millions, except for Number of Employees)	Appropriate Exhibit	Appropriate Regression Equation		Smoothed Premia Over Risk-Free Rate RP_{m+s}
Market Value of Equity	$120	A-1	Smoothed Premium = 21.363% − 3.525% * Log(Market Value)	=	14.0%
Book Value of Equity	$100	A-2	Smoothed Premium = 16.589% − 2.401% * Log(Book Value)	=	11.8%
5-year Average Net Income	$10	A-3	Smoothed Premium = 14.722% − 2.565% * Log(Net Income)	=	12.2%
Market Value of Invested Capital	$180	A-4	Smoothed Premium = 20.607% − 3.226% * Log(MVIC)	=	13.3%
Total Assets	$300	A-5	Smoothed Premium = 18.786% − 2.732% * Log(Assets)	=	12.0%
5-year Average EBITDA	$30	A-6	Smoothed Premium = 15.593% − 2.478% * Log(EBITDA)	=	11.9%
Sales	$250	A-7	Smoothed Premium = 17.796% − 2.442% * Log(Sales)	=	11.9%
Number of Employees	200	A-8	Smoothed Premium = 18.534% − 2.368% * Log(Employees)	=	13.1%

After the "custom" interpolated *smoothed average risk premia* have been calculated for all of the available size measures for the subject, the subject company's cost of equity capital can be estimated, as shown in Exhibit 10.10.

Exhibit 10.10: Build-up 1 Method Cost of Equity Capital Estimate (using regression equations)

	Size Measure (in $millions, except for Number of Employees)	Appropriate Exhibit	Risk-Free Rate, R_f	Smoothed Premia Over Risk-Free Rate, RP_{m+s}	ERP Adjustment	Cost of Equity Capital k_e
Market Value of Equity	$120	A-1	3.5% +	14.0% +	0.5% =	**18.0%**
Book Value of Equity	$100	A-2	3.5% +	11.8% +	0.5% =	**15.8%**
5-year Average Net Income	$10	A-3	3.5% +	12.2% +	0.5% =	16.1%
Market Value of Invested Capital	$180	A-4	3.5% +	13.3% +	0.5% =	17.3%
Total Assets	$300	A-5	3.5% +	12.0% +	0.5% =	16.0%
5-year Average EBITDA	$30	A-6	3.5% +	11.9% +	0.5% =	15.9%
Sales	$250	A-7	3.5% +	11.9% +	0.5% =	15.9%
Number of Employees	200	A-8	3.5% +	13.1% +	0.5% =	17.1%
	Mean (average) values		3.5% +	12.5% +	0.5% =	**16.5%**
	Median (typical) values		3.5% +	12.1% +	0.5% =	**16.1%**

The cost of equity capital for the hypothetical subject company in this example has an estimated cost of capital ranging from 15.8% to 18.0%, with a mean (average) and median (typical) cost of equity capital of 16.5% and 16.1%, respectively.

Unlevered Cost of Equity Capital

Unlevered premia are used to estimate cost of equity capital assuming a firm is financed 100% with equity and 0% debt. Generally, as the percentage of leverage (debt) in a company's capital structure increases, the cost of equity capital increases.

The C exhibits provide *unlevered* "risk premia over the risk-free rate", and enable the valuation analyst to estimate an unlevered cost of equity estimate for the subject company. The C exhibits' unlevered premia are informative in that they generally indicate that the market views smaller companies' operations to be riskier than the operations of larger companies (i.e., unlevered risk premia *increase* as size *decreases*).

The C exhibits also enable a second important capability. The C exhibits provide "comparative risk statistics" that enable the valuation analyst to gauge how "alike or different" the subject company is from the average company that comprises the portfolios in the A and B exhibits. This is an important capability that forms the basis of the Comparative Risk Study. The Comparative Risk Study helps the valuation analyst to potentially "fine tune" the risk premia over the risk-free rate and size premia in the A and B exhibits, respectively, and thus further refine his or her overall cost of equity capital estimate. Examples of using this capability to further refine cost of equity capital estimates are discussed later in this chapter under the section entitled "Comparative Risk Study".

In this section, we first discuss the Risk Premium Report's unlevering and levering methodology, and then provide examples of estimating unlevered cost of equity capital.

Overview of the Methodology and Assumptions Used to Unlever Risk Premia

The average (levered) risk premia presented in Exhibits A-1 through A-8 are unlevered as follows:[10.15]

$$RP_{m+s,\,unlevered} = RP_{m+s,\,levered} - ((W_d / W_e) x (\beta_u - \beta_d) x RP_m)$$

Where:

$RP_{m+s,\,unlevered}$	=	Unlevered realized risk premium over the risk-free rate
$RP_{m+s,\,levered}$	=	Levered realized risk premium over the risk-free rate
β_u	=	Unlevered equity beta
β_d	=	Debt beta, assumed equal to 0.1
RP_m	=	Equity risk premium (ERP) estimate for the "market", represented by the average historical risk premium since 1963
W_d	=	Percent of debt capital in capital structure
W_e	=	Percent of equity capital in capital structure

The average debt to equity (W_d/W_e) ratio of the portfolio is based on the average debt to MVIC for the portfolio since 1963. A debt beta (β_d) of 0.1 is assumed, which is the average estimated debt beta for the companies included in portfolios 1 through 25 over the years 1963 through 2016 after excluding high-financial-risk companies.

A debt beta greater than zero indicates debt capital bears risk of variability of operating net cash flow because interest payments and principal repayments may not be made when owed, implying that tax deductions on the interest expense may not be realized in the period in which the interest is paid. Preferred capital is included with debt capital in measuring the effect of leverage on the risk of equity capital, which is consistent with recent research.

For a detailed discussion about debts betas, see Chapter 5, "Basic Building Blocks of the Cost of Equity Capital – Betas and Industry Risk Premia".

An example of unlevering the average risk premia from the A exhibits is demonstrated using the information found in Exhibit 10.11, 10.12, and 10.13 (these are abbreviated versions of Exhibits A-2, B-2, and C-2, respectively).

[10.15] Derived from R.S. Harris and J. J. Pringle, "Risk-Adjusted Discount Rates – Extensions from the Average Risk Case", *Journal of Financial Research* (Fall 1985) 237–244. Also see: Arzac, Enrique R., and Lawrence R. Glosten. "A Reconsideration of Tax Shield Valuation". *European Financial Management* (2005): 453–461. For a more complete discussion see chapter 12 in *Cost of Capital: Applications and Examples* 5th ed. by Shannon Pratt and Roger Grabowski, Wiley (April 2014).

The average unlevered risk premium of Portfolio 25 in Exhibit C-2 (abbreviated in Exhibit 10.13) is 10.88%, calculated using the following information from Exhibits 10.11, 10.12, and 10.13:

- The arithmetic average risk premium of Portfolio 25 in Exhibit A-2 (see Exhibit 10.11) is 12.22%.

- The debt to market value of equity (W_d/W_e) of Portfolio 25 in Exhibit C-2 (see Exhibit 10.13) is 29.98%.

- The unlevered sum beta (β_u) of Portfolio 25 in Exhibit C-2 (see Exhibit 10.13) is 0.99.

- The debt beta (β_d) is an assumed 0.1, as discussed previously.

The market premium (RP_m) used to calculate the data in the 2017 Risk Premium Report exhibits is the historical ERP from 1963–2016, 5.0%.

Unlevering the average (levered) risk premium in Exhibit A-2 (12.22%), can be accomplished as follows (difference due to rounding):

$$RP_{m+s,unlevered} = RP_{m+s,levered} - ((W_d / W_e) \times (\beta_u - \beta_d) \times RP_m)$$

$$10.88\% = 12.22\% - (29.98\% \times (0.99 - 0.1) \times 5.0\%)$$

Exhibit 10.11: Risk Premium Report Exhibit A-2 (abbreviated)
Companies Ranked by Book Value of Equity
Risk Premia Over the Risk-Free Rate (RP_{m+s})
1963–2016

Portfolio Rank by Size	Average Book Val. (in $millions)	Beta (SumBeta) Since '63	Arithmetic Average Risk Premium
1	67,532	0.78	6.32%
2	21,719	0.84	5.45%
←——— /// ———→			
25	76	1.25	12.22%

Exhibit 10.12: Risk Premium Report Exhibit B-2 (abbreviated)
Companies Ranked by Book Value of Equity
Size Premia
1963–2016

Portfolio Rank by Size	Average Book Val. (in $millions)	Premium over CAPM
1	67,532	2.39%
2	21,719	1.23%
←	///	→
25	76	5.93%

Exhibit 10.13: Risk Premium Report Exhibit C-2 (abbreviated)
Companies Ranked by Book Value of Equity
Comparative Risk Characteristics
1963–2016

Portfolio Rank by Size	Average Book Value (in $millions)	Average Debt to Market Value of Equity	Average Unlevered Risk Premium	Average Unlevered Beta
1	67,532	34.22%	5.45%	0.61
2	21,719	42.75%	4.34%	0.62
←		///		→
25	76	29.98%	10.88%	0.99

Unlevered Risk Premia – Reconciliation of the A, B, and C Exhibits

The levered and unlevered betas for use in CAPM (found in Exhibits B-2 and C-2, respectively) reconcile with the levered and unlevered arithmetic average risk premia for the build-up (found in Exhibits A-2 and C-2, respectively), as demonstrated on the next page using the values from the previous example and the premium over CAPM shown in Exhibit 10.13 (differences due to rounding):

Levered risk premium = Levered beta x Historical market risk premium + Premium over CAPM (i.e., "size premum")

12.22% = 1.25 x 5.0% + 5.93%

Unlevered risk premium = Unlevered beta x Historical market risk premium + Premium over CAPM (i.e., "size premum")

10.88% = 0.99 x 5.0% + 5.93%

Levering

What if the debt-to-market-value-of-equity ratio (W_d/W_e) of the subject company is different from the average (W_d/W_e) of the companies making up Portfolio 25 (29.98% in this case)? It may be possible to adjust the (levered) risk premia over the risk-free rate (RP_{m+s}) from Exhibits A-1 through A-8 for differences in financial leverage between the subject company and the given guideline portfolio. Again, the average (levered) risk premia presented in Exhibits A-1 through A-8 are unlevered as follows:

$$RP_{m+s, unlevered} = RP_{m+s, levered} - ((W_d / W_e) \times (\beta_u - \beta_d) \times RP_m)$$

The unlevered risk premia over the risk-free rate in the C exhibits, which assume a firm is financed 100% with equity and 0% debt, are calculated by unlevering the average risk premia in the A exhibits. In the example, the unlevered risk premium over the risk-free rate ($RP_{m+s, unlevered}$) for Portfolio 25 in Exhibit C-2 (10.88%) was calculated by unlevering the average risk premium over the risk-free rate (RP_{m+s}) for Portfolio 25 in Exhibit A-2 (12.22%). This calculation was performed assuming the 29.98% average debt-to-market-value-of-equity ratio (W_d/W_e) of the companies making up Portfolio 25. The percentage of debt in the capital structure went from 29.98% to 0%, and the unlevered risk premia is lower than the levered risk premium.

This formula can be rearranged to "lever":

$$RP_{m+s, levered} = RP_{m+s, unlevered} + ((W_d / W_e) \times (\beta_u - \beta_d) \times RP_m)$$

If the subject company has a W_d/W_e ratio that is less (say 20%) than the average W_d/W_e of the guideline portfolio (29.98%), the unlevered risk premium may be levered at the subject company's lower ratio:

11.77% = 10.88% + ((20.0%) x (0.99 – 0.1) x 5.0%)

The subject company has less debt relative to equity than the average company in the guideline portfolio (20.0% versus 29.98%), and the relevered risk premium is lower than the average levered risk premium of the guideline portfolio (11.77% versus 12.22%). Generally, as the percentage of leverage (debt) in a company's capital structure decreases, risk to equity investors decreases (and vice versa).

Estimating Cost of Equity Capital Using the "Build-up 1-Unlevered" Method

Estimating cost of equity capital with the "Build-up 1-unlevered" method is identical to estimating cost of equity capital with the Build-up 1 method, with one exception: instead of using the *levered* risk premia over the risk-free rate (RP_{m+s}) found in Exhibits A-1 through A-8, the *unlevered* risk premia over the risk-free rate ($RP_{m+s,\ unlevered}$) found in Exhibits C-1 through C-8 are used. These unlevered risk premia can then be added to a risk-free rate to estimate unlevered cost of equity capital ($k_{e,\ unlevered}$).

Because the unlevered risk premia presented in the C exhibits have an embedded measure of market (i.e., "*beta*") risk, they are not appropriate for use in models (e.g., CAPM) that already have a measure of market (beta) risk.

Examples of both the guideline portfolio method and the regression equation method follow, starting with the guideline portfolio method.

Example 2a: Build-up 1-Unlevered Method (using guideline portfolios)

The Build-up 1-unlevered equation is:

$$k_{e\ build-up\,1} = R_f + RP_{m+s,unlevered} + ERP\ Adjustment$$

Note that the "ERP Adjustment" is a necessary adjustment when using Build-up 1-unlevered. For a detailed discussion of the ERP Adjustment, see the section in Chapter 9 entitled, "Proper Application of the Equity Risk Premium (ERP) Adjustment".

To estimate an unlevered cost of equity capital ($k_{e,\ unlevered}$) with the Build-up 1-unlevered using the "guideline portfolio" method, three pieces of information are needed:

- Risk-free rate (R_f)

- Risk premium over the risk-free rate ($RP_{m+s,\ unlevered}$)

- Equity risk premium adjustment *(ERP Adjustment)*

We have assumed a risk-free rate of 3.5% for all examples, and the ERP Adjustment has been calculated as 0.5% in a previous example, so the only missing input is the risk premium over the risk-free rate ($RP_{m+s,\ unlevered}$):

$$k_{e\ build-up\,1} = 3.5\% + RP_{m+s,\ unlevered} + 0.5\%$$

Gathering the $RP_{m+s,unlevered}$ premia is straightforward. Match the various size measures of the subject company with the guideline portfolios composed of companies of similar size in Exhibits C-1 through C-8, and identify the corresponding *smoothed average unlevered risk premium*.

For example, according to Exhibit 10.5, our hypothetical subject company has a market value of equity of $120 million, and the appropriate data exhibit is Exhibit C-1 (25 portfolios sorted by market value of equity). An abbreviated version of Exhibit C-1 is shown in Exhibit 10.14. Of the 25 portfolios, the portfolio that has an average market value *closest* to the subject company's $120 million market value is Portfolio 25 ($121 million). The corresponding *smoothed average unlevered risk premium* is 12.39% (12.4%, rounded).

Exhibit 10.14: Exhibit C-1 (abbreviated)
Companies Ranked by Market Value of Equity
Unlevered Risk Premia Over the Risk-Free Rate (RP_{m+s})
1963–2016

Portfolio Rank by Size	Average Mkt. Value (in $millions)	Log of Average Mkt. Value	Number of Firms	Arithmetic Average Risk Premium	Average Debt to MVIC	Average Debt to Market Value of Equity	Average Unlevered Risk Premium	Smoothed Average Unlevered Risk Premium
1	238,299	5.38	45	5.20%	14.59%	17.09%	4.67%	1.75%
2	60,613	4.78	36	4.18%	19.02%	23.49%	3.36%	3.67%
3	35,630	4.55	38	5.24%	20.92%	26.46%	4.38%	4.42%
				///				
24	370	2.57	86	12.89%	24.92%	33.19%	11.46%	10.83%
25	121	2.08	249	17.94%	27.08%	37.14%	16.32%	**12.39%**

This process is continued for each of the eight size characteristics that are available for the subject company. After all of the available size measures for the subject company have been matched to the closest guideline portfolio in the appropriate exhibit and the corresponding *smoothed average unlevered risk premium* has been identified for each, the subject company's cost of equity capital can be estimated, as shown in Exhibit 10.15.

Exhibit 10.15: Build-up 1-Unlevered Method Cost of Equity Capital Estimate (using guideline portfolios)

Size Measure (in $millions, except for Number of Employees)		Appropriate Exhibit	Guideline Portfolio	Risk-Free Rate, R_f	Smoothed Unlevered Premia Over Risk-Free Rate, $RP_{m+s,\ unlevered}$	ERP Adjustment	Cost of Equity Capital k_e
Market Value of Equity	$120	C-1	25	3.5% +	12.4% +	0.5% =	**16.4%**
Book Value of Equity	$100	C-2	25	3.5% +	10.7% +	0.5% =	14.6%
5-year Average Net Income	$10	C-3	24	3.5% +	10.3% +	0.5% =	14.3%
Market Value of Invested Capital	$180	C-4	25	3.5% +	11.9% +	0.5% =	15.9%
Total Assets	$300	C-5	24	3.5% +	10.2% +	0.5% =	**14.2%**
5-year Average EBITDA	$30	C-6	25	3.5% +	11.1% +	0.5% =	15.1%
Sales	$250	C-7	25	3.5% +	11.2% +	0.5% =	15.2%
Number of Employees	200	C-8	25	3.5% +	11.2% +	0.5% =	15.2%
		Mean (average) values		3.5% +	11.1% +	0.5% =	**15.1%**
		Median (typical) values		3.5% +	11.1% +	0.5% =	**15.1%**

The unlevered cost of equity capital for the hypothetical subject company in this example has an estimated unlevered cost of capital ranging from 14.2% to 16.4%, with a mean (average) and median (typical) cost of equity capital of 15.1%.

Note that the *unlevered* cost of equity capital estimates calculated in this example are *less* than the *levered* cost of equity capital estimates calculated in Examples 1a and 1b. Again, this is because the unlevered risk premia used to estimate unlevered cost of equity capital are developed assuming a firm is financed 100% with equity and 0% debt. Generally, as the percentage of leverage (debt) in a company's capital structure decreases, risk to equity investors decreases (and vice versa).

Example 2b: Build-up 1-Unlevered Method (using regression equations)

The *only* difference between estimating unlevered cost of equity capital ($k_{e,\ unlevered}$) using the build-up 1-unlevered method using "guideline portfolios" method (Example 2a) and using the "regression equation" method (this example) is how the unlevered risk premia over the risk-free rate ($RP_{m+s,\ unlevered}$) are identified.

This example utilizes the same long-term risk-free rate 3.5% and the ERP Adjustment (0.5%) established in a previous example, so the only missing input is the unlevered risk premium over the risk-free rate ($RP_{m+s,unlevered}$). Again, according to Exhibit 10.5, our hypothetical subject company has a market value of equity of $120 million, and the appropriate data exhibit is Exhibit C-1 (25 portfolios sorted by market value of equity).

The regression equation provided in Exhibit C-1 is:

*Smoothed Unlevered Premium = 19.122% − 3.230% * Log(Market Value)*

To calculate an interpolated smoothed unlevered risk premium, simply substitute the subject company's $120 million market value into the regression equation as follows:

*Smoothed Unlevered Premium (RP$_{m+s, unlevered}$) = 19.122% − 3.230% * Log(120)*

The interpolated smoothed unlevered risk premium over the risk-free rate for "market value of equity" is therefore 12.4%:

*12.4% = 19.122% − 3.230% * 2.079*

This process is continued for each of the eight size characteristics that are available for the subject company. Exhibit 10.16 shows the calculations for each of the eight size measure's "custom" interpolated smoothed average unlevered risk premia over the risk-free rate (RP$_{m+s, unlevered}$).

Exhibit 10.16: Calculation of RP$_{m+s, unlevered}$ Premia (using regression equations)

	Size Measure (in $millions, except for Number of Employees)	Appropriate Exhibit	Appropriate Regression Equation		Smoothed Unlevered Premia Over Risk-Free Rate, RP$_{m+s, unlevered}$
Market Value of Equity	$120	C-1	Smoothed Unlevered Premium = 19.122% − 3.230% * Log(Market Value)	=	12.4%
Book Value of Equity	$100	C-2	Smoothed Unlevered Premium = 14.959% − 2.281% * Log(Book Value)	=	10.4%
5-year Average Net Income	$10	C-3	Smoothed Unlevered Premium = 13.074% − 2.367% * Log(Net Income)	=	10.7%
Market Value of Invested Capital	$180	C-4	Smoothed Unlevered Premium = 18.630% − 3.030% * Log(MVIC)	=	11.8%
Total Assets	$300	C-5	Smoothed Unlevered Premium = 17.337% − 2.694% * Log(Assets)	=	10.7%
5-year Average EBITDA	$30	C-6	Smoothed Unlevered Premium = 13.973% − 2.345% * Log(EBITDA)	=	10.5%
Sales	$250	C-7	Smoothed Unlevered Premium = 16.168% − 2.352% * Log(Sales)	=	10.5%
Number of Employees	200	C-8	Smoothed Unlevered Premium = 16.907% − 2.285% * Log(Employees)	=	11.6%

After the custom interpolated *smoothed average unlevered risk premia* have been calculated for all of the available size measures for the subject company, the subject company's unlevered cost of equity capital can be estimated, as shown in Exhibit 10.17.

Exhibit 10.17: Build-up 1-Unlevered Method Cost of Equity Capital Estimate (using regression equations)

	Size Measure (in $millions, except for Number of Employees)	Appropriate Exhibit	Risk-Free Rate, R_f	Smoothed Unlevered Premia Over Risk-Free Rate, $RP_{m+s,\ unlevered}$	ERP Adjustment	Cost of Equity Capital k_e
Market Value of Equity	$120	C-1	3.5% +	12.4% +	0.5% =	**16.4%**
Book Value of Equity	$100	C-2	3.5% +	10.4% +	0.5% =	**14.4%**
5-year Average Net Income	$10	C-3	3.5% +	10.7% +	0.5% =	14.7%
Market Value of Invested Capital	$180	C-4	3.5% +	11.8% +	0.5% =	15.8%
Total Assets	$300	C-5	3.5% +	10.7% +	0.5% =	14.6%
5-year Average EBITDA	$30	C-6	3.5% +	10.5% +	0.5% =	14.5%
Sales	$250	C-7	3.5% +	10.5% +	0.5% =	14.5%
Number of Employees	200	C-8	3.5% +	11.6% +	0.5% =	15.6%
Mean (average) values			3.5% +	11.1% +	0.5% =	**15.1%**
Median (typical) values			3.5% +	10.7% +	0.5% =	**14.7%**

The unlevered cost of equity capital for the hypothetical subject company in this example has an estimated cost of capital ranging from 14.4% to 16.4%, with a mean (average) and median (typical) cost of equity capital of 15.1% and 14.7%, respectively.

Estimating Cost of Equity Capital Using the Capital Asset Pricing Model (CAPM)

The CAPM is the most widely used method for estimating the cost of equity capital. The Risk Premium Report Size Study calculates average "risk premia over CAPM" (i.e., beta adjusted size premia) for each of the 25 size-ranked portfolios. These size premia (RP_s) are found in Exhibits B-1 through B-8, and can be added to the CAPM as an adjustment for the higher expected returns of smaller companies.

The modified CAPM formula is:[10.16]

$$k_{e\ CAPM} = R_f + (\beta x\ ERP) + RP_s$$

Example 3a: CAPM (using guideline portfolios)

To estimate the cost of equity capital (k_e) with the CAPM method using "guideline portfolios", four pieces of information are needed:

- Risk-free rate (R_f)

- Beta (β)

[10.16] The basic (i.e., "Textbook") CAPM formula is $k_{e.\ CAPM} = R_f + (\beta \ x\ ERP)$. "Modified" CAPM usually refers to the CAPM "modified" to account for risk not captured in the basic CAPM (in this case, "size" risk).

- Equity risk premium (RP_m, otherwise known as ERP)

- Risk premium over CAPM (RP_s, otherwise known as a beta-adjusted "size premium")

We have assumed a risk-free rate of 3.5% and an ERP of 5.5% for all examples. A beta of 1.2 is assumed for the CAPM examples. The ERP Adjustment is *not* needed when estimating cost of equity capital using the Risk Premium Report exhibits' size premia.[10.17] The only missing input is the size premium (RP_s):

$$k_{e\ CAPM} = 3.5\% + (1.2 \times 5.5\%) + RP_s$$

Gathering the *size* premia (RP_s) is straightforward. Match the various size measures of the subject company with the guideline portfolios composed of companies of similar size in Exhibits B-1 through B-8, and identify the corresponding *smoothed average size premium*.

For example, according to Exhibit 10.5, our hypothetical subject company has a market value of equity of $120 million, and the appropriate data exhibit is Exhibit B-1 (25 portfolios sorted by market value of equity). An abbreviated version of Exhibit B-1 is shown in Exhibit 10.18. Of the 25 portfolios, the portfolio that has an average market value *closest* to the subject company's $120 million market value is Portfolio 25 ($121 million). The corresponding *smoothed average size premium* is 7.22% (7.2%, rounded).

Exhibit 10.18: Exhibit B-1 (abbreviated)
Companies Ranked by Market Value of Equity
Size Premia
Data for Year Ending December 31, 2016

Portfolio Rank by Size	Average Mkt. Value (in $millions)	Log of Average Mkt. Value	Beta (SumBeta) Since '63	Arithmetic Average Return	Arithmetic Average Risk Premium	Indicated CAPM Premium	Premium over CAPM	Smoothed Premium over CAPM
1	238,299	5.38	0.83	11.66%	5.20%	4.15%	1.05%	-1.78%
2	60,613	4.78	0.96	10.64%	4.18%	4.84%	-0.65%	-0.16%
3	35,630	4.55	0.92	11.70%	5.24%	4.63%	0.61%	0.47%
←				///				→
24	370	2.57	1.24	19.35%	12.89%	6.22%	6.66%	5.89%
25	121	2.08	1.29	24.39%	17.94%	6.47%	11.47%	**7.22%**

This process is continued for each of the eight size characteristics that are available for the subject company. After all of the available size measures for the subject company have been matched to the closest guideline portfolio in the appropriate exhibit and the corresponding *smoothed average size premium* has been identified for each, the subject company's cost of equity capital can be estimated, as shown in Exhibit 10.19.

[10.17] For a detailed discussion of the ERP Adjustment, see the section entitled "Proper Application of the Equity Risk Premium (ERP) Adjustment" in Chapter 9.

Exhibit 10.19: CAPM Cost of Equity Capital Estimate (using guideline portfolios)

Size Measure (in $millions, except for Number of Employees)		Appropriate Exhibit	Guideline Portfolio	Risk-Free Rate, R_f	Beta β	ERP	Smoothed Risk Premia over CAPM (size premium) RP_s	Cost of Equity Capital k_e
Market Value of Equity	$120	B-1	25	3.5% +	(1.2 x	5.5%) +	7.2% =	**17.3%**
Book Value of Equity	$100	B-2	25	3.5% +	(1.2 x	5.5%) +	5.2% =	15.3%
5-year Average Net Income	$10	B-3	24	3.5% +	(1.2 x	5.5%) +	5.2% =	15.3%
Market Value of Invested Capital	$180	B-4	25	3.5% +	(1.2 x	5.5%) +	6.5% =	16.6%
Total Assets	$300	B-5	24	3.5% +	(1.2 x	5.5%) +	5.1% =	**15.2%**
5-year Average EBITDA	$30	B-6	25	3.5% +	(1.2 x	5.5%) +	5.6% =	15.7%
Sales	$250	B-7	25	3.5% +	(1.2 x	5.5%) +	6.0% =	16.1%
Number of Employees	200	B-8	25	3.5% +	(1.2 x	5.5%) +	6.3% =	16.4%
		Mean (average) values		3.5% +	(1.2 x	5.5%) +	5.9% =	**16.0%**
		Median (typical) values		3.5% +	(1.2 x	5.5%) +	5.8% =	**15.9%**

The hypothetical subject company in this example has an estimated cost of capital ranging from 15.2% to 17.3%, with a mean (average) and median (typical) cost of equity capital of 16.0% and 15.9%, respectively.

Example 3b: CAPM (using regression equations)

The *only* difference between estimating cost of equity capital (k_e) using the CAPM method using "guideline portfolios" (Example 3a) and using "regression equations" is how the size premia (RP_s) are identified.

In the previous example, the smoothed size premia *published* in the Risk Premium Report exhibits for the appropriate guideline portfolios were used to estimate cost of equity capital. In this example, however, the regression equations found in each of the data exhibits will be used to calculate "custom" interpolated smoothed size premia, based upon the specific size measures of the subject company.

This example utilizes the same long-term risk-free rate of 3.5%, ERP of 5.5%, and beta of 1.2 used in a previous example, so the only missing input is the size premium (RP_s). Again, according to Exhibit 10.5, our hypothetical subject company has a market value of equity of $120 million, and the appropriate data exhibit is Exhibit B-1 (25 portfolios sorted by market value of equity).

The regression equation provided in Exhibit B-1 is:

*Smoothed Size Premium = 12.911% − 2.733% * Log (Market Value)*

To calculate an interpolated smoothed size premium for the subject company's $120 million market value, simply substitute the market value into the regression equation as follows:

*Smoothed Size Premium (RP_s) = 12.911% − 2.733% * Log (120)*

The interpolated smoothed size premium for "market value of equity" is therefore 7.2%:

7.2% = 12.911% − 2.733% * 2.079

This process is continued for each of the eight size characteristics that are available for the subject company. Exhibit 10.20 shows the calculations for each of the eight size measure's custom interpolated smoothed size premium (RP_s).

Exhibit 10.20: Calculation of Size Premia (RP_s) (using regression equations)

Size Measure (in $millions, except for Number of Employees)	Appropriate Exhibit	Appropriate Regression Equation		Smoothed Risk Premia over CAPM (size premium) RP_s
Market Value of Equity	$120	B-1	Smoothed Premium = 12.911% − 2.733% * Log(Market Value) =	7.2%
Book Value of Equity	$100	B-2	Smoothed Premium = 7.887% − 1.430% * Log(Book Value) =	5.0%
5-year Average Net Income	$10	B-3	Smoothed Premium = 7.144% − 1.648% * Log(Net Income) =	5.5%
Market Value of Invested Capital	$180	B-4	Smoothed Premium = 11.680% − 2.332% * Log(MVIC) =	6.4%
Total Assets	$300	B-5	Smoothed Premium = 9.744% − 1.771% * Log(Assets) =	5.4%
5-year Average EBITDA	$30	B-6	Smoothed Premium = 7.506% − 1.526% * Log(EBITDA) =	5.3%
Sales	$250	B-7	Smoothed Premium = 9.598% − 1.711% * Log(Sales) =	5.5%
Number of Employees	200	B-8	Smoothed Premium = 11.083% − 1.925% * Log(Employees) =	6.7%

After the custom interpolated *smoothed size premia* have been calculated for all of the available size measures for the subject company, the subject company's cost of equity capital can be estimated, as shown in Exhibit 10.21.

Exhibit 10.21: CAPM Cost of Equity Capital Estimate (using regression equations)

Size Measure (in $millions, except for Number of Employees)	Appropriate Exhibit	Risk-Free Rate, R_f	Beta β	ERP	Smoothed Risk Premia over CAPM (size premium) RP_s	Cost of Equity Capital k_e
Market Value of Equity	$120	B-1	3.5% +	(1.2 x | 5.5%) +	7.2% =	**17.3%**
Book Value of Equity	$100	B-2	3.5% +	(1.2 x | 5.5%) +	5.0% =	**15.1%**
5-year Average Net Income	$10	B-3	3.5% +	(1.2 x | 5.5%) +	5.5% =	15.6%
Market Value of Invested Capital	$180	B-4	3.5% +	(1.2 x | 5.5%) +	6.4% =	16.5%
Total Assets	$300	B-5	3.5% +	(1.2 x | 5.5%) +	5.4% =	15.5%
5-year Average EBITDA	$30	B-6	3.5% +	(1.2 x | 5.5%) +	5.3% =	15.4%
Sales	$250	B-7	3.5% +	(1.2 x | 5.5%) +	5.5% =	15.6%
Number of Employees	200	B-8	3.5% +	(1.2 x | 5.5%) +	6.7% =	16.8%
Mean (average) values			3.5% +	(1.2 x | 5.5%) +	5.9% =	**16.0%**
Median (typical) values			3.5% +	(1.2 x | 5.5%) +	5.5% =	**15.6%**

The cost of equity capital for the hypothetical subject company in this example has an estimated cost of capital ranging from 15.1% to 17.3%, with a mean (average) and median (typical) cost of equity capital of 16.0% and 15.6%, respectively.

Estimating Cost of Equity Capital Using the "Build-up 2" Method

The Risk Premium Report's Size Study can be used in conjunction with the industry risk premia previously published in the *SBBI Valuation Edition Yearbook*, and now published in the *2017 Valuation Handbook – U.S. Guide to Cost of Capital* in Appendix 3a.[10.18]

The "Build-up 1" method presented previously in Examples 1a and 1b utilizes a risk premia over the risk-free rate that are a measure of risk in terms of the combined effect of *market* risk and *size* risk. Build-up 2, however, adds the equity risk premium and a *separate* beta-adjusted size premium to the risk-free rate, and *then* accounts for market (i.e., beta) risk by adding an industry risk premium. As such, Build-up 2 is a hybrid of the CAPM method and Build-up 1 method, with beta risk taking the form of an industry risk premium (RP_i).[10.19]

Because Risk Premium Report size premia are "beta adjusted"[10.20], without the addition of an industry risk premium (RP_i), beta risk is not accounted for:

$$\underbrace{k_{e\,build\text{-}up\,2} = R_f + ERP + RP_s}_{\text{No Beta Risk}} + \underbrace{RP_i}_{\text{Beta Risk}}$$

An industry risk premium is just a beta "scaled around zero" so that it becomes a simple up or down adjustment when used within the context of a build-up method. To create industry risk premia in the *2017 Valuation Handbook – U.S. Guide to Cost of Capital*, we transform what are known as "full-information" (industry) betas into industry risk premia using the formula (FIB x ERP) – ERP. The result is:

- A full-information beta = 1 (which matches the "market's" beta) will become an industry risk premium of "0" (*equal* in risk to the market);

- A full-information beta > 1 will become an industry risk premium *greater* than zero (*riskier* than the market); and

- A full-information beta < 1 will become an industry risk premium less than zero (*less* risky than the market).

[10.18] A detailed discussion of betas and industry risk premia is in Chapter 5, "Basic Building Blocks of the Cost of Equity Capital – Betas and Industry Risk Premia".

[10.19] The industry risk premia previously published in the *SBBI Valuation Yearbook's* Table 3-5 were denoted as "IRP" in equations. In the *2017 Valuation Handbook – U.S. Guide to Cost of Capital* industry risk premia are denoted as "RP_i" in equations. This change in nomenclature was done to match the nomenclature used in *Cost of Capital: Applications and Examples* 5th ed. (Wiley, 2014).

[10.20] All Risk Premium Report size premia *and* CRSP Deciles Size Premia published in the *2017 Valuation Handbook – U.S. Guide to Cost of Capital* are "beta-adjusted". A beta-adjusted size premium has been adjusted to remove that portion of excess return that is attributable to beta, leaving only the size effect's contribution to excess return.

Example 4a: Build-up 2 Method (using guideline portfolios)

To estimate the cost of equity capital (k_e) with the Build-up 2 method using "guideline portfolios", four pieces of information are needed:

- Risk-free rate (R_f)

- Equity risk premium (RP_m, otherwise known as ERP),

- Risk premium over CAPM (RP_s, otherwise known as a beta-adjusted "size premium")

- Industry Risk Premium (RP_i)

We have assumed a risk-free rate of 3.5%, an ERP of 5.5%, and an industry risk premium of 1.1% for all Build-up 2 examples.[10.21] The only missing input is the size premium (RP_s):

$$k_{e\ build-up\ 2} = 3.5\% + 5.5\% + RP_s + 1.1\%$$

The ERP Adjustment is *not* needed when estimating cost of equity capital using the Risk Premium Report exhibits' size premia.[10.22]

Gathering the *size* premia (RP_s) is straightforward. Match the various size measures of the subject company with the guideline portfolios composed of companies of similar size in Exhibits B-1 through B-8, and identify the corresponding *smoothed average size premium*.

For example, according to Exhibit 10.5, our hypothetical subject company has a market value of equity of $120 million, and the appropriate data exhibit is Exhibit B-1 (25 portfolios sorted by market value of equity). An abbreviated version of Exhibit B-1 is shown in Exhibit 10.22. Of the 25 portfolios, the portfolio that has an average market value *closest* to the subject company's $120 million market value is Portfolio 25 ($121 million). The corresponding *smoothed average size premium* is 7.22% (7.2%, rounded).

[10.21] The assumed industry risk premium of 1.1% is derived by a transformation of the assumed beta of 1.2 that was used for the CAPM examples, using the Duff & Phelps recommended ERP of 5.5%. 1.1% = (1.2 x 5.5%) − 5.5%.

[10.22] For a detailed discussion of the ERP Adjustment, see the section entitled "Proper Application of the Equity Risk Premium (ERP) Adjustment" in Chapter 9.

Exhibit 10.22: Exhibit B-1 (abbreviated)
Companies Ranked by Market Value of Equity
Size Premia
Data for Year Ending December 31, 2016

Portfolio Rank by Size	Average Mkt. Value (in $millions)	Log of Average Mkt. Value	Beta (SumBeta) Since '63	Arithmetic Average Return	Arithmetic Average Risk Premium	Indicated CAPM Premium	Premium over CAPM	Smoothed Premium over CAPM
1	238,299	5.38	0.83	11.66%	5.20%	4.15%	1.05%	-1.78%
2	60,613	4.78	0.96	10.64%	4.18%	4.84%	-0.65%	-0.16%
3	35,630	4.55	0.92	11.70%	5.24%	4.63%	0.61%	0.47%
←				///				→
24	370	2.57	1.24	19.35%	12.89%	6.22%	6.66%	5.89%
25	121	2.08	1.29	24.39%	17.94%	6.47%	11.47%	**7.22%**

This process is continued for each of the eight size characteristics that are available for the subject company. After all of the available size measures for the subject company have been matched to the closest guideline portfolio in the appropriate exhibit and the corresponding *smoothed average size premium* has been identified for each, the subject company's cost of equity capital can be estimated, as shown in Exhibit 10.23.

Exhibit 10.23: Build-up 2 Method Cost of Equity Capital Estimate (using guideline portfolios)

	Size Measure (in $millions, except for Number of Employees)	Appropriate Exhibit	Guideline Portfolio	Risk-Free Rate, R_f	ERP	Smoothed Risk Premia over CAPM (size premium) RP_s	Industry Risk Premia RP_i	Cost of Equity Capital k_e
Market Value of Equity	$120	B-1	25	3.5% +	5.5% +	7.2% +	1.1% =	**17.3%**
Book Value of Equity	$100	B-2	25	3.5% +	5.5% +	5.2% +	1.1% =	15.3%
5-year Average Net Income	$10	B-3	24	3.5% +	5.5% +	5.2% +	1.1% =	15.3%
Market Value of Invested Capital	$180	B-4	25	3.5% +	5.5% +	6.5% +	1.1% =	16.6%
Total Assets	$300	B-5	24	3.5% +	5.5% +	5.1% +	1.1% =	**15.2%**
5-year Average EBITDA	$30	B-6	25	3.5% +	5.5% +	5.6% +	1.1% =	15.7%
Sales	$250	B-7	25	3.5% +	5.5% +	6.0% +	1.1% =	16.1%
Number of Employees	200	B-8	25	3.5% +	5.5% +	6.3% +	1.1% =	16.4%
		Mean (average) values		3.5% +	5.5% +	5.9% +	1.1% =	**16.0%**
		Median (typical) values		3.5% +	5.5% +	5.8% +	1.1% =	15.9%

The hypothetical subject company in this example has an estimated cost of capital ranging from 15.2% to 17.3%, with a mean (average) and median (typical) cost of equity capital of 16.0% and 15.9%, respectively.

Example 4b: Build-up 2 Method (using regression equations)

The *only* difference between estimating cost of equity capital (k_e) using the Build-up 2 method using "guideline portfolios" and using "regression equations" is how the size premia (RP_s) are identified.

In the previous example, the smoothed size premia *published* in the Risk Premium Report exhibits for the appropriate guideline portfolios were used to estimate cost of equity capital. In this example, however, the regression equations found in each of the data exhibits will be used to calculate "custom" interpolated smoothed size premia, based upon the specific size measures of the subject company.

This example utilizes the same long-term risk-free rate of 3.5%, ERP of 5.5%, and RP_i of 1.1% used in the previous example, so the only missing input is the size premium (RP_s). Again, according to Exhibit 10.5, our hypothetical subject company has a market value of equity of $120 million, and the appropriate data exhibit is Exhibit B-1 (25 portfolios sorted by market value of equity).

The regression equation provided in Exhibit B-1 is:

*Smoothed Size Premium = 12.911% − 2.733% * Log (Market Value)*

To calculate an interpolated smoothed size premium for the subject company's $120 million market value, simply substitute the market value into the regression equation as follows:

*Smoothed Size Premium (RP_s) = 12.911% − 2.733% * Log (120)*

The interpolated smoothed size premium for "market value of equity" is therefore 7.2%:

*7.2% = 12.911% − 2.733% * 2.079*

This process is continued for each of the eight size characteristics that are available for the subject company. Exhibit 10.24 shows the calculations for each of the eight size measure's "custom" interpolated smoothed size premium (RP_s).

Exhibit 10.24: Calculation of Size Premia (RP_s) (using regression equations)

	Size Measure (in $millions, except for Number of Employees)	Appropriate Exhibit	Appropriate Regression Equation		Smoothed Risk Premia over CAPM (size premium) RP_s
Market Value of Equity	$120	B-1	Smoothed Premium = 12.911% − 2.733% * Log(Market Value)	=	7.2%
Book Value of Equity	$100	B-2	Smoothed Premium = 7.887% − 1.430% * Log(Book Value)	=	5.0%
5-year Average Net Income	$10	B-3	Smoothed Premium = 7.144% − 1.648% * Log(Net Income)	=	5.5%
Market Value of Invested Capital	$180	B-4	Smoothed Premium = 11.680% − 2.332% * Log(MVIC)	=	6.4%
Total Assets	$300	B-5	Smoothed Premium = 9.744% − 1.771% * Log(Assets)	=	5.4%
5-year Average EBITDA	$30	B-6	Smoothed Premium = 7.506% − 1.526% * Log(EBITDA)	=	5.3%
Sales	$250	B-7	Smoothed Premium = 9.598% − 1.711% * Log(Sales)	=	5.5%
Number of Employees	200	B-8	Smoothed Premium = 11.083% − 1.925% * Log(Employees)	=	6.7%

After the "custom" interpolated *smoothed size premia* have been calculated for all of the available size measures for the subject company, the subject company's cost of equity capital can be estimated, as shown in Exhibit 10.25.

Exhibit 10.25: Build-up 2 Method Cost of Equity Capital Estimate (using regression equations)

	Size Measure (in $millions, except for Number of Employees)	Appropriate Exhibit	Risk-Free Rate, R_f	ERP	Smoothed Risk Premia Over CAPM (size premium), RP_s	Industry Risk Premia RP_i	Cost of Equity Capital k_e
Market Value of Equity	$120	B-1	3.5% +	5.5% +	7.2% +	1.1% =	**17.3%**
Book Value of Equity	$100	B-2	3.5% +	5.5% +	5.0% +	1.1% =	**15.1%**
5-year Average Net Income	$10	B-3	3.5% +	5.5% +	5.5% +	1.1% =	15.6%
Market Value of Invested Capital	$180	B-4	3.5% +	5.5% +	6.4% +	1.1% =	16.5%
Total Assets	$300	B-5	3.5% +	5.5% +	5.4% +	1.1% =	15.5%
5-year Average EBITDA	$30	B-6	3.5% +	5.5% +	5.3% +	1.1% =	15.4%
Sales	$250	B-7	3.5% +	5.5% +	5.5% +	1.1% =	15.6%
Number of Employees	200	B-8	3.5% +	5.5% +	6.7% +	1.1% =	16.8%
	Mean (average) values		3.5% +	5.5% +	5.9% +	1.1% =	**16.0%**
	Median (typical) values		3.5% +	5.5% +	5.5% +	1.1% =	**15.6%**

The cost of equity capital for the hypothetical subject company in this example has an estimated cost of capital ranging from 15.1% to 17.3%, with a mean (average) and median (typical) cost of equity capital of 16.0% and 15.6%, respectively.

Risk Study

The Risk Premium Report's Risk Study is an extension of the Size Study. The main difference between the Risk Study and the Size Study is that the Size Study analyzes the relationship between *size* and return, and the Risk Study analyzes the relationship between *fundamental risk measures* (based on accounting data) and return. These are called "fundamental" measures of company risk to distinguish these risk measures from a stock market based measure of equity risk such as beta. A variety of academic studies have examined the relationship between financial statement data and various aspects of business risk.[10.23] Research has shown that measures of earnings volatility can be useful in explaining credit ratings, predicting bankruptcy, and explaining the CAPM beta.

As in the Size Study, 25 portfolios are created, but instead of being ranked by eight alternative measures of size as is done in the Size Study, the Risk Study portfolios are ranked by three fundamental risk measures:

- Five-year average operating income margin

- Coefficient of variation in operating income margin

- Coefficient of variation in return on book equity[10.24]

The first statistic measures profitability and the other two statistics measure volatility of earnings. Companies with *lower* operating margins tend to be *riskier* (and vice versa). Companies with *greater* coefficient of variation of earnings (as measured by operating income margin and return on book equity) tend to be *riskier* (and vice versa).

Size and Risk

Traditionally, valuation analysts have used company size as a factor in determining discount rates for smaller companies. The historical data as presented in the Risk Premium Report studies and in the CRSP Deciles Size Premia studies, verify that small companies have, in fact, earned higher rates of return over long-run periods.

Some have pointed that researchers may be mixing a "size" effect with a "risk" effect when measuring company size by market value, but market value is not just a function of size; it is also a function of the discount rate.[10.25] In other words, some companies might be small because they are risky, rather than risky because they are small.

The Risk Study goes *beyond* size and investigates the relationship between equity returns and fundamental risk measures. Does the evidence support the claim that smaller companies inherently have greater risk? The Risk Study analyzes this question, and demonstrates that as company size decreases, measures of risk calculated from financial statement data do, as a matter of fact, tend to

---

[10.23] A survey of the academic research can be found in *The Analysis and Use of Financial Statements*, 3rd edition, White et al., Wiley (2003), Chapter 18.

[10.24] Coefficient of variation is defined here as the standard deviation divided by the mean.

[10.25] "A Critique of Size Related Anomalies", Jonathan Berk, *Review of Financial Studies*, vol. 8, no. 2 (1995).

increase. The data clearly show that as fundamental risk increases in the form of lower profitability or greater variability of earnings, the return over the risk-free rate tends to increase.

Previously, it was demonstrated in the Risk Premium Report's Size Study that there is a clear inverse relationship between size and historical rates of return (as size *decreases*, returns tend to *increase*). In the Risk Premium Report's Risk Study, the data show a clear *direct* relationship between accounting-data-based fundamental risk measures and historical rates of return (as fundamental risk *increases*, returns tend to *increase*).

In Exhibit 10.26, the average annual return of the 25 portfolios of *each* of the three fundamental risk measures analyzed in the Risk Study is calculated over the time horizon 1963–2016, with risk increasing from left to right. For example, the portfolios comprised of companies with the *highest* operating margins and *least* coefficient of variation for operating income margin and return on book equity are on the left side of the graph; the portfolios comprised of companies with the *lowest* operating margins and *greatest* coefficient of variation for operating income margin and return on book equity are on the *right* side of the graph

In the Risk Premium Report exhibits, the average annual return of the portfolios made up of companies with the *lowest* risk as measured by each of the three fundamental risk measures was 13.9%, while the average annual return of the portfolios made up of companies with the *highest* risk was 19.6%, as shown in Exhibit 10.26.

Exhibit 10.26: Average Annual Return, Risk Study's Three Measures of Fundamental Risk 1963–2016

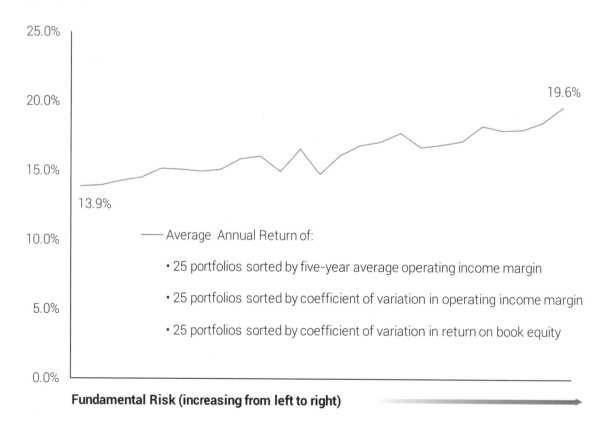

— Average Annual Return of:

• 25 portfolios sorted by five-year average operating income margin

• 25 portfolios sorted by coefficient of variation in operating income margin

• 25 portfolios sorted by coefficient of variation in return on book equity

Fundamental Risk (increasing from left to right)

Reasons for Using Fundamental Measures of Risk in Addition to Measures of Size

First, certain measures of size (such as market value of equity) may be imperfect measures of the risk of a company's operations in some situations. For example, a company with a large and stable operating margin may have a small and unstable market value of equity if it is highly leveraged. In this case the risk of the underlying operations is low while the risk to equity is high. Second, while small size may indicate greater risk, some small companies may maintain near economic monopolies by holding a geographic niche or market niche such that their true riskiness is less than what would be indicated by their size.

Alternatively, while larger size (as measured by sales, for example) may indicate less risk, some companies may be riskier than the average of companies with similar sales. For example, assume the subject company was expecting to emerge from reorganization following bankruptcy. The risk premium appropriate for this company may be more accurately imputed from the pro forma operating profit (after removing non-recurring expenses incurred during the bankruptcy) than from its size as measured by sales. In other words, the subject company may be riskier than companies with similar sales volumes.

Use of fundamental accounting measures of risk allows for direct assessment of the riskiness of the subject company. For example, if the appropriate risk premium for the subject company when measuring risk by one or more fundamental risk measures is different from the risk premium based on size measures, this difference may be an indication of the "company-specific" differences of the subject company's fundamental risk and the average fundamental risk of companies that make up the portfolios from which the risk premia are derived.[10.26]

[10.26] *Valuing a Business*, 4th ed., Pratt et. Al., McGraw-Hill (2000), p. 181. Examples of risks that are typically referred to as "company-specific" risk can include concentration of customer base, key person dependence, key supplier dependence, or any number of other factors that are perceived as unique to the subject company.

The D Exhibits: Summary of Data Presented

Exhibits D-1, D-2, and D-3: The D exhibits provide risk premia over the risk-free rate in terms of the combined effect of market risk and company-specific risk, as represented by the differences in three alternative accounting-based measures of fundamental risk (RP_{m+c}).

Each of the exhibits D-1 through D-3 present 25 portfolios ranked by three fundamental risk factors (based on accounting data), as described in Exhibit 10.27.[10.27]

Exhibit 10.27: Three Measures of Fundamental Risk in the Risk Study's D Exhibits

---

Exhibit D-1

Operating Margin: The mean operating income for the prior five years divided by the mean sales for the prior five years. Operating income is defined as sales minus (cost of goods sold plus selling, general, and administrative expenses plus depreciation). Note that this composite ratio is usually very close to a simple average of the annual ratios of operating income to sales, except in extreme cases generally involving companies with high growth rates.

Exhibit D-2

Coefficient of Variation of Operating Margin: The standard deviation of operating margin over the prior five years divided by the average operating margin for the same years. Note that for calculating this coefficient, average operating margin is a simple average of the annual ratios of operating income to sales rather than the composite ratio used in exhibit D-1.

Exhibit D-3

Coefficient of Variation of Return on Book Value of Equity: The standard deviation of return on book equity for the prior five years divided by the mean return on book equity for the same years. Return on book equity is defined as net income before extraordinary items minus preferred dividends divided by book value of common equity.

[10.27] For a detailed description of the Standard & Poor's *Compustat* data items used as inputs in the calculation of the data in the Risk Premium Report exhibits, please see Appendix 1.

The D exhibits include the statistics outlined in Exhibit 10.28 for each of the risk measures outlined in Exhibit 10.27. For comparative purposes, the average returns from the SBBI series for large companies (essentially the S&P 500 Index), small companies, and long-term government bond income returns for the period 1963 through the latest year are also reported on each exhibit.[10.28]

Exhibit 10.28: Statistics Reported for 25 fundamental-risk-ranked portfolios in the Risk Study's D Exhibits

- The average of the sorting criteria for the latest year (e.g., the average operating margin for the latest five years ending 2015). Note that the reported average risk statistics in exhibits D-1, D-2, and D-3 are *not* the same numbers as reported in exhibits C-1 through C-8. In exhibits C-1 through C-8, the reported statistics are calculated for portfolios of companies grouped according to size and are averages since 1963. In exhibits D-1, D-2, and D-3, the reported statistics are calculated for portfolios grouped according to risk, independent of the "size" of the companies, and are not averages since 1963.

- Log (base-10) of the median of the sorting criteria.

-
  The number of companies in each portfolio as of 2016.

-
  Standard deviation of annual historical equity returns.

- Beta calculated using the "sum beta" method applied to monthly returns for 1963 through the latest year.

- Unlevered beta calculated using the "sum beta" method applied to monthly returns for 1963 through the latest year.

- Geometric average historical equity return since 1963.

- Arithmetic average historical equity return since 1963.

- Arithmetic average historical risk premium over long-term Treasuries (average return on equity in excess of long-term Treasury bonds) since 1963. (RP_{m+s+c}).

- Average Debt as a percent of the MVIC since 1963.

- Smoothed average historical risk premium over long-term Treasuries (average return on equity in excess of long-term Treasury bonds) since 1963: the fitted premium from a regression with the historical "risk premium over long-term Treasuries" as dependent variable and the logarithm of the average sorting criteria as independent variable. (RP_{m+s+c}).

- Unlevered arithmetic average historical risk premium over long-term Treasuries (average return on equity in excess of long-term Treasury bonds) since 1963. ($RP_{m+s+c, unlevered}$).

[10.28] Source: Morningstar *Direct* database.

Is Size Correlated with Market and Fundamental Risk Measures?

The *same* universe of companies used to create the A, B, and C exhibits is the *same* universe of companies used to create the D exhibits. However, the *composition* of any of the 25 portfolios in the D exhibits is *different* from the composition of the 25 portfolios in the A, B, C exhibits.

In the case of the A and B exhibits, the portfolios are sorted (largest to smallest) by each of eight alternative measures of *size*, and *then* the fundamental risk characteristics of each portfolio are calculated and reported in the C exhibits. In the case of the D exhibits, the *same* set of companies that are in the A, B, and C exhibits are sorted by each of the three *fundamental risk measures* (from highest to lowest) to form 25 risk-ranked portfolios, and then the average risk characteristics of each portfolio are calculated.

Why the composition of any one of the D exhibit's 25 portfolios is likely different from the composition of any one of the A, B, and C exhibits 25 portfolios can be illustrated with a simple example. Say you have 10 companies and you sort them by *size* (from largest to smallest). Then (using the *same* 10 companies), you sort them again by a *fundamental risk measure* like operating margin (from highest to lowest). Will the order necessarily be the same? Probably not.

Nonetheless, the Risk Premium Exhibits do suggest that size is correlated with market measures. For example, as size measures decrease in Exhibit 10.29 (from left to right), the beta (both levered and unlevered) of the portfolios increase (as expected).[10.29]

Exhibit 10.29: Average Levered and Unlevered Sum Beta (all eight size measures)

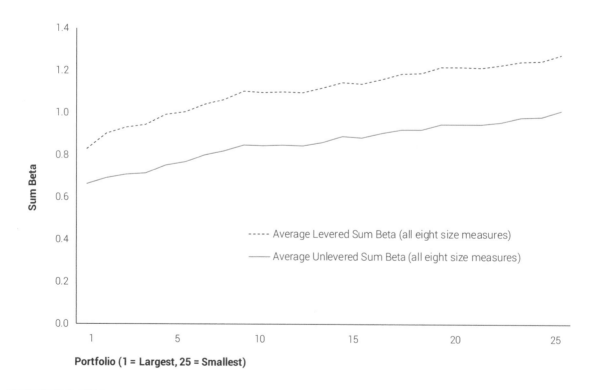

[10.29] In the research on "size" as reported in this report, we have determined that, in the context of the CAPM, the higher betas of the small companies explain some but not all of the higher average historical equity returns in these portfolios.

The data also suggest that this correlation extends to the three fundamental measures of risk. For example, in Exhibit 10.30, as size measures *decrease* (from left to right), operating margin of the portfolios *decreases* (indicating increased risk).

Exhibit 10.30: Average Operating Margin (all eight size measures)
1963–2016

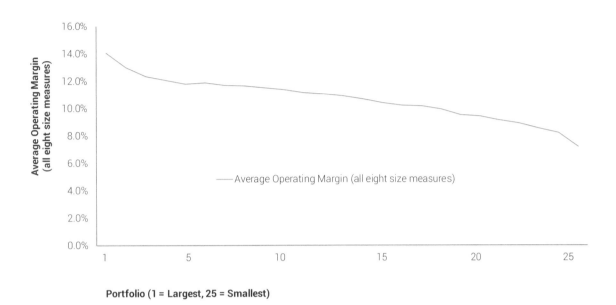

And in Exhibit 10.31, as size measures *decrease* (from left to right), average coefficient of operating margin and average coefficient of variation of ROE of the portfolios *increase* (indicating increased risk).

Exhibit 10.31: Average Coefficient of Operating Margin and Average Coefficient of Variation of ROE
All 8 Size Measures
1963–2016

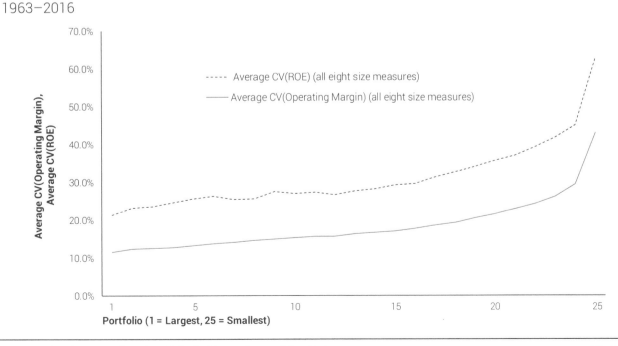

While the correlation between fundamental measures of risk and size demonstrated in Exhibits 10.30 and 10.31 implies that there may be an embedded "size effect" component in the Risk Study's RP_{m+c} premia, the magnitude of this embedded size effect is difficult to quantify. In any case, the size effect embedded in the Risk Study's RP_{m+c} premia are in all likelihood not equivalent to the size effect embedded in the Size Study's RP_{m+s} premia, which are a measure of risk in terms of the combined effect of *market* risk and *size* risk.

Overview of Methods Used to Estimate Cost of Equity Capital Using the Risk Study

The Risk Premium Report's Risk Study provides one method of estimating cost of equity capital for a subject company, Build-up 3, and one method for estimating *unlevered* cost of equity capital (the cost of equity capital assuming a firm is financed 100% with equity and 0% debt), Build-up 3-unlevered.

These two methods are summarized in Exhibit 10.32:

Exhibit 10.32:

Method	Cost of Equity Capital Formula
Build-up 3	$k_e = R_f + RP_{m+c} + ERP\ Adjustment$
Build-up 3-Unlevered	$k_e = R_f + RP_{m+c,\ unlevered} + ERP\ Adjustment$

Risk Study Examples: Assumptions Used

The Risk Study's D exhibits provide "risk premia over the risk-free rate" in terms of the combined effect of market risk and company-specific risk. As such, the same assumptions that were used in the Build-up 1 examples (which utilized "risk premia over the risk-free rate" from the A exhibits) can be used:

- **Valuation Date:** December 31, 2016[10.30]

- **ERP:** 5.5% [10.31]

- **Risk-free Rate:** 3.5% (normalized rate)

- **ERP Adjustment:** 0.5%[10.32]

[10.30] The "data through" date of the *2017 Valuation Handbook – U.S. Guide to Cost of Capital* is December 31, 2016.

[10.31] The Duff & Phelps recommended ERP as of December 31, 2016 is 5.5%, and is intended to be used in conjunction with a 3.5% normalized risk-free rate, as reported in Exhibit 3.19, "Duff & Phelps Recommended ERP and Corresponding Risk-Free Rate January 2008–Present". For detailed information about the ERP and risk-free rates, see Chapter 3, "Basic Building Blocks of the Cost of Equity Capital – Risk-free Rate and Equity Risk Premium".

[10.32] The ERP adjustment is *never* necessary when using size premia, but is *always* necessary when using "risk premia over the risk-free rate", such as are found in the D exhibits. The ERP adjustment in this example is calculated as the difference between the ERP selected to use in these examples (5.5%) and the historical 1963–2016 ERP (5.0%) that was used as a convention to calculate the 2017 Risk Premium Report exhibits. For detailed information about the ERP Adjustment, see the section entitled "Proper Application of the Equity Risk Premium (ERP) Adjustment" in Chapter 9, "Risk Premium Report Exhibits – General Information".

Gathering Accounting Information to Calculate Fundamental Risk Measures

The first step in using the Risk Study to estimate cost of equity capital is to gather the accounting-based information for the subject company that is needed to calculate the three fundamental risk measures analyzed in the Risk Study.

To calculate "operating margin" and "coefficient of variation of operating margin", net sales and operating income are needed.

To calculate "coefficient of variation of ROE", book value and net income before extraordinary items are needed. The accounting information for the last five years needed to calculate the three fundamental risk measures for our hypothetical subject company is summarized in Exhibits 10.33 and 10.34.

Hypothetical Subject Company Fundamental Risk Characteristics

The three fundamental risk measures (five-year average operating income margin, coefficient of variation in operating margin, coefficient of variation in return on book equity) that will be used in the two Risk Study examples are calculated in Exhibits 10.33 and 10.34, and summarized in Exhibit 10.35.

It is important to note that the subject company information necessary to calculate all three of these measures may not be available. In these cases, it is generally acceptable to use the fundamental risk measures that are available. It is recommended, however, that users calculate available risk measures for the subject company using *at least* the three most recent years of data, and the five most recent years of data for best results.

All the examples herein are calculated using full precision decimals. Differences may arise if the user were to hand calculate the examples due to rounding differences.

Exhibit 10.33: Subject Company Operating Margin and Coefficient of Variation of Operating Margin (used in all Risk Study examples)

	2016	**2015**	**2014**	**2013**	**2012**
Net Sales	$900	$800	$850	$750	$900
Operating Income	$150	$120	$130	$80	$140
Operating Margin	16.7% = $150/$900	15.0% = $120/$800	15.3% = $130/$850	10.7% = $80/$750	15.6% = $140/$900
Standard Deviation of Operating Margin	2.3%				
Average Operating Margin	**14.6%**				
Coefficient of Variation of Operating Margin	**15.8%** = 2.3%/14.6%				

Exhibit 10.34: Subject Company Coefficient of Variation of ROE (used in all Risk Study examples)

	2016	**2015**	**2014**	**2013**	**2012**
Book Value	$820	$710	$630	$540	$500
Net Income before extraordinary items	$110	$80	$90	$40	$100
Return on Book Equity (ROE)	13.4% = $110/$820	11.3% = $80/$710	14.3% = $90/$630	7.4% = $40/$540	20.0% = $100/$500
Standard Deviation of ROE	4.6%				
Average ROE	13.3%				
Coefficient of Variation of ROE	**34.7%** = 4.6%/13.3%				

The hypothetical subject company has an average operating margin of 14.6%, a coefficient of variation of operating margin of 15.8%, and a coefficient of variation of ROE of 34.7%, as summarized in Exhibit 10.35.

Exhibit 10.35: Subject Company Fundamental Risk Characteristics
(used in all Risk Study examples)

| | Risk Measure | Appropriate Exhibit | |
		Buildup 3	Buildup 3-Unlevered
Average Operating Margin	14.6%	D-1	D-1
Coefficient of Variation of Operating Margin	15.8%	D-2	D-2
Coefficient of Variation of ROE	34.7%	D-3	D-3

Exhibit 10.35 also includes the data exhibits in which the appropriate risk premia for each of the size measures can be found. For example, for use in the Build-up 3 method, risk premia over the risk-free rate (RP_{m+c}) for "coefficient of variation of operating margin" are found in Exhibit D-2. For use in the Build-up 3-unlevered method, unlevered risk premia over the risk-free rate ($RP_{m+c, unlevered}$) for "coefficient of variation of operating margin" are *also* found in Exhibit D-2.

Risk Study Examples

Build-up 3

The Build-up 3 method is an additive model used for calculating the required rate of return on equity capital. As the name implies, successive "building blocks" are summed, each representing the additional risk inherent to investing in alternative assets.

Examples of both the guideline portfolio method and the regression equation method follow, starting with the simpler guideline portfolio method. In general, the regression equation method is preferred because this method allows for interpolation between the individual guideline portfolios, although the guideline portfolio method is less complicated, and more direct.

Example 5a: Build-up 3 Method (using guideline portfolios)

The Build-up 3 equation is:

$$k_{e\,build-up\,3} = R_f + RP_{m+c} + ERP\ Adjustment$$

Note that the "ERP Adjustment" is a necessary adjustment when using Build-up 3. For a detailed discussion of the ERP Adjustment, see the section in Chapter 9 entitled, "Proper Application of the Equity Risk Premium (ERP) Adjustment".

To estimate the cost of equity capital (k_e) with the Build-up 3 using the "guideline portfolio" method, three pieces of information are needed:

- Risk-free rate (R_f)

- Risk premium over the risk-free rate (RP_{m+c})

- Equity risk premium adjustment (ERP Adjustment)

We have assumed a risk-free rate of 3.5% for all examples, and the ERP Adjustment has been calculated as 0.5% in a previous example, so the only missing input is the risk premium over the risk-free rate (RP_{m+c}):

$$k_{e\ build-up\ 3} = 3.5\% + RP_{m+c} + 0.5\%$$

Gathering the RP_{m+c} premia is straightforward. Match the various fundamental risk measures of the subject company with the guideline portfolios composed of companies of similar size in Exhibits D-1, D-2, and D-3, and identify the corresponding *smoothed average risk premium*.

For example, according to Exhibit 10.35, our hypothetical subject company has an average operating margin of 14.6%, and the appropriate data exhibit is Exhibit C-1 (25 portfolios sorted by operating margin). An abbreviated version of Exhibit D-1 is shown in Exhibit 10.36. Of the 25 portfolios, the portfolio that has an average operating margin *closest* to the subject company's 14.6% is Portfolio 10 (14.62%). The corresponding *smoothed average risk premium* is 9.02% (9.0%, rounded).

Exhibit 10.36: Exhibit D-1 (abbreviated)
Companies Ranked by Operating Margin
Risk Premia over the Risk-Free Rate (RP_{m+c})
1963–2016

Portfolio Rank	Average Operating Margin	Log of Average Op Margin	Number as of 2016	Beta (SumBeta) Since '63	Arithmetic Average Unlevered Risk Premium	Smoothed Average Risk Premium	Average Debt to Market Value of Equity
1	38.24%	-0.42	76	0.90	6.22%	6.23%	31.17%
2	28.34%	-0.55	64	0.84	4.92%	7.10%	35.29%
3	24.42%	-0.61	51	0.87	6.42%	7.54%	33.21%
4	21.81%	-0.66	47	0.94	6.15%	7.86%	28.59%
5	20.20%	-0.69	47	0.98	7.72%	8.09%	24.81%
6	18.66%	-0.73	38	1.06	7.69%	8.32%	21.76%
7	17.56%	-0.76	54	1.10	7.50%	8.49%	23.32%
8	16.50%	-0.78	45	1.10	6.95%	8.67%	23.59%
9	15.47%	-0.81	44	1.14	8.84%	8.86%	24.05%
10	14.62%	-0.84	42	1.16	8.19%	**9.02%**	26.04%

This process is continued for each of the fundamental risk characteristics that are available for the subject company. After all of the available fundamental risk measures for the subject company have been matched to the closest guideline portfolio in the appropriate exhibit and the corresponding *smoothed average risk premium* has been identified for each, the subject company's cost of equity capital can be estimated, as shown in Exhibit 10.37.

Exhibit 10.37: Build-up 3 Method Cost of Equity Capital Estimate (using guideline portfolios)

	Risk Measure	Appropriate Exhibit	Guideline Portfolio	Risk-Free Rate, R_f		Smoothed Premium Over Risk-Free Rate, RP_{m+c}		ERP Adjustment		Cost of Equity Capital k_e
Average Operating Margin	14.6%	D-1	10	3.5%	+	9.0%	+	0.5%	=	**13.0%**
Coefficient of Variation of Operating Margin	15.8%	D-2	12	3.5%	+	9.7%	+	0.5%	=	13.7%
Coefficient of Variation of ROE	34.7%	D-3	12	3.5%	+	9.8%	+	0.5%	=	**13.8%**
		Mean (average) values		3.5%	+	9.5%	+	0.5%	=	**13.5%**
		Median (typical) values		3.5%	+	9.7%	+	0.5%	=	**13.7%**

The hypothetical subject company in this example has an estimated cost of capital ranging from 13.0% to 13.8%, with a mean (average) and median (typical) cost of equity capital of 13.5% and 13.7%, respectively.

Example 5b: Build-up 3 Method (using regression equations)

The *only* difference between estimating cost of equity capital (k_e) using the Build-up 3 method using "guideline portfolios" and using "regression equations" is how the risk premia over the risk-free rate (RP_{m+c}) are identified.

In the previous example, the smoothed risk premia over the risk-free rate *published* in the Risk Premium Report exhibits for the appropriate guideline portfolios were used to estimate cost of equity capital. In this example, however, the regression equations found in each of the data exhibits will be used to calculate "custom" interpolated smoothed risk premia, based upon the specific fundamental risk measures of the subject company.

This example utilizes the same long-term risk-free rate of 3.5%, ERP of 5.5%, and subject company fundamental risk factors as shown in Exhibit 10.35 that were used in the previous example, so the only missing input is the risk premium over the risk-free rate (RP_{m+c}). Again, according to Exhibit 10.35, our hypothetical subject company has an average operating margin of 14.8%, and the appropriate data exhibit is Exhibit D-1 (25 portfolios sorted by operating margin).

The regression equation provided in Exhibit D-1 is:

*Smoothed Size Premium (RP_{m+c}) = 3.445% − 6.681% * Log (Operating Margin)*

To calculate an interpolated smoothed risk premium for the subject company's 14.6% operating margin, simply substitute the operating margin into the regression equation as follows:

Smoothed Size Premium (RP$_{m+c}$) = 3.445% − 6.681% ∗ Log (14.6%)

The interpolated smoothed risk premium for "operating margin" is therefore 9.0%:

9.0% = 3.445% − 6.681% ∗ -0.835

This process is continued for each of the three fundamental risk characteristics that are available for the subject company. Exhibit 10.38 shows the calculations for each of the three fundamental risk measure's custom interpolated smoothed risk premium (RP$_{m+c}$).

Exhibit 10.38: Build-up 3 Calculation of RP$_{m+c}$ Premia (using regression equations)

	Risk Measure	Appropriate Exhibit	Appropriate Regression Equation		Smoothed Premium Over Risk-Free Rate, RP$_{m+c}$
Average Operating Margin	14.6%	D-1	Smoothed Premium = 3.445% − 6.681% ∗ Log(Op. Margin)	=	9.0%
Coefficient of Variation of Operating Margin	15.8%	D-2	Smoothed Premium = 11.956% + 2.766% ∗ Log(CV(Op. Margin))	=	9.7%
Coefficient of Variation of ROE	34.7%	D-3	Smoothed Premium = 10.976% + 2.482% ∗ Log(CV(ROE))	=	9.8%

After the "custom" interpolated *smoothed average risk premia* have been calculated for all of the available fundamental risk measures, the subject company's cost of equity capital can be estimated, as shown in Exhibit 10.39.

Exhibit 10.39: Build-up 3 Method Cost of Equity Capital Estimate (using regression equations)

	Risk Measure	Appropriate Exhibit	Risk-Free Rate, R$_f$		Smoothed Premium Over Risk-Free Rate, RP$_{m+c}$		ERP Adjustment		Cost of Equity Capital k$_e$
Average Operating Margin	14.6%	D-1	3.5%	+	9.0%	+	0.5%	=	**13.0%**
Coefficient of Variation of Operating Margir	15.8%	D-2	3.5%	+	9.7%	+	0.5%	=	13.7%
Coefficient of Variation of ROE	34.7%	D-3	3.5%	+	9.8%	+	0.5%	=	**13.8%**
		Mean (average) values	3.5%	+	9.5%	+	0.5%	=	**13.5%**
		Median (typical) values	3.5%	+	9.7%	+	0.5%	=	**13.7%**

The hypothetical subject company in this example has an estimated cost of capital ranging from 13.0% to 13.8%, with a mean (average) and median (typical) cost of equity capital of 13.5% and 13.7%, respectively.

Build-up 3-Unlevered

The Build-up 3-unlevered method is an additive model used for calculating the required rate of return on equity capital. As the name implies, Build-up-3 is used for estimating *unlevered* cost of equity capital (the cost of equity capital assuming a firm is financed 100% with equity and 0% debt).

Example 6: Build-up 3-Unlevered Method (using guideline portfolios)

The Build-up 3 equation is:

$$k_{e\ Build\text{-}up\ 3\text{-}unlevered} = R_f + RP_{m+c,\ unlevered} + ERP\ Adjustment$$

Note that the "ERP Adjustment" is a necessary adjustment when using Build-up 3-Unlevered method. For a detailed discussion of the ERP Adjustment, see the section in Chapter 9 entitled, "Proper Application of the Equity Risk Premium (ERP) Adjustment".

To estimate the cost of equity capital (k_e) with the Build-up 3 using the "guideline portfolio" method, three pieces of information are needed:

- Risk-free rate (R_f)

- Unlevered Risk premium over the risk-free rate ($RP_{m+c,\ unlevered}$)

- Equity risk premium adjustment (*ERP Adjustment*)

We have assumed a risk-free rate of 3.5% for all examples, and the ERP Adjustment has been calculated as 0.5% in a previous example, so the only missing input is the unlevered risk premium over the risk-free rate ($RP_{m+c,\ unlevered}$):

$$k_{e\ Build\text{-}up\ 3\text{-}unlevered} = 3.5\% + RP_{m+c,\ unlevered} + 0.5\%$$

Gathering the $RP_{m+c,\ unlevered}$ premia is straightforward. Match the various fundamental risk measures of the subject company with the guideline portfolios composed of companies of similar size in Exhibits D-1, D-2, and D-3, and identify the corresponding *average unlevered risk premium*.

For example, according to Exhibit 10.35, our hypothetical subject company has an average operating margin of 14.6%, and the appropriate data exhibit is Exhibit D-1 (25 portfolios sorted by operating margin). An abbreviated version of Exhibit D-1 is shown in Exhibit 10.40. Of the 25 portfolios, the portfolio that has an average operating margin *closest* to the subject company's 14.6% is Portfolio 10 (14.62%). The corresponding *average unlevered risk premium* is 8.19% (8.2%, rounded).

Exhibit 10.40: Exhibit D-1 (abbreviated)
Companies Ranked by Operating Margin
Risk Premia over the Risk-Free Rate ($RP_{m+c,\ unlevered}$)
1963–2016

Portfolio Rank	Average Operating Margin	Log of Average Op Margin	Number as of 2014	Beta (SumBeta) Since '63	Arithmetic Average Unlevered Risk Premium	Smoothed Average Risk Premium	Average Debt to Market Value of Equity
1	38.24%	-0.42	76	0.90	6.22%	6.23%	31.17%
2	28.34%	-0.55	64	0.84	4.92%	7.10%	35.29%
3	24.42%	-0.61	51	0.87	6.42%	7.54%	33.21%
4	21.81%	-0.66	47	0.94	6.15%	7.86%	28.59%
5	20.20%	-0.69	47	0.98	7.72%	8.09%	24.81%
6	18.66%	-0.73	38	1.06	7.69%	8.32%	21.76%
7	17.56%	-0.76	54	1.10	7.50%	8.49%	23.32%
8	16.50%	-0.78	45	1.10	6.95%	8.67%	23.59%
9	15.47%	-0.81	44	1.14	8.84%	8.86%	24.05%
10	14.62%	-0.84	42	1.16	**8.19%**	9.02%	26.04%

This process is continued for each of the fundamental risk characteristics that are available for the subject company. After all of the available fundamental risk measures for the subject company have been matched to the closest guideline portfolio in the appropriate exhibit and the corresponding *average unlevered risk premium* has been identified for each, the subject company's unlevered cost of equity capital can be estimated, as shown in Exhibit 10.41.

Exhibit 10.41: Build-up 3 Method Unlevered Cost of Equity Estimate (using guideline portfolios)

	Risk Measure	Appropriate Exhibit	Guideline Portfolio	Risk-Free Rate, R_f	Unlevered Premium Over Risk-Free Rate, $RP_{m+c,\ unlevered}$	ERP Adjustment	Cost of Equity Capital k_e
Average Operating Margin	14.6%	D-1	10	3.5% +	8.2% +	0.5% =	**12.2%**
Coefficient of Variation of Operating Margin	15.8%	D-2	12	3.5% +	8.9% +	0.5% =	12.9%
Coefficient of Variation of ROE	34.7%	D-3	12	3.5% +	7.3% +	0.5% =	**11.3%**
		Mean (average) values		3.5% +	8.1% +	0.5% =	**12.1%**
		Median (typical) values		3.5% +	8.2% +	0.5% =	**12.2%**

The hypothetical subject company in this example has an estimated unlevered cost of capital ranging from 11.3% to 12.2%, with a mean (average) and median (typical) cost of equity capital of 12.1% and 12.2%, respectively.

High-Financial-Risk Study

The Risk Premium Report exhibits are primarily designed to be used to develop cost of equity capital estimates for the majority of companies that are fundamentally healthy, and for which a "going concern" assumption is appropriate. A set of "high-financial-risk" companies is set aside and analyzed separately in the High-Financial-Risk Study.[10.33]

The companies analyzed in the High-Financial-Risk Study are identified in a two-step process. First, companies that are losing money, have high leverage, or are in bankruptcy are identified and eliminated from the base set of companies used in the Size Study and Risk Study.[10.34] It is possible to imagine companies that don't have any of these characteristics but could still be classified as high-financial-risk (i.e., "distressed"), and it is also possible to imagine companies which do have one or more of these characteristics but are not distressed. For this reason, these companies are further scrutinized in a second test where they are ranked by the appropriate Altman z-Score (for "manufacturing" companies or for "service" companies).[10.35,10.36]

Those companies identified as being in the "safe zone" (as defined by their z-Score) failed the first test, but passed the second test (z-Score), and are set aside and not used in any further analysis due to the inconclusive results. The remaining companies failed both the first test and the second test, and are placed in either the "gray" or "distressed" zone (as defined by their z-Score). The resulting base set of high-financial-risk companies is composed largely of companies whose financial condition is significantly inferior to the average, financially "healthy" public company. The results of the High-Financial-Risk Study are presented in the H exhibits. The H exhibits provide risk premia that may be used in both build-up and CAPM estimates of cost of equity capital if the individual analyst has determined that the subject company is "high-financial-risk".[10.37]

In cases in which the individual analyst has determined that the subject company is "high-financial-risk", the high-financial-risk premia reported in the H exhibits should be used instead of the returns reported in the Size Study, and not added to those returns.

[10.33] For detailed information on the types of companies excluded from the Risk Premium Report Study's portfolios, see the section entitled "Risk Premium Report Portfolios" in Chapter 7, "The CRSP Decile Studies and the Risk Premium Report Studies – A Comparison".

[10.34] The number of companies eliminated in this screen varies from year to year. These companies represented up to 25% of the data set in recent years, but less than 5% in 1963. Certain technical changes in methodology have resulted in a greater number of companies falling into the high-financial-risk database than in versions of this study published prior to 2000.

[10.35] Altman z-Score is an accounting-data-based method designed to assess financial condition and developed originally for assessing the likelihood of bankruptcy. E. I. Altman, "Financial Ratios, Discriminant Analysis and the Prediction of Corporate Bankruptcy", *The Journal of Finance*, Vol. 23, No. 4 (Sep., 1968), pp. 589–609; "Predicting Financial Distress of Companies: Revisiting the z-Score and Zeta Models", July 2000; "Revisiting Credit Scoring Models in a Basel 2 Environment", May 2002.

[10.36] Service industry companies are those in SIC codes: 7200, 7300, 7500, 7600, 8000, 8100, 8200, 8300, 8400, 8700. Manufacturing companies are in all other SIC codes, with the exception of SICs beginning with "6" (financial institutions) or "9" (government). SIC 6 and SIC 9 are not included in the Report's analysis.

[10.37] The decision to apply a high-financial-risk premium is ultimately dependent on the valuation analyst's professional judgment, based upon the analyst's detailed knowledge of the subject company.

The High-Financial-Risk "H" Exhibits

Exhibit H-A: The high-financial-risk equivalent of the A exhibits. "High-financial-risk premia over the risk-free rate" for use in the build-up method are found in the H-A exhibits. These premia can be added to the risk-free rate to estimate the cost of equity capital for a company that has been judged by the analyst to be high-financial-risk.

Exhibit H-B: The high-financial-risk equivalent of the B exhibits. "High-financial-risk premia over CAPM" (i.e., "size premia") for use with the CAPM method are found in the H-B exhibits. These premia can be used in the CAPM to estimate the cost of equity capital for a company that has been judged by the analyst to be high-financial-risk.

Exhibit H-C: The high-financial-risk equivalent of the C exhibits. The H-C exhibits can be used to *compare* the subject company's fundamental risk characteristics to the fundamental risk characteristics of portfolios made up of companies with similar z-Scores.

Why isn't there an H-D exhibit? In the Risk Premium Report D exhibits, operating margin and two other measures of risk are examined (coefficient of variation in operating margin and coefficient of variation in return on equity). Because the denominators of the latter two ratios are often negative for companies in the high-financial-risk portfolio (as a result of either negative earnings or negative book value of equity), developing comparable "high-financial-risk" premia for these frequently results in meaningless statistics.

Altman z-Score

Altman's z-Score was originally designed as a measure to predict the risk of failure up to two years prior to distress for a sample of manufacturing companies using financial data prepared according to the standards of the day. The accuracy of predicting the risk of failure diminished substantially as the lead time increased. The z-Score resulted from a statistical analysis of company data using the statistical technique of multiple discriminant analysis.

Altman has since offered improvements on the original z-Score, but the original z-Score is still frequently calculated as a convenient metric that captures within a single statistic a number of disparate financial ratios measuring liquidity, profitability, leverage, and asset turnover.[10.38]

Manufacturing Companies and z-Score

Z-Score ratios are not strictly comparable across industries or across time (for instance, one would expect large differences in asset turnover among an industrial company or a retailer), and as such, are not used here as a predictor of bankruptcy per se, but as mechanism for ranking the high-financial-risk companies by their relative levels of distress. The following z-Score model for publicly traded "manufacturing" companies (i.e., excluding service industry companies) is used in preparing the analyses presented in the H-A, H-B, and H-C exhibits:

[10.38] In applying any of the z-Score equations cited here, express the ratios in terms of their decimal equivalents (e.g., x_1 = working capital / total assets = 0.083).

$$z = 1.2x_1 + 1.4x_2 + 3.3x_3 + 0.6x_4 + 0.999x_5$$

where:

z = Overall index

x_1 = Net working capital/total assets

x_2 = Retained earnings/total assets

x_3 = Earnings before interest and income taxes/total assets

x_4 = Market value of common equity/book value of total liabilities

x_5 = Sales/total assets

The companies are then sorted by z-Score into three portfolios:

$z > 2.99$ = "safe zone"

$1.80 < z < 2.99$ = "gray zone"

$z < 1.80$ = "distress zone"

Companies in the "safe" zone (z-Score greater than 2.99) are set aside and not used in any further analysis. Companies in the "gray" zone (z-Score between 1.80 and 2.99) and companies in the "distressed" zone (z-Score less than 1.80) are used to form the portfolios from which the statistics presented in H-A, H-B, and H-C exhibits are calculated. Portfolios are rebalanced annually (i.e., the companies are re-ranked and sorted at the beginning of each year). Portfolio rates of return were calculated using an equal-weighted average of the companies in the portfolio.

Service Companies and z''-Score

The following z''-Score model for publicly traded "service" industry high-financial-risk companies is used in preparing the analyses presented in the H-A, H-B, and H-C exhibits:

$$z'' = 6.56x_1 + 3.26x_2 + 6.72x_3 + 1.05x_4$$

where:

z'' = Overall index

x_1 = Net working capital/total assets

x_2 = Retained earnings/total assets

x_3 = Earnings before interest and income taxes/total assets

x_4 = Book value of common equity/book value of total liabilities

The companies are then sorted by z"-Score into three portfolios:

z" > 2.60 = "safe zone"

1.10 < z" < 2.60 = "gray zone"

z" < 1.10 = "distress zone"

Companies in the "safe" zone (z"-Score greater than 2.60) are set aside and not used in any further analysis. Companies in the "gray" zone (z"-Score between 1.10 and 2.60) and companies in the "distressed" zone (z"-Score less than 1.10) are used to form the portfolios from which the statistics presented in H-A, H-B, and H-C exhibits are calculated. Portfolios are rebalanced annually (i.e., the companies are re-ranked and sorted at the beginning of each year). Portfolio rates of return were calculated using an equal-weighted average of the companies in the portfolio.

Again, in both cases (manufacturing and service), we are not using the z-Score or z"-Score as a predictor of bankruptcy. Rather, companies are ranked in the High-Financial-Risk Study based on their relative levels of distress, using z-Score and z"-Score as proxies for "distress".

Non-Public Companies and z'-Score

The traditional z-Score was developed using data for publicly traded companies, and one of the statistics utilizes stock price. This creates problems for application of the data to non-public companies. Altman developed a similar model using only the financial statement data for non-public companies. If the subject company is not publicly traded and not in the service industry, then the analyst can calculate a z-Score for non-public companies (the z'-Score) to compare with the data in the accompanying exhibits:

$z' = 0.717x_1 + 0.847x_2 + 3.107x_3 + 0.420x_4 + 0.998x_5$

where:

z' = Overall index

x_1 = Working capital/total assets

x_2 = Retained earnings/total assets

x_3 = Earnings before interest and income taxes/total assets

x_4 = Book value of common equity/book value of total liabilities

x_5 = Sales/total assets

The z'-Score's "zones of discrimination" loosely approximate the boundaries used to separate the z-Score and z"-Score ranked companies into portfolios, and are as follows:

z' > 2.90 = "safe zone"

1.23 < z' < 2.90 = "gray zone"

z' < 1.23 = "distress zone"

While the H-A, H-B, and H-C exhibits are sorted by using the publicly traded company equations (z-Score for manufacturing companies and z"-Score for service companies) and are not strictly comparable to the z'-Score for non-public companies, the returns reported in these exhibits can be useful in developing cost of equity estimates based on the relative zones of discrimination.

Measurement of Historical Risk Premia

As with the *2017 Valuation Handbook – U.S. Guide to Cost of Capital's* Risk Premium Report A, B, C, and D exhibits, the High-Financial-Risk Study's H exhibits report average historical risk premia for the period 1963–2016 (1963 is the year that the Standard & Poor's *Compustat* database was inaugurated). A long-run average historical risk premium is often used as an indicator of the expected risk premium of a typical equity investor. Returns are based on dividend income plus capital appreciation and represents returns after corporate taxes (but before owner level taxes).

To estimate historical risk premia, an average rate of return is first calculated for each portfolio over the sample period. Portfolios with fewer than six companies in any given year are excluded in the averages. Lastly, the average income return earned on long-term U.S. government bonds is subtracted from the portfolios' returns over the same period (using SBBI data) to arrive at an average historical risk premium for investments in equity.

The "H" Exhibits – Summary of Data Presented

Each of the exhibits H-A, H-B, and H-C displays one line of data for each of the z-Score- and z"-Score-ranked portfolios. For comparative purposes, the average returns from the SBBI series for large companies (essentially the S&P 500 Index), small companies, and long-term government bond income returns for the period 1963 through the latest year are also reported on each exhibit.[10.39]

The H-A, H-B, and H-C exhibits include the statistics outlined in Exhibit 10.42.

[10.39] Source: Morningstar *Direct* database.

Exhibit 10.42: Statistics Reported for the z-Score- and z"-Score-ranked High-Financial-Risk Study's H-A, H-B, and H-C Exhibits

Exhibit H-A	Exhibit H-B	Exhibit H-C
• Beta calculated using the "sum beta" method applied to monthly returns for 1963 through 2016.	• Beta calculated using the "sum beta" method applied to monthly returns for 1963 through 2016.	• Arithmetic average historical risk premium over long-term Treasuries (average return on equity in excess of long-term Treasury bonds) since 1963 ($RP_{m+s,\ high\ financial\ risk}$).
• Standard deviation of annual historical equity returns.	• Arithmetic average historical equity return since 1963.	• Average carrying value of preferred stock plus long-term debt (including current portion) plus notes payable ("Debt") as a percent of MVIC since 1963.
• Geometric average historical equity return since 1963.	• Arithmetic average historical risk premium over long-term Treasuries (average return on equity in excess of long-term Treasury bonds) since 1963 ($RP_{m+s,\ high\ financial\ risk}$).	• Average debt to market value of equity.
• Arithmetic average historical equity return since 1963.	• Indicated CAPM premium, calculated as the beta of the portfolio multiplied by the average historical market risk premium since 1963 (measured as the difference between SBBI Large Stock total returns and SBBI income returns on long-term Treasury bonds).	• Beta calculated using the "sum beta" method applied to monthly returns for 1963 through 2016.
• Arithmetic average historical risk premium over long-term Treasuries (average return on equity in excess of long-term Treasury bonds) since 1963 ($RP_{m+s,\ high\ financial\ risk}$).	• Premium over CAPM, calculated by subtracting the "Indicated CAPM Premium" from the "Arithmetic Risk Premium" ($RP_{s,\ high\ financial\ risk}$).	• Operating Margin: The median operating income for the prior five years divided by the mean sales for the prior five years. Operating income is defined as sales minus cost of goods sold plus selling, general, and administrative expenses plus depreciation.
• Average carrying value of preferred stock plus long-term debt (including current portion) plus notes payable ("Debt") as a percent of MVIC since 1963.		

Overview of Methods Used to Estimate Cost of Equity Capital Using the High-Financial-Risk Study

The cost of equity capital estimation methods provided by the Risk Premium Report's High-Financial-Risk Study are summarized in Exhibit 10.43.

Exhibit 10.43: Methods of Estimating Cost of Equity Capital Using the Risk Premium Report's High-Financial-Risk Study

Method	Cost of Equity Capital Formula
Build-up 1-High-Financial-Risk	$k_e = R_f + RP_{m+s,\ high\text{-}financial\text{-}risk} + ERP\ Adjustment$
CAPM-High-Financial-Risk	$k_e = R_f + (\beta * ERP) + RP_{s,\ high\text{-}financial\text{-}risk}$

Note that the ERP Adjustment *is* a necessary adjustment when using the Build-up 1-High-Financial-Risk method. The ERP Adjustment is *not* necessary when using the CAPM-High-Financial-Risk method. For a detailed discussion of the ERP Adjustment, see the section in Chapter 9 entitled, "Proper Application of the Equity Risk Premium (ERP) Adjustment".

Hypothetical Subject Company Size Characteristics

The information in Exhibit 10.44 will be used to estimate cost of equity capital for a hypothetical non-service (i.e., "manufacturing") subject company.

Exhibit 10.44: Subject Company Characteristics (used in all examples)

	(in $millions)		(in $millions)
Market value of equity	$80	Sales	$250
Book value of equity	$100	Current assets	$75
Total assets	$300	Current liabilities	$50
Most recent year EBIT	-$5	Retained earnings	$75

The z-Score equation for a publicly traded, non-service (i.e., "manufacturing") subject company is:

$z = 1.2x_1 + 1.4x_2 + 3.3x_3 + 0.6x_4 + 0.999x_5$

The inputs (x_1, x_2, x_3, x_4, and x_5) needed for the z-Score equation are calculated as shown in Exhibit 10.45.

Exhibit 10.45: z-Score Inputs Calculation

x_1	=	Net working capital / total assets	=	(\$75 current assets - \$50 current liabilities) / (\$300 total assets)	=	0.0833
x_2	=	Retained earnings / total assets	=	(\$75 retained earnings) / (\$300 total assets)	=	0.2500
x_3	=	Earnings before interest and taxes / total assets	=	(-\$5 EBIT) / (\$300 total assets)	=	-0.0167
x_4	=	Market value of common equity / book value of total liabilities	=	(\$80 market value of equity) / (\$300 total assets - \$100 book value of equity)	=	0.4000
x_5	=	Sales / total assets	=	(\$250 sales) / (\$300 total assets)	=	0.8333

Substituting these inputs into the z-Score equation yields a z-Score of 1.47:

$z = 1.2(0.0833) + 1.4(0.2500) + 3.3(-0.0167) + 0.6(0.4000) + 0.999(0.8333)$

$1.47 = 0.1000 + 0.3500 + (-0.0551) + 0.2400 + 0.8325$

Estimating Cost of Equity Capital Using the "Build-up 1-High-Financial-Risk" Method

The Build-up 1-High-Financial-Risk equation is:

$$k_{e\ build-up\ 1-HFR} = R_f + RP_{m+s,HFR} + ERP\ Adjustment$$

This example utilizes the same long-term risk-free rate (3.5%) and ERP Adjustment (0.5%) established in a previous example, so the only missing input is the high-financial-risk risk premium over the risk-free rate ($RP_{m+s,HFR}$):

$$k_{e\ build-up\ 1-HFR} = 3.5\% + RP_{m+s,\ HFR} + 0.5\%$$

The determination of the high-financial-risk premium in Exhibit H-A is a three-step process:

Step 1: Determine whether the characteristics of the subject company better match the characteristics of the companies included in Exhibits A-1 through A-8 (the 25 portfolios) or the characteristics of the high-financial-risk portfolios. The most straightforward way of doing this is to answer the following *five questions* about the subject company:[10.40]

- Is the subject company in bankruptcy or in liquidation?

- Is the subject company's "5-year average net income available to common equity" less than zero for the previous five years?

- Is the subject company's "5-year-average operating income" less than zero for the previous five years?

- Has the subject company had a negative book value of equity at any one of the company's previous five fiscal year-ends?

- Does the subject company have a debt-to-total capital ratio of more than 80%?

If you answered "Yes" to one or more of the five questions, it may suggest that the subject company's characteristics are more like the companies that make up the "high-financial-risk" portfolios rather than like the "healthy" companies that make up the standard 25 portfolios, but this is not necessarily so. It is, after all, possible to imagine companies which do have one or more of these characteristics, but are not distressed. Alternatively, it is also possible to imagine companies that do not have any of these characteristics, but could still be classified as high-financial-risk (i.e., "distressed").

For example, a company may have a debt-to-total capital ratio greater than 80%, but this does not automatically imply that the company is distressed. Alternatively, a company may have a debt-to-total capital ratio less than 80%, but could still be in a distressed state due to other factors.

A decision by the individual analyst that a company should be treated as "high-financial-risk" should be based on a detailed evaluation of the company's current financial condition and circumstances, and will generally involve more than a review of historical financial statistics and ratios. This decision ("distressed" or "not distressed") is ultimately dependent on the individual analyst's professional judgment and detailed knowledge of the subject company.

[10.40] These five questions mirror the five criteria by which high-financial-risk companies are identified in (and eliminated from) the universe of U.S. companies to form the base set of companies used in the Risk Premium Report's Size Study and Risk Study.

Step 2: If the individual analyst determines that the subject company's characteristics better match the characteristics of the companies comprising the high-financial-risk portfolios, calculate the z-Score of the subject company using the appropriate z-Score equation:[10.41]

- z-Score is for publicly traded, non-service, (i.e., "manufacturing") companies[10.42]

- z"-Score is for publicly traded, "service" companies

- z'-Score is non-public, non-service companies.

Step 3: Lastly, if the z-Score[10.43] of the subject company indicates that it is in the "gray zone" or "distress zone", match the z-Score of the subject company with the zone composed of companies with similar z-Scores in Exhibits H-A, and identify the corresponding average high-financial-risk premium over the risk-free rate ($RP_{m+s, HFR}$). For this example, the subject company is a manufacturing company with a z-Score of 1.47, placing it in the "distressed" zone (z-Scores <1.8) of Exhibit 10.46. The corresponding high-financial-risk arithmetic average risk premium is 16.66% (16.7% rounded).

Exhibit 10.46: Build-up 1-HFR Cost of Equity Input
Exhibit H-A, High-Financial-Risk Premia Over the Risk-Free Rate
Companies Ranked by z-Score
Historical Equity Risk Premium: Average Since 1963
High-Financial-Risk Company Data for Year Ending December 31, 2016

Portfolio	Beta (Sum Beta) Since '63	Standard Deviation of Returns	Geometric Average Return	Arithmetic Average Return	Arithmetic Average Risk Premium	Average Debt/ MVIC
Manufacturing (z-Score)						
1.8 to 2.99 (gray zone)	1.56	35.17%	12.82%	19.29%	12.83%	44.74%
< 1.8 (distress zone)	1.65	38.47%	15.87%	23.12%	**16.66%**	57.82%
Service (z"-Score)						
1.1 to 2.59 (gray zone)	1.57	42.39%	15.88%	28.02%	21.56%	40.00%
< 1.1 (distress zone)	1.72	43.93%	19.00%	31.58%	25.12%	46.76%

Estimate a high-financial-risk cost of equity for the subject company by adding the average high-financial-risk premium over the risk-free rate ($RP_{m+s, HFR}$) to the risk-free rate and the ERP Adjustment.

[10.41] In all examples here, the z-Score for publicly traded, non-service (i.e., "manufacturing") companies is used.

[10.42] While the H-A, H-B, and H-C exhibits are ranked by z-Score and z"-Score and are not strictly comparable to the z'-Score for non-public companies, the returns reported in these exhibits can be useful in developing cost of equity estimates based on the relative zones of discrimination.

[10.43] Or, as appropriate, z"-Score or z'-Score.

$$k_{e\ build-up\ 1-HFR} = R_f + RP_{m+s,HFR} + ERP\ Adjustment$$

$$20.7\% = 3.5\% + 16.7\% + 0.5\%$$

The "high-financial-risk" cost of equity capital estimate for the hypothetical subject company in this example is 20.7%.

Estimating Cost of Equity Capital Using the "CAPM-High-Financial-Risk" Method

The CAPM-High-Financial-Risk equation is:

$$k_{e,CAPM-HFR} = R_f + (\beta \times ERP) + RP_{s,HFR}$$

This example utilizes the same long-term risk-free rate (3.5%), ERP (5.5%), and beta (1.2) established in a previous example, so the only missing input is the high-financial-risk size premium ($RP_{s,HFR}$):

$$k_{e,CAPM-HFR} = 3.5\% + (1.2 \times 5.5\%) + RP_{s,HFR}$$

Note that the ERP Adjustment is *not* needed when estimating cost of equity capital using the Risk Premium Report exhibits' size premia.[10.44]

Determination of the high financial size premium ($RP_{s,HFR}$) in Exhibit H-B follows the same three-step process as was followed in the previous example:

Step 1: Ask the same *five questions* as were asked in the previous example to determine whether the characteristics of the subject company better match the characteristics of the companies included in Exhibits B-1 through B-8 (the 25 portfolios) or the characteristics of the high-financial-risk portfolios.

Step 2: If the individual analyst determines that the subject company's characteristics better match the characteristics of the companies comprising the high-financial-risk portfolios, calculate the z-Score of the subject company using the appropriate z-Score equation.

Step 3: Lastly, if the z-Score[10.45] of the subject company indicates that it is in the "gray zone" or "distress zone", match the z-Score of the subject company with the zone composed of companies with similar z-Scores in Exhibits H-B, and identify the corresponding high-financial-risk size premium ($RP_{s,HFR}$). For this example, the subject company is a manufacturing company with a z-Score of 1.47, placing it in the "distressed" zone (z-Scores <1.8) of Exhibit 10.47. The corresponding high-financial-risk size premium is 8.37% (8.4% rounded).

[10.44] For a detailed discussion of the ERP Adjustment, see the section entitled "Proper Application of the Equity Risk Premium (ERP) Adjustment" in Chapter 9.

[10.45] Or, as appropriate, z''-Score or z'-Score.

Exhibit 10.47: CAPM-High-Financial-Risk Cost of Equity Capital Input
Exhibit H-B, High-Financial-Risk Premia Over CAPM (i.e., "High-Financial-Risk Size Premia")
Companies Ranked by z-Score
Historical Equity Risk Premium: Average Since 1963
High-Financial-Risk Company Data for Year Ending December 31, 2016

Portfolio	Beta (Sum Beta) Since '63	Arithmetic Average Return	Arithmetic Average Risk Premium	Indicated CAPM Premium	Premium over CAPM
Manufacturing (z-Score)					
1.8 to 2.99 (gray zone)	1.56	19.29%	12.83%	7.86%	4.97%
< 1.8 (distress zone)	1.65	23.12%	16.66%	8.29%	**8.37%**
Service (z"-Score)					
1.1 to 2.59 (gray zone)	1.57	28.02%	21.56%	7.88%	13.68%
< 1.1 (distress zone)	1.72	31.58%	25.12%	8.66%	16.46%

Estimate a high-financial-risk cost of equity for the subject company by adding the average high-financial-risk premium over CAPM identified in Step 3 ($RP_{s,\,HFR}$) to the CAPM equation:

$$k_{e,CAPM-HFR} = R_f + (\beta \times ERP) + RP_{s,HFR}$$

18.5% = 3.5% + (1.2 x 5.5%) + 8.4%

The "high-financial-risk" cost of equity capital estimate for the hypothetical subject company in this example is 18.5%.

Comparative Risk Study

Previously the Risk Premium Report's C exhibits were used in the calculation of "unlevered" cost of equity capital estimates. The C exhibits have another important capability, however. The C exhibits, when used in conjunction with the D exhibits, enable valuation analysts to potentially further refine their cost of equity estimate by gauging how "alike or different" the subject company is when compared to the companies that make up the Risk Premium Report's guideline portfolios in the A and B exhibits. These elements, used in tandem, form the basis of the "Comparative Risk Study".

The Risk Premium Report exhibits include information about the characteristics of the companies that make up the portfolios that are used to calculate the "risk premia over the risk-free rate" and the size premia. The Risk Premium Report's C exhibits can be used to gauge whether an increase or decrease adjustment to a risk premium or size premium (and thus, cost of equity capital) is indicated, based upon the "company-specific" differences of the subject company's fundamental risk and the average fundamental risk of companies that make up the portfolios from which the risk premia or size premia are derived.

Valuation is an Inherently Comparative Process

Just about any analysis boils down to trying to comparing one thing to another. For example, when "analyzing" the merits of a house we are thinking about purchasing, it's common to compare it to other houses with similar characteristics. While houses that are exactly the same may be available in certain instances, typically what we end up with is a "peer group" of comparable houses that may be similar in many respects, but may still have some differences. If the house we are looking at is the only one in the neighborhood without a swimming pool, we could probably make a pretty good argument that a downward adjustment in price is justified. On the other hand, if the house we are looking at has a two-car garage while all the other houses in the neighborhood have one-car garages, an upward adjustment in price may be unavoidable.

Just as we oftentimes make decisions based upon the alikeness (or difference) between alternatives, the use of a portfolio's average historical rate of return to estimate a discount rate for a subject company is also based upon the implicit assumption that the risks of the subject company are quantitatively similar to the risks of the average company in the portfolio. If the risks of the subject company differ materially from the average company in the portfolio, then the estimated discount rate may be less than (or greater than) the discount rate derived using the risk premium or size premium associated with the given portfolio.

Company-specific Risk

Using the term "company-specific" might be confusing for some readers, because another use of the term "company-specific" implies risks that in the theoretical sense can be diversified away.[10.46] Having said that, the intended meaning of the term "company-specific risk" can vary from person to person. For example, is a "company-specific" risk adjustment necessary in a hypothetical case in which the comparison peer group and the subject company are *identical* in every way? Many valuation analysts would contend that the answer to this question is "no" – although this answer probably has very little to do with the theoretical definition of company-specific risk. What is probably intended is that no further adjustment may be necessary because the peer group in this hypothetical case (being identical to the subject company) acts as a "perfect" proxy.

We see valuation analysts regularly make adjustments to cost of equity capital estimates made under the heading "company-specific" risk, including (but not limited to):

- Adjustments to cost of equity capital estimates derived from a sample of guideline public companies to account for a subject company having risk characteristics that differ from the peer group.

- Adjustments to cost of equity capital estimates to account for biased cash flow projections provided to the valuation analyst.

- Adjustments to cost of equity capital estimates to account for risks accepted by investors that may not hold diversified portfolios of investments.

The third case (the diversified versus undiversified investor) likely comes up often with valuators, since in many cases the owner of the asset being valued may be an investor who is otherwise "undiversified". Businesses and interests in businesses (any asset) sell in various markets made up of pools of likely buyers. The marginal investors in the pool of likely buyers set the market price. No market, other than possibly the pool of buyers for the smallest businesses, is comprised of fully undiversified investors. In preparing the *Cost of Capital* 5th ed., Pratt and Grabowski investigated the extent to which private equity investors have expanded the market for closely held businesses. The responses from interviews of business brokers was that private equity investors are active market participants for smaller businesses today than they were only several years earlier. For example, whenever the company for sale has EBITDA over $1 million, the pool of likely buyers includes private equity investors. These investors are surely diversified.

Risk of an investment and value must be developed based on the risks (and pricing) perceived by investors that comprise the pool of likely buyers for the subject asset – not based on the diversification or non-diversification of the current owner. As we noted in Chapter 1, "The cost of capital is a function of the investment, not the investor". The cost of capital should reflect the risk of the investment, not the cost of funds to a particular investor.

[10.46] The models used to estimate cost of equity generally assume that risks that can be "diversified away" are not compensable. This type of risk is properly called "unsystematic risk".

Using the C Exhibits to Refine Cost of Capital Estimates

The Risk Premium Report exhibits are designed to assist the valuation analyst in estimating the cost of equity capital for the subject company as if it were publicly traded. That is, the returns reflect the risks and the liquidity of publicly traded stocks. However, discounting expected net cash flows for a closely held business using an "as if public" cost of capital may not be an accurate estimate of value to the extent that market participants consider other risks associated with investments in closely held businesses. In other words, when estimating the cost of equity capital for a subject company, the risks of the subject company more than likely differ in some respects from the risks of the sample of guideline public companies it is being compared to (i.e., the "peer group").

When we use the Risk Premium Report's risk premia over the risk-free rate from the A exhibits or the size premia from the B exhibits, the "peer group" is the guideline portfolio in which the subject company falls. Remember that the cost of equity capital estimates developed using the Risk Premium Report exhibits are still "as if public", even *after* using the C exhibits to gauge the company-specific differences of the subject company and the portfolio(s) to which the subject company is being compared. However, this refined estimate likely better reflects the risk of the subject company as if the stock of the company was publicly traded, and had been discounted by the market's assessment of its company-specific risk characteristics (as measured by its accounting-based fundamental risk measures).

The C exhibits provide the following three comparative risk characteristics (i.e., "accounting-based fundamental risk measures") for each of the 25 portfolios and for each of the 8 size measures of size included on the A and B exhibits, each of which can be useful in assessing how "alike or different" the subject company is to the companies that make up the respective guideline portfolio:

- Average operating margin

- Average coefficient of variation of operating margin

- Average coefficient of variation of ROE

To calculate the statistics included in Exhibits C-1 through C-8, the fundamental risk characteristics are calculated for the same size-ranked portfolios that are created in the Size Study's A and B exhibits. For example, Exhibit A-1 is comprised of 25 portfolios ranked by market value of equity. To calculate the fundamental risk characteristics found in Exhibit C-1, the three fundamental risk measures used to rank the portfolios in the Risk Study (operating margin, coefficient of variation of operating margin, coefficient of variation of ROE) are calculated for *each* of the 25 (market-value-of-equity-ranked) portfolios in Exhibit A-1. These calculations are made in the same fashion for each of the 25 size-ranked portfolios created for Exhibits A-2 through A-8, (and thus for B-1 through B-8, since the portfolio composition in the B exhibits is identical to the portfolios composition in the A exhibits).

The C Exhibits – Summary of Data Presented

In addition to various statistical information repeated from the A and B exhibits, the C exhibits report the additional data points for each of the 25 portfolios described in Exhibit 10.48.

Exhibit 10.48: Statistics Reported for 25 Size-Ranked Portfolios in Exhibits C-1 through C-8 (and not otherwise reported in the A and B Exhibits)

- Average unlevered beta calculated using the "sum beta" method applied to monthly returns for 1963 through the 2016.

- Arithmetic average historical unlevered risk premium over long-term Treasuries (average return on equity in excess of long-term Treasury bonds) since 1963. $(RP_{m+s, \ unlevered})$.

- "Smoothed" average historical unlevered risk premium: the fitted premium from a regression with the average historical unlevered risk premium as dependent variable and the logarithm of the average sorting criteria as independent variable $(RP_{m+s, \ unlevered})$ (The coefficients and constants from this regression analysis are in the top right hand corner of the exhibits).

- Average debt to market value of equity.

- Operating Margin: The mean operating income for the prior five years divided by the mean sales for the prior five years. Operating income is defined as sales minus cost of goods sold plus selling, general, and administrative expenses plus depreciation.

- Coefficient of Variation of Operating Margin: The standard deviation of operating margin over the prior five years divided by the average operating margin for the same years.

- Coefficient of Variation of Return on Book Value of Equity: The standard deviation of return on book equity for the prior five years divided by the mean return on book equity for the same years. Return on book equity is defined as net income before extraordinary items minus preferred dividends divided by book value of common equity.

The "C" exhibits provides users of the Risk Premium Report the information they need to compare their subject company to the average company in the guideline portfolio in which their company falls in the A and B exhibits.

For example, the C exhibits report the operating margin of each of the 25 portfolios in the A and B exhibits. If the operating margin of the subject company is significantly *less* than the average operating margin of the companies that make up the A or B exhibit guideline portfolio, then (all things held the same) this may be an indication that the subject company is *riskier* than the average company in the guideline portfolio (and vice versa). This analysis may indicate the direction of an adjustment (increase or decrease), but not the magnitude of adjustment needed. Gauging the "magnitude" of the potential adjustment needed is easier said than done, simply because there is the potential for so much overlap between size risk and accounting-based fundamental risk factors (e.g., as size decreases, variability of earnings tends to increase, and vice versa (see Exhibits 10.30 and 10.31). For now, the best one might hope for is establishing a *range* in which the adjustment likely falls.

In this section two examples of using the Risk Premium Report's Comparative Risk Study to further refine a cost of equity capital estimate are provided. In the first example, the build-up method (and the A exhibits) is used, in the second example, the CAPM (and the B exhibits) is used.

The output of using the Comparative Risk Study is two-fold: (i) whether an adjustment (*upward* or *downward*) is indicated in the risk premium over the risk-free rate (RP_{m+s}) used in the build-up method or in the size premium (RP_s) used in the CAPM, and (ii) the *range* in which the adjustment likely falls.

In both examples *any* (or all) of the average fundamental risk measures (operating margin, coefficient of variation of operating margin, and coefficient of variation of ROE) of the companies that comprise *any* of the A and B exhibits' 25 portfolios can be are used. For simplicity, however, these examples use "operating margin" (for the build-up example) and then "coefficient of variation of operating margin" (for the CAPM example). In both examples, a *single* A exhibit and a *single* B exhibit are used (A-3 and B-3, which are 25 portfolios sorted by 5-year average net income).[10.47]

Using the Comparative Risk Study to Refine Build-up Method Estimates

Step 1: Identify the equivalent C *exhibit*, per Exhibit 10.49.

Exhibit A-3 (net income) is being used in this example, so the "equivalent C exhibit" is Exhibit C-3. Exhibit C-3 is where the fundamental risk characteristics of the companies that comprise the 25 portfolios in Exhibit A-3 are found.[10.48]

[10.47] While these examples make use of only the fundamental risk measure "operating margin" and only a single A exhibit and B exhibit (i.e., only a single "size" measure, 5-year average net income), we suggest the valuation analyst use as many of the three fundamental risk measures that are available for the subject company, and as many of the size measures that are available for the subject company.

[10.48] Alternatively, if we were using Exhibit A-1 in this example, you would go to Exhibit C-1 to find the average fundamental risk characteristics of the companies that comprise the 25 portfolios Exhibit A-1, etc.

Exhibit 10.49: Identifying the Equivalent C Exhibit

	Build-up Method: Use A Exhibits		CAPM: Use B Exhibits		Equivalent: C Exhibit
Market Value of Equity	A-1	or	B-1	→	C-1
Book Value of Equity	A-2	or	B-2	→	C-2
5-Year Average Net Income	A-3	or	B-3	→	C-3
MVIC	A-4	or	B-4	→	C-4
Total Assets	A-5	or	B-5	→	C-5
5-Year Average EBITDA	A-6	or	B-6	→	C-6
Sales	A-7	or	B-7	→	C-7
Number of Employees	A-8	or	B-8	→	C-8

Step 2: Identify the fundamental risk characteristics (in this example, average "operating margin") of the equivalent *portfolio* in the equivalent C exhibit.

For example, say the subject company fell into portfolio 24 in Exhibit A-3. The smoothed average risk premium for portfolio 24 in Exhibit A-3 is 11.70%. The "equivalent portfolio" in Exhibit C-3 is *also* portfolio 24.[10.49] We are using the fundamental risk measure "operating margin". The average operating margin reported for portfolio 24 in Exhibit C-3 is 7.84% (7.8%, rounded).

Step 3: Identify the guideline portfolio in the D-1 exhibit (25 portfolios sorted by operating margin) which has the most *similar* operating margin as was identified in Step 2 for portfolio 24 in Exhibit C-3 (7.8%).[10.50]

The portfolio in Exhibit D-1 that has the closest average operating margin to 7.8% is portfolio 19, which has an average operating margin of 7.61%. The smoothed average risk premium for portfolio 19 in Exhibit D-1 is 10.92% (10.9%, rounded).

Step 4: Identify the guideline portfolio in the D-1 exhibit (25 portfolios sorted by operating margin) which has the most *similar* operating margin to the subject company.

Say the subject company has an operating margin of 4.0%. The portfolio in Exhibit D-1 that has the closest average operating margin to 4.0% is portfolio 24, which has an average operating margin of 3.63%. The smoothed average risk premium for portfolio 24 in Exhibit D-1 is 13.06% (13.1%, rounded).

[10.49] Alternatively, if the subject company fell into portfolio 22 in Exhibit A-3, the "equivalent portfolio" in Exhibit C-3 would then be portfolio 22, etc.

[10.50] Exhibit D-1 is 25 portfolios sorted by average operating margin; Exhibit D-2 is 25 portfolios sorted by average coefficient of variation of operating margin; Exhibit D-3 is 25 portfolios sorted by average coefficient of variation of ROE.

Step 5: Apply an *upward* or *downward* adjustment to the risk premium over the risk-free rate (and thus the overall cost of equity capital) as indicated.

In this example, the subject company's net income most closely matched the average net income of portfolio 24 in Exhibit A-3 (25 portfolios sorted by net income). The "risk premium over the risk-free rate" for portfolio 24 in Exhibit A-3 is 11.7% (identified in Step 2).

The operating margin of the subject company (4.0%) is *lower* than the average operating margin of the companies that comprise Exhibit A-3's portfolio 24 (7.8%) (identified in Step 2). All things held the same, this suggests that the subject company may be *riskier* than the average company in Exhibit A-3's portfolio 24 (the *lower* the operating margin, the *riskier* the company may be, and vice versa), and an *upward* adjustment to the smoothed average "risk premium over the risk-free rate" of Exhibit A-3's portfolio 24 (11.7%) may be appropriate.

The upward adjustment likely falls into a range of 0% to 2.2%, which is the difference between the smoothed average "risk premium over the risk-free rate" of Exhibit D-1's Portfolio 24 (13.1%) and the smoothed average "risk premium over the risk-free rate" of Exhibit D-1's Portfolio 19 (10.9%).[10.51]

Using the Comparative Risk Study to Refine CAPM Estimates

Step 1: Identify the equivalent C exhibit, per Exhibit 10.49.

Exhibit B-3 (net income) is being used in this example, so the "equivalent C exhibit" is Exhibit C-3. Exhibit C-3 is where the fundamental risk characteristics of the companies that comprise the 25 portfolios in Exhibit B-3 are found.[10.52]

Step 2: Identify the fundamental risk characteristics (in this example, average "coefficient of variation of operating margin") of the equivalent portfolio in the equivalent C exhibit.

For example, say the subject company fell into portfolio 22 in Exhibit B-3. The smoothed *size* premium for portfolio 22 in Exhibit B-3 is 4.62% (4.6%, rounded). The "equivalent portfolio" in Exhibit C-3 is *also* portfolio 22.[10.53] We are using the fundamental risk measure "coefficient of variation of operating margin". The average coefficient of variation of operating margin reported for portfolio 22 in Exhibit C-3 is 23.61% (23.6%, rounded).[10.54]

Step 3: Identify the guideline portfolio in the D-2 exhibit (25 portfolios sorted by coefficient of variation of operating margin) which has the most *similar* coefficient of variation of operating margin as was identified in Step 2 for portfolio 22 in Exhibit C-3 (23.6%).

[10.51] (13.1% - 10.9%) = 2.2%. Thus the likely range of the adjustment is 0.0% to 2.2%.

[10.52] Alternatively, if we were using Exhibit B-1 in this example, you would go to Exhibit C-1 to find the average fundamental risk characteristics of the companies that comprise the 25 portfolios Exhibit B-1, etc.

[10.53] Alternatively, if the subject company fell into portfolio 25 in Exhibit B-3, the "equivalent portfolio" in Exhibit C-3 would then be portfolio 25, etc.

[10.54] Exhibit D-1 is 25 portfolios sorted by average operating margin; Exhibit D-2 is 25 portfolios sorted by average coefficient of variation of operating margin; Exhibit D-3 is 25 portfolios sorted by average coefficient of variation of ROE.

The portfolio in Exhibit D-2 that has the closest average coefficient of variation of operating margin to 23.6% is portfolio 8, which has an average coefficient of variation of operating margin of 22.69% (22.7% rounded). The smoothed average risk premium for portfolio 8 in Exhibit D-2 is 10.17% (10.2%, rounded).

Step 4: Identify the guideline portfolio in the D-2 exhibit (25 portfolios sorted by coefficient of variation of operating margin) which has the most *similar* coefficient of variation of operating margin to the subject company.

Say the subject company has a coefficient of variation of operating margin of 15.0%. The portfolio in Exhibit D-2 that has the closest average coefficient of variation of operating margin to 15.0% is portfolio 12, which has an average coefficient of variation of operating margin of 15.37% (15.4% rounded). The smoothed average risk premium for portfolio 12 in Exhibit D-2 is 9.71% (9.7%, rounded).

Step 5: Apply an *upward* or *downward* adjustment to the size premium (and thus the overall cost of equity capital) as indicated.

In this example, the subject company's net income most closely matched the average net income of portfolio 22 in Exhibit B-3 (25 portfolios sorted by net income). The smoothed size premium for portfolio 22 in Exhibit B-3 is 4.6% (identified in Step 2).

The coefficient of variation of operating margin of the subject company (15.0%) is *lower* than the average coefficient of variation of operating margin of the companies that comprise Exhibit B-3's portfolio 22 (23.6%) (identified in Step 2). All things held the same, this suggests that the subject company may be *less* risky than the average company in Exhibit B-3's portfolio 22 (the *less* volatile operating margin is, the *less* risky the company may be, and vice versa). A *downward* adjustment to the smoothed size premium of Exhibit B-3's portfolio 22 (4.6%) may be appropriate.

The downward adjustment likely falls into a range of 0% to 0.5%, which is the difference between the smoothed average "risk premium over the risk-free rate" of Exhibit D-2's Portfolio 12 (9.7%) and the smoothed average "risk premium over the risk-free rate" of Exhibit D-2's Portfolio 8 (10.2%).[10.55]

[10.55] (9.7% - 10.2%) = −0.5%. Thus the *downward* adjustment likely falls in the range 0.0% to 0.5%.

Chapter 11
Real Estate

In this chapter, we introduce a discussion on real estate (i.e., real property) and associated rates of return.[11.1]

First, we present the reader with some factors to consider when evaluating the risks of individual real estate investments.

Second, the return and volatility characteristics of U.S. real estate as an asset class are compared to the return and volatility characteristics of other U.S. asset classes, followed by a brief discussion of real estate's changing correlation with (i) U.S. equities, and (ii) U.S. government bonds.[11.2]

Lastly, we provide a table of data that could be used as inputs in performing valuations of individual real property investments: (i) pre-tax yield (internal rate of return (IRR), discount rate), (ii) going-in (overall) capitalization rate, and (iii) terminal (residual) capitalization rate (see Exhibit 11.6). These data points are provided for the fourth quarter of 2016.[11.3]

Individual Real Estate Assets

Relative to say, stocks or bonds, direct investment in individual real estate assets can be highly illiquid, require intensive management, and have substantial investment risks that affect the cost of capital. Investors in real estate should be compensated for the additional investment risk over and above the risk-free rate for relative lack of liquidity, and for the additional management burden.[11.4]

[11.1] Chapter 11 is significantly excerpted from Shannon P. Pratt and Roger J. Grabowski, *Cost of Capital: Applications and Examples* 5th edition (John Wiley & Sons, Inc., 2014), Chapter 40, "Cost of Capital of Real Property – Individual Assets", and Chapter 41, "Cost of Capital of Real Estate Entities". Chapter 11 herein is designed to be an introductory discussion of cost of capital as related to real estate. For a comprehensive, detailed discussion of valuing real estate, see Pratt & Grabowski.

[11.2] *The Valuation Handbook – U.S. Guide to Cost of Capital* (this book) is based on U.S. company data, and so we limit our discussion to the U.S. real estate market in this chapter. The *Valuation Handbook – International Guide to Cost of Capital*, also authored by Duff & Phelps and published by Wiley, is based on global company data. The *Valuation Handbook – International Guide to Cost of Capital* includes country-level (i) equity risk premia, (ii) country risk premia, and (iii) relative volatility factors that can be used to estimate country-level cost of equity capital globally, for up to 188 countries, from the perspective of investors based in any one of up to 56 countries. To purchase the *Valuation Handbook – International Guide to Cost of Capital* and its Semi-annual Update, or other Duff & Phelps valuation data resources published by John Wiley & Sons, please go to www.wiley.com/go/ValuationHandbooks.

[11.3] Source for Fourth Quarter 2016 data: RERC LLC, *Situs RERC Real Estate Report, 4q 2016*, Vol. 45, No. 4. All rights reserved. Used with permission. Situs RERC, a Situs company, is a nationally-recognized commercial real estate research, valuation and consulting firm that provides valuation management and fiduciary services, appraisal and litigation services, and research, analytics and research publications for 10 major property types on an institutional, regional, and metro-level basis. To learn more about Situs RERC, visit www.situsrerc.com.

[11.4] The discount for lack of marketability is built into the discount or capitalization rate, as it is in venture capital rates in business appraisals.

Real Estate Investment Trusts (REITs)

Real estate properties can be *directly* owned by individuals (i.e., sole proprietorship), partnerships, corporations (either subchapter C or subchapter S), limited liability company (LLC's) or trusts. An equity investment in real estate can also be made *indirectly* by purchasing shares of an entity holding real property interests. Real estate entities exist substantially for the purpose of holding, directly or indirectly, title to or beneficial interest in real property. The value of a real estate entity includes many components, such as land, buildings, furniture, fixtures and equipment, intangible assets, and often the business operation.

A REIT, "is a company that owns or finances income-producing real estate. Modeled after mutual funds, REITs provide investors of all types regular income streams, diversification and long-term capital appreciation. REITs typically pay out all of their taxable income as dividends to shareholders. In turn, shareholders pay the income taxes on those dividends. REITs allow anyone to invest in portfolios of large-scale properties the same way they invest in other industries – through the purchase of stock".[11.5] One major distinction between equity REITs and other real estate companies is that a REIT must acquire and develop its properties primarily to operate them as part of its own portfolio rather than to resell them once they are developed.[11.6]

To qualify as a REIT, a company must have the bulk of its assets and income connected to real estate investment and must distribute at least 90 percent of its taxable income to shareholders annually in the form of dividends. In addition to paying out at least 90 percent of its taxable income annually in the form of shareholder dividends, a REIT must:[11.7]

- Be an entity that would be taxable as a corporation but for its REIT status.

- Be managed by a board of directors or trustees.

- Have shares that are fully transferable.

- Have a minimum of 100 shareholders after its first year as a REIT.

- Have no more than 50 percent of its shares held by five or fewer individuals during the last half of the taxable year.

- Invest at least 75 percent of its total assets in real estate assets and cash.

- Derive at least 75 percent of its gross income from real estate related sources, including rents from real property and interest on mortgages financing real property.

- Derive at least 95 percent of its gross income from such real estate sources and dividends or interest from any source.

[11.5] Source: The National Association of Real Estate Investment Trusts® (NAREIT) website at: https://www.reit.com.
[11.6] Source: U.S. Securities and Exchange Commission website at: https://www.sec.gov/answers/reits.htm.
[11.7] Source: U.S. Securities and Exchange Commission website at: https://www.sec.gov/answers/reits.htm.

- Have no more than 25 percent of its assets consist of non-qualifying securities or stock in taxable REIT subsidiaries.

REITs can be classified in two broad categories, (i) equity REITs, and (ii) mortgage REITs. These are defined as follows:[11.8]

Equity REITs are real estate companies that acquire commercial properties – such as office buildings, shopping centers and apartment buildings – and lease the space in the structures to tenants. After paying the expenses associated with operating their properties, Equity REITs pay out annually the bulk of the income to their shareholders as dividends. Equity REITs also include capital appreciation from the sale of properties in the dividends they pay. In all cases, this significant dividend distribution is designed to approximate the investment return investors would receive if they owned properties directly.

Mortgage REITs invest in real estate mortgages or mortgage-backed securities, earning income from the interest on these investments, as well as from the sales of mortgages. Mortgage REITs, like other businesses, earn their profit from the difference between the income they receive and their costs, including their funding costs to purchase mortgage investments. They have the same requirement as Equity REITs to distribute the bulk of their income to their shareholders annually.

A third type of REIT is a "hybrid" REIT. Hybrid REITs generally are companies that use the investment strategies of both equity REITs and mortgage REITs.[11.9]

Structure of Real Estate Entities

Real properties are often owned directly (e.g., sole proprietorship) or by a pass-through entity. Pass -through entities (e.g., partnership, limited liability company, master limited partnerships) pay no entity-level income taxes but pass their income through to the investors, thereby avoiding double taxation (i.e., paying income taxes at the entity level and the owner/investor paying taxes on dividends received).

REITs are not technically pass-through entities, but have certain income tax characteristics that are beneficial to their investors. Under U.S. law, the requirements for REITs to maintain their status are quite specific:

For federal tax purposes, REITs are taxed as corporations. That technically means that REITs are taxed first at the entity level and then at the shareholder level. However, REITs are permitted to deduct dividends paid to shareholders from their corporate taxable income. And because REITs are required by U.S. law to distribute at least 90 percent of their taxable income to their shareholders each year, with most REITs distributing 100 percent of their taxable income, this means that REITs effectively pay very little, if any, corporate income tax at the federal level.

REITs will, however, be subject to corporate-level tax on what is left after their annual distributions. That is, if a REIT chooses to distribute 90 percent of its taxable income, it will become subject to

---

[11.8]   Source: The National Association of Real Estate Investment Trusts® (NAREIT) website at: https://www.reit.com.
[11.9]   Source: U.S. Securities and Exchange Commission website at: https://www.sec.gov/answers/reits.htm.

corporate-level tax only on the remaining 10 percent.[11.10]

A portion of the dividends paid to a shareholder also may constitute a nontaxable return of capital, which is not considered income.

Treatment of REIT income at the state level is anything but simple. Some states follow the federal income-taxation rules, whereas other states (e.g., New Hampshire) impose an entity-level tax on REITs. Thus REITs can still be subject to at least some entity-level income taxation, even if profits are fully distributed.

In recent years, companies that were traditionally organized as C corporations have elected to convert to REITs to either mitigate double taxation at the investor level (i.e., to increase the net cash flow in the hands of the investors who invest in their stocks) or enhance shareholder returns in some other form. For example, American Tower, which owns, leases, and operates cellular towers, converted from a C corporation to a REIT.

Correlation of U.S. REITs Compared to Other U.S. Asset Classes

Diversification is "spreading a portfolio over many investments to avoid excessive exposure to any one source of risk".[11.11] Put simply, diversification is "not putting all your eggs in one basket". Diversification offers the potential of higher returns for the same level of risk, or lower risk for the same level of return.

In Exhibit 11.1, the correlation of U.S. REITs and (i) U.S. large company stocks and (ii) long-term U.S. government bonds is shown. Correlation is a measure of the how alternative investments "move" relative to each other, and is thus a measure of potential diversification benefit. The *higher* the correlation (the more investments "move" together), the *less* potential diversification benefit, whereas the *lower* the correlation (the less investments "move" together), the *greater* the potential diversification benefit. The thinking is that by holding a portfolio of assets that do not have high correlation with each other, as some investments decrease in value, others will increase (and vice versa), and thus potentially mitigate overall portfolio losses.

The correlation of U.S. REITs with both stocks and bonds declined during the 1990s, thus increasing the potential diversification benefit.

In the immediate years leading up to and following the 2008–2009 Financial Crisis, the correlation of U.S. REITs with stocks generally *increased*, and the correlation of U.S. REITs and long-term government bonds generally *decreased*. These changes in correlation were likely due, at least in part, to the Federal Reserve's tamping down of interest rates through various market interventions and moral suasion. The publicly stated intention of these interventions by the Federal Reserve was to boost asset prices (e.g., stocks, housing).[11.12]

[11.10] Cara Griffith, "Practical Tax Considerations for Working with REITs", State Tax Notes (October 31, 2011): 315–320, quoting Jennifer Weiss: 316. In 2009, the IRS issued guidance that indicates that the distributions may be in the form of cash or stock in certain instances.

[11.11] Zvi Bodi, Alex Kane, and Alan J. Marcus, Investments (McGraw-Hill, 2002), p. 981.

[11.12] For a broader discussion of monetary intervention and its potential effect on asset prices, see Chapter 3 herein.

Exhibit 11.1: Rolling 60-month Correlation of U.S. Equity REITs and (i) U.S. Large Company Stocks, and (ii) U.S. Long-term Government Bonds
December 1976–December 2016

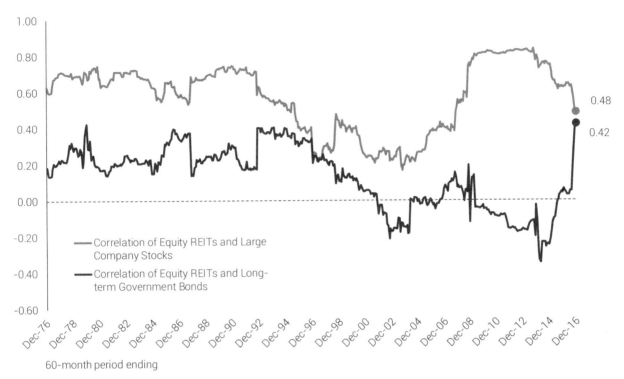

Source of underlying data: (i) Equity REITs: The National Association of Real Estate Investment Trusts® (NAREIT) website at www.reit.com/nareit. Series used: FTSE NAREIT US Real Estate Index Series, "All Equity REITs" total return. All rights reserved. Used with permission. (ii) Stocks, Bonds, Bills, and Inflation (SBBI) total return series from the Morningstar *Direct* database. Series used: Large Company Stocks (IA SBBI US Large Stock TR USD Ext). The "SBBI US Large Stock" total return series is essentially the S&P 500 total return index; Long-term Gov't Bonds (IA SBBI US LT Govt TR USD). All rights reserved. Used with permission. All calculations by Duff & Phelps, LLC.

In more recent periods (2014 to present), these trends seem to have reversed, with the correlation of U.S. REITs with stocks generally *decreasing*, and the correlation of U.S. REITs with long-term government bonds generally *increasing*. This is likely due, at least in part, to the Federal Reserve increasing the federal funds target rate range 0.25% in each of December 2015 and December 2016, and indicating that further rate increases may be on the horizon.[11.13] With the dampening of the exogenous upward pressure on asset prices (e.g., stocks, housing) brought about by the Federal Reserve's tamping down of interest rates, and an outlook that suggests that more rate increases are on the horizon, these correlations *seem* to be regressing to values more typical of pre-financial-crisis levels.

[11.13] The Federal Reserve maintained a target federal funds range of 0.00%–0.25% through open market operations from December 16, 2008 through December 16, 2015. On December 17, 2015, the Federal Reserve raised the target federal funds range 25 bps to 0.25%–0.50%, and again raised the target range another 25 bps to 0.50%–0.75% on December 15, 2016, and has indicated that further increases may occur in 2017 (see the *Wall Street Journal*, January 15, 2016, "Fed Raises Rates for First Time in 2016, Anticipates 3 Increases in 2017").

Summary Statistics of U.S. REITs Compared to Other U.S. Asset Classes

In this chapter, we utilize return data from the National Association of Real Estate Investment Trusts (NAREIT) to examine the performance of U.S. real estate relative to other broad U.S. asset classes, as well as inflation.

In Exhibit 11.2, summary statistics of the annual total returns for U.S. Equity REITs compared to other U.S. asset classes, plus inflation, over the time horizon 1972–2016 are presented. Over this time period, REITs outperformed all other asset classes shown, with the exception of small stocks.

Exhibit 11.2: Summary Statistics of Annual Returns of U.S. Equity REITs and Other U.S. Asset Classes, Plus Inflation
1972–2016

	Geometric Mean (%)	Arithmetic Mean (%)	Standard Deviation (%)
Equity REITs	11.9	13.5	17.9
Large Company Stocks	10.4	11.9	17.5
Small Company Stocks	13.3	15.6	22.7
Long-term Corp. Bonds	8.4	8.8	10.2
Long-term Gov't Bonds	8.2	8.8	12.3
Int.-term Gov't Bonds	7.0	7.2	6.6
T-Bills	4.8	4.9	3.5
Inflation	4.0	4.1	3.1

Source of underlying data: (i) Equity REITs: The National Association of Real Estate Investment Trusts® (NAREIT) website at www.reit.com/nareit. Series used: FTSE NAREIT US Real Estate Index Series, "All Equity REITs" total return. All rights reserved. Used with permission. (ii) Stocks, Bonds, Bills, and Inflation (SBBI) total return series from the Morningstar *Direct* database. Series used: Large Company Stocks (IA SBBI US Large Stock TR USD Ext). The "SBBI US Large Stock" total return series is essentially the S&P 500 total return index; Small Company Stocks (IA SBBI US Small Stock TR USD); Long-term Corp. Bonds (IA SBBI US LT Corp TR USD); Long-term Gov't Bonds (IA SBBI US LT Govt TR USD); Intermediate-term Gov't Bonds (IA SBBI US IT Govt TR USD); T-Bills (IA SBBI US 30 Day T-Bill TR USD); Inflation (IA SBBI US Inflation). All rights reserved. Used with permission. All calculations by Duff & Phelps, LLC.

In Exhibit 11.3, the hypothetical growth of $1.00 over the time horizon 1972–2016 invested in each of the asset classes in Exhibit 11.2 is shown. The value of $1.00 invested in Equity REITs at the end of 1971 grew to $159.15 as of December 31, 2016.

Exhibit 11.3: Terminal Index Values of U.S. Equity REITs and Other U.S. Asset Classes, Plus Inflation; Index (Year-end 1971 = $1.00)
1972–2016

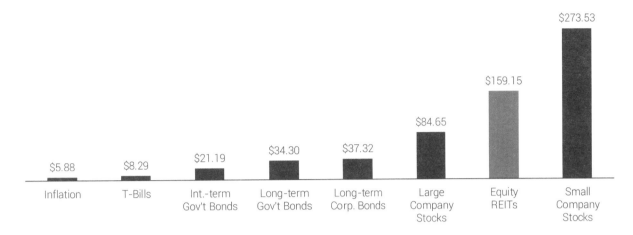

Equity REITs can also be categorized as sectors and sub-sectors. In Exhibit 11.4, summary statistics of the annual total returns for REIT property sectors Industrial, Office, Retail, Apartments, Health Care, and Lodging/Resorts over the time horizon 1994–2016 are presented. Over the 1994–2016 time horizon, the REIT sector Health Care had the highest average annual return (13.9%), while Lodging/Resorts had both the *lowest* average annual return (11.1%), and the *highest* standard deviation (32.6%).

Exhibit 11.4: Summary Statistics of Annual Returns of U.S. Equity REITs Property Sectors
1994–2016

	Geometric Mean (%)	Arithmetic Mean (%)	Standard Deviation (%)
Large Company Stocks	9.2	10.9	18.5
Industrial	9.7	13.0	22.0
Office	11.2	13.6	22.4
Retail	11.2	13.5	21.4
Apartments	12.0	13.7	19.9
Health Care	12.1	13.9	20.7
Lodging/Resorts	5.4	11.1	32.6

In Exhibit 11.5, the hypothetical growth of $1.00 over the time horizon 1994–2016 invested in each of the REIT property sectors shown in Exhibit 11.4 is shown. The value of $1.00 invested in the REIT Health Care sector at the end of 1993 grew to $13.75 as of December 31, 2016, while the value of $1.00 invested in the REIT sector Lodging/Resorts grew to $3.37.

Exhibit 11.5: Terminal Index Values of U.S. Equity REITs Property Sectors, and U.S. Large Company Stocks 1994–2016 (Year-end 1993 = $1.00)

Source of underlying data: (i) Equity REITs: The National Association of Real Estate Investment Trusts® (NAREIT) website at www.reit.com/nareit. Series used: Industrial (FTSE NAREIT Equity Industrial Index); Office (FTSE NAREIT Equity Office Index); Retail (which includes shopping centers and malls) (FTSE NAREIT Equity Retail Index); Apartments (FTSE NAREIT Equity Apartments Index); Health Care (FTSE NAREIT Equity Health Care Index); Lodging/Resorts (FTSE NAREIT Equity Lodging/Resorts Index). All rights reserved. Used with permission. All calculations by Duff & Phelps, LLC.

Real Estate Property Valuation Inputs

The income and cost of capital associated with the ownership of real property are the focus of this section. This is different from the income and cost of capital that might be earned (or required) by a business enterprise operating on the property, such as a marina, hotel, fitness club, or restaurant, or a portfolio of properties, such as a real estate operating company or a REIT.

At the end of this section we will provide examples of data inputs that can be used to estimate the value of real estate property interests, using one of the following methods:

1) Direct Capitalization Method

2) Discounted Cash Flow Method

The following is a brief discussion of each of these methods; our objective is not to provide an all-encompassing guide on real estate valuation and associated discount rates. Rather, it attempts to provide a context for the data exhibits presented at the end of this chapter.[11.14]

[11.14] This discussion is excerpted in part from Pratt Grabowski, Chapter 40, "Cost of Capital of Real Property Individual Assets".

Direct Capitalization Method

In real property valuation, direct capitalization is defined as:

A method used to convert an estimate of a single year's income expectancy into an indication of value in one direct step, either by dividing the income estimate by an appropriate rate or by multiplying the income estimate by an appropriate factor.

A capitalization technique employs capitalization rates and multipliers extracted from the market, mainly in the form of sales. Only the first year's income is considered. Yield and value change are implied, but not identified.[11.12]

Embedded in a market-derived overall capitalization rate are the market-oriented assumptions concerning the future income expectations or the performance of similar properties. The market-oriented assumptions result in changes in projected income and value over time. The expected annual compound rate of change in income and value can be added to the overall capitalization rate to indicate the property yield or discount rate.

Overall Direct Capitalization

In real property valuation, the direct capitalization formula is generally expressed as:

Formula 11.1

$$PV_p = \frac{I_p}{C_p}$$

Where:

PV_p = Overall value or present value of the property

I_p = Overall income to the property, measured before debt service, income taxes, and depreciation

C_p = Overall property capitalization rate

This basic formula can be modified to analyze the financial, physical, or legal interests in real property, provided the appropriate income stream can be estimated. Multipliers are a derivative of the direct capitalization overall rate. The net income multiplier is the reciprocal of the overall rate. Multipliers can be applied to the potential gross income, effective gross income, net operating income, or the equity cash flow. If income factors or multipliers are applied, the formulas generally are used to produce an indication of the property's value based on some form of the property's income. It is of critical importance to adequately define the type of income being estimated in order to employ the correct techniques to estimate proper value. A description of such income relationships is beyond the scope of this chapter.

[11.12] Brueggeman and Fisher, *Real Estate Finance and Investment.* op.cit.

The property yield rate can be estimated at stabilized occupancy if the long-term growth in cash flow and value are stable, as shown in Formula 11.2:

Formula 11.2

$$c = k - g$$

Where:

c	=	Capitalization rate
k	=	Discount or yield rate
g	=	Expected long-term sustainable growth rate in the cash flow available to subject investment

Formula 11.2 uses variable names and terminology as is used earlier in this book. This formula is quite similar to the formula presented in real estate textbooks, which is presented in Formula 11.3:[11.13]

Formula 11.3

$$c = k - A$$

Where:

c	=	Capitalization rate
k	=	Discount or yield rate
A	=	Expected change in income and value (adjustment factor)

The variable A represents the relative change in value and (often expressed as Δ_a). To calculate A, a periodic adjustment factor representing the appropriate time period is multiplied by the total change in value. Subscripts are used to indicate the applicable rates to the various components, such as equity and debt.

Estimating the Capitalization Rate

Although Direct Capitalization is most reliable when a property is stabilized, any real property interest that produces an income stream can be valued using the direct capitalization method. Several approaches are available to estimate the appropriate capitalization rate for the specific real property interest being valued. The approach that is most applicable depends on the quantity, quality, and reliability of the available market information. More than one approach may be necessary to develop the appropriate capitalization rate.

Potential buyers determine the assumptions that are utilized to estimate the transaction price to be paid for real property interests. There are various published surveys indicating the overall rates that

---

[11.13] Charles B. Akerson, *Capitalization Theory and Techniques Study Guide* (Chicago: Appraisal Institute, 1984), 59.

are being applied to estimate value.

Actual transactions provide a clear indication of the market interaction between buyers and sellers. The "going-in" capitalization rate can be extracted from the sale information. The going-in capitalization rate is obtained by dividing a property's expected net operating income (NOI) for the first year after purchase by the sale price of the property.[11.14]

Recent comparable sales provide excellent support for market-derived capitalization rates, if the information has been confirmed by the participants involved in the transaction. The comparable sales must represent a competitive investment with similar risk characteristics to the property that is being evaluated.

The method that should be used to develop the overall rate is based on a number of factors, and the analyst must realize that each approach has certain strengths and weaknesses. More than one method should be employed, whenever possible. The methods applied to develop the overall rate must be supportable and defensible. Market value is estimated based on the actions of typically informed and knowledgeable investors. Therefore, the most appropriate method is the method that reflects the typical actions of the most probable investors. The quantity and quality of data is important to provide support for the indicated overall rate. The information collected must also be reliable.

Discounted Cash Flow Method

The overall value of the property is equal to the present value of the income stream plus the present value of the reversion of the property at the end of the projection period, which is shown in Formula 11.4:

Formula 11.4

$$PV_p = \frac{CF_1}{\left(1+k_p\right)} + \frac{CF_2}{\left(1+k_p\right)^2} + \frac{CF_3}{\left(1+k_p\right)^3} + \dots \frac{CF_n}{\left(1+k_p\right)^n}$$
$$+ \frac{\left\{\left(NOI_{n+1}/c_n\right) - \left[\left(NOI_{n+1}/c_n\right) \times SC\%\right]\right\}}{\left(1+k_p\right)^n}$$

Where:

PV_p	=	Present Value
CF	=	Cash flow for a specific period
k_p	=	Overall rate of return or discount rate for property (property yield rate)
NOI_{n+1}	=	Net operating income in the year following the projection term
c_n	=	Terminal or residual or going-out capitalization rate in final year n used to capitalize NOI_{n+1}
$SC\%$	=	Cost of sale

[11.14] *The Dictionary of Real Estate Appraisal*, 5th ed. (Chicago: Appraisal Institute, 2010)

The last term is the reversion (i.e., proceeds) from the sale of the property. The net operating income is capitalized by the terminal capitalization rate or the so-called "going-out" capitalization rate. The terminal capitalization rate is usually, but not always, greater than the going-in capitalization rate. It is reasonable to assume that this rate will be greater because the improvements are older and the economic life may be reduced accordingly. In addition, there is more risk in forecasting the net operating income in the future. Ideally, the building is stabilized at that point in time. If not, adjustments may be required. The costs associated with selling the property must be deducted from the proceeds of sale at the end of the projection period.

The cash flow and the reversion from the sale of the property are developed before deduction for interest, taxes, depreciation, and amortization. These items are considered if the analyst's objective is to estimate investment value, not market value.

Semi-annual, quarterly, or monthly discounting and capitalization are not typically used in estimating the market value of real property. Application of different time periods can affect the analysis. These conventions were used during the late 1970s when the inflation rate and the returns on money market accounts were quite high in comparison to historical averages. The proper approach would be market oriented, in which case most real property investors expect to receive the cash flows annually. For development properties, a shorter time period is often used.

Different discount rates may be applied to the cash flows and the property reversion. If the real property is leased on a long-term basis to a creditworthy tenant, the risks associated with collecting the related cash flows may be low and warrant a discount rate that might be comparable to the yield on the bonds that are available for a similar time period. The future sale price of the property may be quite speculative and will warrant a substantially higher discount rate to reflect the risk differential. The discount rate is also the weighted average of the yields associated with both components of the cash flow, from operations and the sale of the property.

Estimating the Property Discount Rate

The property (overall) rate of return or discount rate (sometimes called property yield rate) is defined as: the rate of return on the total capital invested, including both debt and equity. Generally, if the objective is to estimate market value, the real property is analyzed on a before-tax basis. The overall yield rate takes into consideration changes in net income over the investment period and net reversion at the end of the holding period. It is applied to cash flow before debt service.[11.15]

The property discount rate is forward looking and, therefore, cannot be abstracted from current comparable sales information without confirmation of the assumptions employed by the buyer to determine the price that was paid for an asset. The discount rate incorporates the investor's compensation for the apparent risks, associated with a specific investment as discussed previously.

[11.15] Peter F. Korpacz, "The Illusive Cap Rate", *Valuation Briefs* (RICS Americas: January 14, 2010).

In theory, the property discount rate should be the sum of its parts: the real rate of return plus the expected inflation rate plus the risk premium (known as the build-up or summation method). The risk premium adjustment includes a variety of risk factors (e.g., market risk, environmental risk, legislative risk, etc.) that are difficult to quantify. Many consider it almost impossible to build up a discount rate by measuring the risks of each component.

The property yield rate can be developed by the "band of investment" method, provided that the assumptions used are market supported.[11.16] The discount rate is the weighted average return on the financial components, equity, and debt. The basic formula is shown on the next page:

Formula 11.5

$$k_p = \left[\left(F_d / PV_p \right) \times k_m \right] + \left[1 - \left(F_d / PV_p \right) \times k_e \right]$$

Where:

k_p	=	Property yield discount rate
k_m	=	Mortgage interest rate
k_e	=	Rate of return on equity investment and all other variables defined in Formula 11.4
$1 - (F_d / PV_p)$	=	Equity to value ratio
F_d / PV_p	=	Loan to value ratio

Formula 11.5 can be modified to include multiple equity investments and mortgages, such as mezzanine loans. The total weights must equal 100%. The typical real property investment includes debt, which provides support for this approach to develop the discount rate. The property discount rate provides for the required return on the mortgage and the expected return on the equity invested.

This method provides only an indication of the property discount rate during the first period. During subsequent periods, the equity component is increasing as the mortgage is amortized. The equity investor is seeking the same yield on the additional equity each year. This approach is widely used despite its shortcomings, which become obvious when interest rates are increasing or decreasing and the terms of any refinancing assumptions are changed.

[11.16] The "band of investment method" is not discussed in detail herein. For a detailed discussion of the band of investment method, see Shannon P. Pratt and Roger J. Grabowski, *Cost of Capital: Applications and Examples* 5th edition (John Wiley & Sons, Inc., 2014), Chapter 40.

The property discount rate can be estimated from overall capitalization rates if the anticipated changes in income and property value are known. Overall rates can be obtained from recent transactions. If the buyers are interviewed, the assumptions concerning the future changes in value and income can be established. If the income and value are expected to increase at a constant compound rate of growth, the formula to estimate the discount rate is derived from Formula 11.3, which we rearrange here in Formula 11.6:

Formula 11.6

$$k = c + A$$

where all variables are as defined in Formula 11.3.

Formula 11.6 can be altered to accommodate level, increasing, or decreasing annuities. The property discount rates and the equity dividend capitalization rates can be extracted from comparable sales if the assumptions developed by the purchaser to prepare the expected cash flows prior to acquisition have been verified.

Discount rates can also be estimated by surveying market participants. Published surveys summarizing the expectations and experience of investors are generally available for purchase or subscription. For example, Exhibit 11.6 shows information obtained from Situs RERC's 4Q 2016 *Real Estate Report* (data through fourth quarter 2016).

This and other similar surveys provide benchmarks that can be used along with other market information to support the discount rate. The discount rates reported can be compared to 10-year U.S. government bonds over time to provide an indication of the risk premium associated with a real estate investment in a central business district (CBD), for example. A wide range is often indicated, and further research is required to support the final selection of an appropriate discount rate.

Cost to Capital Valuation Inputs

Exhibit 11.6 presents data sourced from Situs RERC that can be used as inputs in performing valuations of individual real property investments as of the fourth quarter of 2016.

Situs RERC surveys some of the nation's leading commercial real estate valuation experts each quarter to get their views about the most critical valuation-related trends affecting commercial real estate and then analyzes and interprets their responses and reports them in the quarterly *Situs RERC Real Estate Report*. According to Situs RERC, most of these experts have been through several recessions and business cycles, have worked through several commercial real estate crises, and their independent observations, knowledge, and insights are worth noting.

The primary data points presented in Exhibit 11.6 reflect ex-ante required returns, or goals, of investors contemplating acquisitions, and are defined as follows:

- **Pre-tax Yield (IRR, Discount Rate):** The pre-tax yield is the rate of interest that discounts the pre-income tax cash flows received on an investment back to a present value that is exactly equal to the amount of the original equity investment. (It is in effect a time-weighted average return on equity and, as used here, is synonymous with the term "yield".)

- **Going-In (Overall) Capitalization Rate:** The first-year NOI divided by price or value.

- **Terminal (Residual) Capitalization Rate:** Terminal cap rate is the rate used to estimate resale or reversion value at the end of the holding period. Typically, it is the NOI in the year following the last year of the holding period that is capitalized. Similar to the going-in capitalization rate, but applied at the end of the holding investment period.

The discussion in the preceding sub-section presented a number of methods where these discount and capitalization rates can be used. The Situs RERC rates in Exhibit 11.6 were based on a survey conducted in October, November, and December 2016 and reflect expected returns for fourth quarter 2016 investments by main property type: Office, Industrial, Retail, Apartment, and Hotel.[11.17]

[11.17] As defined by Situs RERC in the quarterly *Situs RERC Real Estate Report*, 4Q 2016 issue, based on 4q 2016 investment criteria and analysis, Scope and Methodology.

2017 Valuation Handbook – U.S. Guide to Cost of Capital

Exhibit 11.6: Required Return Expectations by Property Type – 4Q 2016

Pre-tax Yield Rate (IRR) (%)

| | Office | | Industrial | | | Retail | | | | | |
	CBD*	Suburban	Warehouse	R&D**	Flex***	Regional Mall	Power Center	Neigh/ Comm	Apartment	Hotel	Average All Types
Range	5.3 - 9.0	7.0 - 10.0	5.3 - 9.0	7.0 - 9.5	7.0 - 9.5	7.0 - 9.0	6.8 - 10.0	5.5 - 9.5	4.8 - 9.0	8.5 - 11.5	4.8 - 11.5
Average	7.4	8.2	7.2	8	8.3	7.6	8	7.3	7.2	9.8	7.9
Weighted Average	7.7		7.3			7.6			7.2	9.8	7.9

Going-In Cap Rate (%)

| | Office | | Industrial | | | Retail | | | | | |
	CBD	Suburban	Warehouse	R&D	Flex	Regional Mall	Power Center	Neigh/ Comm	Apartment	Hotel	Average All Types
Range	4.5 - 6.0	5.5 - 7.8	4.5 - 7.5	5.5 - 7.5	5.5 - 8.3	4.0 - 8.0	5.5 - 8.0	5.0 - 7.3	4.0 - 6.5	6.0 - 9.0	4.0 - 9.0
Average	5.3	6.5	5.8	6.5	6.8	6.2	6.7	6	5.2	7.7	6.2
Weighted Average	5.8		5.9			6.2			5.2	7.7	6.2

Terminal Cap Rate (%)

| | Office | | Industrial | | | Retail | | | | | |
	CBD	Suburban	Warehouse	R&D	Flex	Regional Mall	Power Center	Neigh/ Comm	Apartment	Hotel	Average All Types
Range	5.5 - 7.0	6.5 - 9.0	5.0 - 8.0	6.0 - 8.0	6.0 - 9.0	5.0 - 8.5	6.3 - 9.0	5.5 - 8.0	4.3 - 7.0	7.0 - 10.0	4.3 - 10.0
Average	6	7.3	6.3	7.2	7.5	6.8	7.2	6.6	5.7	8.4	6.9
Weighted Average	6.5		6.4			6.8			5.7	8.4	6.9

*CBD: Central Business District ** R&D: Research and Development *** Flex: Can be used for industrial or office space.

Source of underlying data: RERC LLC, *Situs RERC Real Estate Report*, *4q 2016*, Volume 45, No. 4. All rights reserved. Used with permission. Situs RERC, a Situs company, is a nationally-recognized commercial real estate research, valuation and consulting firm that provides valuation management and fiduciary services, appraisal and litigation services, and analytics and research publications for 11 major property types on an institutional, regional, and metro-level basis. Current and historical required pre-tax yield rates, required going-in capitalization rates, and required terminal capitalization rates and other investment criteria are available from Situs RERC. To learn more about Situs RERC, visit www.situsrerc.com.

Key Things to Remember about Real Property Valuation

This section introduced some methods utilized to develop the appropriate returns on individual, income producing, real property investments. The basic concepts are quite similar to business valuation concepts, but additional factors must be considered in the analysis of income-producing real estate and the consideration of external and explicit financial funding.

Furthermore, data used in real estate valuations differ from the traditional sources used to derive discount rates when performing business valuations.

Chapter 12

Answers to Commonly Asked Questions

The authors decided to add this chapter in order to share some of the many thoughtful questions received from valuation analysts about the *Valuation Handbook – U.S. Guide to Cost of Capital*.[12.1]

The questions in this chapter are a sampling of some of the questions we have received since the inaugural *2014 Valuation Handbook – U.S. Guide to Cost of Capital* was published in early 2014. Some of the questions herein refer to specific data found within a specific *Valuation Handbook – U.S. Guide to Cost of Capital* year (and thus are not be updated from year to year), some of the questions are about concepts and ideas which are equally applicable to any *Valuation Handbook – U.S. Guide to Cost of Capital* year (and thus are not necessarily updated from year to year), while some questions do require that we update them annually with the most recent data.

Reader comments, questions, and suggestions are an important source of information for helping us to constantly improve the *Valuation Handbook – U.S. Guide to Cost of Capital* (and our related valuation data resources).[12.2]

[12.1] This chapter is somewhat analogous to the section entitled "Advice to Practitioners" in Shannon P. Pratt and Roger J. Grabowski, *Cost of Capital: Applications and Examples*, 5th edition, where the authors and contributing authors provide their thoughts and insights on handling challenging questions they have received in regards to client engagements, across a wide spectrum of valuation topics. Unlike the "Advice to Practitioners" section therein, Chapter 12 herein focuses on questions that we have received concerning the data and methodology specific to the *Valuation Handbook – U.S. Guide to Cost of Capital*.

[12.2] Other valuation data resources authored by Duff & Phelps, and published by Wiley include: (i) *Valuation Handbook – U.S. Industry Cost of Capital*: this book provides cost of capital estimates (i.e., equity capital, debt capital, and WACC) for approximately 180 U.S. industries and size groupings (i.e., Large-, Mid-, Low-, and Micro-capitalization companies), plus a host of detailed statistics that can be used for benchmarking purposes (over 300 critical industry-level data points calculated for each industry, depending on data availability), (ii) *Valuation Handbook – International Guide to Cost of Capital*: this annual book provides country-level equity risk premia (ERPs), relative volatility (RV) factors, and country risk premia (CRPs) which can be used to estimate country-level cost of equity capital globally, for up to 188 countries, from the perspective of investors based in any one of up to 56 countries (depending on data availability), and (iii) *Valuation Handbook – International Industry Cost of Capital*: this annual book provides the same type of rigorous industry-level analysis published in the U.S.-centric *Valuation Handbook – U.S. Industry Cost of Capital*, on a global scale. The *Valuation Handbook – International Industry Cost of Capital* includes industry-level analyses for four global economic areas: (i) the "World", (ii) the European Union, (iii) the Eurozone, and (iv) the United Kingdom. Each of the four global area's industry analyses are presented in three currencies: (i) the euro (€ or EUR), (ii) the British pound (£ or GBP), and (iii) the U.S. dollar ($ or USD). To learn more about Duff & Phelps valuation data resources published by John Wiley & Sons, please go to: www.wiley.com/go/ValuationHandbooks.

Question 1: Where did Exhibit 5.7 (industry risk premia for use in the Build-up model), Exhibit 5.8 (quarterly debt betas), and Exhibit 5.9 (a graph of rolling debt betas) go? Is this information still in the book?

Response: Yes. All of the information in these former exhibits is in the *2017 Valuation Handbook – U.S. Guide to Cost of Capital*, but is now found in the appendices at the back of the book:

- Starting with the *2016 Valuation Handbook – U.S. Guide to Cost of Capital*, Exhibit 5.7 (industry risk premia for use in the Build-up model) is now presented as Appendix 3a.

- Starting with the *2016 Valuation Handbook – U.S. Guide to Cost of Capital*, Exhibits 5.8 (quarterly debt betas) and 5.9 (graph of 60-month rolling debt betas) are now presented as Appendix 3b.

Question 2: Are the data and methodologies used in the *Valuation Handbook – U.S. Guide to Cost of Capital* the same as those that were used in the (now discontinued) Morningstar/Ibbotson *SBBI Valuation Yearbook*?

Response: This is an important question. The short answer is yes, the historical equity risk premia and size premia data published in the *Valuation Handbook – U.S. Guide to Cost of Capital* is the same exact equity risk premia and size premia data that was published in the former *SBBI Valuation Yearbook*. This continuity is important in any case, but may be especially important in cases when similar valuation analysis is done over a number of years.

The premia in the *Valuation Handbook – U.S. Guide to Cost of Capital* are calculated using the same exact methodology as the former *SBBI Valuation Yearbook*. And, the premia were calculated using the same exact data sources: (i) Standard & Poor's, (ii) the Center for Research in Security Prices at the University of Chicago Booth School of Business (CRSP) and (iii) Morningstar – the actual "SBBI" data series are used in our calculations in the *2017 Valuation Handbook – U.S. Guide to Cost of Capital*.

Question 3: In the *2014 Valuation Handbook – U.S. Guide to Cost of Capital* I could not find the summary statistics of annual returns by asset class that was previously found in Table 2-1 *2013 SBBI Valuation Yearbook* (see page 23 of that book). Will the *2015 Valuation Handbook – U.S. Guide to Cost of Capital* contain information on the income return and capital appreciation components for large-, mid-, and low-cap stocks, or for long-term and intermediate-term government bonds that was previously available in this table?

Response: Yes. Over the course of 2014 we received a number requests to add this information to the *2015 Valuation Handbook – U.S. Guide to Cost of Capital*, and Morningstar graciously granted us permission to use the additional SBBI series needed to produce this table starting with the *2015 Valuation Handbook – U.S. Guide to Cost of Capital*. This information is found in Exhibit 2.3, "Summary Statistics of Total Returns, Income Returns, and Capital Appreciation Returns of Basic U.S. Asset Classes 1926–present" herein. The 1926–present time period in Exhibit 2.3 matches the time horizon over which the size premia, equity risk premia, and other statistics in the CRSP Deciles Size Study exhibits are calculated. Starting with the *2016 Valuation Handbook – U.S. Guide to Cost* *of Capital*, we also added summary statistics of total returns, income returns, and capital appreciation returns of basic U.S. asset classes, as measured over the time period 1963–present. The 1963–present time horizon matches the time horizon over which the size premia, "risk premia over the risk-free rate", and other statistics in the Risk Premium Report Study exhibits are calculated. These data can be found in Exhibit 2.4 herein.

Question 4: According to the Board of Governors of the Federal Reserve website, the risk-free rate of the 20-year U.S. government (constant-maturity) bond yield as of December 31, 2016 is 2.79% (daily rates), whereas the *2017 Valuation Handbook – U.S. Guide to Cost of Capital* reports 2.72%. Why is there a difference?[12.3]

Response: For the long-term (20-year) U.S. government bond yield, the *2017 Valuation Handbook – U.S. Guide to Cost of Capital* uses the same SBBI data that was used in the previously published Morningstar/Ibbotson *SBBI Valuation Yearbooks*.[12.4]

The *2017 Valuation Handbook – U.S. Guide to Cost of Capital's* Appendix 3, which is the direct equivalent of the former "back page" of the *SBBI Valuation Yearbook*, includes all of the critical valuation data (equity risk premia, size premia, etc.) previously published in the *SBBI Valuation Yearbook*, using (i) the same underlying data (S&P, CRSP, and SBBI data), and (ii) using the same methodology, including the risk-free rate information.

For example, in the *2015 Valuation Handbook – U.S. Guide to Cost of Capital*, we reported in Appendix 3 that the (SBBI) long-term (20-year) U.S. government bond yield was 2.40%, which is the identical value that was reported in the Morningstar/Ibbotson *2015 SBBI Classic Yearbook*.[12.5] It is the same data, and the same data source.

This is not to say that there are not differences between the "SBBI" long-term (20-year) government bond series yields and the long-term yields reported by say, the Federal Reserve Bank or the U.S. Treasury websites. These differences are due to slight methodological differences, and are not material. The correlation between these series is 0.999. In other words, the series are nearly identical, and overlap to a very high degree, as illustrated in Exhibit 12.1.

[12.3] This question was originally asked in regard to the *2014 Valuation Handbook – U.S. Guide to Cost of Capital* (data through December 2013), and has been updated with year-end 2016 data.

[12.4] For a description of the construction of the SBBI indices, see the *2017 SBBI Yearbook* (Wiley, 2017) Chapter 3, "Description of the Basic Series". The *SBBI Yearbook* is an analysis of the relative performance of various asset classes in the U.S. and does *not* provide extensive valuation data or methodology.

[12.5] Source: *2015 SBBI Classic Yearbook* (Morningstar, Chicago, 2015), Table A-9, "Long-Term Government Bonds: Yields", pages 212–213. The *SBBI Classic Yearbook* is an analysis of the relative performance of various asset classes in the U.S. and does *not* provide extensive valuation data or methodology. Morningstar previously published two "Ibbotson SBBI" yearbooks: (i) The *SBBI "Classic" Yearbook*, which is now produced by Duff & Phelps and published by John Wiley & Sons as the *"SBBI Yearbook"* starting in 2016 (the word "Classic" was dropped from the title), and (ii) the *SBBI "Valuation" Yearbook*, which was discontinued by Morningstar in 2013. The former *SBBI Valuation Yearbook* was replaced by the *Valuation Handbook – U.S. Guide to Cost of Capital* (this book), also produced by Duff & Phelps and published by John Wiley & Sons, starting in 2014.

Exhibit 12.1: 20-year (constant maturity) U.S. Government Bond Yields from the Board of Governors of the Federal Reserve Website Compared to the SBBI Long-term (20-year) U.S. Government Bond Yield

October 1993–December 2016

Duff & Phelps went to great lengths and cost to secure the same exact underlying data for the *2017 Valuation Handbook – U.S. Guide to Cost of Capital* that was previously used to produce the *Ibbotson SBBI Valuation Yearbook*, including the actual "SBBI" series. This continuity is important in any case, but may be especially important in cases when similar valuation analysis is done over a number of years.

Question 5: In future editions of the *Valuation Handbook – U.S. Guide to Cost of Capital*, is it possible to include in Exhibit 4.7 the market capitalizations of the smallest and the largest company in each of the deciles, since market capitalizations change over time (at least they did in the *Ibbotson SBBI Valuation Yearbooks*)?

Response: The market caps of the companies with the smallest and largest market capitalization can be found in Appendix 3 of the *Valuation Handbook – U.S. Guide to Cost of Capital* (Appendix 3 is the equivalent of the former "back page" of the *SBBI Valuation Yearbook*). Exhibit 4.7, which is in the 2014, 2015, 2016, and 2017 books, has a different purpose. Exhibit 4.7 is a demonstration of how size premia can differ, based on what type of beta is used (OLS beta, Annual beta, or Sum beta).

And yes, you are correct, the smallest and largest companies in the CRSP portfolios *do* change over time (CRSP refers to these as "breakpoints"). The compositions of the CRSP portfolios are reset each quarter, and thus the market caps of the smallest and largest companies in each of the CRSP portfolios can *also* change over time.

Question 6: In the *2014 Valuation Handbook – U.S. Guide to Cost of Capital*, page 2-3, last paragraph, second sentence, states that "The CML is defined as a line used in the capital asset pricing model..." I always thought that the Security Market Line (SML) is used in CAPM. It plots beta on the x-axis. What am I missing?

Response: The Capital Market Line (CML) as referenced in the *2014 Valuation Handbook – U.S. Guide to Cost of Capital* is correct, as is the graph shown in the 2014 book's Exhibit 2.3. However, we can see how someone could have a literal interpretation and focus on the fact that the CAPM equation is based on the Security Market Line (SML).

Both the CML and SML are linear relationships (or equations) defined by the CAPM theory.

The CML depicts the expected relationship of risk (as defined by expected standard deviation of returns) and expected return of portfolios. The point where the CML is tangent to the efficient frontier of the opportunity set of portfolios of investments is denoted as *M*, the market portfolio. Only efficient portfolios that consist of combinations of risk-free assets and the market portfolio can lie on the CML. The expected returns of *portfolios* are a linear function of portfolios' standard deviation of returns.[12.6]

An individual security's risk will consist not only of the systematic risk of portfolios along the CML, but will also contain unsystematic risk. Thus, all individual assets must be more risky than the points on the CML. Individual securities (as opposed to portfolios) will be located *within* the opportunity set instead of directly on the CML.

The SML shows a relationship between covariance (between individual security and the market) and expected return. The expected return of a security is a positive linear function of the security's covariance with the market (increasing function of its systematic risk as measured by covariance).

In equilibrium, every individual security's expected return and risk observation will lie on the SML and off of the CML. But, in equilibrium, portfolios' (rather than individual securities) expected returns and standard deviations will lie on the CML and the SML. Thus, CAPM, the Sharpe/Lintner/Mossin extension of the Markowitz capital market theory of the two-parameter-model, is a function of the CML for portfolios.

Obviously, we can define the SML in terms of the familiar beta (covariance with the market) on the "x" axis.

Exhibit 2.3 is simply a plot of "what happened". It depicts the historical annual returns of certain asset classes, along with their associated "risk" (as measured by standard deviation). It is a

---

[12.6] This explanation is drawn from a great reference book, Jack Clarke Francis and Stephen H. Archer, *Portfolio Analysis* (Prentice Hall, 1971).

depiction of the realized returns versus risk along the observed CML. But historical data play no role in the theory itself.

Question 7: On page 3-14 of the *2014 Valuation Handbook – U.S. Guide to Cost of Capital*, Exhibit 3.6, "Realized Equity Risk Premiums: Stock Market Returns Minus U.S. Government Bonds Through 2013", shows that the 20-year arithmetic average (1994–2013) historical ERP was 6.06%. In contrast, on page 59 of Morningstar's *2013 Ibbotson SBBI Valuation Yearbook,* Table 5-5, "Stock Market Return and Equity Risk Premium Over Time" shows the 20-year arithmetic average (1993–2012) historical ERP was 4.7%.

Why is the difference between the two books so large? If they are comparable sources, any thoughts on how a 20-year average historical ERP increased so significantly when only a single year had passed?

Response: Exhibit 3.6 of the *2014 Valuation Handbook – U.S. Guide to Cost of Capital* and Table 5-5 of the previous year's *2013 Ibbotson Valuation Yearbook* compare the realized equity risk premium (ERP) over various time periods using the same data and methodology. The two ERP measurements refer to the 20-year period ending December 2012 (1993–2012) in the *2013 SBBI Valuation Yearbook,* and the 20-year period ending 2013 (1994–2013) in the *2014 Valuation Handbook – U.S. Guide to Cost of Capital.*

The short answer is that the 4.7% (as reported in the *2013 SBBI Valuation*) and the 6.06% (as reported in the *2014 Valuation Handbook – U.S. Guide to Cost of Capital*) are indeed comparable, and both are <u>correct</u>.

The longer answer is summarized in Exhibit 12.2, which includes the average returns used to calculate both the 4.7% (in the *2013 SBBI Valuation Yearbook*) and the 6.06% (in the *2014 Valuation Handbook – U.S. Guide to Cost of Capital*). The 6.06% reported in the *2014 Valuation Handbook – U.S. Guide to Cost of Capital* is the difference between the average annual S&P 500 total return index return over the 20-year period from 1994–2013 and the average annual income return of long-term U.S. government bonds over the same period (11.13% – 5.07%). Likewise, the 4.7% (rounded from 4.73%) reported in the *2013 SBBI Valuation Yearbook* is the difference between the average annual S&P 500 total return index return over the 20-year period 1993–2012 and the average annual income return of long-term U.S. government bonds over the same period (10.01% – 5.28%).

The main driver of the increase in ERP as measured over these two (different) time periods is the unusually large increase in the S&P 500 total return index in 2013 (32.39%). With the time frame being only 20 years, this large increase acted to significantly *increase* the average total return for "stocks" by 1.12% over the measurement period (from 10.01% to 11.13%). At the same time, the average income return of long-term government bonds *decreased* by 0.21% (from 5.28% to 5.07%). The cumulative effect of these differences (1.12% + 0.21% = 1.33%) accounts for the difference in the ERP as measured over these two periods (6.06% – 4.73% = 1.33%).

Exhibit 12.2: Summary of Average Returns Used to Calculate Equity Risk Premia Over the 1993–2012 and 1994–2013 Periods

	2013 Valuation Yearbook **(Table 5-5)** 20-year period ending 2012 (1993–2012)	*2014 Valuation Handbook* **(Exhibit 3.6)** 20-year period ending 2013 (1994–2013)
S&P 500 Index Total Returns	10.01%	11.13%
Minus: Long-term Government Bond Income Returns	− 5.28%	− 5.07%
Equals: ERP Over 20-year Period	= 4.73%	= 6.06%

Question 8: Why were the size premia calculated for the standard CRSP deciles and size groupings in the Morningstar/Ibbotson *2014 SBBI Classic Yearbook*[12.7] slightly different from those published in the *2014 Valuation Handbook – U.S. Guide to Cost of Capital*?

Response: The *differences* in reported size premia for the CRSP deciles between the *2014 Valuation Handbook – U.S. Guide to Cost of Capital* and the *2014 SBBI Classic Yearbook* are summarized in Exhibit 12.3.[12.8]

Exhibit 12.3: Size Premia (differences only); *Morningstar 2014 Classic Yearbook* versus *2014 Valuation Handbook – U.S. Guide to Cost of Capital*
As of December 31, 2013

As of December 31, 2013	Size Premia (differences)
Mid-Cap (3-5)	0.04%
Low-Cap (6-8)	-0.11%
Micro-Cap (9-10)	-0.03%
Breakdown of CRSP Deciles 1–10	
Decile 1	0.04%
Decile 2	0.05%
Decile 3	0.07%
Decile 4	0.03%
Decile 5	-0.02%
Decile 6	-0.10%
Decile 7	-0.20%
Decile 8	0.12%
Decile 9	-0.05%
Decile 10	0.03%

For example, in Exhibit 12.3, the size premium for Decile 10 published in the *2014 SBBI Classic Yearbook* was approximately 0.03% *greater* than the size premium for Decile 10 published in the *2014 Valuation Handbook – U.S. Guide to Cost of Capital*. Similarly, the size premium for Decile 7 in the *Classic Yearbook* was 0.20% *less* than Decile 7's size premium in the *2014 Valuation Handbook – U.S. Guide to Cost of Capital*.

While these differences are relatively minor in nature, it is nonetheless important to examine and understand the likely source of these differences.

[12.7] The *SBBI Classic Yearbook* was published by Morningstar, Inc. through the 2014 version of the book. Starting with the 2016 version, it has been updated by Duff & Phelps, and published by John Wiley & Sons under the name "*SBBI Yearbook*" (the word "Classic" was dropped from the name). The *SBBI Yearbook* is an analysis of the relative performance of various asset classes in the U.S., and does *not* provide extensive valuation data or methodology. For more information about the SBBI Yearbook and purchasing information, please visit www.wiley.com/go/sbbiyearbook, or call: U.S. (800) 762-2974 International (317) 572-3993 or fax (317) 572-4002.

[12.8] Differences in the two publications' size premia are measured in Exhibit II as: (*2014 SBBI Classic Yearbook* size premia *2014 Valuation Handbook – U.S. Guide to Cost of Capital* size premia). Source: *2014 SBBI Classic Yearbook* (Morningstar, 2014), page 109; *2014 Valuation Handbook – U.S. Guide to Cost of Capital* (Duff & Phelps, 2014), Appendix 3.

Let's start with what we know. The <u>same</u> two primary data sources were used to calculate the size premia in both the *2014 Valuation Handbook – U.S. Guide to Cost of Capital* and in the *2014 Classic Yearbook*:

- SBBI Series from Morningstar's *EnCorr* database[12.9]

- The Center for Research in Security Prices (CRSP) market-cap-based NYSE/NYSE MKT/NASDAQ indices

The specific inputs from these two sources used to calculate the size premia published in the *2014 Valuation Handbook – U.S. Guide to Cost of Capital* and the *2014 Classic Yearbook* are:[12.10]

1. S&P 500 total return index

2. 30-day U.S. T-Bill total return series

3. Long-term income return of 20-year U.S. government bonds

4. CRSP NYSE/NYSE AMEX/NASDAQ Market Capitalization Deciles 1–10 total return indices

To calculate the size premia in the *2014 Valuation Handbook – U.S. Guide to Cost of Capital* and the *2014 SBBI Classic Yearbook*, the following summarizes the elements that are common to both:

- **Identical Market Benchmark:** The *2014 SBBI Classic Yearbook* and the *2014 Valuation Handbook – U.S. Guide to Cost of Capital* both used the S&P 500 total return index as the "market benchmark" when calculating the betas for each of the CRSP deciles and size groupings.[12.11] These betas are important inputs needed to calculate size premia over CAPM.

- **Identical 30-day U.S.** Treasury Bill series: The *2014 SBBI Classic Yearbook* and the *2014 Valuation Handbook – U.S. Guide to Cost of Capital* calculated the CRSP deciles' betas as monthly return data in excess of the <u>same</u> exact 30-day U.S. Treasury bill total return series over the period January 1926–December 2013.[12.12]

[12.9] In 2014, Morningstar discontinued the *EnCorr* database, and transitioned all SBBI series over to the Morningstar *Direct* database. To learn more about the Morningstar *Direct* database, visit corporate.morningstar.com.

[12.10] Source of inputs 1, 2, and 3 in the *2014 Valuation Handbook – U.S. Guide to Cost of Capital* : Morningstar *EnCorr* database. In 2014, Morningstar discontinued the *EnCorr* database, and transitioned all SBBI series over to the Morningstar *Direct* database. To learn more about the Morningstar *Direct* database, visit corporate.morningstar.com. Source of input 4: CRSP U.S. Stock Database and CRSP U.S. Indices Database © 2014 Center for Research in Security Prices (CRSP®), University of Chicago Booth School of Business. To learn more about the Center for Research in Security Prices (CRSP) at the University of Chicago Booth School of Business, visit www.crsp.com.

[12.11] The specific series used in the *2014 SBBI Classic Yearbook* and the *2014 Valuation Handbook – U.S. Guide to Cost of Capital* as the market benchmark when calculating betas for the CRSP deciles and size groupings is "S&P 500 TR (IA Extended)". Source: Morningstar *EnCorr* database. In 2014, Morningstar discontinued the *EnCorr* database, and transitioned all SBBI series over to the Morningstar *Direct* database. To learn more about the Morningstar *Direct* database, visit corporate.morningstar.com.

[12.12] See *2014 SBBI Classic Yearbook* (Morningstar, 2014), page 109; *2014 Valuation Handbook – U.S. Guide to Cost of Capital* (Duff & Phelps, 2014), page 4-10.

- **Identical Long-Term Equity Risk Premium:** The *2014 SBBI Classic Yearbook* and the *2014 Valuation Handbook – U.S. Guide to Cost of Capital* calculated (and used) the same exact values for the arithmetic annual return of the S&P 500 total return index and the long-term income return of 20-year U.S. government bonds over the 1926–2013 time horizon (12.05% and 5.09%, respectively; these two values are used to calculate the long-term equity risk premium, which is an important input needed to calculate size premia).[12.13]

- **Identical Methodology:** Finally, both the *2014 SBBI Classic Yearbook* and the *2014 Valuation Handbook – U.S. Guide to Cost of Capital* use the same methodology to calculate the size premia for the CRSP deciles:

  Size premium = (the excess returns that *actually happened* – the excess returns that CAPM *predicted* would happen)

So, what is different? The *only* set of inputs that we have not examined thus far is the total returns for the CRSP NYSE/NYSE MKT/NASDAQ Market Capitalization Deciles 1–10. Exhibit 12.4 is a summary of the average annual return of each of the standard CRSP deciles over the 1926–2013 period, as published in (i) the *2014 SBBI Classic Yearbook* and (ii) the *2014 Valuation Handbook – U.S. Guide to Cost of Capital*.[12.14] To be clear, note that the "Difference" column in Exhibit 12.4 is not the same as the "Size Premia (differences)" column found in Exhibit 12.3 (even though some of figures may coincide). The latter is adjusted by the beta of each portfolio.

[12.13] See *2014 SBBI Classic Yearbook* (Morningstar, 2014), page 109; *2014 Valuation Handbook – U.S. Guide to Cost of Capital* (Duff & Phelps, 2014), page 4-10.

[12.14] Source of underlying data in Exhibit 12.4: CRSP U.S. Stock Database and CRSP U.S. Indices Database © 2014 Center for Research in Security Prices (CRSP®), University of Chicago Booth School of Business. See *2014 SBBI Classic Yearbook* (Morningstar, 2014), Table 7-6, page 109; *2014 Valuation Handbook – U.S. Guide to Cost of Capital* (Duff & Phelps, 2014), Exhibit 7.3, page 7-10.

Exhibit 12.4: Average Annual Total Returns of the CRSP NYSE/NYSE MKT/NASDAQ Market Capitalization Deciles 1–10 as Published in the *2014 SBBI Classic Yearbook* and the *2014 Valuation Handbook – U.S. Guide to Cost of Capital*
1926–2013

Size Grouping	As published in: *2014 SBBI Classic Yearbook* Arithmetic Annual Average Return (1926–2013)	As published in: *2014 Valuation Handbook* Arithmetic Annual Average Return (1926–2013)	Difference Classic *minus* Handbook
Mid-Cap (3-5)	14.02%	14.01%	0.02%
Low-Cap (6-8)	15.51%	15.57%	-0.07%
Micro-Cap (9-10)	18.38%	18.41%	-0.03%
Breakdown of CRSP Deciles 1–10			
Decile 1	11.13%	11.10%	0.03%
Decile 2	13.09%	13.04%	0.05%
Decile 3	13.68%	13.64%	0.04%
Decile 4	14.12%	14.09%	0.03%
Decile 5	14.88%	14.92%	-0.03%
Decile 6	15.11%	15.12%	-0.01%
Decile 7	15.48%	15.68%	-0.20%
Decile 8	16.62%	16.55%	0.07%
Decile 9	17.23%	17.27%	-0.04%
Decile 10	20.88%	20.85%	0.04%

The slightly different size premia values reported in the *2014 SBBI Classic Yearbook* and the *2014 Valuation Handbook – U.S. Guide to Cost of Capital* are traceable to the slightly different CRSP decile total returns used by the two publications.[12.15] For example, the average annual return of CRSP Decile 7 over the 1926–2013 period as reported in the *2014 SBBI Classic Yearbook* is 15.48%, while the average annual return of Decile 7 as reported in the *2014 Valuation Handbook – U.S. Guide to Cost of Capital* is 15.68%, a difference of -0.20% (15.48% – 15.68%). Note that this difference (-0.20%) is the same as the difference in the size premia reported for Decile 7 in the *2014 SBBI Classic Yearbook* and the *2014 Valuation Handbook – U.S. Guide to Cost of Capital* in Exhibit 12.3, although as mentioned earlier the size premia in Exhibit 12.3 are beta adjusted, whereas the differences in Exhibit 12.4 are not.[12.16]

[12.15] Eight decimals were used in the calculation of the differences in Exhibit12.4; these results were then rounded to two decimals.

[12.16] The *largest* contributing factor to the differences in the size premia reported in the *2014 SBBI Classic Yearbook* and the *2014 Valuation Handbook – U.S. Guide to Cost of Capital* is the difference in the average annual return over the 1926–2013 period (this accounted for 79.8% of the variation). Differences in the betas calculated for each of the deciles were (to a significantly *lesser* degree) a contributing factor to the differences in size premia (this accounted for 20.2% of the variation). However, both the average annual return input and the beta input are a function of the raw monthly annual CRSP returns, and thus the *root* cause is the difference in returns.

Which Size Premia are Correct?

In Exhibit 12.5, the values that $1.00 invested as of December 31, 1925 in each of the CRSP standard market-capitalization-weighted deciles (and three size groupings) would have grown to as of December 31, 2013 are calculated in three alternative ways: (i) by CRSP itself, using their official returns database,[12.17] (ii) using the CRSP returns that were used to calculate the size premia published in the *2014 Valuation Handbook – U.S. Guide to Cost of Capital*, and (iii) as published in the *2014 SBBI Classic Yearbook*.[12.18]

Exhibit 12.5: Terminal Index Values for the CRSP NYSE/NYSE MKT/NASDAQ Market Capitalization Deciles as of December 31, 2013 (i) Calculated by CRSP, (ii) Calculated Using the CRSP Returns Used to Calculate the Size Premia Published in the *2014 Valuation Handbook – U.S. Guide to Cost of Capital*, and (iii) as Published in the *2014 SBBI Classic Yearbook*.
December 31, 1925 = $1.00

Size Grouping/ Decile	Calculated by CRSP	Calculated using the CRSP returns used to calculate the size premia published in the *2014 Valuation Handbook*	Published in the *2014 SBBI Classic Yearbook*
Mid-Cap (3-5)	$11,419	$11,419	$11,728
Low-Cap (6-8)	$17,514	$17,514	$16,606
Micro-Cap (9-10)	$27,771	$27,771	$29,190
Decile 1	$2,510	$2,510	$2,589
Decile 2	$7,704	$7,704	$7,769
Decile 3	$9,846	$9,846	$10,635
Decile 4	$10,606	$10,606	$10,514
Decile 5	$17,141	$17,141	$16,189
Decile 6	$16,115	$16,115	$15,955
Decile 7	$17,175	$17,175	$15,347
Decile 8	$19,675	$19,675	$18,600
Decile 9	$17,440	$17,440	$19,294
Decile 10	$68,670	$68,670	$62,843

Looking to Exhibit 12.5, the following observations can be made:

- The terminal index values calculated by CRSP using their official database <u>match</u> the terminal index values calculated using the CRSP returns used to produce the size premia in the *2014 Valuation Handbook – U.S. Guide to Cost of Capital*, and

- The terminal index values of the CRSP deciles reported in *2014 SBBI Classic Yearbook* do <u>not</u> match CRSP's own calculations.

[12.17] Source: Document "qtr201312.q", prepared by the Center for Research in Security Prices (CRSP), Jan-16-2014/201312 Copyright © 2014

[12.18] Source: *2014 SBBI Classic Yearbook* (Morningstar 2014), Table 7-3, pages 103–104, Table 7-4, pages 105–106. Values have been rounded to nearest dollar.

All other things held the same, the terminal index values in Exhibit 12.5 are dependent on the January 1926–December 2013 monthly returns used to calculate them: if the returns *change*, the terminal index values *change*. The conclusion of this analysis is therefore straightforward:

- The CRSP decile returns used to calculate the size premia in the Morningstar/Ibbotson *2014 SBBI Classic Yearbook* (data through December 31, 2013) do <u>not</u> match the returns in CRSP's own official database as of December 31, 2013, and

- The CRSP decile returns used to calculate the size premia in the *2014 Valuation Handbook – U.S. Guide to Cost of Capital* (data through December 31, 2013) <u>match</u> the returns in CRSP's own official database as of December 31, 2013.

In the *2017 Valuation Handbook – U.S. Guide to Cost of Capital* (this book), we again worked carefully with CRSP to ensure that the size premia in the *2017 Valuation Handbook – U.S. Guide to Cost of Capital* are based upon the <u>exact</u> monthly total return values in CRSP's official database as of December 31, 2016 for the time horizon January 1926–December 2016.

In Exhibit 12.6, the values that $1.00 invested as of December 31, 1925 in each of the CRSP standard market-capitalization-weighted deciles (and three size groupings) would have grown to as of December 31, 2016 are calculated again in two alternative ways: (i) by CRSP itself, using their official returns database,[12.19] and (ii) using the CRSP returns that were used to calculate the size premia published in the *2017 Valuation Handbook – U.S. Guide to Cost of Capital* (this book). The terminal index values again *exactly* match. The conclusion of this analysis is thus again straightforward:

- The CRSP decile returns used to calculate the size premia in the *2017 Valuation Handbook – U.S. Guide to Cost of Capital* (this book) <u>match</u> the returns in CRSP's own official database as of December 31, 2016.

[12.19] Source: Document "qtr201612.q", prepared by the Center for Research in Security Prices (CRSP), Jan-19-2017/201612 Copyright © 2017.

Exhibit 12.6: Terminal Index Values for the CRSP NYSE/NYSE MKT/NASDAQ Market Capitalization Deciles as of December 31, 2016 (i) Calculated by CRSP, (ii) Calculated Using the CRSP Returns Used to Calculate the Size Premia Published in the *2017 Valuation Handbook – U.S. Guide to Cost of Capital* 1926–2016; (December 31, 1925 = $1.00)

Size Grouping/ Decile	Calculated by CRSP	Calculated using the CRSP returns used to calculate the size premia published in the *2017 Valuation Handbook*
Mid-Cap (3-5)	$14,325	$14,325
Low-Cap (6-8)	$20,136	$20,136
Micro-Cap (9-10)	$33,900	$33,900
Decile 1	$3,293	$3,293
Decile 2	$9,285	$9,285
Decile 3	$13,748	$13,748
Decile 4	$11,755	$11,755
Decile 5	$19,943	$19,943
Decile 6	$18,039	$18,039
Decile 7	$21,454	$21,454
Decile 8	$21,077	$21,077
Decile 9	$20,975	$20,975
Decile 10	$86,590	$86,590

Question 9: Can you provide guidance on applying a size premium for a small regulated utility company?

Unlike small companies operating in a non-regulated environment, the small regulated utility company is assured of a certain income stream, and typically operates in a monopoly environment. This would arguably remove a great deal of risk that a typical small company might otherwise face. Furthermore, some of our appraisal firms have concluded that the small electric company could have less risk than their larger counterpart. This could partly be due to the fact that the small utility is often a pure play business, whereas the bigger utilities sometimes venture into areas that are considered riskier.

Given this background, should a small regulated utility company have a similar risk premium to that of a typical small company?

Response: Size premia data are calculated based on a measure of central tendency (i.e., a measure of mid-point) for the sample of firms that comprise a specific size portfolio. Accordingly, the size premia data are reported for the mid-point of the companies included in each of the portfolios. Companies within that same size portfolio can have different risk profiles and, consequently, should have a different cost of capital. The *2017 Valuation Handbook – U.S. Guide to Cost of Capital* provides additional data to help understand risk differences among companies.

For example, let us examine the data in Exhibit B-5 of the *2017 Valuation Handbook – U.S. Guide to Cost of Capital* (this book), Appendix 4. This Exhibit presents size premia data (over CAPM), where size is measured by Total Assets.

Assume that the subject small regulated utility company has $1 billion in total assets placing it in Portfolio 21 in Exhibit B-5. The corresponding smoothed size premium (over CAPM) is shown as 4.38%.

Now, let's further examine the characteristics of the companies that comprise Portfolio 21 of Exhibit B-5. For that information, we turn to the Comparative Risk Characteristics presented in the C Exhibits. The matching Exhibit to Exhibit B-5 is Exhibit C-5.

Upon examination of Exhibit C-5, we observe that the average operating margin of the companies within Portfolio 21 (i.e., the companies comprising that size grouping) equals 8.86% and the average coefficient of variation in operating margin (i.e., how much does the operating margin vary over time) equals 22.46%.

To the extent that a subject company's operating margin is *less* than 8.86%, the risk of that business is likely *greater* than that of the typical company comprising Portfolio 21. Conversely, to the extent that a subject company's operating margin is *greater* than 8.86%, the risk of that business is likely *less* than that of the typical company comprising Portfolio 21.

Now, let's look at Exhibit D-1. Exhibit D-1 is the same companies that are in the A, B, and C exhibits, but instead of being sorted from largest to smallest according to size, the companies are sorted by "operating margin". There is a general relationship between these metrics, such that as operating margin *decreases*, the cost of capital (risk) typically *increases*.

Also, to the extent that a subject company's *variability* of operating margin (as measured by coefficient of variation) is *greater* than 22.46%, the risk of that business is likely *greater* than that of the companies comprising Portfolio 21 (see Exhibit D-2). Alternatively, to the extent that a subject company's variability of operating margin was *less* than 22.46%, the risk of that business is likely *less* than that of the companies comprising Portfolio 21. The relationship in Exhibit D-2 shows that as the coefficient of variation of operating margin decreases, the cost of capital (risk) typically decreases.

Exhibits D-1 and D-2 can help quantify how much less or more from the typical size premium should be the cost of capital for the subject company. For a detailed example of how one might make such an adjustment, consider reviewing The section entitled "Comparative Risk Study" on pages 10-63 to 10-70 in the *2017 Valuation Handbook – U.S. Guide to Cost of Capital.*

The authors believe that the cost of capital needs to reflect the risk characteristics of the subject company, rather than the risks exhibited by the typical firm. The data in the *2017 Valuation Handbook – U.S. Guide to Cost of Capital* will help you make such adjustments.

Question 10: When discussing the Buildup-3 method using the D Exhibits, page 10-45 indicates that the smoothed arithmetic average premia in the D exhibits are "unlevered". Is this correct? By contrast, the "Unlevered Build-up 3" discussion on page 10-49 makes no mention of smoothed premia, and does not use the regression equation method.

Response: The Risk Premium Report D Exhibits include both levered and unlevered risk premia for each portfolio (see columns labeled respectively "Arithmetic Average Risk Premium" and "Arithmetic Average Unlevered Risk Premium"). However, the *Valuation Handbook – U.S. Guide to Cost of Capital* only includes smoothed premia for levered risks premia (see column labeled "Smoothed Average Risk Premium"), but does not provide smoothed unlevered risk premia.

Question 11: I downloaded the full list of companies included in the *2014 Valuation Handbook – U.S. Guide to Cost of Capital* industry risk premia (Exhibit 5.7).[12.20] I noticed that certain SIC codes had the exact *same* listing of companies, but *different* industry risk premia. For example, SIC codes 805 and 8051 were comprised of the same companies, but had different industry risk premia. Same for SIC codes 807 and 8071. Why would this be?

Response: Industry risk premia (RP_i) in the *2014 Valuation Handbook – U.S. Guide to Cost of Capital* (and the *2015, 2016,* and *2017 Valuation Handbook – U.S. Guide to Cost of Capital*) are full-information betas that have been adjusted so that they can be added as a simple "up or down" adjustment in the build-up method. The full-information betas (FIB) published in the *2014 Valuation Handbook – U.S. Guide to Cost of Capital* of the SIC codes that the question references are as follows:

SIC 805, FIB = 1.93
SIC 8051 FIB = 1.87
SIC 807, FIB = 0.65
SIC 8071, FIB = 0.66

The short answer is that SIC 805 and SIC 8051, and SIC 807 and SIC 8071, are (by definition) different "industries". How they come out of the full-information beta calculation in *relation* to all the other industries will likely vary. Full-information betas are designed to measure the *relative* impact on the betas of companies in an industry based on the *relative* exposure (as measured by sales) each company has within the industry.

In Exhibit 12.7, hypothetical values are used in a simplified two-company universe to illustrate how SIC 805 and SIC 8051 can be comprised of *exactly the same companies* (Company ABC and Company DEF), but have *different* industry exposures (vis-à-vis "Sales"), and therefore potentially different full-information betas (and thus different industry risk premia).

[12.20] Starting with the *2016 Valuation Handbook – U.S. Guide to Cost of Capital* Exhibit 5.7 (industry risk premia for use in the Build-up model) is now presented as Appendix 3a.

Exhibit 12.7: Company Exposure to an Industry ("Sales to SIC") for a Hypothetical Two-Company Universe

	SIC'	Sales to SIC'	SIC"	Sales to SIC"
Company ABC	805	$1.00	8051	$0.50
Company ABC	805	–	8052	$0.50
Company DEF	805	$2.00	8051	$2.00
Total Sales		$3.00		$3.00

SIC 8051 and SIC 8052 both "roll up into" SIC 805. Also:

- SIC 805 is comprised *solely* of Company ABC and Company DEF.

- SIC 8051 is comprised *solely* of Company ABC and Company DEF.

However, note that Company ABC <u>also</u> has exposure to SIC 8052, which makes the relationship between Company ABC and Company DEF within the context of SIC 805 *different* from the relationship between Company ABC and Company DEF within the context of SIC 8051.[12.21] This can (and likely will) result in different full-information betas for SIC 805 and SIC 8051.

Question 12: Exhibit 5.7 ("*Industry Risk Premia (RP$_i$) Through Year-end 2013*")[12.22] in the *2014 Valuation Handbook – U.S. Guide to Cost of Capital* does not include an industry risk premium for SIC 0251 (Broiler, Fryer, and Roaster Chickens). What do I do if an industry risk premium is not listed for my industry?

Response: You are correct, an industry risk premium for SIC 0251 (Broiler, Fryer, and Roaster Chickens) is not included in the *2014 Valuation Handbook – U.S. Guide to Cost of Capital*.[12.23] The reason for this is that there were not enough publicly traded companies available to meet the minimum criteria for calculating an industry risk premium (minimum 10).

To answer the broader question of what to do if an industry risk premium is not listed for your industry, there are generally two possible solutions.

The first solution is the easier of the two: use the industry risk premium for the "next level up" SIC code. For example, an industry risk premium is *not* published in the *2014 Valuation Handbook – U.S. Guide to Cost of Capital* for SIC 5141 (Groceries, General Line). However, there *is* an industry risk premium published for SIC 514 (Groceries and Related Products), which is "one level up" SIC code.[12.24] Note that as you move from 4-digit SICs to 3-digit SICs to 2-digit SICs, the industries

---

[12.21] For example, Company ABC's revenues derived from SIC 805 *relative to* Company DEF's revenues derived from SIC 805 is 0.5 ($1.00 / $2.00); Company ABC's revenues derived from SIC 8051 *relative to* Company DEF's revenues derived from SIC 8051 is 0.25 ($0.50 / $2.00).

[12.22] Starting with the *2016 Valuation Handbook – U.S. Guide to Cost of Capital* Exhibit 5.7 (industry risk premia for use in the Build-up model) is now presented as Appendix 3a.

[12.23] An industry risk premium for SIC 0251 does not appear to have been published in *any* edition of the *SBBI Valuation Yearbook* either, from 2000–2013. The *SBBI Valuation Yearbook* was published from 1999–2013; industry risk premia were first published in the 2000 edition.

[12.24] "One level up" from SIC 5141 is SIC 514; "one level up" from SIC 514 is SIC 51).

become *less* specific (i.e., broader), so it is recommended that the analyst examine the full industry descriptions of the SIC codes and make a determination if the SIC code is a suitable proxy for the given subject company.[12.25]

The second solution is to identify a sample of public companies that have comparable risks to the subject company, calculate a custom peer group beta, and then use that peer group beta to calculate a custom industry risk premia. This can be accomplished by applying Formula 5.5 on page 5-13 herein.

Question 13: I downloaded the "Industry Risk Premia Company List" document that is provided at www.duffandphelps.com/CostofCapital, and noticed that there are companies in some of the SICs that look out of place. For example, 3M Company is listed in SIC 26 ("Paper and Allied Products"), SIC 30 ("Rubber and Miscellaneous Plastics Products"), and SIC 384 ("Surgical, Medical, and Dental Instruments and Supplies").

Response: The "Industry Risk Premia Company List" document lists all of the companies used in the calculation of each of the industry risk premium in Appendix 3a (formerly exhibit 5.7) of the *Valuation Handbook – U.S. Guide to Cost of Capital*. The full-information beta analysis employed to form the industry risk premia provided in Appendix 3a uses a cross-sectional regression in which a company's exposure to an industry (as defined by SIC code) is based on a sales-based weighted methodology. Any given company's exposure vis-à-vis "sales" to any given industry can vary from less than 1.0% to 100.0%. The full-information beta approach enables the inclusion of these companies' participation in the industry in the beta calculation.[12.26]

Ideally, one would like to have a sampling of betas from many "pure play" guideline public companies when estimating a proxy beta. "Pure play" companies are companies with say, at least 75.0% of revenue from a single Standard Industrial Classification (SIC) code. In some industries the *largest* participants may be conglomerates for which participation in the given industry is a *small* part of their overall revenues. For example, as of December 2016 (the "data through" date of the *2017 Valuation Handbook – U.S. Guide to Cost of Capital*) the percentage of General Electric's sales in SIC 351 (Engines and Turbines) was less than 25.0% of the company's overall sales, so in a strictly pure-play beta analysis General Electric would be excluded. However, General Electric was arguably the *dominant* participant in this industry, with 61.7% of all sales.[12.27] Companies that have exposure a given industry (even if limited) can be included in the analysis when full-information beta methodology is employed.

To be clear: The companies included in the full-information beta analysis used to create the industry risk premia in the *Valuation Handbook – U.S. Guide to Cost of Capital* are *not* necessarily "pure play" companies:

[12.25] A source of information on SIC codes and their descriptions is the United States Department of Labor Occupational Safety & Health Administration (OSHA) website at: https://www.osha.gov/pls/imis/sicsearch.html.

[12.26] The full-information betas published in the *2014 Valuation Handbook – U.S. Guide to Cost of Capital* (and in the former *SBBI Valuation Yearbook*) are based on an article by Paul D. Kaplan and James D. Peterson: "Full-Information Industry Betas", *Financial Management*, Summer 1998.

[12.27] Source: Standard & Poor's *Research Insight* database.

- You many notice companies included in each industry that may seem *out of place*. However, these companies only impact the full-information betas (and thus the industry risk premia) by the weighted sales exposure the company has to the given industry.

- You may also notice companies listed in *multiple* industries. For example, General Electric was a participant in SIC 351 (Engines and Turbines), but was also a participant in SIC 363 (Household Appliances), and SIC 384 (Surgical, Medical, and Dental Instruments and Supplies).

To learn more, see Chapter 5, "Basic Building Blocks of the Cost of Equity Capital – Betas and Industry Risk Premia" herein.

Question 14: In Exhibit 5.7 ("Industry Risk Premia") in the *2014 Valuation Handbook – U.S. Guide to Cost of Capital*, there are fewer companies in some of the SIC 6xxx codes than there are in the subsequent March, June, and September 2014 quarterly updates to this table.[12.28, 12.29]

Response: A significant number of SIC 6xxx companies were excluded from the analysis in the full-information beta analysis which is used to calculate the industry risk premia provided in Exhibit 5.7 for the *2014 Valuation Handbook – U.S. Guide to Cost of Capital*. In the quarterly updates to the former Exhibit 5.7, these excluded companies were added back. The primary result of the exclusions were that certain SIC 6xxx codes were not reported in the December 31, 2013 analysis (i.e., the *2014 Valuation Handbook – U.S. Guide to Cost of Capital*), but are reported in the subsequent 2014 quarterly updates. For the SIC 6xxx codes that were reported in *both* the December 31, 2013 analysis (i.e., the *2014 Valuation Handbook – U.S. Guide to Cost of Capital*) and the subsequent 2014 quarterly updates, the industry risk premia calculated are not significantly different.

Question 15: What caused the significant volatility in the industry risk premium (RP_i) for SIC 78 *Motion Pictures*? I note that most industry risk premia are relatively stable from period to period, but some appear to be somewhat instable from period to period.

Response: Industry risk premia are a special form of beta that has been adjusted so that it can be employed as a simple up or down adjustment in the build-up method of estimating cost of equity capital. Just like the betas that they are based upon, industry risk premia change from period to period.

All things held the same, however, the *smaller* the number of companies included in the calculations of an RP_i for an SIC ("industry") code, the *greater* the chance of variability from period to period. Specifically, in regards to SIC 78, the industry risk premia calculated using the historical 1926-present ERP over the last 17 years (2000–2016) have been relatively unstable (see Exhibit 12.8).

[12.28] The "Industry Risk Premia Quarterly Updates" includes March, June, and September updates to the approximately 250 U.S. industry risk premia that are published in the *Valuation Handbook – U.S. Guide to Cost of Capital*. Industry risk premia are a necessary cost of capital input that can be used within the context of the build-up method to estimate the cost of equity capital. The industry risk premia in the *Valuation Handbook – U.S. Guide to Cost of Capital* and in these quarterly updates are the equivalent of the industry risk premia formerly published in the Morningstar/Ibbotson *SBBI Valuation Yearbook's* Table 3-5.

[12.29] Starting with the *2016 Valuation Handbook – U.S. Guide to Cost of Capital* Exhibit 5.7 (industry risk premia for use in the Build-up model) is now presented as Appendix 3a.

Exhibit 12.8: SIC 78 (Motion Pictures) Industry Risk Premium (*RP$_i$*) as Published in the *2000–2013 SBBI Valuation Yearbook*, and the *2014–2017 Valuation Handbook – U.S. Guide to Cost of Capital*

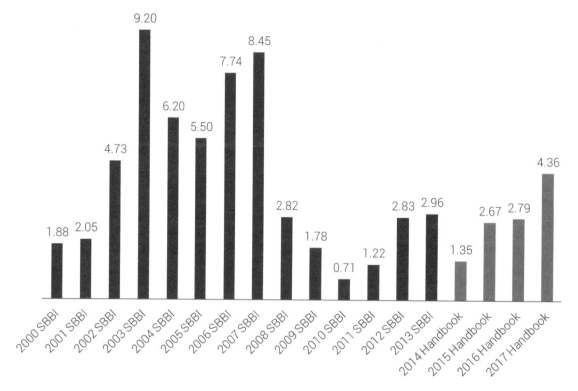

Note that for the comparison across time to be "apples to apples", the industry risk premia in Exhibit 12.8 are calculated using a long-term historical ERP. For example, the 1.35% industry risk premium published in the *2014 Valuation Handbook – U.S. Guide to Cost of Capital* and the 2.67% published in the *2015 Valuation Handbook – U.S. Guide to Cost of Capital* are calculated in the same fashion in this regard as the 2.96% premia reported in the *Ibbotson SBBI* 2013 *Valuation Yearbook*.[12.30, 12.31]

The methodology used to calculate the full information betas (and thus the industry risk premia) in the *2014 and 2015 Valuation Handbook – U.S. Guide to Cost of Capitals'* Exhibit 5.7[12.32], and Appendix 3a in the *2016* and *2017 Valuation Handbook – U.S. Guide to Cost of Capital*, is nearly identical with how they were calculated in the former *SBBI Valuation Yearbook*.[12.33] However, there are some differences with the *Valuation Handbook – U.S. Guide to Cost of Capitals'* methodology for calculating industry risk premia compared to the former *SBBI Valuation Yearbook's*

[12.30] <u>All</u> industry risk premia published in the *2000–2013 SBBI Valuation Yearbooks* were calculated using only the long-term "historical" ERP. In the *Valuation Handbook – U.S. Guide to Cost of Capital*, industry risk premia are also calculated using the long-term "historical" ERP, but are *also* calculated using the supply-side ERP and the Duff & Phelps recommended "conditional" ERP.

[12.31] The *2015 Valuation Handbook – U.S. Guide to Cost of Capital's* Exhibit 12.8 erroneously showed the December 31, 2014 <u>full-information beta</u> for SIC 78 (1.38), instead of showing the December 31, 2014 <u>industry risk premia</u> (as calculated using the "historical" long-term ERP and full-information beta, in concert) for SIC 78 (2.67). Please note that the full information beta, and the associated industry risk premia, for SIC 78 (2.67, 2.37, and 1.91, calculated using the "historical" long-term ERP, the long-term supply-side ERP, and the Duff & Phelps recommended ERP, respectively) were correctly reported in the 2015 book's industry risk premium table.

[12.32] Starting with the *2016 Valuation Handbook – U.S. Guide to Cost of Capital* Exhibit 5.7 (industry risk premia for use in the Build-up model) is now presented as Appendix 3a.

[12.33] The full-information betas published in the *Valuation Handbook – U.S. Guide to Cost of Capital* (and in the former *SBBI Valuation Yearbook*) are based on an article by Paul D. Kaplan and James D. Peterson: "Full-Information Industry Betas", *Financial Management*, Summer 1998.

methodology that were implemented to *increase* the statistical quality and the stability of the industry risk premia.

First, instead of requiring that each company had to have "36 months of [return] data in the previous 60 months", we required "36 months of *contiguous* return data", ending December 31st of the "data through date" year (e.g., December 31, 2013 for *2014 Valuation Handbook – U.S. Guide to Cost of Capital*). The goal of our more stringent criteria was to *lessen* the threshold for excluding companies that had "spotty" data, and thus *increase* the data quality of the overall set.

Second, the minimum number of companies participating in an industry (by SIC code) required in order to be included in the full-information beta regression analysis. We required a minimum of 10 participants in each industry; the former SBBI required 5 participants. The goal of this more stringent requirement was to eliminate SICs that have few participant companies, and are prone to high volatility from period to period.

Question 16: I purchased the *2017 Valuation Handbook – U.S. Guide to Cost of Capital*. Do I also need the *2017 Valuation Handbook – U.S. Industry Cost of Capital* (available in late May / early June 2017)?

Response: The *Valuation Handbook – U.S. Guide to Cost of Capital* provides the key year-end data previously published in (i) the Morningstar/Ibbotson *SBBI Valuation Yearbook* and (ii) the Duff & Phelps *Risk Premium Report*, and can be used to develop cost of equity capital estimates for an *individual* business, business ownership interest, security, or intangible asset.

Valuation is an inherently comparative process – just about any analysis boils down to trying to compare one thing to another. For example, once the valuation practitioner has developed his or her own custom cost of equity estimate for the subject company, a natural first question *is "How does my own analysis of the subject company compare to the subject company's peers (i.e., the industry)?"* It is a normal and prudent step in *any* analysis is to perform some benchmarking as a "reasonableness" test.

The *Valuation Handbook – U.S. Industry Cost of Capital* includes cost of capital estimates (equity capital, debt capital, and WACC) for approximately 180 U.S. industries, plus a host of detailed statistics that can be used for benchmarking purposes.

The industry-level statistics in the *Valuation Handbook – U.S. Industry Cost of Capital* do not replace the valuation practitioner's own custom analyses of the subject company, business ownership interest, security, or intangible asset. However, the valuation analyst will likely find the statistics presented to be a useful indicator for (i) benchmarking, (ii) augmenting, and (iii) providing additional support for his or her own custom analyses of the industry in which a subject business, business ownership interest, security, or intangible asset resides.[12.34]

[12.34] To purchase the *2017 Valuation Handbook – U.S. Industry Cost of Capital* (to be released in late May / early June 2017), or other valuation data sources authored by Duff & Phelps and published by Wiley, please go to www.wiley.com/go/ValuationHandbooks.

Question 17: In Appendix 3 ("*CRSP Deciles Size Premia Study: Key Variables*") of the *2017 Valuation Handbook – U.S. Guide to Cost of Capital,* there are small gaps in the market caps between the deciles.[12.35, 12.36]

For example, the *upper* boundary of decile 10 is $262.891 million, but the *lower* boundary of decile 9 is $263.715 million. This also occurs in the Mid-, Low-, and Micro-Cap size groupings. For example, the *upper* boundary of the Low-cap size grouping is $2,390.899 million, but the *lower* boundary of Mid-Cap size grouping is $2,392.689 million. While these gaps aren't material, we are doing a fairly vigorous valuation exercise where this question could come up. Can you explain why these gaps exist?

Response: The breakpoints of the deciles and size groupings in Appendix 3 of the *2017 Valuation Handbook – U.S. Guide to Cost of Capital* are the *actual* market caps of *actual* companies, as of the time of portfolio formation. The upper and lower boundaries of these portfolios are determined by the Center for Research in Security Prices at the University of Chicago Booth School of Business (CRSP). CRSP creates these portfolios, and reports the boundaries to us. These gaps have always existed between the CRSP portfolios (e.g., the gaps were also present in the former Morningstar/ Ibbotson *SBBI Valuation Yearbook*).

The way to handle this is demonstrated with an example, using only the *upper* market caps of the Mid-, Low-, and Micro-cap size groupings shown in Exhibit 12.9 (Exhibit 12.9 is an excerpt of Appendix 3 from the *2017 Valuation Handbook – U.S. Guide to Cost of Capital*).

Exhibit 12.9: Largest and Smallest Companies in CRSP Standard Market-Cap-Weighted Size Groupings Mid-Cap, Low-Cap, and Micro-Cap (size premia not shown)

CRSP Deciles Size Premium

Decile	Market Capitalization of Smallest Company (in millions)	Market Capitalization of Largest Company (in millions)	Size Premium (Return in Excess of CAPM)
Mid-Cap 3-5	$2,392.689 –	$10,711.194	1.02%
Low-Cap 6-8	569.279 –	2,390.899	1.75%
Micro-Cap 9-10	2.516 –	567.843	3.67%

To identify which of the size groupings the subject falls in:

- Large-capitalization companies have equity capitalizations *greater* than $10,711.194 million.

- Mid-capitalization companies have equity capitalizations *equal* to or *less* than $10,711.194 million, but *greater* than $2,390.889 million.

[12.35] Question 17 (as originally received) was in reference to the CRSP breakpoints in last the *2015 Valuation Handbook – U.S. Guide to Cost of Capital*. We have updated this question to reflect the CRSP breakpoints in the *2017 Valuation Handbook – U.S. Guide to Cost of Capital* (this book) for Reader convenience.

[12.36] Appendix 3 of the *Valuation Handbook – U.S. Guide to Cost of Capital* includes the "key variables in estimating the cost of capital" that were previously published in the Morningstar/Ibbotson *Stocks, Bonds, Bills, and Inflation (SBBI) Valuation Yearbook*.

- Low-capitalization companies have equity capitalizations *equal* to or *less* than $2,390.899 million, but *greater* than $567.843 million.

- Micro-capitalization companies have equity capitalizations *equal* to or *less* than $567.843 million.

The same regimen can be applied to any of the other CRSP portfolios 1-10 and 10th decile sub-deciles as well.

Question 18: We have been using the CAPM to estimate the cost of capital for each division annually. We search for "pure play" companies to estimate a beta. For some divisions we find no "pure play" betas and end up guessing. Any suggestions?

Response: Yes. One option would be to use the "full-information" industry betas from Appendix 3a in the *2017 Valuation Handbook – U.S. Guide to Cost of Capital.*

Ideally, one would like to have a sampling of betas from many "pure play" guideline public companies when estimating a proxy beta. In some industries, however, the *largest* participants may be conglomerates for which participation in the given industry is a *small* part of their overall revenues. In a strictly pure-play analysis, these companies would be *excluded*, even though they may be the dominant participant in the industry. The full-information beta approach enables the inclusion of these companies' participation in the industry in the beta calculation.

Another option is to refer to the *Valuation Handbook – U.S. Industry Cost of Capital*, which provides industry and peer group betas for approximately 180 U.S. industries.[12.37, 12.38]

In addition to industry and peer group betas (both levered and unlevered), the *Valuation Handbook – Industry Cost of Capital* provides eight (8) cost of equity capital estimates for each of the industries covered in the book (depending on data availability), cost of debt capital and weighted average cost of capital (WACC) estimates, plus capital structure, valuation multiples, industry betas, and more. The analyst can use this information to (i) benchmark, (ii) supplement, and (iii) strengthen his or her own custom cost of capital analysis.[12.39]

[12.37] The *Valuation Handbook – U.S. Industry Cost of Capital* provides cost of capital estimates (i.e., equity capital, debt capital, and WACC) for approximately 180 U.S. industries and size groupings (i.e., Large-, Mid-, Low-, and Micro-capitalization companies), plus a host of detailed statistics that can be used for benchmarking purposes (over 300 critical industry-level data points calculated for each industry, depending on data availability). The *Valuation Handbook – U.S. Industry Cost of Capital* has been published since 2014 (2014, 2015, and 2016 editions are available with data through March 31, 2014, March 31, 2015, and March 31, 2016, respectively; the 2017 edition, with data through March 31, 2017, became available in June 2017). This book includes three optional quarterly updates (June, September, and December). To order additional copies of the *2017 Valuation Handbook – U.S. Guide to Cost of Capital* (this book), or other Duff & Phelps valuation data resources published by John Wiley & Sons, please go to: www.wiley.com/go/ValuationHandbooks.

[12.38] See Exhibit 1.4 herein for a sample industry analysis page from the *2016 Valuation Handbook – U.S. Industry Cost of Capital.*

[12.39] A normal and prudent step in any analysis is to perform some benchmarking as a "reasonableness" test. The information in the *Valuation Handbook – U.S. Industry Cost of Capital* helps the analyst answer the question, "How does my own analysis of the subject company compare to the subject company's peers (i.e., the industry)?"

Question 19: My question is about the Risk Premium Report Study exhibits in the *2017 Valuation Handbook – U.S. Guide to Cost of Capital.*[12.40] I noticed that the smoothed "risk premium over the risk-free rate" seemed to have changed since last year. For example, the smoothed risk premium over the risk-free rate for portfolio 25 in Exhibit A-1 increased to 14.02% from 13.07%?

Response: Changes in the premia published in the Risk Premium Report exhibits from one year to the next is not unusual (it would actually be *more* unusual if they did *not* change). This is true for both "risk premium over the risk-free rate" (RP_{m+s}), and also "risk premia over CAPM", which are otherwise known as size premia (RP_s).

In Exhibit 12.10, the RP_{m+s} values are shown for portfolio 25 (comprised of the smallest companies) for both Exhibit A-1 (size measure = market capitalization) and Exhibit A-3 (size measure = 5-year average net income). Note that the premia vary over time.[12.41]

Exhibit 12.10: Risk Premia Over the Risk-free Rate for Exhibit A-1 (size measure = market capitalization) and Exhibit A-3 (size measure = 5-year average net income)
1996 Risk Premium Report Study – 2017 Risk Premium Report Study

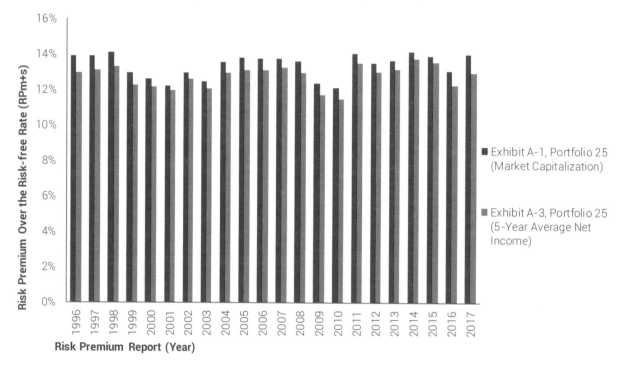

The Risk Premium Report Study exhibits' size premia (see Exhibits B-1 through B-8) *also* vary over time, as do the CRSP Deciles Size Study exhibits' size premia (see Exhibit 4.6 in the *2017 Valuation Handbook – U.S. Guide to Cost of Capital*, which shows the size premium for CRSP decile 10, from year-end 1962 to year-end 2016).

[12.40] The Risk Premium Report Study exhibits are in Appendix 4 of the *2017 Valuation Handbook – U.S. Guide to Cost of Capital*. The Duff & Phelps *Risk Premium Report* is no longer published as a stand-alone publication.

[12.41] Over the 1996–2016 period, the risk premium over the risk-free rate for portfolio 25 in Exhibit A-1 and Exhibit A-3 have varied 2.03% (max 14.17% - min 12.14%) and 2.32% (max 13.77% - min 11.45%), respectively.

Question 20: Which Size Premium should be used when the Subject Company falls in a different CRSP decile from the Guideline Companies?

Note: for purposes of this discussion, we will refer to the data as published in the *2014 Valuation Handbook – U.S. Guide to Cost of Capital*

The practitioner described the following scenario: The CRSP decile (and associated size premia) in the *2014 Valuation Handbook – U.S. Guide to Cost of Capital* which best matched his Subject Company, a non-public company, was Decile 8. At the same time, when trying to calculate a beta in the context of applying the modified capital asset pricing model (MCAPM), he could only identify Guideline Public Companies that were comparable in size to CRSP Decile 4, and therefore significantly *larger* than his Subject Company.[12.42, 12.43]

He went on to ask which size premium should he use, and was considering the following options:

1. The size premium from Decile 8, in which his Subject Company falls.

2. The size premium for Decile 4, which is the decile into which his selected Guideline Public Companies used to calculate his MCAPM beta fall.

3. The difference (or the average) of the Decile 8 size premium and the Decile 4 size premium.

4. Something else.

Response: The short answer is that Option 1 is correct (using the size premium from Decile 8, into which his Subject Company falls).

In Option 2 and Option 3, the practitioner is proposing adjustments to the Decile 8 size premium to make up for the fact that the Guideline Companies he is using to estimate a beta in a MCAPM estimate of cost of equity capital are much *larger* than his Subject Company (the only available Guideline Companies fall in Decile 4). We do not recommend this.

The reason we do not recommend the adjustments proposed in Option 2 and Option 3 is straightforward: All of the size premia reported in the *Valuation Handbook – U.S. Guide to Cost of Capital's* "CRSP Deciles Size Premia Study" and the "Risk Premium Report Study" are already "beta-adjusted". This means that they have been adjusted to remove the portion of excess returns attributable to a textbook CAPM beta, thereby leaving the incremental (or residual) excess returns as the contribution made by the size effect alone.

In this example, the Subject Company falls into CRSP Decile 8, and by using the size premium associated with CRSP Decile 8 you are properly keeping the measurement of "size risk" separate from the measurement of "beta risk". In summary, the appropriate size premium to use in this example is the Decile 8 size premium. So what should the practitioner do in these circumstances?

[12.42] CRSP" stands for the Center for Research in Security Pricing at the University of Chicago Booth School of Business.

[12.43] The CRSP standard market-capitalization-weighted "deciles" are 10 portfolios comprised of different-sized companies (based on market capitalization). Decile 1 is comprised of the largest companies; Decile 10 is comprised of the smallest companies.

An alternative solution might be to adjust the estimated CAPM beta.

Ideally, we would like to locate Guideline Public Companies of the same size as the Subject Company in order to estimate a "proxy beta". Had we been successful in locating such Guideline Companies of similar size to the Subject Company, one would first have unlevered the betas of the Guideline Public Companies (i.e., remove the impact in beta risk caused by differences in financial leverage). But in this case, the Guideline Public Companies were much larger.

Using CRSP size data (i.e., size measured by Market Value of Equity) from the "CRSP deciles Size Premia Study: Key Variables" exhibit (Appendix 3) and Exhibit 4.7 (see page 4-10), we get the following information:

Table 1: The OLS Beta and Sum Beta for CRSP Decile 4 and CRSP Decile 8, as Reported in the *2014 Valuation Handbook – U.S. Guide to Cost of Capital* (data through December 31, 2013).

CRSP Decile	Market Capitalization (in millions)		Using OLS Beta		Using Sum Beta		Unlevered Beta
	Smallest Company	Largest Company	Beta	Size Premium	Beta	Size Premium	
Decile 4	$3,581.547	$5,569.840	1.13	1.16%	1.20	0.65%	–
Decile 8	$636.747	$1,055.320	1.31	2.36%	1.49	1.12%	–

	$(1.31 \div 1.13) - 1$	$(1.49 \div 1.20) - 1$
% Difference between CRSP Decile 8 beta and CRSP Decile 4 beta	15.9%	24.2%

The betas published for the CRSP deciles (and used to calculate the size premia associated with the CRSP Deciles Size Premium Study) are "levered" betas. The CRSP deciles Size Study does *not* provide "unlevered" betas for the CRSP Deciles.[12.44]

The Risk Premium Report Size Study, however, *does* provide both levered *and* unlevered betas for each of the 25 portfolios presented within each of the eight size measures included in that study.[12.45] Using data from the Risk Premia Report Study's Exhibit B-1 (25 portfolios sorted by market value of equity from Appendix 4 in the *2014 Valuation Handbook – U.S. Guide to Cost of Capital*), and Exhibit C-1 (which includes unlevered betas for each of the 25 portfolios in Exhibit B-1), we gathered the guideline information shown in Table 2.[12.46]

[12.44] An "unlevered" beta is the beta of a company as if it were capitalized by 100% equity. Unlevered betas are also called "asset" betas.

[12.45] The CRSP Deciles Size Study includes 10 portfolios (i.e., deciles) sorted from largest to smallest by market capitalization; the Risk Premium Report Study includes 25 portfolios, also sorted from largest to smallest, based on eight measures of "size": (i) market capitalization, (ii) book value of equity, (iii) 5-year average net income, (iv) market value of invested capital (MVIC), (v) total assets, (vi) 5-year average EBITDA, (vii) sales, and (viii) number of employees.

[12.46] On the date as of which the data for the *2014 Valuation Handbook – U.S. Guide to Cost of Capital* (December 31, 2013) was compiled, the closest equivalent portfolio to CRSP Decile 4 in Exhibit B-1 of the Risk Premium Report Study could arguably be Portfolio 11; likewise, the *proximate* of CRSP Decile 8 equivalent to Exhibit B-1 of the Risk Premium Report Study could arguably be Portfolio 21.

Table 2: Risk Premium Report Study Data from Exhibit B-1 (25 Portfolios sorted by market value of equity) and Exhibit C-1 ("Comparative Risk Characteristics" of the portfolios in Exhibit B-1). Source: *2014 Valuation Handbook – U.S. Guide to Cost of Capital* (data through December 31, 2013)

Portfolio	Market Capitalization (in millions)	Using Sum Beta		Unlevered Beta from Exhibit C-1
	Average	Beta	Size Premium	
Portfolio 11	$4,259.000	1.10	3.05%	0.87
Portfolio 21	$826.000	1.26	5.00%	0.98
		$(1.26 \div 1.10) - 1$		$(0.98 \div 0.87) - 1$
% Difference between Portfolio 21 beta and Portfolio 11 beta		↓ 14.5%		↓ 12.6%

Assuming that the observed Guideline Companies have a median beta similar to the beta of CRSP Decile 4 (or Risk Premium Report Study's Portfolio 11), they would have a median OLS (ordinary least squares) beta approximately equal to 1.13. Remember, these betas are reported in the form of a *levered* beta; that is, the observed betas are measures of both operating and financial risk for companies comprising the deciles (or portfolios).

One would expect that companies that were of a similar size as those ranked in CRSP Deciles Size Premium Study Decile 8 (or Risk Premium Report Study Portfolio 21) would typically have unlevered betas greater (on the average) than the unlevered betas of the larger Guideline Public Companies of a size ranked in Decile 4 (or Portfolio 11). In fact, we do observe that the unlevered beta for portfolio 21 is greater than that of portfolio 11 (12.6% greater – see Table 2). The availability of unlevered beta estimates for the portfolios is one of the benefits of using the Risk Premium Report data.

Assuming that (i) the unlevered betas of the companies with a size ranked in CRSP Decile 8 (or Risk Premium Report Study Portfolio 21) were in fact greater than the unlevered betas of the Guideline Public Companies with a size ranked in Decile 4 (or Portfolio 11); and that (ii) the financial leverage of the Guideline Public Companies approximately matches the leverage of other companies comprising those respective deciles (portfolios), one would then use an OLS beta equal to 1.31, and the Decile 8 size premium of 2.36% in the MCAPM (using the CRSP size data – see Table 1).

However, the identified Guideline Companies had betas similar to the betas of the companies comprising Decile 4 (or Portfolio 11). Do we use a beta equal to 1.13 or do we adjust the beta to one that more closely approximates the beta one would observe for companies of a similar size to that of the Subject Company?

Without further analysis, one might adjust upward the unlevered betas of the identified Guideline Companies by 12.6%, the relative difference in the unlevered beta of Portfolios 21 and 11 (see Table 2), and then relever the beta using the iterative method to determine the debt-to-equity ratio of the closely-held Subject Company.

One can do further analysis of the relative risk of the Subject Company using data in the Comparative Risk Exhibits (the "C" Exhibits) of the Risk Premium Report Study to determine if the risks faced by the Subject Company are more similar to the risks of companies comprising those in Decile 4 (or Portfolio 11) or those in Decile 8 (or Portfolio 21). The goal of this analysis is to support the case for increasing the beta estimate.

As illustrated in Table 3, companies comprising Portfolio 11 have fundamental risks evidenced by average operating margin equal to 11.91% and coefficient of variation (COV) of operating margin equal to 14.88%, while companies comprising Portfolio 21 have fundamental risks evidenced by average operating margin equal to 8.90% (lower operating margin reflects greater risk) and COV of operating margin equal to 23.97% (greater COV reflects greater risk).

Table 3: Risk Premium Report Study Data (abbreviated) from Exhibit C-1 ("Comparative Risk Characteristics" of the portfolios in Exhibit B-1). Source: *2014 Valuation Handbook – U.S. Guide to Cost of Capital* (data through December 31, 2013)

Companies Ranked by Market Value of Equity				Exhibit C-1 (abbreviated)
Data for Year Ending December 31, 2013				

Portfolio Rank by Size	Average Mkt. Value (in $millions)	*Various datapoints not shown:*	Average Operating Margin	Average CV(Operating Margin)
1	143,782	-//-	16.41%	9.61%
2	41,383	-//-	14.05%	11.03%
3	26,386	-//-	13.33%	11.46%
(portfolios 5–10 not shown)	-//-	-//-	-//-	-//-
11	4,259	-//-	**11.91%**	**14.88%**
12	3,752	-//-	12.09%	14.36%
(portfolios 13–20 not shown)	-//-	-//-	-//-	-//-
21	826	-//-	**8.90%**	**23.97%**
22	646	-//-	8.53%	24.95%
23	497	-//-	7.94%	26.27%
24	339	-//-	7.80%	30.35%
25	107	-//-	6.11%	42.85%

If the fundamental risk characteristics of the Subject Company approximate those of companies comprising Portfolio 21, then one could make two adjustments in developing the cost of equity capital using the MCAPM (drawing on the data from the Risk Premium Report Study size premia data): (i) use an increased unlevered beta (increase the unlevered beta by 12.6% to match the beta for companies with fundamental risk characteristics similar to those of companies in Portfolio 21); and (ii) use a size premium equal to 5.00% (using the Risk Premium Report data – see Table 2).

If one desires to use the CRSP size data, one may increase the median observed OLS beta of the Guideline Companies by 15.9% (the difference in beta of the typical companies comprising those two deciles) and use a size premium of 2.36% (see Table 1). Alternatively, one may increase the median observed sum beta of the Guideline Companies by 24.2% and use a size premium of 1.12% (see Table 1).

Alternative adjustments may be considered reasonable by valuation professionals. The foregoing illustrates a possible approach to deal with the problem by using data from either the CRSP Deciles Size Premia Study or the Risk Premium Report Study (or both).

Question 21: The *Valuation Handbook – U.S. Guide to Cost of Capital* indicates that the returns presented therein are computed in the following basis: after tax to the corporation, and before tax to the investor. The book also says that the returns are based on capital appreciation and on the dividend income earned and the reinvestment of those dividends. I don't disagree that the dividend income component or the reinvestment component of total return is after tax to the corporation and before tax to the investor.

But what about the capital appreciation component of total return? One could argue that investor anticipation of taxes is impounded in the price. For example, if a company declares a dividend on its stock of $1, you would expect the price of the stock to increase by that dollar until the dividend is paid out. Typically, 90% of the time, it goes up by 65 cents, the difference being the tax to the investor. Another example was that when tax paradigms were changed, the price of the stock changed. That is, when capital gains tax code was changed, stock prices reflected the change. There are several academic studies that prove the point as well (that taxes to the investor are considered when pricing a stock).

So if tax to the investor is impounded in the price of the stock, does it follow that the returns are after tax to the corporation and *after tax to the investor* since capital appreciation is part of the returns presented?

Response: The capital appreciation component of the total returns series used in the *Valuation Handbook – U.S. Guide to Cost of Capital* is after tax to the corporation and before tax to the investor (i.e., prior to shareholder-level taxes).[12.47]

Granted, taxes at the corporate and personal level are, of course, factors that are taken into account by investors. For example, after the passage of the *Patient Protection and Affordable Health Care Act* (i.e., "ObamaCare") the share prices of some medical device manufacturers declined, likely (at least in part) because investors expected the new "medical device excise tax" (which was one of the measures introduced by ObamaCare) to *adversely* affect these companies' future expected cash flows.

Likewise, the level of taxes on capital gains and dividends can certainly be material, and thus certainly something that impacts investor decisions to buy, hold, or sell.

[12.47] This is also how these returns were/are described in the former Morningstar/Ibbotson *SBBI Valuation Yearbook*, the Morningstar/Ibbotson *SBBI Classic Yearbook*, and by the data vendors who create the indices that are used in these resources (e.g., the Center for Research Security Prices (CRSP) and Standard & Poor's).

But your question is not whether taxes affect stock prices, and we agree that they do. Your question is which of the following is true:

- The capital appreciation component of total return is *after* taxes to the corporation, and *before* taxes to the investor, or

- The capital appreciation component of total return is *after* taxes to the corporation, and *after* taxes to the investor.

Your argument is that (i) investors consider taxes when investing, and (ii) investors' consideration of taxes impacts their decisions to buy/hold/sell, which in turn impacts price, then it follows that (iii) the capital appreciation component of returns is after investor-level taxes.

Our opinion is that (i) and (ii) are true, but (iii) is *not* true.

This reasoning improperly conflates (a) the concept of taxes impacting stock prices; and (b) the individual taxes owed on the realized (i.e., "money-in-pocket") returns by the individual investor. In other words, the fact that taxes affect the price of a stock does not mean that the investor has "already paid his individual taxes" on capital gains.

For example, consider the following two scenarios:[12.48]

Scenario 1: The capital gains tax is 10%, and the price of Company ABC's stock goes from $100 to $110 over the course of the year.

Scenario 2: The capital gains tax is 50%, and fewer investors buy Company ABC's stock, so Company ABC's stock price goes from $100 to only $102 over the course of the year.

At the end of the year, investors in Company ABC will *still* owe individual taxes on capital gains in both Scenario 1 and Scenario 2, notwithstanding the fact that the share price in each scenario was impacted by the capital gains tax rate.

So when we say in the *Valuation Handbook – U.S. Guide to Cost of Capital* that the returns presented are "*after tax* to the corporation and *before tax* to the investor":

- We are saying that the realized (i.e., "money-in-pocket") returns to the investor (capital appreciation, dividends, and reinvestment returns) are typically taxed after being received by the investor.

- We are *not* saying that investor level taxes do not affect stock prices. Of course they do, but that is a completely separate, and different discussion.

[12.48] These "scenarios" are highly simplified, and do not represent all possible scenarios. Also, we assume here for purposes of this example that the differences in ending stock price between the scenarios is completely due to differences in the level of taxation.

Question 22: In the *2017 Valuation Handbook – U.S. Guide to Cost of Capital*, does the "historical" equity risk premium (ERP) in Appendix 3, "CRSP Deciles Size Premia Study: Key Variables", have to be used in conjunction with the published risk-free rate in Appendix 3?

Response: The 2.72% risk-free rate displayed in the 2017 "Key Variables" in Appendix 3 represents the spot yield-to-maturity on U.S. long-term Treasury bonds as of December 31, 2016.

ERPs are, by definition, developed in relation to the risk-free rate, and likely should be used in conjunction (to be consistent) with the risk-free rate they were developed in relation to.

For example, as is noted in Appendix 3 of the *2017 Valuation Handbook – U.S. Guide to Cost of Capital*, "the Duff & Phelps recommended ERP was developed in relation to (and should be used in conjunction with), a 'normalized' risk-free rate of 3.5%". The Duff & Phelps recommended ERP as of December 31, 2016 (the "data through" date of the *2017 Valuation Handbook – U.S. Guide to Cost of Capital*) is 5.5%. This implies a base country-level base cost of equity capital in the U.S. of 9.0% (3.5% + 5.5%).[12.49]

Alternatively, Appendix 3 of the *2017 Valuation Handbook – U.S. Guide to Cost of Capital* also lists the "historical" ERP (as measured over the time period 1926–2016) you refer to in your question. The historical ERP is based on the historical (i.e., realized) average difference between equities (i.e., "stocks") and the income return on a long-term (20-year) U.S. government bonds. Therefore, the risk-free rate one could use in conjunction with the historical ERP is arguably the spot (20-year) U.S. Treasury yield. But it's not quite that simple.

During *some* of the 91 years in the 1926–2016 time period over which the historical ERP is calculated, the spot rates used to measure the ERP were "controlled" (at least in part) by non-market forces (e.g., the WWII interest rate bias years from 1942–1951, during which the U.S. Treasury department decreed that interest rates had to be kept at artificially low levels in order to reduce government financing costs during the war, or more recently, the massive central bank interventions seen since the 2008 Financial Crisis that artificially depressed yields). It follows that using the spot rate will likely give you an incorrect base cost of capital because the spot rate on a long-term government bond as of December 2016 is a mismatch with the realized ERP data from 1926–2016 (at least to the degree it is artificially low due to the non-market forces during certain periods).

Having said that, however, *most* of the 91 years in the 1926–2016 time period over which the historical ERP is calculated did not experience the high level of non-market interventions that occurred during the WWII interest rate bias years and the post 2008 Financial Crisis years; therefore, adding the spot U.S. Treasury yield to the historical ERP of 6.94% calculated over the 1926–2016 period will likely cause a lesser distortion in the base cost of equity than using the D&P normalized rate in conjunction with the "historical" ERP. Remember, the Duff & Phelps "normalized" risk-free rate (3.5%) as of December 31, 2016 is designed to match with the Duff & Phelps recommended ERP 5.5% as of December 31, 2016 and should likely not be matched with the historical (i.e., realized) ERP data from 1926–2016.

[12.49] To ensure you are always using Duff & Phelps' most recent ERP recommendation, visit: www.DuffandPhelps.com/CostofCapital.

One could argue, for example, that if a "historical" ERP were adjusted for periods in which non-market forces artificially depressed Treasury yields, then matching the Duff & Phelps normalized risk-free rate with this "adjusted" historical ERP might be appropriate. We agree, but with *significant* qualifications. For example, in Exhibit 3.13 and Exhibit 3.14 we report what the long-term "historical" ERP and the long-term "supply-side" ERP would be if the WWII interest rate bias were subtracted from each. The differences are significant: these analyses suggest (for example) that the long-term historical ERP as measured over the 1926–2016 period is *overstated* by up to 1.08%. While this analysis is compelling, and adjusting the "historical" ERP in this fashion likely does make the concept of matching the Duff & Phelps normalized risk-free rate with an "adjusted" historical ERP more correct, the reality is that this approach is not as internally consistent as compared to that of matching the Duff & Phelps normalized risk-free rate with the Duff & Phelps recommended ERP.

Question 23: In last year's *2016 Valuation Handbook – U.S. Guide to Cost of Capital*, I noticed in Appendix 3 "CRSP Deciles Size Premia Study: Key Variables" that the size premium for Decile 7 (1.62%) was smaller than the size premium for Decile 6 (1.63%). Is this correct?

Response: Yes, that is correct. In the *2016 Valuation Handbook – U.S. Guide to Cost of Capital* the size premium for Decile 7 is 1.63%, and the size premium for Decile 7 is 1.62%.

CRSP Deciles 6 and 7 have tended to have an irregularity in terms of Decile 7 having a lower size premium sometimes than Decile 6. In fact, Decile 7's size premium has been *lower* than the Decile 6 size premium 13 out of the last 19 years, or (about 68% of the time). Exhibit 12.9 provides a summary of the differences between Deciles 6 and 7 size premia since 1999.

Exhibit 12.11: Summary of Decile 6 and 7 Differences over time

Edition Year	Decile 6 Size Premia	Decile 7 Size Premia		
1999	Higher	Lower	Numer of times Decile 7 Size Premia has been lower than Decile 6	13
2000	Higher	Lower	Numer of times Decile 7 Size Premia has been higher than Decile 6	5
2001	Higher	Lower	Numer of times Decile 7 Size Premia has been the same as Decile 6	1
2002	Higher	Lower		
2003	Higher	Lower	Average difference (Decile 7–Decile 6)	-0.04%
2004	Higher	Lower	Average difference of absolute value (Decile 7–Decile 6)	0.01%
2005	Higher	Lower	Median difference (Decile 7–Decile 6)	-0.02%
2006	Higher	Lower		
2007	Higher	Lower		
2008	Higher	Lower		
2009	Higher	Lower		
2010	Same	Same		
2011	Lower	Higher		
2012	Lower	Higher		
2013	Lower	Higher		
2014	Lower	Higher		
2015	Higher	Lower		
2016	Higher	Lower		
2017	Lower	Higher		

Question 24: I'm valuing a small company over a long horizon. The company is currently small (Decile 10 in terms of the CRSP Decile), but the company is expected to grow quickly and will likely to be grouped in Decile 9 or 8 soon. What is the appropriate choice of size premium in this situation? Specifically, should the size premium selected be based on the current size of company, or should the size premium be based upon the expected size of the company in the future?

Response: The size premium should reflect its current size as of the valuation date, since there is a certain degree of risk associated with growing and becoming a larger company in the future, on a permanent basis.

In other words, in the context of using a single discount rate to present value all projected/future cash flows into perpetuity, there is a significant risk that the company may not become a larger going-concern business. Alternatively said, the size premium *already* has an embedded consideration for risk related to future size – the risk that the small company may not be able to become larger is high, and therefore the higher size premium takes into consideration some of that risk.

For more information regarding size premium, please refer to Chapter 14: Size Effect in the *Cost of Capital,* 5th Edition.

Question 25: My valuation date is December 31, 2009. Where can I get the historical CRSP Deciles Size Premia Studies and Risk Premium Report Studies data?

Response: You can purchase the *Valuation Handbook – 2010 U.S. Essentials Edition* (data through December 31, 2009).

Since first publishing the Duff & Phelps *Valuation Handbook – U.S. Guide to Cost of Capital* in 2014, the authors have received many requests for historical (2013 and earlier) *Risk Premium Report* and Morningstar/Ibbotson *SBBI Valuation Yearbook* valuation data. These requests are typically from individual valuation analysts or firms who wish to build a complete, multi-year library of valuation data, or individual valuation analysts or firms involved in a retrospective valuation.

Fulfilling requests for historical *Risk Premium Report* valuation data was always possible (the *Risk Premium Report* data is proprietary to Duff & Phelps).

Fulfilling requests for historical *SBBI Valuation Yearbook* valuation data became possible in 2015, when Duff & Phelps acquired the rights from Morningstar to republish the historical equity risk premia data, size premia data, industry risk premia data, risk-free rate data, and other essential valuation data from the 1999–2013 *SBBI Valuation Yearbooks*.

"Essentials" Years Available

The *Valuation Handbook – U.S. Essentials Editions* are available for publication years *common* to both the CRSP Deciles Size Study and the *Risk Premium Report* (specifically, from 1999 and forward, annually). *U.S. Essentials Editions* are made available for all but the most recent two years, on a rolling basis.

For example, the most recent hardcover *Valuation Handbook – U.S. Guide to Cost of Capital* available at the time of the authors created the initial set of *Valuation Handbook – U.S. Essentials Editions* was the *2016 Valuation Handbook – U.S. Guide to Cost of Capital,* and so the "most recent two years" at that time were 2015 and 2016. The initial set of *Valuation Handbook – U.S. Essentials Editions* made available was therefore years 1999–2014:

> *2016 Valuation Handbook – U.S. Guide to Cost of Capital* (hardcover)
> *2015 Valuation Handbook – U.S. Guide to Cost of Capital* (hardcover)
>
> 1999–2014 *U.S. Essentials Editions* (PDF)

In subsequent years, the same pattern is followed. For example, if the most recent hardcover *Valuation Handbook – U.S. Guide to Cost of Capital* available were the *2017 Valuation Handbook – U.S. Guide to Cost of Capital,* the "most recent two years" at that time would be 2016 and 2017, and the set of U.S. Essentials Editions available would be for years 1999–2015:

> *2017 Valuation Handbook – U.S. Guide to Cost of Capital* (hardcover)
> *2016 Valuation Handbook – U.S. Guide to Cost of Capital* (hardcover)
>
> 1999–2015 *U.S. Essentials Editions* (PDF)

Etc.

To Purchase any of the *Valuation Handbook – U.S. Essentials Editions* or other Duff & Phelps valuation data resources published by John Wiley & Sons, please go to: www.wiley.com/go/ValuationHandbooks.

Question 26: Some commentators have questioned whether the size effect is still applicable. Should one continue to apply a size premium in estimating the cost of equity?

Response: If one holds that the analyst should not apply a size premium in estimating the cost of equity capital (for example in applying the Modified CAPM as shown in Formula 2.6), then one must be contending that beta should be used as the only measure of risk. But that cannot be correct as the literature clearly demonstrates that the pure textbook CAPM is flawed.[12.50]

Some commentators contend that the size effect has disappeared after the early 1980's. As we explain in Chapter 4, "Basic Building Blocks of the Cost of Equity Capital – Size Premium", the 1980's were not kind to small-cap companies as too many start-ups that went public failed (clearly not expected by investors). We agree that there are periods when large company stocks outperform small company stocks even after adjusting for the differences in beta. That is, the size effect is cyclical.

In Exhibit 4.12 in the *2017 Valuation Handbook – U.S. Guide to Cost of Capital,* we display the periods in which small-cap companies outperform large-cap companies and vice-versa in several periods since the 1980's. One sees that small-cap companies do outperform large-cap companies

---

[12.50] See Shannon P. Pratt and Roger J. Grabowski, Chapter 13, "Criticism of CAPM and Beta versus Other Risk Measures," *Cost of Capital: Applications and Examples* 5th ed. (John Wiley & Sons, 2014).

over longer periods, even after 1982.

In a recent paper, additional support is provided for the size effect in the period since 1990.[12.51] That author summarizes: "...the cost of equity capital should be based on expected returns. In developing a cost of equity capital estimate when valuing a non-publicly traded business, the valuation professional is estimating an expected return over a long holding period. Size premia help the analyst correct the pure textbook CAPM for the risks of smaller companies not captured by beta."

Question 27: Some commentators suggest that the returns reported in the Risk Premium Report Study are the result of embodying hindsight.

Response: All categorization of companies for the Risk Premium Report Study dataset and portfolios is based on data known before the beginning of each year for which returns are calculated.

In determining companies to exclude from the base dataset, (e.g., companies lacking 5 years of publicly traded price history or companies with a negative 5-year average EBITDA for the previous five years) all data for the selection process are known before the beginning of any year. The exclusion of companies based on historical financial performance does not imply any unusual foresight on the part of hypothetical investors in these portfolios. In forming portfolios to calculate returns for a given year, we exclude companies on the basis of performance during previous years (e.g., average net income for the five prior fiscal years), rather than current or future years. For instance, to form portfolios for 1963, we take into account the average net income for the five fiscal years preceding September 1962. We repeat this procedure for each year from 1963 through the latest available year.

Thus, investors choosing to apply the methodology employed in the Risk Premium Report Study could select companies to include in their portfolios using the same selection criteria as is used in building the portfolios as are reported in the Risk Premium Report Study each year.

Question 28: Some commentators claim that the average returns reported in the Risk Premium Report Study differ from those of some funds targeted at investing in small-cap companies and therefore are unrealistic estimates of expected returns.

Response: In estimating the expected return from an investment in the stock market, one can summarize historic returns by calculating a geometric average return or an arithmetic average return. The arithmetic average of prior period returns is always greater than the geometric average of returns during the same period because it captures the volatility of the realized returns. Both are correct summaries of observed return data.

In cases where an analyst is estimating the expected accumulated wealth at a point in the future, the preferred estimate of the rate of return on an investment in the stock market is the geometric mean of prior period returns or the implied forward return. But if the analyst is estimating the discount rate that should be used in discounting expected cash flows in future years, the preferred statistic is the arithmetic average of realized returns (realized risk premiums) or the arithmetic

---

[12.51] Roger J. Grabowski, "The Size Effect–It is Still Relevant," *Business Valuation Review*, 35(2): 62–71.

average equivalent of implied future returns.[12.52]

The returns reported in the Risk Premium Report Study each year are equal weighted returns for the companies comprising the size-ranked portfolio. The analyst is not building an investment portfolio. Rather the analyst is estimating the return for the typical company with certain size characteristics. The analyst is using those returns actually realized over time as a proxy for the expected return.

The Risk Premium Report Study presents the arithmetic average of prior period returns because the data is intended to be used in developing discount rates to be used in discounting expected cash flows in future years.

One commentator compares the arithmetic average returns reported in the Risk Premium Report Study for 1963 through 2012 to the geometric average returns reported for the DFA micro-cap fund (DFSCX), a fund which invests in small-cap stocks for the period 1981 through 2015. Any analyst will recognize that this this is a flawed comparison.

The more proper comparison would be to compare the arithmetic average return on the DFA micro-cap fund for the period 1963 through 2012 with the arithmetic average returns reported in the Risk Premium Report Study for the same period.

First, to obtain the returns for the period 1963 through 2012, we will use the "Ibbotson Associates SBBI US Small Stock TR USD" index which is constructed as follows (Source: *2017 SBBI Yearbook*, Chapter 3, "Description of the Basic Series", pages 3-2 and 3-3):

- DFA U.S. Micro Cap Portfolio (April 2001 to December 2016), the small-cap stock return series is the total return achieved by the net of fees and expenses. At year-end 2016, the DFA U.S. Micro Cap Portfolio contained 1,546 stocks, with a weighted average market cap of $1.128 billion.

- DFA U.S. 9–10 Small Company Portfolio (January 1982–March 2001; renamed the DFA U.S. Micro Cap Portfolio in April 2001). The fund's target buy range was a market-cap-weighted universe of the ninth and 10th deciles of the New York Stock Exchange, plus stocks listed on the NYSE Amex (now the NYSE MKT) and NASDAQ National Market.

- The equities of smaller companies from 1926 to 1980 are represented by the historical series developed by Professor Rolf W. Banz.

We can more properly compare the returns for the Ibbotson Associates SBBI US Small Stock TR USD index (essentially the DFA fund used in the commentator's critique) to the returns reported in the Risk Premium Report Study.

Second, we can compare the size of the companies included in each. The average market capitalization reported in Appendix A-1 for portfolio 25 in the *2013 Risk Premium Report* is $94 million. At year-end 2012 (the data-through date of the *2013 Risk Premium Report* is December 31,

---

[12.52] See "Using the Geometric Average for Compounding and the Arithmetic Average for Discounting," in *Cost of Capital: Applications and Examples* 5th ed.: 153–159.

2012), the DFA U.S. Micro Cap Portfolio contained 1,957 stocks, with a weighted average market capitalization of $682 million (Source: *2013 SBBI "Classic" Yearbook*, Chapter 3, "Description of the Basic Series", page 54) (the data-through date of the *2013 SBBI "Classic" Yearbook* is also December 31, 2012).

The average market capitalization reported in Appendix A-1 for portfolio 21 in the *2013 Risk Premium Report* is $811 million. The average annual arithmetic return reported in Appendix A-1 for portfolio 21 in the *2013 Risk Premium Report* is 16.78%.

The average market capitalization reported Appendix A-1 for portfolio 22 in the *2013 Risk Premium Report* is $615 million. The average annual arithmetic return reported in Appendix A-1 for portfolio 22 in the *2013 Risk Premium Report* is 17.12%.

The average annual returns reported for the Risk Premium Report portfolios (21 and 22; 16.78% and 17.12%, respectively) that have similar average market capitalizations ($811 million and $615 million, respectively) as the DFA average market capitalization as of Dec 31, 2012 ($682 million) are similar (the DFA series' arithmetic average annual return 1963–2012 is 16.3%).

The small differences in returns (16.3% versus 16.78% and 17.12%) may be attributed to many factors (e.g., the Risk Premium Report portfolio returns are equal weighted, so the smaller companies' intra-portfolio are given equal weight as the larger companies' intra-portfolio; this will tend to make the Risk Premium Report portfolios have greater returns, all other things held the same than the market weighted returns reported for the DFA micro-cap fund).

Question 29: Some readers have asked whether they should use a size premium for Decile 10z in developing the discount rate for small companies.

Response: In Exhibit 4.10 in the *2017 Valuation Handbook – U.S. Guide to Cost of Capital* we provide the breakdown of the characteristics of companies that comprise 10z. Remember, the analyst is trying to match characteristics of the subject company with the characteristics of the companies included in the dataset. Therefore, before the analyst chooses to use the size premium for Decile 10z, the analyst should compare the subject firm characteristics to those of firms comprising Decile 10z. The analyst should also consider the size premia reported in the Risk Premium Report.

In Exhibit 4.11 in the *2017 Valuation Handbook – U.S. Guide to Cost of Capital* we provide the breakdown of the characteristics companies that comprise the 25th portfolio. The differences between the CRSP Deciles and the Risk Premium Report portfolios is discussed in detail in Chapter 7, "The CRSP Decile Studies and the Risk Premium Report Studies – A Comparison".

Glossary

Altman z-Score
Widely used formula used to predict the probability that a firm will go into bankruptcy. In the Risk Premium Report's "High-Financial-Risk Study", companies are ranked based on the relative levels of distress, using z-Score as a proxy for "distress".

Arbitrage Pricing Theory
A multi-variate model for estimating the cost of equity capital, which incorporates several systematic risk factors.

Asset Based Approach
A method of indicating the value of a business, business or business interest based on a summation of the net value of the individual assets and liabilities. Since each of the assets and liabilities will have been valued using either the market, income or cost approaches, it is not a distinct valuation approach.

Beta
A measure of systemic risk of a stock; the tendency of a stock's price to correlate with changes in a specific index.

Capital Appreciation Return
The return resulting from a price change of an investment over a given period.

Capital Asset Pricing Model (CAPM)
A model in which the cost of capital for any stock or portfolio of stocks equals a risk-free rate plus a risk premium that is proportionate to the systematic risk of the stock or portfolio.

Capital Structure
The composition of the invested capital of a business enterprise; the mix of debt and equity financing.

Company-Specific-Risk
Company-specific risk may have different meanings to different people. Oftentimes valuation analysts think of company-specific risk as an adjustment made to account for the differences between the subject company and the peer group to which it is being compared. In this sense, company-specific risk is differentiated from idiosyncratic risk (also known as "unsystematic" risk), which specifically refers to the uncertainty of expected returns arising from factors other than those factors correlated with the investment market as a whole.

Cost of Capital
The expected rate of return that the market requires in order to attract funds to a particular investment.

Discount Cash Flow Method
A method within the income approach in which a discount rate is applied to future expected income streams to estimate the present value.

Enterprise Value
The total value of the equity in a business plus the value of its debt or debt-related liabilities, minus any cash or cash equivalents available to meet those liabilities.

Equity Risk Premium (ERP)
The ERP is the rate of return added to a risk-free rate to reflect the additional risk of equity instruments over risk-free instruments. Also known as the market risk premium.

Going Concern
Business enterprise that is expected to continue operations for the foreseeable future.

Idiosyncratic Risk
Idiosyncratic risk (also known as "unsystematic" risk) refers to the uncertainty of expected returns arising from factors other than those factors correlated with the investment market as a whole. In this sense, idiosyncratic risk is differentiated from "company-specific" risk, which valuation analysts oftentimes think of as an adjustment made to account for the differences between the subject company and the peer group to which it is being compared.

Income Return
That portion of total return attributable to periodic cash flows (e.g., dividends).

Industry Risk Premium (*RPi*)
A measure of beta (market) risk scaled around 0. Industry risk premia are appropriately used in "build-up" methods of estimating cost of equity that do not otherwise have a measure of beta. Industry risk premia are not appropriate for use in the CAPM model.

Inflation
The overall general upward price movement of goods and services in an economy. In the U.S., usually measured as change in the Consumer Price Index (CPI).

Levered Beta
A beta reflecting a capital structure that includes debt.

Liquidity
A measure of the ease with which an asset may be converted into cash. A highly liquid asset can be easily converted into cash; an illiquid asset is difficult to convert into cash.

Market Approach
A valuation approach which provides an indication of value by comparing the subject asset with identical or similar assets for which price information is available.

Market Value of Invest Capital (MVIC)
The sum of equity and debt in a business enterprise. Debt can be either (i) all interest-bearing debt or (ii) long-term, interest-bearing debt. When the term is used, it should be supplemented by the appropriate qualifying words.

Net Present Value
The value, as of a specified date, of future cash inflows less all cash outflows (including the cost of investment) calculated using an appropriate discount rate.

Portfolio Premium
The historical observed return over the risk-free rate (i.e., "excess return") earned by a given portfolio.

Reinvestment Return
That portion of total return attributable to the reinvestment of dividends, interest and capital gains. It is usually assumed that the reinvestment is in the same asset.

Risk Premia Over CAPM (i.e., size premium) (RP_s)

The difference between historical (observed) excess return and the excess return predicted by the CAPM. Because the difference between the historical excess return and CAPM-predicted excess return of portfolios comprised of *smaller* companies is typically *greater* than the difference between the historical excess return and CAPM-predicted excess return of portfolios comprised of *larger* companies, this difference is commonly referred to as a "beta-adjusted size premium".

Risk Premia Over Risk-Free Rate (RP_{m+s})
Risk premia over the risk-free rate represent the difference between the historical (observed) return of equities over the risk-free rate. This difference is a measure of risk in terms of the combined effect of **market risk** and **size risk.**

Risk-Free Rate
The return available, as of the valuation date, on a security that the market generally regards as free of the risk of default.

Risk Study
The *Risk Study* analyzes the relationship between three fundamental measures of risk (operating margin, coefficient of variation on operating margin, and coefficient of variation on ROE) and return. The *Risk Study* finds that as risk increases, required returns tend to increase.

Size Premium
The difference in historical excess returns observed and the excess returns otherwise predicted by CAPM. *See "Risk Premia Over CAPM".*

Size Study

The *Size Study* analyzes the relationship between size and return using 25 size-ranked portfolios using eight alternate measures of company size (market value of equity, book value of equity, 5 year average net income, MVIC, total assets, 5 year average EBITDA, sales, number of employees). The *Size Study* finds as size decreases, required return tend to increase.

Smoothed Premia

"Smoothed" premia is generally the most appropriate indicator for most of the portfolio groups when using the Risk Premium Report exhibits. Smoothing the premia essentially averages out the somewhat scattered nature of the raw average premia. Smoothed Premia is calculated using regression analysis. The CRSP Deciles Size Premia are not presently smoothed.

Subject Company

The subject company is the entity being valued.

Supply-side Model

Adapted by Roger Ibbotson and Peng Chen to estimate a forward-looking, long-term equity risk premium. The model analyzes historical equity return into the following factors; inflation, earnings, dividends, P/E, dividend payout ratio, book value of equity, return on equity, and GDP per capita. The model normalizes the growth in P/E ratio that is embedded in historical returns deeming it unsustainable and is removed for the model.

Systematic Risk

Risk that affects an entire market and not just a specific company or asset. Within the framework of the CAPM and other cost of capital estimation models, systematic risk is the only risk that is compensable because (unlike "unsystematic" risk) it cannot be "diversified away".

Unlevered Beta

An *unlevered beta* is the beta a company would have if it had no debt (i.e., financed only with equity capital). Also known as an "asset" beta.

Unsystematic Risk

Function of uncertainty of future returns due to the characteristics of the industry, the individual company, and the type of investment interest, and is unrelated to a variation of returns in the market as a whole. Within the framework of the CAPM and other cost of capital estimation models, unsystematic risk is not compensable because (unlike "systematic" risk) it can be "diversified away".

Valuation Date

The date on which the opinion of value applies. The valuation date shall also include the time at which it applies if the value of the type of asset can change materially in the course of a single day.

Weighted Average Cost of Capital (WACC)

A discount rate estimated by the weighted average, at market values, of the cost of all financing sources in a business enterprise's capital structure.

Yield

In terms of a bond, yield is the rate of return that equates future expected cash flows to the bond's market price.

Index

Appendix 1

Definitions of Standard & Poor's *Compustat* Data Items Used to Calculate the Risk Premium Report Exhibits[A.1]

Current Assets – Total: Data Item A4, Units: Millions of dollars

This item represents cash, and other assets which, in the next 12 months, are expected to be realized in cash or used in the production of revenue. This item is the sum of:

1. Cash and Short-Term Investments

2. Current Assets – Other

3. Inventories – Total

4. Receivables – Total

Current Liabilities – Total: Data Item A5, Units: Millions of dollars

This item represents liabilities due within one year, including the current portion of long-term debt. This item is the sum of:

1. Accounts Payable

2. Current Liabilities – Other

3. Debt in Current Liabilities

4. Income Taxes

Assets – Total: Data Item A6, Units: Millions of dollars

This item represents current assets plus net property, plant, and equipment plus other noncurrent assets (including intangible assets, deferred items and investments and advances). Total liabilities and stockholders' equity represents current liabilities plus long-term debt plus other long-term liabilities plus stockholders' equity.

Long-Term Debt – Total: Data Item A9, Units: Millions of dollars

The item represents debt obligations due more than one year from the company's balance sheet date.
This item includes

1. Purchase obligations and payments to officers (when listed as long-term liabilities)

2. Notes payable, due within one year and to be refunded by long-term debt when carried as a non-current liability

3. Long-term lease obligations (capitalized lease obligations)

4. Industrial revenue bonds

5. Advances to finance construction

6. Loans on insurance policies

7. Indebtedness to affiliates

8. Bonds, mortgages, and similar debt

9. All obligations that require interest payments

10. Publishing companies' royalty contracts payable

    1. Timber contracts for forestry and paper

    2. Extractive industries' advances for exploration and development

    3. Production payments and advances for exploration and development

This item excludes

1. Subsidiary preferred stock (included in Minority Interest)

2. The current portion of long-term debt (included in Current Liabilities)

3. Accounts payable due after one year (included in Liabilities – Other)

[A.1] Source: Standard & Poor's Research Insight *Compustat* North America Data Guide

4. Accrued interest on long-term debt (included in Liabilities – Other)

5. Customers' deposits on bottles, kegs and cases (included in Liabilities – Other)

6. Deferred compensation

Long-term debt should be reported net of premium or discount. Standard & Poor's *Compustat* will collect the net figure.

Sales (Net): Data Item A12, Units: Millions of dollars

This item represents gross sales (the amount of actual billings to customers for regular sales completed during the period) reduced by cash discounts, trade discounts, and returned sales and allowances for which credit is given to customers. This item is scaled in millions. For example the 1999 annual sales for GM is 173215.000 (or 173 billion, 215 million dollars).

This item includes

1. Any revenue source that is expected to continue for the life of the company

2. Other operating revenue

3. Installment sales

4. Franchise sales (when corresponding expenses are available) Special cases (by industry) include

Special cases (by industry) include

1. Royalty income when considered operating income (such as, oil companies, extractive industries, publishing companies, etc.)

2. Retail companies' sales of leased departments when corresponding costs are available and included in expenses (if costs are not available, the net figure is included in Nonoperating Income [Expense])

3. Shipping companies' operating differential subsidies and income on reserve fund securities when shown separately

1. Airline companies, net mutual aid assistance and federal subsidies

2. Cigar, cigarette, oil, rubber, and liquor companies' net sales are after deducting excise taxes

3. Income derived from equipment rental is considered part of operating revenue

4. Utilities' net sales are total current operating revenue

5. Advertising companies' net sales are commissions earned, not gross billings

6. Franchise operations' franchise and license fees

7. Hospitals' sales net of provision for contractual allowances (will sometimes include doubtful accounts)

This item excludes

1. Nonoperating income

2. Interest income (included in Nonoperating Income ([Expense])

3. Equity in earnings of unconsolidated subsidiaries (included in Nonoperating Income [Expense])

4. Other income (included in Nonoperating Income [Expense])

5. Rental income (included in Nonoperating Income [Expense])

6. Gain on sale of securities or fixed assets (included in Special Items)

7. Discontinued operations (included in Special Items)

8. Excise taxes (excluded from sales and also deducted from Cost of Goods Sold)

9. Royalty income (included in Nonoperating Income [Expense])

Operating Income Before Depreciation: Data Item A13, Units: Millions of dollars

This item represents Net Sales less Cost of Goods Sold and Selling, General, and Administrative Expenses before deducting Depreciation, Depletion and Amortization. This item includes the effects of adjustments for Cost of Goods Sold and Selling, General, and Administrative Expenses. A partial listing of items which comprise Cost of Goods Sold and Selling, General, and Administrative Expenses is as follows:

This item includes

1. Cost of Goods Sold

· Rent and royalty expense

· General taxes (other than income taxes)

· Profit sharing contributions

· Pension costs, including past service pension costs (except when written off in one year)

· Motion picture and entertainment companies' amortization of film costs

1. Selling General, and Administrative Expense

· Research and development expense

· Strike expense

· Bad debt expense (provisions for doubtful accounts)

· Exploration expense

· Parent company charges for administrative service

The following items, when separately listed, are treated as Nonoperating Income (Expense) rather than as operating expenses:

1. Moving expenses

2. Recurring foreign exchange adjustments

3. Idle plant expenses

4. Profit on sales of properties (except for securities, etc.) for the companies in the oil, coal, airline, and other industries where

these transactions are considered a normal part of doing business

5. Amortization of negative intangibles

The current year's results of discontinued operations are not considered operating expenses and are shown as an extraordinary item.

Income Before Extraordinary Items: Data Item A18, Units: Millions of dollars

This item represents the income of a company after all expenses, including special items, income taxes, and minority interest – but before provisions for common and/or preferred dividends. This item does not reflect discontinued operations (appearing below taxes) or extraordinary items.

This item includes (when reported below taxes):

1. Amortization of intangibles
2. Equity in earnings of unconsolidated subsidiaries
3. Gain or loss on the sale of securities when they are a regular part of a company's operations
4. Shipping companies' operating differential subsidies (current and prior years)

Cash Dividends – Preferred: Data Item A19, Units: Millions of dollars

This item represents the total amount of the preferred dividend requirement on cumulative preferred stock and dividends paid on noncumulative preferred stock of the company during the year.

1. The amount of dividend requirements used by the company in calculating Available for Common
1. Preferred dividends of a merged company accounted for by the pooling of interest method are included for the year of the merger, unless the preferred stock was exchanged for common stock of the acquiring company (included in Cash Dividends – Common)

Utility companies' subsidiary preferred dividends are included

This item excludes

1. Preferred dividends deducted only for that portion of the year the stock was outstanding, if an entire issuance of convertible preferred stock is converted into common during the year
2. The dividends on the old preferred stock treated as common dividends, if common stock is issued by the company in exchanges for preferred stock of another company
3. Subsidiary preferred dividends (included in Minority Interest)

Price – Calendar Year – Close: Data Item A24, Units: Dollars and cents

This item represents the absolute close transactions during the year for companies on national stock exchanges and bid prices for over-the-counter issues. Prices are reported on a calendar-year basis. Prices are adjusted for all stock splits and stock dividends that occurred in the fiscal year, except for 06-11 fiscal year companies which have declared stock splits and stock dividends between the end of their fiscal year and the end of the calendar year. In those instances, that stated prices are not adjusted. When a 01-05 fiscal year company has a stock split or a stock dividend after the calendar year-end but before the fiscal year-end, prices will be adjusted. If a company suspends trading, the close price of the stock will be presented as of the last trading day.

Common Shares Outstanding – Company: Data Item A25, Units: Millions

This item represents the net number of all common shares outstanding at year-end, excluding treasury shares and scrip.

Common treasury shares carried on the asset side of the balance sheet are netted against the number of common shares issued.

Common shares paid in stock dividends are included when the ex-dividend date falls within the year and the payment date the next year.

Common shares will be excluded when a company nets shares held by a consolidated subsidiary against the capital account.

Employees: Data Item A29, Units: Thousands

This item represents the number of company workers as reported to shareholders. This is reported by some firms as an average number of employees and by some as the number of employees at year-end. No attempt has been made to differentiate between these bases of reporting. If both are given, the year-end figure is used.

This item, for banks always represents the number of year-end employees.

This item includes:

1. All part-time and seasonal employees
2. All employees of consolidated subsidiaries, both domestic and foreign

This item excludes:

1. Contract workers
2. Consultants
3. Employees of unconsolidated subsidiaries

Debt Due in 1st Year: Data Item A44, Units: Millions of dollars

This item represents the current portion of long-term debt (included in Current Liabilities).

This item includes

1. The installments son a loan
2. The sinking fund payments

3. The current portion of any item defined as long-term debt (for example, the current portion of a long-term lease obligation)

Common Equity − Total: Data Item A60, Units: Millions of dollars
This item represents the common shareholders' interest in the company.
This item includes
      1. Common stock outstanding (including treasury stock adjustments)
      2. Capital surplus
      3. Retained earnings
      4. Treasury stock adjustments for both common and non-redeemable preferred tock
This figure is not adjusted for excess liquidating value over carrying value of preferred stock or for intangibles.

Nonoperating Income (Expense): Data Item A61, Units: Millions of dollars
This item represents any income or expense items resulting from secondary business-related activities, excluding those considered part of the normal operations of the business. Non-operating income and expense will be reported as a net figure with non-operating income treated as a positive number and non-operating expense treated as a negative number.
This item includes
    1. Income
        · Discount on debt reacquired
        · Dividend income
        · Equity in earnings of a nonconsolidated subsidiary
        · Franchise income when corresponding expenses are not included in the Income Statement
        · Interest charged to construction (interest capitalized)
        · Leased department income when corresponding expenses are not included in the Income Statement
        · Other income, Rental income, Royalty income, Interest income
    2. Expense
        · Amortization of deferred credit
        · Amortization of negative intangibles
        · Foreign exchange adjustments
        · Idle plant expense
        · Miscellaneous expense
        · Moving expense
        · Other expense

Preferred Stock: Data Item A130, Units: Millions of dollars
This item represents the net number of preferred shares at year-end multiplied by the par or stated value per share as presented in the company's Balance Sheet.
This item includes
      1. Preferred stock subscriptions
      2. Utilities subsidiary preferred stock
      3. Redeemable preferred stock
          1. Preference stock
          2. Receivables on preferred stock
This item excludes
      1. Preferred stock sinking funds reported in current liabilities
      2. Secondary classes of common stock
      3. Subsidiary preferred stock
This item is reduced by the effects of
      1. Par or carrying value of nonredeemable preferred treasury stock which was nettled against this item prior to annual and quarterly fiscal periods of 1982 and 1986, 1st quarter, respectively
      2. Cost of redeemable preferred treasury stock which is netted against Preferred Stock − Redeemable

Operating Income After Depreciation: Data Item A178, Units: Millions of dollars
This item represents the operating income of a company after deducting expenses for cost of goods sold, selling, general, and administrative expenses, and depreciation.

Liabilities − Total: Data Item A181, Units: Millions of dollars
This item represents the sum of:
      1. Current Liabilities − Total
      2. Deferred Taxes and Investment Tax Credit (Balance Sheet)
      3. Liabilities − Other
      4. Long-Term Debt − Total

5. Minority Interest (Balance Sheet)

Notes Payable: Data Item A206, Units: Millions of dollars
This item represents the total amount of short-term notes.
This item includes
      1. Bank acceptances
      2. Bank overdrafts
      3. Loans payable to officers of the company
      4. Loans payable to parents, and consolidated and unconsolidated subsidiaries
            1. Loans payable to stockholders
            2. Notes payable – banks, others
            3. Telephone companies' interim notes payable and advances from parent company
            4. Commercial paper
This item excludes
      1. Current portion of long-term notes payable (included in Debt Due in One Year)
      2. Due to factor (included in Current Liabilities – Other) This item is not available for utilities.

Appendix 2
Changes to the Risk Premium Report Over Time

Now in its 22nd year of publication (1996–2016), the Risk Premium Report Study continues to be at the forefront in providing comprehensive valuation methodology and data.

The most significant recent change to the Risk Premium Report Study is its incorporation into the *Valuation Handbook – U.S. Guide to Cost of Capital* in 2014, along with the CRSP Deciles Size Premia Study. The "CRSP Deciles Size Premia Study" is the valuation data previously published in the (now discontinued) Morningstar/Ibbotson *SBBI Valuation Yearbook* from 1999–2013. The Risk Premium Report Study, previously published as the Duff & Phelps Risk Premium Report, is no longer published as a stand-alone publication. Both the Risk Premium Report Study data set and CRSP Deciles Size Premia Study data set (the former SBBI data) now published in the *Valuation Handbook – U.S. Guide to Cost of Capital* by Wiley & Sons.

The development of the online *Risk Premium Toolkit* by Business Valuation Resources (BVR) in 2011 (originally introduced as the "*Risk Premium Calculator*" in 2011; renamed the *Risk Premium Toolkit* in 2015), and the development of the *Cost of Capital Analyzer* by ValuSource remain important milestones.[A.1]

The online *Risk Premium Toolkit* from BVR is a web-based application that makes using the *Valuation Handbook – U.S. Guide to Cost of Capital's* Risk Premium Report Study data and CRSP Deciles Size Premia Data even easier.[A.1] The *Risk Premium Toolkit* instantly delivers a fully customizable "Executive Summary" in Microsoft Word format that includes sourcing, key inputs, and a concluded range of cost of equity capital estimates using both the buildup and CAPM methods. In addition, a detailed record of all inputs, outputs, and calculations is exported to a "Support and Detail" Microsoft Excel workbook.[A.2]

The online "*Cost of Capital Analyzer*" by ValuSource is also designed to help the valuation analyst use the *Valuation Handbook – U.S. Guide to Cost of Capital's* data as efficiently as possible. Both the CRSP Deciles Size Premia Studies and the Risk Premium Report Studies data are included in the *Cost of Capital Analyzer*. The *Cost of Capital Analyzer* can be used by Excel users and will download directly in ValuSource valuation software, including *ValuSource Pro, Business Valuation Manager Pro* and *Express Business Valuation*.

Readers may be interested in the difference between the data presented herein and analogous data published in articles that appeared in 1996 and 1997 (cited above), a 1995 article ("The Size Effect and Equity Returns", *Business Valuation Review*, June 1995), as well as annual updates previously published on the Morningstar (formerly Ibbotson Associates) website from 1998–2012. These changes over time are summarized in the following sections.

Changes from Previously Published Versions of the Risk Premium Report's Size Study

- The 1995 article reported 30-year historical averages. We currently report averages since 1963.

- The 1995 article looked only at the market value of equity as a measure of size. We currently look at eight alternate measures of size.

- The current report includes Total Assets as one of the measures of size. This replaces a Book Value of Invested Capital measure that appeared in the 1996 and 1997 articles.

- The current report excludes newly listed companies, places many companies into a separate high-financial-risk database, includes AMEX and NASDAQ companies, and includes only companies covered by *Compustat*. The 1995 article used all operating NYSE companies found in the CRSP database.

- The 1995 article used market-weighted averaging to calculate the portfolio rates of return. The current report uses equal weighted averaging.

[A.1] The online "Risk Premium Toolkit" is available from BVR at www.bvresources.com/valuationhandboook or by calling 1 (503) 291-7963 ext 2. The "Cost of Capital Analyzer" is available from ValuSource at www.valuationhandbook.com or by calling 1 (800) 825-8763.

[A.2] The CRSP Deciles Size Premia Study data was added to the online Risk Premium Toolkit in mid-2014.

- The 1995 article used natural logarithms, while the current report uses base-10 logarithms. This makes no difference in the calculation of the "smoothed" premia, but we have found that base-10 logs are easier to explain than natural logs.

- The 1995 and 1996 articles included financial companies. The current report excludes financial companies (though in our currently published versions of prior years' reports we exclude financial companies).

- The current report corrects for possible "delisting bias" in the CRSP database. The 1995, 1996, and 1997 articles did not make this adjustment (though in our currently published versions of prior years' reports we include this correction).

- The current report includes tables showing "Premia over CAPM". Versions of this study before 2000 did not include these tables (though our currently published versions of prior years' reports include these data).

- Certain revisions in methodology (made for technical reasons) expanded the number of companies categorized as high-financial-risk relative to versions published before 2000 (though our currently published versions of prior years' reports incorporate this changed methodology).

- The current report changes the method of using financial data such that no data is considered for fiscal years ending less than three months before the formation of portfolios. Versions of this study prior to 2001 allowed use of financial data through the previous month end (though our currently published versions of prior years' reports incorporate this changed methodology).

- The current report uses the "sum beta" method applied to monthly returns to estimate portfolio betas. Versions before 2003 estimated betas using ordinary least squares with annual data (though our currently published versions of prior years' reports incorporate the "sum beta" methodology).

- The current report includes un-levered average risk premia and sum betas for each portfolio. Versions of this study prior to 2005 as originally published did not include this data (though our currently published versions of prior years' reports include these data). The Reports through 2007 used an un-levering formula commonly referred to as the Hamada formula. The current report uses the un-levering formula commonly referred to as the Harris-Pringle formula. See Chapter 12 in *Cost of Capital: Applications and Examples* 5th ed. by Shannon Pratt and Roger Grabowski, Wiley (April, 2014). In the current report the methodology and assumptions for un-levering risk premia reported in Exhibits C-1 through C-8 were updated. Exhibits C-1 through C-8 for the prior report (2010) were also updated using the updated un-levering methodology.

- The current report incorporates various corrections and other changes that have affected the CRSP and *Compustat* databases since the data in the earlier articles was generated. We now use CRSP as the source for all stock prices and number of shares outstanding.

- The current report is the result of a complete reprogramming of the software used in the analyses and may result in differences from prior versions.

- The current report includes information about the size of the companies that comprise Portfolio 25 by percentile (5th, 25th, 50th, 75th, and 95th percentiles) for each of the eight size measures. In the 2013 Report, we started reporting the *smallest* and *largest* companies' size characteristics as well.

- The current report uses the methodology and assumptions for un-levering risk premia reported in Exhibits C-1 through C-8 were updated. Exhibits C-1 through C-8 for the prior report (2010) were also updated using the updated un-levering methodology.

- In the 2013 Report, an expanded section about using the Report to value small companies was added. This new section provides a listing of the smallest and largest companies in "Portfolio 25" (Portfolio 25 is comprised of the smallest companies) for each of the eight size measures (see Table 2 on page 22). This was added to give the valuation analyst greater capability to gauge the size characteristics of his or her subject company relative to the size characteristics of companies that comprise Portfolio 25, and also provides support for adjustments to premia made by utilizing the "regression equation method" to estimate custom "interpolated" risk premia or size premia.

Changes from Previously Published Versions of the Risk Study

- Versions of our study published after 1999 have included the three separate measures of risk described in Part II of this report and presented in Exhibits C-1 through C-8 and Exhibits D-1 through D-3 (our currently published versions of prior years' reports include these data).

- Various changes in methodology over the last several years have affected the underlying database, and these are summarized at the end of Part I.

- In the current version of Exhibits D-1 through D-3, we report averages of the sorting criteria for the most recent year, while versions before 2003 reported the average of the averages for all years since 1963 (though our currently published versions of prior years' reports incorporate this change).

- The current report incorporates various corrections and other changes that have affected the CRSP and Compustat databases since the data in the earlier articles was generated. We now use CRSP as the source for all stock prices and number of shares outstanding.

- The current report is the result of a complete reprogramming of the software used in the analyses and may result in differences from prior versions.

- The current report uses the methodology and assumptions for unlevering risk premia reported in Exhibits C-1 through C-8 were updated; these updated methodologies were used to add average unlevered risk premia over the risk-free rate to the D exhibits.

Changes from Previously Published Versions of the High-Financial-Risk Study

- In reports before 2008 we presented data on the high-financial-risk companies as a single portfolio.

- We first published the data on high-financial-risk companies ranked by z-Score as a Supplemental Report to the Risk Premium Report 2009. We also published characteristics of the companies comprising the high-financial-risk portfolios.

- This is the first time we are publishing data for high-financial-risk service industry companies separated from all other high-financial- risk companies. We also exclude from the averages and the returns for any years in which the portfolio of high-financial-risk companies is fewer than 6 companies.

- In the current report's H exhibits, "safe zone" statistics are not reported. "Safe zone" companies are companies which were classified as "high-financial-risk" in an initial screen, but were not classified as "high-financial-risk" in the second (z-Score) screen. These companies are set aside and not considered in any further analysis due to the inconclusive testing. In the current report "Gray zone " and "distressed zone" statistics are reported; in previous reports "safe zone", "gray zone", and "distressed zone" were reported.

Appendix 3
CRSP Deciles Size Premia Study: Key Variables

Appendix 3 includes the "key variables in estimating the cost of capital" that were previously published in the *Ibbotson Stocks, Bonds, Bills and Inflation (SBBI) Valuation Yearbook*.[A3.1]

The equity risk premium, size premium, and other valuation data reported in Appendix 3 of the *2017 Valuation Handbook – U.S. Guide to Cost of Capital*:

- Was calculated using the same data sources that were used to calculate the equity risk premium, size premium, and other valuation data previously published in the former *SBBI Valuation Yearbook*, and

- Was calculated using the same methodology that was used to calculate the equity risk premium, size premium, and other valuation data previously published in the former *SBBI Valuation Yearbook*.

For detailed examples of using the equity risk premium, size premium, and other valuation data reported in Appendix 3 to estimate cost of equity capital using the capital asset pricing model (CAPM) and the build-up method, see Chapter 8, "CRSP Deciles Size Premia Examples".

[A3.1] The *Ibbotson SBBI Valuation Yearbook* was previously published by Morningstar, Inc. (Chicago). The *SBBI Valuation Yearbook* was discontinued in 2013.

CRSP Deciles Size Premia Study: Key Variables

As of December 31, 2016

Yield (Risk-free Rate)

Long-term (20-year) U.S. Treasury Coupon Bond Yield	2.72%

Equity Risk Premium[1]

Long-horizon expected equity risk premium (historical) : large company stock total returns minus long-term government bond income returns	6.94
Long-horizon expected equity risk premium (supply-side) : historical equity risk premium minus price-to-earnings ratio calculated using three-year average earnings	5.97
Duff & Phelps recommended equity risk premium (conditional) : The Duff & Phelps recommended ERP was developed in relation to (and should be used in conjunction with) a 3.5% "normalized" risk-free rate.[2]	5.50

CRSP Deciles Size Premium[3]

Decile	Market Capitalization of Smallest Company (in millions)		Market Capitalization of Largest Company (in millions)	Size Premium (Return in Excess of CAPM)
Mid-Cap 3-5	$2,392.689	–	$10,711.194	1.02%
Low-Cap 6-8	569.279	–	2,390.899	1.75
Micro-Cap 9-10	2.516	–	567.843	3.67
Breakdown of CRSP Deciles 1-10				
1-Largest	$24,361.659	–	$609,163.498	-0.35%
2	10,784.101	–	24,233.747	0.61
3	5,683.991	–	10,711.194	0.89
4	3,520.566	–	5,676.716	0.98
5	2,392.689	–	3,512.913	1.51
6	1,571.193	–	2,390.899	1.66
7	1,033.341	–	1,569.984	1.72
8	569.279	–	1,030.426	2.08
9	263.715	–	567.843	2.68
10-Smallest	2.516	–	262.891	5.59
Breakdown of CRSP 10th Decile				
10a	$127.296	–	$262.891	4.09%
10w	190.553	–	262.891	3.10
10x	127.296	–	190.383	5.33
10b	$2.516	–	$127.279	8.64%
10y	73.561	–	127.279	7.21
10z	2.516	–	73.504	11.63

[1] See Chapter 3 for complete methodology.

[2] See Exhibit 3.19.

[3] See Chapter 7 for complete methodology.

Note: Examples on how these variables can be used are found in Chapter 8.

Sources of underlying data: 1.) CRSP U.S. Stock Database and CRSP U.S. Indices Database © 2017 Center for Research in Security Prices (CRSP®), University of Chicago Booth School of Business. 2.) Morningstar *Direct* database. Used with permission. All rights reserved. Calculations performed by Duff & Phelps, LLC.

Appendix 3a
Industry Risk Premium (RP_i)

Appendix 3a provides industry risk premia (RP_i) for use within Build-up methods that do not already have a measure of beta risk.[3a.1]

- The industries for which industry risk premia are calculated are based on Standard Industrial Classification (SIC) codes.

- Each company's contribution to the adjustment shown is based on a full-information beta with each company's contribution to the full-information beta based on the segment sales reported in the company's 10-K for that SIC code.

The industry risk premia previously published in Table 3-5 of the *SBBI Valuation Yearbook* were full-information betas converted to industry risk premia using only the long term "historical" ERP as an input in Formula 5.5. In recognition that valuation analysts may use different ERP estimates, we have pre-calculated industry risk premia using two additional ERP estimates in Appendix 3a: (i) the long-term "supply-side" ERP, and (ii) the Duff & Phelps Recommended ERP.

Please refer to the section entitled "Industry Risk Premia" in Chapter 5 for detailed methodology and proper use of industry risk premia.

[3a.1] In the 2014 and 2015 editions of the *Valuation Handbook – U.S. Guide to Cost of Capital*, industry risk premia were presented within Chapter 5 in Exhibit 5.7.

SIC Code	Short Description	Number of Companies*	Full-Information Beta (FIB)	Industry Risk Premia (%) using:		
				Long-term Historical ERP (6.94%)	Long-term Supply-Side ERP (5.97%)	Duff & Phelps Recommended ERP (5.50%)†
	Mining					
12	Coal Mining	10	0.88	-0.80	-0.69	-0.64
13	Oil And Gas Extraction	142	1.22	1.54	1.32	1.22
131	Crude Petroleum And Natural Gas	109	1.28	1.95	1.68	1.55
138	Oil And Gas Field Services	40	1.01	0.06	0.05	0.05
1381	Drilling Oil and Gas Wells	12	0.84	-1.08	-0.93	-0.85
1389	Oil and Gas Field Services, Not Elsewhere Classified	24	1.23	1.61	1.38	1.28
14	Mining And Quarrying Of Nonmetallic Minerals, Except Fuels	16	1.51	3.55	3.05	2.81
	Construction					
15	Building Construction General Contractors And Operative Builders	28	1.20	1.36	1.17	1.08
153	Operative Builders	20	1.23	1.59	1.37	1.26
16	Heavy Construction Other Than Building Construction Contractors	25	1.55	3.82	3.28	3.03
162	Heavy Construction, Except Highway And Street	21	1.28	1.97	1.70	1.57
1623	Water, Sewer, Pipeline, and Communications and Power Line Construction	13	1.01	0.07	0.06	0.06
1629	Heavy Construction, Not Elsewhere Classified	10	1.69	4.79	4.12	3.80
17	Construction Special Trade Contractors	14	0.93	-0.46	-0.39	-0.36
	Manufacturing					
20	Food And Kindred Products	82	0.63	-2.56	-2.20	-2.03
203	Canned, Frozen, And Preserved Fruits, Vegetables, and Food Specialties	14	0.36	-4.47	-3.85	-3.54
204	Grain Mill Products	13	0.67	-2.28	-1.96	-1.81
208	Beverages	25	0.62	-2.67	-2.30	-2.11
2086	Bottled and Canned Soft Drinks and Carbonated Waters	11	0.60	-2.78	-2.39	-2.20
209	Miscellaneous Food Preparations And Kindred	16	0.53	-3.24	-2.79	-2.57
22	Textile Mill Products	10	1.06	0.39	0.34	0.31
23	Apparel And Other Finished Products Made From Fabrics And Similar Materials	26	0.62	-2.67	-2.30	-2.11
24	Lumber And Wood Products, Except Furniture	26	1.70	4.85	4.17	3.84
25	Furniture And Fixtures	23	1.25	1.73	1.49	1.37
251	Household Furniture	14	1.15	1.02	0.88	0.81
26	Paper And Allied Products	29	0.83	-1.17	-1.01	-0.93
262	Paper Mills	10	1.07	0.48	0.42	0.38
267	Converted Paper And Paperboard Products, Except Boxes	11	0.54	-3.16	-2.72	-2.51
27	Printing, Publishing, And Allied Industries	29	1.43	2.99	2.57	2.37
28	Chemicals And Allied Products	366	1.07	0.46	0.39	0.36
281	Industrial Inorganic Chemicals	32	1.04	0.29	0.25	0.23
2819	Industrial Inorganic Chemicals, Not Elsewhere Classified	18	1.22	1.53	1.32	1.21
282	Plastics Materials And Synthetic Resins, Synthetic	22	1.42	2.92	2.51	2.32
2821	Plastics Materials, Synthetic Resins, and Nonvulcanizable Elastomers	17	1.50	3.47	2.99	2.75
283	Drugs	248	1.07	0.45	0.39	0.36
2834	Pharmaceutical Preparations	93	0.93	-0.47	-0.40	-0.37
2835	In Vitro and In Vivo Diagnostic Substances	35	1.09	0.60	0.51	0.47
2836	Biological Products, Except Diagnostic Substances	118	1.29	2.01	1.73	1.60
284	Soap, Detergents, And Cleaning Preparations; Perfumes, Cosmetics, and Other Toilet Preparations	23	0.56	-3.06	-2.64	-2.43
2844	Perfumes, Cosmetics, and Other Toilet Preparations	15	0.53	-3.23	-2.78	-2.56

* To view the full list of companies, download the Industry Risk Premia Company List Report at www.DuffandPhelps.com/CostofCapital.

† The Duff & Phelps recommended ERP as of December 31, 2016 (5.5%) was developed in relation to a 3.5% "normalized" risk-free rate. The Duff & Phelps recommended ERP should be used with the risk-free rate that it was developed in relation to, per the schedule provided in Exhibit 3.19 in the 2017 Valuation Handbook – U.S. Guide to Cost of Capital.

SIC Code	Short Description	Number of Companies*	Full-Information Beta (FIB)	Industry Risk Premia (%) using:		
				Long-term Historical ERP (6.94%)	Long-term Supply-Side ERP (5.97%)	Duff & Phelps Recommended ERP (5.50%)†
	Manufacturing (continued)					
286	Industrial Organic Chemicals	31	1.39	2.72	2.34	2.16
2869	Industrial Organic Chemicals, Not Elsewhere Classified	27	1.31	2.14	1.84	1.70
287	Agricultural Chemicals	16	1.35	2.43	2.09	1.93
289	Miscellaneous Chemical Products	19	1.32	2.19	1.88	1.73
2899	Chemicals and Chemical Preparations, Not Elsewhere Classified	10	1.39	2.72	2.34	2.16
29	Petroleum Refining And Related Industries	37	1.15	1.07	0.92	0.85
291	Petroleum Refining	27	1.13	0.91	0.78	0.72
30	Rubber And Miscellaneous Plastics Products	43	0.75	-1.73	-1.49	-1.37
308	Miscellaneous Plastics Products	30	1.24	1.69	1.46	1.34
3089	Plastics Products, Not Elsewhere Classified	20	1.25	1.71	1.47	1.36
32	Stone, Clay, Glass, And Concrete Products	30	1.44	3.08	2.65	2.44
327	Concrete, Gypsum, And Plaster Products	13	1.40	2.78	2.39	2.21
329	Abrasive, Asbestos, And Miscellaneous	12	1.40	2.78	2.40	2.21
33	Primary Metal Industries	50	2.04	7.24	6.23	5.74
331	Steel Works, Blast Furnaces, And Rolling And Finishing Mills	23	1.98	6.77	5.82	5.37
3312	Steel Works, Blast Furnaces (Including Coke Ovens), and Rolling Mills	11	1.87	6.05	5.21	4.80
335	Rolling, Drawing, And Extruding Of Nonferrous	19	1.29	2.00	1.72	1.59
34	Fabricated Metal Products, Except Machinery And Transportation Equipment	76	0.95	-0.34	-0.30	-0.27
342	Cutlery, Handtools, And General Hardware	15	1.09	0.60	0.52	0.48
344	Fabricated Structural Metal Products	29	1.19	1.34	1.16	1.07
3443	Fabricated Plate Work (Boiler Shops)	13	1.13	0.89	0.77	0.71
349	Miscellaneous Fabricated Metal Products	13	1.34	2.35	2.02	1.86
35	Industrial And Commercial Machinery And Computer Equipment	193	1.27	1.88	1.62	1.49
351	Engines And Turbines	11	1.80	5.55	4.78	4.41
352	Farm And Garden Machinery And Equipment	10	0.67	-2.32	-2.00	-1.84
353	Construction, Mining, And Materials Handling	35	1.55	3.84	3.30	3.04
3531	Construction Machinery and Equipment	11	1.92	6.39	5.50	5.07
3533	Oil and Gas Field Machinery and Equipment	16	1.54	3.72	3.20	2.95
354	Metalworking Machinery And Equipment	13	1.15	1.01	0.87	0.80
355	Special Industry Machinery, Except Metalworking	28	1.63	4.35	3.75	3.45
3559	Special Industry Machinery, Not Elsewhere Classified	19	1.66	4.55	3.91	3.61
356	General Industrial Machinery And Equipment	38	1.23	1.58	1.36	1.25
3561	Pumps and Pumping Equipment	10	1.32	2.24	1.93	1.78
357	Computer And Office Equipment	53	1.24	1.67	1.44	1.32
3577	Computer Peripheral Equipment, Not Elsewhere Classified	14	1.49	3.38	2.91	2.68
358	Refrigeration And Service Industry Machinery	18	1.15	1.05	0.90	0.83
3585	Air-Conditioning and Warm Air Heating Equipment and Commercial and Industrial Refrigeration Equipment	12	1.10	0.66	0.57	0.53
36	Electronic And Other Electrical Equipment And Components, Except Computer Equipment	248	1.28	1.94	1.67	1.54
362	Electrical Industrial Apparatus	24	1.23	1.58	1.36	1.25
3621	Motors and Generators	14	1.40	2.77	2.38	2.20
364	Electric Lighting And Wiring Equipment	13	1.30	2.06	1.77	1.63
365	Household Audio And Video Equipment, And Audio	10	1.93	6.44	5.54	5.11
366	Communications Equipment	55	1.28	1.92	1.65	1.52
3661	Telephone and Telegraph Apparatus	12	1.59	4.10	3.53	3.25

* To view the full list of companies, download the Industry Risk Premia Company List Report at www.DuffandPhelps.com/CostofCapital.
† The Duff & Phelps recommended ERP as of December 31, 2016 (5.5%) was developed in relation to a 3.5% "normalized" risk-free rate. The Duff & Phelps recommended ERP should be used with the risk-free rate that it was developed in relation to, per the schedule provided in Exhibit 3.19 in the 2017 Valuation Handbook – U.S. Guide to Cost of Capital.

Appendix 3a: Industry Risk Premia (RP_i)
Through Year-end 2016

SIC Code	Short Description	Number of Companies*	Full-Information Beta (FIB)	Industry Risk Premia (%) using:		
				Long-term Historical ERP (6.94%)	Long-term Supply-Side ERP (5.97%)	Duff & Phelps Recommended ERP (5.50%)†
	Manufacturing (continued)					
3663	Radio and Television Broadcasting and Communications Equipment	29	1.23	1.57	1.35	1.24
3669	Communications Equipment, Not Elsewhere Classified	14	0.98	-0.11	-0.10	-0.09
367	Electronic Components And Accessories	123	1.35	2.43	2.09	1.93
3672	Printed Circuit Boards	12	1.07	0.48	0.42	0.38
3674	Semiconductors and Related Devices	75	1.36	2.52	2.17	2.00
3679	Electronic Components, Not Elsewhere Classified	24	1.15	1.07	0.92	0.84
369	Miscellaneous Electrical Machinery, Equipment, and Supplies	18	1.47	3.26	2.80	2.58
37	Transportation Equipment	103	1.10	0.72	0.62	0.57
371	Motor Vehicles And Motor Vehicle Equipment	57	1.36	2.49	2.14	1.97
3711	Motor Vehicles and Passenger Car Bodies	12	1.29	2.01	1.73	1.60
3714	Motor Vehicle Parts and Accessories	41	1.38	2.61	2.25	2.07
372	Aircraft And Parts	32	0.78	-1.54	-1.32	-1.22
3728	Aircraft Parts and Auxiliary Equipment, Not Elsewhere Classified	18	0.92	-0.53	-0.46	-0.42
38	Measuring, Analyzing, And Controlling Instruments; Photographic, Medical And Optical Goods; Watches And Clocks	207	0.91	-0.59	-0.51	-0.47
381	Search, Detection, Navigation, Guidance, Aeronautical, and Nautical Systems, Instruments, and Equipment	17	0.70	-2.10	-1.80	-1.66
382	Laboratory Apparatus And Analytical, Optical, Measuring, and Controlling Instruments	76	1.17	1.17	1.01	0.93
3823	Industrial Instruments for Measurement, Display, and Control of Process Variables; and Related Products	14	1.08	0.56	0.48	0.44
3825	Instruments for Measuring and Testing of Electricity and Electrical Signals	17	1.14	0.95	0.82	0.75
3826	Laboratory Analytical Instruments	16	1.06	0.41	0.35	0.33
3829	Measuring and Controlling Devices, Not Elsewhere Classified	20	1.77		4.58	4.22
384	Surgical, Medical, And Dental Instruments And Supplies	116	0.87	5.32	-0.75	-0.69
3841	Surgical and Medical Instruments and Apparatus	36	0.88	-0.87	-0.73	-0.67
3842	Orthopedic, Prosthetic, and Surgical Appliances and Supplies	34	0.88	-0.86	-0.74	-0.68
3845	Electromedical and Electrotherapeutic Apparatus	50	0.98	-0.11	-0.10	-0.09
39	Miscellaneous Manufacturing Industries	31	0.90	-0.67	-0.58	-0.53
394	Dolls, Toys, Games And Sporting And Athletic	14	0.95	-0.36	-0.31	-0.29
	Transportation, Communications, Electric, Gas, and Sanitary Services					
40	Railroad Transportation	11	0.91	-0.59	-0.51	-0.47
4011	Railroads, Line-Haul Operating	10	0.90	-0.68	-0.59	-0.54
42	Motor Freight Transportation And Warehousing	29	0.93	-0.46	-0.40	-0.37
4213	Trucking, Except Local	21	1.10	0.72	0.62	0.57
44	Water Transportation	12	1.22	1.52	1.31	1.21
45	Transportation By Air	24	1.28	1.97	1.69	1.56
451	Air Transportation, Scheduled, And Air Courier	13	1.30	2.11	1.81	1.67
4512	Air Transportation, Scheduled	10	1.35	2.40	2.06	1.90
46	Pipelines, Except Natural Gas	27	1.09	0.63	0.55	0.50
4612	Crude Petroleum Pipelines	20	1.05	0.36	0.31	0.29
47	Transportation Services	29	0.81	-1.33	-1.15	-1.06
473	Arrangement Of Transportation Of Freight And Cargo	24	0.94	-0.45	-0.38	-0.35
48	Communications	91	0.66	-2.35	-2.02	-1.86

* To view the full list of companies, download the Industry Risk Premia Company List Report at www.DuffandPhelps.com/CostofCapital.

† The Duff & Phelps recommended ERP as of December 31, 2016 (5.5%) was developed in relation to a 3.5% "normalized" risk-free rate. The Duff & Phelps recommended ERP should be used with the risk-free rate that it was developed in relation to, per the schedule provided in Exhibit 3.19 in the 2017 Valuation Handbook – U.S. Guide to Cost of Capital.

SIC Code	Short Description	Number of Companies*	Full-Information Beta (FIB)	Industry Risk Premia (%) using:		
				Long-term Historical ERP (6.94%)	Long-term Supply-Side ERP (5.97%)	Duff & Phelps Recommended ERP (5.50%)†
	Transportation, Communications, Electric, Gas, and Sanitary Services (continued)					
481	Telephone Communications	31	0.43	-3.95	-3.40	-3.13
4812	Radiotelephone Communications	11	0.19	-5.63	-4.84	-4.46
4813	Telephone Communications, Except Radiotelephone	26	1.10	0.67	0.58	0.53
483	Radio And Television Broadcasting Stations	32	1.34	2.36	2.03	1.87
4832	Radio Broadcasting Stations	13	1.33	2.30	1.98	1.83
4833	Television Broadcasting Stations	24	1.37	2.57	2.21	2.04
484	Cable And Other Pay Television Services	15	0.91	-0.64	-0.55	-0.51
489	Communications Services, Not Elsewhere	23	0.91	-0.59	-0.51	-0.47
49	Electric, Gas, And Sanitary Services	137	0.42	-4.00	-3.44	-3.17
491	Electric Services	52	0.18	-5.70	-4.91	-4.52
492	Gas Production And Distribution	61	0.93	-0.47	-0.40	-0.37
4922	Natural Gas Transmission	31	1.03	0.21	0.18	0.17
4923	Natural Gas Transmission and Distribution	16	1.16	1.13	0.97	0.90
4924	Natural Gas Distribution	25	0.17	-5.73	-4.93	-4.55
494	Water Supply	14	0.32	-4.72	-4.06	-3.74
495	Sanitary Services	23	0.64	-2.51	-2.16	-1.99
	Wholesale Trade					
50	Wholesale Trade-durable Goods	100	1.08	0.55	0.47	0.43
504	Professional And Commercial Equipment And Supplies	24	1.03	0.20	0.17	0.16
5045	Computers and Computer Peripheral Equipment and Software	16	1.02	0.13	0.11	0.10
505	Metals And Minerals, Except Petroleum	15	1.25	1.76	1.52	1.40
5051	Metals Service Centers and Offices	11	1.26	1.78	1.53	1.41
506	Electrical Goods	21	1.58	4.05	3.48	3.21
5065	Electronic Parts and Equipment, Not Elsewhere Classified	13	1.54	3.75	3.23	2.98
508	Machinery, Equipment, And Supplies	18	0.89	-0.75	-0.64	-0.59
51	Wholesale Trade-non-durable Goods	94	1.01	0.10	0.08	0.08
514	Groceries And Related Products	13	0.66	-2.38	-2.05	-1.89
517	Petroleum And Petroleum Products	40	1.31	2.15	1.85	1.70
5171	Petroleum Bulk stations and Terminals	19	0.88	-0.81	-0.69	-0.64
5172	Petroleum and Petroleum Products Wholesalers, Except Bulk Stations and Terminals	25	1.54	3.75	3.23	2.98
	Retail Trade					
53	General Merchandise Stores	17	0.43	-3.98	-3.43	-3.16
533	Variety Stores	10	0.28	-4.96	-4.27	-3.93
54	Food Stores	16	0.81	-1.32	-1.14	-1.05
55	Automotive Dealers And Gasoline Service Stations	23	0.95	-0.37	-0.32	-0.29
565	Family Clothing Stores	13	1.18	1.22	1.05	0.97
566	Shoe Stores	10	0.62	-2.66	-2.29	-2.11
57	Home Furniture, Furnishings, And Equipment Stores	19	0.92	-0.58	-0.50	-0.46
571	Home Furniture And Furnishings Stores	11	0.72	-1.93	-1.67	-1.53
58	Eating And Drinking Places	55	0.67	-2.29	-1.97	-1.81
59	Miscellaneous Retail	70	1.16	1.13	0.97	0.89
591	Drug Stores And Proprietary Stores	10	0.91	-0.60	-0.51	-0.47
594	Miscellaneous Shopping Goods Stores	12	1.34	2.33	2.01	1.85
596	Nonstore Retailers	29	1.46	3.17	2.73	2.52
5961	Catalog and Mail-Order Houses	28	1.47	3.23	2.78	2.56
598	Fuel Dealers	12	0.60	-2.75	-2.37	-2.18
599	Retail Stores, Not Elsewhere Classified	10	0.78	-1.56	-1.34	-1.23

* To view the full list of companies, download the Industry Risk Premia Company List Report at www.DuffandPhelps.com/CostofCapital.

† The Duff & Phelps recommended ERP as of December 31, 2016 (5.5%) was developed in relation to a 3.5% "normalized" risk-free rate. The Duff & Phelps recommended ERP should be used with the risk-free rate that it was developed in relation to, per the schedule provided in Exhibit 3.19 in the 2017 Valuation Handbook – U.S. Guide to Cost of Capital.

SIC Code	Short Description	Number of Companies*	Full-Information Beta (FIB)	Industry Risk Premia (%) using:		
				Long-term Historical ERP (6.94%)	Long-term Supply-Side ERP (5.97%)	Duff & Phelps Recommended ERP (5.50%)†
	Finance, Insurance, and Real Estate					
60	Depository Institutions	486	1.20	1.38	1.18	1.09
602	Commercial Banks	359	1.24	1.67	1.44	1.32
603	Savings Institutions	118	0.70	-2.09	-1.79	-1.65
6035	Savings Institutions, Federally Chartered	89	0.72	-1.97	-1.70	-1.57
6036	Savings Institutions, Not Federally Chartered	29	0.67	-2.27	-1.95	-1.80
61	Non-depository Credit Institutions	85	1.53	3.70	3.18	2.93
614	Personal Credit Institutions	21	1.21	1.48	1.27	1.17
615	Business Credit Institutions	29	1.13	0.91	0.78	0.72
6153	Short-Term Business Credit Institutions, Except Agricultural	17	1.29	1.99	1.72	1.58
6159	Miscellaneous business Credit Institutions	13	0.59	-2.82	-2.43	-2.24
616	Mortgage Bankers And Brokers	29	1.26	1.83	1.58	1.45
	Finance, Insurance, and Real Estate (continued)					
6162	Mortgage Bankers and Loan Correspondents	26	1.37	2.55	2.19	2.02
62	Security And Commodity Brokers, Dealers, Exchanges, And Services	84	1.61	4.21	3.62	3.34
621	Security Brokers, Dealers, And Flotation	30	1.82	5.71	4.91	4.53
628	Services Allied With The Exchange Of Securities	57	1.63	4.36	3.75	3.46
6282	Investment Advice	54	1.64	4.44	3.82	3.52
63	Insurance Carriers	94	0.99	-0.09	-0.08	-0.07
631	Life Insurance	36	1.69	4.77	4.11	3.78
632	Accident And Health Insurance And Medical	22	0.73	-1.84	-1.58	-1.46
6324	Hospital and Medical Service Plans	10	0.65	-2.45	-2.10	-1.94
633	Fire, Marine, And Casualty Insurance	50	0.81	-1.33	-1.15	-1.06
635	Surety Insurance	13	2.01	7.01	6.04	5.56
64	Insurance Agents, Brokers, And Service	18	0.83	-1.17	-1.01	-0.93
65	Real Estate	69	1.64	4.46	3.84	3.54
651	Real Estate Operators (except Developers) And Lessors	31	0.98	-0.12	-0.11	-0.10
6512	Operators of Nonresidential Buildings	17	0.96	-0.26	-0.23	-0.21
653	Real Estate Agents And Managers	18	1.61	4.20	3.62	3.33
6531	Real Estate Agents and Managers	17	1.57	3.97	3.42	3.15
655	Land Subdividers And Developers	24	1.59	4.09	3.52	3.24
6552	Land Subdividers and Developers, Except Cemeteries	23	1.73	5.07	4.36	4.02
67	Holding And Other Investment Offices	335	0.74	-1.81	-1.56	-1.43
679	Miscellaneous Investing	333	0.69	-2.17	-1.87	-1.72
6792	Oil Royalty Traders	14	0.84	-1.11	-0.95	-0.88
6794	Patent Owners and Lessors	54	0.89	-0.79	-0.68	-0.63
6798	Real Estate Investment Trusts	188	0.67	-2.29	-1.97	-1.82
6799	Investors, Not Elsewhere Classified	31	1.27	1.86	1.60	1.48
	Services					
70	Hotels, Rooming Houses, Camps, And Other Lodging Places	22	1.26	1.83	1.58	1.45
701	Hotels And Motels	21	1.27	1.87	1.61	1.48
72	Personal Services	10	0.83	-1.18	-1.02	-0.94
73	Business Services	448	1.08	0.55	0.47	0.44
731	Advertising	12	1.36	2.51	2.16	1.99
735	Miscellaneous Equipment Rental And Leasing	22	2.17	8.15	7.01	6.46
7359	Equipment Rental and Leasing, Not Elsewhere Classified	19	1.80	5.53	4.76	4.38
736	Personnel Supply Services	24	1.30	2.10	1.80	1.66

* To view the full list of companies, download the Industry Risk Premia Company List Report at www.DuffandPhelps.com/CostofCapital.

† The Duff & Phelps recommended ERP as of December 31, 2016 (5.5%) was developed in relation to a 3.5% "normalized" risk-free rate. The Duff & Phelps recommended ERP should be used with the risk-free rate that it was developed in relation to, per the schedule provided in Exhibit 3.19 in the 2017 Valuation Handbook – U.S. Guide to Cost of Capital.

SIC Code	Short Description	Number of Companies*	Full-Information Beta (FIB)	Industry Risk Premia (%) using:		
				Long-term Historical ERP (6.94%)	Long-term Supply-Side ERP (5.97%)	Duff & Phelps Recommended ERP (5.50%)†
	Services (continued)					
7361	Employment Agencies	15	0.92	-0.53	-0.45	-0.42
7363	Help Supply Services	15	1.47	3.27	2.81	2.59
737	Computer Programming, Data Processing, And Other Computer Related Services	352	1.05	0.36	0.31	0.28
7372	Prepackaged Software	121	1.13	0.93	0.80	0.74
7373	Computer Integrated Systems Design	50	1.15	1.01	0.87	0.80
7374	Computer Processing and Data Preparation and Processing Services	41	0.88	-0.86	-0.74	-0.68
7375	Information Retrieval Services	124	0.98	-0.12	-0.10	-0.09
7379	Computer Related Services, Not Elsewhere Classified	39	0.92	-0.52	-0.45	-0.42
738	Miscellaneous Business Services	36	1.20	1.39	1.20	1.11
75	Automotive Repair, Services, And Parking	10	1.53	3.66	3.15	2.90
78	Motion Pictures	18	1.63	4.36	3.75	3.46
79	Amusement And Recreation Services	42	1.67	4.64	3.99	3.68
799	Miscellaneous Amusement And Recreation	32	1.60	4.18	3.60	3.32
7999	Amusement and Recreation Services, Not Elsewhere Classified	16	1.57	3.98	3.43	3.16
80	Health Services	66	0.88	-0.82	-0.71	-0.65
807	Medical And Dental Laboratories	19	0.88	-0.80	-0.69	-0.64
808	Home Health Care Services	10	1.13	0.93	0.80	0.74
809	Miscellaneous Health And Allied Services, Not	19	0.85	-1.03	-0.89	-0.82
82	Educational Services	21	0.74	-1.77	-1.53	-1.41
822	Colleges, Universities, Professional Schools, And	14	1.22	1.51	1.30	1.20
8221	Colleges, Universities, and Professional Schools	10	1.10	0.67	0.58	0.53
87	Engineering, Accounting, Research, Management, And Related Services	91	0.91	-0.61	-0.53	-0.49
871	Engineering, Architectural, And Surveying	27	1.31	2.18	1.88	1.73
873	Research, Development, And Testing Services	30	0.83	-1.17	-1.01	-0.93
874	Management And Public Relations Services	33	1.05	0.33	0.29	0.26
8742	Management Consulting Services	24	1.01	0.10	0.09	0.08

---

* To view the full list of companies, download the Industry Risk Premia Company List Report at www.DuffandPhelps.com/CostofCapital.

† The Duff & Phelps recommended ERP as of December 31, 2016 (5.5%) was developed in relation to a 3.5% "normalized" risk-free rate. The Duff & Phelps recommended ERP should be used with the risk-free rate that it was developed in relation to, per the schedule provided in Exhibit 3.19 in the 2017 Valuation Handbook – U.S. Guide to Cost of Capital.

Appendix 3b
Debt Betas

Appendix 3b provides debt betas. The risk of debt capital can be measured by the beta of the debt capital (β).[3b.1]

- Betas of debt generally correlate with credit ratings.

- Debt betas by debt rating can be used in conjunction with the equity beta unlevering and levering formulas which require debt beta estimates.

[3b.1] In the 2014 and 2015 editions of the *Valuation Handbook – U.S. Guide to Cost of Capital*, debt betas, and a graph of rolling 60-month debt betas, were presented in Exhibit 5.8 and Exhibit 5.9, respectively, within Chapter 5.

Appendix 3b: Debt Betas
Through Year-end 2016
Quarterly Debt Betas
March 2015–December 2016, Quarterly

Moody's Ratings	2015				2016			
	Mar	Jun	Sep	Dec	Mar	Jun	Sep	Dec
Aaa	-0.41	-0.39	-0.33	-0.29	-0.25	-0.26	-0.13	-0.14
Aa	-0.19	-0.17	-0.13	-0.10	-0.08	-0.09	0.00	-0.05
A	-0.14	-0.13	-0.09	-0.07	-0.04	-0.06	0.02	-0.03
Baa	0.01	0.02	0.05	0.08	0.13	0.11	0.18	0.13
Ba	0.29	0.29	0.30	0.31	0.36	0.35	0.34	0.33
B	0.52	0.55	0.56	0.61	0.59	0.58	0.54	0.47
Caa	0.76	0.80	0.85	0.83	0.87	0.86	0.82	0.70
Ca–D	0.78	0.86	0.95	0.88	1.06	1.04	1.00	1.00

Source of Underlying data: Barclays Global Family of Indices. Copyright 2017: Barclays Risk Analytics and Index Solutions Limited, Used with permission. Barclays Risk Analytics and Index Solutions Limited and its affiliates ("Barclays") are not responsible and shall have no liability for any conclusions, results or derived data created or otherwise from the use of any of the Barclays Indices. Corporate bond series used in analysis herein: Barclays US Corp Aaa Long TR USD, Barclays US Corp Aa Long TR USD, Barclays US Corp A Long TR USD, Barclays US Corp Baa Long TR USD , Barclays US Corp Ba Long TR USD, Barclays US Corp B Long TR USD, Barclays US Corp Caa Long TR USD, Barclays US HY Ca to D TR USD. Source: Morningstar *Direct*. Calculations by Duff & Phelps, LLC.

60-month Rolling Average Debt Beta of Aaa–Baa and Debt Beta of Ba–D
December 2008–December 2016

Source of Underlying data: Barclays Global Family of Indices. Copyright 2017: Barclays Risk Analytics and Index Solutions Limited, Used with permission. Barclays Risk Analytics and Index Solutions Limited and its affiliates ("Barclays") are not responsible and shall have no liability for any conclusions, results or derived data created or otherwise from the use of any of the Barclays Indices. Corporate bond series used in analysis herein: (i) Investment grade: Barclays US Corp Aaa Long TR USD, Barclays US Corp Aa Long TR USD, Barclays US Corp A Long TR USD, Barclays US Corp Baa Long TR USD , (ii) Non-investment grade: Barclays US Corp Ba Long TR USD, Barclays US Corp B Long TR USD, Barclays US Corp Caa Long TR USD, Barclays US HY Ca to D TR USD. Source: Morningstar *Direct*. Calculations by Duff & Phelps, LLC.

Example: Unlevering an Equity Beta Using a Formula that Requires a Debt Beta as an Input

Unlevering and levering betas using the Miles-Ezzell, Harris-Pringle or Fernandez formulas is often a superior method than using the simple (and often inappropriately applied) Hamada formula to unlever and lever betas.[3b.2]

$$\beta_u = \frac{\beta_L + \beta_d \times \dfrac{W_d}{W_e}}{1 + \dfrac{W_d}{W_e}}$$

where:

β_U	=	Unlevered beta of equity capital
β_L	=	Levered beta of equity capital
β_d	=	Beta of debt capital
W_d	=	Percent debt in the capital structure
W_e	=	Percent equity in the capital structure

The debt betas on the previous page can be used in conjunction with an equity beta in an unlevering and levering formula, which requires a debt beta estimate. For example, the Harris-Pringle formula requires a debt beta estimate:

On the previous page, the debt beta for a Moody's Rating of "Ba" is 0.33 as of December 2016. If you have concluded that (i) your subject company's levered equity beta is 1.09 and (ii) the capital structure of your subject company is 80% equity and 20% debt, an unlevered equity beta can be calculated using the Harris-Pringle formula as follows:

$$0.94 = \frac{1.09 + 0.33 \times \dfrac{0.20}{0.80}}{1 + \dfrac{0.20}{0.80}}$$

[3b.2] The Risk Premium Report Study in the *2017 Valuation Handbook – U.S. Guide to Cost of Capital* uses the unlevering formula commonly referred to as the Harris-Pringle formula to estimate the unlevered risk premia reported in Exhibits C-1 through C-8 and D-1 through D-3, and so we use the Harris-Pringle formula in the example herein. There are several options available to the analyst for unlevering and levering equity betas, including the Hamada formulas, the Miles-Ezzell formulas, the Harris-Pringle formulas, the Practitioners' method formulas, and the Fernandez formulas. For a detailed discussion (with additional examples), see Shannon P. Pratt and Roger J. Grabowski, *Cost of Capital: Applications and Examples* 5th ed. (John Wiley & Sons, 2014), Chapter 12, "Unlevering and Levering Equity Betas".

Appendix 4
Risk Premium Report Study Exhibits

The Risk Premium Report exhibits include the Size Study, the Risk Study, the High-Financial-Risk Study, and the Comparative Risk Study.

- **Size Study:** Comprised of Exhibits A-1 through A-8 (used in the build-up method) and Exhibits B-1 through B-8 (used in CAPM). Analyzes the relationship between equity returns and company size, using eight measures of company size.

- **Risk Study:** Comprised of Exhibits D-1, D-2, and D-3 (fundamental measures of risk based on accounting data). Analyzes the relationship between equity returns and three accounting-based fundamental risk measures.

- **High-Financial-Risk Study:** Comprised of Exhibits H-A, H-B, and H-C. Exhibit H-A is the high-financial-risk equivalent to the A exhibits, Exhibit H-B is the high-financial-risk equivalent to the B exhibits, and Exhibit H-C is the high-financial-risk equivalent to the C exhibits. Analyzes the relationship between equity returns and high-financial-risk, as measured by the Altman z-Score.

- **Comparative Risk Study:** Comprised of the C exhibits, when used in conjunction with the D exhibits. The C Exhibits can help valuation analysts further refine their cost of equity capital estimates by comparing their subject company's fundamental risk factors to the fundamental risk factors of the companies that comprise the 25 Size Study portfolios.

For detailed examples of using the valuation data reported in Appendix 4 to estimate cost of equity capital using the capital asset pricing model (CAPM) and various build-up methods, see Chapter 9, "Risk Premium Report Exhibits – General Information" and Chapter 10, "Risk Premium Report Exhibits Examples".

Risk Premium Report – Exhibits A-1 through A-8 Premia Over the Risk-Free Rate (RP_{m+s})

Risk premia over the risk-free rate reflect risk in terms of the combined effect of *market* risk and size risk in excess of the risk-free rate. These premia are added to the risk-free rate, within the context of the build-up method. An ERP Adjustment is required when using the A exhibits.

The A Exhibits are used in the following method to estimate a cost of equity capital:

- Build-up 1

Size Measures:

A-1: Market value of equity

A-2: Book value of equity

A-3: 5-year average net income

A-4: Market value of invested capital (MVIC)

A-5: Total assets

A-6: 5-year average EBITDA

A-7: Sales

A-8: Number of employees

Companies Ranked by Market Value of Equity

Historical Equity Risk Premium: Average Since 1963
Data for Year Ending December 31, 2016

Exhibit A-1

Premia Over the Risk-Free Rate (RP_{m+s})

Portfolio Rank by Size	Average Mkt. Value (in $millions)	Log of Average Mkt. Value	Number as of 2016	Beta (Sum Beta) Since '63	Standard Deviation of Returns	Geometric Average Return	Arithmetic Average Return	Arithmetic Average Risk Premium	Smoothed Average Risk Premium	Average Debt/MVIC
1	238,299	5.38	45	0.83	15.90%	9.64%	11.66%	5.20%	2.41%	14.59%
2	60,613	4.78	36	0.96	16.96%	8.52%	10.64%	4.18%	4.50%	19.02%
3	35,630	4.55	38	0.92	15.90%	9.62%	11.70%	5.24%	5.32%	20.92%
4	23,756	4.38	39	0.93	16.65%	10.30%	12.50%	6.05%	5.94%	23.13%
5	17,471	4.24	35	0.98	17.21%	10.10%	12.39%	5.93%	6.41%	23.48%
6	13,871	4.14	37	1.02	17.70%	10.26%	12.67%	6.21%	6.76%	22.72%
7	11,594	4.06	37	1.01	18.97%	10.74%	13.30%	6.84%	7.04%	23.58%
8	9,463	3.98	37	1.07	19.47%	11.78%	14.56%	8.10%	7.35%	22.54%
9	7,822	3.89	37	1.09	18.29%	12.56%	15.20%	8.74%	7.64%	22.63%
10	6,482	3.81	35	1.12	19.77%	11.47%	14.28%	7.82%	7.93%	23.10%
11	5,637	3.75	35	1.09	20.14%	11.11%	13.93%	7.47%	8.14%	22.85%
12	4,791	3.68	47	1.11	19.59%	11.13%	13.90%	7.44%	8.39%	23.06%
13	3,915	3.59	45	1.12	18.92%	11.59%	14.24%	7.78%	8.70%	23.72%
14	3,329	3.52	42	1.14	20.24%	11.81%	14.74%	8.28%	8.95%	23.27%
15	2,897	3.46	40	1.14	20.30%	13.44%	16.52%	10.06%	9.16%	23.58%
16	2,508	3.40	52	1.16	20.76%	12.95%	16.03%	9.57%	9.38%	22.89%
17	2,130	3.33	44	1.20	21.64%	12.69%	15.91%	9.45%	9.63%	22.59%
18	1,842	3.27	53	1.21	20.70%	11.47%	14.52%	8.06%	9.85%	23.30%
19	1,584	3.20	53	1.21	21.97%	12.64%	15.95%	9.49%	10.08%	22.96%
20	1,313	3.12	73	1.19	21.71%	12.08%	15.26%	8.80%	10.37%	24.11%
21	1,023	3.01	76	1.24	22.20%	13.09%	16.47%	10.01%	10.75%	23.60%
22	731	2.86	82	1.24	23.19%	12.59%	16.17%	9.71%	11.27%	24.47%
23	532	2.73	75	1.25	30.21%	15.00%	19.23%	12.77%	11.75%	23.71%
24	370	2.57	86	1.24	24.14%	15.71%	19.35%	12.89%	12.31%	24.92%
25	121	2.08	249	1.29	36.29%	18.48%	24.39%	17.94%	14.02%	27.08%
Large Stocks (Ibbotson SBBI data)						10.13%	11.48%	5.02%		
Small Stocks (Ibbotson SBBI data)						13.63%	16.27%	9.81%		
Long-Term Treasury Income (Ibbotson SBBI data)						6.43%	6.46%			

Equity Risk Premium Study: Data through December 31, 2016
Data Smoothing with Regression Analysis
Dependent Variable: Arithmetic Average Risk Premium
Independent Variable: Log of Average Market Value of Equity

Regression Output:

Constant	21.363%
Standard Error of Y Estimate	1.311%
R Squared	80%
No. of Observations	25
Degrees of Freedom	23
X Coefficient(s)	-3.525%
Standard Error of Coefficient	0.365%
t-Statistic	-9.67

*Smoothed Premium = 21.363% - 3.525% * Log(Market Value)*

Smoothed Premium vs. Arithmetic Premium

Premia Over the Risk-Free Rate (RP_{m+s})

Historical Equity Risk Premium: Average Since 1963

Data for Year Ending December 31, 2016

Equity Risk Premium Study: Data through December 31, 2016

Data Smoothing with Regression Analysis

Dependent Variable: Arithmetic Average Risk Premium

Independent Variable: Log of Average Book Value of Equity

Portfolio Rank by Size	Average Book Val. (in $millions)	Log of Average Book Val.	Number as of 2016	Beta (Sum Beta) Since '63	Standard Deviation of Returns	Geometric Average Return	Arithmetic Average Return	Arithmetic Average Risk Premium	Smoothed Average Risk Premium	Average Debt/ MVIC
1	67,532	4.83	40	0.78	15.49%	10.72%	12.78%	6.32%	5.00%	25.50%
2	21,719	4.34	33	0.84	15.91%	9.87%	11.91%	5.45%	6.18%	29.95%
3	14,074	4.15	33	0.92	16.78%	10.68%	12.93%	6.47%	6.63%	28.42%
4	9,200	3.96	35	0.90	16.72%	12.00%	14.32%	7.86%	7.07%	29.30%
5	6,875	3.84	36	0.98	17.70%	10.96%	13.42%	6.96%	7.38%	27.67%
6	5,488	3.74	34	1.01	17.56%	11.65%	14.09%	7.63%	7.61%	25.90%
7	4,590	3.66	31	1.04	20.45%	11.91%	14.90%	8.44%	7.80%	25.75%
8	3,716	3.57	34	1.07	18.61%	10.54%	13.01%	6.55%	8.02%	25.55%
9	3,112	3.49	40	1.12	19.45%	11.22%	14.01%	7.55%	8.20%	25.40%
10	2,586	3.41	37	1.07	20.03%	11.62%	14.45%	7.99%	8.40%	25.49%
11	2,266	3.36	41	1.08	19.09%	11.74%	14.48%	8.02%	8.53%	25.51%
12	2,012	3.30	33	1.10	20.26%	11.52%	14.39%	7.93%	8.66%	25.04%
13	1,751	3.24	45	1.07	18.24%	13.53%	16.25%	9.79%	8.80%	25.38%
14	1,500	3.18	39	1.17	20.82%	11.57%	14.57%	8.11%	8.96%	23.52%
15	1,303	3.11	43	1.12	18.75%	12.89%	15.60%	9.15%	9.11%	22.48%
16	1,174	3.07	42	1.17	21.56%	13.35%	16.63%	10.17%	9.22%	23.42%
17	1,030	3.01	50	1.18	21.41%	13.01%	16.28%	9.82%	9.36%	23.19%
18	861	2.93	59	1.17	19.96%	13.49%	16.50%	10.04%	9.54%	23.16%
19	711	2.85	62	1.26	24.26%	11.84%	15.17%	8.72%	9.74%	23.87%
20	577	2.76	67	1.25	21.41%	12.05%	15.22%	8.76%	9.96%	22.56%
21	479	2.68	59	1.22	23.28%	15.99%	19.29%	12.84%	10.16%	22.75%
22	385	2.59	74	1.21	22.30%	12.47%	15.90%	9.44%	10.38%	23.44%
23	303	2.48	77	1.26	23.50%	13.56%	17.21%	10.76%	10.63%	22.86%
24	207	2.32	135	1.27	24.71%	13.87%	17.89%	11.43%	11.03%	22.68%
25	76	1.88	249	1.25	25.42%	14.47%	18.68%	12.22%	12.07%	23.06%

Large Stocks (Ibbotson SBBI data)						10.13%	11.48%	5.02%		
Small Stocks (Ibbotson SBBI data)						13.63%	16.27%	9.81%		
Long-Term Treasury Income (Ibbotson SBBI data)						6.43%	6.46%			

Regression Output:

Constant	16.589%
Standard Error of Y Estimate	0.953%
R Squared	75%
No. of Observations	25
Degrees of Freedom	23
X Coefficient(s)	-2.401%
Standard Error of Coefficient	0.292%
t-Statistic	-8.22

Smoothed Premium = 16.589% − 2.401% ∗ Log(Book Value)

Smoothed Premium vs. Arithmetic Premium

Premia Over the Risk-Free Rate (y-axis: 0% to 20%)
Log of Average Book Value of Equity (x-axis: 1.0 to 6.0)

Companies Ranked by 5-Year Average Net Income

Premia Over the Risk-Free Rate (RP _m+s_)

Historical Equity Risk Premium: Average Since 1963
Data for Year Ending December 31, 2016

Portfolio Rank by Size	Average Net Inc. (in $millions)	Log of Average Net Inc.	Number as of 2016	Beta (Sum Beta) Since '63	Standard Deviation of Returns	Geometric Average Return	Arithmetic Average Return	Arithmetic Average Risk Premium	Smoothed Average Risk Premium	Average Debt/ MVIC
1	10,101	4.00	39	0.77	15.79%	10.82%	12.92%	6.46%	4.45%	20.90%
2	2,747	3.44	33	0.87	15.79%	10.44%	12.51%	6.05%	5.90%	24.62%
3	1,735	3.24	37	0.85	15.89%	11.34%	13.48%	7.02%	6.41%	26.82%
4	1,183	3.07	33	0.90	16.36%	11.19%	13.42%	6.96%	6.84%	27.36%
5	853	2.93	37	0.96	17.25%	10.49%	12.81%	6.35%	7.20%	26.08%
6	627	2.80	37	0.99	18.56%	11.32%	13.85%	7.39%	7.55%	24.70%
7	516	2.71	34	1.04	18.29%	10.90%	13.42%	6.96%	7.76%	24.89%
8	408	2.61	37	1.09	19.38%	11.65%	14.40%	7.94%	8.02%	24.55%
9	340	2.53	35	1.05	17.77%	11.08%	13.54%	7.08%	8.23%	24.35%
10	295	2.47	36	1.06	18.46%	11.91%	14.50%	8.04%	8.39%	24.01%
11	244	2.39	38	1.09	19.99%	11.61%	14.42%	7.96%	8.60%	23.88%
12	213	2.33	37	1.08	19.77%	13.04%	15.98%	9.53%	8.75%	24.38%
13	185	2.27	39	1.07	19.06%	13.06%	15.87%	9.41%	8.90%	23.73%
14	160	2.20	41	1.14	20.10%	11.46%	14.36%	7.90%	9.07%	23.99%
15	141	2.15	33	1.12	21.96%	12.43%	15.67%	9.21%	9.21%	23.40%
16	119	2.07	49	1.13	20.31%	13.24%	16.29%	9.83%	9.40%	23.10%
17	100	2.00	43	1.18	21.15%	12.10%	15.22%	8.76%	9.59%	22.64%
18	84	1.92	46	1.20	20.69%	13.76%	16.95%	10.49%	9.78%	22.93%
19	67	1.82	77	1.24	21.69%	12.30%	15.57%	9.11%	10.04%	23.05%
20	52	1.72	64	1.23	21.51%	13.74%	17.06%	10.60%	10.32%	23.66%
21	42	1.62	70	1.22	21.58%	12.94%	16.21%	9.75%	10.56%	24.45%
22	34	1.53	56	1.21	22.44%	13.13%	16.62%	10.16%	10.80%	23.97%
23	24	1.39	113	1.25	23.02%	13.73%	17.32%	10.87%	11.17%	22.56%
24	15	1.18	111	1.26	25.90%	15.43%	19.27%	12.81%	11.70%	23.38%
25	5	0.68	253	1.31	30.97%	16.38%	21.44%	14.98%	12.97%	24.59%

						Geometric Average Return	Arithmetic Average Return	Arithmetic Average Risk Premium		
Large Stocks (Ibbotson SBBI data)						10.13%	11.48%	5.02%		
Small Stocks (Ibbotson SBBI data)						13.63%	16.27%	9.81%		
Long-Term Treasury Income (Ibbotson SBBI data)						6.43%	6.46%			

Equity Risk Premium Study: Data through December 31, 2016
Data Smoothing with Regression Analysis
Dependent Variable: Arithmetic Average Risk Premium
Independent Variable: Log of Average Net Income

Regression Output:

Constant	14.722%
Standard Error of Y Estimate	0.901%
R Squared	82%
No. of Observations	25
Degrees of Freedom	23
X Coefficient(s)	-2.565%
Standard Error of Coefficient	0.247%
t-Statistic	-10.39

Smoothed Premium = 14.722% − 2.565% * Log(Net Income)

Smoothed Premium vs. Arithmetic Premium

Premia Over the Risk-Free Rate (y-axis: 0% to 20%)
Log of Average 5-Year Avereage Net Income (x-axis: 0.0 to 6.0)

Historical Equity Risk Premium: Average Since 1963
Data for Year Ending December 31, 2016

Equity Risk Premium Study: Data through December 31, 2016
Data Smoothing with Regression Analysis
Dependent Variable: Arithmetic Average Risk Premium
Independent Variable: Log of Average MVIC

Regression Output:

Constant	20.607%
Standard Error of Y Estimate	1.237%
R Squared	79%
No. of Observations	25
Degrees of Freedom	23
X Coefficient(s)	-3.226%
Standard Error of Coefficient	0.348%
t-Statistic	-9.26

$Smoothed\ Premium = 20.607\% - 3.226\% * Log(MVIC)$

Smoothed Premium vs. Arithmetic Premium

Portfolio Rank by Size	Average MVIC (in $millions)	Log of Average MVIC	Number as of 2016	Beta (Sum Beta) Since '63	Standard Deviation of Returns	Geometric Average Return	Arithmetic Average Return	Arithmetic Average Risk Premium	Smoothed Average Risk Premium	Average Debt/ MVIC
1	277,921	5.44	44	0.80	16.06%	9.62%	11.67%	5.21%	3.04%	19.20%
2	77,365	4.89	34	0.87	15.60%	9.14%	11.10%	4.65%	4.83%	25.42%
3	46,877	4.67	36	0.89	16.05%	9.44%	11.49%	5.03%	5.54%	26.98%
4	32,471	4.51	37	0.93	17.37%	10.52%	12.87%	6.41%	6.05%	27.25%
5	24,248	4.38	33	0.98	16.77%	10.81%	13.07%	6.61%	6.46%	26.77%
6	18,506	4.27	37	1.00	16.88%	10.33%	12.62%	6.16%	6.84%	25.93%
7	15,426	4.19	35	1.00	18.37%	11.27%	13.77%	7.31%	7.09%	24.67%
8	13,457	4.13	36	1.05	19.38%	11.41%	14.13%	7.67%	7.28%	24.38%
9	10,762	4.03	42	1.10	19.36%	10.46%	13.15%	6.69%	7.60%	24.70%
10	8,658	3.94	34	1.11	19.23%	12.65%	15.44%	8.98%	7.90%	24.25%
11	7,453	3.87	35	1.11	19.31%	12.09%	14.92%	8.47%	8.11%	25.47%
12	6,455	3.81	41	1.07	19.72%	11.65%	14.42%	7.96%	8.31%	25.08%
13	5,466	3.74	43	1.15	19.47%	11.42%	14.16%	7.71%	8.55%	25.01%
14	4,718	3.67	39	1.17	20.72%	11.94%	14.98%	8.52%	8.75%	23.74%
15	4,043	3.61	39	1.16	21.98%	12.07%	15.36%	8.90%	8.97%	24.73%
16	3,541	3.55	44	1.19	20.69%	12.73%	15.85%	9.39%	9.16%	23.40%
17	3,075	3.49	46	1.22	21.82%	12.57%	15.87%	9.41%	9.35%	24.28%
18	2,587	3.41	54	1.16	20.86%	13.37%	16.53%	10.08%	9.60%	23.60%
19	2,109	3.32	67	1.20	21.42%	11.01%	14.06%	7.60%	9.88%	23.92%
20	1,696	3.23	64	1.24	21.40%	12.29%	15.50%	9.04%	10.19%	24.98%
21	1,323	3.12	89	1.25	22.26%	12.12%	15.47%	9.01%	10.54%	24.16%
22	1,014	3.01	64	1.25	22.44%	13.73%	17.16%	10.70%	10.97%	24.04%
23	738	2.87	75	1.26	23.50%	13.63%	17.35%	10.89%	11.35%	23.89%
24	513	2.71	95	1.24	24.06%	14.57%	18.11%	11.65%	11.86%	23.83%
25	163	2.21	265	1.28	35.97%	18.30%	24.05%	17.59%	13.47%	22.92%
Large Stocks (Ibbotson SBBI data)						10.13%	11.48%	5.02%		
Small Stocks (Ibbotson SBBI data)						13.63%	16.27%	9.81%		
Long-Term Treasury Income (Ibbotson SBBI data)						6.43%	6.46%			

Companies Ranked by Total Assets

Historical Equity Risk Premium: Average Since 1963
Data for Year Ending December 31, 2016

Premia Over the Risk-Free Rate (RP_{m+s})

Equity Risk Premium Study: Data through December 31, 2016
Data Smoothing with Regression Analysis
Dependent Variable: Arithmetic Average Risk Premium
Independent Variable: Log of Total Assets

Portfolio Rank by Size	Average Total Assets (in $millions)	Log of Average Assets	Number as of 2016	Beta (Sum Beta) Since '63	Standard Deviation of Returns	Geometric Average Return	Arithmetic Average Return	Arithmetic Average Risk Premium	Smoothed Average Risk Premium	Average Debt/ MVIC
1	161,117	5.21	36	0.80	16.00%	9.62%	12.39%	5.94%	4.56%	29.09%
2	51,936	4.72	38	0.84	15.81%	9.14%	12.17%	5.71%	5.91%	34.00%
3	35,110	4.55	33	0.92	16.84%	9.44%	13.10%	6.64%	6.37%	31.15%
4	25,351	4.40	29	0.90	17.47%	10.52%	13.07%	6.61%	6.76%	31.09%
5	18,141	4.26	32	0.95	17.61%	10.81%	14.25%	7.79%	7.15%	30.07%
6	14,376	4.16	34	0.96	16.97%	10.33%	14.86%	8.40%	7.43%	28.55%
7	11,035	4.04	34	1.04	18.87%	11.27%	14.34%	7.88%	7.74%	27.67%
8	9,004	3.95	33	1.04	18.00%	11.41%	13.41%	6.95%	7.98%	27.85%
9	7,861	3.90	31	1.10	20.27%	10.46%	14.69%	8.23%	8.14%	28.11%
10	6,771	3.83	38	1.10	19.10%	12.65%	13.23%	6.77%	8.32%	27.35%
11	5,710	3.76	39	1.12	21.27%	12.09%	14.89%	8.43%	8.52%	27.88%
12	4,998	3.70	35	1.10	20.52%	11.65%	14.88%	8.42%	8.68%	26.33%
13	4,290	3.63	43	1.14	19.53%	11.42%	15.72%	9.27%	8.86%	26.18%
14	3,661	3.56	40	1.14	21.05%	11.94%	15.26%	8.80%	9.05%	25.17%
15	3,160	3.50	40	1.15	19.75%	12.07%	15.28%	8.82%	9.23%	25.77%
16	2,735	3.44	38	1.19	21.06%	12.73%	15.68%	9.22%	9.40%	24.55%
17	2,345	3.37	48	1.17	19.76%	12.57%	15.81%	9.35%	9.58%	24.95%
18	1,927	3.28	64	1.20	21.99%	13.37%	16.44%	9.99%	9.81%	25.03%
19	1,621	3.21	46	1.22	21.56%	11.01%	15.44%	8.98%	10.02%	25.22%
20	1,363	3.13	59	1.24	22.95%	12.29%	15.92%	9.47%	10.22%	24.46%
21	1,069	3.03	87	1.22	21.05%	12.12%	15.66%	9.20%	10.51%	23.56%
22	801	2.90	78	1.25	27.66%	13.73%	19.11%	12.66%	10.85%	23.24%
23	600	2.78	79	1.25	22.67%	13.63%	17.08%	10.62%	11.20%	22.19%
24	429	2.63	97	1.26	23.62%	14.57%	17.51%	11.05%	11.59%	21.56%
25	161	2.21	297	1.28	31.98%	18.30%	21.91%	15.45%	12.76%	19.50%
Large Stocks (Ibbotson SBBI data)						10.13%	11.48%	5.02%		
Small Stocks (Ibbotson SBBI data)						13.63%	16.27%	9.81%		
Long-Term Treasury Income (Ibbotson SBBI data)						6.43%	6.46%			

Regression Output:

Constant	18.786%
Standard Error of Y Estimate	0.977%
R Squared	80%
No. of Observations	25
Degrees of Freedom	23
X Coefficient(s)	-2.732%
Standard Error of Coefficient	0.288%
t-Statistic	-9.47

*Smoothed Premium = 18.786% − 2.732% * Log(Assets)*

Smoothed Premium vs. Arithmetic Premium

Sources of underlying data: 1.) © 201702 CRSP®, Center for Research in Security Prices. University of Chicago Booth School of Business used with permission. All rights reserved. 2.) Morningstar *Direct* database. Used with permission. All rights reserved. Calculations performed by Duff & Phelps LLC.

Companies Ranked by 5-Year Average EBITDA

Historical Equity Risk Premium: Average Since 1963

Data for Year Ending December 31, 2016

Premia Over the Risk-Free Rate (RP_{m+s})

Equity Risk Premium Study: Data through December 31, 2016
Data Smoothing with Regression Analysis
Dependent Variable: Arithmetic Average Risk Premium
Independent Variable: Log of Average EBITDA

Regression Output:

Constant	15.593%
Standard Error of Y Estimate	0.897%
R Squared	80%
No. of Observations	25
Degrees of Freedom	23
X Coefficient(s)	-2.478%
Standard Error of Coefficient	0.259%
t-Statistic	-9.55

$Smoothed\ Premium = 15.593\% - 2.478\% * Log(EBITDA)$

Smoothed Premium vs. Arithmetic Premium

(Y-axis: Premia Over the Risk-Free Rate; X-axis: Log of Average 5-Year Average EBITDA)

Portfolio Rank by Size	Average EBITDA (in $millions)	Log of Average EBITDA	Number as of 2016	Beta (Sum Beta) Since '63	Standard Deviation of Returns	Geometric Average Return	Arithmetic Average Return	Arithmetic Average Risk Premium	Smoothed Average Risk Premium	Average Debt/MVIC
1	22,452	4.35	37	0.79	15.87%	10.42%	12.49%	6.03%	4.81%	23.88%
2	6,905	3.84	33	0.84	15.86%	10.97%	13.10%	6.65%	6.08%	28.87%
3	4,343	3.64	34	0.88	16.09%	10.91%	13.07%	6.62%	6.58%	29.53%
4	3,136	3.50	34	0.90	16.68%	11.13%	13.36%	6.90%	6.93%	29.08%
5	2,192	3.34	36	0.98	18.43%	11.06%	13.63%	7.17%	7.31%	27.83%
6	1,632	3.21	36	0.93	16.83%	11.89%	14.25%	7.79%	7.63%	28.59%
7	1,338	3.13	30	1.03	18.95%	11.27%	13.85%	7.39%	7.85%	26.60%
8	1,133	3.05	35	1.06	17.65%	11.42%	13.88%	7.42%	8.02%	25.64%
9	934	2.97	34	1.11	19.87%	10.32%	13.04%	6.58%	8.23%	25.45%
10	799	2.90	41	1.08	18.65%	11.35%	13.92%	7.46%	8.40%	25.93%
11	667	2.82	37	1.02	18.54%	12.84%	15.56%	9.10%	8.59%	24.80%
12	578	2.76	36	1.09	20.97%	12.89%	16.11%	9.66%	8.75%	26.00%
13	478	2.68	41	1.07	20.44%	12.74%	15.80%	9.34%	8.95%	25.69%
14	411	2.61	36	1.16	20.64%	13.54%	16.63%	10.18%	9.12%	24.28%
15	371	2.57	40	1.14	20.95%	11.27%	14.38%	7.92%	9.22%	24.70%
16	327	2.51	43	1.18	20.41%	12.77%	15.81%	9.36%	9.36%	23.83%
17	287	2.46	32	1.19	21.53%	12.81%	16.05%	9.59%	9.50%	24.47%
18	253	2.40	44	1.20	22.47%	13.12%	16.51%	10.05%	9.64%	25.00%
19	211	2.32	57	1.23	20.42%	12.98%	16.07%	9.62%	9.84%	24.88%
20	164	2.22	79	1.23	21.45%	11.72%	14.93%	8.47%	10.10%	24.53%
21	125	2.10	88	1.20	21.80%	13.56%	16.86%	10.40%	10.40%	24.08%
22	94	1.97	62	1.22	21.58%	14.12%	17.45%	11.00%	10.70%	23.34%
23	74	1.87	70	1.23	22.57%	14.01%	17.60%	11.14%	10.96%	23.27%
24	51	1.71	109	1.25	22.94%	13.29%	16.87%	10.41%	11.36%	23.02%
25	17	1.23	304	1.30	30.97%	16.20%	21.13%	14.67%	12.55%	21.55%
Large Stocks (Ibbotson SBBI data)						10.13%	11.48%	5.02%		
Small Stocks (Ibbotson SBBI data)						13.63%	16.27%	9.81%		
Long-Term Treasury Income (Ibbotson SBBI data)						6.43%	6.46%			

Sources of underlying data: 1.) © 201702 CRSP®, Center for Research in Security Prices, University of Chicago Booth School of Business used with permission. All rights reserved. 2.) Morningstar *Direct* database. Used with permission. All rights reserved. Calculations performed by Duff & Phelps LLC.

Companies Ranked by Sales

Historical Equity Risk Premium: Average Since 1963
Data for Year Ending December 31, 2016

Premia Over the Risk-Free Rate (*RP* RP_{m+s})

Portfolio Rank by Size	Average Sales (in $millions)	Log of Average Sales	Number as of 2016	Beta (Sum Beta) Since '63	Standard Deviation of Returns	Geometric Average Return	Arithmetic Average Return	Arithmetic Average Risk Premium	Smoothed Average Risk Premium	Average Debt/ MVIC
1	123,791	5.09	38	0.89	16.81%	10.67%	12.94%	6.49%	5.36%	24.45%
2	38,382	4.58	32	0.96	18.35%	10.36%	12.85%	6.39%	6.60%	24.97%
3	22,044	4.34	35	1.00	17.42%	10.97%	13.32%	6.87%	7.19%	27.14%
4	17,114	4.23	33	0.98	16.45%	12.17%	14.47%	8.02%	7.46%	27.98%
5	13,286	4.12	33	1.01	18.08%	12.16%	14.72%	8.26%	7.73%	28.94%
6	10,376	4.02	35	1.02	18.18%	11.55%	14.06%	7.61%	7.99%	27.99%
7	8,400	3.92	36	1.08	19.45%	12.71%	15.51%	9.05%	8.21%	25.73%
8	6,977	3.84	36	1.04	18.83%	10.72%	13.31%	6.85%	8.41%	27.23%
9	5,938	3.77	36	1.10	20.48%	11.48%	14.36%	7.91%	8.58%	26.46%
10	5,106	3.71	35	1.11	20.48%	11.64%	14.57%	8.11%	8.74%	26.88%
11	4,435	3.65	42	1.11	19.08%	12.76%	15.59%	9.13%	8.89%	26.56%
12	3,740	3.57	37	1.11	21.25%	13.05%	16.23%	9.77%	9.07%	26.65%
13	3,184	3.50	44	1.20	20.79%	13.85%	17.12%	10.66%	9.24%	26.23%
14	2,771	3.44	41	1.11	21.04%	13.00%	16.13%	9.67%	9.39%	25.22%
15	2,509	3.40	40	1.12	19.17%	13.07%	15.84%	9.39%	9.49%	25.36%
16	2,276	3.36	37	1.15	20.79%	11.68%	14.74%	8.28%	9.60%	26.20%
17	1,980	3.30	49	1.15	21.46%	13.55%	16.84%	10.38%	9.75%	25.99%
18	1,670	3.22	56	1.19	21.66%	12.87%	16.18%	9.72%	9.93%	25.74%
19	1,412	3.15	52	1.23	21.11%	11.27%	14.36%	7.90%	10.10%	25.63%
20	1,181	3.07	58	1.18	22.12%	13.92%	17.34%	10.88%	10.29%	24.50%
21	969	2.99	57	1.18	22.57%	12.40%	15.76%	9.30%	10.50%	24.36%
22	797	2.90	73	1.25	22.56%	13.69%	17.19%	10.73%	10.71%	23.29%
23	589	2.77	102	1.23	23.79%	13.69%	17.42%	10.96%	11.03%	22.71%
24	407	2.61	115	1.24	23.86%	14.28%	17.81%	11.35%	11.42%	20.07%
25	129	2.11	276	1.26	29.91%	16.50%	21.11%	14.65%	12.64%	
Large Stocks (Ibbotson SBBI data)						10.13%	11.48%	5.02%		
Small Stocks (Ibbotson SBBI data)						13.63%	16.27%	9.81%		
Long-Term Treasury Income (Ibbotson SBBI data)						6.43%	6.46%			

Equity Risk Premium Study: Data through December 31, 2016
Data Smoothing with Regression Analysis
Dependent Variable: Arithmetic Average Risk Premium
Independent Variable: Log of Average Sales

Regression Output:

Constant	17.796%
Standard Error of Y Estimate	0.970%
R Squared	74%
No. of Observations	25
Degrees of Freedom	23
X Coefficient(s)	-2.442%
Standard Error of Coefficient	0.302%
t-Statistic	-8.09

*Smoothed Premium = 17.796% − 2.442% * Log(Sales)*

Smoothed Premium vs. Arithmetic Premium

2017 Valuation Handbook – U.S. Guide to Cost of Capital

Companies Ranked by Number of Employees

Historical Equity Risk Premium: Average Since 1963
Data for Year Ending December 31, 2016

Premia Over the Risk-Free Rate (RP_{m+s})

Exhibit A-8

Equity Risk Premium Study: Data through December 31, 2016
Data Smoothing with Regression Analysis
Dependent Variable: Arithmetic Average Risk Premium
Independent Variable: Log of Average Employees

Regression Output:

Constant	18.534%
Standard Error of Y Estimate	1.131%
R Squared	68%
No. of Observations	25
Degrees of Freedom	23
X Coefficient(s)	-2.368%
Standard Error of Coefficient	0.338%
t-Statistic	-7.01

*Smoothed Premium = 18.534% - 2.368% * Log(Employees)*

Smoothed Premium vs. Arithmetic Premium

Portfolio Rank by Size	Average Number of Employees	Log of Number of Employees	Number as of 2016	Beta (Sum Beta) Since '63	Standard Deviation of Returns	Geometric Average Return	Arithmetic Average Return	Arithmetic Average Risk Premium	Smoothed Average Risk Premium	Average Debt/MVIC
1	341,434	5.53	35	0.98	18.39%	10.10%	12.53%	6.07%	5.43%	24.64%
2	107,466	5.03	38	1.03	18.08%	10.68%	13.12%	6.66%	6.62%	23.58%
3	64,944	4.81	34	1.05	18.99%	10.75%	13.38%	6.92%	7.14%	24.54%
4	46,747	4.67	37	1.09	19.43%	11.75%	14.50%	8.04%	7.47%	23.46%
5	34,256	4.53	42	1.08	19.84%	12.13%	15.01%	8.55%	7.79%	25.04%
6	26,595	4.42	34	1.11	20.76%	12.01%	14.96%	8.50%	8.06%	23.95%
7	22,447	4.35	38	1.06	20.42%	10.83%	13.67%	7.22%	8.23%	24.90%
8	18,590	4.27	44	1.07	18.17%	11.10%	13.62%	7.16%	8.42%	25.25%
9	15,489	4.19	37	1.15	21.30%	12.50%	15.68%	9.23%	8.61%	27.19%
10	13,344	4.13	39	1.13	21.27%	12.84%	15.93%	9.47%	8.76%	25.40%
11	11,841	4.07	41	1.17	21.04%	12.94%	16.07%	9.61%	8.89%	25.67%
12	10,389	4.02	36	1.11	20.83%	13.23%	16.32%	9.86%	9.02%	25.43%
13	9,004	3.95	49	1.13	20.13%	12.20%	15.20%	8.74%	9.17%	26.01%
14	7,588	3.88	48	1.14	19.27%	10.73%	13.49%	7.03%	9.34%	26.19%
15	6,511	3.81	57	1.17	21.33%	12.99%	16.23%	9.77%	9.50%	26.97%
16	5,710	3.76	47	1.12	19.98%	12.04%	14.93%	8.48%	9.64%	26.51%
17	4,908	3.69	51	1.20	20.84%	11.46%	14.51%	8.05%	9.79%	26.22%
18	4,194	3.62	47	1.19	20.62%	13.56%	16.76%	10.30%	9.95%	26.59%
19	3,507	3.54	60	1.16	21.68%	12.93%	16.15%	9.70%	10.14%	25.14%
20	2,908	3.46	65	1.18	21.29%	11.58%	14.70%	8.24%	10.33%	24.56%
21	2,328	3.37	70	1.18	22.59%	13.99%	17.58%	11.12%	10.56%	24.87%
22	1,797	3.25	68	1.20	24.13%	15.63%	19.12%	12.66%	10.83%	24.97%
23	1,281	3.11	91	1.22	28.43%	15.47%	19.71%	13.25%	11.17%	23.95%
24	871	2.94	84	1.21	23.44%	14.83%	18.63%	12.18%	11.57%	23.31%
25	305	2.48	236	1.22	24.47%	14.79%	18.75%	12.29%	12.65%	20.33%
Large Stocks (Ibbotson SBBI data)						10.13%	11.48%	5.02%		
Small Stocks (Ibbotson SBBI data)						13.63%	16.27%	9.81%		
Long-Term Treasury Income (Ibbotson SBBI data)						6.43%	6.46%			

Risk Premium Report – Exhibits B-1 through B-8 Premia Over CAPM (RP_s)

Premia over CAPM (commonly referred to as "size premia") represent the difference between historical (observed) excess return and the excess return predicted by the capital asset pricing model (CAPM). Size premia can be added to cost of capital estimation models as an adjustment for the additional risk of small companies relative to large companies.

The B Exhibits are used in the following method to estimate a cost of equity capital:

- CAPM
- Build-up 2

Size Measures:

B-1: Market value of equity

B-2: Book value of equity

B-3: 5-year average net income

B-4: Market value of invested capital (MVIC)

B-5: Total assets

B-6: 5-year average EBITDA

B-7: Sales

B-8: Number of employees

Companies Ranked by Market Value of Equity

Premia over CAPM (Size Premia, RP_s)

Historical Equity Risk Premium: Average Since 1963

Data for Year Ending December 31, 2016

Equity Risk Premium Study: Data through December 31, 2016

Data Smoothing with Regression Analysis

Dependent Variable: Premium over CAPM

Independent Variable: Log of Average Market Value of Equity

Portfolio Rank by Size	Average Mkt. Value (in $millions)	Log of Average Mkt. Value	Beta (Sum Beta) Since '63	Arithmetic Average Return	Arithmetic Average Risk Premium	Indicated CAPM Premium	Premium over CAPM	Smoothed Premium over CAPM
1	238,299	5.38	0.83	11.66%	5.20%	4.15%	1.05%	-1.78%
2	60,613	4.78	0.96	10.64%	4.18%	4.84%	-0.65%	-0.16%
3	35,630	4.55	0.92	11.70%	5.24%	4.63%	0.61%	0.47%
4	23,756	4.38	0.93	12.50%	6.05%	4.68%	1.37%	0.95%
5	17,471	4.24	0.98	12.39%	5.93%	4.94%	0.99%	1.32%
6	13,871	4.14	1.02	12.67%	6.21%	5.14%	1.07%	1.59%
7	11,594	4.06	1.01	13.30%	6.84%	5.06%	1.77%	1.80%
8	9,463	3.98	1.07	14.56%	8.10%	5.37%	2.73%	2.04%
9	7,822	3.89	1.09	15.20%	8.74%	5.49%	3.25%	2.27%
10	6,482	3.81	1.12	14.28%	7.82%	5.62%	2.21%	2.49%
11	5,637	3.75	1.09	13.93%	7.47%	5.47%	1.99%	2.66%
12	4,791	3.68	1.11	13.90%	7.44%	5.57%	1.87%	2.85%
13	3,915	3.59	1.12	14.24%	7.78%	5.61%	2.17%	3.09%
14	3,329	3.52	1.14	14.74%	8.28%	5.74%	2.54%	3.28%
15	2,897	3.46	1.14	16.52%	10.06%	5.70%	4.36%	3.45%
16	2,508	3.40	1.16	16.03%	9.57%	5.83%	3.75%	3.62%
17	2,130	3.33	1.20	15.91%	9.45%	6.01%	3.43%	3.81%
18	1,842	3.27	1.21	14.52%	8.06%	6.06%	2.01%	3.99%
19	1,584	3.20	1.21	15.95%	9.49%	6.08%	3.40%	4.17%
20	1,313	3.12	1.19	15.26%	8.80%	5.98%	2.82%	4.39%
21	1,023	3.01	1.24	16.47%	10.01%	6.21%	3.81%	4.69%
22	731	2.86	1.24	16.17%	9.71%	6.23%	3.48%	5.08%
23	532	2.73	1.25	19.23%	12.77%	6.27%	6.49%	5.46%
24	370	2.57	1.24	19.35%	12.89%	6.22%	6.66%	5.89%
25	121	2.08	1.29	24.39%	17.94%	6.47%	11.47%	7.22%

Large Stocks (Ibbotson SBBI data)				11.48%	5.02%			
Small Stocks (Ibbotson SBBI data)				16.27%	9.81%			
Long-Term Treasury Income (Ibbotson SBBI data)				6.46%				

Regression Output:

Constant	12.911%
Standard Error of Y Estimate	1.386%
R Squared	69%
No. of Observations	25
Degrees of Freedom	23
X Coefficient(s)	-2.733%
Standard Error of Coefficient	0.386%
t-Statistic	-7.09

*Smoothed Premium = 12.911% - 2.733% * Log(Market Value)*

Smoothed Premium vs. Unadjusted Premium

(y-axis: Premia over CAPM, -4% to 10%; x-axis: Log of Average Market Value of Equity, 0.0 to 6.0)

2017 Valuation Handbook – U.S. Guide to Cost of Capital

Companies Ranked by Book Value of Equity

Exhibit B-2

Historical Equity Risk Premium: Average Since 1963
Data for Year Ending December 31, 2016

Premia over CAPM (Size Premia, RP_s)

Equity Risk Premium Study: Data through December 31, 2016
Data Smoothing with Regression Analysis
Dependent Variable: Premium over CAPM
Independent Variable: Log of Average Book Value of Equity

Portfolio Rank by Size	Average Book Val. (in $millions)	Log of Average Book Val.	Beta (Sum Beta) Since '63	Arithmetic Average Return	Arithmetic Average Risk Premium	Indicated CAPM Premium	Premium over CAPM	Smoothed Premium over CAPM
1	67,532	4.83	0.78	12.78%	6.32%	3.93%	2.39%	0.98%
2	21,719	4.34	0.84	11.91%	5.45%	4.23%	1.23%	1.68%
3	14,074	4.15	0.92	12.93%	6.47%	4.64%	1.83%	1.95%
4	9,200	3.96	0.90	14.32%	7.86%	4.52%	3.35%	2.22%
5	6,875	3.84	0.98	13.42%	6.96%	4.94%	2.02%	2.40%
6	5,488	3.74	1.01	14.09%	7.63%	5.05%	2.58%	2.54%
7	4,590	3.66	1.04	14.90%	8.44%	5.21%	3.22%	2.65%
8	3,716	3.57	1.07	13.01%	6.55%	5.38%	1.17%	2.78%
9	3,112	3.49	1.12	14.01%	7.55%	5.64%	1.91%	2.89%
10	2,586	3.41	1.07	14.45%	7.99%	5.39%	2.60%	3.01%
11	2,266	3.36	1.08	14.48%	8.02%	5.43%	2.59%	3.09%
12	2,012	3.30	1.10	14.39%	7.93%	5.55%	2.39%	3.16%
13	1,751	3.24	1.07	16.25%	9.79%	5.36%	4.44%	3.25%
14	1,500	3.18	1.17	14.57%	8.11%	5.86%	2.25%	3.34%
15	1,303	3.11	1.12	15.60%	9.15%	5.63%	3.52%	3.43%
16	1,174	3.07	1.17	16.63%	10.17%	5.88%	4.29%	3.50%
17	1,030	3.01	1.18	16.28%	9.82%	5.93%	3.89%	3.58%
18	861	2.93	1.17	16.50%	10.04%	5.86%	4.18%	3.69%
19	711	2.85	1.26	15.17%	8.72%	6.35%	2.36%	3.81%
20	577	2.76	1.25	15.22%	8.76%	6.25%	2.51%	3.94%
21	479	2.68	1.22	19.29%	12.84%	6.14%	6.70%	4.05%
22	385	2.59	1.21	15.90%	9.44%	6.07%	3.37%	4.19%
23	303	2.48	1.26	17.21%	10.76%	6.31%	4.44%	4.34%
24	207	2.32	1.27	17.89%	11.43%	6.37%	5.07%	4.57%
25	76	1.88	1.25	18.68%	12.22%	6.29%	5.93%	5.19%

Large Stocks (Ibbotson SBBI data)				11.48%	5.02%			
Small Stocks (Ibbotson SBBI data)				16.27%	9.81%			
Long-Term Treasury Income (Ibbotson SBBI data)				6.46%				

Regression Output:

Constant	7.887%
Standard Error of Y Estimate	1.036%
R Squared	47%
No. of Observations	25
Degrees of Freedom	23
X Coefficient(s)	-1.430%
Standard Error of Coefficient	0.318%
t-Statistic	-4.50

*Smoothed Premium = 7.887% – 1.430% * Log(Book Value)*

Smoothed Premium vs. Unadjusted Premium

(y-axis: Premia over CAPM; x-axis: Log of Average Book Value of Equity)

2017 Valuation Handbook – U.S. Guide to Cost of Capital

Companies Ranked by 5-Year Average Net Income

Exhibit B-3

Historical Equity Risk Premium: Average Since 1963
Data for Year Ending December 31, 2016

Equity Risk Premium Study: Data through December 31, 2016
Data Smoothing with Regression Analysis
Dependent Variable: Premium over CAPM
Independent Variable: Log of Average Net Income

Portfolio Rank by Size	Average Net Inc. (in $millions)	Log of Average Net Inc.	Beta (Sum Beta) Since '63	Arithmetic Average Return	Arithmetic Average Risk Premium	Indicated CAPM Premium	Premium over CAPM	Smoothed Premium over CAPM
1	10,101	4.00	0.77	12.92%	6.46%	3.88%	2.58%	0.54%
2	2,747	3.44	0.87	12.51%	6.05%	4.38%	1.66%	1.48%
3	1,735	3.24	0.85	13.48%	7.02%	4.29%	2.73%	1.81%
4	1,183	3.07	0.90	13.42%	6.96%	4.53%	2.43%	2.08%
5	853	2.93	0.96	12.81%	6.35%	4.80%	1.55%	2.37%
6	627	2.80	0.99	13.85%	7.39%	4.96%	2.43%	2.53%
7	516	2.71	1.04	13.42%	6.96%	5.23%	1.73%	2.67%
8	408	2.61	1.09	14.40%	7.94%	5.49%	2.45%	2.84%
9	340	2.53	1.05	13.54%	7.08%	5.27%	1.81%	2.97%
10	295	2.47	1.06	14.50%	8.04%	5.32%	2.72%	3.07%
11	244	2.39	1.09	14.42%	7.96%	5.48%	2.48%	3.21%
12	213	2.33	1.08	15.98%	9.53%	5.42%	4.11%	3.31%
13	185	2.27	1.07	15.87%	9.41%	5.37%	4.04%	3.41%
14	160	2.20	1.14	14.36%	7.90%	5.71%	2.19%	3.51%
15	141	2.15	1.12	15.67%	9.21%	5.60%	3.61%	3.60%
16	119	2.07	1.13	16.29%	9.83%	5.67%	4.16%	3.73%
17	100	2.00	1.18	15.22%	8.76%	5.95%	2.81%	3.85%
18	84	1.92	1.20	16.95%	10.49%	6.01%	4.48%	3.97%
19	67	1.82	1.24	15.57%	9.11%	6.22%	2.89%	4.14%
20	52	1.72	1.23	17.06%	10.60%	6.17%	4.43%	4.37%
21	42	1.62	1.22	16.21%	9.75%	6.11%	3.64%	4.47%
22	34	1.53	1.21	16.62%	10.16%	6.06%	4.10%	4.62%
23	24	1.39	1.25	17.32%	10.87%	6.27%	4.60%	4.86%
24	15	1.18	1.26	19.27%	12.81%	6.33%	6.48%	5.20%
25	5	0.68	1.31	21.44%	14.98%	6.60%	8.39%	6.02%

Large Stocks (Ibbotson SBBI data)				11.48%	5.02%			
Small Stocks (Ibbotson SBBI data)				16.27%	9.81%			
Long-Term Treasury Income (Ibbotson SBBI data)				6.46%				

Regression Output:

Constant	7.144%
Standard Error of Y Estimate	0.999%
R Squared	61%
No. of Observations	25
Degrees of Freedom	23
X Coefficient(s)	-1.648%
Standard Error of Coefficient	0.274%
t-Statistic	-6.02

$Smoothed\ Premium = 7.144\% - 1.648\% * Log(Net\ Income)$

Smoothed Premium vs. Unadjusted Premium

x-axis: Log of Average 5-Year Average Net Income (0.0 – 6.0)
y-axis: Premia over CAPM (-2% – 10%)

Premia over CAPM (Size Premia, RP_s)

Companies Ranked by Market Value of Invested Capital

Historical Equity Risk Premium: Average Since 1963
Data for Year Ending December 31, 2016

Equity Risk Premium Study: Data through December 31, 2016
Data Smoothing with Regression Analysis
Dependent Variable: Premium over CAPM
Independent Variable: Log of Average MVIC

Portfolio Rank by Size	Average MVIC (in $millions)	Log of Average MVIC	Beta (Sum Beta) Since '63	Arithmetic Average Return	Arithmetic Average Risk Premium	Indicated CAPM Premium	Premium over CAPM	Smoothed Premium over CAPM
1	277,921	5.44	0.80	11.67%	5.21%	4.03%	1.18%	-1.02%
2	77,365	4.89	0.87	11.10%	4.65%	4.37%	0.28%	0.28%
3	46,877	4.67	0.89	11.49%	5.03%	4.49%	0.54%	0.79%
4	32,471	4.51	0.93	12.87%	6.41%	4.67%	1.74%	1.16%
5	24,248	4.38	0.98	13.07%	6.61%	4.94%	1.67%	1.45%
6	18,506	4.27	1.00	12.62%	6.16%	5.03%	1.13%	1.73%
7	15,426	4.19	1.00	13.77%	7.31%	5.02%	2.29%	1.91%
8	13,457	4.13	1.05	14.13%	7.67%	5.25%	2.41%	2.05%
9	10,762	4.03	1.10	13.15%	6.69%	5.52%	1.17%	2.28%
10	8,658	3.94	1.11	15.44%	8.98%	5.57%	3.41%	2.50%
11	7,453	3.87	1.11	14.92%	8.47%	5.58%	2.88%	2.65%
12	6,455	3.81	1.07	14.42%	7.96%	5.38%	2.58%	2.79%
13	5,466	3.74	1.15	14.16%	7.71%	5.76%	1.94%	2.96%
14	4,718	3.67	1.17	14.98%	8.52%	5.87%	2.65%	3.11%
15	4,043	3.61	1.16	15.36%	8.90%	5.82%	3.08%	3.27%
16	3,541	3.55	1.19	15.85%	9.39%	5.98%	3.41%	3.40%
17	3,075	3.49	1.22	15.87%	9.41%	6.15%	3.27%	3.55%
18	2,587	3.41	1.16	16.53%	10.08%	5.83%	4.25%	3.72%
19	2,109	3.32	1.20	14.06%	7.60%	6.02%	1.58%	3.93%
20	1,696	3.23	1.24	15.50%	9.04%	6.23%	2.81%	4.15%
21	1,323	3.12	1.25	15.47%	9.01%	6.29%	2.72%	4.40%
22	1,014	3.01	1.25	17.16%	10.70%	6.26%	4.45%	4.67%
23	738	2.87	1.26	17.35%	10.89%	6.32%	4.56%	4.99%
24	513	2.71	1.24	18.11%	11.65%	6.23%	5.42%	5.36%
25	163	2.21	1.28	24.05%	17.59%	6.42%	11.17%	6.52%

Large Stocks (Ibbotson SBBI data)				11.48%	5.02%			
Small Stocks (Ibbotson SBBI data)				16.27%	9.81%			
Long-Term Treasury Income (Ibbotson SBBI data)				6.46%				

Regression Output:

Constant	11.680%
Standard Error of Y Estimate	1.345%
R Squared	62%
No. of Observations	25
Degrees of Freedom	23
X Coefficient(s)	-2.332%
Standard Error of Coefficient	0.379%
t-Statistic	-6.16

Smoothed Premium = 11.680% − 2.332% * Log(MVIC)

Smoothed Premium vs. Unadjusted Premium

(x-axis: Log of Average Market Value of Invested Capital, 0.0 to 6.0; y-axis: Premia over CAPM, -2% to 10%)

Premia over CAPM (Size Premia, RP_s)

Historical Equity Risk Premium: Average Since 1963
Data for Year Ending December 31, 2016

Equity Risk Premium Study: Data through December 31, 2016
Data Smoothing with Regression Analysis
Dependent Variable: Premium over CAPM
Independent Variable: Log of Average Total Assets

Regression Output:

Constant	9.744%
Standard Error of Y Estimate	1.084%
R Squared	57%
No. of Observations	25
Degrees of Freedom	23
X Coefficient(s)	-1.771%
Standard Error of Coefficient	0.320%
t-Statistic	-5.53

Smoothed Premium = 9.744% - 1.771% * Log(Total Assets)

Smoothed Premium vs. Unadjusted Premium

Portfolio Rank by Size	Average Total Assets (in $millions)	Log of Average Assets	Beta (Sum Beta) Since '63	Arithmetic Average Return	Arithmetic Average Risk Premium	Indicated CAPM Premium	Premium over CAPM	Smoothed Premium over CAPM
1	161,117	5.21	0.80	12.39%	5.94%	4.02%	1.92%	0.52%
2	51,936	4.72	0.84	12.17%	5.71%	4.20%	1.52%	1.39%
3	35,110	4.55	0.92	13.10%	6.64%	4.63%	2.01%	1.69%
4	25,351	4.40	0.90	13.07%	6.61%	4.54%	2.08%	1.95%
5	18,141	4.26	0.95	14.25%	7.79%	4.77%	3.02%	2.20%
6	14,376	4.16	0.96	14.86%	8.40%	4.81%	3.59%	2.38%
7	11,035	4.04	1.04	14.34%	7.88%	5.24%	2.64%	2.59%
8	9,004	3.95	1.04	13.41%	6.95%	5.24%	1.71%	2.74%
9	7,861	3.90	1.10	14.69%	8.23%	5.52%	2.71%	2.85%
10	6,771	3.83	1.10	13.23%	6.77%	5.52%	1.25%	2.96%
11	5,710	3.76	1.12	14.89%	8.43%	5.65%	2.78%	3.09%
12	4,998	3.70	1.10	14.88%	8.42%	5.51%	2.91%	3.19%
13	4,290	3.63	1.14	15.72%	9.27%	5.73%	3.53%	3.31%
14	3,661	3.56	1.14	15.26%	8.80%	5.71%	3.09%	3.43%
15	3,160	3.50	1.15	15.28%	8.82%	5.76%	3.06%	3.55%
16	2,735	3.44	1.19	15.68%	9.22%	5.97%	3.25%	3.66%
17	2,345	3.37	1.17	15.81%	9.35%	5.86%	3.50%	3.78%
18	1,927	3.28	1.20	16.44%	9.99%	6.03%	3.95%	3.93%
19	1,621	3.21	1.22	15.44%	8.98%	6.13%	2.85%	4.06%
20	1,363	3.13	1.24	15.92%	9.47%	6.23%	3.24%	4.19%
21	1,069	3.03	1.22	15.66%	9.20%	6.14%	3.06%	4.38%
22	801	2.90	1.25	19.11%	12.66%	6.25%	6.40%	4.60%
23	600	2.78	1.25	17.08%	10.62%	6.26%	4.36%	4.82%
24	429	2.63	1.26	17.51%	11.05%	6.32%	4.73%	5.08%
25	161	2.21	1.28	21.91%	15.45%	6.41%	9.05%	5.83%

Large Stocks (Ibbotson SBBI data)				11.48%	5.02%			
Small Stocks (Ibbotson SBBI data)				16.27%	9.81%			
Long-Term Treasury Income (Ibbotson SBBI data)				6.46%				

Companies Ranked by 5-Year Average EBITDA

Historical Equity Risk Premium: Average Since 1963

Data for Year Ending December 31, 2016

Premia over CAPM (Size Premia, RP_s)

Equity Risk Premium Study: Data through December 31, 2016

Data Smoothing with Regression Analysis

Dependent Variable: Premium over CAPM

Independent Variable: Log of Average EBITDA

Portfolio Rank by Size	Average EBITDA (in $millions)	Log of Average EBITDA	Beta (Sum Beta) Since '63	Arithmetic Average Return	Arithmetic Average Risk Premium	Indicated CAPM Premium	Premium over CAPM	Smoothed Premium over CAPM
1	22,452	4.35	0.79	12.49%	6.03%	3.99%	2.05%	0.87%
2	6,905	3.84	0.84	13.10%	6.65%	4.23%	2.42%	1.65%
3	4,343	3.64	0.88	13.07%	6.62%	4.44%	2.18%	1.96%
4	3,136	3.50	0.90	13.36%	6.90%	4.54%	2.35%	2.17%
5	2,192	3.34	0.98	13.63%	7.17%	4.94%	2.23%	2.41%
6	1,632	3.21	0.93	14.25%	7.79%	4.65%	3.14%	2.60%
7	1,338	3.13	1.03	13.85%	7.39%	5.18%	2.21%	2.74%
8	1,133	3.05	1.06	13.88%	7.42%	5.32%	2.10%	2.85%
9	934	2.97	1.11	13.04%	6.58%	5.59%	0.99%	2.97%
10	799	2.90	1.08	13.92%	7.46%	5.43%	2.03%	3.08%
11	667	2.82	1.02	15.56%	9.10%	5.13%	3.98%	3.20%
12	578	2.76	1.09	16.11%	9.66%	5.47%	4.19%	3.29%
13	478	2.68	1.07	15.80%	9.34%	5.36%	3.97%	3.42%
14	411	2.61	1.16	16.63%	10.18%	5.81%	4.36%	3.52%
15	371	2.57	1.14	14.38%	7.92%	5.73%	2.19%	3.59%
16	327	2.51	1.18	15.81%	9.36%	5.91%	3.45%	3.67%
17	287	2.46	1.19	16.05%	9.59%	5.98%	3.61%	3.76%
18	253	2.40	1.20	16.51%	10.05%	6.02%	4.03%	3.84%
19	211	2.32	1.23	16.07%	9.62%	6.16%	3.46%	3.96%
20	164	2.22	1.23	14.93%	8.47%	6.20%	2.27%	4.13%
21	125	2.10	1.20	16.86%	10.40%	6.04%	4.36%	4.31%
22	94	1.97	1.22	17.45%	11.00%	6.15%	4.84%	4.49%
23	74	1.87	1.23	17.60%	11.14%	6.15%	4.99%	4.66%
24	51	1.71	1.25	16.87%	10.41%	6.27%	4.14%	4.90%
25	17	1.23	1.30	21.13%	14.67%	6.55%	8.12%	5.63%

Large Stocks (Ibbotson SBBI data)				11.48%	5.02%			
Small Stocks (Ibbotson SBBI data)				16.27%	9.81%			
Long-Term Treasury Income (Ibbotson SBBI data)				6.46%				

Regression Output:

Constant	7.506%
Standard Error of Y Estimate	1.009%
R Squared	54%
No. of Observations	25
Degrees of Freedom	23
X Coefficient(s)	-1.526%
Standard Error of Coefficient	0.292%
t-Statistic	-5.23

*Smoothed Premium = 7.506% - 1.526% * Log(EBITDA)*

Smoothed Premium vs. Unadjusted Premium

Historical Equity Risk Premium: Average Since 1963
Data for Year Ending December 31, 2016

Equity Risk Premium Study: Data through December 31, 2016
Data Smoothing with Regression Analysis
Dependent Variable: Premium over CAPM
Independent Variable: Log of Average Sales

Portfolio Rank by Size	Average Sales (in $millions)	Log of Average Sales	Beta (Sum Beta) Since '63	Arithmetic Average Return	Arithmetic Average Risk Premium	Indicated CAPM Premium	Premium over CAPM	Smoothed Premium over CAPM
1	123,791	5.09	0.89	12.94%	6.49%	4.45%	2.03%	0.88%
2	38,382	4.58	0.96	12.85%	6.39%	4.83%	1.56%	1.75%
3	22,044	4.34	1.00	13.32%	6.87%	5.00%	1.86%	2.17%
4	17,114	4.23	0.98	14.47%	8.02%	4.94%	3.08%	2.35%
5	13,286	4.12	1.01	14.72%	8.26%	5.08%	3.18%	2.54%
6	10,376	4.02	1.02	14.06%	7.61%	5.10%	2.50%	2.73%
7	8,400	3.92	1.08	15.51%	9.05%	5.40%	3.65%	2.88%
8	6,977	3.84	1.04	13.31%	6.85%	5.21%	1.64%	3.02%
9	5,938	3.77	1.10	14.36%	7.91%	5.54%	2.37%	3.14%
10	5,106	3.71	1.11	14.57%	8.11%	5.57%	2.54%	3.25%
11	4,435	3.65	1.11	15.59%	9.13%	5.57%	3.56%	3.36%
12	3,740	3.57	1.11	16.23%	9.77%	5.58%	4.19%	3.48%
13	3,184	3.50	1.20	17.12%	10.66%	6.03%	4.63%	3.60%
14	2,771	3.44	1.11	16.13%	9.67%	5.59%	4.08%	3.71%
15	2,509	3.40	1.12	15.84%	9.39%	5.63%	3.75%	3.78%
16	2,276	3.36	1.15	14.74%	8.28%	5.78%	2.50%	3.85%
17	1,980	3.30	1.15	16.84%	10.38%	5.78%	4.60%	3.96%
18	1,670	3.22	1.19	16.18%	9.72%	5.97%	3.75%	4.08%
19	1,412	3.15	1.23	14.36%	7.90%	6.17%	1.74%	4.21%
20	1,181	3.07	1.18	17.34%	10.88%	5.93%	4.95%	4.34%
21	969	2.99	1.18	15.76%	9.30%	5.95%	3.35%	4.49%
22	797	2.90	1.25	17.19%	10.73%	6.28%	4.45%	4.63%
23	589	2.77	1.23	17.42%	10.96%	6.20%	4.77%	4.86%
24	407	2.61	1.24	17.81%	11.35%	6.21%	5.14%	5.13%
25	129	2.11	1.26	21.11%	14.65%	6.33%	8.32%	5.99%

Large Stocks (Ibbotson SBBI data)				11.48%	5.02%			
Small Stocks (Ibbotson SBBI data)				16.27%	9.81%			
Long-Term Treasury Income (Ibbotson SBBI data)				6.46%				

Regression Output:

Constant	9.598%
Standard Error of Y Estimate	1.009%
R Squared	56%
No. of Observations	25
Degrees of Freedom	23
X Coefficient(s)	-1.711%
Standard Error of Coefficient	0.314%
t-Statistic	-5.46

*Smoothed Premium = 9.598% − 1.711% * Log(Sales)*

Smoothed Premium vs. Unadjusted Premium

(y-axis: Premia over CAPM; x-axis: Log of Average Sales)

Companies Ranked by Number of Employees

Historical Equity Risk Premium: Average Since 1963
Data for Year Ending December 31, 2016

Premia over CAPM (Size Premia, RP_s)

Equity Risk Premium Study: Data through December 31, 2016
Data Smoothing with Regression Analysis
Dependent Variable: Premium over CAPM
Independent Variable: Log of Average Employees

Portfolio Rank by Size	Average Number of Employees	Log of Average Employees	Beta (Sum Beta) Since '63	Arithmetic Average Return	Arithmetic Average Risk Premium	Indicated CAPM Premium	Premium over CAPM	Smoothed Premium over CAPM
1	341,434	5.53	0.98	12.53%	6.07%	4.90%	1.17%	0.43%
2	107,466	5.03	1.03	13.12%	6.66%	5.15%	1.51%	1.40%
3	64,944	4.81	1.05	13.38%	6.92%	5.29%	1.63%	1.82%
4	46,747	4.67	1.09	14.50%	8.04%	5.46%	2.58%	2.09%
5	34,256	4.53	1.08	15.01%	8.55%	5.42%	3.12%	2.35%
6	26,595	4.42	1.11	14.96%	8.50%	5.59%	2.92%	2.57%
7	22,447	4.35	1.06	13.67%	7.22%	5.35%	1.87%	2.71%
8	18,590	4.27	1.07	13.62%	7.16%	5.37%	1.79%	2.86%
9	15,489	4.19	1.15	15.68%	9.23%	5.76%	3.47%	3.02%
10	13,344	4.13	1.13	15.93%	9.47%	5.66%	3.81%	3.14%
11	11,841	4.07	1.17	16.07%	9.61%	5.90%	3.71%	3.24%
12	10,389	4.02	1.11	16.32%	9.86%	5.56%	4.30%	3.35%
13	9,004	3.95	1.13	15.20%	8.74%	5.69%	3.05%	3.47%
14	7,588	3.88	1.14	13.49%	7.03%	5.70%	1.33%	3.61%
15	6,511	3.81	1.17	16.23%	9.77%	5.89%	3.88%	3.74%
16	5,710	3.76	1.12	14.93%	8.48%	5.62%	2.85%	3.85%
17	4,908	3.69	1.20	14.51%	8.05%	6.01%	2.04%	3.98%
18	4,194	3.62	1.19	16.76%	10.30%	5.99%	4.32%	4.11%
19	3,507	3.54	1.16	16.15%	9.70%	5.82%	3.87%	4.26%
20	2,908	3.46	1.18	14.70%	8.24%	5.94%	2.30%	4.42%
21	2,328	3.37	1.18	17.58%	11.12%	5.95%	5.17%	4.60%
22	1,797	3.25	1.20	19.12%	12.66%	6.04%	6.62%	4.82%
23	1,281	3.11	1.22	19.71%	13.25%	6.13%	7.12%	5.10%
24	871	2.94	1.21	18.63%	12.18%	6.10%	6.08%	5.42%
25	305	2.48	1.22	18.75%	12.29%	6.15%	6.14%	6.30%

Large Stocks (Ibbotson SBBI data)				11.48%	5.02%			
Small Stocks (Ibbotson SBBI data)				16.27%	9.81%			
Long-Term Treasury Income (Ibbotson SBBI data)				6.46%				

Regression Output:

Constant	11.083%
Standard Error of Y Estimate	1.105%
R Squared	60%
No. of Observations	25
Degrees of Freedom	23
X Coefficient(s)	-1.925%
Standard Error of Coefficient	0.330%
t-Statistic	-5.83

*Smoothed Premium = 11.083% − 1.925% * Log(Employees)*

Smoothed Premium vs. Unadjusted Premium

Premia over CAPM (vertical axis: −2%, 0%, 2%, 4%, 6%, 8%, 10%)
Log of Average Number of Employees (horizontal axis: 0.0, 1.0, 2.0, 3.0, 4.0, 5.0, 6.0)

2017 Valuation Handbook – U.S. Guide to Cost of Capital

Risk Premium Report – Exhibits C-1 through C-8

The "C" exhibits provide information about the companies that comprise the 25 portfolios that are used to create the various risk premia and size premia published in the Report. The "C" exhibits provide the following three comparative risk characteristics (i.e., "accounting-based fundamental risk measures") for each of the 25 portfolios and for each of the 8 size measures of size, each of which can be useful in assessing how "alike or different" the subject company is to the companies that make up the respective guideline portfolio:

- Operating Margin
- Coefficient of variation in operating income margin
- Coefficient of variation in return on book equity

The C Exhibits are used in the following method to estimate an unlevered cost of equity capital:

- Build-up 1-Unlevered

Size Measures:

     C-1: Market value of equity

     C-2: Book value of equity

     C-3: 5-year average net income

     C-4: Market value of invested capital (MVIC)

     C-5: Total assets

     C-6: 5-year average EBITDA

     C-7: Sales

     C-8: Number of employees

Exhibit C-1

Companies Ranked by Market Value of Equity
Data for Year Ending December 31, 2016

Comparative Risk Characteristics

Data Smoothing with Regression Analysis
Dependent Variable: Average Unlevered Risk Premium
Independent Variable: Log of Average Market Value of Equity

Constant	19.122%
X Coefficient(s)	-3.230%

*Smoothed Unlevered Premium = 19.122% - 3.230% * Log(Market Value)*

Portfolio Rank by Size	Average Mkt. Value (in $millions)	Log of Average Mkt. Value	Number of Firms	Arithmetic Average Risk Premium	Average Debt to MVIC	Average Debt to Market Value of Equity	Average Unlevered Risk Premium[1]	Smoothed Average Unlevered Risk Premium	Beta (Sum Beta) Since '63	Average Unlevered Beta	Average Operating Margin	Average CV(Operating Margin)	Average CV(ROE)
1	238,299	5.38	45	5.20%	14.59%	17.09%	4.67%	1.75%	0.83	0.72	17.01%	9.72%	18.30%
2	60,613	4.78	36	4.18%	19.02%	23.49%	3.36%	3.67%	0.96	0.80	13.84%	11.19%	22.72%
3	35,630	4.55	38	5.24%	20.92%	26.46%	4.38%	4.42%	0.92	0.75	13.54%	11.68%	21.91%
4	23,756	4.38	39	6.05%	23.13%	30.10%	5.08%	4.99%	0.93	0.74	13.21%	12.76%	23.66%
5	17,471	4.24	35	5.93%	23.48%	30.69%	4.89%	5.42%	0.98	0.78	12.78%	12.90%	23.44%
6	13,871	4.14	37	6.21%	22.72%	29.39%	5.16%	5.74%	1.02	0.81	12.78%	13.68%	25.05%
7	11,594	4.06	37	6.84%	23.58%	30.85%	5.76%	5.99%	1.01	0.79	12.76%	13.65%	22.82%
8	9,463	3.98	37	8.10%	22.54%	29.10%	7.00%	6.28%	1.07	0.85	12.79%	14.52%	25.41%
9	7,822	3.89	37	8.74%	22.63%	29.25%	7.61%	6.55%	1.09	0.87	12.60%	14.43%	25.99%
10	6,482	3.81	35	7.82%	23.10%	30.03%	6.64%	6.81%	1.12	0.88	11.48%	14.85%	27.67%
11	5,637	3.75	35	7.47%	22.85%	29.61%	6.33%	7.01%	1.09	0.86	11.73%	14.97%	28.54%
12	4,791	3.68	47	7.44%	23.06%	29.97%	6.27%	7.23%	1.11	0.88	12.12%	14.74%	24.95%
13	3,915	3.59	45	7.78%	23.72%	31.10%	6.57%	7.52%	1.12	0.88	11.30%	15.36%	26.70%
14	3,329	3.52	42	8.28%	23.27%	30.32%	7.06%	7.74%	1.14	0.90	11.03%	17.41%	28.27%
15	2,897	3.46	40	10.06%	23.58%	30.85%	8.83%	7.94%	1.14	0.89	10.86%	17.34%	29.08%
16	2,508	3.40	52	9.57%	22.89%	29.68%	8.36%	8.14%	1.16	0.92	10.52%	18.09%	28.98%
17	2,130	3.33	44	9.45%	22.59%	29.19%	8.20%	8.37%	1.20	0.95	10.57%	18.52%	29.71%
18	1,842	3.27	53	8.06%	23.30%	30.38%	6.77%	8.57%	1.21	0.95	9.97%	20.31%	33.13%
19	1,584	3.20	53	9.49%	22.96%	29.80%	8.21%	8.79%	1.21	0.96	9.48%	21.44%	35.31%
20	1,313	3.12	73	8.80%	24.11%	31.77%	7.48%	9.05%	1.19	0.93	9.20%	22.57%	36.85%
21	1,023	3.01	76	10.01%	23.60%	30.89%	8.67%	9.40%	1.24	0.97	8.87%	24.21%	39.06%
22	731	2.86	82	9.71%	24.47%	32.40%	8.31%	9.87%	1.24	0.96	8.61%	25.53%	40.79%
23	532	2.73	75	12.77%	23.71%	31.08%	11.40%	10.32%	1.25	0.98	8.06%	26.83%	43.98%
24	370	2.57	86	12.89%	24.92%	33.19%	11.46%	10.83%	1.24	0.96	7.87%	30.50%	46.60%
25	121	2.08	249	17.94%	27.08%	37.14%	16.32%	12.39%	1.29	0.97	6.21%	43.90%	66.07%

CV(X) = Standard deviation of X divided by mean of X, calculated over 5 fiscal years.

[1] Unlevered risk premiums and unlevered betas are calculated using methodology described in Chapter 10 with an average assumed debt beta = 0.1.

Sources of underlying data: 1.) © 201702 CRSP®, Center for Research in Security Prices. University of Chicago Booth School of Business used with permission. 2.) Morningstar Direct database. Used with permission. All rights reserved. Calculations performed by Duff & Phelps LLC.

Companies Ranked by Book Value of Equity

Data for Year Ending December 31, 2016

Exhibit C-2

Comparative Risk Characteristics

Data Smoothing with Regression Analysis
Dependent Variable: Average Unlevered Risk Premium
Independent Variable: Log of Average Book Value

Constant	14.959%
X Coefficient(s)	-2.281%

Smoothed Unlevered Premium = 14.959% - 2.281% * Log(Book Value)

Portfolio Rank by Size	Average Book Value (in $millions)	Log of Average Book Value	Number of Firms	Arithmetic Average Risk Premium	Average Debt to MVIC	Average Debt to Market Value of Equity	Average Unlevered Risk Premium[1]	Smoothed Average Unlevered Risk Premium	Beta (Sum Beta) Since '63	Average Unlevered Beta	Average Operating Margin	Average CV(Operating Margin)	Average CV(ROE)
1	67,532	4.83	40	6.32%	25.50%	34.22%	5.45%	3.94%	0.78	0.61	14.94%	12.51%	22.66%
2	21,719	4.34	33	5.45%	29.95%	42.75%	4.34%	5.07%	0.84	0.62	14.24%	12.81%	21.70%
3	14,074	4.15	33	6.47%	28.42%	39.71%	5.30%	5.50%	0.92	0.69	12.36%	13.78%	25.71%
4	9,200	3.96	35	7.86%	29.30%	41.44%	6.69%	5.92%	0.90	0.67	12.15%	13.15%	25.96%
5	6,875	3.84	36	6.96%	27.67%	38.25%	5.74%	6.21%	0.98	0.74	12.97%	13.31%	26.19%
6	5,488	3.74	34	7.63%	25.90%	34.96%	6.45%	6.43%	1.01	0.77	12.43%	14.14%	26.17%
7	4,590	3.66	31	8.44%	25.75%	34.68%	7.22%	6.61%	1.04	0.80	11.73%	15.26%	27.33%
8	3,716	3.57	34	6.55%	25.55%	34.32%	5.31%	6.82%	1.07	0.82	11.77%	15.01%	26.59%
9	3,112	3.49	40	7.55%	25.40%	34.05%	6.24%	6.99%	1.12	0.86	12.14%	15.21%	26.27%
10	2,586	3.41	37	7.99%	25.49%	34.20%	6.75%	7.18%	1.07	0.82	11.68%	14.68%	25.78%
11	2,266	3.36	41	8.02%	25.51%	34.25%	6.76%	7.31%	1.08	0.83	11.32%	15.39%	27.09%
12	2,012	3.30	33	7.93%	25.04%	33.40%	6.67%	7.42%	1.10	0.85	11.22%	15.36%	27.41%
13	1,751	3.24	45	9.79%	25.38%	34.02%	8.56%	7.56%	1.07	0.82	11.03%	15.78%	24.78%
14	1,500	3.18	39	8.11%	23.52%	30.76%	6.85%	7.72%	1.17	0.92	11.13%	15.85%	26.69%
15	1,303	3.11	43	9.15%	22.48%	29.01%	7.99%	7.86%	1.12	0.89	10.74%	16.46%	30.18%
16	1,174	3.07	42	10.17%	23.42%	30.58%	8.91%	7.96%	1.17	0.92	10.37%	17.55%	29.46%
17	1,030	3.01	50	9.82%	23.19%	30.19%	8.56%	8.09%	1.18	0.93	9.94%	18.16%	31.79%
18	861	2.93	59	10.04%	23.16%	30.15%	8.80%	8.27%	1.17	0.92	9.97%	18.75%	31.03%
19	711	2.85	62	8.72%	23.87%	31.36%	7.32%	8.45%	1.26	0.99	9.48%	19.73%	34.85%
20	577	2.76	67	8.76%	22.56%	29.13%	7.47%	8.66%	1.25	0.99	9.14%	21.65%	36.43%
21	479	2.68	59	12.84%	22.75%	29.45%	11.55%	8.85%	1.22	0.97	8.57%	23.80%	39.14%
22	385	2.59	74	9.44%	23.44%	30.62%	8.14%	9.06%	1.21	0.95	8.64%	24.54%	40.33%
23	303	2.48	77	10.76%	22.86%	29.63%	9.43%	9.30%	1.26	0.99	8.12%	26.39%	42.83%
24	207	2.32	135	11.43%	22.68%	29.34%	10.10%	9.68%	1.27	1.00	8.34%	27.64%	41.96%
25	76	1.88	249	12.22%	23.06%	29.98%	10.88%	10.66%	1.25	0.99	7.11%	40.43%	58.69%

CV(X) = Standard deviation of X divided by mean of X, calculated over 5 fiscal years.

[1] Unlevered risk premiums and unlevered betas are calculated using methodology described in Chapter 10 with an average assumed debt beta = 0.1.

Companies Ranked by 5-Year Average Net Income

Data for Year Ending December 31, 2016

Data Smoothing with Regression Analysis
Dependent Variable: Average Unlevered Risk Premium
Independent Variable: Log of Average Net Income

| Constant | 13.074% |
| X Coefficient(s) | -2.367% |

Smoothed Unlevered Premium = 13.074% - 2.367% * Log(Net Income)

Portfolio Rank by Size	Average Net Inc. (in $millions)	Log of Average Net Inc.	Number of Firms	Arithmetic Average Risk Premium	Average Debt to MVIC	Average Debt to Market Value of Equity	Average Unlevered Risk Premium[1]	Smoothed Average Unlevered Risk Premium	Average Unlevered Beta	Beta (Sum Beta) Since '63	Average Operating Margin	Average CV(Operating Margin)	Average CV(ROE)
1	10,101	4.00	39	6.46%	20.90%	26.43%	5.75%	3.59%	0.63	0.77	16.51%	10.21%	18.37%
2	2,747	3.44	33	6.05%	24.62%	32.65%	5.09%	4.93%	0.68	0.87	14.36%	10.65%	20.11%
3	1,735	3.24	37	7.02%	26.82%	36.64%	6.00%	5.41%	0.65	0.85	13.34%	11.79%	21.35%
4	1,183	3.07	33	6.96%	27.36%	37.66%	5.86%	5.80%	0.68	0.90	12.99%	12.03%	21.96%
5	853	2.93	37	6.35%	26.08%	35.28%	5.23%	6.13%	0.73	0.96	12.47%	12.95%	23.76%
6	627	2.80	37	7.39%	24.70%	32.80%	6.29%	6.45%	0.77	0.99	12.56%	13.04%	22.90%
7	516	2.71	34	6.96%	24.89%	33.14%	5.78%	6.65%	0.81	1.04	12.70%	12.89%	22.52%
8	408	2.61	37	7.94%	24.55%	32.53%	6.71%	6.89%	0.85	1.09	12.62%	13.88%	24.35%
9	340	2.53	35	7.08%	24.35%	32.19%	5.92%	7.08%	0.82	1.05	11.86%	14.75%	26.39%
10	295	2.47	36	8.04%	24.01%	31.60%	6.89%	7.23%	0.83	1.06	12.17%	14.10%	24.40%
11	244	2.39	38	7.96%	23.88%	31.38%	6.77%	7.42%	0.85	1.09	11.83%	15.04%	24.79%
12	213	2.33	37	9.53%	24.38%	32.24%	8.33%	7.56%	0.84	1.08	11.40%	15.22%	24.95%
13	185	2.27	39	9.41%	23.73%	31.12%	8.26%	7.71%	0.84	1.07	11.37%	15.71%	25.60%
14	160	2.20	41	7.90%	23.99%	31.56%	6.65%	7.85%	0.89	1.14	11.15%	14.81%	24.67%
15	141	2.15	33	9.21%	23.40%	30.55%	8.02%	7.98%	0.88	1.12	10.86%	15.63%	25.58%
16	119	2.07	49	9.83%	23.10%	30.04%	8.64%	8.16%	0.89	1.13	10.77%	16.73%	27.18%
17	100	2.00	43	8.76%	22.64%	29.26%	7.53%	8.34%	0.94	1.18	10.47%	18.24%	31.59%
18	84	1.92	46	10.49%	22.93%	29.75%	9.23%	8.52%	0.95	1.20	10.33%	18.50%	31.32%
19	67	1.82	77	9.11%	23.05%	29.95%	7.79%	8.75%	0.98	1.24	9.66%	19.53%	31.18%
20	52	1.72	64	10.60%	23.66%	31.00%	9.26%	9.01%	0.96	1.23	9.51%	20.98%	35.36%
21	42	1.62	70	9.75%	24.45%	32.37%	8.38%	9.23%	0.94	1.22	9.25%	22.81%	34.64%
22	34	1.53	56	10.16%	23.97%	31.53%	8.83%	9.45%	0.94	1.21	8.82%	23.61%	37.80%
23	24	1.39	113	10.87%	22.56%	29.13%	9.57%	9.79%	0.99	1.25	8.72%	26.11%	41.16%
24	15	1.18	111	12.81%	23.38%	30.51%	11.45%	10.29%	0.99	1.26	7.84%	29.91%	47.51%
25	5	0.68	253	14.98%	24.59%	32.60%	13.49%	11.46%	1.02	1.31	6.05%	49.66%	81.18%

CV(X) = Standard deviation of X divided by mean of X, calculated over 5 fiscal years.

[1] Unlevered risk premiums and unlevered betas are calculated using methodology described in Chapter 10 with an average assumed debt beta = 0.1.

Companies Ranked by Market Value of Invested Capital

Exhibit C-4

Data for Year Ending December 31, 2016

Comparative Risk Characteristics

Data Smoothing with Regression Analysis
Dependent Variable: Average Unlevered Risk Premium
Independent Variable: Log of Average MVIC

Constant	18.630%
X Coefficient(s)	-3.030%

Smoothed Unlevered Premium = 18.630% - 3.030% * Log(MVIC)

Portfolio Rank by Size	Average MVIC (in $millions)	Log of Average MVIC	Number of Firms	Arithmetic Average Risk Premium	Average Debt to MVIC	Average Debt to Market Value of Equity	Average Unlevered Risk Premium[1]	Smoothed Average Unlevered Risk Premium	Beta (Sum Beta) Since '63	Average Unlevered Beta	Average Operating Margin	Average CV(Operating Margin)	Average CV(ROE)
1	277,921	5.44	44	5.21%	19.20%	23.77%	4.53%	2.13%	0.80	0.67	16.85%	10.14%	18.94%
2	77,365	4.89	34	4.65%	25.42%	34.08%	3.66%	3.82%	0.87	0.67	15.58%	11.53%	22.17%
3	46,877	4.67	36	5.03%	26.98%	36.95%	3.96%	4.48%	0.89	0.68	14.23%	12.14%	22.36%
4	32,471	4.51	37	6.41%	27.25%	37.46%	5.28%	4.96%	0.93	0.70	12.89%	12.40%	23.68%
5	24,248	4.38	33	6.61%	26.77%	36.55%	5.42%	5.34%	0.98	0.75	12.53%	12.70%	24.46%
6	18,506	4.27	37	6.16%	25.93%	35.01%	4.98%	5.70%	1.00	0.77	12.43%	13.72%	26.95%
7	15,426	4.19	35	7.31%	24.67%	32.74%	6.19%	5.94%	1.00	0.78	12.60%	13.97%	24.52%
8	13,457	4.13	36	7.67%	24.38%	32.23%	6.51%	6.12%	1.05	0.82	12.61%	13.89%	24.77%
9	10,762	4.03	42	6.69%	24.70%	32.81%	5.45%	6.41%	1.10	0.85	12.21%	14.38%	25.81%
10	8,658	3.94	34	8.98%	24.25%	32.02%	7.75%	6.70%	1.11	0.86	12.21%	14.88%	26.82%
11	7,453	3.87	35	8.47%	25.47%	34.18%	7.17%	6.90%	1.11	0.85	12.16%	15.09%	27.03%
12	6,455	3.81	41	7.96%	25.08%	33.47%	6.74%	7.09%	1.07	0.83	11.78%	15.01%	26.39%
13	5,466	3.74	43	7.71%	25.01%	33.34%	6.39%	7.30%	1.15	0.89	11.70%	15.93%	27.86%
14	4,718	3.67	39	8.52%	23.74%	31.13%	7.25%	7.50%	1.17	0.92	11.04%	16.22%	27.77%
15	4,043	3.61	39	8.90%	24.73%	32.85%	7.58%	7.70%	1.16	0.90	10.25%	17.55%	30.54%
16	3,541	3.55	44	9.39%	23.40%	30.55%	8.11%	7.88%	1.19	0.94	10.37%	18.51%	30.36%
17	3,075	3.49	46	9.41%	24.28%	32.06%	8.04%	8.06%	1.22	0.95	10.40%	18.69%	31.04%
18	2,587	3.41	54	10.08%	23.60%	30.89%	8.82%	8.29%	1.16	0.91	9.86%	18.93%	31.32%
19	2,109	3.32	67	7.60%	23.92%	31.44%	6.28%	8.56%	1.20	0.94	9.38%	20.96%	33.84%
20	1,696	3.23	64	9.04%	24.98%	33.30%	7.61%	8.84%	1.24	0.96	9.28%	21.73%	38.02%
21	1,323	3.12	89	9.01%	24.16%	31.87%	7.61%	9.17%	1.25	0.97	8.98%	22.90%	38.11%
22	1,014	3.01	64	10.70%	24.04%	31.64%	9.32%	9.52%	1.25	0.97	8.56%	25.87%	41.56%
23	738	2.87	75	10.89%	23.89%	31.39%	9.50%	9.94%	1.26	0.98	8.21%	26.03%	42.28%
24	513	2.71	95	11.65%	23.83%	31.28%	10.29%	10.42%	1.24	0.97	7.77%	29.88%	46.22%
25	163	2.21	265	17.59%	22.92%	29.73%	16.23%	11.93%	1.28	1.01	6.46%	43.53%	62.28%

CV(X) = Standard deviation of X divided by mean of X, calculated over 5 fiscal years.

[1] Unlevered risk premiums and unlevered betas are calculated using methodology described in Chapter 10 with an average assumed debt beta = 0.1.

Sources of underlying data: 1.) © 201702 CRSP®, Center for Research in Security Prices. University of Chicago Booth School of Business used with permission. All rights reserved. 2.) Morningstar *Direct* database. Used with permission.

Companies Ranked by Total Assets
Data for Year Ending December 31, 2016

Exhibit C-5

Comparative Risk Characteristics

Data Smoothing with Regression Analysis
Dependent Variable: Average Unlevered Risk Premium
Independent Variable: Log of Average Total Assets

Constant	17.337%
X Coefficient(s)	-2.694%

Smoothed Unlevered Premium = 17.337% − 2.694% * Log(Assets)

Portfolio Rank by Size	Average Total Assets (in $millions)	Log of Average Total Assets	Number of Firms	Arithmetic Average Risk Premium	Average Debt to MVIC	Average Debt to Market Value of Equity	Average Unlevered Risk Premium[1]	Smoothed Average Unlevered Risk Premium	Beta (Sum Beta) Since '63	Average Unlevered Beta	Average Operating Margin	Average CV(Operating Margin)	Average CV(ROE)
1	161,117	5.21	36	5.94%	29.09%	41.03%	4.91%	3.31%	0.80	0.60	14.27%	13.04%	22.98%
2	51,936	4.72	38	5.71%	34.00%	51.51%	4.46%	4.63%	0.84	0.59	14.01%	13.83%	25.11%
3	35,110	4.55	33	6.64%	31.15%	45.24%	5.36%	5.09%	0.92	0.67	12.53%	13.32%	24.74%
4	25,351	4.40	29	6.61%	31.09%	45.11%	5.36%	5.47%	0.90	0.65	12.50%	12.33%	24.41%
5	18,141	4.26	32	7.79%	30.07%	43.01%	6.51%	5.87%	0.95	0.69	11.39%	12.78%	26.78%
6	14,376	4.16	34	8.40%	28.55%	39.96%	7.17%	6.14%	0.96	0.71	12.56%	13.87%	28.42%
7	11,035	4.04	34	7.88%	27.67%	38.26%	6.57%	6.45%	1.04	0.78	11.47%	15.03%	29.70%
8	9,004	3.95	33	6.95%	27.85%	38.59%	5.63%	6.68%	1.04	0.78	11.76%	14.54%	25.96%
9	7,861	3.90	31	8.23%	28.11%	39.10%	6.82%	6.84%	1.10	0.82	11.34%	15.09%	27.90%
10	6,771	3.83	38	6.77%	27.35%	37.65%	5.40%	7.02%	1.10	0.83	11.58%	15.30%	28.73%
11	5,710	3.76	39	8.43%	27.88%	38.66%	6.99%	7.22%	1.12	0.84	11.51%	15.51%	27.37%
12	4,998	3.70	35	8.42%	26.33%	35.74%	7.10%	7.37%	1.10	0.83	10.83%	16.39%	27.53%
13	4,290	3.63	43	9.27%	26.18%	35.47%	7.90%	7.55%	1.14	0.87	11.13%	16.41%	28.13%
14	3,661	3.56	40	8.80%	25.17%	33.63%	7.49%	7.74%	1.14	0.88	10.53%	17.41%	29.97%
15	3,160	3.50	40	8.82%	25.77%	34.72%	7.46%	7.91%	1.15	0.88	9.88%	17.38%	30.47%
16	2,735	3.44	38	9.22%	24.55%	32.55%	7.88%	8.08%	1.19	0.92	9.54%	17.44%	31.67%
17	2,345	3.37	48	9.35%	24.95%	33.24%	8.01%	8.26%	1.17	0.90	10.28%	18.15%	30.02%
18	1,927	3.28	64	9.99%	25.03%	33.39%	8.60%	8.49%	1.20	0.93	9.71%	18.63%	31.71%
19	1,621	3.21	46	8.98%	25.22%	33.72%	7.56%	8.69%	1.22	0.94	9.71%	19.73%	33.05%
20	1,363	3.13	59	9.47%	24.46%	32.38%	8.07%	8.89%	1.24	0.96	9.48%	20.66%	34.62%
21	1,069	3.03	87	9.20%	23.56%	30.81%	7.87%	9.18%	1.22	0.96	8.86%	22.46%	36.94%
22	801	2.90	78	12.66%	23.24%	30.28%	11.32%	9.51%	1.25	0.98	8.59%	24.39%	39.50%
23	600	2.78	79	10.62%	22.19%	28.51%	9.35%	9.85%	1.25	0.99	8.37%	25.70%	41.12%
24	429	2.63	97	11.05%	21.56%	27.49%	9.80%	10.24%	1.26	1.01	8.10%	28.24%	44.58%
25	161	2.21	297	15.45%	19.50%	24.22%	14.30%	11.39%	1.28	1.05	7.31%	40.06%	56.49%

CV(X) = Standard deviation of X divided by mean of X, calculated over 5 fiscal years.

[1] Unlevered risk premiums and unlevered betas are calculated using methodology described in Chapter 10 with an average assumed debt beta = 0.1.

Exhibit C-6

Companies Ranked by 5-Year Average EBITDA
Data for Year Ending December 31, 2016

Comparative Risk Characteristics
Data Smoothing with Regression Analysis
Dependent Variable: Average Unlevered Risk Premium
Independent Variable: Log of Average EBITDA

Constant	13.973%
X Coefficient(s)	-2.345%

Smoothed Unlevered Premium = 13.973% - 2.345% * Log(EBITDA)

Portfolio Rank by Size	Average EBITDA (in $millions)	Log of Average EBITDA	Number of Firms	Arithmetic Average Risk Premium	Average Debt to MVIC	Average Debt to Market Value of Equity	Average Unlevered Risk Premium[1]	Smoothed Average Unlevered Risk Premium	Beta (Sum Beta) Since '63	Average Unlevered Beta	Average Operating Margin	Average CV(Operating Margin)	Average CV(ROE)
1	22,452	4.35	37	6.03%	23.88%	31.37%	5.20%	3.77%	0.79	0.63	15.31%	11.70%	21.43%
2	6,905	3.84	33	6.65%	28.87%	40.58%	5.57%	4.97%	0.84	0.63	14.20%	12.68%	24.90%
3	4,343	3.64	34	6.62%	29.53%	41.91%	5.45%	5.44%	0.88	0.65	13.22%	11.42%	22.28%
4	3,136	3.50	34	6.90%	29.08%	41.00%	5.72%	5.78%	0.90	0.67	12.10%	12.28%	24.84%
5	2,192	3.34	36	7.17%	27.83%	38.57%	5.93%	6.14%	0.98	0.74	12.02%	13.24%	26.15%
6	1,632	3.21	36	7.79%	28.59%	40.04%	6.60%	6.44%	0.93	0.69	12.34%	13.50%	26.56%
7	1,338	3.13	30	7.39%	26.60%	36.24%	6.15%	6.64%	1.03	0.78	12.29%	13.07%	23.66%
8	1,133	3.05	35	7.42%	25.64%	34.48%	6.18%	6.81%	1.06	0.81	11.91%	14.49%	25.45%
9	934	2.97	34	6.58%	25.45%	34.14%	5.28%	7.01%	1.11	0.85	12.12%	14.75%	27.98%
10	799	2.90	41	7.46%	25.93%	35.01%	6.18%	7.17%	1.08	0.83	12.14%	15.12%	26.75%
11	667	2.82	37	9.10%	24.80%	32.97%	7.96%	7.35%	1.02	0.79	11.30%	15.37%	26.43%
12	578	2.76	36	9.66%	26.00%	35.14%	8.36%	7.50%	1.09	0.83	11.57%	15.29%	25.98%
13	478	2.68	41	9.34%	25.69%	34.56%	8.09%	7.69%	1.07	0.82	11.11%	16.12%	29.11%
14	411	2.61	36	10.18%	24.28%	32.07%	8.89%	7.85%	1.16	0.90	10.66%	16.81%	27.65%
15	371	2.57	40	7.92%	24.70%	32.80%	6.63%	7.95%	1.14	0.88	10.71%	16.36%	28.70%
16	327	2.51	43	9.36%	23.83%	31.28%	8.07%	8.08%	1.18	0.92	10.32%	16.86%	26.83%
17	287	2.46	32	9.59%	24.47%	32.39%	8.25%	8.21%	1.19	0.92	10.13%	17.71%	30.28%
18	253	2.40	44	10.05%	25.00%	33.34%	8.67%	8.34%	1.20	0.92	10.01%	18.98%	33.66%
19	211	2.32	57	9.62%	24.88%	33.12%	8.21%	8.53%	1.23	0.95	9.75%	18.51%	30.68%
20	164	2.22	79	8.47%	24.53%	32.50%	7.07%	8.78%	1.23	0.96	9.47%	20.42%	33.24%
21	125	2.10	88	10.40%	24.08%	31.71%	9.07%	9.06%	1.20	0.94	9.33%	21.93%	35.34%
22	94	1.97	62	11.00%	23.34%	30.44%	9.68%	9.35%	1.22	0.96	8.92%	22.64%	36.54%
23	74	1.87	70	11.14%	23.27%	30.33%	9.82%	9.59%	1.23	0.96	8.34%	26.12%	40.41%
24	51	1.71	109	10.41%	23.02%	29.90%	9.08%	9.97%	1.25	0.98	8.20%	29.17%	43.45%
25	17	1.23	304	14.67%	21.55%	27.46%	13.37%	11.09%	1.30	1.04	6.73%	44.20%	63.10%

CV(X) = Standard deviation of X divided by mean of X, calculated over 5 fiscal years.

[1] Unlevered risk premiums and unlevered betas are calculated using methodology described in Chapter 10 with an average assumed debt beta = 0.1.

Sources of underlying data: 1.) © 201702 CRSP®, Center for Research in Security Prices. University of Chicago Booth School of Business used with permission. 2.) Morningstar *Direct* database. Used with permission. All rights reserved. Calculations performed by Duff & Phelps LLC.

Companies Ranked by Sales

Data for Year Ending December 31, 2016

Exhibit C-7

Comparative Risk Characteristics

Data Smoothing with Regression Analysis
Dependent Variable: Average Unlevered Risk Premium
Independent Variable: Log of Average Sales

Constant	16.168%
X Coefficient(s)	-2.352%

Smoothed Unlevered Premium = 16.168% - 2.352% * Log(Sales)

Portfolio Rank by Size	Average Sales (in $millions)	Log of Average Sales	Number of Firms	Arithmetic Average Risk Premium	Average Debt to MVIC	Average Debt to Market Value of Equity	Average Unlevered Risk Premium[1]	Smoothed Average Unlevered Risk Premium	Beta (Sum Beta) Since '63	Average Unlevered Beta	Average Operating Margin	Average CV(Operating Margin)	Average CV(ROE)
1	123,791	5.09	38	6.49%	24.45%	32.37%	5.52%	4.19%	0.89	0.69	9.19%	13.27%	24.53%
2	38,382	4.58	32	6.39%	24.97%	33.27%	5.31%	5.39%	0.96	0.75	8.80%	13.85%	25.46%
3	22,044	4.34	35	6.87%	27.14%	37.26%	5.64%	5.95%	1.00	0.75	10.02%	14.17%	25.60%
4	17,114	4.23	33	8.02%	27.98%	38.86%	6.77%	6.21%	0.98	0.74	11.05%	12.33%	22.83%
5	13,286	4.12	33	8.26%	28.94%	40.73%	6.94%	6.47%	1.01	0.75	10.53%	14.06%	28.82%
6	10,376	4.02	35	7.61%	27.99%	38.87%	6.32%	6.72%	1.02	0.76	10.52%	14.58%	28.08%
7	8,400	3.92	36	9.05%	25.73%	34.64%	7.79%	6.94%	1.08	0.82	10.27%	14.59%	26.74%
8	6,977	3.84	36	6.85%	27.23%	37.42%	5.57%	7.13%	1.04	0.78	9.74%	15.28%	25.41%
9	5,938	3.77	36	7.91%	26.46%	35.97%	6.57%	7.29%	1.10	0.84	9.85%	15.19%	29.24%
10	5,106	3.71	35	8.11%	26.88%	36.76%	6.75%	7.45%	1.11	0.84	9.88%	16.19%	27.40%
11	4,435	3.65	42	9.13%	26.68%	36.40%	7.78%	7.59%	1.11	0.84	9.81%	16.01%	29.20%
12	3,740	3.57	37	9.77%	26.56%	36.17%	8.42%	7.77%	1.11	0.84	9.69%	16.83%	28.10%
13	3,184	3.50	44	10.66%	26.65%	36.34%	9.19%	7.93%	1.20	0.91	9.64%	17.88%	29.36%
14	2,771	3.44	41	9.67%	26.23%	35.55%	8.34%	8.07%	1.11	0.85	9.89%	17.57%	29.71%
15	2,509	3.40	40	9.39%	25.22%	33.73%	8.09%	8.17%	1.12	0.86	10.26%	17.32%	28.23%
16	2,276	3.36	37	8.28%	25.36%	33.98%	6.94%	8.27%	1.15	0.89	10.11%	17.90%	30.46%
17	1,980	3.30	49	10.38%	26.20%	35.50%	9.00%	8.42%	1.15	0.88	9.68%	18.40%	31.65%
18	1,670	3.22	56	9.72%	25.99%	35.12%	8.30%	8.59%	1.19	0.91	10.21%	19.11%	33.43%
19	1,412	3.15	52	7.90%	25.74%	34.67%	6.45%	8.76%	1.23	0.94	9.24%	21.80%	38.50%
20	1,181	3.07	58	10.88%	25.63%	34.46%	9.49%	8.94%	1.18	0.90	9.63%	21.28%	34.24%
21	969	2.99	57	9.30%	24.50%	32.45%	7.97%	9.15%	1.18	0.92	9.31%	22.46%	36.12%
22	797	2.90	73	10.73%	24.36%	32.20%	9.32%	9.34%	1.25	0.97	9.52%	22.96%	37.40%
23	589	2.77	102	10.96%	23.29%	30.36%	9.64%	9.65%	1.23	0.97	9.34%	25.22%	40.40%
24	407	2.61	115	11.35%	22.71%	29.39%	10.05%	10.03%	1.24	0.98	8.86%	27.96%	43.17%
25	129	2.11	276	14.65%	20.07%	25.11%	13.48%	11.20%	1.26	1.03	8.50%	41.44%	57.47%

CV(X) = Standard deviation of X divided by mean of X, calculated over 5 fiscal years.

[1] Unlevered risk premiums and unlevered betas are calculated using methodology described in Chapter 10 with an average assumed debt beta = 0.1.

Sources of underlying data: 1.) © 201702 CRSP®, Center for Research in Security Prices. University of Chicago Booth School of Business used with permission. All rights reserved. 2.) Morningstar *Direct* database. Used with permission.
All rights reserved. Calculations performed by Duff & Phelps LLC.

Comparative Risk Characteristics

Data Smoothing with Regression Analysis
Dependent Variable: Average Unlevered Risk Premium
Independent Variable: Log of Average Employees

| Constant | 16.907% |
| X Coefficient(s) | -2.285% |

Smoothed Unlevered Premium = 16.907% - 2.285% * Log(Employees)

Portfolio Rank by Size	Average Number of Employees	Log of Average Employees	Number of Firms	Arithmetic Average Risk Premium	Average Debt to MVIC	Average Debt to Market Value of Equity	Average Unlevered Risk Premium[1]	Smoothed Average Unlevered Risk Premium	Beta (Sum Beta) Since '63	Average Unlevered Beta	Average Operating Margin	Average CV(Operating Margin)	Average CV(ROE)
1	341,434	5.53	35	6.07%	24.64%	32.70%	4.99%	4.26%	0.98	0.76	8.36%	12.20%	23.54%
2	107,466	5.03	38	6.66%	23.58%	30.86%	5.57%	5.41%	1.03	0.81	9.02%	12.28%	23.74%
3	64,944	4.81	34	6.92%	24.54%	32.51%	5.74%	5.91%	1.05	0.82	9.65%	13.04%	25.39%
4	46,747	4.67	37	8.04%	23.46%	30.65%	6.88%	6.24%	1.09	0.86	9.60%	14.63%	29.67%
5	34,256	4.53	42	8.55%	25.04%	33.41%	7.32%	6.54%	1.08	0.83	9.53%	14.60%	26.51%
6	26,595	4.42	34	8.50%	23.95%	31.49%	7.29%	6.80%	1.11	0.87	9.49%	14.36%	26.97%
7	22,447	4.35	38	7.22%	24.90%	33.15%	6.01%	6.96%	1.06	0.82	9.53%	14.15%	26.45%
8	18,590	4.27	44	7.16%	25.25%	33.77%	5.93%	7.15%	1.07	0.82	9.82%	15.32%	27.25%
9	15,489	4.19	37	9.23%	27.19%	37.35%	7.80%	7.33%	1.15	0.86	10.00%	16.36%	31.35%
10	13,344	4.13	39	9.47%	25.40%	34.05%	8.16%	7.48%	1.13	0.87	9.71%	17.40%	29.39%
11	11,841	4.07	41	9.61%	25.67%	34.54%	8.22%	7.60%	1.17	0.90	9.45%	17.99%	29.41%
12	10,389	4.02	36	9.86%	25.43%	34.10%	8.58%	7.73%	1.11	0.85	9.71%	17.08%	28.29%
13	9,004	3.95	49	8.74%	26.01%	35.15%	7.39%	7.87%	1.13	0.87	9.75%	17.56%	30.16%
14	7,588	3.88	48	7.03%	26.19%	35.49%	5.67%	8.04%	1.14	0.86	9.79%	17.87%	31.88%
15	6,511	3.81	57	9.77%	26.97%	36.93%	8.32%	8.19%	1.17	0.88	9.41%	18.43%	32.09%
16	5,710	3.76	47	8.48%	26.51%	36.08%	7.12%	8.32%	1.12	0.85	9.80%	19.23%	32.65%
17	4,908	3.69	51	8.05%	26.22%	35.55%	6.60%	8.47%	1.20	0.91	9.60%	21.03%	34.22%
18	4,194	3.62	47	10.30%	26.59%	36.23%	8.84%	8.63%	1.19	0.90	9.25%	21.54%	35.74%
19	3,507	3.54	60	9.70%	25.14%	33.59%	8.36%	8.81%	1.16	0.89	9.28%	22.34%	35.63%
20	2,908	3.46	65	8.24%	24.56%	32.55%	6.91%	8.99%	1.18	0.92	9.54%	22.65%	37.15%
21	2,328	3.37	70	11.12%	24.87%	33.10%	9.76%	9.21%	1.18	0.91	10.09%	23.18%	37.13%
22	1,797	3.25	68	12.66%	24.97%	33.28%	11.28%	9.47%	1.20	0.93	9.56%	24.95%	39.99%
23	1,281	3.11	91	13.25%	23.95%	31.49%	11.90%	9.81%	1.22	0.95	8.89%	27.78%	42.61%
24	871	2.94	84	12.18%	23.31%	30.40%	10.87%	10.19%	1.21	0.95	8.77%	32.86%	48.10%
25	305	2.48	236	12.29%	20.33%	25.52%	11.14%	11.23%	1.22	1.00	9.15%	41.56%	57.78%

CV(X) = Standard deviation of X divided by mean of X, calculated over 5 fiscal years.
[1] Unlevered risk premiums and unlevered betas are calculated using methodology described in Chapter 10 with an average assumed debt beta = 0.1.
Sources of underlying data: 1.) © 201702 CRSP®, Center for Research in Security Prices. University of Chicago Booth School of Business used with permission. 2.) Morningstar Direct database. Used with permission.
All rights reserved. Calculations performed by Duff & Phelps LLC.

Risk Premium Report — Exhibits D-1 through D-3

The D exhibits used in the *Risk Study* present 25 portfolios ranked by three fundamental accounting measures: five-year average operating income margin, the coefficient of variation in operating income margin, and the coefficient of variation in return on book equity. Use of fundamental accounting measures of risk allows for direct assessment of the riskiness of the subject company.

The D Exhibits are used in the following method to estimate a cost of equity capital:

- Build-up 3
- Build-up 3-Unlevered

Risk Measures:

D-1: Operating Margin

D-2: Coefficient of variation in operating income margin

D-3: Coefficient of variation in return on book equity

Companies Ranked by Operating Margin

Historical Equity Risk Premium: Average Since 1963
Data for Year Ending December 31, 2016

Equity Risk Premium Study: Data through December 31, 2016
Data Smoothing with Regression Analysis
Dependent Variable: Arithmetic Average Risk Premium
Independent Variable: Log of Average Operating Margin

Regression Output:	
Constant	3.445%
Standard Error of Y Estimate	0.995%
R Squared	80%
No. of Observations	25
Degrees of Freedom	23
X Coefficient(s)	-6.681%
Standard Error of Coefficient	0.692%
t-Statistic	-9.66

*Smoothed Premium = 3.445% - 6.681% * Log(Operating Margin)*

Smoothed Premium vs. Arithmetic Premium

Portfolio Rank	Average Operating Margin	Log of Average Op Margin	Number as of 2016	Beta (Sum Beta) Since '63	Average Unlevered Beta	Standard Deviation of Returns	Geometric Average Return	Arithmetic Average Return	Arithmetic Average Risk Premium	Arithmetic Average Unlevered Risk Premium	Smoothed Average Risk Premium	Average Debt to Market Value of Equity	Average Debt/ MVIC
1	38.24%	-0.42	76	0.90	0.71	16.99%	11.34%	13.63%	7.17%	6.22%	6.23%	31.17%	23.76%
2	28.34%	-0.55	64	0.84	0.65	17.50%	10.05%	12.35%	5.89%	4.92%	7.10%	35.29%	26.08%
3	24.42%	-0.61	51	0.87	0.68	17.53%	11.44%	13.84%	7.38%	6.42%	7.54%	33.21%	24.93%
4	21.81%	-0.66	47	0.94	0.76	16.78%	11.22%	13.55%	7.09%	6.15%	7.86%	28.59%	22.23%
5	20.20%	-0.69	47	0.98	0.81	18.57%	12.38%	15.06%	8.60%	7.72%	8.09%	24.81%	19.88%
6	18.66%	-0.73	38	1.06	0.89	17.96%	12.45%	15.01%	8.55%	7.69%	8.32%	21.76%	17.87%
7	17.56%	-0.76	54	1.10	0.91	18.88%	12.21%	14.91%	8.45%	7.50%	8.49%	23.32%	18.91%
8	16.50%	-0.78	45	1.10	0.91	19.94%	11.54%	14.36%	7.90%	6.95%	8.67%	23.59%	19.09%
9	15.47%	-0.81	44	1.14	0.94	19.36%	13.45%	16.31%	9.85%	8.84%	8.86%	24.05%	19.39%
10	14.62%	-0.84	42	1.16	0.94	20.40%	12.77%	15.75%	9.29%	8.19%	9.02%	26.04%	20.66%
11	13.69%	-0.86	53	1.16	0.94	20.82%	11.51%	14.45%	7.99%	6.89%	9.22%	26.12%	20.71%
12	12.84%	-0.89	60	1.18	0.95	20.03%	12.01%	14.90%	8.44%	7.28%	9.40%	27.29%	21.44%
13	11.92%	-0.92	50	1.20	0.97	20.74%	11.19%	14.16%	7.70%	6.53%	9.62%	26.82%	21.15%
14	11.13%	-0.95	48	1.19	0.95	21.95%	13.19%	16.67%	10.22%	9.02%	9.82%	28.11%	21.94%
15	10.46%	-0.98	43	1.23	0.97	22.86%	13.14%	16.64%	10.19%	8.90%	10.00%	29.28%	22.65%
16	9.87%	-1.01	54	1.18	0.92	21.97%	14.48%	17.95%	11.49%	10.19%	10.16%	31.36%	23.87%
17	9.17%	-1.04	65	1.26	0.97	24.41%	14.55%	18.12%	11.67%	10.24%	10.38%	32.49%	24.52%
18	8.36%	-1.08	56	1.22	0.95	23.53%	13.52%	17.28%	10.82%	9.46%	10.64%	31.87%	24.17%
19	7.61%	-1.12	49	1.27	0.97	23.77%	13.09%	16.85%	10.39%	8.87%	10.92%	34.80%	25.81%
20	7.10%	-1.15	58	1.25	0.94	23.80%	13.67%	17.45%	10.99%	9.43%	11.12%	37.01%	27.01%
21	6.38%	-1.19	67	1.26	0.95	24.18%	15.31%	19.24%	12.78%	11.19%	11.43%	37.37%	27.21%
22	5.56%	-1.25	72	1.24	0.93	28.78%	15.59%	19.89%	13.43%	11.86%	11.83%	37.81%	27.44%
23	4.71%	-1.33	76	1.29	0.94	25.63%	15.21%	19.55%	13.09%	11.36%	12.31%	41.12%	29.14%
24	3.63%	-1.44	70	1.26	0.91	24.89%	14.28%	18.37%	11.91%	10.16%	13.06%	42.83%	29.99%
25	1.96%	-1.71	99	1.28	0.94	28.20%	15.29%	20.10%	13.64%	11.93%	14.85%	40.77%	28.96%

						Geometric Average Return	Arithmetic Average Return	Arithmetic Average Risk Premium					
Large Stocks (Ibbotson SBBI data)						10.13%	11.48%	5.02%					
Small Stocks (Ibbotson SBBI data)						13.63%	16.27%	9.81%					
Long-Term Treasury Income (Ibbotson SBBI data)						6.43%	6.46%						

Companies Ranked by CV(Operating Margin)

Historical Equity Risk Premium: Average Since 1963
Data for Year Ending December 31, 2016

Equity Risk Premium Study: Data through December 31, 2016
Data Smoothing with Regression Analysis
Dependent Variable: Arithmetic Average Risk Premium
Independent Variable: Log of Average CV(Operating Margin)

Portfolio Rank	Average CV(Op Margin)	Log of Average CV(Op Margin)	Number as of 2016	Beta (Sum Beta) Since '63	Average Unlevered Beta	Standard Deviation of Returns	Geometric Average Return	Arithmetic Average Return	Arithmetic Average Risk Premium	Arithmetic Average Unlevered Risk Premium	Smoothed Average Risk Premium	Average Debt to Market Value of Equity	Average Debt/ MVIC
1	168.86%	0.23	115	1.44	1.14	28.86%	13.49%	18.41%	11.95%	10.44%	12.58%	28.94%	22.45%
2	78.75%	-0.10	72	1.38	1.05	26.87%	13.80%	18.14%	11.68%	10.05%	11.67%	34.00%	25.37%
3	59.50%	-0.23	76	1.35	1.02	27.75%	13.61%	17.88%	11.42%	9.78%	11.33%	35.28%	26.08%
4	43.87%	-0.36	90	1.33	1.01	24.96%	12.45%	16.42%	9.96%	8.35%	10.97%	35.05%	25.95%
5	34.72%	-0.46	82	1.25	0.96	24.47%	13.32%	17.26%	10.80%	9.36%	10.68%	33.25%	24.96%
6	28.10%	-0.55	80	1.27	0.97	24.48%	12.63%	16.44%	9.98%	8.47%	10.43%	34.71%	25.76%
7	24.90%	-0.60	47	1.25	0.96	22.86%	13.74%	17.40%	10.94%	9.48%	10.29%	33.96%	25.35%
8	22.69%	-0.64	51	1.26	0.97	22.90%	13.27%	16.85%	10.39%	8.94%	10.17%	33.19%	24.92%
9	20.44%	-0.69	53	1.18	0.91	22.75%	14.41%	18.09%	11.63%	10.28%	10.05%	33.21%	24.93%
10	18.43%	-0.73	45	1.16	0.90	21.68%	13.94%	17.27%	10.81%	9.51%	9.92%	32.61%	24.59%
11	16.92%	-0.77	61	1.15	0.89	21.10%	13.63%	16.81%	10.36%	9.07%	9.82%	32.50%	24.53%
12	15.37%	-0.81	49	1.14	0.87	20.11%	13.64%	16.69%	10.23%	8.92%	9.71%	33.62%	25.16%
13	13.72%	-0.86	55	1.12	0.87	19.45%	12.07%	14.90%	8.44%	7.21%	9.57%	31.67%	24.05%
14	12.82%	-0.89	38	1.11	0.86	20.37%	12.96%	15.95%	9.50%	8.28%	9.49%	31.72%	24.08%
15	11.76%	-0.93	47	1.08	0.85	18.82%	12.74%	15.47%	9.01%	7.85%	9.38%	30.91%	23.61%
16	10.80%	-0.97	47	1.06	0.83	20.46%	12.57%	15.55%	9.09%	7.93%	9.28%	31.62%	24.02%
17	9.52%	-1.02	55	1.01	0.79	18.04%	13.26%	15.89%	9.43%	8.35%	9.13%	31.05%	23.69%
18	8.42%	-1.07	50	1.00	0.79	18.81%	13.38%	16.13%	9.67%	8.60%	8.98%	30.78%	23.53%
19	7.64%	-1.12	40	1.00	0.78	18.09%	12.31%	14.92%	8.46%	7.38%	8.87%	31.60%	24.01%
20	6.89%	-1.16	51	0.99	0.79	17.70%	12.71%	15.27%	8.81%	7.83%	8.74%	28.20%	22.00%
21	5.89%	-1.23	51	0.90	0.72	16.87%	12.35%	14.72%	8.26%	7.36%	8.55%	28.89%	22.41%
22	5.16%	-1.29	45	0.88	0.71	15.80%	11.85%	14.05%	7.59%	6.70%	8.40%	29.39%	22.71%
23	4.51%	-1.35	42	0.90	0.72	17.40%	11.96%	14.40%	7.94%	7.05%	8.23%	28.73%	22.32%
24	3.64%	-1.44	39	0.86	0.70	16.62%	11.92%	14.22%	7.76%	6.94%	7.98%	27.24%	21.41%
25	2.26%	-1.65	47	0.82	0.68	15.35%	11.84%	13.99%	7.53%	6.82%	7.40%	24.25%	19.52%

							Geometric Average Return	Arithmetic Average Return	Arithmetic Average Risk Premium				
Large Stocks (Ibbotson SBBI data)							10.13%	11.48%	5.02%				
Small Stocks (Ibbotson SBBI data)							13.63%	16.27%	9.81%				
Long-Term Treasury Income (Ibbotson SBBI data)							6.43%	6.46%					

Regression Output:

Constant	11.956%
Standard Error of Y Estimate	0.626%
R Squared	79%
No. of Observations	25
Degrees of Freedom	23
X Coefficient(s)	2.766%
Standard Error of Coefficient	0.293%
t-Statistic	9.43

Smoothed Premium = 11.956% + 2.766% * Log(CV Op Inc)

Smoothed Premium vs. Arithmetic Premium

(Premium vs. Log of Median CV(Operating Margin))

Companies Ranked by CV(ROE)
Historical Equity Risk Premium: Average Since 1963
Data for Year Ending December 31, 2016

Portfolio Rank	Average CV(ROE)	Log of Average CV(ROE)	Number as of 2016	Beta (Sum Beta) Since '63	Average Unlevered Beta	Standard Deviation of Returns	Geometric Average Return	Arithmetic Average Return	Arithmetic Average Risk Premium	Arithmetic Average Unlevered Risk Premium	Smoothed Average Risk Premium	Average Debt to Market Value of Equity	Average Debt/ MVIC
1	989.06%	1.00	65	1.42	1.01	31.40%	15.22%	20.33%	13.87%	11.82%	13.45%	44.87%	30.97%
2	288.06%	0.46	63	1.40	1.02	27.16%	14.48%	19.04%	12.58%	10.70%	12.12%	40.66%	28.91%
3	176.91%	0.25	67	1.35	1.01	26.07%	12.51%	16.68%	10.22%	8.49%	11.59%	38.05%	27.56%
4	136.56%	0.14	76	1.32	0.99	25.58%	13.44%	17.65%	11.19%	9.51%	11.31%	37.46%	27.25%
5	99.89%	0.00	64	1.31	0.98	25.42%	14.15%	18.26%	11.80%	10.19%	10.97%	36.27%	26.62%
6	81.20%	-0.09	75	1.31	0.99	23.70%	13.88%	17.66%	11.20%	9.63%	10.75%	35.08%	25.97%
7	66.90%	-0.17	68	1.28	0.97	24.32%	12.69%	16.45%	10.00%	8.45%	10.54%	35.34%	26.11%
8	59.23%	-0.23	51	1.23	0.95	22.19%	12.63%	16.00%	9.54%	8.16%	10.41%	32.01%	24.25%
9	51.83%	-0.29	65	1.26	0.98	23.12%	13.36%	17.08%	10.62%	9.22%	10.27%	31.65%	24.04%
10	44.35%	-0.35	67	1.20	0.95	22.89%	12.68%	16.19%	9.73%	8.48%	10.10%	29.29%	22.66%
11	38.82%	-0.41	63	1.18	0.93	20.72%	13.95%	17.14%	10.68%	9.44%	9.96%	29.73%	22.92%
12	34.35%	-0.46	62	1.17	0.92	21.81%	11.85%	15.00%	8.54%	7.32%	9.82%	29.75%	22.93%
13	30.77%	-0.51	48	1.14	0.92	19.32%	12.44%	15.24%	8.78%	7.64%	9.71%	27.93%	21.83%
14	28.25%	-0.55	51	1.13	0.90	25.12%	15.39%	18.87%	12.41%	11.28%	9.61%	28.21%	22.00%
15	25.61%	-0.59	49	1.12	0.90	20.23%	12.08%	15.04%	8.58%	7.47%	9.51%	27.82%	21.77%
16	23.45%	-0.63	49	1.10	0.89	20.46%	13.76%	16.90%	10.44%	9.37%	9.41%	27.16%	21.36%
17	21.22%	-0.67	55	1.07	0.86	19.23%	12.69%	15.51%	9.05%	8.02%	9.30%	27.16%	21.36%
18	19.38%	-0.71	36	1.02	0.82	17.72%	12.36%	14.89%	8.43%	7.43%	9.21%	27.81%	21.76%
19	17.77%	-0.75	47	0.98	0.79	18.61%	12.40%	15.05%	8.59%	7.65%	9.11%	27.21%	21.39%
20	15.99%	-0.80	45	0.94	0.76	18.62%	12.42%	15.09%	8.63%	7.71%	9.00%	27.74%	21.71%
21	14.16%	-0.85	55	0.96	0.79	18.12%	13.12%	15.78%	9.32%	8.43%	8.87%	25.95%	20.60%
22	12.25%	-0.91	48	0.90	0.73	18.26%	13.68%	16.02%	9.56%	8.68%	8.71%	27.91%	21.82%
23	10.06%	-1.00	47	0.84	0.68	16.06%	12.37%	14.62%	8.16%	7.38%	8.50%	26.96%	21.24%
24	8.11%	-1.09	62	0.80	0.66	16.26%	12.93%	15.23%	8.77%	8.07%	8.27%	24.93%	19.95%
25	4.87%	-1.31	50	0.79	0.65	14.82%	11.92%	13.97%	7.51%	6.85%	7.72%	24.06%	19.99%

	Geometric Average Return	Arithmetic Average Return	Arithmetic Average Risk Premium
Large Stocks (Ibbotson SBBI data)	10.13%	11.48%	5.02%
Small Stocks (Ibbotson SBBI data)	13.63%	16.27%	9.81%
Long-Term Treasury Income (Ibbotson SBBI data)	6.43%	6.46%	

Equity Risk Premium Study: Data through December 31, 2016
Data Smoothing with Regression Analysis
Dependent Variable: Arithmetic Average Risk Premium
Independent Variable: Log of Average CV(ROE)

Regression Output:

Constant	10.976%
Standard Error of Y Estimate	0.925%
R-Squared	67%
No. of Observations	25
Degrees of Freedom	23
X Coefficient(s)	2.482%
Standard Error of Coefficient	0.364%
t-Statistic	6.81

*Smoothed Premium = 10.976% + 2.482% * Log(CV ROE)*

Smoothed Premium vs. Arithmetic Premium

Risk Premium Report – Exhibits H-A through H-C

The High-Financial-Risk Study includes Exhibits H-A, H-B, and H-C. The companies in the H exhibits are companies that are losing money, have high leverage, or are in bankruptcy. These companies were eliminated from the base set of companies used in the *Size Study* and *Risk Study*. The H exhibits provide risk premia that may be used in both build-up and CAPM estimates of cost of equity capital.

The H Exhibits are used in the following method to estimate a cost of equity capital:

- Build-up 1-High-Financial-Risk
- CAPM-High-Financial-Risk

Historical Equity Risk Premium: Average Since 1963
High-Financial-Risk Company Data for Year Ending December 31, 2016

Portfolio	Beta (Sum Beta) Since '63	Standard Deviation of Returns	Geometric Average Return	Arithmetic Average Return	Arithmetic Average Risk Premium	Average Debt/ MVIC
Manufacturing (z-Score)						
1.8 to 2.99 (*gray zone*)	1.56	35.17%	12.82%	19.29%	12.83%	44.74%
< 1.8 (*distress zone*)	1.65	38.47%	15.87%	23.12%	16.66%	57.82%
Service (z''-Score)						
1.1 to 2.59 (*gray zone*)	1.57	42.39%	15.88%	28.02%	21.56%	40.00%
< 1.1 (*distress zone*)	1.72	43.93%	19.00%	31.58%	25.12%	46.76%
Large Stocks (Ibbotson SBBI data)			10.13%	11.48%	5.02%	
Small Stocks (Ibbotson SBBI data)			13.63%	16.27%	9.81%	
Long-Term Treasury Income (Ibbotson SBBI data)			6.43%	6.46%		

Sources of underlying data: 1.) © 201702 CRSP®, Center for Research in Security Prices. University of Chicago Booth School of Business used with permission. All rights reserved. 2.) Morningstar *Direct* database. Used with permission. All rights reserved. Calculations performed by Duff & Phelps LLC.

Premia Over CAPM ($RP_{s,\,high\text{-}financial\text{-}risk}$)

Historical Equity Risk Premium: Average Since 1963
High-Financial-Risk Company Data for Year Ending December 31, 2016

Portfolio	Beta (Sum Beta) Since '63	Arithmetic Average Return	Arithmetic Average Risk Premium	Indicated CAPM Premium	Premium over CAPM
Manufacturing (z-Score)					
1.8 to 2.99 (gray zone)	1.56	19.29%	12.83%	7.86%	4.97%
< 1.8 (distress zone)	1.65	23.12%	16.66%	8.29%	8.37%
Service (z''-Score)					
1.1 to 2.59 (gray zone)	1.57	28.02%	21.56%	7.88%	13.68%
< 1.1 (distress zone)	1.72	31.58%	25.12%	8.66%	16.46%
Large Stocks (Ibbotson SBBI data)		11.48%	5.02%		
Small Stocks (Ibbotson SBBI data)		16.27%	9.81%		
Long-Term Treasury Income (Ibbotson SBBI data)		6.46%			

Sources of underlying data: 1.) © 201702 CRSP®, Center for Research in Security Prices. University of Chicago Booth School of Business used with permission. All rights reserved. 2.) Morningstar *Direct* database. Used with permission. All rights reserved. Calculations performed by Duff & Phelps LLC.

Premia Over the Risk-Free Rate ($RP_{m+s, high-financial-risk}$)

Historical Equity Risk Premium: Average Since 1963
High-Financial-Risk Company Data for Year Ending December 31, 2016

Portfolio	Arithmetic Average Risk Premium	Average Debt to MVIC	Average Debt to Market Value of Equity	Beta (Sum Beta) Since '63	Average Operating Margin
Manufacturing (z-Score)					
1.8 to 2.99 (gray zone)	12.83%	44.74%	80.95%	1.56	2.52%
< 1.8 (distress zone)	16.66%	57.82%	137.10%	1.65	5.49%
Service (z''-Score)					
1.1 to 2.59 (gray zone)	21.56%	40.00%	66.66%	1.57	4.14%
< 1.1 (distress zone)	25.12%	46.76%	87.83%	1.72	3.66%

Sources of underlying data: 1.) © 201702 CRSP®, Center for Research in Security Prices. University of Chicago Booth School of Business used with permission. All rights reserved. 2.) Morningstar *Direct* database. Used with permission. All rights reserved. Calculations performed by Duff & Phelps LLC.